Strategic and Practical Approaches for Information Security Governance:

Technologies and Applied Solutions

Manish Gupta
State University of New York, Buffalo, USA

John Walp
M&T Bank Corporation, USA

Raj Sharman
State University of New York, Buffalo, USA

Information Science
REFERENCE

Managing Director: Lindsay Johnston
Senior Editorial Director: Heather Probst
Book Production Manager: Sean Woznicki
Development Manager: Joel Gamon
Development Editor: Myla Harty
Acquisitions Editor: Erika Gallagher
Typesetter: Adrienne Freeland
Cover Design: Nick Newcomer, Lisandro Gonzalez

Published in the United States of America by
Information Science Reference (an imprint of IGI Global)
701 E. Chocolate Avenue
Hershey PA 17033
Tel: 717-533-8845
Fax: 717-533-8661
E-mail: cust@igi-global.com
Web site: http://www.igi-global.com

Library of Congress Cataloging-in-Publication Data

Strategic and practical approaches for information security governance: technologies and applied solutions / Manish Gupta, John Walp, Raj Sharman, editors.
p. cm.
Includes bibliographical references and index.
Summary: "This book provides organizations with insights into practical and applied solutions, frameworks, technologies and practices on technological and organizational factors in information security"--Provided by publisher.
ISBN 978-1-4666-0197-0 (hardcover) -- ISBN 978-1-4666-0198-7 (ebook) -- ISBN 978-1-4666-0199-4 (print & perpetual access) 1. Computer networks--Security measures. 2. Information networks--Security measures. 3. Data protection--Security measures. I. Gupta, Manish, 1978- II. Walp, John, 1967- III. Sharman, Raj.
TK5105.59.S766 2012
005.8--dc23
2011042029

British Cataloguing in Publication Data
A Cataloguing in Publication record for this book is available from the British Library.

All work contributed to this book is new, previously-unpublished material. The views expressed in this book are those of the authors, but not necessarily of the publisher.

Table of Contents

Preface xvii

Chapter 1
Investigating the Concept of Information Security Culture 1
Daniel Oost, University of Technology, Australia
Eng Chew, University of Technology, Australia

Chapter 2
Assessing Market Compliance of IT Security Solutions: A Structured Approach Using Diffusion of Innovations Theory 13
Heiko Roßnagel, Fraunhofer IAO, Germany
Jan Zibuschka, Fraunhofer IAO, Germany

Chapter 3
Identity Assurance in Open Networks 34
Ivonne Thomas, Hasso-Plattner-Institute, Germany
Christoph Meinel, Hasso-Plattner-Institute, Germany

Chapter 4
Information Security Governance 53
Janne J. Korhonen, Aalto University, Finland
Kari Hiekkanen, Aalto University, Finland
Juha Mykkänen, University of Eastern Finland, Finland

Chapter 5
Enterprise Information Security Policies, Standards, and Procedures: A Survey of Available Standards and Guidelines 67
Syed Irfan Nabi, Institute of Business Administration, Pakistan & Center of Excellence in Information Assurance (CoEIA), King Saud University, Saudi Arabia
Ghmlas Saleh Al-Ghmlas, Center of Excellence in Information Assurance (CoEIA), King Saud University, Saudi Arabia
Khaled Alghathbar, Center of Excellence in Information Assurance (CoEIA), King Saud University, Saudi Arabia

Chapter 6
ISMS Building for SMEs through the Reuse of Knowledge 90
Luís Enrique Sánchez, SICAMAN NT, Spain
Antonio Santos-Olmo, SICAMAN NT, Spain
Eduardo Fernandez-Medina, University of Castilla-La Mancha, Spain
Mario Piattini, University of Castilla-La Mancha, Spain

Chapter 7
Information Security and Management in Social Network 117
Alkesh Patel, Rediff.com, India
Ajit Balakrishnan, Rediff.com, India

Chapter 8
Music is the Key: Using our Enduring Memory for Songs to Help Users Log On 137
Marcia Gibson, Institute for Research in Applicable Computing, University of Bedfordshire, UK
Karen Renaud, University of Glasgow, UK
Marc Conrad, Institute for Research in Applicable Computing, University of Bedfordshire, UK
Carsten Maple, Institute for Research in Applicable Computing, University of Bedfordshire, UK

Chapter 9
Information System Integrated Security 158
Milena Tvrdíková, VSB-Technical University Ostrava, Czech Republic

Chapter 10
Surveillance Communities of Practice: Supporting Aspects of Information Assurance for Safeguards and Compliance Monitoring 170
Peter Goldschmidt, The University of Western Australia, Australia

Chapter 11
Not Every Cloud Brings Rain: Legal Risks on the Horizon 181
Sylvia Kierkegaard, International Association of IT Lawyers, Denmark

Chapter 12
Securing the Extended Enterprise: A Method for Analyzing External Insider Threat 195
Virginia N. L. Franqueira, University of Twente, The Netherlands
André van Cleeff, University of Twente, The Netherlands
Pascal van Eck, University of Twente, The Netherlands
Roel Wieringa, University of Twente, The Netherlands

Chapter 13
Information Security Management Systems Cybernetics 223
Wolfgang Boehmer, Technische Universität Darmstadt, Germany

Chapter 14
Fraud and Identity Theft Issues 245
Ranaganayakulu Dhanalakshmi, Anna University, India
Chenniappan Chellappan, Anna University, India

Chapter 15
Information Security Governance and Standard Based Management Systems 261
Margareth Stoll, University of Innsbruck, Austria
Ruth Breu, University of Innsbruck, Austria

Chapter 16
A Construct Grid Approach to Security Classification and Analysis 283
Michael Van Hilst, Florida Atlantic University, USA
Eduardo B. Fernandez, Florida Atlantic University, USA

Chapter 17
Towards an Organizational Culture Framework for Information Security Practices 296
Joo Soon Lim, The University of Melbourne, Australia
Shanton Chang, The University of Melbourne, Australia
Atif Ahmad, The University of Melbourne, Australia & SECAU – Security Research Centre, Edith Cowan University, Australia
Sean Maynard, The University of Melbourne, Australia

Chapter 18
Establishment of Enterprise Secured Information Architecture 316
Shyh-Chang Liu, I-Shou University, Taiwan
Tsang- Hung Wu, I-Shou University, Taiwan

Chapter 19
Information Security Management Based on Adaptive Security Policy Using User Behavior Analysis 326
Ines Brosso, Mackenzie Presbyterian University, Brazil
Alessandro La Neve, Centro Universitário da FEI, Brasil

Chapter 20
Detecting Credit Fraud in E-Business System: An Information Security Perspective on the Banking Sector in UK 346
Md Delwar Hussain Mahdi, Applied Research Centre for Business and Information Technology (ARCBIT), UK
Karim Mohammed Rezaul, Centre for Applied Internet Research (CAIR), Glyndŵr University, UK

Chapter 21
Safeguarding Australia from Cyber-Terrorism: A SCADA Risk Framework 369
Christopher Beggs, Security Infrastructure Solutions, Australia
Matthew Warren, Deakin University, Australia

Detailed Table of Contents

The concept of an "information security culture" is relatively new. A review of published research on the topic suggests that it is not the information security panacea that has been suggested. Instead it tends to refer to a range of existing techniques for addressing the human aspect of information security, oversimplifying the link between culture and behaviour, exaggerating the ease with which a culture can be adjusted, and treating culture as a monolith, set from the top. Evidence for some of the claims is also lacking. This chapter finds that the term "information security culture" is ambiguous and vague enough to suggest the possibility of achieving an almost mystical state, whereby behaviour consistent with information security is second nature to all employees, but when probed, does not deliver. Instead, future research should be clear about what it considers information security culture to be, should provide evidence for claims, and should take complexity and context seriously.

In this work, the authors discuss the diffusion of IT security solutions. The authors base their research on Roger's diffusion of innovations theory, and derive a model for holistic ex-ante analysis of the market potential of such systems based on generic factors influencing the diffusion of security solutions. After giving an overview of the relevant aspects of diffusion of innovations theory, and presenting the approach to use it as a structuring tool in ex-ante analysis, the authors present case study analyses for three IT security solutions, demonstrating the applicability of the method, and the alignment of results produced by the method with actual market results.

Identity assurance is the degree of confidence another party, such as a service provider, can have in the belief that identity in the digital world actually matches with "real-life" identity. In open networks, establishing this confidence is not an easy task, as participants are often located in different trust domains. Moreover, with the spread of open identity management systems, identity information is often held by designated identity provisioning services, so called identity providers. If another party shall be enabled to rely on received information, it ought to know how much confidence it can put into the assertions of the sender. In the intent to create a global standard, governments, commercial organizations, and academia alike have published common guidelines for identity assurance as part of so-called identity assurance frameworks. This chapter provides a state-of-the-art overview of identity assurance frameworks and describes them along important trust factors of identity providers. Furthermore, limitations of identity assurance frameworks are identified and highlighted as potential fields for further research. As an outlook to future developments, a small case study is presented that introduces trust levels for attributes in order to enable a service provider to distinguish between different qualities of trust, thus providing more flexibility in the way identity assurance is achieved in open networks.

In today's economic, regulatory, and social environment, information security governance and management are topics of great interest to practitioners and researcher alike. In response to the increasingly interconnected, information intensive business landscape, legal pressures and ongoing scrutiny to transparency and overall governance, organizations are increasingly interested in frameworks and methodologies for security governance and management. As the traditional view of governance as a control and conformance mechanism turns out to be inadequate in changing environments, a specifically contrived, more encompassing and design-oriented approach to information security governance is called for. In this chapter, the authors subscribe to the design science approach in order to outline a prescriptive reference model for information security governance that aims to help institute cross-functional information security management throughout the organization and build it into the organizational design.

This chapter explores enterprise information security policies, standards, and procedures. It examines the existing resources, analyses the available options, and offers recommendations to the CIOs and other people that have to make decisions about policies, standards, and procedures to ensure informa-

Social networking sites (SNSs) have gained significant attention in last few years. Most Internet users are associated with at least one popular SNS depending on their personal and professional preferences. Users have, in general, trusted the SNSs with personal data, and assumed that their privacy preferences are correctly enforced. Users of SNSs often want to manage the sharing of information and content with different groups of people based on their differing relationships. Configuring settings for each user is a great burden for a user, and most of the time, settings are not evident to users, and hence some automatic or semi-automatic mechanism should be available to reduce the privacy configuration efforts. Increasing user-driven contribution has also led to other kinds of problems, like spam and abusive message contents. The authors refer both of these types as social spam, which not only consumes extra resources of site, but also spoils the user experience and creates legal issues. In large scale SNS, human moderation becomes out of hand, and there is a need for machine intelligence to get rid of such spammers in an effective way. In social networks, users' actions, contributions, demographic details, et cetera can be tracked, and necessary measures can be taken if unwanted behavior about a particular user is detected. One can make a user model of reputation to identify troublesome users and ban their activities temporarily or permanently whenever needed. User reputation systems help to improve the user experience of a site, enrich content quality, and provide incentives for users to become better, more active participants. In this chapter, authors describe issues related to privacy, social spamming, and show the measures to handle them by nearly automatic ways. The chapter also shows the making of a user reputation system and its applicability in social network.

Devising access control systems to support needs and capabilities of users, as well as the security requirements of organisations, is a key challenge faced in many of today's business environments. If users are to behave securely, they must not be overburdened with unworkable authentication policies and methods. Yet the prevailing alphanumeric password can be a double-edged sword: secure passwords are inherently difficult to recall and vice-versa. Consequentially, a growing number of alternatives are emerging. In this chapter, the authors describe one novel scheme - a musical password. Musipass was designed with the user in mind and is tailored toward the task of authentication on the Web, where biometric and token-based systems have proved unsuccessful in replacing the flawed, yet prevalent traditional password. This chapter, which includes discussion on current thinking in the field of authentication, will be of interest to information managers, security practitioners, and HCI professionals.

A comprehensive and integrated view on the security of an Information System considering all its parts (hardware, software, human factor, data, and the impact of real world) is presented in the chapter. The security of information systems cannot be solved only by management of Information Technologies,

In extended enterprises, the traditional dichotomy between insiders and outsiders becomes blurred: consultants, freelance administrators, and employees of business partners are both inside and outside of the enterprise. As a consequence, traditional controls to mitigate insider and outsider threat do not completely apply to this group of indivuduals, and additional or improved solutions are required. The ISO 27002 security standard, recognizing this need, proposes third-party agreements to cover security requiremens in B2B relationships as a solution, but leaves open how to realize them to counter security problems of inter-organizational collaboration. To reduce this gap, this chapter presents a method for identifying external insiders and analyzing them from two perspectives: as threats and as possible mitigation. The output of the method provides input for further engineering of third-party agreements related to non-measurable IT security agreements; the authors illustrate the method using a manufacturer-retailer example. This chapter also provides an overview of the external insider threat, consisting of a review of extended enterprises and of challenges involved with external insiders.

With the widespread dissemination of Information Technology in enterprises and households in the mid-90s, discussions began on how to manage it. Meanwhile, in the area of enterprise security management systems worldwide, enforced use of the Deming cycle initially worked against the implementation of policies. Standard management systems include ISMS (Information Security Management System) as specified in ISO 27001, BCM (Business Continuity Management System) as specified in BS 25999, and ITSM (Information Technology Service Management System) as specified in ISO 20000. In contrast to policies, these best-practice management systems continue to operate today with no formal method. Management systems have, however, some advantages that policies do not have. In this chapter, the authors present possible uses of policies with respect to management systems and identify potential applications. Furthermore, the atuhors present a field study, cited here, which highlights the advantages of management systems in practice. Moreover, this chapter shows how a formal description of an information security management system can be created by means of discrete-event systems theory and how an objective function for management systems can be defined.

Identity theft and identity fraud are terms used to refer to all types of crime in which someone wrongfully obtains and uses another person's personal data in some way that involves fraud or deception, typically for economic gain. In spite of the different possible attacks discussed in later chapters, this chapter can focus on phishing attacks – a form of indirect attacks– such as an act of sending an e-mail to a user falsely claiming to be an established legitimate enterprise in an attempt to scam the user into surrendering private information that will be used for identity theft. The e-mail directs the user to visit a Web site where they are asked to update personal information, such as passwords and credit card, social security, and bank account numbers, that the legitimate organization already has. Phishing attacks use 'spoofed' e-mails and fraudulent websites designed to fool recipients into divulging personal financial data such as credit card numbers, account usernames and passwords, social security numbers, et cetera. The vulnerabilities on various phishing methods such as domain name spoofing, URL obfuscation, susceptive e-mails, spoofed DNS and IP addresses, and cross site scripting are analyzed, and the chapter concludes that an integrated approach is required to mitigate phishing attacks.

The importance of information and Information Systems for modern organizations as a key differentiator is increasingly recognized. Sharpened legal and regulatory requirements have further promoted to see information security governance as part of corporate governance. More than 1.37 million organizations worldwide are implementing a standards based management system, such as ISO9001 or others. To implement information security governance and compliance in an effective, efficient, and sustainable way, the authors integrate these standard based management systems with different information security governance frameworks and the requirements of the international ISO/IEC 27001 information security management standard to a holistic information security governance model. In that way information security is part of all strategic, tactical, and operational business processes promotes corporate governance and living information security. The implementation of this innovative holistic model in several organizations and the case studies results are described.

This chapter presents a method of mapping solution elements to regions of the problem space. Security requires complete, effective, and comprehensive coverage. Existing methodologies can enumerate known weaknesses and common solution elements. But not every solution is right for every situation. Moreover, any weakness in any component, phase, or activity can compromise the entire system. The method presented here helps map solutions to problems, and also brings attention to what might be missing. The approach, called a construct grid, divides the conceptual problem space along multiple dimensions. The space along each dimension is defined as a continuum with identifiable regions of concern. The chapter provides examples of several dimensions and the types of concerns used to define the regions of concern.

In organizations, employee behaviour has a considerable impact on information security. The organizational culture (OC) that shapes acceptable employee behaviours is therefore significant. A large body of literature exists that calls for the cultivation of security culture to positively influence information security related behaviour of employees. However, there is little research examining OC that enables the implementation of information security. The authors address the unsubstantiated claim that there is an important relationship between OC and the ability to successfully implement information security. Findings suggest that security practices can be successfully implemented within eight organizational culture characteristics. Investigation of these organizational culture characteristics from a security perspective is an important step toward future empirical research aimed at understanding the relationship between OC and the implementation of systematic improvement of security practices. The research and practical implications of these findings are discussed, and future research areas are explored.

Due to the fast progressing of the Information Technology, the issues of the information security became more important for the industry recently. Since the scopes of the information security are so broad, it hardly can be absolutely safety, not to mention only the limited resources are provided. The possible solution to enhance the security of present IT environment is to plan the safe and sound information flow (includes the strategy flow, risk management flow, and logistic flow) by integrated planning, based on the company integrated operation modes.

This chapter presents a system for information security management based on adaptative security policy using user's behavior analysis in Information Technology. This system must be able to acquire information about the environment, space, time, equipment, hardware, and software. This information is used in the user behavior analysis. This work proposes that, based on the evidence of the user behavior, it is possible to trust or not trust the user. Levels of trust are released according to the user behavior and the rules that were previously established for the parameters, which help to establish the evidences of

management framework is explained. The effect of using automated auditing tools to detect compliance failures against internal control points in unmanaged business processes is investigated. Risk exposure of a business process due to compliance failures is analyzed, and the factors that affect the risk exposure of a business process are evaluated.

Chapter 23
Loss of Data: Reflective Case Studies 405
Ian Rosewall, Deakin University, Australia
Matt Warren, Deakin University, Australia

This chapter will focus upon the impact of Generation F - the Facebook Generation - and their attitudes to security. The chapter is based around discussing the loss of data, the prevention approaches and enforcement policies that are currently being investigated, and the implications that this has upon the modern, working environment. The changing landscape of work presents the issue of the Need to Know against the modern, working practises of Need to Share, a conflict that needs to be resolved as a matter of urgency. Many hold the view that it would be wrong to return to the Cold War scenario, however the modern position of Need to Share leads to a steadily rising fear of Information Insecurity. Accepting this situation means that working practises within large organisations need to be reviewed without ignoring the benefits of the new and emerging technologies and yet still be vigilant with regards to Information security.

Compilation of References 421

About the Contributors 451

Index 464

Preface

In today's rapidly changing and evolving environment, IT and security executives have to make difficult calculations and decisions about security with limited information. They need to make decisions that are based on analyzing opportunities, risks, and security. In such an environment, information security management and governance issues are at the forefront of any discussions for security organization's information assets, which includes considerations for managing risks, data, and costs. Organizations worldwide have adopted practical and applied approaches for mitigating risks and managing information security program. Considering complexities of a large-scale, distributed IT environments, security should be proactively planned for and prepared ahead, rather than as used as reactions to changes in the landscape.

Security governance framework should provide alignment of decisions regarding safeguarding information with the strategy, objectives, and culture of an organization (Dallas & Bell, 2004). Also, security governance should include what, who, and how decisions regarding information security (Weill and Woodham, 2002). *What* decisions should focus on assessment and decisions, *who* decisions should focus on people, roles, and structures in an organization, including responsibilities and accountability, responsible for business and security accordingly (Korac-Kakabadse & Kakabadse, 2001), and *how* decisions on processes and technology. Active participation of individuals from across an enterprise in assessments and decision making is also suggested as one of critical success factors of an information security governance (Williams, 2008). Security culture, thereby, emerges as a vital area to inculcate proper user security behavior and responsibility (Schlienger & Teufel, 2002; von Solms, 2000; Nosworthy, 2000). Not realizing that information security is a corporate governance responsibility and that a information security governance structure (organization) is absolutely essential are some of the most common mistakes made by organizations today (von Solms & von Solms, 2004).

Alongside people and cultural factor, lack of security decisions alignment with business strategy has been researched to be the one of the biggest factors in ineffective security governance (Kim and Leem, 2004; Kim and Leem, 2005). Absence of communication of security goals and objectives is also another factor in weak implementation of any security governance initiatives. Measuring and monitoring effectiveness of security governance structure and processes has also been articulated as one of the areas where organizations fail.

Role and importance of information security culture in establishing a successful information security program has never been higher. Technical and procedural controls effectively support information security objectives of an organization through awareness of organizational security culture. Cultural aspects in understanding security goals and enforcing them play vital role in any business setting. In Chapter 1, *Investigating the Concept of Information Security Culture,* Dr. Daniel Oost and Dr. Eng Chew of University of Technology, Sydney, Australia explore the concept of information security culture and find that information security culture is a new concept and should not be treated as a panacea for information security problems. They also call for future research on information security culture, staying clear on definition and constituents of information security culture, while providing evidence for such claims. They also suggest that both and complexity and context of the culture be considered while findings and assertions are discussed. They also suggest that research be wary of distinction between behavior and culture from an information security culture standpoint.

In Chapter 2, *Assessing Market Compliance of IT Security Solutions: A Structured Approach Using Diffusion of Innovations Theory*, Dr. Heiko Roßnagel and Dr. Jan Zibuschka from Fraunhofer IAO, Germany present a theory based model for understanding diffusion of IT security solutions. Using Roger's diffusion of innovations theory, authors suggest a model for holistic ex-ante analysis of the market potential of such systems based on generic factors influencing the diffusion of security solutions. Authors provide introductions to pertinent aspects of diffusion of innovations theory, and present their model that uses theoretical elements as structuring tool in ex-ante analysis. They present case study analyses for three IT security solutions, demonstrating the applicability of their method. They also compare the results yielded by application of their model with the actual market results.

Need for services and frameworks for identity assurance has increased last few years due to propagation of open networks used for identity assertion and trust. Identity assurance is a concept defined as "the degree of confidence" that one party (usually the one receiving identity information about participants) can have about the veracity of the information as well as its closeness in portraying the intended attributes of the participant. With growth of communication over open networks, establishing this confidence has never been more challenging. With recent upsurge in use of open identity management systems, establishing trust with the identity provider is of utmost importance in instilling confidence in the assertions made by them about participant's identity. Dr. Ivonne Thomas and Dr. Christoph Meinel from Hasso-Plattner-Institute, Germany, in the chapter titled *Identity Assurance in Open Networks* (Chapter 3), provide a state-of-the-art overview of identity assurance frameworks and describe them along important trust factors of identity providers. Authors also call for research into the areas that they identify and highlight as limitations of identity assurance frameworks. To demonstrate suitability of future research, authors present a small case study to enable a service provider to distinguish between different qualities of trust, providing more flexibility in the way identity assurance is achieved in open networks.

With fast evolving technological and business landscapes, managing information security has never been more challenging and rewarding. Information security governance has emerged as one of the most effective ways to effectively manage information security while also aiding immensely on corporate governance. There are several frameworks and standards available that can enable companies to incorporate information security governance in their structures, processes, and culture. However, they need to be contextualized for effective management and implementation while ensuring alignment with corporate objectives. In chapter 4, titled *Information Security Governance*, authors, Janne J. Korhonen and Kari Hiekkanen of Aalto University, Finland and Juha Mykkänen of University of Eastern Finland, Finland use design science approach to present a prescriptive reference model for information security governance that aims to incorporate cross-functional information security management throughout the organization and frame it within the overall organizational design.

Chapter 5, *Enterprise Information Security Policies, Standards, and Procedures: A Survey of Available Standards and Guidelines*, surveys enterprise information security policies, standards, and procedures while examining the existing resources, analyzing available options. Authors of the chapter, Syed Irfan Nabi, Ghmlas Saleh AlGhmlas, and Khaled Alghathbar, King Saud University, Riyadh, Saudi Arabia offer recommendations to decision makers about policies, standards, and procedures to establish effective information security management. Authors evaluate the need, requirements, and audience for different types of security documents and their relationships with one another. This research in the chapter involved identifying the relevant documents and analyzing the various well-known and established international, as well as national, information security standards and guidelines. Authors, based on their research presented in the chapter, recommend appropriate information security standards and guidelines based on the sector to which an organization belongs.

Information Security Management Systems (ISMSs) have emerged as a valid and proven systems for effective management of information security in all levels of organization. These systems offer richer value to Small and Medium-size Enterprises (SMEs), where resource availability and selective deployments are the norm. In Chapter 6 (*ISMS Building for SMEs through the Reuse of Knowledge*), Luís Enrique Sánchez and Antonio Santos-Olmo of Departament of R+D, Ciudad Real, Spain and Eduardo Fernandez-Medina and Mario Piattini of University of Castilla-La Mancha, Ciudad Real, Spain present strategy to manage and reuse security information in Information System security management. This strategy is framed within a methodology that is designed for integral security management and its information systems maturity, described as "Methodology for Security Management and Maturity in Small and Medium-size Enterprises (MSM2-SME)," and it is defined in a reusable model that authors have called "Reusable Pattern for Security Management (RPSM)." Authors, during the last 10 years, have obtained considerable experience in the establishment of ISMSs, and during this time they have observed that the structure and characteristics of different SMEs as they do security management is more similar than not. Authors have leveraged this finding to construct patterns for ISMSs which can be reused and refined.

Social networking sites (SNSs) have gain significant attention in last few years. With a diverse demographics participating in the SNSs, users have traditionally entrusted SNSs with confidential and personal information. While users have some control over their information, the implications surrounding security and privacy are real and severe. SNSs have used a wide variety of systems to mitigate risks from information sharing on these sites, but the threats are fast evolving. In chapter 7 (*Information Security and Management in Social Network*), authors Ajit Balakrishnan and Alkesh Patel describe issues related with privacy and social spamming, and show the measures to handle them by semi-automatic ways. They also navigate through construction of user reputation system and its applicability in social network.

Effective access management is a growing concern for most organizations. Authentication plays a central role in managing access to information in an organization. Stronger authentication on one hand tends to improve security due to complex (and hard to guess) passwords, but at same time, they are difficult to recall, which encourages users to write down the password, thereby undermining security or impacts availability and productivity due to forgotten passwords. Due to importance of authentication mechanism in ensuring integrity and confidentiality of information, there are many newer and innovative methods emerging to supplement or replace passwords. As an unique alternative to secure passwords, Marcia Gibson, Marc Conrad, and Carsten Maple of University of Bedfordshire, Luton, United Kingdom and Karen Renaud of University of Glasgow, Glasgow, United Kingdom present a novel scheme - a musical password in Chapter 8, titled *Music is the Key: Using our Enduring Memory for Songs to Help Users Log On*. Their method - Musipass – is designed for user authentication to Web resources and proposes to replace passwords. The chapter presents one the most promising and innovative authentication mechanisms proposed for replacing passwords for user authentication.

Chapter 9, *Information System Integrated Security*, presents a comprehensive and integrated view on the security of Information System that includes considering hardware, software, human factor, data, and the impact of real world. Author, Milena Tvrdíková of VSB-Technical University Ostrava, Czech Republic, asserts that the security of Information Systems cannot be solved only by management of Information Technologies alone, because they are just part of a larger and more integrated system. The chapter presents an integrated approach to the security of Information System, while providing recommendations for managing the security of Information System.

Surveillance is an important and critical aspect of compliance and threat monitoring. In today's complex and high traffic environments, continuous monitoring and response, with cost management, is a daunting task due to highly evolving contexts with time and location based sensitivities. Complete automatic detection, without human intervention and decision-making, from results produced by these surveillance systems, is not possible. Introduction of human element to verify alarms generated by surveillance systems and to respond to alarms is not only necessary but required for assurance of the process. This entails impact on performance. In Chapter 10, Dr. Peter Goldschmidt, of The University of Western Australia, Australia, discusses support and assurance of surveillance monitoring outcomes and processes. The aim of this chapter, *Surveillance Communities of Practice: Supporting Aspects of Information Assurance for Safeguards and Compliance Monitoring,* is to manage and operationalize information assurance real time alarm identification and verification, by tracking the parameters monitored by the existing information assurance monitoring infrastructure and operating work systems, and then leveraging that data/knowledge to create useful and actionable information. The ultimate objective of this research is to expedite decision making process to enable accurate and rapid operational execution.

The prospects of cloud-based computing are highly promising. Companies have a lot to gain by adopting cloud based services and products to not only enhance their own capabilities while focusing on their core competencies, but also allowing for agility and scalability while effectively managing costs. The trend towards this phenomenon is strong and encouraging. It has been researched and found that while there are proven benefits to cloud computing there are inherent risks that are inadequately, at best, managed by existing safeguards. Particularly concerns around risks and compliance cannot be ignored and haven't found an established strategies or frameworks for effective management. Chapter 11, titled *Not Every Cloud Brings Rain: Legal Risks on the Horizon*, authored by Dr. Sylvia Kierkegaard of International Association of IT Lawyers, Denmark, provides an introduction and discusses different kinds of legal risks associated with cloud computing. Dr. Kierkegaard asserts "Cloud computing opens numerous legal, privacy and security implications, such as copyright, data loss, destruction of data, identity theft, third-party contractual limitations, e-discovery, risk/insurance allocation and jurisdictional issues." The chapter presents special coverage on the international data transfer between the EU and non- EU states.

In current organizational environment where collaboration and partnerships with strategic service providers are key to sustaining competitive advantages, organizational processes are managed by individuals from within company as well as from outside including a varied sources of companies such as contractors, employees of partners, etc. This raises unique challenges in maintaining integrity and confidentiality of enterprise information without hampering collaboration and information sharing. Standards such as ISO27001 do provision for work agreements and contracts to serve as basis of trust and ensuring security of information, but actual implementation and enforcement is left to companies to decide. To address this challenging situation, chapter 12, *Securing the Extended Enterprise: A Method for Analyzing External Insider Threat*, presents a method to identify external insiders and to categorize them as a threat or as a possible mitigation. The results of the method can be further used to help companies design third-party agreements to include and address non-measurable IT security agreements. The authors of the chapter, Virginia N. L. Franqueira, André van Cleeff, Pascal van Eck, and Roel Wieringa of University of Twente, Enschede, The Netherlands, illustrate the above-mentioned method using a manufacturer-retailer example, while giving an overview of the external insider threat and showing challenges involved with external insiders.

Management of different aspects of information security is an overwhelming challenge. Effective management usually entails use of a standard framework or structure for ensuring success and continuous monitoring of overall performance. Some of the most common standard security management systems include ISO 27001, BS 25999, and ISO 20000. Each organization can evaluate strengths and weaknesses of each of these available and widely adopted standard based on their own unique requirements and environmental impositions. Guiding through the process of selection and eventual adoption of a standard and its structures is a significant undertaking for most organizations. In chapter 13, *Information Security Management Systems Cybernetics*, Dr. Wolfgang Boehmer of Technische Universität Darmstadt, Germany presents standard management systems as they relate to prescribed policies while suggesting valuable potential applications. Dr. Boehmer also presents a field study that highlights the advantages of management systems in practice, while demonstrating how a formal description of an information security management system can be created by means of discrete-event systems theory and how an objective function for management systems can be defined.

Identity theft is one of the major upcoming threats in cybercrime, which could be defined as an unlawful activity where the identity of an existing person is used as a target without that person's consent. There are obvious direct financial losses, e.g. the amounts directly extracted by criminals from the accounts etc, but also indirect costs for businesses, governments, and consumers in terms of loss of reputation. In Chapter 14, *Fraud and Identity Theft Issues*, authors Ranaganayakulu Dhanalakshmi and Chenniappan Chellappan of Anna University, India present contemporary issues and challenges with fraud and identity theft prevention while proving an overview of different modes of launching identity theft. The chapter presents methods of fraud and identity theft while evaluating the impact on consumers and businesses. The chapter discusses defense mechanisms for phishing attacks and presents a content based statistical filter for thwarting phishing emails.

In recent years, with a spurt in growth of legal and regulatory requirements surrounding protecting consumer interests, companies have embraced information security governance as part of corporate governance for meeting their due diligence efforts. Several security governance frameworks and models have come to commercial successful adoption at millions of companies across globe. Use of a governance framework allows companies to leverage some of the best practices in the industry while following standard based systems for monitoring and enforcement. Chapter 15, *Information Security Governance and Standard Based Management Systems*, by Margareth Stoll and Ruth Breu of University of Innsbruck, Austria, presents an effective and efficient method to implement information security governance and compliance. The presented holistic information security governance model integrates standard based management systems with different information security governance frameworks while meeting the requirements of the international ISO/IEC 27001 information security management standard. The model has been implemented in various organizations, and the chapter discusses the case studies results as well.

Implementation of effective security solutions requires availability of and interaction amongst several solution elements, each element of which a component can be posed as a potential weakness, thereby threatening effectiveness and objectives of the complete security coverage and system. Chapter 16, *A Construct Grid Approach to Security Classification and Analysis*, presents a method to map solutions to problems while identifying gaps and weaknesses. The authors of the chapter, Michael Van Hilst and Eduardo B. Fernandez of Florida Atlantic University, Boca Raton, Florida, USA, call the suggested method a construct grid, which divides the conceptual problem space along multiple dimensions, where each dimension is defined as a continuum with identifiable regions of concern. The chapter also provides examples of several dimensions and the types of concerns used to define the regions of concern.

Employee motivations and behaviour significantly impact implementation of security measures in an organization. There are a lot of factors that influence employee behaviour towards security practices and their own intention to proactively safeguard company's information assets. The development of a security culture in an organization that promotes positive compliance and security behaviour from employees is utmost critical to success of any information security program. Chapter 17, *Towards an Organizational Culture Framework for Information Security Practices*, analyses the important relationship between organizational culture and its role in successful implementation of information security system. Authors, Joo Soon Lim, Shanton Chang, Atif Ahmad, and Sean Maynard of The University of Melbourne, Australia, identify eight organizational culture characteristics that any security practice can be successfully implemented within. The chapter presents research and practical implications of the findings and future research areas are discussed.

Despite the fact that need for IT security architecture has never been higher in recent years, there is a lack of comprehensive and proven models or frameworks for security architecture development. Literature on applied and practical aspects of the architectural design is even more lacking. Architecture for Information Security that is modular and flexible allows for changes in it as landscape for threats, and risks change over time. This not only allows for more organizations to adapt such architectural blueprint, but also allows them to effectively mitigate new risks that emerge over time. Development of an architecture that is based on industry best practices, as well as well understood and deployed standards such as ISO27001, further adds validity to the components of the architecture while allowing companies to fit their objectives and requirements with the architecture. Shyh-Chang Liu and Tsang- Hung Wu of I-Shou University, Taiwan, Republic of China, in chapter 18, *Establishment of Enterprise Secured Information Architecture*, present a unique solution to enhance the overall security of IT environment by designing and incorporating information flows (including the strategy flow, risk management flow and logistic flow) based on the company's own integrated operational modes.

Ines Brosso of Mackenzie Presbyterian University, Brazil and Alessandro La Neve of Centro Universitário da FEI, Brazil, present a system for information security management based on adaptive security policy using user's behavior analysis in Information Technology. Chapter 19, titled *Information Security Management Based on Adaptive Security Policy using User Behavior Analysis*, presents a system that analyzes user behavior based on information accessed about different systemic components such as hardware, software, time, policies, et cetera. The output of the system provides different levels of trust that can be assigned to each user, which can determine if the user can be trusted or not. The dynamic nature of the system continuously gathers information from environment and performs updated assessments for the trust levels, in an effort to keep current with changes in environment and in user behavior.

Credit fraud is one of the fastest emerging threats in electronic commerce domain, which affects both consumers and businesses alike. While e-commerce is thriving due to its convenience and choices that it offers consumers and businesses, it also poses untraditional risks that are undermining the trust and validity of the channel. Banks are increasingly investing in detection and prevention technologies and procedures for mitigating risks from credit card fraud. However, with recent data breaches are most high profile transaction processors, the use of credit card information (without having to have physical possession of the card) via Internet to make fraudulent charges are increasing at an alarming rate. The techniques for effective detection and deterrence have never been more needed for security of the electronic commerce channel. Chapter 20, Dete*cting Credit Fraud in E-Business System: An Information Security Perspective on the Banking Sector in UK*, investigates the current debate regarding the credit fraud and vulnerabilities in online banking and discusses some possible remedial actions to detect and prevent credit fraud. Authors, Md Delwar Hussain Mahdi of Applied Research Centre for Business and Information Technology (ARCBIT), London, UK and Karim Mohammed Rezaul of Glyndŵr University, Wrexham, UK, conduct a comprehensive study of online banking and e-business, paying special attention to credit fraud detection. They find that there are specific channels of credit fraud that are increasing, while imposing significant barrier to growth of e-business in the banking sector.

Use of cyber attacks and threats are increasingly gaining attention from terrorism experts. Recently, threats in cyber space have been highlighted as upcoming and most challenging channel of launching cyber terrorism attacks. Given the interconnectedness of the communications media and reliance of them for business and national defense alike, cyber terrorism has taken a central position in cyber terrorism discussions. Christopher Beggs of Security Infrastructure Solutions, Australia and Matthew Warren of Deakin University, Australia in Chapter 21, *Safeguarding Australia from Cyber-Terrorism: A SCADA Risk Framework*, suggest that cyber-terrorism capabilities are an integral, imperative, yet under-researched component in establishing and enhancing cyber-terrorism risk assessment models for SCADA systems. In their chapter, they propose a cyber-terrorism SCADA risk framework that has been adopted and validated by SCADA industry practitioners. The chapter presents a high level managerial framework designed to measure and protect SCADA systems from the threat of cyber-terrorism within Australia. The chapter presents the findings and results of an industry focus group in support of the developed framework for SCADA industry acceptance.

Yurdaer N. Doganata of IBM T. J. Watson Research, USA discusses the importance and challenges of detecting compliance failures in unmanaged business processes in Chapter 22, *Detecting Compliance Failures in Unmanaged Processes*. The chapter also explains the process of creating and verifying internal controls as a requirement of enterprise risk management framework while investigating use and effectiveness of automated auditing tools to detect compliance failures against internal control points in unmanaged business processes. The chapter also analyzes risk exposure of a business process due to compliance failure and the factors that affect the exposure.

Chapter 23, *Loss of Data: Reflective Case Studies*, by Ian Rosewall and Matthew Warren, Deakin University, Australia presents a number of real life case studies: Wikileaks, Ministry of Defence - Burton Report (UK), and disclosure issues within the Victorian Police (Australia). The chapter discusses organizational loss of data, prevention approaches, enforcement policies, and need to know versus need to share policies in a modern working environment. The chapter focuses on the impact of "Generation F - the Facebook Generation" and their attitudes to security, while discussing the issues surrounding the compliance /non compliance with enforcement policies and the dilemma facing current work practices of need to know versus need to share.

The primary audience for the book is professionals, scholars, researchers, and academicians working in this field that is fast evolving and growing as an area of information assurance. Practitioners and managers working in Information Technology or information security area across all industries would vastly improve their knowledge and understanding of critical human and social aspects of information security. Auditors and lawyers from organizations from across industries will also find this book as a very helpful resource. Often the managers are overwhelmed with solutions and technologies for information security while squandering a lot of resources on trying to understand what would work for them and what not. While there are a few publications in the area, the proposal of this edited book is quite unique and different from current offerings. By keeping the focus of the chapters to the practices and solutions that are practical and implementable, it will add huge value to the extant literature while helping organizations around the world understand and effectively improve their overall security posture. Based on the contributors' collective experience in information security and allied domains, they are highly confident that the focus and approach of this book is nothing like the ones already published. The editors anticipate huge response from information security community due to practicality and applicability of issues and solutions that are included in the book.

Manish Gupta
State University of New York, Buffalo, USA

John Walp
M&T Bank Corporation, USA

Raj Sharman
State University of New York, Buffalo, USA

REFERENCES

Dallas, S., & Bell, M. (2004). *The need for IT governance: Now more than ever*. Gartner Inc.

Kim, S., & Leem, C. S. (2004). *Information strategy planning methodology for the security of information systems.* ICCIE 2004, Cheju (2004).

Kim, S., & Leem, C. S. (2005). Security of the Internet-based Instant Messenger: Risks and safeguards. *Internet Research: Electronic Networking Applications and Policy, 15*(1).

Korac-Kakabadse, N., & Kakabadse, A. (2001). IS/IT governance: Need for an integrated model. *Corporate Governance*, *1*(4), 9–11. doi:10.1108/EUM0000000005974

Nosworthy, J. (2000). Implementing information security in the 21st century – Do you have the balancing factors? *Computers & Security*, *19*(4), 337–347. doi:10.1016/S0167-4048(00)04021-9

Schlienger, T., & Teufel, S. (2002). *Information security culture - The socio-cultural dimension in information security management.* IFIP TC11 International Conference on Information Security, Cairo, Egypt, 7-9 May 2002.

Von Solms, B. (2000). Information security – The third wave? *Computers & Security*, *19*(7), 615–620. doi:10.1016/S0167-4048(00)07021-8

Von Solms, B., & Von Solms, R. (2004). The 10 deadly sins of information security management. *Computers & Security*, *23*(5), 371–376. doi:10.1016/j.cose.2004.05.002

Weill, P., & Woodham, R. (2002). *Don't lead, govern: Implementing effective IT governance*. MIT Sloan CISR Working Paper no 326, April 2002.

Williams, P. (2008). *In a trusting environment, everyone is responsible for information security*. Information Security Technical Report.

Chapter 1
Investigating the Concept of Information Security Culture

Daniel Oost
University of Technology, Australia

Eng Chew
University of Technology, Australia

ABSTRACT

The concept of an "information security culture" is relatively new. A review of published research on the topic suggests that it is not the information security panacea that has been suggested. Instead, it tends to refer to a range of existing techniques for addressing the human aspect of information security, oversimplifying the link between culture and behaviour, exaggerating the ease with which a culture can be adjusted, and treating culture as a monolith, set from the top. Evidence for some of the claims is also lacking. This chapter finds that the term "information security culture" is ambiguous and vague enough to suggest the possibility of achieving an almost mystical state, whereby behaviour consistent with information security is second nature to all employees, but when probed does not deliver. Instead, future research should be clear about what it considers information security culture to be, should provide evidence for claims, and should take complexity and context seriously.

INTRODUCTION

Information security culture has been defined in different ways. Some authors see an information security culture as a goal to be achieved. For example, von Solms (2000) calls for the creation of a culture of information security within organizations, "by instilling the aspects of information security to every employee as a natural way of performing his or her daily job" (p. 618). Similarly, Schlienger and Teufel (2002) suggest that "Security culture should support all activities in a way, that information security becomes a natural aspect in the daily activities of every employee" (p. 7). Other researchers with definitions along these lines include Vroom and von Solms (2004) and

DOI: 10.4018/978-1-4666-0197-0.ch001

Thomson et al (2006). In contrast, Ngo et al (2005) allow for information security culture to refer to "how things are done (i.e. accepted behaviour and actions) by employees and the organisation as a whole, in relation to information security" (p. 68), not just a situation where behaviour is 'naturally' consistent with information security principles.

For Martins and Eloff (2002) an information security culture emerges from employee behaviour in relation to information security, which over time ends up being equated with the 'ways things are done around here'. May (2003) equates an information security culture with internal acceptance of the idea that information security is vital for a successful business. Knapp et al (2006) build a security culture construct based on the extent to which employees value the importance of security, how the culture promotes good security practices, whether security has traditionally been considered an important organizational value that fosters security-minded thinking, and whether practicing good security is the accepted way of doing business and a key norm shared by organizational members.

As Ruighaver et al (2007) point out some authors' use the term 'information security culture' without clarifying exactly what they mean by it. Despite this criticism Ruighaver et al do not go on to provide a definition. Instead, they declare that the concept of a security culture is too complex to be explained by a single framework, and hence are hesitant to even define it. In place of such a definition, Ruighaver et al recommend the use of Detert et al's (2000) organizational culture framework for studying an organization's security culture. This framework was developed as a synthesis of different organizational culture research, and consists of eight dimensions of organizational culture: 1) the basis of truth and rationality, 2) the nature of time and time horizon, 3) motivation, 4) stability versus change/innovation/personal growth, 5) orientation to work, task, co-workers, 6) isolation versus collaboration/cooperation, 7) control, coordination and responsibility, and 8) orientation and focus – internal and/or external.

The use of Detert et al's framework as a theoretical resource by Ruighaver et al (and Chia et al 2002) is a deviation from the more frequent reference to Edgar Schein's work on organizational culture (e.g. Schein, 1992) by information security culture researchers (e.g. Schlienger and Teufel 2002, 2003a, 2003b; Thomson et al 2006; Thomson and von Solms 2005; Vroom and von Solms 2004; Zakaria 2004). These researchers relate elements of information security culture to Schein's distinction between three aspects of organizational culture: 'artefacts and creations', 'collective values, norms and knowledge', and 'basic assumptions and beliefs'. Each of these aspects is seen as being interrelated with the next, and increasingly difficult for a researcher to access.

The variety of opinions on what defines information security culture, reference to the concept without explaining what is meant by it and the different theoretical resources authors draw upon to investigate it, creates some confusion when trying to review research on the concept. The variety of approaches is not a problem in of itself, as it may well lead to new insights that a single unified way of looking at the concept could not do, but it does leave the question of what is being addressed somewhat in abeyance. In this context, this paper outlines and critiques published research on the relatively new concept of an 'information security culture'. Specifically, it suggests that rather than providing new avenues to address the human aspect of information security, the research tends to refer to a range of existing techniques, oversimplifies the link between culture and behaviour, and exaggerates the ease with which a culture may be adjusted. Further, evidence for the claims made by the authors is frequently lacking. The paper concludes by highlighting the importance of taking context into account when researching information security culture, and points to how a *phronetic* approach to research might one way to do this.

What Does Information Security Culture add to the Understanding of Information Security?

Despite information security culture researchers attempting to approach information security problems from new angles, informed by theorists such as Schein and Detert et al, it is questionable whether their suggestions are new or distinctly 'cultural'. Indeed, the normative responses to information security culture needs reflect a range of actions that relate to well established and conventional managerial practices. In some cases the response is to implement new policies. For example in the form of information security management standards (e.g. May 2003) or policies and procedures on how to act securely (Thomson et al 2006; Thomson and von Solms 2005; von Solms and von Solms 2004). Researchers have also promoted particular human resource management solutions, whether they be the provision of education/training on how to behave securely (e.g. Leach 2003; Lewandowski 2005; Schlienger and Teufel 2002; Thomson et al 2006; von Solms and von Solms 2004) or the screening of potential employees (Kuusisto et al 2004; Schlienger and Teufel 2002). Other 'solutions' have included 'motivating' employees to encourage them to behave in a secure way (Leach 2003; Schlienger and Teufel 2002) and emphasising the importance of top management support for information security practices (e.g. Dutta and McCrohan 2002; Knapp et al 2006; Kuusisto 2004; Leach 2003; May 2003; Thomson et al 2006; Thomson and von Solms 2005; von Solms and von Solms 2004). While the actions listed above may well prove to be beneficial to organizations that carry them out, what is questionable is whether it is useful or appropriate to label them as constitutive of a new information security culture project.

The simplicity and lack of innovation inherent in the information security culture approach is exemplified by Schlienger and Teufel's (2003b) statement that "[o]n the basis of internal communication, training, education and exemplary acting of managers, a culture can be developed step by step" (p. 8). The recommended elements – communication, training, education, and management support have been associated with good information security practices, long before the notion of 'culture' was mobilized. It is difficult to see what is distinct about the notion of an information security culture from Siponen's (2000) definition of security awareness. Siponen defines this as "a state where users in an organization are aware of – ideally committed to – their security mission (often expressed in end-user security guidelines)" (p. 31). If we compare this with, for example, Thomson et al's (2006) discussion on the cultivation of an organizational information security culture whereby "employees learn about, and integrate, acceptable information security skills into their daily behaviour" (p. 7), the differences are far from significant. Security culture in these terms looks very much like the established notion of information security awareness. Indeed, it is telling that Dhillon (1999) can write about the management and control of computer misuse without invoking the term 'information security culture'. Similarly Nosworthy (2000) suggests a range of ways to "educate the people of the organization to successfully implement the requirements of the information security policy" (p. 337) without mentioning the need for an information security culture. Another example is Trompeter and Eloff's (2001) paper on 'socio-ethical controls' in information security which is also without reference to culture.

To make a case for the distinctiveness of the information security culture approach is particularly difficult if you consider that, as noted above, Ruighaver et al (2007) reviewed the literature on the topic, yet hesitated to provide a definition of a security culture. This is not to claim that all the suggestions by information security culture researchers can be easily folded into prior research on good information security practices, but rather that the notion of culture is not itself the source of distinction or contribution in thinking about information security. This literature on information security culture can thus be best regarded as having made some contribution to understanding how to promote information security; it is just that this contribution is not particularly cultural in character. Key contributions here include:

- Koh et al (2005) recommendation for the formalisation of social participation activities in relation to security governance – an increase in a sense of responsibility and ownership of security issues by security personnel should result
- Kuusistio (2004) suggestion that a unified image of how security should be conducted and thought about must be communicated to customers and other organisations
- Leach (2003) promotion of the creation of a strong psychological contract with the employer
- Schlienger and Teufel (2002) suggestion to involve the users in security decisions, with the how's and why's to be explained
- von Solms (2000) call for changing of awareness programs into "continuous corporate information security plans, starting from the moment an employee is taken on board" (p. 618)

Despite these suggestions not being easy to pigeon hole into existing information security research topics, they do not they appear to cohere as distinctly 'cultural'. Even if an argument were made for their unity, the question remains as to what the cultural label adds to the understanding of information security problems, over and above the long recognised 'human factor'. The creation of a new term for an existing problem area does nothing to advance understanding of the existing area, and could potentially create confusion and divide efforts.

An Oversimplified Link between Culture and Behaviour

One effect of referring to an information security culture is to give the impression that if you know an organization's security culture you will know how its members will behave in relation to security issues. However, the idea that organizational culture should only be conceptualised as something so uniform and deterministic has been criticised by organization studies researchers.

Martin (2002) distinguishes three perspectives on organizational culture. The first is the integration perspective. This perspective

focuses on those manifestations of a culture that have mutually consistent interpretations. An integration portrait of a culture sees consensus (although not necessarily unanimity) throughout an organization. From the integration perspective, culture is like a solid monolith that is seen the same way by most people, no matter which angle they view it (p. 94).

Second, the differentiation perspective

focuses on cultural manifestations that have inconsistent interpretations, such as when top executives announce a policy and then behave in a policy-inconsistent manner. From the differentiation perspective, consensus exists within an organization – but only at lower levels of analysis, labelled "subcultures." Subcultures may exist in harmony, independently, or in conflict with each other. Within a subculture all is clear; ambiguity is banished to the interstices between subcultures (p. 94).

Third, the fragmentation perspective

conceptualises the relationship among cultural manifestations as neither clearly consistent nor clearly inconsistent. Instead, interpretations of cultural manifestations are ambiguously related to each other, placing ambiguity, rather than clarity, at the core of culture. In the fragmentation view, consensus is transient and issue specific (p. 94).

Martin advocates examining all of the perspectives in a single study in order to gain a fuller understanding of the complexities involved in studying organizational culture. Despite this, the literature on information security culture is dominated by the integration perspective. Following Martin, this suggests not only that the information security culture literature is lacking in distinctiveness, but also that it is blinded to the possibility of differences and ambiguities that are inherent in cultural phenomena.

Suggestive of a bias towards avoiding ambiguity, the assumption that an employee only belongs to one culture has been highlighted by Straub et al (2002). However, some information security culture researchers highlight the possibility of multiple cultures existing within one organization (e.g. Helokunnas and Kuusisto 2003; Kuusito et al 2004). Acknowledgement of this complexity suggests a more realistic treatment of the possibility (or otherwise) of creating an information security culture. There is still, however, the danger recently highlighted by Leidner and Kayworth (2006):

the assumption that all individuals within a given cultural unit will respond in a consistent fashion based on the group's cultural values. The potential problem with this view is it does not take into account the possibility for individual differences within the particular cultural unit that may lead to different behavioural outcomes (p. 381)

An example of this assumption is Thomson and von Solms (2005) statement that:

Since, the corporate culture of an organisation determines the behaviour of employees in an organisation; it should be used to influence these behaviour patterns of employees towards the protection of information as envisioned by the Board of Directors (p. 72)

The possibility that an organization has a variety of subcultures that do not share the same view of information security, and that even within these culturally consistent groups some individuals may respond differently to the same stimulus seems lost in this simplistic view whereby culture determines behaviour. Culture trumping individual agency is a peculiar conceptual problem within a discipline that deals with the problem of the 'insider', the disgruntled or devious employee who takes advantage of their position to break the rules, who surely epitomises the exercise of agency in the face of structures set to limit it. Creating awareness of information security policies is one thing, consistently determining what an employee will do with this awareness seems quite another. Even if a consistent organization-wide set of responses to stimuli that related to information security (potentially a wide range of stimuli) could be instituted, this also raises the question of what happens to employees' innovative and creative instincts which by definition transcend existing rules. Perhaps information security research that considers consistent responses to stimuli should be confined to that which deals with hard measures that leave little room for the exercise of agency. For example, more than merely a desire to break policy is required to decrypt a file without the required credentials.

EASE WITH WHICH TO CHANGE A CULTURE EXAGGERATED

Another implication of the current literature on information security culture is that it gives the impression that culture is a variable that can be adjusted by management, which will in turn lead to a consistent and uniform change in employee behaviour that reflects organizational security policy. As an example, Ernst & Young's 2004 Global Information Security Survey contains statements that reflect this sentiment: "We expect that incidents – particularly internal ones – will proliferate unless senior management makes information security a core management and governance function – a cultural imperative" (p. 3). This assumption of the cultural potency of senior managers continues throughout the report: "There is no factor more influential than senior management setting the tone that information security is important and that individuals – including senior and middle management – will be held accountable for their actions" (p. 6). The received wisdom is that senior management "must lead the charge in creating a security-conscious culture based on individual awareness and personal accountability for conduct" (p. 7).

Whilst Ernst and Young's report can be expected to appeal to the perceived needs and anxieties of their managerial clients, information security culture researchers have drawn similar conclusions. For example, Ruighaver et al's (2007) comment that "[i]nformation security is, in general, a management problem and the security culture reflects how management handles this problem" (p. 56). von Solms and von Solms (2004) provide another example when they claim:

if management wants their employees to act in a specific way that is beneficial to the organization, they need to dictate the behaviour of the employees. This can be done by expressing collective values, norms and knowledge, through defining specific policies and procedures. These policies and procedures should reflect the underlying assumptions and beliefs of management (p. 277)

Perhaps the best example of an information security researcher suggesting security culture can be adjusted by management is provided by Leach (2003) when he writes that: "It is a simple matter of leadership. Strong leadership creates a strong culture, and a strong culture gives clear direction to staff at all levels" (p. 692)

These statements are reminiscent of the over-simplified promises that some organizational researchers started offering in the 1980s. As Martin (2002) critiques:

Organizations could supposedly develop 'strong' cultures, becoming havens of harmony in which employees shared their leader's beliefs, assumptions, and vision for the company [...] It offered a leader-focused way to achieve agreement, on issues where it mattered most, in organizational domains that seemed riddled with misunderstanding, confusion, unspoken dissent, and sometimes, overt conflict (p. 8)

Martin describes this as a Lazarus of an idea that is periodically resurrected, despite its over-simplified and managerial fad nature, the lack of evidence for some claims, and the financial woes that beset the companies initially held up as exemplars of strong culture success. Complexity and ambiguity are ignored in favour of the integrative view of culture, as discussed in the previous section. This is not to suggest that management does not have an important part to play in influencing the behaviour of employees, but rather that is problematic that management can 'control' culture unilaterally. Indeed Knapp et al (2006) have found survey based evidence for their impact on 'security culture' (as they construct it). What is warranted, however, is caution when deciding whether to accept statements that propose that an information security culture is a 'simple matter of leadership' (e.g Leech, 2003). If there is a safe assumption, it is that culture is not simple.

The need for caution is also pertinent in the face of research by Leidner and Kayworth (2006) which found that: "the overwhelming focus in both national and organizational culture IS research has been to treat culture as being stable, persistent, and difficult to change" (p. 370). Indeed, several information security publications have given primacy to existing organizational culture by suggesting security policies be adapted to suit it. For example, Dhillon (1999) writes: "Since the security policy of an enterprise largely depends on the prevalent organizational culture, the choice of individual elements is case specific" (p. 174). Another example is contained within ISO 17799, a de jure information security management standard (Backhouse et al 2006). This standard refers to "an approach and framework to implementing, maintaining, monitoring, and improving information security that is consistent with the organizational culture" (p. ix) as a critical success factor. Some further examples include: Nosworthy's (2000) claim that culture can determine what is practical or otherwise to implement in terms of information security policy, Siponen's (2000) suggestion that creating information security awareness (arguably security culture related) is dependent on the organization in question, and requires an understanding of its culture, and Spurling's (1995) description of the need for computer security awareness and commitment efforts to suit the culture of his organization

If organizational culture is typically difficult to change and not as monolithic as some researchers assume, then suggestions on how to go about building a security culture should be quite nuanced and complex. Despite this, researchers continue to claim that cultural management is quite simple. For example May (2003) suggests that "[i]f security is gradually incorporated into the daily processes and procedures it becomes part of the culture of the business and not an expensive overhead" (p. 12) and, as referred to previously, Schlienger and Teufel (2003b) suggest that "[o]n the basis of internal communication, training, education and exemplary acting of managers, a culture can be developed step by step" (p. 8). An extreme example of this tendency can be found in Vroom and Von Solms' (2004) claim that:

> *[O]rganizational culture can be changed. Firstly, organizational behaviour is used to change the shared values and knowledge of the group. Once group behaviour begins to alter, it would influence the individual employees and likewise have an eventual effect on the formal organization. The artifacts of the organization would reflect these changes that have been put in place. Slowly but surely, by changing one aspect, it will filter through the organization at a formal and individual level and the culture will eventually change into a more secure one (p. 197)*

Note that 'organizational behaviour' is the key to changing organizational culture according to Vroom and Von Solms, yet what they mean by either term is unclear, hence any potential complexity is glossed over. The examples of information security researchers suggesting that information security culture is a variable to be tweaked by top management given previously are similarly simplistic. When compexities are acknowledged, it is commonly in respect to the length of time that cultural change can be expected to take. For example, Kuusito et al (2004) note that even if organisational members share the same values it could take a few years to form a united security culture. Ngo et al (2005) look closer at the change process, suggesting that beyond establishing, fostering and managing information security culture there is also a need to understand the transition process.

It is also worth commenting that given the days of lifelong employment at a single organization are over for most people, the time organisations have to impose a culture has been reduced. Also, as Dhillon (1999) discussed: "Traditionally, employees of a particular concern had strong ties with the principle concern employing them, as opposed to today where employees may have strong ties with other outside organizations and businesses" (p. 173). Both of these factors suggest increased difficulty involved in security culture indoctrination.

Given the difficulties noted above, empirical evidence for how to create or modify an information security culture is particularly needed. However, empirical evidence within information security culture papers tends to be limited to small case studies of existing information security cultures (e.g. Chia et al 2002; Koh et al 2005; Kuusisto et al 2004; Schlienger and Teufel 2003a, 2003b, 2003c; Zakaria 2004; Zakaria 2006), often published as conference papers. Put simply, the existing literature does not provide evidence for declarations on how a security culture might be transformed into one where all employees share information security awareness as second nature in their daily activities. Despite this, as noted above, the possibility of an ideal information security culture is claimed or implied, and in some cases instructions for how to go about obtaining one are given. Empirical evidence for information security related research in general is limited, in part due to the sensitivities involved (Kotulic and Clark 2004). Given this, making the case for information security culture research as a unique niche splits an already small pie of empirical research. Justification for this split needs to be provided, above and beyond the current state of information security culture research.

The Need for Context to be Taken Seriously

In this paper, we have argued that the current literature on information security culture is limited by its lack of conceptual clarity, its lack of unique contribution, and its assumption that cultural change is simple and programmatic. What this calls for is a more complex, empirically informed and nuanced understanding of how culture is actually practiced in relation to information security. Following Flyvbjerg (2001), one methodological direction that can be pursued in order to remedy this situation is to study information security culture in relation to phronesis – that is the 'practical wisdom' that informs people's actions and behaviour.

For Flyvberg, studying objects which are also subjects (i.e. self reflexive people) will never result in the types of context-independent predictive theory currently favoured in information security culture research. Aiming for such theories is ultimately a fruitless exercise due to the contingent nature of social circumstance – it is always dependent upon context. Nevertheless, research on information security culture tends not to take context into account, particularly those that come to definitive conclusions without reference to empirical evidence. The search for a general theory of information security culture – how to consistently predict information security related behaviour, and how to tweak this determining force to suit the needs of management no matter the situation – is hoping for a lot, particularly given that others' attempting similar general theories over time have persistently failed. As an alternative Flyvbjerg develops Aristotle's concept of *phronesis* as an appropriate approach for the social sciences, given their inability to successfully produce cumulative predictive theory, in contrast to the physical sciences. The development of the concept has been recognized as a legitimate approach to academic research (see Greenwood and Levin 2005).

To understand what we mean by phronesis, it needs to be considered in relation to what Aristotle identified as the intellectual virtues: *episteme*, *techne,* and *phronesis*. *Episteme* is equated with scientific knowledge, and *techne* is considered technical know-how, and phronesis is defined as practical wisdom. Flyvbjerg suggests that the study of people should aim for phronesis, a virtue equated with commonsense, or prudence. Flyvbjerg defines Aristotle's three intellectual virtues as follows:

"Episteme: Scientific knowledge. Universal, invariable, context-independent. Based on general analytical rationality. The original concept is known today from the terms "epistemology" and "epistemic."

Techne: Craft/art. Pragmatic, variable, context-dependent. Oriented towards production. Based on practical instrumental rationality governed by a conscious goal. The original concept appears today in terms such as "technique," "technical," and "technology."

Phronesis: Ethics. Deliberation about values with reference to praxis. Pragmatic, variable, context-dependent. Oriented toward action. Based on practical value-rationality. The original concept has no analogous contemporary term." (p. 57).

The epistemological status of the answers provided by *phronetic* research is purposefully context-dependent. Context-dependent does not mean relativistic or nihilistic. Flyvbjerg suggests that the main objective of such research is to "produce input for ongoing social dialogue and social praxis rather than definitive, empirically verifiable knowledge, even though rigorous empirical study and verification of data are central" (p. 115). Confirmation, revision and rejection of such research is still very much possible; one interpretation is not just as good as any other – validity still needs to be established and defended. Challenges to an interpretation must seek to provide a *better* explanation:

If a better interpretation demonstrates the previous interpretation to be "merely interpretation", this new interpretation remains valid until another, still better interpretation is produced which can reduce the previous interpretation to "merely" interpretation (p. 131).

In phronesis based research, rules for identifying the "ultimate" or "final" interpretation based on fundamental values and facts do not yet exist, and this will likely remain the case – rules must be interpreted by subjects, they cannot provide for their own (single) interpretation (Clegg 1989). In the absence of such rules, the process described above of interpretations competing on the basis of testable validity claims is the only basis for discriminating between interpretations. The goal of *phronetic* research is "to produce input into the ongoing social dialogue and praxis in a society, rather than to generate ultimate, unequivocally verified knowledge" (p. 139). Perhaps a *phronetic* approach to the study of information security culture (or 'awareness', or 'the human problem of information security', or however it happens specifically to be defined), closely tied to detailed empirical evidence and context, will result in more fruitful research on the topic.

CONCLUSION

In our review of the literature we have found that the term 'information security culture' is ambiguously defined. Despite this, such research offers the exaggerated promises that culture is a means of predicting security related behaviour, which can be unproblematically adjusted to suit the needs of management. Perhaps this ambiguity concerning what an 'information security culture' is allows it to promise so much, given that the mechanisms by which such promises might be delivered are not clear. Indeed, as this review has shown, in many cases it is difficult to distinguish what is new about the term at all. On the basis of such limitations, we propose that future research needs to be clear about what it considers information security culture to refer to, and how this is distinct from or additional to existing research on the human factor of information security, often couched in terms of 'security awareness'. If the research is closely tied to empirical research, this may avoid researchers treating the concept in an ambiguous way. As a means of addressing this, we have suggested that it might help researchers to take context and complexity into account and that the *phronetic* approach to research as explained by Flyvbjerg (2001) may result in more useful outcomes.

Martin's (2002) warning seems apt:

An oversimplified theory, however comforting and appealing, is not likely to be useful if it ignores important complexities in the world it attempts, imperfectly, to represent. Application of an over-simplified theory is not only a potential waste of organizational resources; it can also undermine society's shaky commitments to the academic enterprises of education and research (p. 9)

Presenting practitioners, who are faced with a complex context dependent reality every day, with a simplistic information security culture theory does not serve anyone's purposes: the theory will not deliver results, and the esteem with which researchers are held will suffer.

REFERENCES

Backhouse, J., Hsu, C. W., & Silva, L. (2006). Circuits of power in creating *de jure* standards: Shaping an international information systems security standard. *Management Information Systems Quarterly*, *30*, 413–438.

Chia, P. A., Maynard, S. B., & Ruighaver, A. B. (2003). Understanding organizational security culture. In Hunter, M. G., & Dhanda, K. K. (Eds.), *Information Systems: The challenges of theory and practice* (pp. 335–365). Las Vegas, NV: Information Institute.

Clegg, S. R. (1989). *Frameworks of power*. London, UK: Sage.

Detert, J., Schroeder, R., & Mauriel, J. (2000). A framework for linking culture and improvement initiatives in organisations. *Academy of Management Review*, *25*(4), 850–863.

Dhillon, G. (1999). Managing and controlling computer misuse. *Information Management & Computer Security*, *7*(4), 171–175. doi:10.1108/09685229910292664

Dutta, A., & McCrohan, K. (2002). Management's role in information security in a cyber economy. *California Management Review*, *45*(1), 67–87.

Ernst & Young LLP. (2004). *Global information security survey*.

Flyvbjerg, B. (2001). *Making social science matter: why social inquiry fails and how it can count again*. Cambridge, UK: Cambridge University Press.

Greenwood, D. J., & Levin, M. (2005). Reform of the social sciences and of universities through action research. In Denzin, N. K., & Lincoln, Y. S. (Eds.), *Handbook of qualitative research* (3rd ed., pp. 43–64). London: Sage.

Helokunnas, T., & Kuusisto, R. (2003). Information security culture in a value net. In *Proceedings of the International Engineering Management Conference*, New York, USA, November 2003.

ISO/IEC 17799. (2005). *Information technology – Security techniques – Code of practice for information security management.*

Knapp, K. J., Marshall, T. E., Rainer, R. K., & Ford, F. N. (2006). Information security: Management's effect on culture and policy. *Information Management & Computer Security*, *14*(1), 24–36. doi:10.1108/09685220610648355

Koh, K., Ruighaver, A. B., Maynard, S. B., & Ahmad, A. (2005). Security governance: Its impact on security culture. In *Proceedings of the third Australian Information Security Management Conference*, Perth, Australia, September 2005.

Kotulic, A. G., & Clark, J. G. (2004). Why there aren't more information security research studies. *Information & Management*, *41*(5), 597–607. doi:10.1016/j.im.2003.08.001

Kuusisto, R., Nyberg, K., & Virtanen, T. (2004). Unite security culture: May a unified security culture be plausible? In *Proceedings of the 3rd European conference on information warfare and security,* London, United Kingdom. 2004.

Leach, J. (2003). Improving user security behaviour. *Computers & Security*, *22*(8), 685–692. doi:10.1016/S0167-4048(03)00007-5

Leidner, D., & Kayworth, T. (2006). A review of culture in information systems research: toward a theory of information technology culture conflict. *Management Information Systems Quarterly*, *30*(2), 357–399.

Lewandowski, J. O. (2005). Creating a culture of technical caution: Addressing the issues of security, privacy protection and the ethical use of technology. In *Proceedings of the 33rd Annual ACM SIGUCCS Conference on User Services*, Monterey, USA, 2005.

Martin, J. (2002). *Organizational culture: mapping the terrain*. London, UK: Sage.

Martins, A., & Eloff, J. (2002). Information security culture. In IFIP TC11 International Conference on Information Security, Cairo, Egypt, 7-9 May 2002.

May, C. (2003). Dynamic corporate culture lies at the heart of effective security strategy. *Computer Fraud & Security*, *5*, 10–13. doi:10.1016/S1361-3723(03)05011-5

Ngo, L., Zhou, W., & Warren, M. (2005). Understanding transition towards information security culture change. In *Proceedings of the Third Australian Information Security Management Conference*, Perth, Australia, 30 September 2005.

Nosworthy, J. D. (2000). Implementing information security in the 21st century – Do you have the balancing factors? *Computers & Security*, *19*(4), 337–347. doi:10.1016/S0167-4048(00)04021-9

Ruighaver, A. B., Maynard, S. B., & Chang, S. (2007). Organisational security culture: Extending the end-user perspective. *Computers & Security*, *26*(1), 56–62. doi:10.1016/j.cose.2006.10.008

Schein, E. (1992). *Organisational culture and leadership* (2nd ed.). San Francisco, CA: Jossey-Bass.

Schlienger, T., & Teufel, S. (2002). Information security culture – The socio-cultural dimension in information security management. In IFIP TC11 International Conference on Information Security, Cairo, Egypt; 7-9 May 2002.

Schlienger, T., & Teufel, S. (2003a). *Analyzing information security culture: Increased trust by an appropriate information security culture*. In 14th International Workshop on Database and Expert Systems Applications (DEXA'03), Prague, Czech Republic.

Schlienger, T., & Teufel, S. (2003b). Information security culture – From analysis to change. In *Proceedings of the 3rd Annual Information Security South Africa Conference* (ISSA 2003), Johannesburg, South Africa, 9-11 July.

Siponen, M. T. (2000). A conceptual foundation for organizational information security awareness. *Information Management & Computer Security*, *8*(1), 31–41. doi:10.1108/09685220010371394

Spurling, P. (1995). Promoting security awareness and commitment. *Information Management & Computer Security*, *3*(2), 20–26. doi:10.1108/09685229510792988

Straub, D., Loch, K., Evaristo, R., Karahanna, E., & Strite, M. (2002). Toward a theory-based measurement of culture. *Journal of Global Information Management*, *10*(1), 13–23. doi:10.4018/jgim.2002010102

Thomson, K., & Von Solms, R. (2005). Information security obedience: A definition. *Computers & Security*, *24*(1), 69–75. doi:10.1016/j.cose.2004.10.005

Thomson, K., Von Solms, R., & Louw, L. (2006). Cultivating an organizational information security culture. *Computer Fraud & Security*, *10*, 7–11. doi:10.1016/S1361-3723(06)70430-4

Trompeter, C. M., & Eloff, J. H. P. (2001). A framework for the implementation of socio-ethical controls in information security. *Computers & Security*, *20*(5), 384–391. doi:10.1016/S0167-4048(01)00507-7

Von Solms, B. (2000). Information security – The third wave? *Computers & Security*, *19*(7), 615–620. doi:10.1016/S0167-4048(00)07021-8

Von Solms, R., & Von Solms, B. (2004). From policies to culture. *Computers & Security*, *23*(4), 275–279. doi:10.1016/j.cose.2004.01.013

Vroom, C., & Von Solms, R. (2004). Towards information security behavioural compliance. *Computers & Security*, *23*(3), 191–198. doi:10.1016/j.cose.2004.01.012

Zakaria, O. (2004). Understanding challenges of information security culture: A methodological issue. In *Proceedings of the Second Australian Information Security Management Conference*, Perth, Australia, 26 November 2004.

Zakaria, O. (2006). *Internalisation of information security culture amongst employees through basic security knowledge*. In IFIP TC11 International Conference on Information Security, Karlstad, Sweden, 22-24 May 2006.

Chapter 2
Assessing Market Compliance of IT Security Solutions:
A Structured Approach Using Diffusion of Innovations Theory

Heiko Roßnagel
Fraunhofer IAO, Germany

Jan Zibuschka
Fraunhofer IAO, Germany

ABSTRACT

In this chapter, the authors discuss the diffusion of IT security solutions. The authors base their research on Roger's diffusion of innovations theory, and derive a model for holistic ex-ante analysis of the market potential of such systems based on generic factors influencing the diffusion of security solutions. After giving an overview of the relevant aspects of diffusion of innovations theory, and presenting the approach to use it as a structuring tool in ex-ante analysis, the authors present case study analyses for three IT security solutions, demonstrating the applicability of the method, and the alignment of results produced by the method with actual market results.

INTRODUCTION

Contemporary IT security solutions often appear disconnected from markets, user needs and economic contexts. Several security and privacy technologies have become market failures in recent years, for example advanced electronic signatures (Roßnagel, 2006) or web anonymity services (Feigenbaum, Freedman, Sander, & A. Shostack, 2002). Economic issues are often neglected by technology developers. Instead, security solutions continue to be designed with technological factors in mind, valuing marginal increases in security

DOI: 10.4018/978-1-4666-0197-0.ch002

guarantees and even technical complexity over practical relevance. The underlying assumption is that these technologies will become a market success based on their technological sophistication and the elegance of their algorithmic design. The resulting business models are usually poorly aligned with real market demands, and fail to address important success factors appropriately.

As a quick literature review illustrates, this failure can not be attributed to a single factor. Costs and benefits of security solutions are often not distributed fairly, leading to a lack of incentive for users to adopt. Also, vendors of security technology often fail to consider the users' willingness to pay when creating their price models, which results in overprizing and eventually a lack of market success. In addition, these technologies often fail to address user requirements, such as usability and accessibility by individuals and organizations (Greenwald, Olthoff, Raskin, & Ruch, 2004). Furthermore, the success of several security solutions might be increased if vendors were to market their solutions to different customer groups (Roßnagel, Zibuschka, Pimenides, & Deselaers, 2009).

Factors that influence the market success of information technology have been well researched in the economics and information systems domains. This has led to the development of widely accepted and used theories such as the diffusion of innovations theory (Rogers, 2003) and the technology acceptance model (Davis, 1989). Also numerous theories exist that enable researchers to deal with economic factors that influence the success of technologies such as network effects (Katz & Carl Shapiro, 1994), information asymmetries (Akerlof, 1970) and competition (Porter, 1998). However, the focus of these theories is on innovations in general and only little work has been done on the economics of information and communication security and privacy technologies. Therefore, the special economic properties of such solutions have not been considered in depth.

In this paper we propose a structured approach to assess the market compliance of security solutions, grounded in the Diffusion of Innovations theory (Rogers, 2003). We will demonstrate the feasibility of our approach on three different case studies of security solutions: electronic signatures, web anonymizers and federated identity management solutions. In each case study we try to identify driving factors and major obstacles and to provide recommendations on how to design and deploy security solutions in order to achieve higher acceptance in the future.

BACKGROUND

Ex-Ante Valuation of Security

When companies are faced with a security investment decision, the management has to assess the amount of the security investment, which is a challenging task. One possible approach is determined by the costs of the security investment. Using this approach, the decision makers within an organisation define a fixed budget to be spent on security. Then, the responsible management aims at achieving the optimal amount of security for that budget appropriated. Thereby, the benefits of the security investment are simply assumed to be overhead costs and will not be quantified. A limitation of this approach is that it does not help to decide on the optimal amount of money to be spent on security (Cavusoglu, Mishra, & Raghunathan, 2004).

The alternative is to rely on the traditional risk or decision analysis framework. Therefore, an expected loss is estimated for a security breach on the basis of potential risk factors identified, expected losses and their likelihoods (Cavusoglu et al., 2004) (Matsuura, 2003) (Tsiakis & Stephanides, 2005) (Lawrence A. Gordon & Martin P. Loeb, 2002). The major challenge of the approach is to estimate the probabilities, which are required to calculate the expected losses. Unfortunately, only little data are available upon to base such an estimate (J. J. Ryan & D. J. Ryan, 2006). One possibility is to rely on statistical reports such as (L. A Gordon, M. P Loeb, Lucyshyn, & Richardson, 2005) and (Ernst & Young, 2004). Unfortunately, none of these existing data sources is without problems. Governments and security vendors have repeatedly suggested that firms under-report computer security incidents in order to avoid loss of confidence, while other observers have suggested that companies over-report the value of incidents in order to get the police interested (R. Anderson, Böhme, Clayton, & Moore, 2008).

To make things even more challenging, a successful attack's likelihood can increase through technological progress, for example by someone automating an exploit. Furthermore, the likelihood of an attack could also increase because the system's assets have become more attractive, making the security breach's impact much higher (Peeters & Dyson, 2007).

Several methods to address these challenges have been proposed (J. J. Ryan & D. J. Ryan, 2006) (V. C. Lee & Shao, 2006) (Chaudhury, Rao, & Wang, 2005).

However, when applying these models to privacy breaches, new challenges arise. First, unlike the security domain, the privacy domain bears risks that are not only relevant to the affected company but rather involve further risks to the subject's privacy (Fritsch & Abie, 2008). These risks can lead to further long term indirect costs, which comprise loss of existing customers, increased difficulty in recruiting new customers and measures to cover the brand damage (Ponemon Institute, LLC, 2010). These indirect costs are especially hard to quantify (Fritsch & Abie, 2008).

Consequently, these quantitative ex-ante valuations of security are not broadly applied in practice. Since quantitative data is hard acquire or difficult to estimate we rather promote a qualitative approach for assessing the value of security solutions.

Diffusion of Innovations Theory

In information systems literature, a variety of theoretical perspectives have been advanced to provide an understanding of the determinants of usage. An important line of research has examined the adoption and usage of information technology from a diffusion of innovation perspective (Rogers, 2003). This research examines a variety of factors, which have been shown to be determinants of IT adoption and usage, and further has been applied to explain the adoption and diffusion of a great variety of innovations ranging from new methods of agriculture to modern communication technology. In his seminal work Rogers defines five attributes of innovations, as perceived by the members of the social system that determine the rate of adoption of an innovation (Rogers, 2003): Relative Advantage, Compatibility, Complexity, Triability and Observability.

Relative advantage is the degree to which an innovation is perceived as better than the idea it supersedes. It is not so important if the innovation has an objective advantage, but rather if the individual perceives the innovation as advantageous. Advantages can be measured in economic terms, but social prestige, convenience, and satisfaction also can play an important role.

Compatibility is the degree to which an innovation is perceived as being consistent with the existing values, past experiences, and needs of potential adopters. An Innovation that is consistent with the existing values will diffuse more rapidly than one that is incompatible with the norms and values of the social system.

Complexity is the degree to which an innovation is perceived as difficult to understand and use. Innovations that are easier to understand will be adopted more rapidly than those which require the adopter to develop new skills and understandings.

Triability is the degree to which an innovation may be experimented with on a limited basis. New ideas that can be tried before the potential adopter has to make a significant investment in the innovation are adopted more quickly.

Observability is the degree to which the results of an innovation are visible to others. The easier it is for individual to observe the results of an innovation, the more likely they are to adopt (Rogers, 2003).

In addition to the main attributes, it is also important to consider the diffusion process. As Rogers characterizes it: "The innovation-decision process is the process through which an individual passes from gaining initial knowledge of an innovation, to forming an attitude toward the innovation, to making a decision to adopt or reject, to implementation of the new idea, and to confirmation of this decision" (Rogers, 2003). A model of the innovation-decision process is illustrated in Figure 1. The start and speed of the innovation-decision process varies between the different members of the social system. Therefore, the various decisions to adopt or reject the innovation are also spread over time. The dynamic of this process is a result of the changes in the information the individual acquires and possesses about the innovation (Litfin, 2000).

Another important aspect of diffusion of innovations theory to consider in information technology are interactive innovations. An interactive innovation is an innovation that is of little use to an adopting individual unless other individuals with whom the adopter wants to communicate also adopt. Thus a critical mass of individuals has to adopt the innovation before it is of use for the average member of the system (Mahler & Rogers, 1999). The individuals who have adopted an innovation form a network and with each new member the overall value of the network increases (Mahler & Rogers, 1999). This fundamental value proposition is being called network effects, network externalities, and demand side economics of scale (C. Shapiro & Varian, 1999). Until a critical mass occurs in the diffusion

Figure 1. The innovation-decision process (Rogers, 2003)

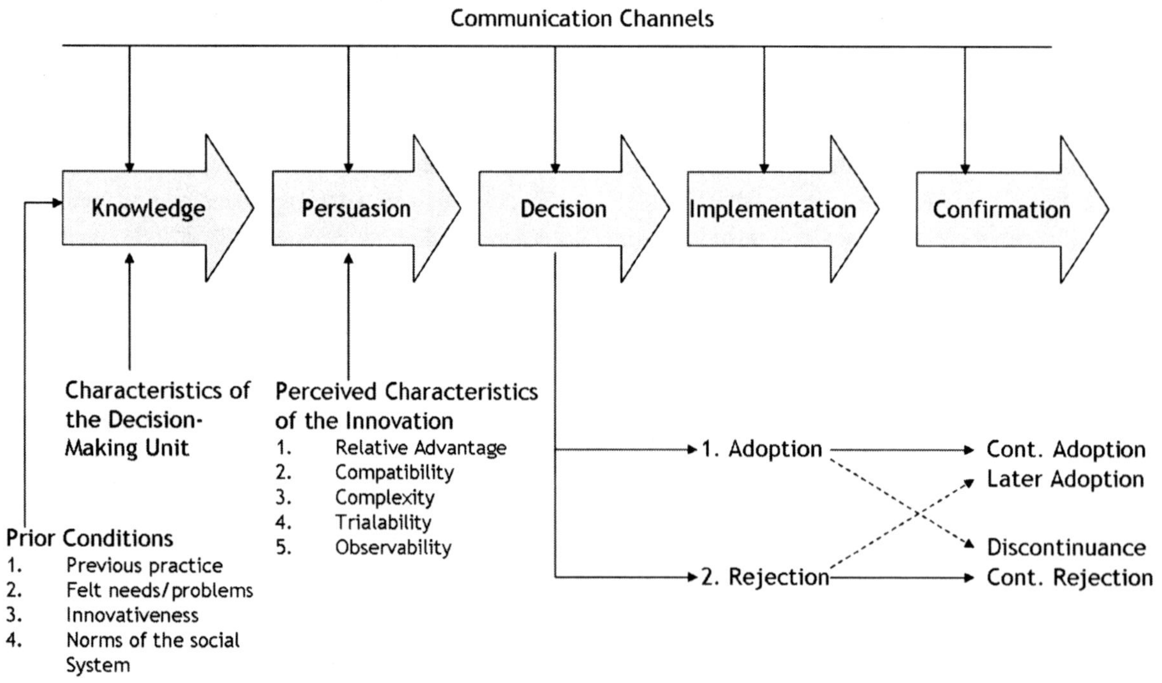

process the rate of adoption is relatively slow (Mahler & Rogers, 1999). After the critical mass is achieved the rate of adoption accelerates and leads to a take off in the adoption curve.

A STRUCTURED APPROACH

Structuring Ex-Ante Analyses Using Diffusion Theory

The adoption and diffusion of information technology has been well researched in the economics and information systems domains. This has led to the development of widely accepted and used theories such as the diffusion of innovations theory (Rogers, 2003) and the technology acceptance model (Davis, 1989). However, the adoption of security technology has not enjoyed similar attention. Instead, IT security technologies continue to be designed with technological factors in mind.

We propose using Rogers' five attributes that determine the diffusion of innovations (Relative Advantage, Compatibility, Complexity, Triability and Observability, see previous section) to structure ex-ante evaluations of IT security technology, specifically in the phase of system design. This is especially helpful in the context of security, as it directly addresses several fields where security solutions have had problems, such as usability/complexity (Dhamija & Dusseault, 2008) or observability (Ross Anderson, 2001). In addition to the perceived attributes of innovations, innovation process and interactiveness of the innovation can also be considered to make decisions about initiatives, as for example (R. Dingledine & Mathewson, 2005) consider network effects in the context of Tor ("Tor Project: Anonymity Online," 2010).

While this approach is not meant to discover new empirical evidence of a system's chances of success, it may be used by system designers to structure the knowledge available to them from different sources, such as IT security-related surveys performed by consultancies or public bodies, or academic sources. It is also not meant to improve the security of a system, in contrast to approaches such as (Jürjens, 2002). Instead, it can be used by designers of IT security systems to assess the market compliance of their systems, identify non-security-related factors that may impact the success of the system, and adapt the high-level design of the system accordingly. System designers do not need the specific numbers that form the basis for empirical analyses but rather need business requirements they can consider in their designs, while marketing often is not aware of technological affordances. Our proposed structure can serve as an interface between the two functions.

The proposed framework is rather loose, and of course to reach a reliable forecast, more specific investigations, e.g. surveys of consumer preferences, will have to be performed. However, as the case studies presented in the next section demonstrate, the framework can help to conceptualize reasons for systems' failures in the marketplace for a broad range of IT security solutions. In addition, being generic also makes the structure flexible enough to be applied in a wide range of cases.

CASE STUDIES

We have applied our structured method of analysis to three different case studies of security solutions. These cases are electronic signatures (Roßnagel, 2006), web anonymizers (Roßnagel, 2010), and federated identity management (Hühnlein et al., 2010). For each of the cases we will identify hindrances and success factors using diffusion theory for structuring our analysis. We also provide recommendations on how to improve the market compliance of each solution.

Case Study 1: Electronic Signatures

In the last couple of years several efforts in Europe have been started to increase the diffusion of qualified electronic signatures. Some examples are described in (De Cock, Wouters, & Preneel, 2004) (Hvarre, 2004) (J. V. Hoff & F. V. Hoff, 2010). Common to these initiatives is that they focus on achieving a high penetration rate of signature cards within the complete population. As has been seen with other innovations the pure presence and availability does not necessarily lead to adoption of the innovation. One example is the German “Geldkarte”. This smart card enables small electronic payments and is included on most German ATM-cards. Despite 60 million cards being distributed in Germany only 38 million transactions have been made in 2004 (0,63 transaction per user per year) (Koppe, 2005). Therefore, a high penetration rate of signature cards will not automatically lead to the adoption of qualified signatures, especially if costs and benefits are not fairly distributed and prices remain as high as they are. In addition, the network for qualified signatures does not increase with the distribution of signature cards but with the adoption of the signature. So simply distributing signature cards is not enough to obtain a critical mass. Therefore, it might be better to specifically target early adopters instead of trying to reach everyone. Also none of these initiatives has been able to provide some sort of triability of qualified electronic signatures.

Based on the market penetration rate of qualified electronic signatures up to now (Dumortier, Kelm, Nilsson, Skouma, & Van Eecke, 2003), we assume that only a fraction of the innovators has adopted the innovation.

So far the lack of an awareness policy and missing marketing efforts, as have been undertaken for other preventive innovations like HIV prevention and seat belt usage, has hurt the diffusion process. Even worse, political signals such as allowing non-qualified electronic signatures for e-government applications are counterproductive especially in the persuasion phase (Rogers, 2003). Even if potential adopters develop a favorable attitude towards qualified electronic signatures and decide to adopt, it is actually pretty hard to obtain them, because the personnel at the registration authorities is often badly informed and not aware that they even offer these products. And even for individuals who actually have adopted, the lack of applications for qualified electronic signatures and the resulting negative feedback could eventually lead to discontinuance of the innovation.

Relative Advantage and Perceived Usefulness

Actually there are two ideas being superseded: manuscript signatures and electronic transactions without signatures. Qualified electronic signatures enable users to conduct legally binding contracts with relying parties that are physically at a different location at any time by communicating over the internet. However, the user is forced to make these transactions at his PC using his signature card and card reader. So while the location of the relying party becomes unimportant, the location of the user making the transaction is fixed. Therefore, qualified electronic signatures will be a supplement of manuscript signatures (when conducting transactions over the internet) and not a substitute. The perceived relative advantage will most likely be the freedom of choice with whom to conduct business, the time independence and the possibility to conduct business at home instead of the necessity to show up at a specific location as for example in dealing with public administration.

In superseding electronic transactions without signatures, qualified electronic signatures take the role of a preventive innovation. Preventive innovations are ideas that are adopted by an individual at one point in time in order to lower the probability that some future unwanted event will occur (Rogers, 2003). Preventive innovations usually have a very slow rate of adoption, because the unwanted event might not happen even without the adoption of the innovation. Therefore, the relative advantage is not very clear cut. Furthermore, qualified electronic signatures can only be used if they are accepted by the relying party. Therefore, the relative advantage is dependent on the size of the network of accepting parties, increasing the network effects. In order to determine the relative advantage perceived by potential adopters, it is important to take a look at the costs and benefits of qualified electronic signatures. Table 1 provides an overview of the distribution of costs and benefits[1]. Obviously the costs and benefits are not evenly distributed. While public administrations are the major gainers they only marginally contribute to the costs of the infrastructure. On the other hand private customers have to carry the majority of the costs, while almost not gaining any benefits. Therefore, the relative advantage will probably be perceived as very low by private customers.

All of these trust centers are using a fixed price strategy instead of practicing price differentiation (Alessandro Acquisti, 2008) for different customer groups. The prices can be regarded as being rather high if you consider that almost no applications for qualified electronic signatures exist. This leads to further reduction of the perceived usefulness.

Compatibility

Most signature providers use a personal identification number (PIN) to authenticate the signatory. The usage of PINs has a high degree of compatibility since PINs are commonly used to authorize financial transactions for example in online banking or at Automatic Teller Machines (ATM). However, some individuals may not perceive a contract signed by means of qualified electronic signatures as a legal binding transaction, even if this is the case. Therefore, the potential adopter should be informed about the legal consequences of using qualified electronic signatures.

Complexity and Ease of Use

We cannot expect the average user to be able to understand the principles of public key cryptography (Whitten & Tygar, 1999). This, however, might not be necessary. By using qualified electronic signatures the perceived security is rather high and a complete understanding of the underlying principles is not required. For example the use of

Table 1. Distribution of costs and benefits of electronic signatures (Lippmann & Roßnagel, 2005)

	Private Customers		Companies		Public Administration	
	Costs	**Benefits**	**Costs**	**Benefits**	**Costs**	**Benefits**
Electronic bid invitations			■	■		■
Electronic tax declaration	■		■			■
Access to public archives	■		■	■		■
Electronic elections	■					■
Application for public documents	■					■
Notifying change of residence	■					■
Electronic dunning procedures			■	■	he	■
Electronic marketplaces	■	■	■	■	■	■
Automated orderings			■	■	■	■
Online-Banking	■		■	■	■	
Alteration of contracts online	■			■		
Electronic billing			■	■		
Archiving			■	■	■	■
Total	8	1	9	9	4	10

ATMs is quite common, despite the fact that most users don't understand the underlying processes and security measures. Of course it is of utmost importance that the signature application is easy to use and to comprehend and does not allow the user to give away his private key. On the other hand, the usage of a chip card reader will likely be new to most potential adopters and installment and maintenance could lead to problems (Fritsch & Rossnagel, 2005).

Triability

The way qualified electronic signatures are offered today, there is no triability. Customers are charged upfront with an initial fee and have to pay for certification services before they can create qualified electronic signatures. Therefore, potential adopters have to invest a considerable amount, before being able to test potential benefits of the innovation. However, it is possible to test electronic signatures in general by using free software like Pretty Good Privacy (PGP). But in this case different software with different look and feel, as well as a different certification structure would be tested than the one to adopt.

Observability

By being able to verify the own signature the adopter can demonstrate the validity to others. However, individuals who have not obtained a qualified electronic signature themselves are not able to verify the signature leading to missing observability. Furthermore, by being a preventive innovation the unwanted prevented event, by definition, does not occur, and thus can not be observed or counted.

Recommendations

Based on our previous analysis we now present some recommendations on how to structure the future market of qualified electronic signatures:

- **Shift costs and benefits in order to achieve a fair distribution:** In order to increase the relative advantage of qualified electronic signatures, it is necessary to have a fair distribution of costs and benefits. Price discrimination could be used to specifically target different customer groups. Also, a new price model as proposed in (Lippmann & Roßnagel, 2005) is necessary, that collects fees for signature verification instead of only charging the signatory, leading to reduced annual cost for the signatory. Furthermore, the acceptance of qualified electronic signatures could be increased by providing monetary benefits for its users. For example fees for public administration processes could be omitted for users that choose to conduct these transactions online using a qualified electronic signature.
- **Try to reach a critical mass:** Using dumping prices in the early phases of the diffusion process could help to reach a critical mass. These early losses can be compensated by profiting on the ensuing lock-in effects (C. Shapiro & Varian, 1999). An example of such a business model is the distribution of video game consoles. Vendors of video consoles sell their product with prices below their production costs in order to increase the size of their networks and to create lock-in effects. Later on they profit from selling games to their customer base (C. Shapiro & Varian, 1999). The same thing could be applied to qualified electronic signatures and the complementary product of signature verification.
- **Increase the knowledge:** A large marketing campaign is essential to increase the awareness of the technology. This campaign could be financed by either the trust centers or public administration. As stated earlier the awareness of the new technology could trigger a need for it. Also, the

gained benefits for public administration could finance the efforts to host such a campaign.

- **Specifically target early adopters:** Early adopters are the most influential group of potential adopters. Therefore it is of utmost importance to place the product within this group in order to reach a critical mass.
- **Reduce complexity:** In order to reduce complexity mobile qualified electronic signatures might be very helpful (Roßnagel, 2009). Also, for conventional signatures every effort to make the signature application as easy to use as possible, like for example including chip card reader in PCs, should be undertaken.
- **Increase triability:** By, for example, issuing free 14 day certificates, certification service providers could enable potential customers to experience the product on a limited basis.

Case Study 2: Anonymity Services

Since Chaum proposed a method for anonymous and unobservable delivery of electronic messages (Chaum, 1981) technologies for anonymous communication have been thoroughly researched. The concept has been adapted to internet data traffic (A. Pfitzmann & M. Waidner, 1986), ISDN call routing (A. Pfitzmann, B. Pfitzmann, & M. Waidner, 1991) or mobile technology (H. Federrath, Jerichow, Kesdogan, A. Pfitzmann, & Spaniol, 1997). Furthermore, several protection services that provide anonymous communications such as TOR ("Tor Project: Anonymity Online," 2010) or JonDo ("JonDonym software downloads," 2010) are offered without financial charges[2]. However, the deployment of such technology and services has not yet reached the mass market of end users.

So far only a small fraction of users are using anonymity services (D. McCoy, Bauer, Grunwald, Kohno, & Sicker, 2008) and early adopters, which are necessary to reach a critical mass of adopters, have not been attracted (Feigenbaum et al., 2002). Consequently, there is no beneficial market today for providers of anonymity services. Only as of late there is a growing body of research in the area of economics of privacy enhancing technologies. Most of the work, however, is concerned with the willingness of users to pay for privacy services (Adam Shostack, 2003) or under which circumstances users are willing to disclose private information (Alessandro Acquisti, 2004a). What seems to be missing is an analysis on possible reasons for the slow diffusion of anonymity services, despite having been available and useable for free such as the TOR service ("Tor Project: Anonymity Online," 2010).

Relative Advantage and Perceived Usefulness

An awareness of the privacy risks associated with unprotected online behavior is required to perceive a relative advantage of using anonymity services. Also, anonymity services are preventive innovations, which are ideas that are adopted by an individual at one point in time to lower the probability that some future unwanted event (i.e. Surveillance of the users traffic) will occur (Rogers, 2003). Preventive innovations usually have a very slow rate of adoption, because the unwanted event might not happen even without the adoption of the innovation (i.e. no surveillance occurs despite not using anonymity services). Therefore, the relative advantage is not very clear cut. Furthermore, bounded rationality and optimistic biases diminish the perceived usefulness of this technology (Alessandro Acquisti, 2004b). In addition, being able to surf anonymously will not necessarily lead to an advantage by itself. The usefulness is dependent on the context of the accessed information and the actual situation of the user. For example there should be usually a higher demand to anonymously access adult entertainment material than to anonymously access news or weather reports. Also individuals might wish to be anonymous when accessing some information such as sports results while being at work; they might not be concerned about their anonymity when performing the same task at home. Even reading the website of the New York Times might require different degrees of anonymity depending on the country from which you access the website. Also as stated in (R. Dingledine & Mathewson, 2005), anonymity services can also be classified as interactive innovations that are subject to network effects. For example it has been shown that the size of the anonymity sets of web anonymizers and therefore their usefulness is dependent on the number of users of the system (R. Dingledine & Mathewson, 2005). Therefore, the adoption of PETs will be rather slow until a critical mass of users will be reached. In some cases the usage of an anonymity service might even lead to the opposite of the intended effect by reducing the number of potential suspects due to the small number of people who posses the required knowledge to use such a system. Network effects also influence the performance of the system. The more users are active on a system, the better the performance of the systems becomes. This in turn influences usability, and specifically in the case of web sites, loading speeds have been shown to be a major usability factor (Galetta, Henry, S. McCoy, & Polak, 2004). Such reductions in performance and loading speeds will form costs that the individuals will weigh against the perceived benefits of adopting, which have been shown to be rather nebulous. However, the relative advantage of using anonymity services could be improved by bundling the use of the technology with different services that particularly require or benefit from anonymous communications.

Compatibility

Usage of privacy measures is quite common in the offline world. We use curtains to protect the privacy of our homes (Adam Shostack, 2003). Caller-ID blocking, voice mail services, and unlisted numbers are used to protect ourselves against unwanted phone calls (Adam Shostack, 2003). Traditional mail is usually sent in an envelope and cash has been a widely used form of anonymous payment. In the online world, however, we are used to identifying ourselves in order to access particular services. Online shopping is rarely anonymous and users usually do not encrypt their mail (A. Acquisti & Grossklags, 2005). On the other hand, users are starting to undertake steps to protect their online privacy. Spam filters are used to block unwanted mails and people supply no or false information in online forms (A. Acquisti & Grossklags, 2005). Therefore, a high degree of compatibility could be achieved, especially if the anonymity service is able to motivate its usage by paralleling similar applications in the offline world.

Complexity and Ease of Use

Complexity and missing user-friendliness of anonymity solutions can pose a major barrier for their adoption. The correct installation and usage of local proxies and related browser configuration is often too hard for users to be properly carried out (Clark, van Oorschot, & Adams, 2007). Also the time required to install the software, the added complexity of maintaining the additional software, the complexity of uninstalling software one doesn't like, and the risk that any software downloaded from the Internet may contain malware add to the complexity and limit the ease of use. Technical problems include possible information leakages due to DNS, browser plug-ins, or plain configuration faults during installation (Berthold, Hannes Federrath, & Köpsell, 2001). However, there have been major improvements in this regard. The JonDoFox-browser ("JonDonym software downloads," 2010) for example is a modification of the popular Firefox browser, readily packaged with a client for the JonDo network that is usable out of the box without requiring any complicated configurations. The limited popularity of this software might be attributed, apart from the problems stated above, to the (necessary) deactivation of several features such as Javascript and Active-X due to security reasons.

Triability

Since several anonymity services are available for testing without financial charges the degree of triability is quite good. If the trend to commercialize these services continues, the degree of triability might decrease in the near future. However, it seems to be very likely that there will be free solutions available that can be tested even years from now.

Observability

A lack of observability or missing ability to demonstrate the effects of anonymous communications is a major concern for the adoption of such services. While confidentiality can be achieved by the sender using encryption, anonymity cannot be created by the sender or receiver. Instead users have to trust the infrastructure to provide protection (Alessandro Acquisti, Roger Dingledine, & Syverson, 2003). Furthermore, without some technical expertise users are not able to reliably detect if they are really communicating anonymously. There might be indications like a symbol or message in the browser or a decreased performance when accessing web sites, but still users have to trust their systems configuration and the used infrastructure. In the context of malicious nodes this asymmetric information about the reliability of the used technology could lead to a lemons market (Fritsch & Abie, 2008). The consequence of such practice will lead to a continuous fall of both quality and value of services.

Recommendations

A successful adoption of anonymity services without some additional stimulation seems to be very unlikely. Vendors of anonymity services should try to bundle their technology and services with complementary goods in order to increase the relative advantage of their solution. Furthermore, specifically targeting subnetworks which have an obvious demand for anonymous access and ideally have a large percentage of early adopters could be a promising approach to bootstrap the adoption.

- **Information Provisioning.** One possibility to facilitate the adoption of privacy technology is to increase the awareness of users about the risks of unprotected online communications. Similar campaigns have been carried out for other preventive innovations like seat belt usage, designated drivers and safer sex. The rationale behind such campaigns is that when individuals are aware of the associated risks and the possibilities of protection they will apply the respective protection measures. Such campaigns, however, often fail to achieve the desired effectiveness.
- **Mandatory Adoption.** The most invasive form to stimulate adoption is to mandate the usage of the technology and to impose this mandate by issuing fines for noncompliance. Users who adopt will receive the relative advantage of not being subjected to the fines (Ozment & Schechter, 2006). One example of a partial mandate to adopt anonymity technology can be found in the German 'Teledienstedatenschutzgesetz' (TDDSG). According to 4 par. 6 TDDSG, service providers are required to provide anonymous or pseudononymous access to their service, if this is technically possible and economic reasonable. However, this mandate has not been enforced so far, although there are cases where this reasonability exists (Fritsch, Roßnagel, Schwenke, & Stadler, 2005).
- **Bundling Complements.** Another way to increase the relative advantage of adopting a technology is to bundle it with comple-

mentary goods (Ozment & Schechter, 2006). In the case of anonymity services one such complementary good could be to provide access to websites that are blocked for particular user groups.

- **Facilitating Subnetwork Adoption.** Adoption may start within a subnetwork. If this group is large enough and well coordinated this could lead to natural adoption (Ozment & Schechter, 2006). Privacy technology could be selectively offered to users of services which have a more obvious demand for anonymity. For example users of pornographic material could be a promising target group for the deployment of anonymous services (Roßnagel et al., 2009), since they usually have a high demand for anonymity, a high level of innovativeness and a high willingness to pay and have been drivers of technological innovation in the past (Coopersmith, 1998). However, technology designers might have ethical issues directly promoting the usage of their technology to access pornographic material. Dating services are another example where privacy technology could be tailored to a specific target group (Fritsch et al., 2005).
- **Coordination.** Coordination is a related approach in which individuals and organisations try to adopt together. For example different service providers could form a single network of anonymous users in order to increase the anonymity set and therefore the usefulness of their services. Of course such an approach will also create costs for recruiting, drafting contracts and other coordination activities (Ozment & Schechter, 2006).
- **Subsidization.** Another approach is to decrease the costs associated with the adoption by subsidizing the technology. Since some anonymity services can be used without service charges a decrease of monetary costs on the user side is not possible. Nevertheless, generating incentives for service providers to handle personal information in a new way, can allow the growth of the market (Alessandro Acquisti, 2004b).

Case Study 3: Web Identity Management

Identity Management (IdM) has emerged as a promising technology to distribute identity information across security domains (Maler & Reed, 2008). In e-business scenarios, federated identity management is used to connect enterprises along the value chain and enables them to reduce transaction costs significantly. On the web it offers the promise of single sign on for different domains and service providers, offering a common authentication and authorization infrastructure that eliminates the necessity of using passwords. This would on one hand provide improved ease of use for the users and at the same time eliminate problems that are caused by password management issues, password reuse (Ives, Walsh, & Schneider, 2004), and passwords' security flaws (Neumann, 1994). Therefore, it could make a major contribution to improvement of security on the web. In the e-government domain, Identity Management Systems (IMS) could help to introduce the necessary security infrastructure enabling online services that so far could not have been offered by public administration due to security constraints. Several different solutions for Federated Identity Management (FIM) have emerged over the last couple of years such as Microsofts Passport and Cardspace, Liberty Alliance and OpenID. The success of these systems in the marketplace has been very diverse. Some Systems, such as Passport, have not been successful and have been replaced (Cameron & Jones, 2007).

Relative Advantage

In the context of identity management, relative advantage is the utility that an IMS can offer to its stakeholders, including both end users, SPs, enterprises, and other players, compared to the previous state of the art (e.g. passwords on the Web). Examples of how an IMS can offer utility include:

- Reduced sign on is one of the main benefits provided by IMS. In the enterprise case, it lowers help desk costs, while on the web, it unburdens users of password management worries.
- Privacy is also often mentioned as one of the issues IMS can help address. Integration of anonymization and privacy-enhancing technologies into an IMS (Hansen et al., 2001) offers value to privacy-sensitive users.
- Reduction of user interaction Form-filling reduces the time users have to spend while registering. e-government applications may enable users to carry out administrative tasks online, rather than at the local authority offices. In the context of Web services, this may also lead to a larger registered user base, as the effort necessary for registration is lowered.
- Security IMS have the potential to alleviate common security risks of passwords (Neumann, 1994). However, as SSO also adds a single point of failure, IMS also have higher security requirements than analogous decentralized password systems.
- Identity Intermediation Identity intermediation, the outsourcing of user identity storage and part of the authentication process, offers cost reductions, compliance risk reduction, and increased identity quality to service providers (Zibuschka, Fritsch, Radmacher, Scherner, & Rannenberg, 2007).
- So, all in all, IMS can offer competitive advantage on several levels. However, an IMS may also decrease utility for several reasons:
- Liability: Depending on contract, an identity provider may be held liable for the identities it provides. A user employing a signature card rather than a password may find himself bound by contracts and held liable in a way that would not be possible with password-based authentication.
- Costs of certification, implementation and other IdM processes may eat up the advantage gained from the other factors.

It should be noted that network effects play a huge role in each scenario because FIM is by nature an interactive innovation. It is quite obvious that a system with a larger user base would be more appealing to service providers, while a system supported by a larger set of services would be of a higher utility to users, offering a meaningful reduction of sign-on processes.

Compatibility

In the context of IMS, compatibility refers mainly to privacy/trust questions. Trust is a key inhibitor of the broader success of e-business systems, which may be addressed using privacy-enhancing IMS (Hansen, Schwartz, & Cooper, 2008). However, trust-related previous work shows that technical measures providing trust through security are dominated by user interface issues: a user may distrust even a secure system because it is very complicated to use, it appeals less to him visually, or it produces errors during usage. Those influences have an impact that is at least as strong as technical security across all user groups (D. Lee, Park, & Ahn, 2001). Also, trust in the SP influences the trust in the system much stronger than the trustworthiness of the system influences trust towards the SP (McKnight, Choudhury, & Kacmar, 2002). With regard to compatibility with user expectations, passwords are still dominant. Especially in the web case, passwords will have to be offered simultaneously to reach compatibility with users' authentication expectations. Compatibility could also be an issue for service providers depending on the business model of the IdP.

Complexity

Usability also has a major influence on the perceived complexity of an innovation by users. Many systems require the users to learn a new authentication interaction paradigm, causing new usability problems (Maler & Reed, 2008). If the users have the impression that the system is difficult to use or to obtain, they are unlikely to adopt unless the perceived relative advantage significantly outweighs these hindrances. On the other hand, IMS have the potential to offer a significant reduction of complexity to end users, with SSO relieving the users of password management problems, and form filling reducing the time spent while registering. For SPs the perceived complexity of FIM is not a question of using this technology but rather a question on how easily such systems can be implemented on the server side. This includes potential sunk cost for installing the infrastructure and the operation of several different authentication systems. Even if SPs switch to FIM for user authentication they will still have to support password authentication, because otherwise they would exclude a huge amount of potential customers of using their services. For enterprises that want to adopt a IMS, a major factor influencing the perceived complexity will be how easily the system can be adapted to and integrated in existing business processes. If major adjustments to existing processes have to be made, the complexity of adopting the innovation increases significantly and the costs of adoption will also increase.

Triability

Triability is generally not an issue, as many IMS can be experimented with on a limited basis. However, there are also areas where triability is problematic. In the context of enterprise identity management, complete deployments cannot be easily evaluated, and assumptions about the cost savings have to be made. In national e-government IMS, such as eIDs, ex ante costs such as the price of card readers may inhibit users from trying out the system. On the SP side, it may not be trivial to integrate IMS. Even where modular encapsulated interoperable IMS modules for SPs exist, usability issues add another layer of cost and risk to lose users.

Observability

Signalling quality is a problem for FIM (Hsu, Baptista, Tseng, & Backhouse, 2003). It's hard to understand and to see the differences in applied security solutions for users. This could lead to a lemons market, which was defined in (Akerlof, 1970). In this pioneering article the author argues that information asymmetry and uncertainty about the product quality will lead to a market failure, unless appropriate counteracting mechanisms are undertaken. In a market that contains good and bad (lemons) FIMs, imperfect information about service quality causes the user to average the quality and price of the service used. The information gap enables the opportunistic behavior of the owner of a lemon to sell it at average price. As a result, the better quality service will not be used since the price it deserves cannot be obtained. The consequence of such practice will lead to a continuous fall of both quality and value of services. On the other hand, the advantages of SSO are easily observed by users. The same applies for cost reductions in the helpdesk area reached through enterprise SSO systems. However, the lemon market problem applies, at the very least, to certification authorities acting as a stakeholder in IMS.

FUTURE RESEARCH DIRECTIONS

We have presented a holistic and pragmatic approach to assessment of market potentials of IT security technologies. Going further, it would be beneficial to integrate interdisciplinary research and develop a well-structured model of viable security solutions that provides a framework to integrate the different research streams, i.e. technological, economic, psychological, legal and societal aspects. This could be used to more clearly identify key inhibitors of existing security solutions and adapt the designs. We strongly believe that following such a pragmatic approach for designing security solutions will lead to systems that when applied in practice are more secure and more successful than existing solutions.

CONCLUSION

We presented an approach that uses diffusion of innovations theory to structure ex-ante assessment of IT security technologies' market compliance, to inform system designers about potentials and limitations of the systems they are envisioning and allow dialogue with other functions, i.e. marketing, and adaptation of the system design. We applied our approach to three cases of security technologies, demonstrating its viability. Those case studies may also serve as a template of how our approach can be instantiated for individual technologies.

ACKNOWLEDGMENT

This work is an abstraction and synthesis of (Hühnlein, Roßnagel, & Zibuschka, 2010), (Roßnagel, 2010), (Roßnagel, 2006).

REFERENCES

Acquisti, A. (2004a). Privacy in electronic commerce and the economics of immediate gratification. In *Proceedings of the 5th ACM Conference on Electronic Commerce - EC '04* (p. 21). Presented at the 5th ACM Conference, New York, NY, USA. doi:10.1145/988772.988777

Acquisti, A. (2004b). Privacy and security of personal information. In L. Camp & S. Lewis (Eds.), *Economics of Information Security, Advances in Information Security* (Vol. 12, pp. 179-186). Springer US. Retrieved from http://dx.doi.org/10.1007/1-4020-8090-5_14

Acquisti, A. (2008). Identity management, privacy, and price discrimination. *IEEE Security & Privacy Magazine*, *6*(2), 46–50. doi:10.1109/MSP.2008.35

Acquisti, A., Dingledine, R., & Syverson, P. (2003). On the economics of anonymity. In *Financial cryptography* (pp. 84-102). Retrieved from http://www.springerlink.com/content/cbyufprgwjgubhlb

Acquisti, A., & Grossklags, J. (2005). Privacy and rationality in individual decision making. *Security & Privacy, IEEE*, *3*(1), 26–33. doi:10.1109/MSP.2005.22

Akerlof, G. A. (1970). The market for "lemons": Quality uncertainty and the market mechanism. *The Quarterly Journal of Economics*, *84*(3), 488–500. doi:10.2307/1879431

Anderson, R. (2001). Why information security is hard - An economic perspective. In *Computer Security Applications Conference* (pp. 358-365). Las Vegas.

Anderson, R., Böhme, R., Clayton, R., & Moore, T. (2008). *Security economics and the internal market*. ENISA.

Berthold, O., Federrath, H., & Köpsell, S. (2001). Web MIXes: A system for anonymous and unobservable Internet access. In H. Federrath (Ed.), *Designing Privacy Enhancing Technologies, Lecture Notes in Computer Science* (Vol. 2009, pp. 115-129). Berlin, Germany: Springer. Retrieved from http://dx.doi.org/10.1007/3-540-44702-4_7

Cameron, K., & Jones, M. B. (2007). Design rationale behind the identity metasystem architecture. In *ISSE/SECURE 2007 Securing Electronic Business Processes* (pp. 117-129). Retrieved from http://dx.doi.org/10.1007/978-3-8348-9418-2_13

Cavusoglu, H., Mishra, B., & Raghunathan, S. (2004). A model for evaluating IT security investments. *Communications of the ACM, 47*(7), 87–92. doi:10.1145/1005817.1005828

Chaudhury, A., Rao, R., & Wang, J. (2005). An extreme value approach to Information Technology security investment. *ICIS 2005 Proceedings*. Retrieved from http://aisel.aisnet.org/icis2005/29

Chaum, D. L. (1981). Untraceable electronic mail, return addresses, and digital pseudonyms. *Communications of the ACM, 24*(2), 84–90. doi:10.1145/358549.358563

Clark, J., van Oorschot, P. C., & Adams, C. (2007). Usability of anonymous Web browsing. In *Proceedings of the 3rd Symposium on Usable Privacy and Security - SOUPS '07* (p. 41). Presented at the 3rd symposium, Pittsburgh, Pennsylvania. doi:10.1145/1280680.1280687

Coopersmith, J. (1998). Pornography, technology and progress. *Icon, 4*, 94–125.

Davis, F. D. (1989). Perceived usefulness, perceived ease of use, and user acceptance of Information Technology. *Management Information Systems Quarterly, 13*(3), 319–340. doi:10.2307/249008

De Cock, D., Wouters, K., & Preneel, B. (2004). Introduction to the Belgian EID Card. In *Public Key Infrastructure* (pp. 621-622). Retrieved from http://www.springerlink.com/content/rqm391495220px5n

Dhamija, R., & Dusseault, L. (2008). The seven flaws of identity management: Usability and security challenges. *IEEE Security & Privacy Magazine, 6*(2), 24–29. doi:10.1109/MSP.2008.49

Dingledine, R., & Mathewson, N. (2005). Anonymity loves company: Usability and the network effect. In *Designing security systems that people can use*. O'Reilly Media.

Dumortier, J., Kelm, S., Nilsson, H., Skouma, G., & Van Eecke, P. (2003). *The legal and market aspects of electronic signatures*. Interdisciplinary Centre for Law & Information Technology, Katholieke Universiteit Leuven.

Ernst & Young. (2004). *Global information security survey 2004*. Retrieved from www.ey.com/global/download.nsf/International/2004_Global_Information_Security_Survey/$file/2004_Global_Information_Security_Survey_2004.pdf

Federrath, H., Jerichow, A., Kesdogan, D., Pfitzmann, A., & Spaniol, O. (1997). Mobilkommunikation ohne Bewegungsprofile. In Pfitzmann, A., & Mueller, G. (Eds.), *Mehrseitige Sicherheit in der Kommunikationstechnik* (pp. 169–180). Boston, MA: Addison Wesley.

Feigenbaum, J., Freedman, M. J., Sander, T., & Shostack, A. (2002). Economic barriers to the deployment of existing privacy technologies (position paper). In *Proceedings of the Workshop on Economics of Information Security*.

Fritsch, L., & Abie, H. (2008). Towards a research road map for the management of privacy risks in Information Systems. In *Sicherheit 2008: Sicherheit, Schutz und Zuverlässigkeit. Konferenzband der 4. Jahrestagung des Fachbereichs Sicherheit der Gesellschaft für Informatik e. V. (GI)* (pp. 1-15).

Fritsch, L., & Rossnagel, H. (2005). Die Krise des Signaturmarktes: Lösungsansätze aus betriebswirtschaftlicher Sicht. In *SICHERHEIT 2005* (pp. 315–327). GI.

Fritsch, L., Roßnagel, H., Schwenke, M., & Stadler, T. (2005). Die Pflicht zum Angebot anonym nutzbarer Dienste: Eine technische und rechtliche Zumutbarkeitsbetrachtung. *Datenschutz und Datensicherheit*, *29*(10), 592–596.

Galetta, D. F., Henry, R., McCoy, S., & Polak, P. (2004). Web site delays: How tolerant are users? *Journal of the Association for Information Systems*, *5*(1). Retrieved from http://aisel.aisnet.org/jais/vol5/iss1/1

Gordon, L. A., & Loeb, M. P. (2002). The economics of information security investment. *ACM Transactions on Information and System Security*, *5*(4), 438–457. doi:10.1145/581271.581274

Gordon, L. A., Loeb, M. P., Lucyshyn, W., & Richardson, R. (2005). CSI/FBI computer crime and security survey. *Computer Security Institute, 25.*

Greenwald, S. J., Olthoff, K. G., Raskin, V., & Ruch, W. (2004). The user non-acceptance paradigm: INFOSEC's dirty little secret. In *Proceedings of the 2004 Workshop on New Security Paradigms* (pp. 35-43). Nova Scotia, Canada: ACM. doi:10.1145/1065907.1066032

Hansen, M., Berlich, P., Camenisch, J., Clauß, S., Pfitzmann, A., & Waidner, M. (2001). Privacy-enhancing identity management. *Information Security Technical Report*, *9*(1), 35–44. doi:10.1016/S1363-4127(04)00014-7

Hansen, M., Schwartz, A., & Cooper, A. (2008). Privacy and identity management. *IEEE Security & Privacy Magazine*, *6*(2), 38–45. doi:10.1109/MSP.2008.41

Hoff, J. V., & Hoff, F. V. (2010). The Danish eID case: Twenty years of delay. *Identity in the Information Society*, *3*(1), 155–174. doi:10.1007/s12394-010-0056-9

Hsu, C., Baptista, J., Tseng, J., & Backhouse, J. (2003). The key to trust? Signalling quality in the PKI market. In *ECIS 2003 Proceedings*. Retrieved from http://aisel.aisnet.org/ecis2003/64

Hühnlein, D., Roßnagel, H., & Zibuschka, J. (2010). *Diffusion of federated identity management*. In SICHERHEIT 2010. Berlin, Germany: GI.

Hvarre, J. (2004). Electronic signatures in Denmark: Free for all citizens. *E-Signature and Law Journal*, *1*(1), 12–17.

Ives, B., Walsh, K. R., & Schneider, H. (2004). The domino effect of password reuse. *Communications of the ACM*, *47*(4), 75–78. doi:10.1145/975817.975820

JonDonym. (2010). *Software downloads*. Retrieved November 30, 2010, from https://anonymous-proxy-servers.net/en/software.html

Jürjens, J. (2002). UMLsec: Extending UML for secure systems development. In J. Jézéquel, H. Hussmann, & S. Cook (Eds.), *UML 2002 — The Unified Modeling Language, Lecture Notes in Computer Science* (vol. 2460, pp. 1-9). Berlin, Germany: Springer. Retrieved from http://dx.doi.org/10.1007/3-540-45800-X_32

Katz, M. L., & Shapiro, C. (1994). Systems competition and network effects. *The Journal of Economic Perspectives*, *8*(2), 93–115. doi:10.1257/jep.8.2.93

Koppe, V. (2005). *Die Geldkarte der deutschen Kreditwirtschaft: Aktuelle Situation und Ausblick*. Retrieved February 28, 2005, from www.geldkarte.de

Lee, D., Park, J., & Ahn, J. (2001). *On the explanation of factors affecting e-commerce adoption* (pp. 109–120).

Lee, V. C., & Shao, L. (2006). Estimating potential IT security losses: An alternative quantitative approach. *IEEE Security and Privacy*, *4*(6), 44–52. doi:10.1109/MSP.2006.151

Lippmann, S., & Roßnagel, H. (2005). Geschäftsmodelle für signaturgesetzkonforme Trust Center. In O. K. Ferstl, E. J. Sinz, S. Eckert, & T. Isselhorst (Eds.), *Wirtschaftsinformatik 2005* (pp. 1167-1186). Physica-Verlag HD. Retrieved from http://dx.doi.org/10.1007/3-7908-1624-8_61

Litfin, T. (2000). *Adoptionsfaktoren*. Deutscher Universitäts-Verlag.

Mahler, A., & Rogers, E. M. (1999). The diffusion of interactive communication innovations and the critical mass: the adoption of telecommunications services by German banks. *Telecommunications Policy*, *23*(10-11), 719–740. doi:10.1016/S0308-5961(99)00052-X

Maler, E., & Reed, D. (2008). The Venn of identity: Options and issues in federated identity management. *IEEE Security & Privacy Magazine*, *6*(2), 16–23. doi:10.1109/MSP.2008.50

Matsuura, K. (2003). *Information security and economics in computer networks: An interdisciplinary survey and a proposal of integrated optimization of investment* (Computing in Economics and Finance 2003 No. 48). Society for Computational Economics. Retrieved from http://econpapers.repec.org/RePEc:sce:scecf3:48

McCoy, D., Bauer, K., Grunwald, D., Kohno, T., & Sicker, D. (2008). Shining light in dark places: Understanding the Tor Network. In N. Borisov & I. Goldberg (Eds.), *Privacy Enhancing Technologies, Lecture Notes in Computer Science* (vol. 5134, pp. 63-76). Berlin, Germany: Springer. Retrieved from http://dx.doi.org/10.1007/978-3-540-70630-4_5

McKnight, D. H., Choudhury, V., & Kacmar, C. (2002). Developing and validating trust measures for e-commerce: An integrative typology. *Information Systems Research*, *13*(3), 334–359. doi:10.1287/isre.13.3.334.81

Neumann, P. G. (1994). Risks of passwords. *Communications of the ACM*, *37*(4), 126. doi:10.1145/175276.175289

Ozment, A., & Schechter, S. E. (2006). *Bootstrapping the adoption of Internet security protocols*. In Fifth Workshop on the Economics of Information Security. Presented at the WEIS 2006, Cambridge, UK.

Peeters, J., & Dyson, P. (2007). Cost-effective security. *IEEE Security and Privacy*, *5*(3), 85–87. doi:10.1109/MSP.2007.56

Pfitzmann, A., Pfitzmann, B., & Waidner, M. (1991). ISDN-mixes: Untraceable communication with very small bandwidth overhead. In *Proceedings of the GI/ITG-Conference "Kommunikation in Verteilten Systemen" (Communication in Distributed Systems)* (pp. 451–463).

Pfitzmann, A., & Waidner, M. (1986). Networks without user observability — Design options. In F. Pichler (Ed.), *Advances in Cryptology — EUROCRYPT' 85, Lecture Notes in Computer Science* (vol. 219, pp. 245-253). Berlin, Germany: Springer. Retrieved from http://dx.doi.org/10.1007/3-540-39805-8_29

Ponemon Institute. LLC. (2010). *2009 annual study: Cost of a data breach - Understanding financial impact, customer turnover, and preventive solutions*. Retrieved from http://www.ponemon.org/local/upload/fckjail/generalcontent/18/file/US_Ponemon_CODB_09_012209_sec.pdf

Porter, M. E. (1998). *Competitive advantage: Creating and sustaining superior performance*. Free Press.

Rogers, E. M. (2003). *Diffusion of Innovations* (5th ed.). Free Press.

Roßnagel, H. (2006). On diffusion and confusion – Why electronic signatures have failed. In *Trust and privacy in digital business* (pp. 71-80). Retrieved from http://dx.doi.org/10.1007/11824633_8

Roßnagel, H. (2009). *Mobile qualifizierte elektronische Signaturen*. Gabler Verlag. doi:10.1007/978-3-8349-8182-0

Roßnagel, H. (2010). The market failure of anonymity services. In *Information Security Theory and Practices, Security and Privacy of Pervasive Systems and Smart Devices, 4th IFIP WG 11.2 International Workshop, WISTP 2010, Passau, Germany, April 12-14, 2010. Proceedings, Lecture Notes in Computer Science* (vol. 6033, pp. 340-354).

Roßnagel, H., Zibuschka, J., Pimenides, L., & Deselaers, T. (2009). Facilitating the adoption of Tor by focusing on a promising target group. In *Identity and privacy in the Internet age* (pp. 15-27). Retrieved from http://dx.doi.org/10.1007/978-3-642-04766-4_2

Ryan, J. J., & Ryan, D. J. (2006). Expected benefits of information security investments. *Computers & Security*, *25*(8), 579–588. doi:10.1016/j.cose.2006.08.001

Shapiro, C., & Varian, H. R. (1999). *Information rules: A strategic guide to the network economy*. Boston, MA: Harvard Business School Press.

Shostack, A. (2003). *People won't pay for privacy: Reconsidered*. In 2nd Annual Workshop on Economics and Information Security. Robert H. Smith School of Business.

Tor Project. (2010). *Anonymity online*. Retrieved November 30, 2010, from http://www.torproject.org/

Tsiakis, T., & Stephanides, G. (2005). The economic approach of information security. *Computers & Security*, *24*(2), 105–108. doi:10.1016/j.cose.2005.02.001

Whitten, A., & Tygar, J. D. (1999). *Why Johnny can't encrypt: A usability evaluation of PGP 5.0, 169-184.*

Zibuschka, J., Fritsch, L., Radmacher, M., Scherner, T., & Rannenberg, K. (2007). Enabling privacy of real-life LBS: A platform for flexible mobile service provisioning. In *New Approaches for Security, Privacy and Trust in Complex Environments: Proceedings of the 22nd IFIP TC-11 International Information Security Conference* (vol. 232, pp. 325-336). Sandton, South Africa.

ADDITIONAL READING

Adams, A., & Sasse, M. A. (1999). Users Are Not the Enemy. *Communications of the ACM*, *42*(12), 41–46. doi:10.1145/322796.322806

Anderson, R., Böhme, R., Clayton, R., & Moore, T. (2008). *Security economics and the internal market*. ENISA.

Backhouse, J., Hsu, C., & McDonnell, A. (2003). Toward Public-Key Infrastructure Interoperability. *Communications of the ACM*, *46*(6), 98–100. doi:10.1145/777313.777345

Beautement, A., & Sasse, A. (2009). The economics of user effort in information security. *Computer Fraud & Security*, *2009*(Oct), 8–12. doi:10.1016/S1361-3723(09)70127-7

Bottomley, P. A., & Fildes, R. (1998). The Role of Prices in Models of Innovation Diffusion. *Journal of Forecasting*, *17*(17), 539–555. doi:10.1002/(SICI)1099-131X(199812)17:7<539::AID-FOR684>3.0.CO;2-S

Fritsch, L. (2007). Privacy-respecting location-based service infrastructures: a socio-technical approach to requirements engineering. *J. Theor. Appl. Electron. Commer. Res.*, *2*, 1–17.

Gefen, D., & Straub, D. (2000). The Relative Importance of Perceived Ease of Use in IS Adoption. *Journal of the Association for Information Systems*, *1*(8), 1–30.

Golder, P. N., & Tellis, G. J. (1997). Will It Ever Fly? *Marketing Science*, *16*(3), 256–270. doi:10.1287/mksc.16.3.256

Greenwald, S. J., Olthoff, K. G., Raskin, V., & Ruch, W. (2004) "The user non-acceptance paradigm: INFOSEC's dirty little secret," *Proceedings of the 2004 workshop on New security paradigms*, Nova Scotia, Canada, pp. 35-43.

Herley, C. (2009) So long, and no thanks for the externalities: the rational rejection of security advice by users, *Proceedings of the 2009 workshop on New security paradigms workshop*, Oxford, United Kingdom, pp. 133-144.

Horsky, D., & Simon, L. S. (1983). Advertising and the Diffusion of New Products. *Marketing Science*, *2*(1), 1–17. doi:10.1287/mksc.2.1.1

Kosta, E., Zibuschka, J., Scherner, T., & Dumortier, J. (2008). Legal considerations on privacy-enhancing Location Based Services using PRIME technology. *Computer Law & Security Report*, *24*, 139–146. doi:10.1016/j.clsr.2008.01.006

Lopez, J., Oppliger, R., & Pernul, G. (2004). Authentication and authorization infrastructrures (AAIs). *Computers & Security*, (23): 578–590. doi:10.1016/j.cose.2004.06.013

Lopez, J., Oppliger, R., & Pernul, G. (2005). Why Have Public Key Infrastructures Failed So Far? *Internet Research*, *15*(5), 544–556. doi:10.1108/10662240510629475

Lutes, M. (2000). Privacy and security compliance in the E-healthcare marketplace. *Healthcare Financial Management: Journal of the Healthcare Financial Management Association*, *54*(Mar), 48–50.

Moore, G. C., & Benbasat, I. (1991). Development of an Instrument to Measure the Perceptions of Adopting an Information Technology Innovation. *Information Systems Research*, *2*(3), 173–191. doi:10.1287/isre.2.3.192

Muntermann, J., & Roßnagel, H. (2009). On the Effectiveness of Privacy Breach Disclosure Legislation in Europe: Empirical Evidence from the US Stock Market. *Identity and Privacy in the Internet Age*, *2009*, 1–14. doi:10.1007/978-3-642-04766-4_1

Oren, S. S., & Schwartz, R. G. (1988). Diffusion of New Products in Risk-sensitive Markets. *Journal of Forecasting*, *7*(4), 273–287. doi:10.1002/for.3980070407

Pavlou, P. A. (2003). Consumer Acceptance of Electronic Commerce. *International Journal of Electronic Commerce*, *7*(3), 101–134.

Rodríguez, E. (2007). Fernández-Medina, and M. Piattini, "A BPMN Extension for the Modeling of Security Requirements in Business Processes," *IEICE - Trans. Inf. Syst.*, vol. *E (Norwalk, Conn.)*, *90-D*, 745–752.

Roßnagel, H., & Hinz, O. (2007). Zahlungsbereitschaft für elektronische Signaturen. In Oberweis, A., Weinhardt, C., Gimpel, H., Koschmider, A., Pankratius, V., & Schnizler, B. (Eds.), *Wirtschaftsinformatik 2007 - eOrganisation: Service-, Prozess-, Market-Engineering* (*Vol. 8*, pp. 163–180). Karlsruhe: Universitätsverlag.

Roßnagel, H., & Royer, D. (2005). Investing in Security Solutions: Can Qualified Electronic Signatures be Profitable for Mobile Operators, In *Proceedings of the 11th Americas Conference on Information Systems (AMCIS 05)*, August, Omaha, Nebraska, AIS, 3248-3257.

Roßnagel, H., & Royer, D. (2005). Making Money with Mobile Qualified Electronic Signatures. In S. Katsikas, J. Lopez & G. Pernul (Ed.), *Trust, Privacy, and Security in Digital Business; Proceedings of the 2nd International Conference on Trust, Privacy, and Security in Digital Business (TrustBus 05)* (Vol.3592, pp. 110-118). Berlin Heidelberg: Springer-Verlag.

Roßnagel, H., & Zibuschka, J. (2010). Tragfähige IT-Sicherheitslösungen. *digma. Zeitschrift für Datenrecht und Informationssicherheit*, *10*(2), 68–72.

Saloner, G., & Shepard, A. (1995). Adoption of Technologies with Network Effects. *The Rand Journal of Economics*, *26*(3), 479–501. doi:10.2307/2555999

Sasse, M. A. (2003) Computer security: Anatomy of a usability disaster, and a plan for recovery, In: *Proceedings of CHI 2003 Workshop on HCI and Security Systems*.

Smetters, D. K., & Grinter, R. E. (2002) Moving from the design of usable security technologies to the design of useful secure applications, In *Proceedings of the 2002 workshop on New security paradigms*, Virginia Beach, Virginia: ACM, 2002, pp. 82-89.

Xiaojuan Ou, C., & Sia, C. L. (2009). To Trust or to Distrust, that is the Question. *Communications of the ACM*, *52*(5), 135–139. doi:10.1145/1506409.1506442

KEY TERMS AND DEFINITIONS

Compatibility: Social compatibility, measuring how easy it is to assimilate he innovation into an individual's life (Rogers, 2003).

Complexity: High complexity innovations may be too difficult to use and an individual will be less likely to adopt it (Rogers, 2003).

Innovation: "an idea, practice, or object that is perceived as new by an individual or other unit of adoption" (Rogers, 2003).

Observability: The extent that an innovation is visible to others. Higher visibility drives communication and thus diffusion (Rogers, 2003).

Preventive Innovation: A new idea that an individual adopts in order to lower the probability of some unwanted future event (Rogers, 2003).

Relative Advantage: The level of improvement an innovation offers over the previous generation (Rogers, 2003).

Triability: How easily an innovation may be experimented with, e.g. whether trial versions are available.

ENDNOTES

1 This only considers benefits that are not achievable without the use of electronic signatures

2 JonDos has both a free base version and a non-free premium version of the service

Chapter 3
Identity Assurance in Open Networks

Ivonne Thomas
Hasso-Plattner-Institute, Germany

Christoph Meinel
Hasso-Plattner-Institute, Germany

ABSTRACT

Identity assurance is the degree of confidence another party, such as a service provider, can have in the belief that identity in the digital world actually matches with "real-life" identity. In open networks, establishing this confidence is not an easy task as participants are often located in different trust domains. Moreover, with the spread of open identity management systems, identity information is often held by designated identity provisioning services, so called identity providers. If another party shall be enabled to rely on received information, it ought to know how much confidence it can put into the assertions of the sender. In the intent to create a global standard, governments, commercial organizations, and academia alike have published common guidelines for identity assurance as part of so-called identity assurance frameworks. This chapter provides a state-of-the-art overview of identity assurance frameworks and describes them along important trust factors of identity providers. Furthermore, limitations of identity assurance frameworks are identified and highlighted as potential fields for further research. As an outlook to future developments, a small case study is presented that introduces trust levels for attributes in order to enable a service provider to distinguish between different qualities of trust, thus providing more flexibility in the way identity assurance is achieved in open networks.

INTRODUCTION

Today, many transactions in the online world require the sharing of identity information. Consider an online shop that requires our name, address and payment information to process an order. This sharing comes along with substantial trust demands for both, the party releasing identity information, such as the user, and the party that is receiving and using this identity information, such as the online shop. Users need to trust that their personal data is kept private and that it is not disclosed to unauthorized parties. Service

DOI: 10.4018/978-1-4666-0197-0.ch003

providers on the other side need to trust that the information received from a foreign source is accurate and does not pose a risk on the intended transaction.

In the traditional isolated or application-centric identity management model (cf. (Jøsang, Fabre, Hay, Dalziel, & Pope, 2005)), service providers gain this confidence by setting up reasonable technical, operational and legal safeguards that ensure that a user is who he claims to be and he can be held liable in case anything bad happens. However, when applied in the open environment of the web, this approach comes along with the creation of identity islands (Jøsang, Zomai, & Suriadi, 2007). Every service provider forms a separate "island" in which its users' identity information is stored. For users, this usually results in a multitude of user accounts, each holding duplicate identity information and requiring authentication.

To overcome the limitations of the isolated approach, so called open identity management models (Jøsang & Pope, 2005) emerged in recent years to explicitly address the open nature of the Internet. Open identity management models add an additional entity to the process of sharing identity information. So called identity providers (IPs) take the role of managing digital identities of users for the purpose of provisioning this data to parties willing to rely on it. Identity provider services can be operated by an independent service organization or can be a functional unit that is part of a larger organization such as a commercial entity or university. Figure 1 illustrates the three parties that are usually involved in the exchange of identity information when applying open identity management models (Maler, Nadalin, Reed, Rundle, & Thibeau, 2010).

Identity providers are the entities holding identity data and relying parties are the entities using this data. The user is in the middle of all transactions and controls the flow of his private data ((Rieger, 2009), (Ahn, Ko, & Shehab, 2009)). The benefit of this approach is a reduced number of user accounts, as users register with an identity provider of their choice once and use the resulting account to log in to various service providers.

However, open identity management also adds a new dimension to the trust issue as the identity provider, as an additional party, needs to be trusted by both the user and the service provider. If a service provider has to rely on the information received from another trust domain such as the identity provider's domain, it requires

Figure 1. The traditional triangle of parties involved in an exchange of identity information

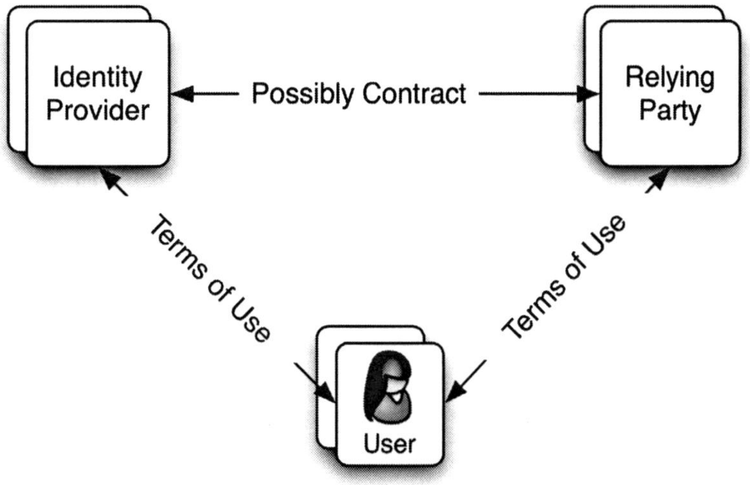

the same assurance about the user's identity as in the traditional isolated model ((Baldwin, Casassa Mont, Beres, & Shiu, 2010), (Madsen & Itoh, 2009)). This means, it ought to know about all the technical, operational and legal safeguards in place to assess the confidence it can put into the assertions made by this identity provider.

This degree of confidence another party can have in the belief that an identity in the digital world actually matches with the corresponding real-life identity is referred to as identity assurance (IAAC, 2005), (Madsen & Itoh, 2009). A lot of effort has been made to standardize identity assurance. Many governmental organizations as well as commercial initiatives have defined so-called identity assurance frameworks that identify and cluster certain security and trust criteria into levels of trust or levels of assurance (LoA) ((Kantara Initiative, 2010), (InCommon Federation, 2010)). The basic idea is to describe identity providers in open networks by a level of trust that allows instant assessment with regard to their ability to make reliable assertions. Each level of trust comes along with a number of security requirements that need to be fulfilled in order to reach the level. Companies and organizations of identity provider services can pass through an independent audit process that certifies their compliance with a certain trust level. Upon successful certification, an identity provider can use the certification in its daily businesses.

As part of this chapter, existing identity assurance frameworks are presented and their shortcomings and limitations are discussed. A closer look is taken on the factors that influence the trust level of identity data, such as the authentication process or the technical infrastructure of an identity provider. To overcome the limitations of current frameworks, the second part of the chapter suggests trust levels for identity attributes as an emerging trend in future research ((Chadwick & Inman, 2009), (Thomas & Meinel, 2010)). Attribute verification classes are defined and presented, which contain information about the verification process of an attribute. At the end of the chapter, we provided a case study to illustrate how these attribute verification classes can be used by a reliant party, such as an online shop, to express its identity data needs.

BACKGROUND

Identity Management and Digital Identity

Identity management broadly refers to the establishment and controlled use of identity. In the context of IT, the term identity is often prefixed with the attribute digital, because "IT identities" are a digital representation of the concept of a "real–world" identity. This concept manifests identity as a concrete set of attributes characterizing an entity ((Bertocci, Serack, & Baker, 2007), (Windley, 2005)). For example, the identity conveyed in your passport describes you in terms of name, address, citizenship, and so on. The set is normally only a partial set of all identity attributes. Hence, it is called partial identity and should not be confused with the concept of identity itself, which is the characteristic trait that makes an individual or entity unique. Particularly, someone else cannot assume your identity. You will always be you and he or she will always be someone else. In contrast, your passport can be stolen and/or forged, for example, to commit identity fraud.

Concrete identities, including digital identities, follow an inherent management life cycle, and it is the purpose of identity management to facilitate this life cycle (Windley, 2005). At the beginning identities are provisioned/created, which entails collecting and persisting identity information. Once provisioned, identities are ready for use. Usage comprises three stages: identity verification (authentication), identity propagation (supplying applications with identity information) and operating on the identity. Parallel to usage, identities are maintained, i.e. kept up–to–date. Finally, if an identity is no longer needed, it should be de–provisioned/destroyed.

Open Identity Management

Identity Management can be broadly divided into the traditional identity management models as the isolated and the centralized model and into the open identity management models, which emerged in recent times to address the needs of open networks as the Web and Service-oriented Architectures (Jøsang, Fabre, Hay, Dalziel, & Pope, 2005). For decades the user account was the central building block of almost all identity management systems. Being a necessity at the beginning, accounts later evolved into a valuable asset for organizations. Directories with customer, employee and partner data denotes one of the core requirements of organizations. Information stored in these directories is used to communicate with customers and partners in the outside world.

However, at the same time, an account-based organisation of identity management implies that for an organisation only those subjects exist which are currently held in the organization's directory. This means, every user is required to register before s/he is able to make a transaction with the organisation.

In the growing open world of the Internet, in which new players enter the online service market each day, such an approach slows down businesses, as customers need to create additional accounts before they can use a service.

Therefore, new approaches that supplement the traditional identity management solutions have been developed in recent years. So-called token- or claim-based systems add a functional layer on top of existing IDM systems (Cameron, 2005), which abstracts from their specific characteristics and allows expressing identity data in a common format. Standards define a common data format to express identity data as sets of attributes (also called claims) (e.g. SAML (Cantor, Kemp, Maler, & Philpott, 2005)), as well as a common language to request and send identity attributes as part of security tokens between independent identity management systems (e.g. WS-Trust (Nadalin, Goodner, Gudgin, Barbir, & Granqvist, 2007)). It is worth noting, that the user account, which represents a digital identity inside a trust domain, has been supplemented by the notion of a claim or identity attribute, which has become the unit of sharing identity information in the open world.

Open identity management systems exist in different flavours. While the underlying mechanisms to request and receive identity information are almost the same, the way in which trust is established between the partners differs. The user-centric identity management model puts the user in the centre of all trust decisions while in the federated identity management the organisation that holds the user accounts mainly manages the trust relations.

User-Centric Identity Management

The user-centric identity management uses an approach to identity management that is very similar to the way identities are used in the real world. In our daily life, every one of us possesses a number of identity cards to prove certain claims upon request. Consider a driver's license to prove that one is eligible to drive a car, a passport to prove our citizenship or an ATM card to prove our ownership to a bank account. All these cards are issued by different authorities, our real-world identity providers. We carry them around and show them upon request. For example, in order to retrieve a discount in the movie theater, our student card is requested by the ticket sales person as a proof of us being a student.

User-centric identity management works exactly this way. Every user in the online world has his identity data stored with one or more identity providers. Instead of using one identity provider all the time, the user can choose which identity provider he wants to use for a certain application or service. This identity provider is contacted to assert a certain claim, such as "This user's name is Bob." This assertion, the counterpart of the real-world identity card, is given to the requesting application. As in the real world, the application provider now decides whether it trusts assertions by this identity provider and either accepts the information or requests further proof for the same claim.

The clear benefit is, that the user enjoys more privacy and has full control over his data and knows who is using it and when. In fact, in the user-centric model the identity providers typically do not know where and what a user is using his identity for. Only the reliant parties, such as a service or an application, know about the identity provider(s); otherwise they would have no basis for making a decision to trust an assertion.

Popular technologies include OpenID (The OpenId Foundation, 2007) and Information Card (OASIS, 2009).

Federated Identity Management

Federated identity management is primarily a way to allow single-sign-on (SSO) between partner organizations regardless of organizational borders. Members of one organization such as employees of a company can link their account with accounts they might have with other organizations in the same federation. Once linked, a member can access all connected accounts by authenticating just once, allowing him to sign in to a number of applications at the same time.

The basic principle to make this happen is the trusted federation relationship established between identity providers and service providers. Identity providers and service providers affiliate into federations by agreeing upon common obligations and policies that each federation member needs to adhere to. This process is usually accompanied by contracts each federation member signs. As a result, a circle of trust forms, in which assertions about the authentication of users and attributes are shared among the federation members.

Technically, each federation member stays in control of its own identity management system, but augments this with additional federation features that allow users to link (federate) their digital identities between the federation members. Certain identity management functions like authentication or provision of identity attributes are then offloaded to the identity provider(s) in the federation. Identity consumers on the other side receive this identity and authentication information from the providers and use it as if it was coming from their own identity management system.

The downside to the federated identity management concerns the privacy of the users. In a federation the identity provider "sees all"; that means it knows which relying parties a subject visits. Given this information and the identity data of the user, a malicious identity provider could track the users behavior and would hold a rather comprehensive profile of a user. Also, without proper protection mechanisms, identity providers and service providers are in the position to match different digital identities of the same user for the purpose of creating an even more comprehensive user profile that can be used to provide personalized offers.

Another threat arises from account linkage. Once the user's password is compromised in any of the linked identity providers, an attacker has instant access to all applications and services that are connected with the user's account.

Technologies for federated identity management exist mainly in the field of service-oriented architectures. In the past, two initiatives have formed to develop a standard for the interoperable exchange of identity information across organizational borders on the basis of web services. As a result, we find today on one side the specifications of the Liberty Alliance (now Kantara Initiative (Kantara Initiative, 2010)) with SAML 2.0 (Cantor, Kemp, Maler, & Philpott, 2005) as a standard to describe identity information in an interoperable format and on the other side, WS-

Federation (Lockhart, et al., 2006), a specification developed by IBM and Microsoft.

Originated as two separate specifications, latest efforts have driven a development towards interoperability between both specifications (OASIS Cover Pages, 2008).

IDENTITY ASSURANCE FRAMEWORKS

Identity Assurance Frameworks constitute an effort to unify and standardize the perception of assurance into a digital identity for the purpose of sharing digital identities between independent trust domains.

Each organization usually forms its own trust domain, in which digital identities are maintained and managed. As organizations have very different legal requirements and organizational policies, they usually find it hard to share identity information and in particular to accept identity data from outside their own trust domain. While inside their own domain appropriate organizational structures and processes are set up, that guarantee the adherence to these policies, organizations have little influence on the security processes in other domains. Therefore, subjects within their own domain are usually fully trusted while those from another trust domain are usually not – Even though both trust domains will often follow the same or roughly equivalent security standards.

Contracts are required to align different trust requirements of independent partners and balance the risk for both sides before mutual access and information exchange can take place. However, setting up these contracts is a tedious task, as there are many factors that influence the trust into an identity including the registration of a subject in an identity management system, the type of credential provided to the subject, how this credential was delivered to the subject, as well as all security safeguards in place to protect the storage and management of identity data in the identity management system.

In order to ease this process and allow online partners to set up business relations more easily identity frameworks evolved with the aim to provide a common standard for identity assurance upon which organizations can set up their contracts. One example is the InCommon Identity Assurance Assessment Framework (InCommon Federation, 2008). The InCommon initiative (InCommon Federation, 2010) is a federation of companies, universities and government organizations that follow up the goal to establish a circle of trust between partners that adhere to the trust criteria defined by the initiative. Within this circle of trust each partner trusts assertions received from someone else. This way, customers can access partner services with a single login, which naturally increases customer satisfaction. While the InCommon initiative's approach is one of the later solutions, the idea of defining common criteria to trust on each other and assign trust levels existed before. In fact, most ideas for identity assurance frameworks share a common aim and approach.

General Aim and Approach

The general idea of identity assurance frameworks is to define a common, standardized set of trust criteria to assess an identity provider and its systems. Often these trust criteria are clustered and assigned a level of trust or in case of digital identities a level of assurance (LoA).

Referring to this level of assurance an identity provider can announce its trustworthiness. On the other end, a relying party can define its required degree of assurance. This will depend on the intended transaction and can be accomplished by performing a risk management analysis.

Defining levels of assurance is by no means an easy task due to the vast amount of criteria that influence the assurance that a digital identity of a subject matches with its real-life identity. Basically the whole process, technologies, protections, infrastructure and other safeguards in place at an identity provider, on which the identity provider's assertions are based, need to be taken into consideration. Typical influence categories are for example the procedure followed in enrolling the subject into the identity management system, the credential's nature as well as the processes that manage the credentials. In the following, a brief overview is given on existing identity assurance frameworks. Afterwards we draw out their limitations and open issues.

UK Office of the e-Envoy

The UK Office of the e-Envoy has published a document called "Registration and Authentication – E-government Strategy Framework Policy and Guideline" (Office of the e-Envoy, UK, 2002). In this document the initial registration process of a person with the system as well as the authentication process for a user's engagement in an e-government transaction are defined. Depending on the severity of consequences that might arise from unauthorized access, four authentication trust levels are defined, reaching from Level 0 for minimal damage up to Level 3 for substantial damage. The more severe the likely consequences, the more confidence in an asserted identity will be required when engaging in a transaction. For example, for filing an income tax return electronically, an authentication trust level of two is needed, which is reached when the client can present a credential (preferably a digital certificate) and can prove his right to that credential, e.g. by signing it with his private key.

OMB M-04-04 / NIST 800-63

The e-Authentication Initiative, another approach, is a major project of the e-government program of the US. The core concept is a federated architecture with multiple e-government applications and credential providers. The e-Authentication Initiative provides an architecture that delivers a uniform, government-wide approach for authentication, leaving the choice of concrete authentication technologies with the individual government agencies. In order to assist agencies in determining the appropriate level of identity assurance for electronic transactions, the initiative has published a policy called "E- Authentication Guidance for Federal Agencies" (OMB M-04-04) (e-Authentication Initiative, 2007). The document defines four assurance levels, which are based on the risks associated with an authentication error. The four assurance levels reach from "little or no confidence in the asserted identity" to "very high confidence in the asserted identity". In order to determine the required level of assurance, a risk assessment is accomplished for each transaction. Hereby, the potential harm and their likelihood of occurrence are identified. The categories of potential harm reach from inconvenience to the risk of personal safety and civil violations. Each category is assigned one of the impact values "N/A", "Low", "Medium" or "High".

Which technical requirements apply for each assurance level is described in a recommendation of the National Institute of Standards and Technology (NIST), which is called "Electronic Authentication Guideline" (National Institute of Standards and Technology, 2006). This document states specific technical requirements for each of the four levels for the token type, the authentication protocol as well as the types of attacks that need to be prevented.

InCommon

The Identity Assurance Assessment framework defined by InCommon is by far the most comprehensive approach for identity assurance. InCommon is a federation of more than 100 members from industry, government and the higher education sector (InCommon Federation, 2008). The goal of InCommon is to establish a common standard among the federation members that allows them to assess the trustworthiness of exchanged identity data, rank it and compare it directly to the required quality for an intended transaction. Every partner in the federation that wants to provide identity information (therefore taking the role of an identity provider) offers a technical service that issues upon request assertions about a user's identity that is managed by this partner. InCommon also manages a directory with all services that are known within the federation. For each service, a security level is assigned that tells all federation members about the quality of the assertions they can expect from this service. In order to reach a certain security level, an audit is accomplished in which the identity management system of the partner providing this service is assessed with regard to a set of pre-defined criteria. There are two different Assurance Profiles that specify these criteria: The first one, the *Bronze* profile provides reasonable assurance that the same person is authenticating on subsequent visits. It should be sufficient to manage access to low value services and resources. The second profile is the *Silver* Identity Assurance Profile. It builds upon the Bronze profile requirements and demands for example stronger credential technologies, individual identity proofing as well as certain requirements to secure the business and IT security management processes that manage the digital identities. The Silver profile is intended for medium risk transactions that require individual user accountability.

Limitations and Open Issues

Existing frameworks for identity assurance as described in the previous sections aim at assessing identity providers and their services in a global context. Their goal is to have a global trust semantic that allows any participant instant assessment of a partner's qualities to assert identity claims by referring to a global trust level. Although current frameworks provide a quite comprehensive assessment, a number of limitations exist.

First of all, most consider an identity provider and the digital identities held by it in a combined assessment. Having different trust requirements for specific attributes is usually not in their scope. However, if we look at the current online world, we find varying trust requirements for identity attributes. For some services or web sites, a strong assurance of a digital identity is not required. Often it is not necessary to provide strong proof of a user's name or address as long as it is always the same user that logs on. In other cases, in particular for transactions that carry a risk, a strong identity is a necessity in order to use a service.

Current identity assurance frameworks usually have one requirement for all digital identities that they manage. For example, InCommon requests in-person proofing for the registration of all users of this identity provider. However, it is not possible to manage a strong identity with verified attributes besides an identity that contains self-asserted attributes.

This also implies that it is not possible to change a user's identity trust level over time. As identity proofing processes, in particular such as in-person proofing, are expensive and time-consuming for both, the user and the identity provider, a verification of a user's attributes might not be desired in the first place. Only upon concrete requirement, for example if the user wants to carry out transactions that demand a higher trust level, such a verification step seems to be worth the effort.

Furthermore, information held by identity providers inherently differs due to their affiliation with an organization or institution and might be suitable for asserting certain identity attributes only to a limited extent. For example, a banking identity provider will be in particular suitable to assert that a user can pay for a certain service, but might have weak records of the user's status as a student while for a university's identity provider it would probably be the opposite. Such a diversity of identity provisioning sources is preferable for the open world of the Internet as relying parties can have very different requirements.

FACTORS OF IDENTITY ASSURANCE

Many people have approached the question of what makes a good identity provider and what is needed to safeguard identity information of users. When looking at the specifications and guidelines developed by initiatives and standard organizations such as OASIS (OASIS, 2010), NIST (National institute for standards and technology) or InCommon (InCommon Federation, 2010) and comparing them, it becomes clear that many identified aspects for identity assurance are the same. There are usually two types of factors that influence the trust level of identity data. On one side, those that refer to the digital identity of users themselves, such as the mode of authentication employed, enrollment procedure applied in subject-to-account mapping or the used security token used in transfer between parties. On the other side, there are factors that concern the nature of the identity provider's operator, basically its readiness to support and operate a reliable service. Such factors are the legal situation, laws and guidelines an identity provider adheres to or the storage of user data on its internal systems. In this section, we will have a closer look at these factors to better understand the problem of providing identity assurance across organizational borders.

Operational Factors

First of all, using and trusting an identity service requires having confidence in the processes and actions of the organization that is running the service. An important question here is for example whether the organization is an established legal entity that can be held liable in case anything bad happens. Furthermore, the organization should have sufficient financial and personnel resources to run an identity service in a reliable manner.

Technical Environment

Closely related with the operational factors is the technical environment that the operator of an identity service employs. A secure network, a proper setup of protection mechanisms as firewalls and access control lists are necessary factors to keep data safely guarded. Besides this, also the interoperability to external systems is a factor that should be considered when assessing an identity service.

Token Technologies and Issuance

Identity data is conveyed as security token between the identity provider and a service. A token usually consists of a unique subject identifier and well-structured and typed pairs of attribute names and values. Different formats are possible such as SAML or X.509 Tokens. Besides the token format, also the content of the assertions is of importance. An identity provider should convey only those attributes to service providers that were requested and should allow users to control which attributes are send out in order to respect their privacy.

Registration and Identity Proofing

Besides factors concerning the identity provider operator, it is also important to consider how digital identities of the users are established and managed at an identity service. Registration and identity proofing is the process of establishing a mapping between a particular physical person and the digital identity record in the identity provider operators database. If the identity provider is part of an organization, this organization such as a company or a university, usually has strong records of its members' identities. However, if the identity provider is an independent organization or a user is not affiliated with the provider's organization, more effort is required to establish strong identity records. Often registration is done using an online registration form, which users fill in by themselves. Although additional verification can be demanded as presenting authoritative documents at a registration authority, this usually means more effort than in the first case.

User Authentication, Used Credential Technologies, and Credential Issuance

Another trust factor that concerns the user identity is the used authentication method. User authentication should guarantee to a certain extent that an identity provider associates a specific subject with the correct record in the identity provider database during an authentication event. Authentication mechanisms can differ tremendously in their strength. Multi-factor authentication is often considered to be more secure than using a single one of the aggregate factors alone (Bertino, Paci, & Shang, 2009). Usually a credential is issued as part of the registration process, which is used by the user in subsequent authentication events. Besides the used credential technology, such as a password or smartcard, an important aspect is also how this credential was conveyed to the user. For example, if a smartcard is used and sent to the user by mail, the probability that the card does not reach the appropriate receiver is higher than if the card was given to the user directly. Therefore, it is also important to consider how the identity provider reacts to authentication errors and suspicious activity.

CASE STUDY: TRUST LEVELS FOR ATTRIBUTES

Summing up the previous sections, we have seen that current approaches for identity assurance typically assess digital user identities as a whole. There is no distinction between trusted attributes that have been verified using proper registration processes and attribute values that have been entered online by the user and are therefore self-asserted.

Similar to Chadwick et. al (Chadwick & Inman, 2009), we are introducing trust levels for identity attributes in order to address varying attribute trust requirements of web sites and services. In the heart of our scenario is an identity provider that manages digital identities of users for the purpose of provisioning identity attributes, such as an email address, name or date of birth to applications that are willing to rely on it. Each of these attributes can be used in multiple digital identities and can have different levels of trust. For example, a user can manage an anonymous identity with his nickname and a private email address besides an identity that comprises verified data and matches his real-life identity. While the latter identity is usually required for financial transactions that carry a risk, the anonymous identity guarantees user privacy and can for example be used in low-risk transactions such as forum discussions.

In our case study, which is shown in Figure 2, the service provider is an online web shop of a university, which offers merchandising products. After adding items to the shopping cart, the user proceeds to the checkout. In order to complete the purchase, users are asked to provide their name, address, email-address as well as payment information. Furthermore, a student discount is granted if the user provides a confirmation of enrolment at a university. The online shop requires a valid email address as well as a valid account number. There are two options to provide this data. First a user can create a new account directly using an online registration form. However, the information that is entered by the user is not trusted and needs to be verified by the online shop before the ordered items are sent out. In particular for the student discount, the user needs to upload a confirmation of enrolment, which requires manual checking of an employee of the online shop. The second option is to use identity providers that are trusted by the

Figure 2. Case study - attributes from multiple authoritative sources with different trust qualities

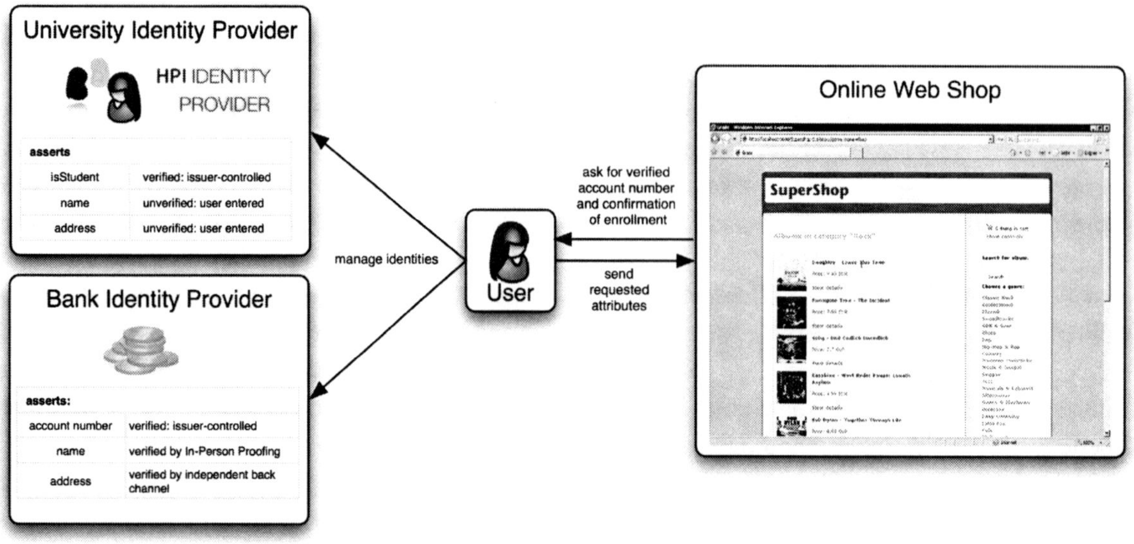

shop. In our example, users can use their existing accounts with the university's identity provider to provide the necessary information. In this case the identity provider can directly assert that the user is a student. Furthermore the identity provider asserts name, address and a verified email. Verification can be done using one of two verification options. The first option is to upload an email certificate and the second option is to have a confirmation email send to the user's email account. Usually a single identity provider is not able to provide all identity attributes that are requested by a relying party. In particular, the account number and payment information is preferably managed by the user's bank. Therefore, it can be useful to have multiple sources for identity attributes. In the scenario, we simultaneously use multiple identity providers and aggregate the identity attributes at the online shop.

The architecture of the scenario is shown in Figure 3. Our architecture is based on the decentralized or user-centric identity management model, which puts the users in the middle of all interactions. Users decide which identity provider they want to use and which attributes are send to a requesting relying party. As can be seen in the figure, the user has an account registered with several identity providers of his choice. Each identity provider manages a selection of his attributes, such as name, address or date of birth. Each attribute is assigned a level of trust, a so-called attribute verification class, which contains information about the verification of this attribute when collected from the user. In our approach, we summarize verification characteristics into various classes, which are described in the next section. The benefit of such a classification is a better comparability of verification mechanisms. As verification methods of identity attributes usually differ depending on the attribute, it is hard to provide a common classification. Consider an email address that is usually verified by a confirmation email as compared to a name or address which requires for example in-person proofing. In our approach, we defined several verification classes in a hierarchical structure to reflect similarities as well as differences of attribute verification. A relying party, such as the online web shop, can state its trust policy for identity attributes using these verification classes. For example, for

Figure 3. Case study architecture

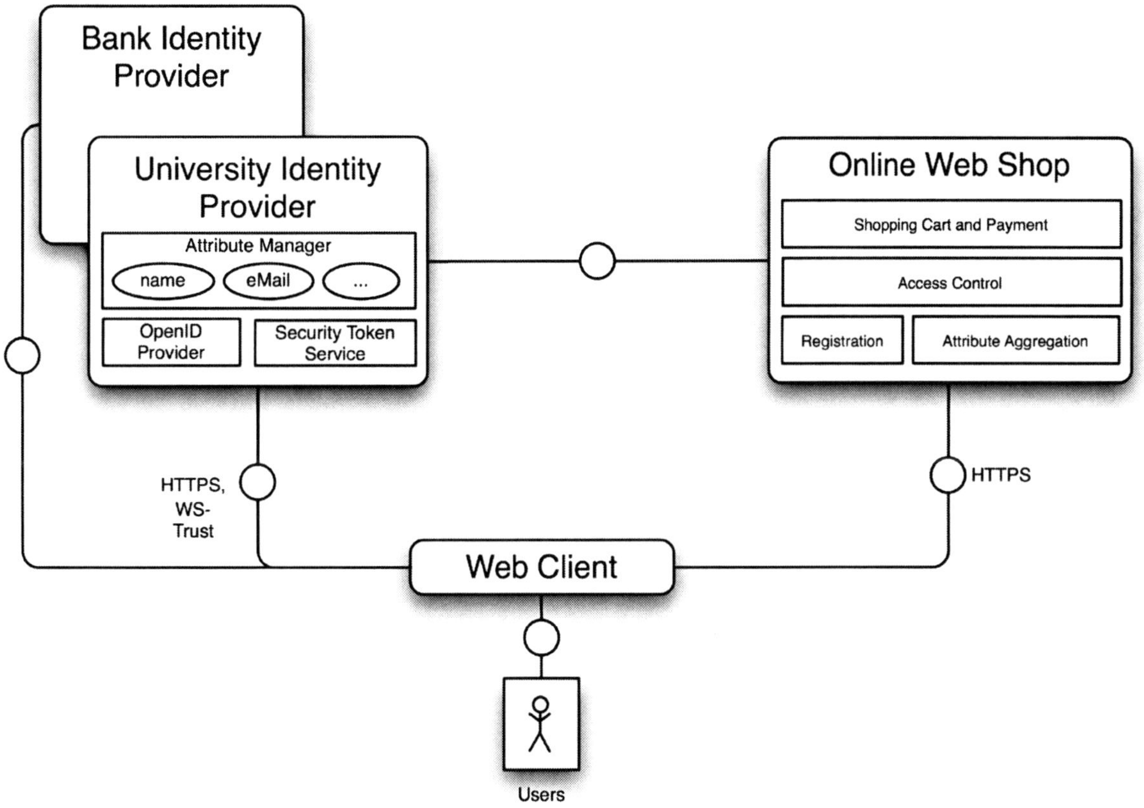

the confirmation of enrolment, the online shop can request that the attribute *isStudent* is verified and that the one who is asserting the attribute is also the one who is in control of this attribute. This means only the university in which the student is enrolled, can assert the attribute. This class is called verified: issuer-controlled.

Now, when the user proceeds to the checkout in the store, the stores policy is used to find suitable identity provider that fulfill the requirements. The user is asked to choose one or more from those identity providers to retrieve the attributes from. Upon successful authentication of the user at his identity provider(s), the requested attributes are send to the web shop and aggregated for further use. In order to implement such a scenario, various technologies can be used. In our approach, the identity provider and online web shop support both, OpenID and web services. OpenID (The OpenId Foundation, 2007) is a very lightweight protocol, which uses HTTP to share identity attributes between OpenID-enabled web sites. Besides OpenID, the identity provider also provides an interface for web services. To be more specific, a security token service based on the WS-Trust (Nadalin, Goodner, Gudgin, Barbir, & Granqvist, 2007) specification is provided which allows SOAP-based relying parties to request identity attributes. Both specifications have been extended to allow the exchange of trust requirements in addition to the attribute data itself.

Verification Classes for Identity Attributes

In our approach, we defined verification classes to allow the online web shop to specify the attribute verification requirements on one side and the identity providers to express their requirements on the other side. These verification classes are shown in Figure 4.

Verification context classes denote general verification schemes that can be applied to several attributes, but might be implemented in different ways. For example, the verification of an attribute by an independent back channel can be done for email addresses by sending an email to the claimed address with a verification link in it. The same scheme can also be used to verify a bank account. In this case a small amount of money (1 cent) is usually transferred to the claimed account with a password in the transaction data, that the user needs to enter later on to prove that s/he is the owner of the account. Figure 4 shows our ontology to describe various verification methods and their applicability to identity attributes. For each verification class, we state the attributes that are eligible to be verified in the given manner. However, for the sake of readability, Figure 4 only shows the suitable verification classes for the two attributes email and last name. A complete assignment for a common set of globally known attributes is given in Table 1. In the following, each of the attribute verification classes depicted in our identity trust ontology in Figure 4 is described in more detail. The list is a proposal based on experience with existing assurance frameworks and can be extended and adapted to match the needs of a given use case.

In-Person Proofing

In-Person Proofing is an attribute verification class that is used in most assurance frameworks. As required evidence for the attribute value, the verifying authority has to ensure that the applicant is in possession of a primary Government ID document that bears a photographic image of the holder and that this image matches with that of the applicant. Furthermore it has to be ensured that the presented document appears to be a genuine document properly issued by the claimed issuing authority and valid at the time of application.

Independent Back Channel

Independent Back Channel denotes a verification method by which a claimed attribute value is proven by sending some information via another communication channel than the one used to claim the value.

Issuer-Controlled

Issuer-Controlled is a verification class that can be used when the holder of the identity information is equal to the creator of the identity information or is in control of this identity information, as for example in case of email providers for email addresses or a company in case of affiliation claims.

Proof by Electronic ID Card

This verification class is used when an electronic ID card has been read by a service approved by the government (in Germany: eID Service Providers).

Proof by X.509 Certificate

This verification class is used when the applicant has presented a certificate and it has been ensured that the presented certificate was valid at the time of application.

User-Entered

This verification class shall be used when identity data is entered by the user or received from a user-like source without any further verification.

Figure 4. Classification of attribute verification

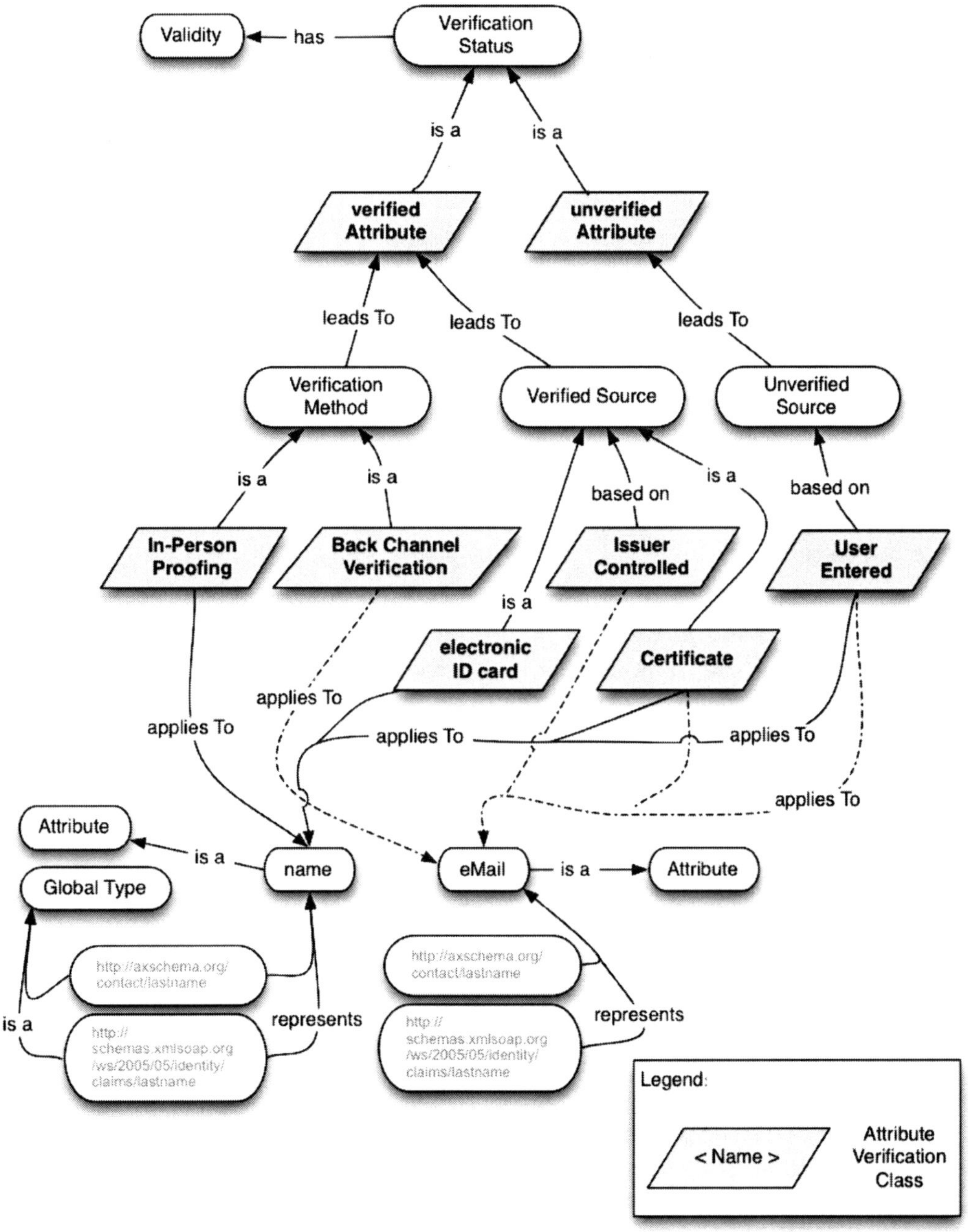

Verified and Unverified

There are two basic classes, verified and unverified. As can be seen in Figure 4, all other verification context classes are derived from these basic classes. These basic classes can be used to express for example that verification is required without defining which verification method has been used.

Table 1. Assignment of attributes to verification context classes

Verification Class	*Applies to*
In-Person Proofing	given name, family name, gender, date of birth, address
Back-channel Proofing	eMail, telephone number, address, credit card num- ber (given name), (family name)
Issuer-controlled	eMail, telephone number, credit card number, (address)
User-entered	eMail, given name, family name, gender, date of birth, telephone number
Proof by electronic ID card	given name, family name, gender, date of birth, ad- dress
Proof by certificate	given name, family name, email, (etc.)

Finally, Table 1 gives an overview of all classes and lists identity attributes that apply to these classes.

CONCLUSION AND FUTURE RESEARCH

Past experiences have shown that trust and in particular trust in digital identities is essential to accept information that was gathered and is managed outside their own control. In this book chapter we describe and compare different frameworks for identity assurance. Identity assurance frameworks aim at assessing identity services on the Internet, so-called identity providers, with regard to their ability to assess certain identity attributes of users. Such criteria are for example operational characteristics of the identity provider operator, the technical infrastructure as well as factors concerning the management of user identities, such as registration and identity proofing, the strength of the authentication process as well as the type of credential technology used. Identity assurance frameworks try to identify these criteria and to cluster them into levels of trust or levels of assurance (LoA). Using global levels of assurance allows service providers as companies and organizations to assess a potential business partner instantly. This eases e–commerce and business collaborations. Although, identity assurance frameworks help to build up circles of trust, there are also some limitations that have been identified and discussed as part of this chapter. In order to overcome these limitations, we introduce trust levels not only for identity providers, but also for identity attributes. In the chapter, we provide a classification of attribute verification processes, so called attribute verification classes, and use a case study to illustrate how these classes can be used to express a service providers need for identity data with finer granularity than can be achieved using existing technologies. Our verification classes are defined in a hierarchical ontology that can be easily extended and adapted to further needs. Additional research is required to find out exactly which factors are relevant to assess the trust level for attributes and in which way the overall trust level of the identity provider relates to the trust levels of attributes.

REFERENCES

Ahn, G.-J., Ko, M., & Shehab, M. (2009). Privacy-enhanced user-centric identity management.

Baldwin, A., Casassa Mont, M., Beres, Y., & Shiu, S. (2010). Assurance for federated identity management. *Journal of Computer Security - Digital Identity Management (DIM2007), 18*(4), 541-572.

Bertino, E., Paci, F., & Shang, N. (2009). *Keynote 2: Digital identity protection - Concepts and issues.* International Conference on Availability, Reliability and Security. IEEE Computer Society.

Bertocci, V., Serack, G., & Baker, C. (2007). *Understanding Windows CardSpace: An introduction to the concepts and challenges of digital identities*. Amsterdam, The Netherlands: Addison-Wesley Longman.

Cameron, K. (2005, 05). *Microsoft's vision for an identity metasystem*. Kim Cameron's Identity Weblog. Retrieved August, 2010, from http://www.identityblog.com/stories/2005/07/05/IdentityMetasystem.html

Cantor, S., Kemp, J., Maler, E., & Philpott, R. (2005). *Assertions and protocols for the OASIS security assertion markup language (SAML) V2.02*. OASIS.

Chadwick, D. W., & Inman, G. (2009, May). Attribute aggregation in federated identity management. *Computer*, *42*(5), 33–40. doi:10.1109/MC.2009.143

e-Authentication Initiative. (2007). *E-authentication guidance for federal agencies*. US.

IAAC. (2005). *IAAC position paper on identity assurance (IdA): Towards a policy framework for electronic identity*. Retrieved August, 2010, from http://www.iaac.org.uk

InCommon Federation. (2008). *Identity assurance assessment framework*. Retrieved August 2010, from http://www.incommonfederation.org/docs/assurance/ InC IAAF 1.0 Final.pdf

InCommon Federation. (2010). Retrieved October, 2010 from http://www.incommonfederation.org/

Jøsang, A., Fabre, J., Hay, B., Dalziel, J., & Pope, S. (2005). *Trust requirements in identity management*. Newcastle: Australasian Information Security Workshop 2005.

Jøsang, A., & Pope, S. (2005). User centric identity management. In A. Clark, K. Kerr, & G. Mohay (Eds.), *AusCERT Asia Pacific Information Technology Security Conference*, (p. 77).

Jøsang, A., Zomai, M. A., & Suriadi, S. (2007). Usability and privacy in identity management architectures. *Proceedings of the Fifth Australasian Symposium on ACSW Frontiers*, vol. 68, (pp. 143-152).

Kantara Initiative. (2010). Retrieved August, 2010, from http://kantarainitiative.org/

Lockhart, H., Andersen, S., Bohren, J., Sverdlov, Y., Hondo, M., Maruyama, H., et al. (2006, December). *Web services federation language* (WS-Federation), version 1.1.

Madsen, P., & Itoh, H. (2009). Challenges to supporting federated assurance. *Computer*, *42*, 42–49. doi:10.1109/MC.2009.149

Maler, E., Nadalin, A., Reed, D., Rundle, M., & Thibeau, D. (2010, March). *The open identity trust framework (OITF) model*.

Nadalin, A., Goodner, M., Gudgin, M., Barbir, A., & Granqvist, H. (2007). *WS-trust 1.3. Organization for the Advancement of Structured Information Standards*. OASIS.

National Institute for Standards and Technology. (2010). Retrieved August, 2010, from http://www.nist.gov

National Institute of Standards and Technology. (2006). *Electronic authentication guideline*.

OASIS. (2009, July). *Identity metasystem interoperability*, version 1.0. OASIS Standards.

OASIS. (2010). *OASIS: Advanced open standards for the global information society*. Retrieved August, 2010 from http://www.oasis-open.org/

OASIS Cover Pages (2008, October). *Microsoft 'Geneva' framework supports SAML 2.0, WS-Federation, and WS-Trust*. Retrieved July 2010, from http://xml.coverpages.org/ni2008-10-29-a.html

Office of the e-Envoy, UK. (2002). *Registration and authentication - e-government strategy framework policy and guidelines*. Retrieved August, 2010 from http://www.cabinetoffice.gov.uk/csia/documents/pdf/ RegAndAuthentn0209v3.pdf

Proceedings of the2009IEEE International Conference on Communications (pp. 998-1002). Piscataway, NJ: IEEE Press.

Rieger, S. (2009). User-centric identity management in heterogeneous federations. *Proceedings of the 2009 Fourth International Conference on Internet and Web Applications and Services* (pp. 527-532). Washington, DC: IEEE Computer Society.

The OpenId Foundation. (2007). *OpenID authentication 2.0 - Final Specification*. Retrieved 2010, from http://openid.net/specs

Thomas, I., & Meinel, C. (2010). *An identity provider to manage reliable digital identities for SOA and the Web*. 9th Symposium on Identity and Trust on the Internet. Gaithersburg, MD: ACM.

Windley, P. J. (2005). *Digital identity*. O'Reilly Media.

ADDITIONAL READING

Baier, D., Bertocci, V., & Brown, K. (2010). *A Guide to Claims-Based Identity and Access Control: Authentication and Authorization for Services and the Web (Patterns & Practices)*. Microsoft Press.

Benantar, M. (2006). *Access Control Systems: Security, Identity Management and Trust Models*. Berlin: Springer.

Berger, A. (2008). *Identity Management Systems: Introducing yourself to the Internet*. Vdm Verlag Dr. Müller.

Bertino, E., Martino, L., Paci, F., & Squicciarini, A. (2009). *Security for Web Services and Service-Oriented Architectures*. Berlin: Springer.

Bertocci, V., Serack, G., & Baker, C. (2007). *Understanding Windows CardSpace: An Introduction to the Concepts and Challenges of Digital Identities*. Amsterdam: Addison-Wesley Longman.

Cameron, K. (2005, 05). *Microsoft's Vision for an Identity Metasystem*. Retrieved 08 2010, from Kim Cameron's Identity Weblog: http://www.identityblog.com/stories/2005/07/05/IdentityMetasystem.html

Cameron, K. (2005, 12 05). *The Laws of Identity*. Retrieved 08 2010, from Kim Cameron's Identity Weblog: http://www.identityblog.com/stories/2005/05/13/TheLawsOfIdentity.pdf

Chadwick, D. W., & Inman, G. (2009, May). Attribute Aggregation in Federated Identity Management. *Computer*, *42*(5), 33–40. doi:10.1109/MC.2009.143

El Maliki, T., & Seigneur, J.-M. (2007). A Survey of User-centric Identity Management Technologies. *The International Conference on Emerging Security Information, Systems, and Technologies (SECURWARE 2007)*. Valencia: IEEE.

Jones, M. B. (2006). The Identity Metasystem: A User-Centric, Inclusive Web Authentication Solution. *W3C Workshop on Transparency and Usability of Web Authentication*. New York City.

Josang, A., Maseng, T., & Knapskog, S. J. (2009). *Identity and Privacy in the Internet Age*. Berlin: Springer.

Jøsang, A., & Pope, S. (2005). User Centric Identity Management. In A. Clark, K. Kerr, & G. Mohay (Ed.), *AusCERT Asia Pacific Information Technology Security Conference*, (p. 77).

Kanneganti, R., & Chodavarapu, P. (2007). *SOA Security*. Manning Publications.

Leeuw, E. D., Fischer-Hubner, S., & Tseng, J. (2008). *Policies and Research in Identity Management: First IFIP WG11.6 Working Conference on Policies and Research in Identity Management (IDMAN'07), RSM... Federation for Information Processing)*. Berlin: Springer.

Madsen, P., & Itoh, H. (2009, May). Challenges to Supporting Federated Assurance. *Computer*, *42*(5), 42–49. doi:10.1109/MC.2009.149

Mercuri, M. (2007). *Beginning Information Cards and CardSpace: From Novice to Professional (Expert's Voice in. Net)*. Apress. doi:10.1007/978-1-4302-0204-2

Pacyna, P., Rutkowski, A., Sarma, A., & Takahashi, K. (2009, May). Trusted Identity for All: Toward Interoperable Trusted Identity Management Systems. *Computer*, *42*(5), 30–32. doi:10.1109/MC.2009.168

Paschoud, J. (2010). *Access and Identity Management: Controlling Access to Online Information*. Facet Publishing.

Recordon, D., Rae, L., & Messina, C. (2010). *The Definitive Guide*. Open, ID: O'Reilly Media.

Recordon, D., & Reed, D. (2006). OpenID 2.0: a platform for user-centric identity management. *Workshop on Digital identity management* (pp. 11-16). ACM.

Rieger, S. User-Centric Identity Management in Heterogeneous Federations. *International Conference on Internet and Web Applications and Services*. IEEE.

Seigneur, J.-M., & Jensen, C. D. (2007). User-Centric Identity, Trust and Privacy. In Song, R., Korba, L., & Yee, G. (Eds.), *Trust in E-Services: Technologies, Practices and Challenges*. IGI Global. doi:10.4018/978-1-59904-207-7.ch012

Sharoni, I., Williamson, G., & Yip, D. (2009). *Identity Management: A Primer*. Mc Pr Llc.

Steel, C. (2005). *Core Security Patterns: Best Practices and Strategies for J2EE(TM), Web Services, and Identity Management*. Prentice Hall International.

Surhone, L. M., Timpledon, M. T., & Marseken, S. F. (2009). *Authentication, Login, Service, Digital Identity, Password, User, Software System, List of OpenID Providers, Yadis, Shared Secret*. Open, ID: Betascript Publishing.

Surhone, L. M., Timpledon, M. T., & Marseken, S. F. (2009). *Security Assertion Markup Language: Security Domain, Single Sign-on, Identity Management, Access Control, OASIS, Liberty Alliance, SAML 1.1, SAML 2.0*. Betascript Publishing.

Thomas, E., Schittko, C., Chou, D., deVadoss, J., King, J., & Wilhelmsen, H. (2010). *SOA with. NET and Windows Azure: Realizing Service-orientation with the Microsoft Platform (Prentice Hall Service-Oriented Computing Series from Thomas ERL)*. Prentice Hall.

KEY TERMS AND DEFINITIONS

Digital Identity: A digital identity represents parts of a person's real-life identity in the digital world. A digital identity is usually comprised in an account that contains a limited set of attributes that characterizes this person.

Federated Identity Management: Federated Identity Management denotes an open identity management model. In Federated Identity Management identity providers and relying parties form a circle of trust in which identity information from each identity provider can be used at any relying party.

Federation: A federation is a circle of trust across independent security domains.

Identity Assurance: A level of identity assurance (LoA) or level of trust reflects the degree of confidence that a relying party can assign to the assertions made by another identity provider with respect to a user's identity information.

Identity Assurance Framework: Identity Assurance Frameworks cluster trust requirements with regard to an identity into levels of assurance (LoA).

Identity Management: Identity management refers to the process of establishing, representing and recognizing a person's identity as digital identities in computer networks.

Identity Provider: An identity provider holds identity information of users for the purpose of provisioning it to parties that are willing to rely on it.

Identity Trust Level: see Identity Assurance.

Open Identity Management: Open Identity Management comprises identity management approaches for open networks involving several independent security domains.

Relying Party: A relying party in the context of identity management is usually a service or application that relies on identity information from a foreign source.

Security Domain: A security domain is a closed area that is administrated independently with regard to security. Often a security domain matches with the domain formed by organizational borders.

Service-Oriented Architecture: Service-oriented architectures describe an architecture paradigm to build software systems from loosely coupled, self-contained components, the services. All services need to adhere to certain design principles and properties as being self-descriptive, re-usable and discoverable.

Single-Sign-On: Single-Sign-On is a concept that allows users by authenticating once in a certain security domain to gain seamless access to services and applications in other domains; synonym: single-logon.

User-Centric Identity Management: User-Centric Identity Management belongs to the open identity management models. In User-Centric Identity Management Systems identity information is passed on demand from an identity provider, chosen by the user, to a relying party. The user is fully controls the flow of information.

Chapter 4
Information Security Governance

Janne J. Korhonen
Aalto University, Finland

Kari Hiekkanen
Aalto University, Finland

Juha Mykkänen
University of Eastern Finland, Finland

ABSTRACT

In today's economic, regulatory, and social environment, information security governance and management are topics of great interest to practitioners and researcher alike. In response to the increasingly interconnected, information intensive business landscape, legal pressures, and ongoing scrutiny to transparency and overall governance, organizations are increasingly interested in frameworks and methodologies for security governance and management. As the traditional view of governance as a control and conformance mechanism turns out to be inadequate in changing environments, a specifically contrived, more encompassing and design-oriented approach to information security governance is called for. In this chapter, the authors subscribe to the design science approach in order to outline a prescriptive reference model for information security governance that aims to help institute cross-functional information security management throughout the organization and build it into the organizational design.

INTRODUCTION

As the amount of information and the number of interconnected organizations and individuals continues to increase, so do the risks and costs of security breaches. The tightening regulations of data privacy, loss prevention and transparency require organizations to demonstrate due care and diligence with respect to security. Information security used to cover technical, and in many cases minor, security issues, but has recently evolved to proactive protection of business assets, reputation, profitability, customer confidence and economic performance. Security risks have evolved respectively from accidental computer worms and

DOI: 10.4018/978-1-4666-0197-0.ch004

viruses to targeted attacks by malevolent parties with specific motivations such as direct economic gain or access to intellectual property. At the same time, an organization's ability to take advantage of new opportunities, create new markets and operate in the emerging service-based economy depends heavily on its ability to provide open, accessible and available network connectivity and services. Security measures, policies and guidelines must simultaneously both protect information and enable its safe passage to interested parties in different business ecosystems.

While the existing information security frameworks range from detailed technical guidance to high-level principles (Federal Information Security Management Act, 2002; International Organization for Standardization, 2005), there are few actionable organization-wide frameworks that would guide in designing and developing security arrangements, incorporating them in the organization's operations and monitoring their implementation. Also, the responsibility for information security is too often delegated to the chief information officer (CIO) or the chief security officer (CSO) who is conflicted with demands and lacks leverage to address the problem across multiple business lines or divisions, while too little attention is given to the issue at the chief executive officer (CEO) or board level.

In this chapter, we outline a reference model for information security governance that aims to help the CIO/CSO a) obtain a clearance from the board to organize information security activities by identifiable organizational loci and b) identify and assign respective key roles with requisite responsibilities and accountabilities. The reference model extends and builds on an abstract meta-level governance structure, Agile Governance Model (AGM) (Korhonen, Hiekkanen and Lähteenmäki, 2009, Korhonen, Yildiz and Mykkänen, 2009) and is instantiated for information security.

In order to outline a pragmatic information security governance model that is both actionable and open to validation, we subscribe to the design science approach (e.g. Simon, 1996; Banathy, 1996; Hevner et al., 2004; van Aken and Romme, 2009). Van Aken (2004) argues that understanding a problem is only halfway to solving it and that in management research description-driven research needs to be complemented with prescription-driven development of field-tested and grounded technological rules applicable as design exemplars to classes of managerial problems. Hevner et al. (2004) promote design approach in the context of information systems research.

BACKGROUND

As information and information technology are of increasing strategic importance, effective management of IT and information assets becomes a critical strategic concern. IT Governance (ITG) deals with the management of an organization's use of IT. According to the IT Governance Institute (2007), it is "an integral part of enterprise governance and consists of the leadership and organizational structures and processes that ensure that the organization's IT sustains and extends the organization's strategies and objectives".

Information security has traditionally been defined as the protection of information and its critical elements, including the systems and hardware that use, store, and transmit that information (Whitman and Mattord, 2008). Traditional viewpoints on information security included access to information systems, securing communications, security management and development of secure information systems (Siponen and Oinas-Kukkonen, 2007). However, while security considerations are an essential part of IT governance, information security governance goes beyond the IT realm. Information security is increasingly a business issue (von Solms and von Solms, 2005) that calls for governance of its own (von Solms, 2006).

In the networked, always-on business environment of today, it may seem futile to try and keep systems patched and protected for viruses, intrusions and other attacks. IT-reliant wall-to-wall defense against all conceivable contingencies renders inadequate in the face of ever-new methods that bypass even the sturdiest firewalls. Thus, information security needs to be adaptive and guided by business objectives and goals as well as to be increasingly tied to the information and its life-cycle. The key elements to be protected include not just information itself but also organizational assets such as trust, reputation, brand, stakeholder value and customer loyalty for which security breaches could have negative effects. Implementing and maintaining adequate security measures in all these facets should be seen as a non-negotiable cost of doing business.

Effective information security governance shall integrate legal, managerial, operational, and technical considerations (Allen and Westby, 2007). It shall specify roles that have the requisite authority, accountability, and resources to implement and enforce policies, standards, awareness programs, security strategies, and other organizational procedures. Thereby, it establishes an appropriate framework for decision making that relies on well-informed decision-making and ensures that decisions are enacted, implemented and monitored consistently.

A number of standards and best practice frameworks for Information Security Management (ISM) have been developed. These frameworks help organizations assess and control their security risks and comply with given regulations and governance requirements.

One such framework is the international information security management standard ISO/IEC 27002:2005, which is published by the International Organization for Standardization (ISO) and International Electrotechnical Commission (IEC) and originally derived from the UK government's BS 7799. The standard defines 133 security controls strategies under 11 major headings. ISO/IEC 27002:2005 pronounces the importance of risk management and advises not to implement every stated guideline but only those that are relevant. The guiding principles rely on either legal requirements or generally accepted best practices and are the initial points for implementing information security.

Another established and comprehensive standard on information security is the business-oriented Standard of Good Practice for Information Security (SOGP) by Information Security Forum (ISF). The standard consists of six different aspects, each of which is broken down into summary areas and detailed sections. The full standard covers 36 summary areas and 166 sections.

We concur with Allen and Westby (2007) that governance and management of security are most effective when they are systemic and when the responsibility for enterprise security is assigned to roles that have the requisite authority, accountability, and resources to implement and enforce it. We also subscribe to Hoogervorst's (2009) notion that change must be addressed from the constructional perspective that entails coherent and consistent design principles and holistically integrates various business and organizational aspects.

While the existing ISM frameworks identify different information security areas and define detailed security controls, they provide limited insight into how information security is systemically built into the organizational design. The frameworks typically lack the notion of organizational levels and horizontal dimensions pertinent to roles, accountabilities and policies, as well as the "organizational connection points horizontally and vertically" (Allen and Westby, 2007), needed for effective enterprise security. In essence, the frameworks are representative of management models rather than governance models.

Von Solms and von Solms (2006; 2009) provide a welcome exception to this observation. Their model for information security governance identifies three levels of management – strategic, tactical and operational – and three distinct "actions" across these levels – direct, execute and control. The strategic level "directives" are expanded into sets of information security policies, company standards and procedures at the tactical level and further to administrative guidelines and administrative procedures at the operational level. Execution then takes place at the lowest level, producing measurement data that is extracted at the operational level, compiled and integrated at the tactical level and finally aggregated and abstracted to perform measurement against the requirements of the directives at the strategic level. Because of this Direct-Control Cycle, the model represents a governance model, not merely a management model (von Solms and von Solms, 2006).

In a similar vein, our approach to governance model design is systemic and structural. Not unlike the von Solms brothers, we distinguish a number of decision-making levels, in our case five, but instead of processes like direct, execute and control flowing across these levels, we identify horizontal dimensions common to the levels. As the horizontal dimensions, we discern design, development, operations and monitoring. Somewhat different from the common convention of some typologies, including the one by von Solms and von Solms, and with respect to the governance principle of "separation of duties", we do not view "control" as a distinct dimension or action, but as being spread out over operations (prevention) and monitoring (detection).

CHANGING LANDSCAPE OF INFORMATION SECURITY

Issues, Controversies, Problems

The executive management's commitment to information security is a key aspect of effectively managing the security exposure and related risks to an organization's digital assets. Executive management should view information security as an essential component of business, equivalent to any other core business asset or function. Building a proper governance structure requires an understanding of the full range of actions and operations involved in creating an enterprise level program, framework and culture for information security. To achieve a sustainable capability, security must be addressed at the governance level by executive management and embraced at all levels of the organization. Contemporary information security is not to be relegated to a technical issue within the IT department (Allen, 2005).

The need for executive level governance of information security flows both a) from legal compliance requirements associated with laws, regulations, treaties and other duties in protecting data and b) from corporate governance practices such as fiduciary duty of care owed by executive management and directors to shareholders in case of business enterprise. Legal compliance requirements originate from domestic and increasingly from international law. Numerous laws require protections for various types of data such as financial, personal and medical information. Furthermore, tightening corporate governance practices impose new requirements for data protection, traceability and transparency, record management and other internal controls.

Addressing security at the enterprise level is often hard to justify. Security measures are typically viewed as disaster prevention and the exact value of such investments is hard to measure. Without adequate executive sponsorship and understanding of the value of information security to business, organizations tend to approach security by fixing the problems as they appear and trying to cope with emerging external threats.

Legislation and regulation increasingly impose administrative, civil, and criminal penalties for security breaches that were made possible due to the lack of supervision or control by someone in a senior managerial or executive position. Examples of such legislation include U.S. Gramm-Leach-Bliley Act (1999), U.S. Health Insurance

Portability and Accountability Act (1996), U.S. Sarbanes-Oxley Act (2002), European Union (EU) Data Protection Directives, etc.

Regulatory requirements for data protection include not only organizations' own information but increasingly also data collected on or stored by customers or consumers – users of the digital services that the organization provides – in different contexts. Such laws include, for example, compliance requirement on organizations to notify individuals in the event of a breach to their personal information such as address, credit card number or email account. Therefore, the information governance practices in today's organizations should not be limited to mere data protection but should also include measures such as active prevention, threat analysis, breach detection, and in the event of breach, damage control, recovery and other reactionary measures.

The current focus on sustainability and corporate social responsibility are also pushing for better information security governance. From the executive management viewpoint, governance should not be seen only as a matter of regulatory compliance and accountability but also as a strategic means to reduce risks, create value and improve the long-term performance of the organization.

Also, several converging IT trends will have a significant impact on existing information governance practices. In the following, we will discuss a few of these trends: cloud computing, proliferation of digital information and consumerization of IT.

In this context, we view cloud computing as a way of delivering computing resources ranging from data storage and processing to software, e.g. instant, commitment-free and on-demand handling of e-mail by external parties. Due to its virtualized, distributed and global nature, cloud computing will place new challenges to effective information security and risk management, as the control of information will be increasingly delegated to third parties. From information security management viewpoint, cloud computing initiatives should have a rigorous set of criteria designed to assess and manage the risk of adopting cloud services, to compare and measure suitable providers, and to monitor their operation and performance. Information security governance models should include a clear division of liabilities and responsibilities between customer and providers in the appropriate areas of security, access, audit control, recovery and incident management.

The proliferation of digital information will also pose new demands for information security practice. The amount of digital information handled and stored by organizations has been increasing continuously for years and, according to a recent study by IDC (Gantz and Reinsel, 2010), it will continue to increase by several tenfolds in the coming decade. IDC predicts that the average growth rate of information will exceed 50 % annually and the amount of sensitive information, both protected and unprotected, is growing even faster. As the amount of information, in general, and sensitive information, in particular, is growing, the importance of governance and management practices becomes ever more pronounced.

In the consumerization of IT, widely available consumer IT technologies, solutions and devices are making their way into workplace. Examples of these new technologies and solutions include smart phones, tablet PCs, social networking, blogs, wikis, etc. These developments have created many more avenues of vulnerability for organizations and have also changed the mindset of employees and technology users in terms of risk. IT departments in organizations no longer have full control over the devices and solutions used in the workplace; downright banning of their use is not an option either. Employees accustomed to using new services will either break the rules or change their job. Organizations need to recognize this trend and accommodate their information security management accordingly. Without proper oversight and governance, the proliferation of consumer technologies presents a serious risk of data leakage, as information increasingly flows through environments that, by default, are more open than the ones organizations have become accustomed to.

In the increasingly networked economy, organizations constitute extended enterprises where even core functions are divided between partners, suppliers and service providers. The continuing trend towards outsourcing and offshoring also increases potential risks and security exposures. Albeit organizations internal security policies and controls are maintained and enforced, these external relationships may pose a significant risk, unless governed and managed properly. As globalization continues, legal and cultural differences across the globe must be understood and taken into account in a proper fashion.

Governance Requirements for Information Security

The increasing risks and mounting security breaches render traditional, IT-oriented approach futile in bringing about the requisite level of security and safety. To cope with the aforementioned challenges of today's information security, organizations are in increasing need for more holistic, business-driven, and change-oriented approaches to govern and manage their information security. Instead of applying unmanaged and unintegrated "point solutions" to meet the minimum regulatory requirements, information security requires a concerted effort, high-level management commitment, and proactive stance to mitigate strategically relevant risks.

The traditional notion of Corporate Governance (CG) is geared to address the "agency problem" (Jensen and Meckling, 1976) of shared ownership apart from executive management. It subscribes to a functional view of an enterprise, where the one-dimensional overriding objective is to minimize the costs and maximize the profit. This teleological stance results in control-oriented behavior that emphasizes short term efficiency and conformance aspect of governance (Hoogervorst, 2009). As this traditional approach falls short in addressing the escalating complexity of the global business landscape, a specifically contrived, more encompassing, and design-oriented Enterprise Governance (EG) will be required (ibid.).

We view that with a proper, up-front design of pertinent policy domains and respective roles, accountabilities and policies, decision-making can be effectively distributed throughout the organization. The governance structure so contrived enables independent yet interconnected decision-making at all levels. Through this structure, the objectives of the company are set, and the means of attaining those objectives and monitoring performance are determined. The deliberate design helps create and sustain the connections among principles, policies, processes, products, people, and performance.

REFERENCE MODEL FOR INFORMATION SECURITY GOVERNANCE

In this section, we outline a reference model for information security governance. The governance model is intended to complement industry standards such as SOGP or ISO/IEC 27002 with the notion of "policy domains". Each policy domain represents a conceptual realm of responsibility that operates within its granted decision-making rights. The identification of policy domains in terms of the organizational level and horizontal dimension promotes clarity in the definition of roles and accountabilities as well as helps in partitioning and positioning the security activities. It helps in specifying and instantiating security policies, principles, standards and guidelines throughout the enterprise.

First, we will identify the horizontal and vertical dimensions of the governance model and outline an exemplary instantiation of the model by populating the policy domains with pertinent roles and descriptions of the domains. Then, we will provide an exemplary mapping of one of the sections of SOGP (Standard of Good Practice) to the governance model, highlighting how the model helps structuring the security activities by the policy domains.

Dimensions and Policy Domains

Characteristic to organizational decision-making is that the knowledge needed for the decision does not occur in centralized, integrated form, but is dispersed among several people. The decisions should be made by those who are familiar with the knowledge important to the decisions (Jensen and Meckling, 1992). Decision-making takes place at different levels of an organization and has different characteristics at each level.

Requisite Organization (Jaques, 1998) provides a useful, absolute yardstick to identify just the right number of levels to provide for effective managerial leadership. The complexity of work in organizations increases discontinuously in specific steps, stratifying different kinds of work into natural layers, or "strata", in the hierarchy. We view that Requisite Organization provides a rigorous, well-justified foundation for prescriptive organizational layering.

Jaques (1998) points out that Stratum V is the natural limit for a self-governing organization such as a middle-size business or an independent business unit of a large corporation and argues that an attempt should be made to organize complex and large-scale work into five-strata "unified complex systems". Accordingly, we limit the scope of the governance model to the lowest five strata that represent mainstream operational work as well as the business-level strategic context in a self-governing organization. Higher-level corporate realm, while relevant in large corporations, will be deliberately scoped out from this analysis.

The five levels of the governance model are, in descending order:

V – Strategic steering, with a planning horizon of more than five years. Decisions at this level pertain to the organization's business models, long-term objectives, future directions as well as formulation of corporate objectives and policies. These decisions are usually made in the face of external influences – technical advances, market shifts, environmental factors, or competition.

Typically, a steering committee ensures that the organization's security endeavors are aligned with its strategic objectives, provides funding for information security governance and is ultimately accountable for the definition, development and monitoring of respective strategy and policies.

IV – Strategic implementation, with a planning horizon of two to five years. Decisions are far-reaching and their implementation requires substantial time and effort: breakthrough innovation of new products and services and discovery of new markets. The strategic intent and demand signals from the strategic steering level are translated into more tangible objectives and concrete plans for operating units to realize.

At this level, organization-wide security policies, standards, guidelines, procedures and best practices are established and enforced, and respective development programs are designed, developed and followed up for compliance.

III – Tactical level with a planning horizon of one to two years. Decisions are limited to the existing asset base. Decision-making authority is limited to short-term core business process efficiencies to maximize the return on investment. Extrapolating from single instances, systems are planned to cope with known or predictable situations on a linear or serial basis.

At this level, information security services are designed, developed, managed and monitored. Specified security requirements are also incorporated in the existing and new work systems and solutions.

II – Operational level with a planning horizon of three months to a year. Operational decision-making is related to concerns of the immediate future, such as resource allocation, priorities, and expenditures. Operational decisions have a direct impact on the conduct of business and typically do not require laborious development efforts. The decisions are made in response to tactical plans or based on operational data and are mostly made by front-line business managers.

At this level, security aspects are integrated in the design and development of information systems in line with respective policies, standards and guidelines. Compliance with architectural and regulatory constraints is monitored, the overall level of security assessed and exceptions to security standards reported and acted upon.

I – Real-time level with an operational time perspective of one day to three months. Real-time decisions pertain to current activities and are an integral part of the modus operandi of the enterprise. They are made within the operations themselves, in line with the operational plans, by automation or people conducting the work.

At this level, information security features are implemented in applications and used in adherence with the policies and guidelines. Audit trails and logs are collected and security breaches and other exceptions reported.

Horizontally, the governance model distinguishes four dimensions:

1. **Design.** This aspect is about producing plans, blueprints and specifications that address security threats, risks, requirements, contingencies, compliance and policies.
2. **Development.** This aspect is about developing information security solutions and services and implementing requisite security features in existing and new solutions and work systems.
3. **Operations.** This aspect is about enforcing security policies in day-to-day operational work and carrying out security-related responsibilities.
4. **Monitoring.** This aspect is about monitoring the execution of established security procedures. The collected data are enriched to support new design and development.

Figure 1. Horizontal and vertical dimensions of the governance model

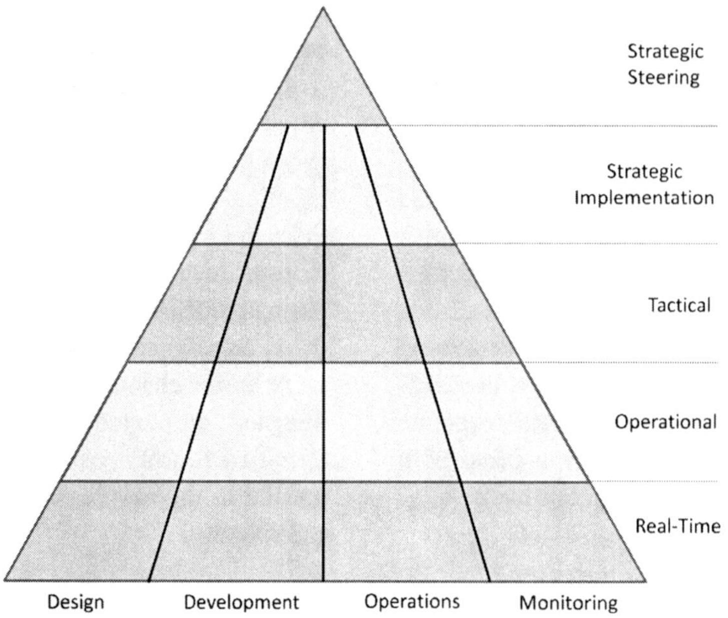

Table 1. Policy domain descriptions and exemplary roles

Strategic Steering	Executive Management, Chief Information Officer (CIO), Chief Security Officer (CSO)	Strategic Steering provides strategic direction and funding for information security governance and is accountable for the definition, development and monitoring of respective strategy and policies. Typically, a steering committee communicates the strategic management's aims and directions and ensures alignment of the security endeavors with organizational objectives. A steering committee of executives may include the chief executive officer (CEO), chief information officer (CIO), chief security officer (CSO), other C-level executives, business unit managers, and executives presenting functions such as human resources, legal, and public relations.						
	Design		**Development**		**Operations**		**Monitoring**	
Strategic Implementation	CIO, Chief Information Security Officer (CISO), Chief Architect, Chief Security Architect	Enterprise-wide authority over security management. Sets policies, standards and guidelines for information security, designs and coordinates respective development programs, and formally approves the information security architecture.	Chief Security Architect	In alignment with the information security strategy, conducts enterprise-wide information security initiatives, each of which is concerned with a particular security area, such as personnel security, data security, compliance, or business continuity management. Specifies high-level security requirements for work systems and solutions being developed.	Business Owners, Function Managers (e.g. Head of IT)	Enforces the specified policies, standards and guidelines and incorporates them with operational business practices. Business owners carry out their assigned information security responsibilities along with their management duties.	External Auditor	Ensures conformance with internal and external security requirements, such as regulatory compliance, and that information security policies and other measures are requisite. Ensures that governance arrangements are properly established and functioning.
Tactical	Domain Architects (e.g. Information Architect)	Identifies pertinent information, processes and applications. Designs and coordinates information security services and IT support to the security management practices in line with the enterprise level standards, guidelines and procedures. Brings IT perspective to information security governance work.	Business Analysts, Solution Architects	Translates high-level security requirements into use cases and "misuse cases" for work systems and solutions being developed. Implements information security services that support the organization's security initiatives.	Business Unit Managers, Process Owners, Service Managers	Ensures adherence to policies, standards and guidelines in processes and services.	Business Controllers	Monitors the use of architectural standards, guidelines, principles, regulatory compliance and other constraints and assesses the overall level of information security. Reporting and exception handling.
Operational	System Architects	Designs and coordinates the implementation of requisite security measures in information systems.	Project Managers, Integration and Application Architects, Subject Matter Experts	Incorporates security aspects in project-based IT development work. Implements security solutions, standards and policies in technical terms.	System Owners, Main Users	Ensures adherence to policies, standards and guidelines in information systems. Day-to-day security administrative activities.	Administrators	Monitors breaches to security policies, standards and guidelines.
Real-Time	Support Engineers	Assists developers and users in security-conscious development and use of technology.	Developers	Security administration tasks, incorporation and enforcement of security features in applications.	Users	Adheres to information security policies, standards and guidelines in using IT.	Operators	Real-time IT audit. Collection of audit trails, logs and reporting of exceptions.

The horizontal and vertical dimensions of the governance model are depicted in Figure 1. Strategic steering provides unity and closure as a separate top-level domain, and each intersection of the horizontal and vertical dimension constitutes a policy domain at lower levels. The policy domains are described and populated in Table 1. The instantiation of domains is exemplary and nonconclusive.

Exemplary SOGP Mapping

The Standard of Good Practice for Information Security (SOGP) by Information Security Forum (ISF) is an established and comprehensive business-oriented framework for information security management. An exemplary mapping of one of its sections, Security Architecture, to the governance model is exhibited in Table 2.

As can be readily noted in Table 2, the varied responsibilities for security architecture are dispersed across organizational levels and governance aspects. The same applies to other sections of SOGP as well and, in our view, is characteristic to ISM frameworks, in general. We view that a structured, more precise identification of policy domains for different information security activities provides clarity to designing and deploying information security governance and management practices into the organization. Our proposed reference model is intended to complement existing standards and frameworks such as SOGP for this part and take the guidance one step towards an actionable framework that would guide in designing and developing security arrangements throughout the organization.

FUTURE RESEARCH DIRECTIONS

This paper represents socio-organizational research that continues to be relevant to information security considerations (Dhillon and Backhouse, 2001). It is also representative of the design science approach (Simon, 1996) that has recently gained conspicuousness, inter alia, in management research (e.g. van Aken, 2004) and in information systems research (Hevner et al., 2004).

The model proposed in this chapter has several limitations that create opportunities for further research. First of all, the model, while rooted in pertinent research, is purely conceptual and needs empirical corroboration.

The first step to validate the model would be its encompassing mapping to existing governance and management frameworks in order to assess its applicability to different contexts. Examples of such mappings would include a full SOGP mapping along the lines outlined in this chapter, a mapping to ISO/IEC 27002:2005, and a mapping against CobiT and/or COSO.

The second step, based on the findings of the first step, would be to test the feasibility and practical applicability of the proposed governance model by applying it as a reference model in conjunction with one or several of the frameworks above in order to institute or enhance information security in case companies.

Further conceptual conjectures could be made for instance of how the model relates to different levels in information security maturity models.

CONCLUSION

As the business landscape is increasingly interconnected, fast-paced, and changing, governance, in general, cannot be based on all-inclusive implementation of detailed controls whose relevance must be frequently revisited. Rather, governance shall set a broad framework for decision-making, accountability and communication that is designed to change when needed. We call for encompassing enterprise governance that embraces all the pertinent aspect-systems and integrates them to a coherent whole.

Likewise, information security governance must transcend the traditional divide between

Table 2. Exemplary mapping of a SOGP section to the reference governance model

SOGP Section 4.1: Security Architecture				
Strategic Steering	Signs off on the development of security architecture [SM4.1.1] and approves the security architecture [SM4.1.5]. Accountable for the design and development of the security architecture.			
	Design	**Development**	**Operations**	**Monitoring**
Strategic	Incorporates the security architecture into the organization's enterprise architecture [SM4.1.1]. Defines security architecture principles [SM4.1.2]. Establishes a layered security architecture model [SM4.1.2]. Segregates environments with different security requirements [SM4.1.7]. Takes ownership of the security architecture [SM4.1.5].	Assesses business security requirements [SM4.1.2]	Approves the security architecture [SM4.1.5].	Introduces a method of measuring the uptake of the security architecture across the organization [SM4.1.3].
Tactical	Identifies security components that may be included in the security architecture (e.g. security controls, security services and security technologies) [SM4.1.2]. Provides architectural expertise and education [SM4.1.3]. Designs a process for implementing coherent and consistent security services and establishing common interfaces [SM4.1.6]. Specifies common naming conventions [SM4.1.7].	Develops tools and resources that will be used to help manage the security architecture (e.g. repositories of solutions, design patterns) [SM4.1.2]. Applies the security architecture in major IT projects [SM4.1.4]. Employs the defined process of implementing coherent and consistent security services [SM4.1.6].		Measures the uptake of security architecture across the organization [SM4.1.3].
Operational	Provides consistent security functionality across different hardware and software platforms [SM4.1.7].	Applies the security architecture in the development of business applications [SM4.1.4]. Integrates security controls at application, computer and network level [SM4.1.7]. Applies consistent cryptographic techniques [SM4.1.7].	Makes sure that consistent cryptographic techniques are used [SM4.1.7].	Controls the flow of information between different environments [SM4.1.7].
Real-Time	Helps managing the IT infrastructure [SM4.14].			

the strategy and governance of the organization and management of its information security. Security shall be woven into the very fabric of the organization and embedded in its culture. As with other aspect-systems, this requires fundamental re-thinking of established business practices. In fact, the biggest impediment to implementing information security governance as outlined herein may be the traditional, deeply rooted way of doing business.

In this chapter, we have outlined a reference model for information security governance. As a pure governance model, it does not prescribe what the actual controls and activities are; these particulars are left to more contingent management models that can be used in conjunction with our model. The model provides particular guidance in partitioning and positioning security controls and activities into "policy domains" at the intersections of vertical levels and horizontal dimensions.

The governance model is also generic enough to be reasonably applicable to business-level organizations of varying size. The population of policy domains will just be different case by case. The model is not meant to be used in corporate-scale organizations at the entire enterprise level, but it can be adapted to its divisional organizations. It is also indifferent to the idiosyncracies of different industries and is intended to be applicable to for-profit as well as non-profit organizations.

REFERENCES

Allen, J. (2005). *Governing for enterprise security*. Pittsburgh: Technical Note. Carnegie Mellon University.

Allen, J. H., & Westby, J. R. (2007). *Governing for enterprise security (GES)- Implementation guide, article 1: Characteristics of effective security governance*. Pittsburgh: Carnegie Mellon University.

Banathy, B. H. (1996). *Designing social systems in a changing world*. Springer.

Dhillon, G., & Backhouse, J. (2001). Current directions in IS security research: Towards socio-organizational perspectives. *Information Systems Journal*, *11*(2), 127–153. doi:10.1046/j.1365-2575.2001.00099.x

Federal Information Security Management Act. (2002). *Federal Information Security Management Act of 2002*.

Gantz, J. F., & Reinsel, D. (Eds.). (2010). *The expanding digital universe: A forecast of worldwide information growth through 2010*. IDC.

Hevner, S., & March, J., Park, & Ram, S. (2004). Design science research in Information Systems. *Management Information Systems Quarterly*, *28*(1), 75–105.

Hoogervorst, J. A. P. (2009). *Enterprise governance and enterprise engineering*. Springer.

Information Security Forum. (2007). *The standard of good practice for information security*. Information Security Forum.

International Organization for Standardization. (2005). *ISO/IEC 27002:2005. Information Technology–Security techniques–Code of practice for information security management*. International Organization for Standardization.

IT Governance Institute. (2007). *CobiT 4.1*. Isaca.

Jaques, E. (1998). *Requisite organization: A total system for effective managerial organization and managerial leadership for the 21st century* (revised 2nd edition). Baltimore, MD: Cason Hall & Co.

Jensen, M. C., & Meckling, W. H. (1976). Theory of the firm: Managerial behavior, agency costs and ownership structure. *Journal of Financial Economics*, *3*(4), 3–24. doi:10.1016/0304-405X(76)90026-X

Jensen, M. C., & Meckling, W. H. (1992). Specific and general knowledge, and organizational structure. In Werin, L., & Wijkander, H. (Eds.), *Contract economics* (pp. 251–274). Oxford, UK: Blackwell. doi:10.1111/j.1745-6622.1995.tb00283.x

Korhonen, J. J., Hiekkanen, K., & Lähteenmäki, J. (2009). EA and IT governance – A systemic approach. In J. Politis (Ed.), *Proceedings of the 5th European Conference on Management, Leadership and Governance* (pp. 66-74). Reading, UK: Academic Publishing Limited.

Korhonen, J. J., Yildiz, M., & Mykkänen, J. (2009). Governance of information security elements in service-oriented enterprise architecture. In R. Bilof (Ed.), *10th International Symposium on Pervasive Systems, Algorithms, and Networks - I-SPAN 2009* (pp. 768-773). Los Alamitos, CA: CPS, IEEE Computer Society.

McGinnis, S. K., Pumphrey, L., Trimmer, K., & Wiggins, C. (2004). Sustaining and extending organization strategy via Information Technology governance. *Proceedings of the 37th Hawaii International Conference on System Sciences*.

Siponen, M. T., & Oinas-Kukkonen, H. (2007). A review of information security issues and respective research. *Association for Computer Machinery SIGMIS Database*, *38*(1), 60–80.

van Aken, J. E. (2004). Management research based on the paradigm of the design sciences: The quest for field-tested and grounded technological rules. *Journal of Management Studies*, *41*, 219–246. doi:10.1111/j.1467-6486.2004.00430.x

van Aken, J. E., & Romme, A. G. L. (2009). Reinventing the future: Adding design science to the repertoire of organization and management studies. *Organization Management Journal*, *6*(1), 5–12. doi:10.1057/omj.2009.1

von Solms, R., & von Solms, S. H. (2006). Information security governance: A model based on the direct-control cycle. *Computers & Security*, *25*(6), 408–412. doi:10.1016/j.cose.2006.07.005

von Solms, S. H. (2006). Information security – The fourth wave. *Computers & Security*, *25*, 165–168. doi:10.1016/j.cose.2006.03.004

von Solms, S. H., & von Solms, R. (2005). From information security to business security? *Computers & Security*, *24*, 271–273. doi:10.1016/j.cose.2005.04.004

von Solms, S. H., & von Solms, R. (2009). *Information security governance*. Springer. doi:10.1007/978-0-387-79984-1

Whitman, M. E., & Mattord, H. J. (2008). *Principles of information security* (3rd ed.). Delmar.

ADDITIONAL READING

American Institute of CPAs. (2004). *Enterprise Risk Management – Integrated Framework*. AICPA.

American Institute of CPAs. (2009). *Guidance on Monitoring Internal Control Systems*. AICPA.

Anderson, R. J. (2008). *Security Engineering: A Guide to Building Dependable Distributed Systems* (2nd ed.). Indianapolis, IN: Wiley.

Brotby, K. (2009). *Information Security Governance: A Practical Development and Implementation Approach*. Hoboken, NJ: John Wiley and Sons.

Calder, A., & Watkins, S. (2008). *IT Governance: A Manager's Guide to Data Security and ISO 27001/ISO 27002* (4th ed.). London: Kogan Page.

Caralli, R. A. (2004). *Managing for Enterprise Security*. Pittsburgh: Carnegie Mellon University.

Egan, M., & Mather, T. (2004). *The Executive Guide to Information Security: Threats, Challenges, and Solutions*. Addison-Wesley Professional.

Hill, D. G. (2009). *Data Protection: Governance, Risk Management, and Compliance*. Boca Raton, FL: CRC Press. doi:10.1201/9781439806937

Information Systems Security Association. (2004). *Generally Accepted Information Security Principles (GAISP), V3.0*. Information Systems Security Association.

IT Governance Institute. (2006). *Information Security Governance: Guidance for Boards of Directors and Executive Management* (2nd ed.). ISACA.

IT Governance Institute. (2007). *Information Security Governance: Guidance for Information Security Managers*. ISACA.

Johnston, A. C., & Hale, R. (2009). Improved Security through Information Security Governance. *Communications of the ACM*, *52*(1), 126–129. doi:10.1145/1435417.1435446

Lacey, D. (2009). *Managing the Human Factor in Information Security: How to win over staff and influence business managers*. Wiley.

Mather, T., Kumaraswamy, S., & Latif, S. (2009). *Cloud Security and Privacy: An Enterprise Perspective on Risks and Compliance (Theory in Practice)*. Sebastopol, CA: O'Reilly Media.

Oram, A., & Viega, J. (Eds.). (2009). *Beautiful Security: Leading Security Experts Explain How They Think*. Sebastopol, CA: O'Reilly Media.

Osborne, M. (2006). *How to Cheat at Managing Information Security*. Rockland, MA: Syngress.

Raggad, B. G. (2010). *Information Security Management: Concepts and Practice*. CRC Press.

Schneier, B. (2004). *Secrets and Lies: Digital Security in a Networked World*. New York, NY: Wiley.

Sherwood, J., Clark, A., & Lynas, D. (2005). *Enterprise Security Architecture: A Business-Driven Approach*. San Fransisco, CA: CMP Books.

Starr, R., Newfrock, J., & Delurey, M. (2003). Enterprise Resilience: Managing Risk in the Networked Economy. *strategy+business*, 30, 1-10.

Tipton, H. F., & Krause, M. (Eds.). (2007). *Information Security Management Handbook* (6th ed.). Boca Raton, FL: Auerbach Publications. doi:10.1201/9781439833032

Vacca, J. R. (Ed.). (2009). *Computer Information Security Handbook*. Burlington, MA: Morgan Kaufmann Publishers.

Vacca, J. R. (Ed.). (2010). *Managing Information Security*. Burlington, MA: Syngress.

Westby, J. R., & Allen, J. H. (2007). *Governing for Enterprise Security (GES); Implementation Guide; Article 2: Defining an Effective Enterprise Security Program (ESP)*. Pittsburgh: Carnegie Mellon University.

Westby, J. R., & Allen, J. H. (2007). *Governing for Enterprise Security (GES); Implementation Guide; Article 3: Enterprise Security Governance Activities*. Pittsburgh: Carnegie Mellon University.

Williams, P. (2001). Information Security Governance. *Information Security Technical Report*, *6*(3), 60–70. doi:10.1016/S1363-4127(01)00309-0

KEY TERMS AND DEFINITIONS

Corporate Governance: The arrangement of controls over an organization that contributes to ensuring that the suppliers of its capital get return on their investment.

Enterprise Governance: The arrangement of roles, accountabilities and policies to effectively design, develop, operate and control an enterprise.

Enterprise Risk Management: Holistic approach to managing risks in an organization.

Information Security: Protection of the confidentiality, integrity and availability of information against the risks of unauthorized access, tampering, and accidental or deliberate eradication through pertinent prevention and detection measures.

Information Security Governance: The arrangement of roles, accountabilities and policies to deliberately design, develop, operate and monitor information security in an organization.

Information Security Management: Management of information security in an organization, typically through security controls.

IT Security: Information security applied to the development, acquisition, use and decommissioning of software and hardware infrastructure, data stores, information systems, networks and other information technology-related resources.

Chapter 5
Enterprise Information Security Policies, Standards, and Procedures:
A Survey of Available Standards and Guidelines

Syed Irfan Nabi
Institute of Business Administration, Pakistan & Center of Excellence in Information Assurance (CoEIA), King Saud University, Saudi Arabia

Ghmlas Saleh Al-Ghmlas
Center of Excellence in Information Assurance (CoEIA), King Saud University, Saudi Arabia

Khaled Alghathbar
Center of Excellence in Information Assurance (CoEIA), King Saud University, Saudi Arabia

ABSTRACT

This chapter explores enterprise information security policies, standards, and procedures. It examines the existing resources, analyses the available options, and offers recommendations to the CIOs and other people that have to make decisions about policies, standards, and procedures to ensure information security in their enterprise. Additionally, the need, requirements, and audience for different types of security documents are scrutinized. Their mutual relationship is examined, and the association among them is illustrated with a diagram supplemented by an example to bring about better comprehension of these documents. It is important to know the sources and organizations that make standards and guidelines. Therefore, the major ones are discussed. This research involved finding all of the relevant documents and analyzing the reasons for the ever-increasing number of newer ones and the revisions of the existing ones. Various well-known and established international, as well as national, information security standards and guidelines are listed to provide a pertinent collection from which to choose. The distinguishing factors and common attributes are researched to make it easier to classify these documents. Finally, the crux of the chapter involves recommending appropriate information security standards and guidelines based on the sector to which an organization belongs. An analysis of the role played by

DOI: 10.4018/978-1-4666-0197-0.ch005

these standards and guidelines in the effectiveness of information security is also discussed, along with some caveats. It is important for practitioners and researchers to know what is available, who the key players are, and the potential issues with information security standards and guidelines; they are all concisely presented in this chapter.

INTRODUCTION

Various facets of human life have undergone tremendous change because of technological advancements, especially in information and communication technologies (ICT). Information systems and communications networks, which are integral parts of these ever increasing information collection, processing, storage, and transmission activities, are becoming more and more attractive targets for malicious attacks by individuals, groups, and even organizations backed by nation states as another arena of warfare–cyberspace and a new type of war–information warfare. A recent example was the cyber attack on Iranian nuclear installations using a worm ("Stuxnet worm hits Iran nuclear plant staff computers," 2010; "Kaspersky Lab provides its insights on Stuxnet worm," 2010). There have been numerous incidents of cyber attacks on information systems and networks and the reported losses from these are increasing (PricewaterhouseCoopers, 2010).

Organizations need to effectively and proactively deal with these risks of potential attacks on their information systems and assets by providing appropriate measures in the form of systems, resources, policies, and programs to counter such risks. Responding to this need, numerous information security-related companies have developed and provided various off-the-shelf solutions. Although this seems to have simplified the tasks faced by organizations by allowing them to pick and choose whatever solutions best suit their needs, the situation is not as comfortable as one would like it to be. To provide information assurance, a plethora of policies, procedures, and standards have emerged in the global market that claim to provide the required protection. Because absolute information security is practically impossible, according to Gene Spafford, professor of computer science at Purdue university (Hagen, Albrechtsen, & Hovden, 2008), and with all of these companies trying to "sell" their products, it is not easy for an organization to make the best choice. The CISO/CIO can choose from numerous international standards and guidelines that are available to implement in their organization. The proponents of each have their own arguments as to why a particular standard or guideline is better for an organization. The purpose of this chapter is to cut through all the jargon, get to the heart of enterprise security, and provide actionable information for establishing appropriate policies, procedures, and standards for enterprise-level security. In this chapter the authors have tried to sieve through the available options and organize them in a fashion that makes it easier to select the most appropriate components for their particular organization. This chapter outlines various major standards and approaches to information security.

Although it is essential to look at the available standards, yet, it is first fundamentally indispensable to understand the concept of enterprise-level information security and how these standards fit into its information security framework. Enterprise information security may be divided into three levels: strategic, tactical, and operational. Based on the classification by Johnson (2003), the information security policy is at the top. This is going to establish the information security stance of an enterprise and steer the whole information security effort. It should be aligned with the business strategy of the enterprise. At the tactical level, the information security policies might be used to define standards that can then be translated into procedures at the operational level.

Before we proceed much further, it would be a good idea to define the various information security related documents that are referred to in the above sentences and throughout the chapter. The next section deals with this. The subsequent two sections discuss various security documents and their relationships with each other, along with an example to illustrate the differences among them. Then, enterprise information security polices, as well as their contents, components, and coverage are examined. This is followed by a survey of the international and some pertinent national information security standards and guidelines, including the relevant laws and regulations. Then comes the essence of the chapter, where these are analyzed for their applicability to various sectors such as banking and finance, corporate, defense, government, health care, and SMEs (Small and Medium Enterprises). In addition, the real world perspective and expectations from the information security standards are assessed for their reasonableness. Finally, we present a conclusion and future research directions.

SECURITY DOCUMENTS

Table 1 lists the main types of security documents. When examining this table and its related text, it is important to remember that the general characteristics of these documents have been put together as described by various researchers and practitioners, as well as institutes and organizations (Johnson, 2003; "Is it a Policy, a Standard or a Guideline?," 2010; Wood, 2008) to allow the reader to distinguish between them. Each of these documents has its own specific audience, which have to be kept in mind when designing/producing it. This list by no means represents the final word on these types of documents but is given to provide a better understanding of the often-used classifications of security related documents and the relationships between them. Different definitions or other characteristics may also exist for these documents.

DIFFERENTIATING BETWEEN POLICIES, STANDARDS, AND GUIDELINES

Information security policies, procedures, guidelines, and standards are put into service through information security controls to ensure that the information is protected (Johnson, 2003). Because the bottom-line operational parts of all these documents are security controls, their boundaries might be blurred. Therefore, it is important not only to know what each of these documents relates to but also to be able to distinguish among them.

Table 1. Type of security documents

Name/ Type	Structure	Purpose	Scope	Audience	Status
Policy	High-level statements	Setting the direction	Across the business	All	Mandatory
Standard	Specifics/ checklist	Compliance with established bench mark	Various (Global/national/ industry/organization)	Middle management	Regulatory
Guideline	Statements/ checklists	Providing best practice	Specific to standards or de facto standard	Middle & front-line managers	Recommendations
Procedure	Step-wise listings	Providing action steps	Specific to controls	Implementer/ user	Instructions

Descriptions of Documents

Policies

At the uppermost level and with the broadest scope are the policies. These are written statements from the leading executives of an organization about their intent in relation to securing information and giving direction and guidance to the workers who are to take actions and resolve any dispute that might arise regarding information security.

While some organizations might prefer a single policy, there are generally at least a few policies. Some organizations have numerous policies, each of which addresses only one specific area. Once again, the size, type, industry, culture, and criticality of the information and information systems often determine what and how many information security policies are adequate, ranging from a single all encompassing policy to several, each directed toward a particular issue, e.g., email policy, network access policy computer use/misuse policy, etc.

Information security policies are like business rules that might be considered as commitments from the top executive regarding the security of information that must be followed and adhered to. Sometimes these are mandated by law, particularly in the case of financial institutions. In those cases, it is all the more important that these be strictly abided by.

According to Wood, "a typical policy document includes a statement of purpose, description of the people affected, history of revisions, a few definitions of special terms and specific policy instructions from management." (Wood, 2008)

Standards

Standards are a "common ground where uniform actions will lead to predictable results" and serve as benchmarks against which a company measures its policies and practices (Kramer, 2003). Standards are means of enforcing information security policies consistently throughout an organization by provisioning appropriate obligatory controls related to specific technology, hardware, and/or software. Compliance with the standards provides uniformity of security controls. Yet, this by no means guarantees that the controls are adequate to provide effective information security (Siponen, 2006a).

Guidelines

According to the SANS Institute, guidelines are derived from best practices (a [best] practice is defined as a "technique or methodology that, through experience and research, has been proven to reliably lead to a desired result" (Visser, Matten, Pohl, & Tolhurst, 2008)) and consist of system specific or procedural specific "suggestions" ("Is it a Policy, a Standard or a Guideline?," 2010). These are highly recommended but non-obligatory controls that either supplement standards or fill-in as de facto standards where none exist.

Procedures

The step-by-step directions on how to apply various policies, standards, and guidelines in the real world on actual systems are called procedures. These are designed to help employees by providing detailed instructions on each step for implementing the controls that are specified in the policies, standards, and guidelines.

Information Security Documents Framework

In order to better understand the mutual relationships between the various information security documents discussed above, it might be better to look at how they are organized with reference to the management structure, as well as each other, as given in Figure 1. This is by no means a definite

Figure 1. Information security documents framework

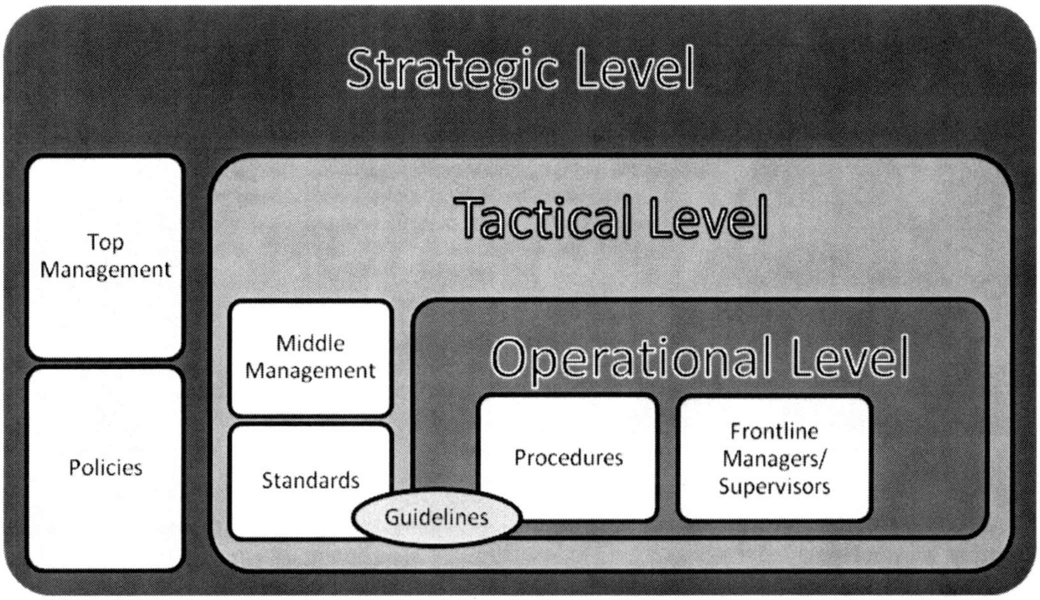

structure because these concepts tend to overlap in the real world based on different perspectives. Nevertheless, they have been put into distinct boundaries to make it easier to comprehend the differences. It might be of interest to note that the boxes in Figure 1 correspond to the scopes of the documents, which have inverse relationships with the sizes of the documents. In other words, a policy document contains all encompassing generalized direction on information security at the strategic level given by the top management, while procedures would be detailed (and perhaps lengthy) documents specific to each control in particular circumstances for particular systems.

To get a better understanding of these documents and how they are related, let's look at the example given in Figure 2. The *policy* here is the access control policy, which states that only authorized persons are to be allowed into the building. This is a clear but very general statement and it is not possible to implement it directly. Who is or is not authorized is a separate policy issue. The focus here is how to authenticate an authorized person. Therefore, there has to be some *standard* for authentication. The standard here mentions the use of a robust authentication technique and suggests the use of two-factor biometric authentication. This is still not directly implementable, and thus a *guideline* is used to help. It gives recommendations on selecting two appropriate biometric features that would be compatible and gives the required robustness. Moreover, it also suggests how the hardware should be installed so that the system could be ready for use. The worker that has to physically install and implement the system needs *procedure* that gives the directly implementable information on the details of installing the hardware, doing the preliminary data acquisition of the biometric features of the users, and making the required data link to ensure that only authorized users are allowed access.

Now that the differences between the various information security documents are clear, it might be a good idea to have a look at what should be included in information security policies at the enterprise level.

Figure 2. Example of information security documents explaining relationships among them

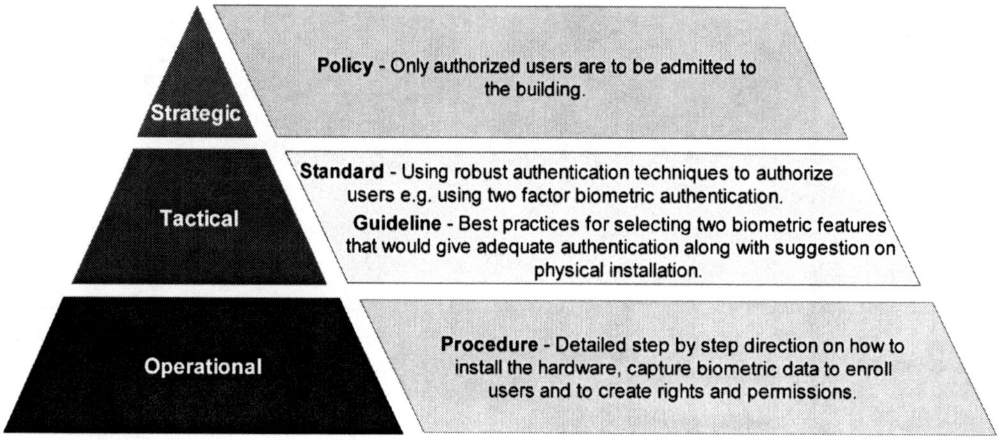

ENTERPRISE INFORMATION SECURITY POLICIES

As discussed above, adherence to security policies is mandatory, and an enterprise needs to specify in the policies the "organization's law" regarding all areas that are critical to it. Different areas could be critical for different organizations, but as a general guideline, the areas that are normally considered critical to an organization are given below.

Areas of Enterprise Information Security Policies

Network

Nowadays, organizations cannot work without networks. With networks comes the risk of unauthorized access–intrusion. This could be from outsiders as well as insiders. Companies need to make certain that their computer network is secure enough to resist any attempt at gaining unauthorized access by intruders.

Systems

By definition, information systems are there to gather, treat, keep, and communicate data important to and required by an organization to remain in business/operation and this whole setup including its processes needs to be secure.

Data Security

An important part of any organization's assets is the data it has. Securing it might be a matter of survival for the organization. Thus, data security, while it is in transit, being processed, or in storage, must be addressed in the policy.

Communications

Unless data and the resulting information are communicated in time and without distortion to the legitimate user that requires it, the whole purpose of an information system fails. Thus, securing communication is a critical aspect of information security.

Physical Security

When considering information security, it might be possible to overlook the security of the actual systems. Physically securing the building/room that contains the information systems and business data is a must. Thus, physical security also needs to be addressed in the policy.

Security from Viruses and Worms

Viruses and worms might be simple nuisances at the least or could be threats to the operations and existence of an organization. A network virus or worm could make its removal a nightmare for the IT people. A virus or worm is not something that an organization would want to have in its enterprise network. With the increasing focus on industrial sabotage through information warfare ("Stuxnet worm hits Iran nuclear plant staff computers," 2010; "Kaspersky Lab provides its insights on Stuxnet worm," 2010), this critical aspect has to be addressed in the policy.

Security from Social Engineering and Spam

Generally, information security is looked at from the technical perspective (Halliday, Badenhorst, & R. V. Solms, 1996), (B. V. Solms & R. V. Solms, 2004), but non-technical aspects are equally vital, if not more important (Spears & Barki, 2010). Users are generally considered to be the weakest link in any information security architecture (Dhillon & Moores, 2001), (Spears & Barki, 2010). The most common risk associated with an unsuspecting user is becoming a subject of social engineering. In addition, spam email can create havoc in a large network, especially if it comes from the users themselves. Both of these risks may be realized without any notice to the company or its workers. User awareness is considered to be a very effective technique in reducing these risks. Because when the going gets tough the budget cuts generally start with educational/training expenses, a policy directive regarding user awareness could reduce a lot of heartburn later.

Coverage

A security policy should cover all of the following aspects:

- **End-users:** This is important because the end-users must realize that information security is very important and that the top management is committed to securing its information.
- **Information owners:** It is imperative that the information owners are aware of their obligation regarding the information they own, including its security.
- **IT department:** The IT department is the key department with regard to information security. Their commitment and the top management's commitment to them in ensuring information security are essential for any effective implementation of information security.
- **Incident response and management:** No system is absolutely secure and a security breach is not a question of "if" but "when." In the case of this eventuality, the prime focus should be on damage control and the resumption of operations. Thus, incident response and management is vital for an organization to remain operational and as such must be addressed in the policy.

Components of Enterprise Information Security Policies

Information security policy documents could be as small as a single comprehensive policy or a collection of policies for all of the various specific aspects of information security. Similarly, there could be a variety of components for an information security policy, but it should contain the following essential components. If any one of these is missing, the policy might be rendered worthless.

- **Managements' stance:** This is where the direction for the whole organization is set.
- **Roles and responsibilities:** This is where the people learn what they are required to do or are responsible for getting done.

- **Disciplinary actions:** This is important to encourage people to adhere to and follow the policies.

SURVEY OF INTERNATIONAL STANDARDS AND GUIDELINES

This section will first discuss the sources of information security standards and guidelines, including some of the noticeable laws and regulations from different countries followed by some of the globally recognized standard forming bodies and professional organizations. Second, the available information security standards and guidelines are classified based on their analysis. Listed here are some of the pertinent national standards and guidelines. In addition, some other standards and guidelines of interest are given. The National Institute of Standards and Technology (NIST) has given a lot of importance to information security standards and guidelines, and thus documents from it are given separately. While there are standards and guidelines specifically dealing with information security, as discussed in the chapter there are other standards and guidelines that are not specifically intended for information security but nevertheless do contain some aspects relevant to information security. Some of these from the ISO are given at the end of this section.

Sources of Information Security Standards and Guidelines

The sources for information security standards and guidelines could be laws and regulations passed by governments and competent authorities, e.g., FISMA in the USA, standard forming bodies like ISO, or professional organizations like ISACA.

Laws and Regulations

Laws and regulations that are passed by the parliament or some other competent authority are by their very nature quite generalized and may be worded in an all-encompassing legal language. Their focus is more on what is to be done (or not to be done) and by whom, with emphasis on the end result rather than how it is to be done. These may then be elaborated using various guidelines for ease in putting these laws and regulations into action. The highly visible laws and regulation are generally those of the USA, UK, EU, Canada, and Australia. This is not to say that other countries are lagging behind in any respect but might be merely because of the language (i.e., English, which is quite widespread in the world in terms of the number of countries in which it is understood, as compared to Chinese, which might be understood by a fairly large number of people but in a relatively small number of countries) and/or the global influence of these countries. Among these, some of the most widely known are given in Table 2.

Standard Forming Bodies and Professional Organizations

There are certain bodies that develop standards and guidelines. Some of these are mandated through relevant legislation, while others are given by professional organizations based on consensus. Table 3 lists some of the significant ones.

Because there are so many standards, it is important to classify them to make it easier for the concerned individuals to understand the available options.

Classification of Standards

There are a variety of ways to classify the available information security standards and guidelines:

Global: These are the standards and guidelines that have been developed/proposed by international bodies that have a global de jure or de facto authority to provide such standards and guidelines. These are accepted by the world at large and are a means of achieving cooperation

Table 2. Prominent laws & regulations related to IS standards and guidelines

Law & Regulations	Name	Owner/ Developer	Focus	Concerned Organizations
EUDPD	European Union Data Protection Directive	EU	Privacy	Organizations keeping personal data
EUDRD	EU Data Retention Directive	EU	Privacy	Data Network and Telecommunication
FERPA	Family Educational Rights and Privacy Act	USA	Privacy	Educational Institutions
FISMA	Federal Information Systems Management Act	USA	IS Management	NIST
GLBA	Gramm–Leach–Bliley Act (Financial Services Modernization Act)	USA	Financial Services	Financial Organizations
HIPPA	Health Insurance Portability and Accountability Act	USA	Electronic Health Data and Transaction	Health Organizations
SOX	Sarbanes–Oxley Act	USA	Auditing	Corporation
UK DPA	UK Data Protection Act	UK	Privacy	Organizations keeping personal data

and communication among countries. At times, the goal of developing and adopting such standards is to facilitate mutual trade, travel, and commerce. The major global information security standards are: ISO 27000 series, CoBIT, ITIL, etc.

Regional/Group: These standards and guidelines are developed and adopted by a certain group of countries that have some common interest. They may (Regional) or may not (Group) be geographically located in proximity to one another.

National: These standards and guidelines are developed by a country to cater to its needs and are specifically suited to it. Sometimes these are a local adaption of prevailing International standards and guidelines, while at other times these may be developed indigenously for national use but are adopted by other countries as well and may even become global standards.

Industry: These are the standards and guidelines that are developed by consensus for an industry so that a baseline is maintained throughout the industry. At times, these are globally accepted/ required, while at other times they are restricted to an industry within a country.

Consortium: These standards and guidelines are developed/promoted by a group of companies belonging to different industries that are stakeholders in a larger project/product, thus forming a consortium.

The major ones are listed in Table 4.

National Standards and Guidelines

The standards and guidelines discussed above are primarily internationally accepted ones from the USA, UK, and EU. To get a broader picture of the global situation, it might be pertinent to look at a few national standards prevailing in some countries such as Australia/New Zealand, Canada, Singapore, Malaysia, and the UAE, as given in Table 5.

Other Standards and Guidelines of Interest

There are numerous information security standards and guidelines and among the leading ones are given above. Apart from the above-mentioned standards and guidelines, there are some other

Table 3. List of bodies that develop and/or provide standards

Source	Authority	Jurisdiction	Applicability	Document Type	Examples Related to Information Security
ISO (International Organization for Standardization)	Consensus (network of the national standards institutes of 163 countries)	Global	Business and Government	Standards and guidelines	ISO 27001
Attorney-General's Department	Government	Australia	Government agencies	Mandatory base-line	PSPF
Defence Signals Directorate (DSD)	Military	Australia	Government agencies	Mandatory base-line	ISM
ANSI (American National Standards Institute)	Government	USA	Government agencies	Technical Security Standards	X.9 Series
BSI (British Standards Institute)	Government	UK	Government agencies	Standards	BS10008, BS25999, BS7799
BSI (Bundesamt fur Sicherheit in der Informationstechnik)	Government	Germany	Government agencies	Standards	BSI 100
ISACA (Formerly IS Audit and Control Association)	Professional	International	General	Framework /Guidelines	CoBIT
ISSA (Information Systems Security Association)	Professional	International	Security Industry	Guidance	GAISP
IEEE (Institute of Electrical and Electronic Engineers)	Professional	International	General	Standards	IEEE1619, IEEE P1363
ITU - T (International Telecommunications Union - Telecommunication Standardization Sector	Professional	International	Telecommunications	Standards	X-Series
NFPA (National Fire Protection Association)	Professional	USA	General	Standard	NFPA 1600
NIST (National Institute of Standards and Technology)	Government	USA	General	Standards & Guidelines	NIST 800 Series
Government Chief Information Office (Department of Commerce, NSW, Australia)	Government	Australia	Government agencies	Guideline	NSW DoC GCIO ISG
OECD (Organization for Economic and Cultural Development)	Professional	OECD	General	Guideline	OECD Guidelines for the Security of Information Systems and Networks
COSO (Committee of Sponsoring Organizations of the Treadway Commission)	Professional	USA	private-sector	Voluntary	COSO Framework
OGC (Office of Government Commerce)	Government	UK	General	Voluntary	ITIL

Table 4. Major IS standards and guidelines

Standard/Guideline	Name/Description	Owner/Developer	Focus	Jurisdiction
ISO 27001	Information security management systems	ISO	ISMS - Framework	Global
ISO 27002	Code of practice for information security management	ISO	IS Controls	Global
COBIT	Control Objectives in IT	ISACA	Audit - Information Systems	Global
ITIL (ISO/IEC 2000)*	Information Technology Infrastructure Library	OGC - UK	Service Level Management	Global
SGP	Standard for Good Practice for Information Security	Information Security Forum (ISF)	Policies & Procedures	Global
SP 800-53	Recommended Security Controls for Federal Information Systems	NIST - USA	ISMS	US
SP 800-53 A	Guide for Assessing the Security Controls in Federal Information Systems	NIST - USA	ISMS	US
ISG	Information Security Guideline	Government Chief Information Office, Department of Commerce, NSW, Australia	ISMS and Controls	Australia
OECD Guidelines for the Security of Information Systems and Networks	OECD Guidelines for the Security of Information Systems and Networks	OECD	Security Culture	OECD

* Related to each other – ITIL provides detailed guidance and best practices on implementing ISO/IEC 20000

relevant ones that are either with a particular focus for some specific purpose or may be classified as supporting standard or guideline. Because these might be of interest to an information security professional these are listed in Table 6.

National Institute of Standards and Technology (NIST) Documents

The National Institute of Standards and Technology (NIST) has developed and provided many valuable guidelines. Some of the important ones are listed in Table 7.

Non-Information Security Specific Standards and Guidelines from International Organization for Standardization (ISO)

While there are specific Information Security standards and guidelines, there are many other standards and guidelines that are not primarily meant for information security but do include one or more aspects related to it. For example, ISO 9000 is known as a quality standard but includes a guideline (ISO 9003:2004) related to information security in software engineering. Thus, these sorts of standards and guidelines have their own value for the security professionals. Table 8 gives a list of some of these ISO standards and guidelines.

Table 5. List of some relevant IS publications from different countries around the world

Country	Standard/Guideline	Name/Description	Focus [§]
Canada	**GO-ITS 25** Series	Government of Ontario Information & Technology Standards	Platform-independent technical security requirements for the protection of the integrity, confidentiality and availability of networks and computer systems.
Singapore	**SS 463** (ICS 35) Series	Singapore Standard National Information Infrastructure (NII) Standards	Establishing open standards that connect various disparate networks to interoperate with each other for information sharing and communication.
Singapore	**SS 493**	Specification For IT Security Standards Framework	IT security standards framework with the aim to facilitate the development and adoption of IT security standards in Singapore
Malaysia	**MS 1536**	Information Technology – Guidelines For The Management of IT Security	Management of IT security
Malaysia	**MS 1537**	Information Security Managements Systems - Specification With Guidance For Use	Establishing, implementing, operating, monitoring, reviewing, maintaining and improving a documented ISMS within the context of the organisation's overall business risks.
UAE	**Information Security Standards**	Abu Dhabi Information Security Standards	Standardization of information security controls to create an environment of trust for stakeholders and secure their operations through risk management process.
UAE	**Information Security Policies and Procedures Guide**	Abu Dhabi Information Security Policies and Procedures Guide	A general overall practical starting point for developing and maintaining the full set of information security policies and procedures.

[§] The **Focus** of each of these documents has been taken from the document/website listed in **Resources**[1].

DISCUSSION AND ANALYSIS

When examining this chapter, information security professionals might feel inundated by the scores of information security standards and guidelines and the numerous options. In fact, it might be unnerving to a novice. To make life easier for information security professionals, especially those tasked with making decisions about information security at a higher level, the following section succinctly summarizes important information about information security standards and guidelines, along with recommendations, that will help them get started. It is imperative that they also go through the next section, "Reality Check," before jumping into action.

Recommended Information Security Standards and Guidelines for Specific Sectors

While there are many standards and guidelines mentioned in this chapter, it is just an introduction to the topic meant to provide a general idea of the types of standards and guidelines available. The relevant sector-wise information security standards and guidelines, which may be better suited and applicable to a particular sector, are discussed below. It is hoped that it is clear by now

Table 6. Other standards and guidelines of interest

Standard/Guideline	Name/Description	Owner/Developer	Focus	Jurisdiction	Applicability
ISM (formerly ACSI 33)	Information Security Manual	Defence Signals Directorate (DSD), Australian Government	Security of Defence ICT systems	Australia	Defence
PSPF	Protective Security Policy Framework	Australian Government	Government Policy on Information Security	Australia	Government
AS/NZS 4360	Risk Management	Australia/New Zealand	Risk Management Process	Australia & New Zealand	General
BS 10008	Evidence Weight and Legal Admissibility of Electronic Information Specification	BSI - UK	Legal Aspects of Authenticity and Integrity	UK	General
BS 25999	Business Continuity Management	BSI - UK	Audit & Compliance of Business Continuity Management System	UK	General
BSI 100 (IT-Grundschutz)	IT Baseline Protection	BSI - Germany	ISMS	Germany	General
OECD Guidelines for Cryptography Policy	Cryptographic Policies Guidelines	OECD	Cryptography	OECD	Data communications and storage
GAIT	Guide to the Assessment of IT Risk	The Institute of Internal Auditors	Risk Management and Audit	Global	General
NFPA 1600	Standard on Disaster Management and Business Continuity	NFPA - USA	Governance of Disaster Management	USA	Government
PAS77	Publicly Accessible Specification 77	BSI - UK	IT Service Continuity Management	UK	Government
PCI DSS	Payment Card Industry Data Security Standard	PCI Security Standard Council	Data Security	Global	Banking & Finance
STIGs	STIGs Security Technical Implementation Guides	NIST, NSA and DISA/DoD	Technical Security	USA	Government Agencies
TickIT	TickIT	BSI Joint TickIT Industry Steering Committee (JTISC)	Software Quality Assurance	UK & Sweden – Global	Software
FIPS 199	Standards for Security Categorization of Federal Information and Information Systems	NIST - USA	Security Categorization	USA	Government Agencies
FIPS 200	Minimum Security Requirements for Federal Information and Information Systems	NIST - USA	Security Baseline	USA	Government Agencies
FIPS 201	Personal Identity Verification for Federal Employees and Contractors	NIST - USA	Authentication	USA	Government Agencies

continued on following page

Table 6. Continued

Standard/Guideline	Name/Description	Owner/Developer	Focus	Jurisdiction	Applicability
ISO 15408 - Common Criteria for IT Security Evaluation		ISO	Evaluation specifications for information Security Assurance of IT	Global	General

that there is no single standard or guideline that would be good enough for all organizations in the various sectors all over the world. It is essential to examine information security from different perspectives to form, as much as possible, a holistic and complete view.

The standards and guidelines that are more pertinent and applicable to various sectors and for specific purposes are given below and listed in Table 9:

Banking and Finance: Although this sector has a variety of laws that govern its operations, from the information security perspective, the relevant portion of these laws is mostly concerned with the privacy of personal data, including Personally Identifiable Information (PII), or the assurance of the correct reporting of financial data pertaining to an organization. Certain standards and guidelines have been developed to ensure compliance with the stipulated laws and regulations, but the regulations as such like GLBA (Gramm–Leach–Bliley Act) or SOX (Sarbanes–Oxley Act) are more commonly known in the industry.

Corporate Sector: Most of the regular comprehensive information security standards and guidelines are targeted toward the corporate sector because corporations have the budget and organizational structure to get these implemented and have a greater risk of potential loss in the case of a security breach. Moreover, at times there are legal information security requirements that the corporate sector has to abide by, and it may be virtually impossible for these corporations to operate without these elaborate, detailed, and voluminous information security standards and guidelines. An exception to this is the first one on the list, CAG (Consensus Audit Guidelines), which contains 20 Critical Security Controls that have been agreed upon so as to provide some ray of hope for smaller organizations because of being fairly simple and easy to understand and implement. It may be used as the bare-minimum essential for any organization and a foundation stone for larger organizations.

Defense: Defense is a special sector because its security is closely guarded by all governments and they would rather live with vulnerabilities in their defense organizations than agree to an independent security audit. Because of its special status, i.e., they might be operating in a hostile environment where it is better to permanently lose an information asset than risk it landing in an adversary's hands, defense organizations must conform to a separate different set of regulations, mostly designated as directives. Because these are numerous, only the names of the issuing organizations are listed in the table.

Government: Governments are run through public funding and generally have a parliamentary body and judiciary to keep an eye on its operations. Thus, there are various legalities that governments have to follow. There are certain directives from various executive offices, as well as legislation, that must be observed, e.g., FISMA. At the same time, the information security standards and guidelines applicable to the corporate sector may also be used by public sector organizations.

Health care: Health care may be considered to be part of the corporate sector. However, the volume of personal information involved and the necessity of all human beings to occasion-

Table 7. List of information security related NIST publications

Number	Name
SP 800-12	An Introduction to Computer Security: The NIST Handbook
SP 800-18	Guide for Developing Security Plans for Information Technology Systems
SP 800-27	Engineering Principles for Information Technology Security
SP 800-28	Guidelines on Active Content and Mobile Code
SP 800-30	Risk Management Guide for Information Technology Systems
SP 800-34	Contingency Planning Guide for Information Technology Systems
SP 800-35	Guide to Information Technology Security Services
SP 800-36	Guide to Selecting Information Security Products
SP 800-37	Guide for the Security Certification and Accreditation of Federal Information Systems
SP 800-39	Managing Risk from Information Systems - An Organizational Perspective
SP 800-40	Creating a Patch and Vulnerability Management Program
SP 800-44	Guidelines on Securing Public Web Servers
SP 800-45	Guidelines on Electronic Mail Security
SP 800-46	Security for Telecommuting and Broadband Communications
SP 800-47	Security Guide for Interconnecting Information Technology Systems
SP 800-48	Wireless Network Security: 802.11, Bluetooth, and Handheld Devices
SP 800-50	Building an Information Technology Security Awareness and Training Program
SP 800-53A	Guide for Assessing the Security Controls in Federal Information Systems
SP 800-55	Performance Measurement Guide for Information Security
SP 800-58	Security Considerations for Voice Over IP Systems
SP 800-60	Guide for Mapping Types of Information and Information Systems to Security Categories
SP 800-61	Computer Security Incident Handling Guide
SP 800-63	Electronic Authentication Guideline
SP 800-64	Security Considerations in the Information System Development Life Cycle
SP 800-65	Integrating Security into the Capital Planning and Investment Control Process
SP 800-66	An Introductory Resource Guide for Implementing the Health Insurance Portability and Accountability Act (HIPAA) Security Rule
SP 800-68	Guidance for Securing Microsoft Windows XP Systems for IT Professionals: A NIST Security Configuration Checklist
SP 800-70	National Checklist Program for IT Products--Guidelines for Checklist Users and Developers
SP 800-72	Guidelines on PDA forensics.
SP 800-82	Guide to Industrial Control Systems (ICS) Security
SP 800-83	Guide to Malware Incident Prevention and Handling
SP 800-88	Guidelines for Media Sanitization
SP 800-92	Guide to Computer Security Log Management
SP 800-95	Guide to Secure Web Services
SP 800-97	Establishing Wireless Robust Security Networks: A Guide to IEEE 802.11i
SP 800-100	Information Security Handbook: a Guide for Managers
SP 800-101	Guidelines on Cell Phone Forensics
SP 800-115	Technical Guide to Information Security Testing

continued on following page

Table 7. Continued

Number	Name
SP800-123	Guide to General Server Security
NISTIR 7298	Glossary of Key Information Security Terms
NISTIR 7564	Directions in Security Metrics Research
NISTIR 7621	Small Business Information Security - The Fundamentals

ally access health care facilities have prompted specific legislation for the health care industry (HIPPA - Health Insurance Portability and Accountability). Like the banking and finance sector, the prime concern here is also the privacy of the PII and other health related information. A good source of information security standards and guidelines for health care facilities could be the Tenet Healthcare Corporation Information security standards, which are freely available at their website and may be modified/customized by other health care providers to their particular needs and requirements.

SMEs (Small and Medium Enterprises): These are numerous and may not per se have a significant dollar amount in terms of loss in the case of a breach in their information assets. Yet, the indiscriminate attacks by cyber criminals and the cumulative effect of such attacks on SMEs might warrant a serious approach by SMEs to better protect their information systems and assets. Applying the widely-known information security standards and guideline like the ISO 27000 series, ITIL, COBIT, and SGP is not only cumbersome but also expensive. However, instead of leaving out information security, the CAG (Consensus Audit Guidelines) 20 Critical Security Controls may be applied by SMEs. The CAG are simple, concise, and easy to implement and maintain, thus allowing SMEs to benefit from having at least minimal base-line protection.

The list of suitable information security standards and guidelines that are appropriate to particular sectors is given in Table 9.

Reality Check

With the whole world apprehensive about the looming menace posed by the realization of any one of several information security threats and working frantically to build security walls around their information resources and systems to fortify them, it is easy to lose sight of the actual goal of all this work. When an individual is so keenly focused on specifics, it is only natural that the big picture of the forest is lost to the uniqueness of the trees. The purpose is to ensure the security of information assets and resources, not to have a particular policy, standard, control, hardware, software, or system. All of these policies, standards, controls, and systems, which are there to ensure the presence of processes (Siponen, 2006b) that adhere to the policies, standards, and controls, are merely tools and techniques for achieving the fundamental goal of effectively securing the information. As such, they ought to be treated just like that, i.e., supporting elements to achieve the principal objective of effective security.

It is pertinent to mention that standards are by no means a guarantee that there is going to be effective security in an organization. An organization that has implemented an information security standard and has a certification to that effect is only making it known to its stakeholders, partners, customers, suppliers, and the world at large that it takes security seriously, and that it has consistently applied security controls all over the organization. The fact that the organization has shown due diligence and is not turning a blind eye to the eventuality of a security incident should

Table 8. List of publications from ISO that have some information security aspect

Standard/Guideline	Name/Description	Owner/Developer	Focus
ISO 9000	Quality management systems	ISO	Relevant to standardization of software and systems with regards to information security.
ISO 12207	Systems and software engineering -- **Software** life cycle processes	ISO	Software life cycle
ISO 15288	Systems and software engineering -- **System** life cycle processes	ISO	System life cycle
ISO/IEC 7498	Open System Interconnect Security Model	ISO	Secure Networks & Communications
ISO/IEC 10181	Security Frameworks	ISO	Security Services Application
ISO/IEC 13335	IT Security Management	ISO	Technical IT Security Controls
ISO TR 13569	Financial Services - Information Security Guidelines	ISO	Information Security Program for Financial Service Providers
ISO/IEC 13888	Non-Repudiation	ISO	Evidence of Communication/Transaction
ISO 15489	Records Management	ISO	Recordkeeping
ISO/IEC 17021	Conformity Assessment	ISO	Audit & Certification Providers
ISO/IEC 18028 (ISO27033)*	IT Network Security	ISO	Specifics of network security mechanisms
ISO/IEC 18043	Selection, Deployment and operations of Intrusion Detection Systems	ISO	Principles to Check Unauthorized Access
ISO/IEC TR 18044 (ISO 27035)*	Security Incident Management	ISO	Incident Management
ISO 19011	Guidelines for Quality and/or Environmental Management Systems Auditing	ISO	Auditing
ISO/IEC 19770	Software Asset Management	ISO	Management of Software
ISO/IEC 2000 (ITIL)**	ITIL- IT Service Management	ISO	IT Service Management
ISO 21827	System Security Engineering Capability Maturity Model (SSE CCM)	ISO	Security Processes in SDLC
ISO/PAS 22399	Societal Security - Guideline for Incident Preparedness and Operational Continuity Management	ISO	Performance criteria for Operational Continuity
ISO/IEC 24762	Guidelines for ICT Disaster Recovery Services	ISO	Resilience of ICT infrastructure
ISO/PAS 28000	Specifications for Security Management for the Supply Chain Management	ISO	Security Management for Supply Chain

continued on following page

Table 8. Continued

Standard/Guideline	Name/Description	Owner/Developer	Focus
ISO 31000 (AS/NZ 4360)	Risk Management	ISO	Comprehensive Risk Management
ISO 31010	Risk Assessment	ISO	Risk Assessment Techniques
ISO 38500 (AS 8015)	Corporate Governance of IT	ISO	Guidance for Top Executives on IT
ISO/IEC Guide 73	Risk Management	ISO	Vocabulary for Risk Management

* New version with a new number

** Related to each other – ITIL provides detailed guidance and best practices on implementing ISO/IEC 20000

calm down any edgy stakeholder that is nervous about possible security lapses.

That is all a policy, standard, or control is going to achieve. A different question is whether those controls are adequate to effectively secure the information assets. The *proof of the pudding is in the eating* and although numerous experts have put time and effort into developing this plethora of standards, yet, unfortunately there are few if any rigorous empirical verifications of the effectiveness of these standards. This may explain why there are so many of them and still more continue to be doled out. Actually, there is a dire need to empirically verify whether or not these numerous information security standards are effective (Siponen & Willison, 2009).

Another important point to remember in this regard is that on the way down from generalized policy statements through standards and guidelines to implementing individual specific controls it all generally becomes technical and the non-technical aspects, including the "dynamic, capricious, and unpredictable" human element, are lost (Nabi et al., 2010), which might hold the key to an effective information security solution (Spears & Barki, 2010; Siponen, 2005; Stanton & Stam, 2006; Whitman, 2008). It is imperative that non-technical elements of information security, including but not limited to organizational culture, corporate ethics, and human behavior, be taken into account along with suitable policies, standards, and controls to establish meaningful and effective security for information assets and systems.

CONCLUSION

It can be seen from the above discussion and analysis of the information security standards and guidelines that these are very much needed to create an environment conducive to effective information security, and that this is more akin to "information security hygiene factor", similar to the "hygiene factor" of Herzberg's Two Factor Theory of Motivation (Herzberg, 1968), which is necessary but not sufficient enough in itself to provide the required effective information security. Thus, this has to be kept in mind when designing any enterprise information security policy and during the selection of any standard to be applied in an organization. There are some of the other factors apart from the technical ones that should also be considered when effective information security is required by an organization.

FUTURE RESEARCH DIRECTIONS

Information security, like any other aspect of security, involves putting controls on operations, which is actually creating hindrances to the operations of an organization. At the same time, a lack of security has the potential to realize any of the many information security risks that can cause huge losses to an organization, to the extent that the organization might cease to operate. Having a better idea of the information security docu-

Table 9. List of information security standards and guidelines relevant to different sectors

Industry	Standard & Guideline	Comments
Banking and Finance	**Basel II** - second report from the Basel Committee on Banking Supervision, Risk Management Principles for Electronic Banking	Dealing with internal controls, financial reporting and insider threat
	COBIT (Control Objectives for Information and related Technology)	Produced by ISACA with focus on controls and auditing
	COSO - Committee of Sponsoring Organizations of the Treadway Commission, Enterprise Risk Management Integrated Framework	A three dimensional framework used for analyzing controls
	FDIC (Federal Deposit Insurance Corporation)	Information security component is privacy of personal information
	GLBA (Gramm-Leach-Bliley Act)	Information security component is privacy, protecting the security and confidentiality of financial institution customers' non-public personal information
	PCI DSS (Payment Card Industry Data Security Standard)	Security and interoperability of various payment cards.
	SOX - The United States' Sarbanes-Oxley law - Section 404 7 302	Integrity of information systems and reports generated by them
Corporate Sector	**CAG** (Consensus Audit Guidelines) 20 Critical Security Controls	Simple and easy
	CISO Toolkit by Fred Cohen	An easy to understand checklist for business managers
	COBIT (Control Objectives for Information and related Technology)	Produced by ISACA with focus on controls and auditing
	ISO 27000 Series	Information Security Management Systems and corresponding controls.
	IT Baseline Protection Catalogues	Produced by German Federal Office for Security in Information Technology – very detailed.
	ITIL (Information Technology Infrastructure Library)	Produced by Office of Government Commerce (OGC), UK. Very comprehensive.
	NIST 800-14 Generally Accepted Principles and Practices for Securing Information Technology Systems	Guidelines for general use
	OCTAVE (Operationally Critical Threat, Asset, and Vulnerability Evaluation)	A risk management method from Carnegie Mellon University
	SGP (Standard of Good Practice) for Information Security	Provided by ISF (Information Security Forum), UK
	SSE-CMM (Systems Security Engineering Capability Maturity Model)	For large enterprises
Defense	Defense Intelligence Agency - IS related directives	Deals mostly with intelligence agencies
	Department of Defense - IS related directives	Must for DoD related departments
	DITSCAP (Defense Information Technology Systems Certification and Accreditation Process)	More focused on certification and assurance of IT Systems
	IT Baseline Protection Catalogues	Produced by German Federal Office for Security in Information Technology – very detailed.
	National Security Agency (NSA) - IS related directives	Deals generally with security agencies
Government	Attorney General of the United States - IS related directives	These are various related to government

continued on following page

Table 9. Continued

Industry	Standard & Guideline	Comments
	CAG (Consensus Audit Guidelines) 20 Critical Security Controls	Simple and easy
	Department of Commerce - IS related directives	These are various related to government
	Department of State - IS related directives	These are various related to government
	FISMA (Federal Information Security Management Act) of 2002 related standard and guidelines	NIST (National Institute of Standards and Technology) has developed standards and guideline for implementing it and are freely available.
	IT Baseline Protection Catalogues	Produced by German Federal Office for Security in Information Technology – very detailed.
	ITIL (Information Technology Infrastructure Library)	Office of Government Commerce (OGC), UK. Very comprehensive
	National Security Decision Directives (NSDs/NSDDs) - IS related directives	These are various related to government
	NIACAP (National Information Assurance Certification and Accreditation Process)	Complementary guideline to DITSCAP for government
	NIST 800-18 Guide for Developing Security Plans for Federal Info Systems	These are various related to government
	NIST 800-53 Recommended Security Controls for Federal Information Systems	These are various related to government
	Standard of Good Practice for Information Security	Provided by ISF (Information Security Forum), UK
Health care	**HIPPA** (Health Insurance Portability and Accountability) Act of 1996	Related to personal data on the patients
	Tenet Healthcare Corporation Information security standards	Available and may be used as guidelines by health care service industry
SMEs	**CAG** (Consensus Audit Guidelines) 20 Critical Security Controls	Simple and easy

ments, the next step is to see how security can be effectively balanced against operations.

Further, there is a need to verify the effectiveness of implementing an information security standard. Perhaps the effectiveness of all of these various standards and guidelines might be compared to provide a more objective basis for selection of the most appropriate one for an organization.

REFERENCES

BBC News Middle East. (2010, September 26). *Stuxnet worm hits Iran nuclear plant staff computers*. Retrieved from http://www.bbc.co.uk/news/world-middle-east-11414483

Dhillon, G., & Moores, S. (2001). Computer crimes: Theorizing about the enemy within. *Computers & Security*, *20*(8), 715–723. doi:10.1016/S0167-4048(01)00813-6

Hagen, J. M., Albrechtsen, E., & Hovden, J. (2008). Implementation and effectiveness of organizational information security measures. *Information Management & Computer Security*, *16*(4), 377–397. doi:10.1108/09685220810908796

Halliday, S., Badenhorst, K., & Solms, R. V. (1996). A business approach to effective information technology risk analysis and management. *Information Management & Computer Security*, *4*(1), 19–31. doi:10.1108/09685229610114178

Herzberg, F. (1968). One more time: How do you motivate employees? *Harvard Business Review*, *46*(1), 53–62.

Is it a Policy, a Standard or a Guideline? (2010). *SANS: Information Security Policy Templates*. Professional Orgnaization. Retrieved November 29, 2010, from http://www.sans.org/security-resources/policies/

Johnson, P. (2003, September 2). *What are policies, standards, guidelines and procedures?* MindfulSecurity.com – The Information Security Awareness Resource. Retrieved November 29, 2010, from http://mindfulsecurity.com/2009/02/03/policies-standards-and-guidelines/

Kaspersky Lab - Virus News. (2010, September 24). *Kaspersky Lab provides its insights on Stuxnet worm*. Antivirus Company. Retrieved November 29, 2010, from http://www.kaspersky.com/news?id=207576183

Kramer, J. (2003). *The CISA prep guide: mastering the certified information systems auditor exam*. New Jersey: John Wiley and Sons.

Nabi, S. I., Nabi, S. W., Tipu, S. A. A., Haqqi, B., Abid, Z., & Alghathbar, K. (2010). Data confidentiality and integrity issues and role of information security management standard, policies and practices – An empirical study of telecommunication industry in Pakistan. In *Security Technology, Disaster Recovery and Business Continuity International Conferences, SecTech and DRBC 2010, Future Generation Information Technology Conference, FGIT 2010,* Jeju Island, Korea, December 13-15, 2010, Communications in Computer and Information Science (CCIS) (vol. 122). Berlin, Germany: Springer.

PricewaterhouseCoopers. (2010). *Information security breaches survey 2010 - Technical report* (p. 22). Earl's Court, UK: PricewaterhouseCoopers.

Siponen, M. (2006a). Information security standards: focus on the existence of process not its content. *Communications of the ACM, 49*(8), 97–100. doi:10.1145/1145287.1145316

Siponen, M. (2006b). Information security standards focus on the existence of process, not its content. *Communications of the ACM, 49*(8), 97–100. doi:10.1145/1145287.1145316

Siponen, M., & Willison, R. (2009). Information security management standards: Problems and solutions. *Information & Management, 46*(5), 267-270. doi:doi: DOI: 10.1016/j.im.2008.12.007

Siponen, M. T. (2005). Analysis of modern IS security development approaches: towards the next generation of social and adaptable ISS methods. *Information and Organization, 15*(4), 339–375. doi:10.1016/j.infoandorg.2004.11.001

Solms, B. V., & Solms, R. V. (2004). The 10 deadly sins of information security management. *Computers & Security, 23*(5), 371–376. doi:10.1016/j.cose.2004.05.002

Spears, J. L., & Barki, H. (2010). User participation in Information Systems security risk management. *Management Information Systems Quarterly, 34*(3), 503–522.

Stanton, J. M., & Stam, K. R. (2006). *The visible employee: Using workplace monitoring and surveillance to protect information assets-without compromising employee privacy or trust*. Medford, NJ: Information Today, Inc.

Visser, W., Matten, D., Pohl, M., & Tolhurst, N. (2008). *The A to Z of corporate social responsibility*. New Jersey: John Wiley and Sons.

Whitman, M. E. (2008). Security policy: From design to maintenance. In *Information Security: Policy, Processes, and Practices, Advances in Management Information Systems* (*Vol. 11*, pp. 123–151). Armonk, NY: M. E. Sharpe Inc.

Wood, C. C. (2008). *Information security policies made easy* (10th ed.). Houston, TX: Information Shield.

KEY TERMS AND DEFINITIONS

Enterprise: A large organization, company, or entire business group spanning various countries that uses computers and computer-based information systems.

Framework: Organization of different components in such a way that their inter-relationships and workings are clearly defined.

Guideline: A document that give the best practices of how to go about doing something.

Law: A statute passed by a competent authority, e.g., a parliament.

Policy: High level statement(s) from the top management that defines the strategic direction of an organization.

Procedure: The step-by-step details of how to do something.

Standard: A consensus document to ensure the presence of certain controls that are supposed to provide consistency in the operations of an organization.

ENDNOTE

[1] **Resources:**

GO-ITS Standards - Government of Ontario (Canada). (n.d.). Mandatory Government of Ontario Information Technology Standards, Guidelines, Policies and Procedures. Government. Retrieved December 6, 2010, from http://www.mgs.gov.on.ca/en/IAndIT/STEL02_047303.html

Information Security Policies and Procedures Guide. (2009, March 15). Abu Dhabi Systems & Information Centre. Retrieved from http://adsic.abudhabi.ae/Sites/ADSIC/Navigation/EN/Projects/information-security.html

Information Security Standards. (2009, March 15). Abu Dhabi Systems & Information Centre. Retrieved from http://adsic.abudhabi.ae/Sites/ADSIC/Navigation/EN/Projects/information-security.html

MS 1536 - Information Technology – Guidelines For The Management of IT Security. (2002). Malaysian Standards. Retrieved from http://www.msonline.gov.my/catalog.php?source=production&score=checked

MS 1537 - Information Security Managements Systems - Specification With Guidance For Use. (2004). Malaysian Standards. Retrieved from http://www.msonline.gov.my/catalog.php

SS 463 - (ICS 35) - National information infrastructure (NII) standards. (1999). SPRING Singapore. Retrieved from http://www.singaporestandardse-shop.sg/data/ECopyFileStore/060424160620Preview%20-%20SS%20463-1-1999.pdf

APPENDIX

Apart from the references cited in the chapter and given above in the **References** section, here is a list of web resources for additional information. There are two sections. The first lists specific documents, while the second lists the websites.

Web-Documents

http://www.cpni.gov.uk/Docs/Sources_of_Guidance_on_Security_in_the_Telecommunications_sector.pdf
http://www-08.nist.gov/groups/SMA/fisma/faqs.html
http://www.isaca.org/Knowledge-Center/cobit/Pages/COBIT-5-Initiative-Status-Update.aspx
http://www.mastercardintl.com/newtechnology/mcommerce/standards/etsi.html
http://fdic.gov/help/faq.html
http://csrc.nist.gov/publications
http://www.isaca.org/Knowledge-Center/COBIT/Pages/Overview.aspx
http://www.dhs.gov/xlibrary/assets/nipp-ssp-information-tech.pdf

Websites

http://www.nist.gov/itl/csd/index.cfm
http://www.issa.org
http://www.bethesda.med.navy.mil/patient/hipaa/security.asp
http://iase.disa.mil/stigs
http://www.isaca.org
http://www.itgovernance.co.uk
http://www.ffiec.gov
http://www.opengroup.org
http://www.gov.on.ca
http://www.mgs.gov.on.ca
http://www.standards.org.sg
http://www.standards.com.au
http://www.bankinfosecurity.com
http://www.iso.org
http://www.itsc.org.sg
http://cio.gov

Chapter 6
ISMS Building for SMEs through the Reuse of Knowledge

Luís Enrique Sánchez
SICAMAN NT, Spain

Antonio Santos-Olmo
SICAMAN NT, Spain

Eduardo Fernandez-Medina
University of Castilla-La Mancha, Spain

Mario Piattini
University of Castilla-La Mancha, Spain

ABSTRACT

The information society is increasingly more dependent upon Information Security Management Systems (ISMSs), and the availability of these systems has become crucial to the evolution of Small and Medium-size Enterprises (SMEs). However, this type of companies requires ISMSs which have been adapted to their specific characteristics, and these systems must be optimized from the point of view of the resources necessary to deploy and maintain them. Over the last 10 years, the authors have obtained considerable experience in the establishment of ISMSs, and during this time, they have observed that the structure and characteristics of SMEs as regards security management are frequently very similar (since they can all be grouped by business size and sector), thus signifying that it is possible to construct patterns for ISMSs that can be reused and refined. In this chapter, the authors present the strategy that they have designed to manage and reuse security information in information system security management. This strategy is framed within a methodology designed for integral security management and its information systems maturity, denominated as "Methodology for Security Management and Maturity in Small and Medium-size Enterprises (MSM2-SME)," and it is defined in a reusable model called "Reusable Pattern for Security Management (RPSM)," which systematically defines, manages, and reuses the aforementioned methodology through a sub-process denominated as "Generation of Security Management Patterns (GSMP)." This model is currently being applied in real cases, and is thus constantly improving.

DOI: 10.4018/978-1-4666-0197-0.ch006

INTRODUCTION

The information society is increasingly more dependent upon Information Security Management Systems (ISMSs), and the availability of these systems has become crucial to the evolution of Small and Medium-size Enterprises (SMEs). However, this type of companies requires ISMSs which have been adapted to their specific characteristics, and these systems must be optimized from the point of view of the resources which are necessary to deploy and maintain them. Our wide experience in the implantation of ISMS over the last 10 years, has allowed us to observe that, with regard to security management, SMEs frequently share many characteristics and structures (which can be grouped by size and business sector), thus making it possible to construct patterns for ISMSs which can be reused and refined. In this paper we show the strategy that we have designed for the management and reuse of security information in the information system security management process. This strategy is set within the framework of a methodology that we have designed for the integral management of information system security and maturity, denominated as "Methodology for Security Management and Maturity in Small and Medium-sized Enterprises (MSM2-SME)". More specifically, this is a reusable model that we have denominated as "Reusable Pattern for Security Management (RPSM)", which is systematically defined, managed and reused through a sub-process of the aforementioned methodology denominated as "Generation of Security Management Patterns (GSMP)". This model is currently being applied in real cases, and is thus constantly improving.

It is extremely important for enterprises to introduce security controls which will allow them to discover and to control the risks that they may be confronted with (Dhillon & Backhouse, 2000; Fernández-Medina, Jurjens, Trujillo, & Jajodia, 2009; Kluge, 2008). However, the introduction of these controls is not sufficient, and systems which manage security in the long term, thus permitting a swift reaction to new risks, vulnerabilities and threats are also necessary (Barlette & Vladislav, 2008; De Capitani, Foresti, & Jajodia, 2008). Unfortunately, present-day companies often do not have security management systems, or those which do exist have been created without the appropriate guidelines or documentation, and with insufficient resources (Vries, Blind, Mangelsdorf, Verheul, & Zwan, 2009; T. Wiander & Holappa, 2006). Moreover, the majority of the security tools available on the market help to solve part of the security problems, but very few tackle the problem of security management in a global and integrated manner. In fact, the enormous diversity of these tools and their lack of integration suppose a huge amount of spending on resources with which to be able to manage them (Alfawaz, Nelson, & Mohannak, 2010; Valdevit, Mayer, & Barafort, 2009).

Therefore, in spite of the fact that real-life has shown that for a business to be able to use information technology and communication with guarantees it needs to have at its disposal guidelines, measures and tools which will allow it to know at all times both the level of its security and those vulnerabilities which have not been covered (T Wiander, 2008), the level of successful deployment of these systems is, in reality, very low. This problem is particularly accentuated in the case of SMEs, which have the additional limitation of not having sufficient human and economic resources to be able to carry out an appropriate management (T. Wiander & Holappa, 2006).

According to recent research (Dojkovski, Lichtenstein, & Warren, 2006; Siponen & Willison, 2009), the success of ISMSs depends mainly upon the following factors: i) the security is focused on the business; ii) the security is implemented in accordance with the company's business culture; iii) the company's management provides unarguable, visible and committed support, iv) there is a good understanding of the security requirements and of risk evaluation and management; v) both management and employees are aware of the necessity for security; vi) training and guidelines exist with regard to the entire organisation's policies and regulations; vii) the definition of a measurement system to evaluate the output of security management and to suggest improvements. In the case of SMEs these factors are important, but the ISMS must, moreover, be optimised with regard to the necessary resources and must also have a sufficient reach which does not neglect security, but which is also not excessive in order to control costs (Bartsch, Sohr, & Bormann, 2009). It is therefore extremely important to be able to rely on information security management methodologies which are especially designed for this type of enterprises, and which also permit knowledge reuse, thus ensuring that their deployment is faster, more certain and more economic.

As we shall show later in this paper, certain proposals already exist for the management of information security (ISO/IEC27001, ISO/IEC21827, ISM3, along with some other proposals such as (Areiza, Barrientos, Rincón, & Lalinde-Pulido, 2005a; Carey-Smith, Nelson, & May, 2007; Eloff & Eloff, 2003; Linares & Paredes, 2007; Tawileh, Hilton, & McIntosh, 2007)), almost all of which have been created by international standardizing organisations, and are mainly oriented towards large enterprises. However, numerous research works ((Barlette & Vladislav, 2008; Coles-Kemp & Overill, 2007)) confirm that these proposals are not appropriate for SMEs, since they offer them processes which are excessively bureaucratic or costly for them.

Of the main weaknesses detected in these proposals, we can highlight the fact that they are excessively oriented towards large businesses and thus ignore fundamental aspects of SMEs such as the reuse of knowledge acquired in different implantations.

Our wide experience in the implantation of ISMSs has led us to detect that, while large companies tend to apply highly diverse and specialised security controls which are oriented towards very specific activities and are of great value in their information systems, the security controls in SMEs tend to share the majority of their characteristics, particularly when these companies belong to the same business sector and are of the same size with regard to turnover and number of employees.

This characteristic, which was obtained and validated through research in action (Dick, 2000; O´Brien, 1998) in real cases, is of great importance to the viability of ISMSs in SMEs, since it permits knowledge reuse in different SMEs through the use of patterns which can be reused and refined in different implantations, thus obtaining tremendous advantages such as those of the following characteristics: economic, since they reduce the time and resources needed for implantation; reliability, since they already have valid solutions; continuous process improvement; adaptability to specific and differentiated aspects of certain companies, etc.

Therefore, and taking into consideration the fact that SMEs represent the vast majority of enterprises, both at a national and at an international level, and are extremely important to business as a whole, we believe that advances in knowledge reuse oriented research to improve security management for this type of enterprises, may make important contributions in this area, and may contribute not only towards improving the security in SMEs, but also towards improving their level of competitiveness. In recent years we have, therefore, created a methodology (MSM2-SME) for security management and for the establishment of a security maturity level in SMEs' information systems (L.E Sánchez, Villafranca, Fernández-Medina, & Piattini, 2006a, 2006b, 2007a, 2007b). We have also developed a tool that completely automates this methodology (L.E Sánchez, Villafranca, Fernández-Medina, & Piattini, 2007c), which has been applied in real cases (L.E. Sánchez, Villafranca, Fernández–Medina, & Piattini, 2008), and which has allowed us to evaluate the methodology, the tool, and the improvement effects produced by knowledge reuse provided by this tool.

We have paid particular attention to the methodology's capacity for knowledge reuse through the definition of reusable patterns, which are a complete customizable configuration that permit the immediate implantation of ISMSs in businesses, taking advantage of the knowledge obtained in the previous implantation of other ISMSs in companies that share similar structural characteristics (business sector and size). In order to validate this methodology we have recently created a single pattern denominated as "Root Pattern" with the intention of it being as generic as possible in order for it to serve as a basis from which to create new more specific patterns. Our objective is to create a pattern for each business sector, which will be obtained from the NACE code (The European standard of industry classification), and the experience of applying this methodology will, therefore, increase with each pattern. This signifies that the implementation of the ISMSs (in each business sector) will be progressively more precise, more economic and faster. We can therefore conclude that the principal contribution of this paper centres on presenting the elements of which the GSMP process in the MSM2-SME methodology is composed MSM2-SME (L.E Sánchez, Santos-Olmo, Fernández-Medina, & Piattini, 2009a, 2009b; L.E. Sánchez et al., 2008). This process is entrusted with the generation of patterns, and a first pattern, denominated as the "Root Pattern", will serve as a basis for the generation of other patterns.

The chapter continues in Section 2, which briefly describes the existing security management methodologies and models and their current tendencies. In Section 3 a brief introduction to our proposal for a security management methodology oriented towards SMEs is provided. In Section 4 we concentrate on knowledge reuse patterns and the activities which permit them to be generated. In section 5, we will show the tool developed to support the methodology and some of the major lessons learned during its development. Finally, in Section 6 we present our conclusions and future work.

RELATED WORK

The aim of reducing both the lacks that ISMSs have proved to have in businesses, and the losses that these lacks occasion, has led to the emergence of a significant amount of processes (Kostina, Miloslavskaya, & Tolstoy, 2009), frameworks and information security method (Ohki, Harada, Kawaguchi, Shiozaki, & Kagaua, 2009), the need to establish/install these is ever-increasingly recognised and considered by organisations, but as has been demonstrated, they are inefficient in the case of SMEs (Siponen & Willison, 2009) and do not consider aspects which we believe to be fundamental, such as knowledge reuse.

With regard to the most outstanding standards, it is possible to state that the majority of security management models have taken the ISO/IEC17799 and ISO/IEC27002 international standards as their basis, and that the security management models which are most successful in large companies are ISO/IEC27001, COBIT and ISM3, but that they are very difficult to implement and require too high an investment for the majority of SMEs (Gupta & Hammond, 2005). This is owing to the fact that they are oriented towards large companies, and aspects such as knowledge reuse, which in the case of SMEs is fundamental if the installation and maintenance costs of these types of systems are to be reduced, take second place.

Although various extremely interesting new proposals oriented towards this type of companies are currently emerging, their approach towards the problem is incomplete.

Among the main security management standards we can find:

- **ISO/IEC27001 (ISO/IEC27001, 2005):** This standard was developed to provide a model for the establishment, implementation, operation, monitoring, review, maintenance and improvement of ISMSs.
- **ISO/IEC20000 (ISO/IEC20000, 2005) e ITIL (ITILv3.0, 2007):** These are a vast set of management procedures created to facilitate organisations' attainment of quality and efficiency in their IT operations.
- **COBIT (COBITv4.0, 2006):** COBIT is a methodology for the appropriate control of technology projects, information flows and risks which imply the lack of suitable controls. The COBIT methodology is used to plan, implement, control and evaluate the government of ITC, and incorporates control objectives, auditory directives, measurements of output and results, critical success factors and maturity models. Its main problem is that it is too complex for deployment in small companies.
- **ISM3 (ISM3, 2007):** This security and maturity management model is oriented towards implementing an ISMS and defining different levels of security, in which each level can be the organisation's final objective.

Numerous bibliographic sources detect and highlight the difficulty that SMEs face with the use of traditional security management methodologies and maturity models which were conceived for use in large enterprises (Batista & Figueiredo, 2000; Calvo-Manzano et al., 2004; Hareton & Terence, 2001; Tuffley, Grove, & G, 2004). It is repeatedly justified that the application of this type of methodology and maturity models to SMEs is difficult and costly. Moreover, organisations, including those which are large, have a greater tendency towards adopting groups of processes which are related as a set rather than dealing with processes independently (Mekelburg, 2005).

The aforementioned methodologies and security management models have not proved to be valid in SMEs for four reasons:

- They were developed for organisations with a larger amount of resources.
- They tackle only part of the security management system and almost none of them tackle the deployment of these systems from a global perspective, which thus obliges companies to acquire, implement, manage and maintain various methodologies, models and tools to manage their security. Additionally, the few applications which have attempted to tackle all aspects of security management are expensive to obtain and require complex management and costly maintenance, signifying that they are not suitable for SMEs.
- Finally, we can conclude that although various standards, norms, guides to good practices, methodologies, and security management and risk analysis models exist, they are not integrated into a global model which can be applied to small and medium-sized enterprises with a guarantee of success.
- The most important point is that none of them are centred on knowledge reuse, which according to our research is fundamental if viability is to be guaranteed, not only during the ISMS implantation phase, but also during its lifecycle.

We can therefore conclude this subsection by stating that it is both pertinent and opportune to tackle the problem of developing a new methodology with which to manage security and its maturity for information systems in SMEs that is capable of reusing the knowledge acquired from previous installations. A further objective is to obtain great reductions in costs which will make the installation of ISMSs in SMEs viable, in addition to a model that will make its functioning valid, and a tool to support this model, taking as a basis the problems that this type of companies confront which have led to continual failures in the attempt to install these systems this type of businesses.

MSM2-SME OVERVIEW

The methodology for the management of security and its maturity in SMEs that we have developed will allow any organisation to manage, evaluate and measure the security of its information systems, but is oriented mainly towards SMEs, since it is these organisations which have the highest level of failure in the deployment of existing security management methodologies.

One of the desired objectives of the MSM2-SME methodology was that it will be easy to apply, and that the model developed on it will permit the greatest possible level of automation and reusability to be obtained with a minimum amount of information collected in a greatly reduced time.

The MSM2-SME methodology will also permit the patterns used in a company to be refined in order to make them more precise, but this refinement reduces the cost-saving that it offers, and SMEs should therefore seek a compromise between precision and the investment that they wish to make.

Knowledge reuse is achieved through a structure of matrices which allow us to relate the various ISMS components (controls, actives, threats, vulnerabilities, risk criteria, procedures, registers, templates, technical instructions, regulations, etc) that the model will use to generate a considerable part of the necessary information, thus notably reducing the time needed to deploy and develop the ISMS. This set of inter-relations between all of the ISMS components signifies that the alteration of any of these objects will change the measurement value of the remaining objects of which the model is composed, so that it is always possible to have an up-to-date evaluation of how the company's security system is evolving.

The entire weight of the knowledge reuse process falls on the first of the three sub-processes of which the MSM2-SME methodology is composed. Figure 1 shows details of these sub-processes and the activities of which they are composed. Each of these sub-processes will be briefly analysed below.

GSMP: Generation of Security Management Patterns

The principal objective of this sub-process is to create the structures that are necessary to store the knowledge obtained from different installments with the objective of being able to reuse it in future installments, thus obtaining great advantages. These structures will contain reusable patterns, and will permit both the time needed to create the ISMS and the maintenance costs to be reduced, signifying that they are suitable for the dimensions of an SME. The use of patterns is of special interest in the case of SMEs since their special characteristics tend to mean that they have simple information systems which are very similar to each other.

Each pattern will contain the knowledge obtained during the installation of an ISMS in a company, and will be suitable for reuse by companies with similar structural characteristics.

- **Activity A1.1. – Generation of Master Tables:** The main objective of this activity is to determine which general elements can be best adapted to the pattern which is being created. The entrance is the knowledge of a group of security domain experts obtained during the ISMS deployment process, which will permit the selection of a subset of elements of which the Root Pattern will be composed. Figure 2 shows the structure created to store both the knowledge from this activity and the charged values in the root pattern, so, for example, 6 elements and various sub-profiles have been initially introduced for the element created to contain the roles and profiles.

Figure 1. The sub-processes of the methodology

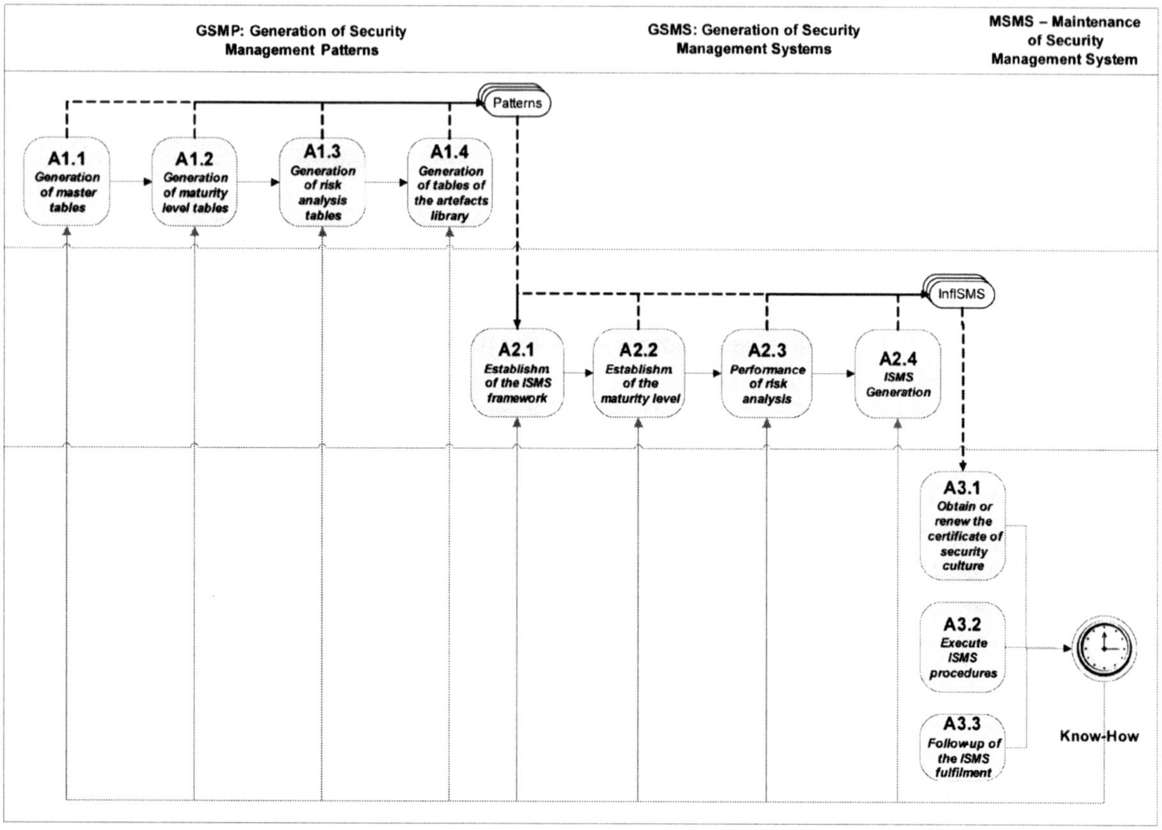

Figure 2. Root pattern elements for activity A1.1

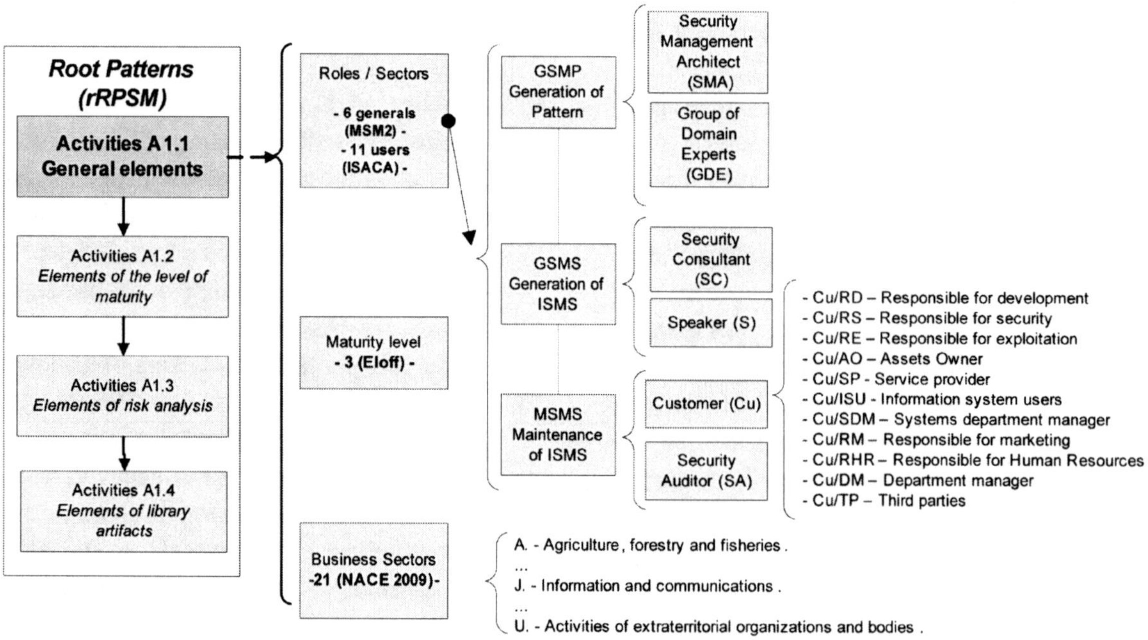

Figure 3. Root pattern elements for activity A1.2

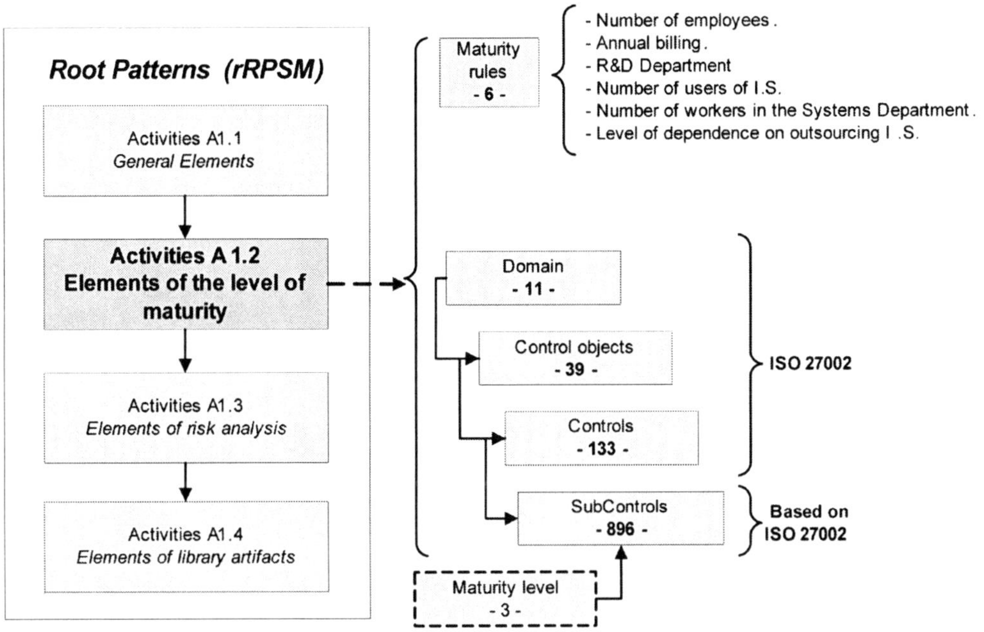

- **Activity1.2. – Generation of maturity level tables:** The main objective of this activity is to determine the controls and maturity rules that can be best adapted to the pattern that is being created, and which will later be used to determine the company's present security maturity level, and the maturity level to which it would be advisable to evolve. The input are the knowledge of a Group of Security Domain Experts obtained during the ISMS deployment process, the maturity levels obtained from task "Establishing the maturity levels" and a set of elements from which the final elements that will form this part of the Root Pattern will be selected. Figure 3 shows the structure created to store both the knowledge from this activity and the charged values in the root pattern, so, for example, 133 controls have initially been introduced for the element created to contain the controls, taking as a basis the ISO/IEC27002 since it is an internationally recognized and prestigious standard. One of the principal advantages of this pattern structure is that it can be easily adapted to other international regulations.
- **Activity A1.3. – Generation of risk analysis tables:** The main objective of this activity is to select those elements which are necessary to be able to carry out a low cost basic risk analysis of the activities of which the company's information system is composed which can be adapted to the requirements of SMEs, in activities subsequent to the methodology. The entrance is the knowledge of the group of security domain experts which was obtained during the ISMS deployment process, the controls selected in task of Establishing Controls which are stored in the patterns repository, and a set of elements (types of activities, threats, vulnerabilities and risk criteria) which are necessary for the creation of the risk analysis. Figure 4 shows the structure created to store both the knowledge for this

Figure 4. Root pattern elements for activity A1.3

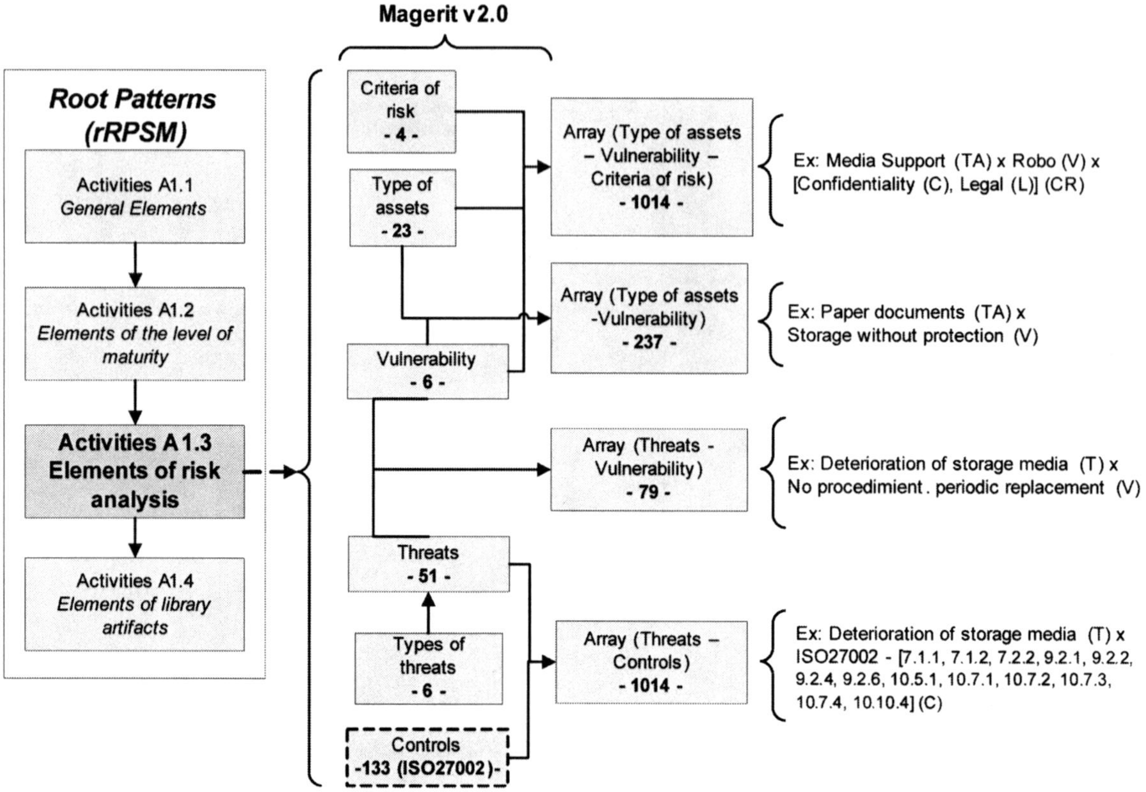

activity and the charged values in the root pattern.

- **Activity A1.4. – Generation artefacts library tables:** The main objective of this activity is to select those elements which are necessary to be able to obtain the subset of those elements of which the ISMS will be composed for a company, and the relationship that exists between them, in subsequent activities to the methodology. Its entrance will be the knowledge of a group of security domain experts obtained during the ISMS deployment process, the controls selected by that pattern, which are stored in the pattern repository, and a set of elements (regulations, procedures, templates, registers, technical instructions and measures) necessary to create an ISMS. The various components from this zone (see Figure 5) are of great importance to the final generation of the ISMS. In the case of the root pattern, they have been extracted from a detailed study of the international standards from the ISO/IEC27000 family, thus guaranteeing that the ISMSs generated from these elements will be very robust.

The entire set of elements, which are necessary to be able to generate the company's information system's management system, are included in the pattern repository for the ISMS, together with the relationships that exist between them which represent part of the practical knowledge provided by the Group of Domain Experts in each new deployment.

The patterns are under constant evaluation and are up-dated with the knowledge obtained from the

Figure 5. Root pattern elements for activity A1.4

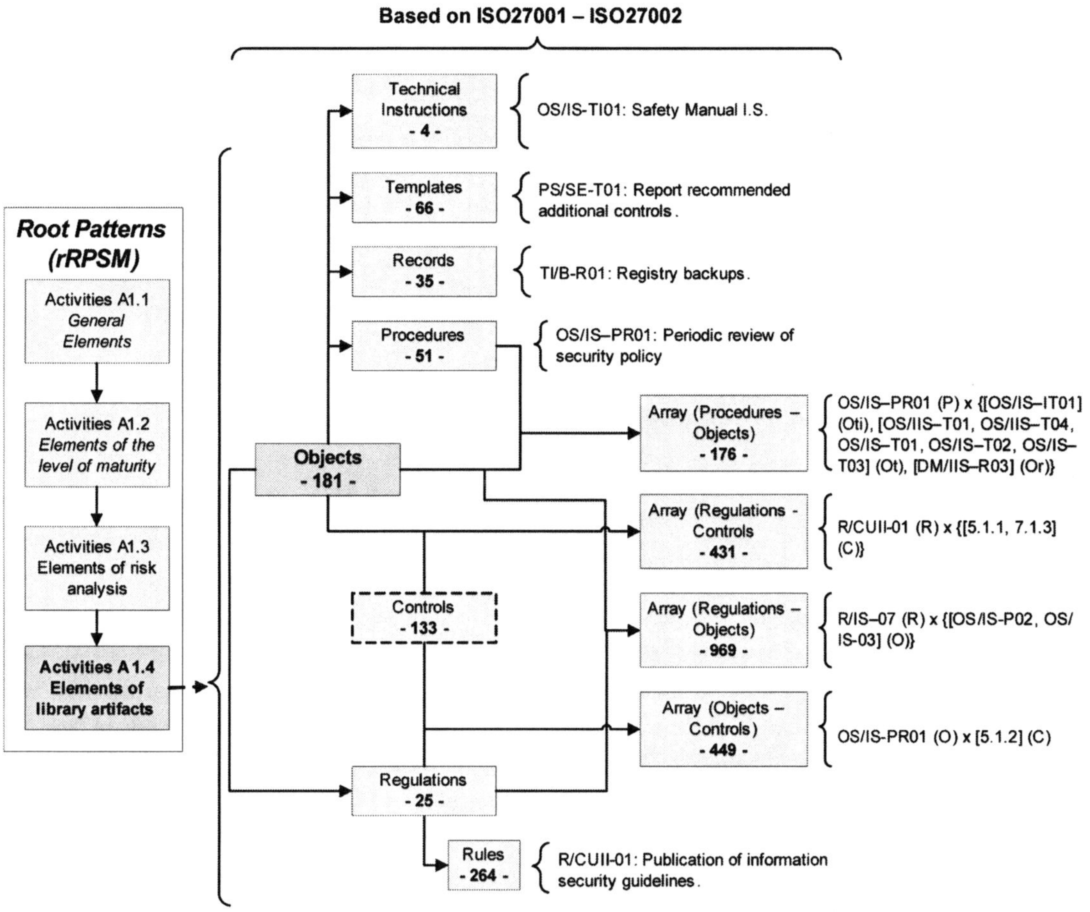

Security Management Architect and the Group of Domain Experts in each new deployment.

GSMS: Generation of Security Management Systems

The principal objective of this sub-process is to permit the generation of those elements of which the security management system (SMS) is formed for a company, from a schema (a structure which is generated from the GSMS sub-process) that is valid for a set of companies, thus carrying out this process at a reduced cost. It is important to mention that this sub-process has been developed from a minimum set of the company's information (organigram, list of information system users, roles, verification lists and activity list) to allow a series of documents (current security level, recommended security level, risk matrix, improvement plan, elements in a GSMS) to be generated which will leave the management system completely defined and functional. This sub-process is formed of four activities:

- **A2.1 – Establishment of the ISMS framework:** The principal objective of this activity is to create an initial framework between the security consultant (SC) in charge of generating the ISMS and the customer (Cu). The input will be: i) a schema of that which is contained in the schema repository, which will be selected

Figure 6. Task-level scheme of activity A2.1

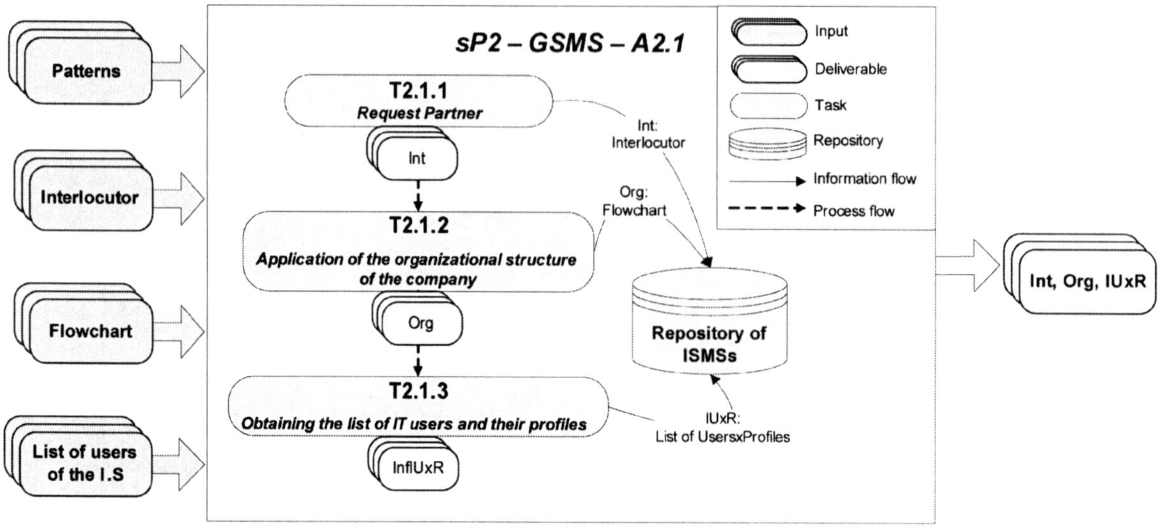

by the security consultant (SC) on the basis of the company's characteristics (its size and sector); ii) the company's information in which it is desired to implant the ISMS. The sub-process will be formed of three tasks which are dependent on each other. These tasks are: i) a valid interlocutor request; ii) a request for the company's organigram; and iii) a request for a list of the information system's users and their roles. Finally, the output produced by this sub-process will consist of a series of deliverable (notification of the company's elected delegate's address, the company's organigram, the information system users' matrix and the roles of these users in the ISMS) to allow the security consultant (SC) to analyse them. The information contained in these deliverables will be stored in the ISMS repository to permit its subsequent use in the generation those elements of which the company's ISMS is composed. Figure 6 shows the schema for the input, task and output of which this activity is composed.

- **A2.2 – Establishment of the maturity level:** The principal objective of this activity is to establish the initial point at which the company finds itself with regard to security management (current maturity level), and the point that it would be desirable for the company to attain (desirable security level). These security levels were established by carrying out two interviews via limited value questionnaires. (Fontana & Frey, 2005) show the advantages of carrying out interviews via questionnaires which have a pre-established series of questions with a limited number of response categories. The input will be: i) a schema of that which is contained in the schema repository, which will be selected by consulting the security consultant (SC) on the basis of the company's characteristics (its size and sector), which will be obtained from the questionnaires (one organizational and one technical) filled in by the customer; ii) the company's elected delegate (Del), who will be in charge of responding to the questionnaires. The sub-process will be formed of three tasks. These tasks are: i) collecting the organisational information; ii) collecting the information system technical information; and iii) obtaining the security maturity level. Tasks T2.2.1 (Collection of organisational information) and T2.2.2 (Collection of technical information are independent and can therefore be carried out in parallel, although, since they depend on the delegate they would normally be processed in series. Task T2.2.3 (Obtain the security maturity level) depends on the results of the previous tasks and cannot therefore be carried out until the other two have been completed. Finally, the outputs resulting from this sub-process consist of a series of deliverables (organisational report, technical report and results of current and desirable security maturity level) that the security consultant (SC) can analyse. The information contained in these deliverables will be stored in the ISMS repository to permit its subsequent use in the generation of those elements of which the company's ISMS is composed. Figure 7 shows the schema for the input, task and output of which this activity is composed.

- **A2.3 – Performance of risk analysis:** The principal objective of this activity is to establish an evaluation of the risks to which the company's information system's main activities are exposed and over which it is desirable to install the GSMS, along with proposing a plan to the person responsible for security (Cu/RS) in order to manage the risks as efficiently as possible. The development of this activity is based on the proposals made by Stephenson which are centred on the synergy between the technical test and the risk analysis (Stephenson, 2004), taking as a reference ISO/IEC27002 (ISO/IEC27002, 2007) and the Magerit v2 risk analysis methodology (MageritV2, 2005). If this activity is to function in a coherent manner, it is necessary to bear in mind the special conditions of SMEs, in which users have neither the time nor sufficient knowledge to apply risk analysis methodologies in an efficient way, or to determine which are the best informa-

Figure 7. Task-level scheme of activity A2.2

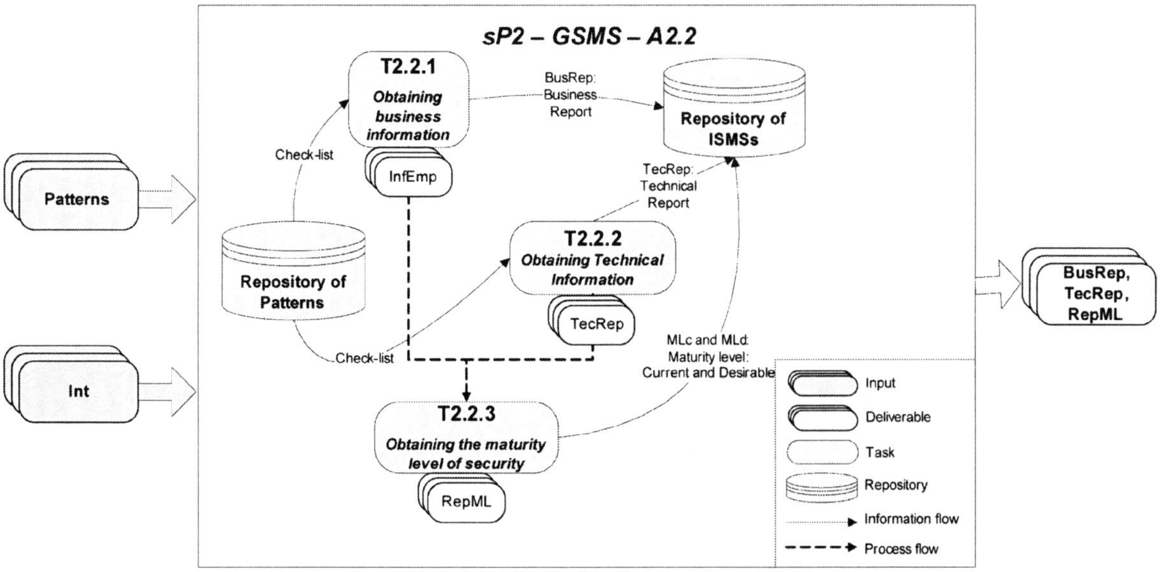

tion system activities. The input will be: i) a schema of that which is contained in the schema repository, which will be selected by the security consultant (SC) on the basis of the company's characteristics (its size and sector), from which those elements which are necessary to carry out the risk analysis will be obtained (control list, list of activity types, list of vulnerabilities, relationships between threats and vulnerabilities, relationships between threats and controls, and the relationships between the types of assets, the vulnerabilities and the risk criteria); ii) the company's elected delegate (Del), who will be in charge of defining the assets; iii) a set of information system assets, which are as general as possible (coarse grained). The sub-process will be formed of two tasks. These tasks are: i) identification of assets; and ii) generation of the risk matrix and improvement plan. Task T2.3.2 (Generation of risk matrix and improvement plan) is dependent on Task T2.3.1 (Identification of assets), and cannot therefore be carried out until the latter has been completed; Finally, the outputs resulting from this sub-process will consist of a series of deliverables (information system assets report, matrix of risks to which the information systems assets are exposed and improvement plan recommended by the methodology to make improvements to security management in the ISMS) so that the security consultant (SC) will be able to analyse them. The information contained in these deliverables will be stored in the ISMS repository for its subsequent use in the generation of those elements of which the company's ISMS is composed. Figure 8 shows the schema for the input, tasks and output of which this activity is composed.

- **A2.4 – ISMS Generation:** The principal objective of this activity is to generate the elements of which the company's ISMS will be composed and to obtain the company's elected delegate's (Del) approval of the results obtained, or if this is not the case, to take the necessary steps to rectify the deficiencies (by altering the schema selected, selecting another more appropriate schema or correcting the input to the sub-process). The input will be: i) a schema of that which is contained in the schema repository, which will be selected by the security consultant (SC) on the basis of the company's characteristics (its size and sector), from which the elements needed to generate the ISMS will be generated (control list, list of regulations, list of procedures, list of registers, list of templates, list of technical

Figure 8. Task-level scheme of activity A2.3

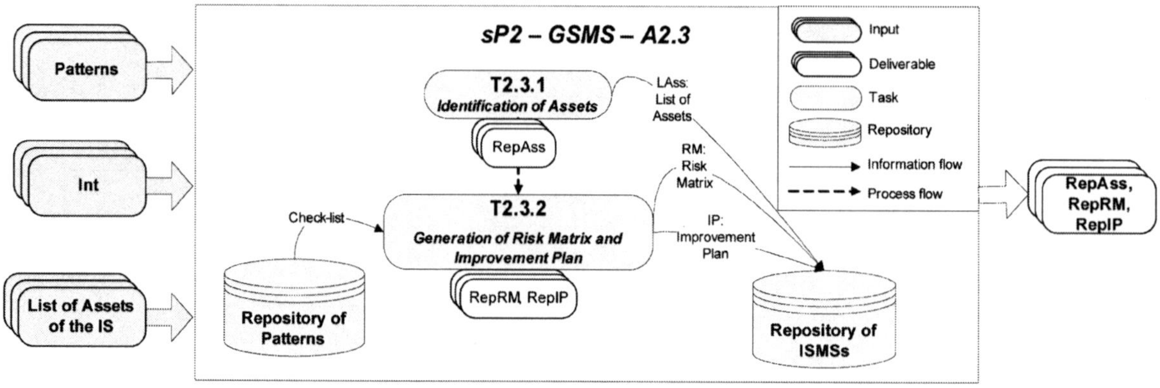

instructions, list of metrics, relationships between regulations and artefacts, relationships between regulations and controls, relationships between artefacts and controls, relationships between procedures and artefacts); ii) the company's elected delegate (Del), who will be in charge of validating and approving the result obtained; iii) the deliverables generated during the previous activities of the ISMS sub-process for the delegate's approval; iv) the content of the ISMS repository which were generated in the activities prior to the GSMS sub-process. The sub-process will be formed of two tasks. These tasks are: i) the generation of the objects from the ISMS; and ii) the presentation of the results to the delegate. Task T2.4.2 (Presentation of results to delegate) is dependent on Task T2.4.1 (Generation of ISMS objects), and cannot therefore be carried out until the latter has been completed. Finally, the output resulting from this sub-process consists of: i) the approval of the deliverables obtained during the previous activities from the GSMS sub-process; ii) knowledge which will allow the group of domain experts (GDE) to refine the schemas from the GSMS sub-process; the elements of which the company's ISMS will be formed (a scoreboard which will indicate the security level for each control related to the company's security management; a set of regulations, templates and technical instructions which are currently valid for the company; a set of metrics; a set of users associated with roles which, according to their profiles, can execute a series of procedures in order to interact with the company's information system; and a set of regulations which must be complied with if the ISMS is to work properly). Figure 9 shows the schema for the input, tasks and output of which this activity is composed:

MSMS: Maintenance of Security Management System

The principal objective of this sub-process is to permit the company to manage the information security system, and support it in this, by using the deliverables generated during the ISMS generation phase. This sub-process is formed of three activities, and has been developed to make

Figure 9. Task-level scheme of activity A2.4

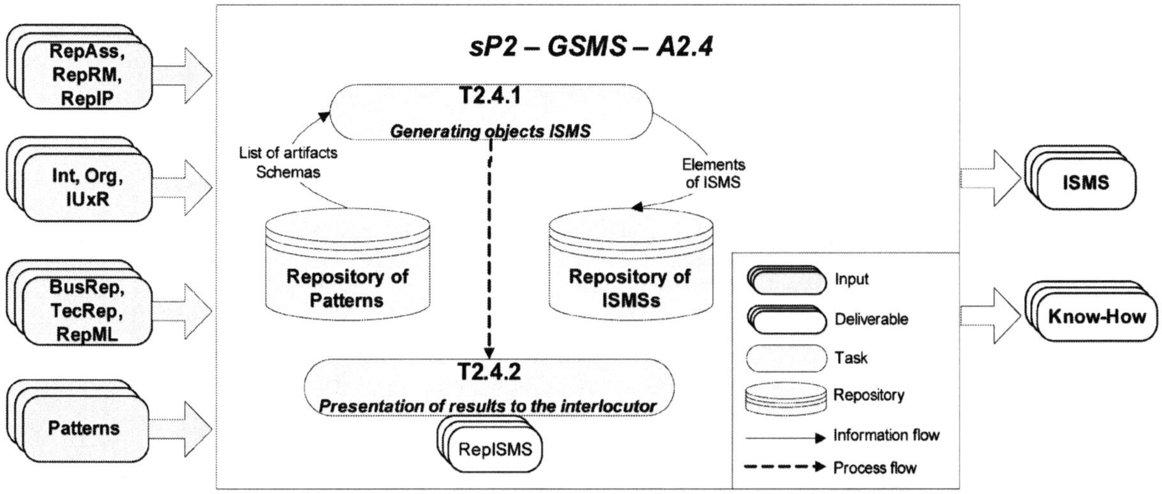

its fulfilment very easy and comfortable for the information system users, by simplifying the tasks of which it is composed.

- **A3.1 – Obtain or renew the certificate of security culture:** The principal objective of this activity is to establish a basic security culture for the users who will have to work with the company's information system, and without which they will not be able to access it. The main idea is that a "certificate of cultural level" will be required by the users of the information system, which can be withdrawn and must be periodically renewed in order to guarantee that the users continue to maintain said level of security culture. The input will be the users' responses to the questionnaire concerning the regulations generated by the system. The sub-process will be formed of a single task which will consist of the issuing of security certificates. Finally, the output resulting from this sub-process will consist of the security culture certificate, all supposing that the mark obtained in the questionnaire is above five, or otherwise the refusal of this certificate. Those users who fail the exam are advised to study the security manual included in the ISMS, or to participate on a security management course in order to increase their knowledge in this subject. Figure 10 shows the schema for the input, tasks and output of which this activity is composed.
- **A3.2 – Execute ISMS procedures:** The principal objective of this activity is to allow the information system users to execute the procedures that contain the processes which are necessary to maintain the company's ISMS. The execution of one of these ISMS procedures will produce a procedure instance, which will be the set of unique data introduced during the execution of this procedure. The input will be: i) the security culture certificate, since without this it will not be possible to access the company's information system; ii) the company's users' input data for the procedure phase which is being executed; iii) the data from the phase previous to the procedure instance that is being executed, which will be obtained from the ISMS information repository. The sub-process is formed of two independent tasks which correspond to the two types of procedure in the system (general and complaint). Finally, the output

Figure 10. Task-level scheme of activity A3.1

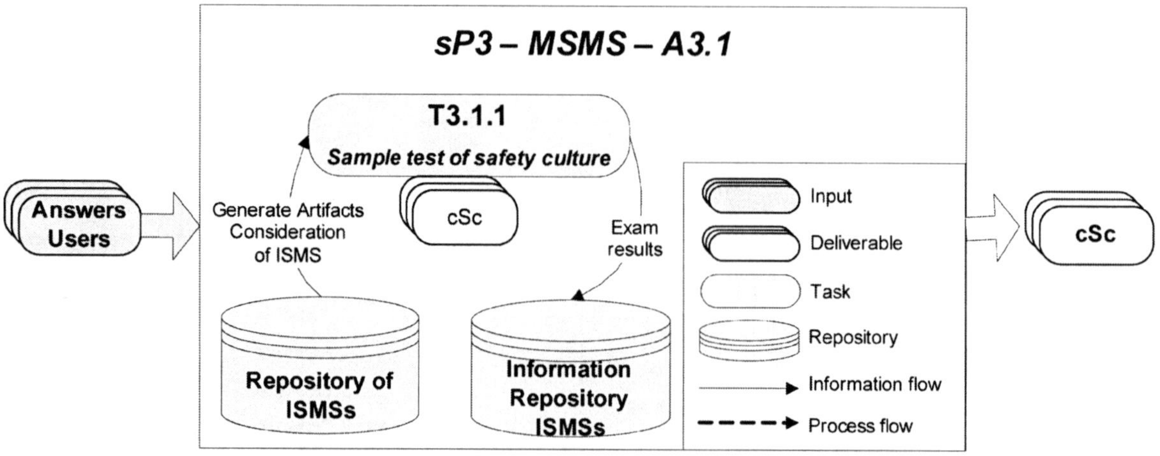

Figure 11. Task-level scheme of activity A3.2

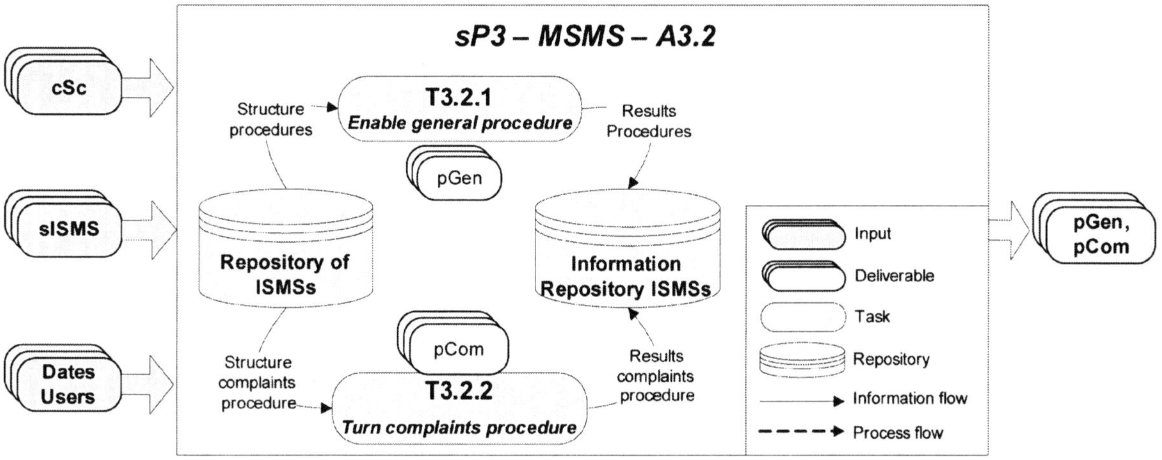

resulting from this sub-process will consist of a report which contains all the information generated in the instance of each phase of the procedure during its execution, with the objective of allowing the security auditor (SAu) and the person responsible for security (Cu/RS) to analyse and determine improvements in the procedures. Figure 11 shows the schema for the input, tasks and output of which this activity is composed.

- **A3.3 – Follow-up of the ISMS fulfilment:** The principal objective of this activity is to maintain the ISMS's maturity level updated and to be constantly aware of the level of fulfilment of the security controls that form part of the company's ISMS. This activity has been designed to allow the ISMS to evolve the level of security control fulfilment in a dynamic manner, without the need for intervention by external auditors, although this would be advisable. The result of each change is reflected in the fulfilment level of the security control panel controls, and is converted in the company's person responsible for security's (Cu/RS) control centre to permit the system's evolution to be analysed and corrective measures to be taken. The input will be: i) the security culture certificate, since without this it will not be possible to access the company's information system; ii) the users' input data (e.g. measures of control fulfilment levels by the security auditor as part of the recalibration process); iii) information on the changes in security control fulfilment levels, which will be obtained from the ISMS information repository. The sub-process will be formed of seven independent tasks which will be executed when necessary, without a time limit (represented by a clock on the schema). These tasks are: i) management of security control panel; ii) management of regularity of procedures; iii) management of security violations; iv) Management of security culture certificates; v) Realisation of periodical auditing; vi) realisation of general metrics; vii) management of warning system. Finally, the output resulting from this sub-process will consist of a series of reports associated with changes in security control fulfilment levels, to allow the security auditor (SAu) and the person responsible for security (Cu/RS) to analyse and determine improvements that can be made to them. Figure 12 shows the schema

Figure 12. Task-level scheme of activity A3.3

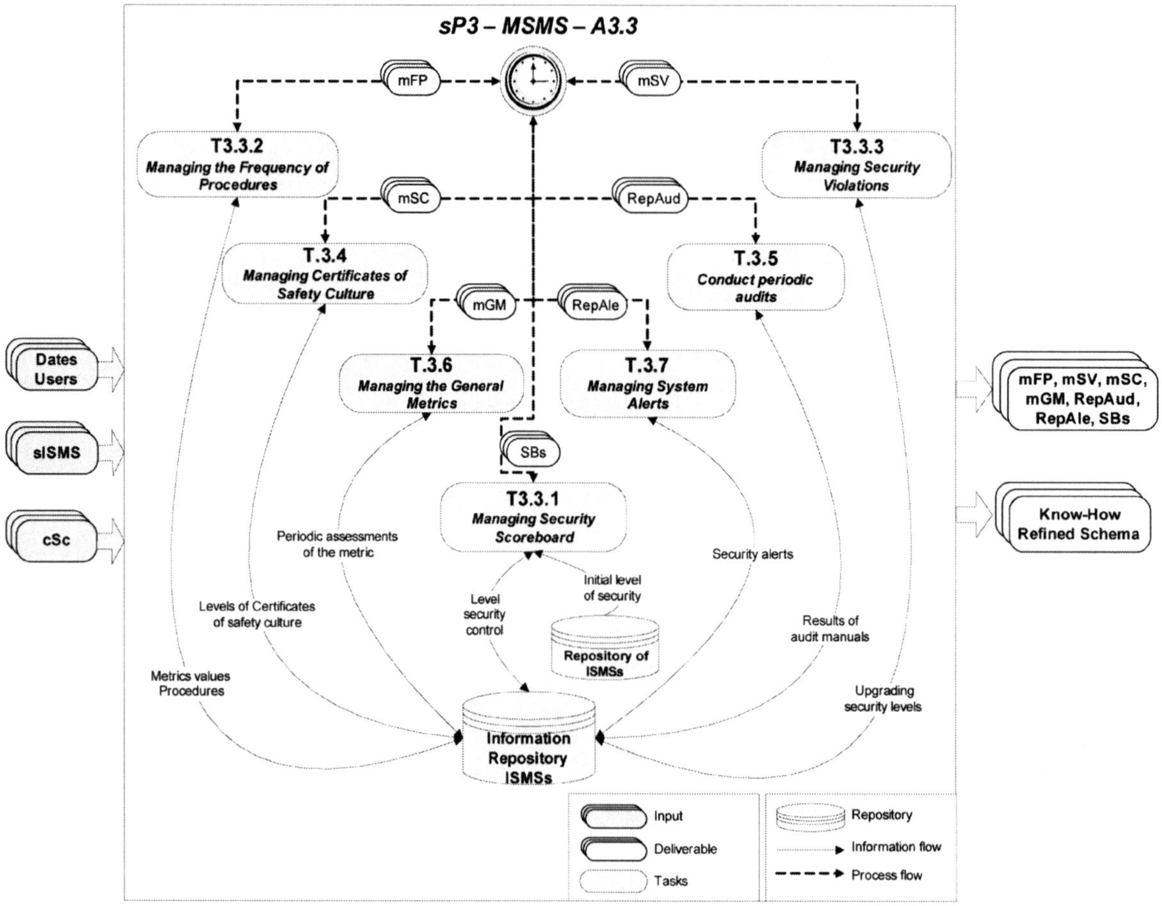

for the input, tasks and output of which this activity is composed.

GENERATION OF PATTERNS AND ROOT PATTERN

In this sub-section we shall describe the different activities in the MSM2-SME methodology's GSMP sub-process that permit the creation of new patterns, analysing the elements of which a pattern is composed and the standards and regulations used in the creation of the "root pattern", with the objective of guaranteeing good quality results. Finally we shall show three sub-sections with some of the most characteristic elements of the "root pattern" in relation to their maturity levels, procedures and profiles.

rRPSM Maturity Levels

This subsection will show the different maturity levels into which the root pattern developed has been divided. These maturity levels have been created on the basis of practical experience and the results of other research (Barrientos & Areiza, 2005; Eloff & Eloff, 2003; SSE-CMM, 2003).

The proposals developed for the maturity levels are based on the ISO/IEC17799:2000 (ISO/IEC17799, 2000) and ISO/IEC27002 good practice guideline domains and controls (ISO/IEC27002, 2007).

The Root Pattern has been developed with three maturity levels, this being the number of levels that received the best reception amongst the companies with which the research was carried out. Nevertheless, the MSM2-SME methodology has been prepared to support any number of maturity levels. The rRPSM proposal has been obtained from the continuous readjustments of the Root Pattern with test cases:

- **Level 1 or minimum protection:** This centres on the weight of the business's evolution in the following domains: i) Domain 5 – Security policy; ii) Domain 6 – Organizational aspects of information security; iii) Domain 7 – activity management; iv) Domain 8 – Security linked to human resources; v) Domain 11 – Access control; vi) Domain 13 – Information security incident management; and vii) Domain 15 – Compliance.
- **Level 2 or reasonable protection:** This centres on the weight of the business's evolution in the following domains: i) Domain 6 – Organizational aspects of information security; ii) Domain 9 – Physical and environmental security; iii) Domain11 – Access control; iv) Domain 12 – Acquisition, development and maintenance of information systems; v) Domain 13 – Information security incident management; and vi) Domain 15 – Compliance.
- **Level 3 or adequate protection:** This centres on the weight of the company's evolution in the following domains: i) Domain 10 – communication and operations management; ii) Domain 12 – Acquisition, development and maintenance of information systems; and iii) Domain 14 – Management of enterprises continuity.

The following objectives have been sought during the development of the structure of maturity levels created for the rRPSM: i) to create a government and consciousness of security in the basic aspects in Level 1, which will advance in the other levels; ii) to attain the organization's evolution in security and the settlement of the security policies in Level 2; and iii) finally, Level 3 will centre on physical aspects and on certain advanced aspects of the business's continuity.

Table 1 shows the association between the maturity levels proposed for the rRPSM and the ISO/IEC27002 standard (ISO/IEC27002, 2007). The domains of the ISO/IEC27002 standard which should be tackled in each maturity level are shown in grey. The domains which are of greatest importance in this maturity level are shown in dark grey, and those levels in which the domain is also important but is not the priority domain in this level are shown in light grey.

rRPSM Procedures

The Root Pattern developed by applying the methodology is supported by a series of elements, among which the procedures have an important mission in that they are in charge of defining

Table 1. rRPSM maturity model

ISO/ IEC27002 Domain	Root Pattern (rRPSM) (Maturity Level)		
	1	2	3
5	100%		
6	73%	27%	
7	100%		
8	100%		
9		100%	
10	3%	16%	81%
11	42%	58%	
12	31%	50%	19%
13	40%	60%	
14			100%
15	60%	40%	
	36%	38%	26%

and sustaining the information system's security management processes.

The procedures of the root pattern were developed by taking the ISO/IEC27002 good practice guideline controls (ISO/IEC27002, 2007) as a basis and simplifying them to adapt them to the requirements of SMEs. The root pattern consists of some 50 procedures which have been grouped into 9 domains and 25 sub-domains. Figure 13 shows the domains of which the rRPSM is composed.

The procedures are composed of a set of phases which are associated with other elements of the ISMS such as templates, regulations, technical instructions, roles. The procedures can thus be modified by adding to or modifying the existing phases, or creating new procedures within the pattern.

rRPSM Profiles

The root pattern developed on the MSM2-SME methodology includes a set of profiles associated with the phases of which each procedure is composed.

In the MSM2-SME methodology all the information system users are associated with one or various roles. The roles defined in the ISMS are associated with the phases of the procedures.

The association of these profiles with the phases of the procedures is of vital importance to the good functioning of the system. In SMEs many of these roles are taken on by the same person, although this does not suppose a problem for the proposed methodology.

Figure 14 shows an example of the procedures which a person with a type Cu/AO profile could access (Customer-Assets Owner).

Figure 13. Pattern of the domains in MSM2-SME

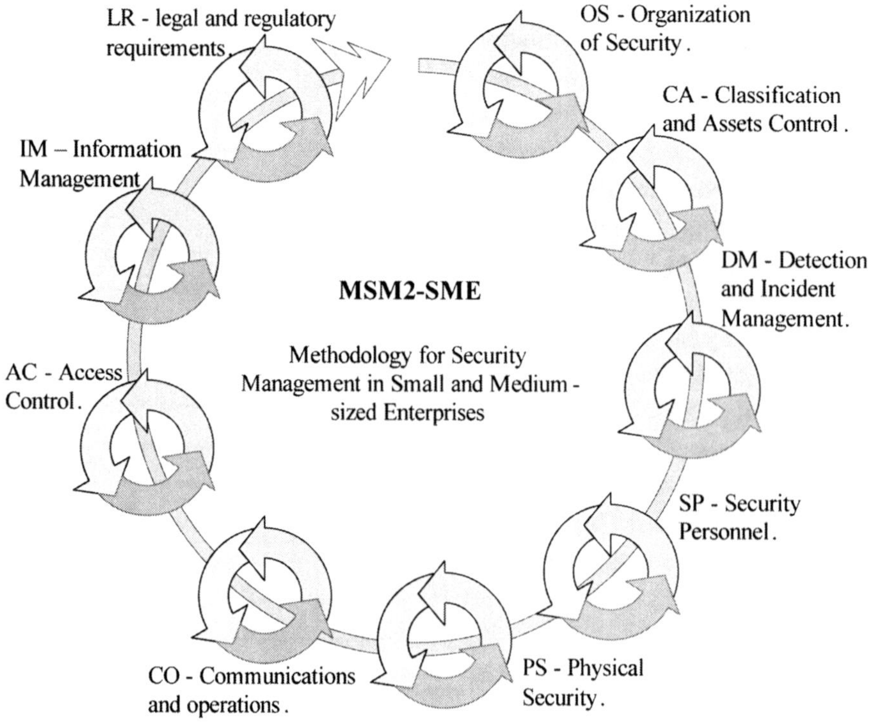

A brief list of the various roles that have been defined for the Root Pattern will be shown as follows: i) Cu/RD – Responsible for development; ii) Cu/RS – Responsible for security; iii) Cu/RE – Responsible for Exploitation; iv) Cu/AO – Assets Owner; v) Cu/SP - Service provider; vi) Cu/ISU - Information system users; vii) Cu/SDM – Systems department manager; viii) Cu/RM – Responsible for marketing; ix) Cu/RHR – Responsible
for Human Resources; x) Cu/DM – Department manager; and xi) Cu/TP – Third parties.

The main advantage of associating the ISMS user roles with the phases of the procedures is that it permits their processing to be automated, so that a user will not have to know how a procedure works, but will only have to carry out a task which s/he will request from within the procedure and decide who among the other users who have been designated roles associated with the next phase of the procedure will be assigned the following task.

APPLICABILITY OF MSM2-SME

To validate the MSM2-SME methodology, a tool called MSM2-TOOL has been developed. This tool allows us to develop simple, inexpensive, fast, automated, progressive and sustainable security management models. These are the main requirements that this type of enterprises have at the time of implementing these models.

From the viewpoint of the user, this tool presents two clear advantages:

- **Simplicity:** All ISMS activities are oriented to reduce the complexity of the process of construction and maintenance of ISMSs, thinking of organizations (SMEs) whose organizational structures are very simple.
- **Automation:** The whole system uses a concept called schemas to be able to automate the necessary steps to build and maintain the ISMS of the enterprise.

The tool is composed of three clearly differentiated parts and that correspond to the subprocesses of the methodology:

- **Patterns Generator (GSMP):** This zone of the tool can only be accessed by the security management architect (SMA) and the group of experts in the Domain (GED) and from this zone, we can carry out three

Figure 14. Procedures accessible by assets owner

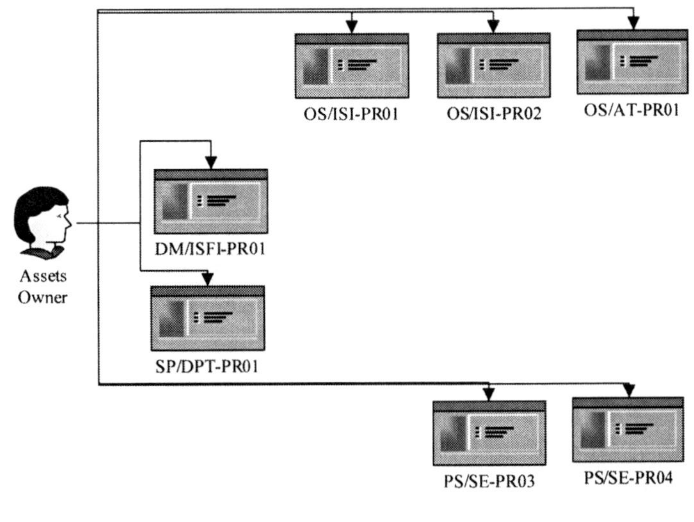

basic operations: i) create new schemas; ii) clone schemas from an existing schema; and iii) modify schemas to improve the ISMS generation.

- **ISMS Generator (GSMS):** This zone of the tool can only be accessed by the security consultant (CoS) and the objective here is that of generating the ISMS for the enterprise.
- **ISMS Support (MSMS):** This zone of the tool can be accessed by the users of the information system. The most relevant profile within this zone is the responsible for security (RS). From this zone, we can carry out three basic operations: i) management of the certificates of security culture; ii) procedure management; and iii) control board management.

Schemas are the nucleus over which the tool is developed because they allow the ISMS automation. These schemas are formed by a set of elements and associations between them, defined from the knowledge acquired by the customers.

The tool has allowed us to reduce the implementation costs of the systems and implies a higher percentage of success in implementations into SMEs. For these reasons, we consider that the results of this research can be very positive for SMEs because this tool allows them to access to the use of security management with a cost of resources reasonable for their size. Also, through the use of this methodology and the tool supporting it, we can obtain short-term results and reduce the costs that the use of other models and tools implies, thus obtaining a higher degree of satisfaction and efficiency in the enterprise.

Additionally, the tool allows us to maintain repositories containing not only information about the specifications of the necessary schemas for the construction of ISMSs but also information about the results obtained in the different use cases, thus allowing the constant improvement of the methodology along with the models.

From the application of the methodology and its tool to practical cases, we have extracted some interesting data: i) Information system users are not reluctant to security when its application is simple and the required knowledge is minimum; ii) In the case of SMEs, it is better to obtain less precise data (although keeping enough quality) if with this we obtain huge cost reductions; iii) The security culture is fundamental for the success of ISMSs in SMES at long term; and iv) The short-term knowledge of the level of fulfilment of the involved security controls is fundamental to maintain the ISMS.

CONCLUSION

In this chapter we have shown the mechanisms defined in the MSM2-SME methodology which make it possible to reuse knowledge acquired in different installations, thus obtaining enormous benefits (reductions in costs, robust results, etc.).We have also analysed the root pattern developed from all the knowledge obtained from a starting point for the creation of new more refined patterns for other companies.

We have shown how the root pattern has been developed by considering internationally recognised and prestigious standards in order to guarantee high quality in the results obtained when installing ISMSs, and how the structure of the patterns allows them to be adapted to any type of regulation, even making it possible to take only part of them, which supposes an enormous potential when applying the methodology.

We have also defined how this model can be used, along with the improvements that it offers in comparison to other models which confront the problem only partially or in a manner which is too costly for SMEs.

The characteristics offered by the model and its orientation towards SMEs has been very well received, and its application is proving to be very positive since it allows this type of enterprises an access to information security management systems which has, until now, only been available to large companies. Moreover, this model permits short term results to be obtained and it reduces the costs supposed by the use of other methodologies, thus leading to greater satisfaction in the business involved.

We are currently analysing the possibility of complementing the model developed on the methodology with other types of standards and recommendations in security material and security management, which could resolve the detected lacks. To do this we would take the guideline used as a basis for the development of the model (ISO/IEC27002), such as is the case of OLDP (OLDP, 1999) or HIPAA (HIPAA, 1996), and we should also take advantage of the ease of the methodology developed to incorporate new elements (more controls, procedures, standards).

All future improvements to the methodology and the model are oriented towards improving its precision, whilst always respecting the principal of the cost of resources, i.e., we seek to improve the model without incurring higher generation and maintenance costs of the ISMS.

REFERENCES

Alfawaz, S., Nelson, K., & Mohannak, K. (2010). *Information security culture: A behaviour compliance conceptual framework.* Paper presented at the Australasian Information Security Conference (AISC), Brisbane, Australia.

Areiza, K. A., Barrientos, A. M., Rincón, R., & Lalinde-Pulido, J. G. (2005a). Hacia un modelo de madurez para la seguridad de la información. *3er Congreso Iberoamericano de seguridad Informática*, (pp. 429–442).

Barlette, Y., & Vladislav, V. (2008). *Exploring the suitability of IS security management standards for SMEs.* Paper presented at the Hawaii International Conference on System Sciences, Proceedings of the 41st Annual, Waikoloa, HI, USA.

Barrientos, A. M., & Areiza, K. A. (2005). *Integration of a safety management system with an information quality management system.* Universidad EAFIT.

Bartsch, S., Sohr, K., & Bormann, C. (2009). *Supporting agile development of authorization rules for SME applications.* Paper presented at the CollaborateCom 2008, LNICST 10, ICST Institute for Computer Sciences, Social-Informatics and Telecommunications Engineering 2009.

Batista, J., & Figueiredo, A. (2000). SPI in very small team: A case with CMM. *Software Process Improvement and Practice*, *5*(4), 243–250. doi:10.1002/1099-1670(200012)5:4<243::AID-SPIP126>3.0.CO;2-0

Calvo-Manzano, J. A., Cuevas, G., San Feliu, T., De Amescua, A., García, L., & Pérez, M. (2004). Experiences in the application of software process improvement in SMES. *Software Quality Journal*, *10*(3), 261–273. doi:10.1023/A:1021638523413

Carey-Smith, M. T., Nelson, K. J., & May, L. J. (2007). *Improving information security management in nonprofit organisations with action research.* Paper presented at the 5th Australian Information Security Management Conference, Perth, Western Australia.

Cobit. (2006). *Guidelines.* Information Security Audit and Control Association.

Coles-Kemp, E., & Overill, R. E. (2007, 2-3 July). *The design of information security management systems for small-to-medium size enterprises.* Paper presented at the ECIW - The 6th European Conference on Information Warfare and Security, Shrivenham, UK.

De Capitani, S., Foresti, S., & Jajodia, S. (2008, October 27, 2008). *Preserving confidentiality of security policies in data outsourcing.* Paper presented at the WPES'08, Alexandria, Virginia, USA.

Department of Defense. (2003). *Systems security engineering capability maturity model* (SSE-CMM), version 3.0.

Dhillon, G., & Backhouse, J. (2000). Information System security management in the new millennium. *Communications of the ACM, 43*(7), 125–128. doi:10.1145/341852.341877

Dick, B. (2000). *Applications.* Sessions of Areol. Action research and evaluation.

Dojkovski, S., Lichtenstein, S., & Warren, M. J. (2006). *Challenges in fostering an information security culture in Australian small and medium sized enterprises.* Paper presented at the 5th European Conference on Information Warfare and Security, Helsinki, Finland.

Eloff, J., & Eloff, M. (2003). Information security management - A new paradigm. *Annual Research Conference of the South African Institute of Computer Scientists and Information Technologists on Enablement through Technology,* SAICSIT´03, (pp. 130-136).

Fernández-Medina, E., Jurjens, J., Trujillo, J., & Jajodia, S. (2009). Model-driven development for secure Information Systems. *Information and Software Technology Journal, 51*(5), 809–814. doi:10.1016/j.infsof.2008.05.010

Fontana, A., & Frey, J. (2005). The interview. In Denzin, N. L. (Ed.), *The SAGE handbook of qualitative research* (3rd ed., pp. 695–727). Thousand Oaks, CA: SAGE Publication.

Gupta, A., & Hammond, R. (2005). Information systems security issues and decisions for small businesses. *Information Management & Computer Security, 13*(4), 297–310. doi:10.1108/09685220510614425

Hareton, L., & Terence, Y. (2001). A process framework for small projects. *Software Process Improvement and Practice, 6,* 67–83. doi:10.1002/spip.137

Health Insurance Portability and Accountability Act, 74 Federal Register 3295-3328 C.F.R. *(1996).*

Information security management maturity model (ISM3 v.2.0). (2007).

ISO/IEC20000. (2005). *Service management IT.*

ISO/IEC 17799. (2000). *Information Technology - Security techniques - Code of practice for information security management.*

ISO/IEC 27001. (2005). *Information Technology - Security techniques information security management systems - Requirements.*

ISO/IEC 27002. (2007). *Information Technology - Security techniques - The international standard code of practice for information security management.*

(2007). *ITIL.* Information Technology Infrastructure Library.

Kluge, D. (2008). *Formal information security standards in German medium enterprises.* Paper presented at the CONISAR: The Conference on Information Systems Applied Research.

Kostina, A., Miloslavskaya, N., & Tolstoy, A. (2009). *Information security incident management process.* Paper presented at the SIN'09.

Linares, S., & Paredes, I. (2007). *IS2ME: Information security to the medium enterprise* [Electronic Version]. Retrieved from http://www.is2me.org/introduccion-en.html

MageritV2. (2005). *Metodología de Análisis y Gestión de Riesgos para las Tecnologías de la Información, V2.* Ministerio de Administraciones Públicaso.

Mekelburg, D. (2005). Sustaining best practices: How real-world software organizations improve quality processes. *Software Quality Professional*, *7*(3), 4–13.

O´Brien, R. (1998). *An overview of the methodological approach of action research.*

Ohki, E., Harada, Y., Kawaguchi, S., Shiozaki, T., & Kagaua, T. (2009). *Information security governance framework.* Paper presented at the WISG'09.

Organic Law Data Personal Protection, 15/1999 C.F.R. (1999).

Siponen, M., & Willison, R. (2009). Information security management standards: Problems and solutions. *Information & Management*, *46*, 267–270. doi:10.1016/j.im.2008.12.007

Stephenson, P. (2004). Forensic Análisis of Risks in Enterprise Systems. *Law, Investigation and Ethics,* Sep/Oct, 20-21.

Tawileh, A., Hilton, J., & McIntosh, S. (2007). Managing information security in small and medium sized enterprises: A holistic approach. In Pohlmann, N. (Ed.), *ISSE/SECURE 2007 Securing Electronic Business Processes* (*Vol. 4*, pp. 331–339). doi:10.1007/978-3-8348-9418-2_35

Tuffley, A., & Grove, B., & G, M. (2004). SPICE for small organisations. *Software Process Improvement and Practice*, *9*, 23–31. doi:10.1002/spip.191

Valdevit, T., Mayer, N., & Barafort, B. (2009). Tailoring ISO/IEC 27001 for SMEs: A guide to implement an information security management system in small settings. In O'Connor, R. V. (Eds.), *EuroSPI 2009, CCIS 42* (pp. 201–212). Berlin, Germany: Springer-Verlag. doi:10.1007/978-3-642-04133-4_17

Vries, H., Blind, K., Mangelsdorf, A., Verheul, H., & Zwan, J. (2009). *SME access to European standardization. Enabling small and medium-sized enterprises to achieve greater benefit from standards and from involvement in standardization.* Rotterdam, the Netherlands. (A. 2009 o. Document Number)

Wiander, T. (2008). *Implementing the ISO/IEC 17799 standard in practice – Experiences on audit phases.* Paper presented at the AISC '08: The Sixth Australasian Conference on Information security, Wollongong, Australia.

Wiander, T., & Holappa, J. (2006). *Theoretical framework of ISO 17799 compliant information security management system using novel ASD method.*

ADDITIONAL READING

Fernández-Medina, E. (2004). *Extending UML for designing secure Data Warehouses. in 23rd ER.* China: Shangai.

Fernández-Medina, E., et al. Extending the UML for Designing Secure Data Warehouses. in International Conference on Conceptual Modeling (ER 2004). 2004. Shangai, China: Springer-Verlag.

Fernández-Medina, E. (2006). Access Control and Audit Model for the Multidimensional Modeling of Data Warehouses. *Decision Support Systems*, *42*, 1270–1289. doi:10.1016/j.dss.2005.10.008

Fernández-Medina, E. (2007). Developing Secure Data Warehouses with a UML extension. *Information Systems*, *32*(6), 826–856. doi:10.1016/j.is.2006.07.003

Fernández-Medina, E., De Capitani di Vimercati, S., et al. (2004). Multimedia security and digital rights management technology. Information Security Policies and Actions in Modern Integrated Systems. M. F. y. C. Bellettini. Estados Unidos y Gran Bretaña, Idea Group Publishing: 230-271.

Fernández-Medina, E., & Jurjens, J. (2008). (in press). Model-Driven Development for secure information systems. *Information and Software Technology*.

Fernández-Medina, E., & Jurjens, J. (2009). Model-Driven Development for secure information systems. *Information and Software Technology*, *51*(5), 809–814. doi:10.1016/j.infsof.2008.05.010

Fernández-Medina, E., & Piattini, M. Designing Secure Database for OLS, in Database and Expert Systems Applications: 14th International Conference (DEXA 2003), V. Marik, W. Retschitzegger, and O. Stepankova, Editors. 2003, Springer. LNCS 2736: Prague, Czech Republic. p. 886-895.

Fernández-Medina, E., & Piattini, M. Extending OCL for Secure Database Design. in International Conference on the Unified Modeling Language (UML 2004). 2004. Lisbon, Portugal: Springer-Verlag. LNCS.

Fernandez-Medina, E., & Piattini, M. (2005). Designing Secure Databases. *Information and Software Technology*, *47*(7), 463–477. doi:10.1016/j.infsof.2004.09.013

Fernández-Medina, E., & Piattini, M. (2005). Designing secure databases. *Information and Software Technology*, *47*(7), 463–477. doi:10.1016/j.infsof.2004.09.013

Fernández-Medina, E., & Rodriguez, A. (2009). Guest Editorial. Special Issue: Security in Information Systems: New Advances and Tendencies. *Journal of Universal Computer Science*, *15*(15), 2912–2915.

Fernández-Medina, E., G. Ruiz, et al. (2003). Implementing an Access Control System for SVG Documents. On the Move to Meaningful Internet Systems 2003: OTM 2003 Workshops, Catania, Sicilia, Italia, Springer-Verlag. LNCS 2889.

Fernández-Medina, E., & Trujillo, J. (2006). Access Control and Audit Model for the Multidimensional Modeling of Data Warehouses. *Decision Support Systems*, *42*, 1270–1289. doi:10.1016/j.dss.2005.10.008

Fernández-Medina, E., & Trujillo, J. (2007). Model Driven Multidimensional Modeling of Secure Data Warehouses. *European Journal of Information Systems*, *16*, 374–389. doi:10.1057/palgrave.ejis.3000687

Fernández-Medina, E., & Trujillo, J. (2007). Developing Secure Data Warehouses with a UML extension. *Information Systems*, *32*(6), 826–856. doi:10.1016/j.is.2006.07.003

Fernández-Medina, E., Trujillo, J., & Piattini, M. (2007). Model Driven Multidimensional Modeling of Secure Data Warehouses. *European Journal of Information Systems*, *16*, 374–389. doi:10.1057/palgrave.ejis.3000687

Mellado, D., & Fernandez-Medina, E. (2007). A common criteria based security requirements engineering process for the development of secure information systems. *Computer Standards & Interfaces*, *29*(2), 244–253. doi:10.1016/j.csi.2006.04.002

Mellado, D., E. Fernández-Medina, et al. (2008). A Systematic Review of Security Requirements Engineering. Computers and Security (Being processed - Under review).

Sánchez, L. E., Ruiz, C., et al. (2010). Managing the asset risk of SMEs. Fifth International Conference on Availability, Reliability and Security (ARES'10). Second International Workshop on Organizational Security Aspects (OSA). Krakow, Poland.

Sánchez, L. E., Santos-Olmo, A., et al. (2010). Security Culture in Small and Medium-Size Enterprise. Conference on ENTERprise Information Systems (CENTERIS'10). Viana do Castelo, Portugal: 315-324.

Sánchez, L. E., Santos-Olmo, A., Fernández-Medina, E., & Piattini, M. (2009a). Managing Security and its Maturity in Small and Medium-Sized Enterprises. Journal of Universal Computer Science (J.UCS), 15(15), 3038-3058.

Sánchez, L. E., Santos-Olmo, A., Fernández-Medina, E., & Piattini, M. (2009b). MMSM-SME: Methodology for the management of security and its maturity in Small and Medium-sized Enterprises. Paper presented at the 11th International Conference on Enterprise Information Systems (WOSIS09).

Sánchez, L. E., Villafranca, D., et al. (2009). Management of Scorecards and Metrics to manage Security in SMEs. The 18th ACM Conference on Information and Knowledge Management (CIKM 2009). International Workshop on Data Quality and Security (DQS'09). Hong Kong, China: 9-16.

Sánchez, L. E., Villafranca, D., Fernández-Medina, E., & Piattini, M. (2006a). Developing a maturity model for information system security management within small and medium size enterprises. Paper presented at the 8th International Conference on Enterprise Information Systems (WOSIS'06), Paphos (Chipre).

Sánchez, L. E., Villafranca, D., Fernández-Medina, E., & Piattini, M. (2006b). Security Management in corporative IT systems using maturity models, taking as base ISO/IEC 17799. Paper presented at the International Symposium on Frontiers in Availability, Reliability and Security (FARES'06) in conjunction with ARES., Viena (Austria).

Sánchez, L. E., Villafranca, D., Fernández-Medina, E., & Piattini, M. (2007a). Developing a model and a tool to manage the information security in Small and Medium Enterprises. Paper presented at the International Conference on Security and Cryptography (SECRYPT'07). Barcelona. Spain.

Sánchez, L. E., Villafranca, D., Fernández-Medina, E., & Piattini, M. (2007b). MMISS-SME Practical Development: Maturity Model for Information Systems Security Management in SMEs. Paper presented at the 9th International Conference on Enterprise Information Systems (WOSIS'07). Funchal, Madeira (Portugal).

Sánchez, L. E., Villafranca, D., Fernández-Medina, E., & Piattini, M. (2007c). SCMM-TOOL: Tool for computer automation of the Information Security Management Systems. Paper presented at the 2nd International conference on Software and Data Technologies (ICSOFT'07)., Barcelona-España

Sánchez, L. E., Villafranca, D., Fernández–Medina, E., & Piattini, M. (2008). Practical Application of a Security Management Maturity Model for SMEs Based on Predefined Schemas. Paper presented at the International Conference on Security and Cryptography (SECRYPT'08). Porto–Portugal.

KEY TERMS AND DEFINITIONS

Information Security Management System (ISMS): Is a set of policies concerned with information security management or IT related risks. The governing principle behind an ISMS is that an organization should design, implement and maintain a coherent set of policies, processes and systems to manage risks to its information assets, thus ensuring acceptable levels of information security risk.

Information Technology Security Assessment: Is an explicit study to locate IT security vulnerabilities and risks.

Risk Management: Risk management is the identification, assessment, and prioritization of risks followed by coordinated and economical application of resources to minimize, monitor, and control the probability and/or impact of unfortunate events or to maximize the realization of opportunities.

Security Culture: Is a set of customs shared by a community whose members may engage in illegal or sensitive activities, the practice of which minimizes the risks of such activities being subverted, or targeted for sabotage.

Security Management: Is a broad field of management related to asset management, physical security and human resource safety functions. It entails the identification of an organization's information assets and the development, documentation and implementation of policies, standards, procedures and guidelines.

Security Metrics: Set of measures to assess the security level of a company.

Small and Medium Size Enterprise (SME): Its current definition categorizes companies with fewer than 10 employees as "micro", those with fewer than 50 employees as "small", and those with fewer than 250 as "medium".

Chapter 7
Information Security and Management in Social Network

Alkesh Patel
Rediff.com, India

Ajit Balakrishnan
Rediff.com, India

ABSTRACT

Social networking sites (SNSs) have gained significant attention in last few years. Most Internet users are associated with at least one popular SNS depending on their personal and professional preferences. Users have, in general, trusted the SNSs with personal data, and assumed that their privacy preferences are correctly enforced. Users of SNSs often want to manage the sharing of information and content with different groups of people based on their differing relationships. Configuring settings for each user is a great burden for a user, and most of the time, settings are not evident to users, and hence some automatic or semi-automatic mechanism should be available to reduce the privacy configuration efforts. Increasing user-driven contribution has also led to other kinds of problems, like spam and abusive message contents. The authors refer both of these types as social spam, which not only consumes extra resources of site, but also spoils the user experience and creates legal issues. In large scale SNS, human moderation becomes out of hand, and there is a need for machine intelligence to get rid of such spammers in an effective way. In social networks, users' actions, contributions, demographic details, et cetera can be tracked, and necessary measures can be taken if unwanted behavior about a particular user is detected. One can make a user model of reputation to identify troublesome users and ban their activities temporarily or permanently whenever needed. User reputation systems help to improve the user experience of a site, enrich content quality, and provide incentives for users to become better, more active participants. In this chapter, authors describe issues related to privacy, social spamming, and show the measures to handle them by nearly automatic ways. The chapter also shows the making of a user reputation system and its applicability in social network.

DOI: 10.4018/978-1-4666-0197-0.ch007

INTRODUCTION

The success and growth of social networking sites like Facebook, Orkut and many other locally dominant sites are very apparent. Such sites provide users various tools to stay in touch with friends, family and colleagues where they can view and share updates, photos or any other interesting life transitions. At the time of registration to these sites, users are asked to provide basic information like name, school, college, company, email ids, phone, city, address etc. Moreover, users also perform lot of other activities e.g. commenting on feeds, photo/video/link sharing, updating profile information etc. There are settings provided to user for what kind of information will be visible to others and who can see that information. There is a tread off between encouraging interactions and enforcing strict privacy settings. Additionally, providing configuration for controlling each friend in the user's network is complex and it rather confuses the users than helping them. In general, user would like to show certain information to everyone, only friends, friends of friends or none other than self. Automated approaches to grouping may have the potential to reduce this burden. However, their use remains largely untested. We shall discuss one of clustering methods in this chapter that group similar friends.

In social network, apart from users' profile pages, there are fan pages where one can become a fan of a celebrity, location, organization or specific event so that he/she can get the updates from followed pages regularly. Many times page owners allow their page follower to post updates about them and discuss about it. Users behave nicely with their friends in online social network so there is hardly any need for moderation of comments but in case of fan pages, allowing users to become a fan, post whatever they like and discuss whatever they feel, can create unwanted situations. Some spammers try to seek attention of users on the most popular fan pages. It has also been seen that some users create fake profiles and try to put abusive remarks in discussion happening on active pages. Both of these cause very bad experience for genuine users and harm the reputation of not only page owner but also overall site. We call this phenomenon as social spamming and show automatic way of tackling them with the help of machine learning techniques in this chapter.

Web is moving from content-centric to user-centric gradually and social networking is the best example of it. In this chapter, we propose making of user reputation system which is capable of managing per user information management in effective manner and opens the doors to build potential related applications in social network.

In summary, the proposed chapter is supposed to provide thorough understanding with implementation details on following:

- Privacy issues and the automated ways to control them in social networks
- Social spamming issues and ways to tackle them
- Building user reputation system and its applications in social network

BACKGROUND

The networks of 'Friends' which users sustain on SNSs often consist of contacts associated with distinct facets of their lives. Presenting information equally across connections from these various implied groups can be problematic, particularly for users who are privacy conscious. Goffman (1959) observed that people attempt to maintain a great deal of control over their personas and minimize the appearance of characteristics that are contrary to an idealized version of them. Lampinen et al. (2009) study revealed that even the most carefree SNS users had attempted to manage group co-presence even when it was not explicitly supported by the system. This required establishing and continually managing group identities to facilitate more contextual sharing. Several studies (DiMicco et al., 2007 and Skeels et al., 2009) have demonstrated users' desire to create groups of contacts that act as a mechanism for multi-level access control when sharing content and thus reducing the burden of employing such strategies. Group-based access control could offer a solution that prevents the inadvertent flow of information between groups within a user's network. Davis et al. (2005) established that people decide with whom to share information based on the type of relationship (e.g. spouse, friend, peer etc). Jones et al. (2004) and Olson et al. (2005) showed that people want to specify groups and basic categories centered on these relationships, for which they can specify an appropriate privacy setting. However, it has also been noted (Lederer et al., 2004) that managing groups can be a significant burden for the user, particularly as the number of contacts and relationship types expands with the growth and popularity of the service. In addition, Ackerman and Mainwaring (2005) stress that, although valued, privacy is not the users' primary task and that making it an explicit task for the user can be problematic. Designing systems that reduce privacy violations without significant configuration effort from the user is therefore an important objective. Researchers have suggested using automated algorithms that use information such as network measures or tie strength to automatically determine distinct groups within a social network, however building and evaluating such system's performance is yet to be figured out. Gilbert and Karahalios (2009) suggest that privacy controls based on tie strength may help to segment a user's social network into meaningful groups. For example, a system could decide which contacts fall into trusted and un-trusted categories and restrict content accordingly. In order to distinguish between strong and weak ties, they examined activity networks in Facebook, i.e. interactions between members of a social network rather than merely 'Friend' connections. They also showed that tie strength may be modeled with high accuracy based on these interactions. There has been considerable research into partitioning networks (Clauset et al., 2004 and Xau et al., 2007) into such clusters by algorithmic analysis of the network structure. Most of these algorithms cluster people within the social network such that there is a set of many ties within each cluster and few ties between clusters. We speculate that such clustering might reasonably predict groups that users wish to create for controlling their privacy within a social network, separating groups representing distinct contexts and relationship types from one another. Although many contextual factors can affect privacy decisions, the findings from Lederer et al. (2002) suggest that the primary index for such decisions should be the identity of the recipient. The exact context surrounding the disclosure is secondary to this and has less influence on the overall decision. Standard network clustering algorithms are unaware to such context and operate only on the structure of the network, i.e. the individuals in the network and their links, yet they provide good starting point. Hence, in this chapter, we shall discuss about one of such basic clustering algorithms for grouping users in SNSs and see how it can be useful in automating privacy setting configuration.

Spamming has been common topic in E-mails and numbers of techniques are suggested for detecting it and preventing spammers. In social network intentions of spammer are similar where they may utilize the social network's search tools to target a certain demographic section of the users, or use popular fan pages or groups to send notes to them from an account disguised as that of a real person. Such notes may include implanted links to pornographic or other product sites designed to sell something. Plenty of automated methods are available (Mertz 2002) like *basic structured text filters*, *whitelist or verification filters*, *distributed adaptive blacklists*, *rule-based or regular expression-based rankings*, *Bayesian word distribution filters* and *Bayesian trigram filters*. Wikpedia—another system focused around user-generated content—has also seen an increase in research interest in automatic approaches to spam detection (Priedhorsky et al. 2007). Heymann et al. (2007) classified the anti-spam strategies commonly adopted in practice into three different categories: prevention, demotion, and detection. Prevention-based approaches are aimed at making it difficult to contribute spam content to the social bookmarking system by restricting certain types of access through the submission interface (such as CAPTCHAs) or through usage limits (such as post or tagging quota). The nofollow HTML attribute of hyperlinks can also serve as a spam deterrent, since it instructs search engines that a hyperlink should not influence the link target's ranking in the search engine's index, thereby removing the main motivation of spammers. Demotion-based strategies focus on reducing the prominence and visibility of content likely to be spam. Rank-based methods, for instance, try to produce orderings of the system's content that are more accurate and more resistant to spam. A demotion-based strategy for combating spam is described by Heymann et al. (2007) where ranking methods are used to lower the rank of the contents. They investigate the influence of various factors on these rankings, such as the proportion and behavior of spam users. Markines et al. (2009) presented a study of automatic detection of spammers in a social tagging system where they described six features that a spam post carry – i) spammer use tags and tag combinations that are statistically unlikely to appear in legitimate posts, ii) spam resource is usually associated with a large number of popular tags that may be unrelated to the resource and are often semantically unrelated to one another, iii) content of annotated resources in social spam often tend to have a similar document structure, possibly due to the fact that many of them are automatically generated by tools that craft web sites from predefined templates, iv) spammers often create pages for the sole purpose of serving ads, v) *plagiarism* i.e. spammers copy original content from all over the Web and vi) similar user profiles created for spam purposes. Mishne et al. (2005) were among the first to address the problem of spam comments in blogs and used language model disagreement between the blog post itself, the comments, and any pages linked to from the comments to identify possible spam comments. In content level spam detection methods, Bayesian filtering is the most widely used and effective method of detecting spam from content of the post itself. Along with different kinds of spam moderation methods, we shall elaborate Bayesian spam filtering technique in this chapter.

The Internet has created enormous new opportunities to interact with strangers. The interactions can be fun, informative, and even profitable. But they also involve risks. In this scenario, if there is some mechanism which tells about user's reputation, then decision for 'whom to trust and whom not to trust' can be easier. According to Resnick et al. (2006), reputation systems must have the following three properties to operate at all: i) Entities must be long lived, so that with every interaction there is always an expectation of future interactions, ii) Ratings about current interactions are captured and distributed and iii) Ratings about past interactions must guide decisions about current interactions. Dingledine et al. (2000) have proposed the following set of basic criteria for judging the quality and soundness of reputation computation engines: a) *Accuracy for long-term performance*- The system must reflect the confidence of a given score. It must also have the capability to discriminate between a new entity of unknown quality and an entity with poor long-term performance. b) *Weighting toward current behavior*- The system must recognize and reflect recent trends in entity performance. For example, an entity that has behaved well for a long time but suddenly goes downward should be quickly recognized as unreliable. c) *Robustness against attacks*- The system should resist attempts of entities to manipulate reputation scores. d) *Smoothness*- Adding any single rating should not influence the score significantly. Randall Farmer and Bryce Glass (2010) in their latest book, have given great depth of their study on building web reputation system. Here, they refer user reputation system as 'Karma'. According to them *Karma* is reputation of user in community in terms of some score. It may be comprised of many components, such as: i) how long has this person been a member of the community? ii) what types of activities has he/she involved in? iii) how well has he/she performed at others in community? iv) what do other people think about this person?. Besides providing a means for trust between users, karma is often used as an incentive to encourage contributions to a service, or to identify specific users for particular action. In this chapter we shall use some of the concepts from their work pertaining to social network and show how user reputation system can be built in social network and what benefits it can offer for enhanced user experience.

PRIVACY CONTROL

Issues, Controversies, Problems

More private data online has lead to growing privacy concerns for the users, and some have faced extreme repercussions for sharing their private information on social networking sites. For example, students have been fined for their online social behavior; a mayor was forced to resign because of a controversial profile picture. There are numerous such cases, and these incidents clearly highlight the importance of privacy control in social networks.

Granular level of privacy control is expected by users in susceptible social networks. E.g. "who can view someone's personal information", "what activities one can perform on someone's updates" and "who should receive specific updates". Facebook and Orkut like SNSs provide exhaustive list of settings to be enforced for different kind of activities and access control of information. Most of the time, users do not even know that they have such settings available or they are too complex for users to make any changes in them and hence end up keeping default settings. To help such users and keeping the things simple, there should be some automated way for employing privacy and access control to certain information.

Solutions and Recommendations

In this chapter, we propose group-based privacy and such grouping done by using automatic approach. We shall see some of the factors mentioned by Jones and O'Neill (2010) that influence users to make group of his friends for particular purpose.

Criteria for Clustering

1. **Social Circles & Cliques:** They refer to tightly knit groups, e.g. a group of friends that are very much connected to one another. People tend to joke around one group more often while with other group they behave more sensible. Users are not only aware of social circles and cliques within their large social network but are influenced by them in their information and content sharing choices, with an inclination not to share information or content or candid behavior that does not conform to the social norms or values of a particular social circle.
2. **Tie Strength:** It indicates the factors relating to their relationship with a contact, such as the closeness, emotional intensity, level of trust and frequency of communication, when assigning them to a group. These factors can be taken as indicators of the strength of an interpersonal tie. It is quite common for users to form groups of 'Close friends' or 'Best friends'. For example, in a typical user's friend list, not all are really his friends. Sometimes they are just people that he knows, perhaps not even very well at all. He doesn't want them knowing everything about himself. But it is different for close friends where he would be willing to share

far more. It was also frequent for participants to create groups exclusively containing weak ties, such as 'People I hardly know', 'Acquaintances', 'Friends of friends' and 'People that randomly added me'. Many times a user have based his groups on the different levels of faith that he placed in people and on his assessment of whether people would "judge" him based on the content he uploaded. Other friends might judge personal content in a negative way. It is not considered very cool to have lots of photos with your Mom and Dad, but user's close friends and family enjoy seeing those photos. On the other hand, people that he doesn't know very well might see things like that and laugh at him. General pattern is that users feel that it would be important to share content differently with people with whom they do not interact a large amount or very often versus people with whom they interact a lot and frequently. Hence, although users are often able to recognize groups of contacts for privacy purposes, there is still a need to specify privacy settings for individuals.

3. **Temporal Episodes:** Many times, users create groups that represented significant parts of their lives called *episodes*. Each episode representing a certain period of time and users used to place contacts that they associated with that episode. Time scales ranged from hours (e.g. the time spent at a certain event) to months or years (e.g. the groups 'Winter 2010' and 'My Childhood'). Temporal Episodes are often closely associated and sometimes mixed with geographical locations. For example, users would interchangeably talk about periods of time by referring to particular locations where that time was spent and vice versa.
4. **Geographical Locations:** It has been seen that classifying contacts into groups is associated with particular locations, for example where users first met or where they spent a significant amount of time during their relationship. Locations varied in scale from particular venues to entire countries. For example, participants created groups such as 'Las Vegas Pub ', for anybody they had met at that place in the gap of only a few hours. 'People I met on holiday in Switzerland' is used to group people met in a certain country during a particular period of a few weeks. Temporal episodes and geographical locations are important to consider for controlling privacy because users expressed concern about their momentary actions having unpredicted consequences if viewed in different contexts. There is a time and a place for certain behavior and if one shares content such as photos, one would be comfortable acting like this in front of people if they were actually there at the time.
5. **Functional Roles:** Although SNSs are primarily a friend networking service in social circle, users sometimes use it to enhance non-social connections. Some contacts are added for professional networking and others are added for functional reasons, providing a particular use or service to the user. For example, user may add as a contact somebody whom he had encountered through a classified advertisement, which he had placed on SNS to sell an item, merely as a way of bookmarking that guy, for when he wanted to communicate about the transaction. There is a concern about making personal information, particularly regarding their social activities, available to such contacts; however, users generally do not take any measures to address such concerns which are inherently there and there is no specific tool to handle it.
6. **Organizational Boundaries:** Users are likely to group contacts based on the institutions or organizations that they belonged to, in order to be able to separate the professional and social aspects of their lives. They create

groups representing particular companies, departments and different roles within their workplace. Here again, user may worry what other people might think when they see his profile since, not everything on there portrays him in a professional light. They do need mechanism to alter privacy preferences for these people, but don't have one.

Structural Clustering Algorithm for Networks (SCAN)

Network clustering appears to capture groups that are formed analogously to several of the 6 criteria that are listed above. Social circles and cliques can readily be derived by algorithmic analysis of the network structure as per Boyd and Heer (2006). The persistence of ties within the network also allows users' network graphs to evolve over time, reflecting a personal history of relationships. Clusters of ties are likely to form as people transition between temporal episodes, distinct geographical locations and organizational boundaries and build new sets of relationships. Such clusters will also be identifiable algorithmically in the network structure. We shall see the SCAN algorithm given by Xu et al. (2007) to cluster people (vertices) within each user's egocentric social network (Figure 1) into groups. This algorithm also detects and isolates two kinds of vertex that play distinctive roles: 'hubs' that bridge clusters and 'outliers' that are marginally connected to a cluster. It has been observed that users struggle to place some contacts into groups because they were either weakly associated with a group (outliers) or strongly associated with multiple groups (hubs). Vertices are grouped into the clusters by how they share neighbors. This is

Figure 1. Result of SCAN clustering algorithm for a user with his social network of friends

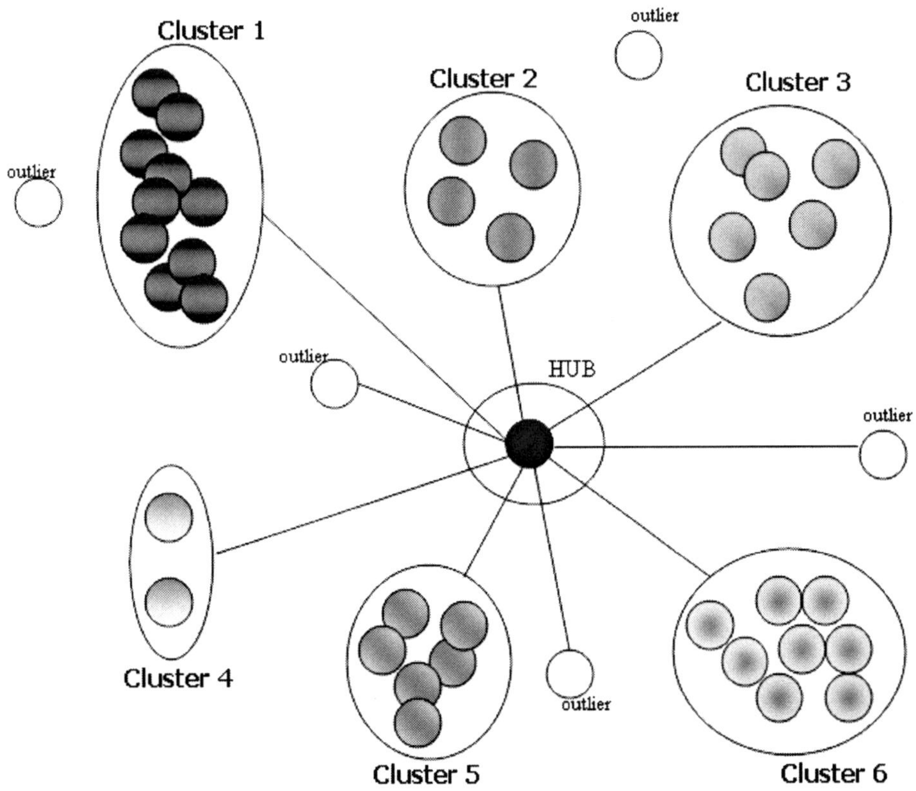

quite obvious thing to do in large social networks, because two people who share many friends should be clustered in the same community. SCAN has the following characteristics:

- It detects clusters, hubs, and outliers by using the structure and the connectivity of the vertices as clustering criteria.
- It is fast. Its running time on a network with n vertices and m edges is $O(m)$. In contrast, the running time of the fastest existing network clustering algorithm i.e. $O(md \log n)$.

Steps Involved in Algorithm

SCAN performs one pass of a network and finds all connected clusters for a given parameter setting.

Step 1: At the beginning all vertices are labeled as unclassified. The SCAN algorithm classifies each vertex either a member of a cluster or a nonmember.

Step 2: For each vertex that is not yet classified, SCAN checks whether this vertex is a core. If the vertex is a core, a new cluster is expanded from this vertex.

Step 3: Otherwise, the vertex is labeled as a non-member. To find a new cluster, SCAN starts with an arbitrary core v and search for all vertices that are structure reachable from v in Step 2. This is sufficient to find the complete cluster containing vertex v. In Step 2, a new cluster ID is generated which will be assigned to all vertices found in Step 2. SCAN begins by inserting all vertices in ε-neighborhood of vertex v into a queue. For each vertex in the queue it computes all directly reachable vertices and inserts those vertices into the queue which are still unclassified. This is repeated until the queue is empty.

Step 4: The non-member vertices can be further classified as hubs or outliers. If an isolated vertex has edges to two or more clusters, it is may be classified as a hub. Otherwise, it is an outlier.

We have proposed the architecture of the entire system as shown in Figure 2. Here, a user with his friends in social network is considered.

Figure 2. System architecture of machine learning framework to cluster similar friends for privacy control

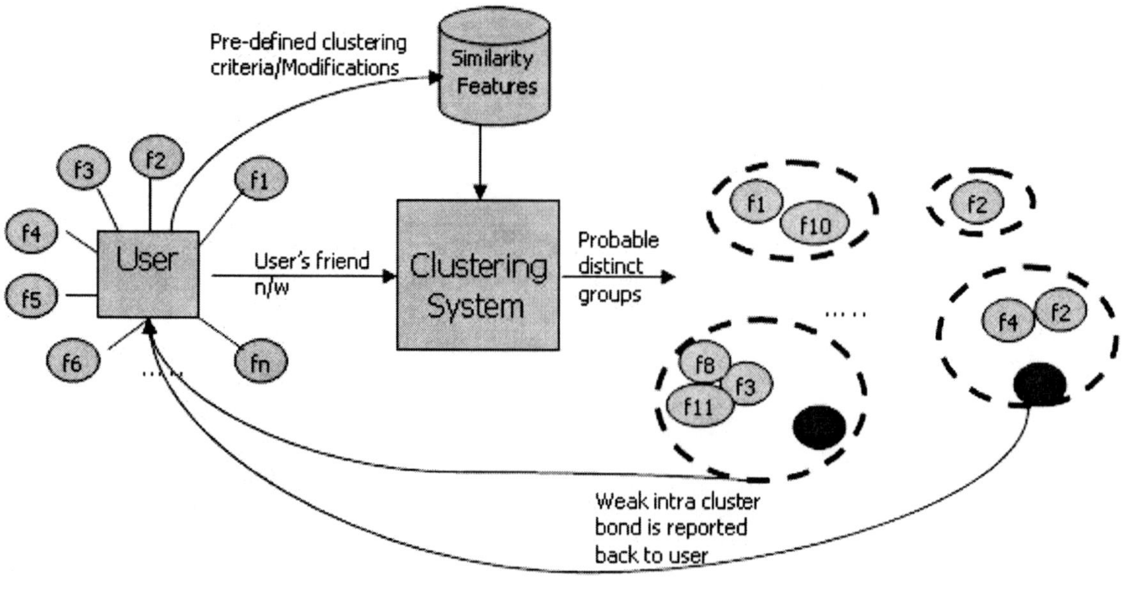

As an input, clustering system has a user's friend network and pre-defined clustering criteria for finding similarity among users. As described earlier, SCAN clustering algorithm outputs probable distinct groups of friends with certain confidence. In a good cluster there is always strong intra-cluster bondage among elements and very weak inter-cluster bondage among elements. Our system also detects such discrepancies if exist and report such clusters to user as a feedback. User can take necessary action which then translated into modification in clustering criteria and hence similarity features' weights. Clustering system continuously learns from the user's feedback for grouping and rearranges clusters in future. User can label resulted clusters on his own way to create groups and apply preferred privacy settings.

Thus, we can handle the problem of users' concern for privacy on different activities for different friends in social network almost automatically by applying machine learning technique.

SOCIAL SPAMMING

Issues, Controversies, Problems

Motivation for spamming can range from advertising and self-promotion to disruption and disparagement of competitors. Spamming is inexpensive because the barrier for entry into the systems that allows user-generated contents is generally low. Moreover, it requires virtually no operating costs beyond the building and managing the automatic spamming software. Also, it is often difficult to catch hold of spammers for their behavior. Any system that relies on user-generated content is vulnerable to spam in one or the other way. Users are contributing more and more content to social networking sites in order to express themselves as part of their profiles and to share to their social circles online. Spam comments are also becoming an increasing problem for websites that allow users to post reactions to content, such as blogs and video and photo sharing websites. While user contribution builds up the online characteristics for the user, it also leaves the data exposed to be misused, as an example, for targeted advertising and sale. In this scenario, many unwanted elements (spammers) become active and try to make money by attracting users to their site. Social spam is a cheap way to attract users and what they need to do is to create some content, place ads, and use social sites to pull traffic. Much of this can be done automatically through a software which: (1) finds relevant keywords using suggestion tools; (2) registers domain names based on the keywords; (3) creates hosting accounts for those domain names; (4) creates complete websites full of fake content using keywords in generic sentences, with embedded ads; (5) uploads these websites to the hosting accounts for the corresponding domain names; and (6) cross-links the websites to boost PageRank. The software allowed the creation of hundreds of sites per hour, each with hundreds of pages, generating significant revenues from advertising. Thus, it generates significant online junk, and consequently to promote it through social spam. Another kind of social spamming which is not for monetary purpose, but has lot to do for any civilized site and it carries legal implications. These contents are bad quality contents and often include abusive, pornographic, religious, using copyrighted material or libelous remarks. See the Figure 3.

Solutions and Recommendations

There are different methods employed on social networking site for controlling social spam or low-quality contents with human aided and automatic measures. There are generally considered to be four major (rough) categories of moderation systems operating on the Internet today:

Pre-moderation: Some sites work on the principle that every piece of user generated content that could go up onto a site should be checked by

Figure 3. Example of social spamming

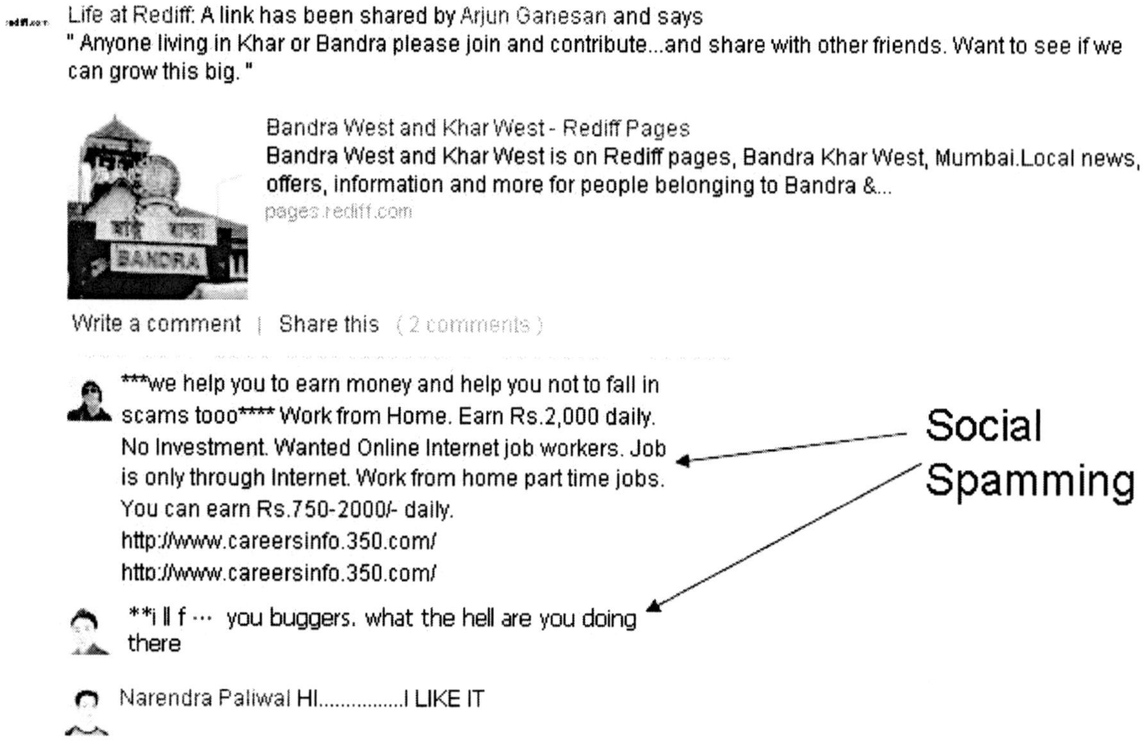

a moderator before it goes live. This is of course not scalable solution as the costs of pre-moderation are too high and bad user experience.

Post-moderation: The immediacy that people want when they press their submit button is primary to all online communities and most sites based around user generated content. That is where post-moderation comes in. Here too, every piece of user-generated content needs to be checked, but rather than checking them all before they go live they are instead checked as soon as possibly afterwards.

Reactive-moderation: Reactive moderation is based on the assumption that if something bad is happening on a site, then the users will spot it quickly and can alert the moderators. This is becoming by far the most common form of moderation for message boards where "Report Abuse" functionality is provided for each post.

Distributed-moderation: Distributed moderation relies on principle, that a community can self-moderate and collectively decide what appropriate and inappropriate behavior is for them. This kind of moderation scheme is yet to be researched.

Apart from moderation, there exist automatic methods for filtering unwanted content with decent accuracy using machine learning techniques. Such methods initially, rely on human moderated training data for making machine understand what should be accepted and what should be rejected. Bayesian classification is the most widely used technique for detecting spam or abusive contents.

Bayesian filtering: Bayesian filtering is predicated on the idea that spam can be filtered out based on the probability that certain words will correctly identify a piece of contents as spam while other words will correctly identify a piece of contents as legitimate and wanted. The advantage of Bayesian spam filtering is that it can be trained on a per-user basis. The spam that a user receives is often related to the specific activities. For example, a user may have followed a fan page or played a game on SNS that are having access to user's basic information. A Bayesian spam filter will eventually assign a higher probability based on the user's specific patterns. The automated system learns over time with corrective training whenever the filter incorrectly classifies message content. Thus, accuracy of Bayesian spam filtering improves after several training cycle and system works superior to pre-defined rules. The architecture of the system is shown in Figure 4.

The system building consists of two phases: a) Training phase and b) Testing phase. In training phase, abusive message filtering system needs to be trained with pre-moderated human judged data. Generally, last few months data is taken as training data where moderators have clearly specified which message content is social spam and which is non-spam. For extraction of features, a pre-processing on the contents is done, where removal of stop words and stemming is performed. Next, statistical significance of the keywords is stored with some normalized score as trained data for both types (i.e. spam and non-spam) of messages. In testing phase, actual un-labeled message is passed through same kind of pre-processing and supplied to the classifier module. Classifier module refers the already trained data and generates spam and non-spam score for given content. A decision making module finds the difference between these scores and finalizes whether to accept or reject given content. In this way, system can filter out un-wanted messages with 80 to 90% accuracy. However, there can be false positive and false negative that are fed back to the system through post moderation or reactive moderation to make the system correct its output in future.

Thus, system continuously learns over the period of time and can do hundreds of moderators' work effectively. Such automated systems are fundamental part of any large scale social networking sites where millions of user content contributions are added everyday to the site.

USER REPUTATION SYSTEM

Issues, Controversies, Problems

One of the main attractions of many online environments is that they facilitate social interactions with others. Because these environments are used by real people, often anonymously, and from diverse backgrounds, social interactions can be

Figure 4. System architecture of machine learning based social spam filtering method

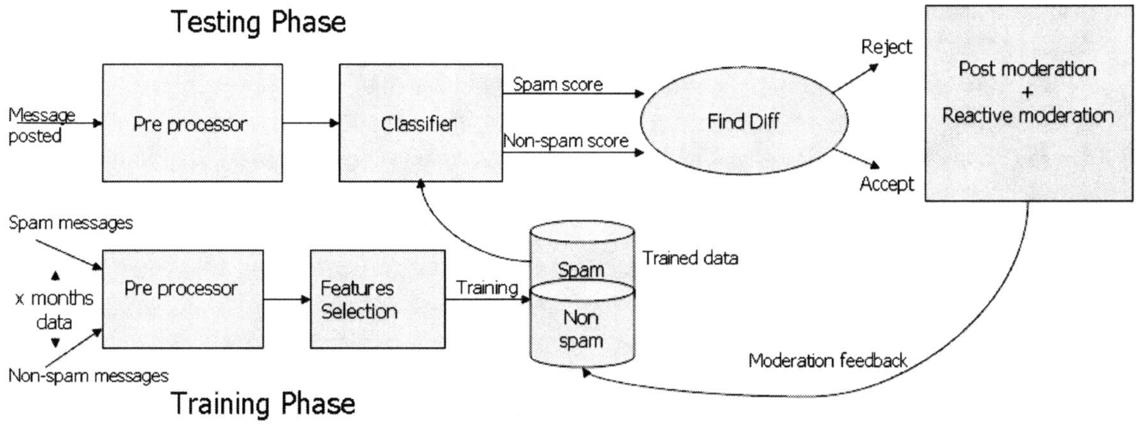

unpredictable and unsafe. Booming popularity of social media has brought with it a whole new set of challenges for online communities or social networks as well as the users who consume those sites:

- Problem of scale i.e. how to manage and present a devastating inflow of user contributions
- Problems of quality i.e. how to tell the good stuff from the bad
- Problems of engagement i.e. how to reward contributors so that they keep coming back
- Problems of moderation i.e. how to filter out the worst stuff quickly and efficiently

To ease the judgment in social network for a user about "Can I trust this person?", "Should I make friendship with this person?", "Is it worth my time to listen to this person?" etc., user reputation system can be built so that other users in network can access person's reputation score and take appropriate decision. Once user reputation system is built and reputation score for each user is calculated, another problem of displaying them properly and contextually comes. For each of reputation created to display or use, following questions should be kept in mind:

1. *Who will be able to see the reputation?* – Reputation can be of several types like *personal* i.e. hidden from other users but visible to the reputation owner, *public* i.e. displayed to friends or outsiders or visible to search engines, *corporate* i.e. limited to internal use - for improving the site or discreetly recognizing outliers in ways that may not be visible to the community.
2. *How will the reputation be used to modify your site's output?* – Reputation can be used in many ways e.g. filtering the lowest or highest quality items in a set, sorting *or* ranking items, making other decisions about how the site is doing or business is operating.

In subsequent section, we have elaborated how reputation system can be designed and how it can be leveraged in SNSs.

Solutions and Recommendations

The architecture of the user reputation system should answer one or more of the questions discussed above depending on the overall objective of the system. Evaluation of reputation score for each user in social network can once again be done through intelligent techniques.

Building Reputation Model

Before we create a simple reputation model, let us understand what reputation statement is and its constituents. Reputation system computes many different reputation values that turn out to possess a single common element: *reputation statement*. Reputation statement is a unit which consists of: *a source, a claim* and *a target*. The exact type and value of these particles depend on the application where it is going to be used. E.g.

A source	makes a claim	about a target
User ("Ramesh")	rates (4 out of 5)	video ("Funny incidents")

Every reputation statement is made by someone or something. A claim whose creator is not known is worthless. E.g. "Some people say Suresh is bad", here 'some people' carries no value. The claim is the value that the source assigned to the target in the reputation statement. Each claim is of particular type and has a claim value. E.g. In above statement 5-star rating is claim type and it has claim value 4 (stars). Claim value can be quantitative or qualitative. Quantitative values are numeric values which needs normalization while qualitative values needs to be converted into numeric value so that software can leverage it. A reputation statement is always focused on

Figure 5. Types of karma systems

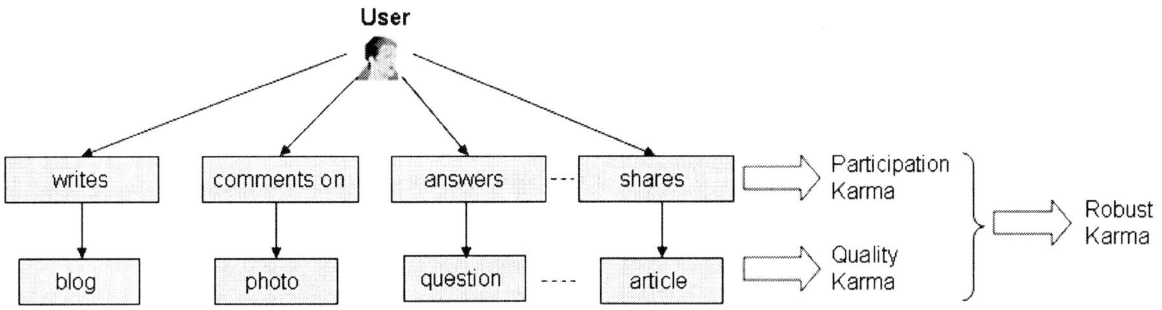

some unique identifiable entity- the target of the claim. Reputations are assigned to targets like users, movies, products, blog posts, videos, tags, companies and IP addresses. Later, application can query to reputation system that "Give me all videos rated above 3 stars". When a user is the reputable entity target of the claim, we call that *karma*, which generally the case in our context of social networks. So, we shall focus in this chapter for building user reputation (karma) system.

Types of Karma System

Karma is built based on the actions of a user within a context, such as a web site, or even as a member a sub-community of a site. And those contributions are often limited to a very narrow range of actions - care must be taken to not over-generalize the value of a karma score. Such actions include commenting on updates (i.e. status message, video, photo, link, etc.), writing blog posts or reviews, answering questions, rating contents and so on. There are two primitive forms of karma models: models that measure the amount of user participation and models that measure the quality of contributions. When these types of karma models are combined, we refer to the combined model as robust. Including both types of measures in the model gives the highest scores to the users who are both active and produce the best content.

Participation karma: As a user engages in various activities, they are recorded, weighted, and tallied. Counting socially and/or commercially noteworthy events by content creators is probably the most common type of participation karma model. This model (Figure 5) is often implemented as a point system, in which each action is worth a fixed number of points and the points accrue. A participation karma model, where the input event represents the number of points for the action and the source of the activity becomes the target of the karma. There is also a negative participation karma model, which counts how many terrible things a user does.

Quality karma: A quality-karma model deals solely with the quality of contributions by users. In a quality-karma model, the number of contributions is not given emphasis (Figure 5). The best quality-karma scores are always calculated as a side effect of other users evaluating the contributions of the target. In case of sites that allow user to comment on an article, bad quality content can be identified by other users' feedback on it by reporting it as abuse. There are several methods which look into the syntactic and semantic features of the contents and assign quality score, however, elaboration on such techniques is beyond the scope of this chapter.

Robust karma: By itself, a participation-based karma score is inadequate to describe the value of a user's contributions to the community. Similarly, you probably don't want a karma score based solely on quality of contributions either. So, there should be decent mix of both these scores to arrive as final conclusion. What you really want to do is to combine quality-karma and participation-karma scores into one score-call it robust karma (Figure 5). The robust-karma score represents the overall value of a user's contributions: the quality component ensures some thought and care in the preparation of contributions, and the participation side ensures that the contributor is very active, that he has contributed recently, and (probably) that he has surpassed some minimal thresholds for user participation-enough that you can reasonably detach the passionate, dedicated contributors from the fly-by post-then-flee crowd.

Karma is complex and built of many indirect inputs. So, some of the obvious mistakes should be avoided:

1. Rating a user directly should be avoided. Typical implementations only require a user to click once to rate another user and are therefore prone to abuse.
2. Asking people to assess others directly is socially awkward. Don't put users in the position of lying about their friends.
3. Using multiple inputs presents a broader picture of the target user's value.
4. Economics research into "revealed preference," or what people actually do, as opposed to what they say, indicates that actions provide a more correct picture of value than elicited ratings.

The simple architecture in context of social networking for a Karma system is shown in Figure 6.

While implementing user reputation (karma) system for any SNS, there are four major aspects of users to be considered to calculate final karma score: *a) Profile richness-* user should have filled good amount of profile information like company, school, college, city, country, interests etc. However, it is to be verified by system that the information is not junk and are real values. Karma system has to determine with intelligent method about the richness of the profile of a user. *b) Social Significance-* a genuine user has always at least few genuine friends in his network. More the number of friends, more socially attached he is. Moreover, depending on the other his friends' reputation score and their past history of interaction with him, social significance of a given user can be determined. *c) Activity Importance-* user's activity level can be figured out from the actions he takes on his friends' updates e.g. commenting/sharing/liking on status message/photos/videos/links shared by friends. Usually, user who often interacts with other users in his network and propagates good contents by sharing it to others is considered to be well-reputed user in social network. *d) Quality of contents-* many SNSs allow user to write blogs or reviews or questions/answers. In this case, the quality of their contribution plays vital role in judging the users characteristics. Good users contribute high quality of contents and hence considered to be reputed ones. All these four features act as basic inputs for user reputation system to calculate karma score.

Displaying Karma

After building user reputation system (karma), equivalently important thing is how to show karma. There are broadly three categories: public (shown to other users), personal (shown only to the owner), and corporate (for company's internal use.) Corporate karma is normally used to identify the very best and the very worst users for special actions, such as PR contact or account termination by the site owner. Personal karma is typically used for reflecting progress against some goal – like completeness of profile information. When karma display becomes public it is more challenging. There are several important things to consider when displaying karma to the public:

- With content reputation, users are easily confused by the display of many reputations on the same page or within the same context.

Figure 6. System architecture of karma computing system in social network

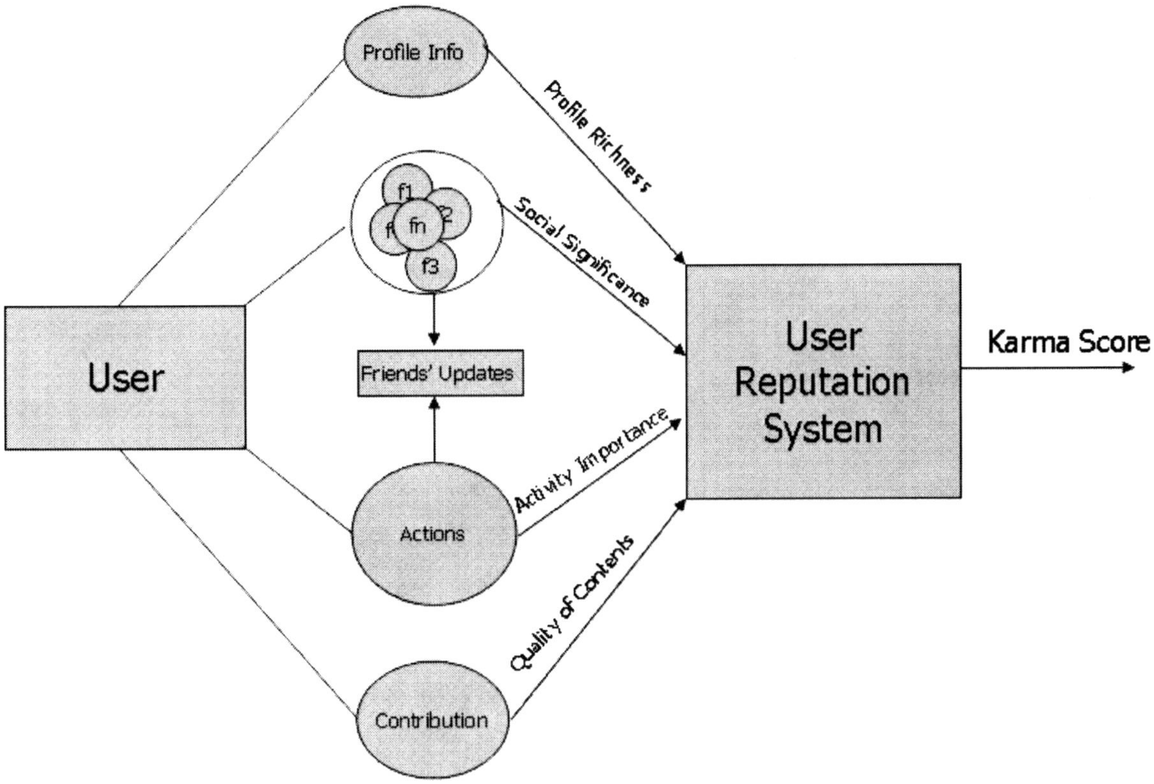

- It can create the wrong incentives for your community. Avoid sorting users by karma.
- It can create confusion between content reputation and user reputation. So, there should be clear distinction made e.g. show content reputation with stars and show karma as excellent, good and bad.
- Nobody expect karma and most of the time it is unnoticed if shown somewhere.

The best places for showing karma publicly in social networks must be contextual. Here are some of the positions where it can be put for public display:

1. Show karma of suggested users in "people you may know". Here, user would like to be friend with recommended users with high karma. (Figure 7(i))
2. Show karma of sender when friend request is sent in social network. Here the receiver on other side can take decision whether to confirm the requester as friend or not. (Figure 7(ii))
3. Show karma of sender when message or mail is sent. Here message receiver can see the public karma of sender and decide whether to respond or not. (Figure 7(iii))
4. In question and answering system, the answer seeker can judge the best answer based on public karma of the answerer. (Figure 7(iv))

Public karma can discourage some contributors. Putting user reputations in a public ranked list creates a competitive environment and some users' motivations are not at all compatible with being publicly recognized. Still others will see high karma as the goal of the activity instead of

Figure 7. (i) Showing user karma in 'people you may know' (ii) Showing user karma when friend requests is to be accepted or ignored (iii) Showing user karma when unknown users communicate through messages (iv) Showing user karma of answerer in question-answer system

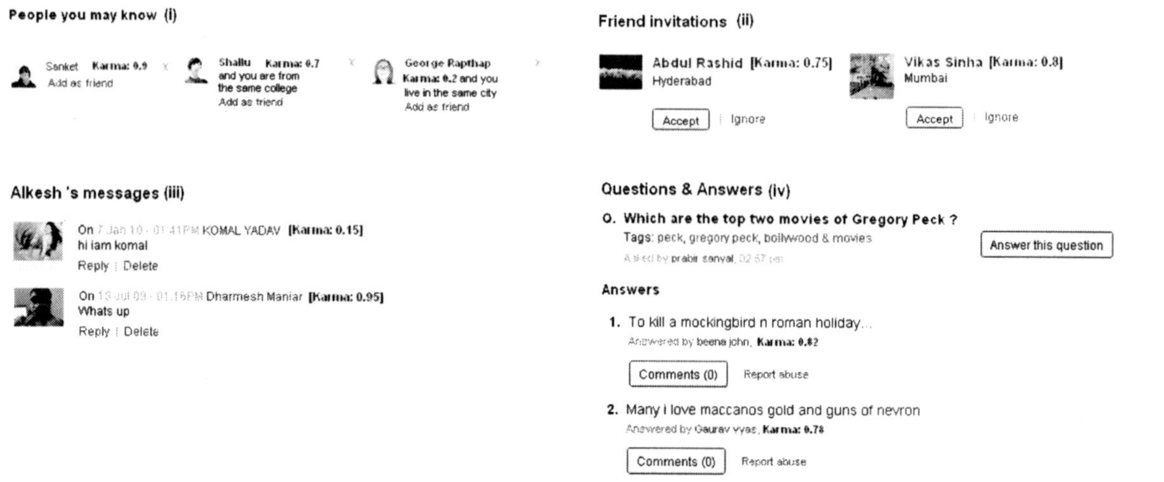

the benefit and start to change their behavior to optimize their actions around their karma instead of using the site as intended.

FUTURE RESEARCH DIRECTIONS

The evaluation of automatic clustering approach for applying privacy settings is still un-tested. In this chapter we have seen few criteria regarding how users actually tend to group their friends in social network. However, there can be more hidden aspects of user behavior as well as preferences and those change from user to user. So, deeper study is required in future to unveil some generic model and evaluate it. Social spamming is ever burning issue in online communities and with growth of social network, spammers or abusers will find different ways to cheat the system. Hence, one needs to keep eyes on the evolving patterns of contents contributed by social spammers. Building user reputation model has enormous potential applications. Social network are the places where social behavior about a user can be tracked and his/her reputation score can be calculated. More features to evaluate karma of user can be identified as a future research task.

CONCLUSION

We have seen that automatic group-base privacy setting can alleviate users' configuration efforts at large extent. Clustering technique can group the similar users with quite a good accuracy, initially. Later, machine learning technique of incorporating user's feedback in clustering criteria can continuously modify grouping logic. User can label groups and apply appropriate privacy settings on each of them. We have also discussed the various ways to combat social spamming with automatic or semi-automatic approaches. Here also, architecture of the system learns from moderation feedback and enhance itself with time. User reputation systems are the necessity of today's Internet. In this chapter, we elaborated on the issues and things to be taken into consideration while building user reputation system and also discussed some of the contextual places in social network where it can be applied. Thus, we have learnt some effective solutions that largely affect information security and management in social network.

REFERENCES

Ackerman, M., & Mainwaring, S. (2005). Privacy issues in human-computer interaction. In Cranor, L., & Garfinkel, S. (Eds.), *Security and usability: Designing secure systems that people can use* (pp. 381–400). Sebastopol, CA: O'Reilly.

Boyd, D., & Heer, J. (2006). *Profiles as conversation: Networked identity performance on Friendster*. In Hawaii International Conference on Systems Science (vol. 39). Kauai, HI: IEEE Computer Society.

Clauset, A., Newman, M., & Moore, C. (2004). Finding community structure in very large networks. *Physical Review E: Statistical, Nonlinear, and Soft Matter Physics*, *70*, 066111. doi:10.1103/PhysRevE.70.066111

Davis, M., & Canny, J. Van House, N., Good, N., King, S., Nair, R., ... Reid, N. (2005). MMM2: Mobile media metadata for media sharing. In *Proceedings of the 13th Annual ACM International Conference on Multimedia* (Hilton, Singapore, November 06 - 11, 2005), MULTIMEDIA '05, (pp. 267-268). New York, NY: ACM.

DiMicco, J. M., & Millen, D. R. (2007). Identity management: Multiple presentations of self in Facebook. In *Proceedings of the 2007 International ACM Conference on Supporting Group Work* (Sanibel Island, Florida, USA, November 04 - 07, 2007*)*, 383–386.

Dingledine, R., Freedman, M. J., & Molnar, D. (2000). Accountability measures for peer-to-peer systems. In *Peer-to-peer: Harnessing the power of disruptive technologies*. O'Reilly Publishers.

Farmer, R., & Glass, B. (2010). *Building Web reputation systems*. O'Reilly Media, Inc.

Gilbert, E., & Karahalios, K. (2009). Predicting tie strength with social media. In *CHI '09: Proceedings of the 27th International Conference on Human Factors in Computing Systems*, New York, NY, USA, (pp. 211-220). ACM.

Goffman, E. (1959). *The presentation of self in everyday life*. New York, NY: Doubleday.

Heymann, P., Koutrika, G., & Garcia-Molina, H. (2007). Fighting Spam on social Web sites: A survey of approaches and future challenges. *IEEE Internet Computing*, *11*(6), 36–45. doi:10.1109/MIC.2007.125

Jones, Q., Gandhi, S. A., Whittaker, S., Chivakula, K., & Terveen, L. (2004). Putting systems into place: A qualitative study of design requirements for location-aware community systems. In *Proceedings of Computer-Supported Cooperative Work* (CSCW '04), Chicago, (pp. 202-211). ACM Press.

Jones, S., & O'Neill, E. (2010). Feasibility of structural network clustering for group-based privacy control in social networks. *Proceedings of the Sixth Symposium on Usable Privacy and Security*. Redmond, Washington.

Jøsang, A., Ismail, R., & Boyd, C. (2007). A survey of trust and reputation systems for online service provision. *Decision Support Systems*, *43*(2). doi:10.1016/j.dss.2005.05.019

Lampinen, A., Tamminen, S., & Oulasvirta, A. (2009). All my people right here, right now: Management of group copresence on a social networking site. In *Proceedings of the ACM 2009 International Conference on Supporting Group Work* (Sanibel Island, Florida, USA, May 10 - 13, 2009), 281–290.

Lederer, S., Dey, A. K., & Mankoff, J. (2002). *A conceptual model and a metaphor of everyday privacy in ubiquitous computing*. Intel Research Berkeley, Tech. Rep. IRB-TR- 02- 017, 2002.

Lederer, S., Hong, J., Dey, A., & Landay, J. (2004). Personal privacy through understanding and action: Five pitfalls for designers. *Personal and Ubiquitous Computing*, *8*(6), 440–454. doi:10.1007/s00779-004-0304-9

Markines, B., Cattuto, C., & Menczer, F. (2009). Social Spam detection. In *Proceedings of the 5th International Workshop on Adversarial Information Retrieval on the Web,* AIRWeb-09.

Mertz, D. (2002). *Spam filtering techniques: Six approaches to eliminating unwanted e-mail.* Retrieved September 01, 2002, from http://www.ibm.com/developerworks/linux/library/l-spamf.html

Mishne, G., Carmel, D., & Lempel, R. (2005). Blocking blog spam with language model disagreement. In *AIRWeb '05: Proceedings of the 1st International Workshop on Adversarial Information Retrieval on the Web*, (pp. 1–6). New York, NY: ACM.

Olson, J., Grudin, J., & Horvitz, E. (2005). A study of preferences for sharing and privacy. In *CHI '05 Extended Abstracts on Human Factors in Computing Systems*, Portland, OR, USA, (pp. 1985–1988).

Priedhorsky, R., Chen, J., Lam, S. K., Panciera, K., Terveen, L., & Riedl, J. (2007). Creating, destroying, and restoring value in Wikipedia. In *Proceedings of GROUP '07.*

Resnick, P., Zeckhauser, R., Swanson, J., & Lockwood, K. (2006). The value of reputation on eBay: A controlled experiment. *Experimental Economics*, *9*(2), 79–101. doi:10.1007/s10683-006-4309-2

Skeels, M. M., & Grudin, J. (2009). When social networks cross boundaries: A case study of workplace use of Facebook and LinkedIn. In *Proceedings of the ACM 2009 International Conference on Supporting Group Work* (Sanibel Island, Florida, USA, May 10 - 13, 2009), 95–104.

Xu, X., Yuruk, N., Feng, Z., & Schweiger, T. A. (2007). SCAN: A structural clustering algorithm for networks. In *Proceedings of the 13th ACM SIGKDD International Conference on Knowledge Discovery and Data Mining*, KDD '07, (pp. 824-833). New York, NY: ACM Press.

ADDITIONAL READING

Ackerman, M. S., & Mainwaring, S. D. (2005). Privacy issues and human-computer interaction. In Garfinkel, S., & Cranor, L. (Eds.), *Security and Usability: Designing Secure Systems that People Can Use* (pp. 381–400). Sebastopol, CA, USA: O'Reilly.

Androulaki, E., Choi, S. G., Bellovin, S. M., & Malkin, T. (2008). Reputation systems for anonymous networks. In: PETS '08: Proceedings of the 8th international symposium on *Privacy Enhancing Technologies*, Berlin, Heidelberg, Springer-Verlag, pp. 202–218.

Benevenuto, F., Rodrigues, T., Almeida, V., Almeida, J., Zhang, C., & Ross, K. (2008). Identifying video spammers in online social networks. In Proc. 4th Intl. Workshop on *Adversarial Information Retrieval on the Web* (AIRWeb), pages 45–52.

Bogers, T., & van den Bosch, A. In Aly, R., Hauff, C., den Hamer, I., Hiemstra, D., Huibers, T. & de Jong, F. (Eds.) (2009). *Using Language Modeling for Spam Detection in Social Reference Manager Websites*, Proceedings of the 9th Belgian-Dutch Information Retrieval Workshop (DIR 2009), pp 87-94. Enschede.

Buchegger, S., Mundinger, J., & Boudec, J.-Y. L. (2007). Lessons Learned. In *IEEE Technology & Society Magazine*. Reputation Systems for Self-Organized Networks.

Erkin, Z., Veugen, T., Toft, T., & Lagendijk, R. L. (2009). Privacy-preserving user clustering in a social network. First *IEEE International Workshop on Information Forensics and Security WIFS (2009)*, pp 96-100.

Fajfrov, L., Sladk, K., Klir, G., & Kramosil, I. (2009). *Clustering Methods for Privacy Preserving* (*Vol. 45*, p. 3). Computer and Information Science.

Farmer, R., & Glass, B. (2010). *On Karma: Topline Lessons on User Reputation Design, Building Web Reputation System.* Retrieved from the Blog-http://buildingreputation.com/writings/2010/02/on_karma.html

Gkanogiannis, A., & Kalamboukis, T. (2008). A novel supervised learning algorithm and its use for spam detection in social bookmarking systems. In Proc. Europ. Conf. on *Machine Learning and Principles and Practice of Knowledge Discovery in Databases (ECML/PKDD).*

Granovetter, M. S. (1973). The Strength of Weak Ties. *American Journal of Sociology*, *78*(6), 1360–1380. doi:10.1086/225469

Guzella, T. S. & Caminhas, W. M. (2009). A Review of machine Learning Approaches to Spam Filtering, Elsever, *Expert System with Applications*.

Hsu, C., Khabiri, E., & Caverlee, J. (2009). Ranking Comments on the Social Web. In Proceedings of International Conference on *Computational Science and Engineering*-Volume 04, pages 90–97.

Jensen, C., Davis, J., & Farnham, S. (2002). Finding others online: reputation systems for social online spaces, Proceedings of the SIGCHI conference on *Human factors in computing systems: Changing our world, changing ourselves*. Minneapolis, Minnesota, USA.

Kaufman, L., & Rousseeuw, P. J. (2005). *Finding Groups in Data: An Introduction to Cluster Analysis*. Wiley.

Kim, C., & Hwang, K. B. (2008) Naive bayes classifier learning with feature selection for spam detection in social bookmarking. In Proc. Europ. Conf. on *Machine Learning and Principles and Practice of Knowledge Discovery in Databases (ECML/PKDD).*

Lam, H., & Yeung, D. (2007). A learning approach to spam detection based on social networks. In 4th Conference on *Email and Anti-Spam (CEAS).*

Lederer, S., Hong, I., Dey, K., & Landay, J. A. (2004). Personal privacy through understanding and action: five pitfalls for designers. *Personal and Ubiquitous Computing*, *8*(6). doi:10.1007/s00779-004-0304-9

McCarty, C. (2002). Structure in personal networks. *Journal of Social Structure*, Vol. 3.

Resnick, P., & Zeckhauser, R. (2001). Trust Among Strangers in Internet Transactions: Empirical Analysis of eBay's Reputation System. In the Economics of the Internet and e-Commerce, M.R. Baye, Ed. *Advances in Applied micronomics*, vol. 11. Elsevier Science, Amsterdam, 127-157.

Sabater, J., & Sierra, C. (2002). Reputation and Social Network Analysis in Multi-Agent Systems. Proceedings of the 1st International Joint Conference on *Autonomous Agents and Multi-agent Systems*. 475-482.

Sabater, J., & Sierra, C. (2002). Reputation and social network analysis in multi-agent systems. In Proceedings of 1st International Joint Conference on *Autonomous Agents and Multiagent Systems*, pages 475–482

Sadlon, E., Sakamoto, Y., Dever, H. J., & Nickerson, J. V. (2008). The Karma of Digg: Reciprocity in Online Social Networks. In Proceedings of the 18th Annual Workshop on *Information Technologies and Systems*.

Sundaresan, N. (2006). *On an Online Reputation System*. eBay Research Labs Technical Report.

Sundaresan, N. (2007). Online trust and reputation systems. Proceedings of the 8th *ACM* conference on *Electronic commerce*. San Diego, California, USA.

Voss, M., Heinemann, A., & Mühlhäuser, M. (2005). A Privacy Preserving Reputation System for Mobile Information Dissemination Networks. In: First International Conference on *Security and Privacy for Emerging Areas in Communications Networks (SECURECOMM'05)*, IEEE, pp. 171–181.

Wang, A. H. (2010). Detecting Spam Bots in Online Social Networking Sites: A Machine Learning Approach. S. Foresti and S. Jajodia(Eds.): *Data and Applications Security XXIV*, LNCS 6166, pp. 335-342.

Wasserman, S., & Faust, K. (1994). *Social Network Analysis*. Cambridge: Cambridge University Press.

Witten, I. H. & Frank, E. (2005). *Data Mining: Practical machine learning tools and techniques*. Morgan Kaufmann, 2nd edition.

Zdziarski, J. A. (2005). *Ending Spam: Bayesian Content Filtering and the Art of Statistical Language Classification*. No Starch Press.

KEY TERMS AND DEFINITIONS

Bayesian Filtering: A statistical technique whereby the system assigns a spam probability based on training from users.

Clustering: A process of grouping a number of similar things.

Karma: Reputation of user in community in terms of some score.

Machine Learning: A scientific discipline that is concerned with the design and development of algorithms that allow computers to evolve behaviors based on empirical data.

Social Network: A social structure made up of individuals (or organizations) called "nodes", which are tied (connected) by one or more specific types of interdependency, such as friendship, kinship, common interest, financial exchange, dislike, sexual relationships, or relationships of beliefs, knowledge or prestige.

Spamming: The use of electronic messaging systems (including most broadcast media, digital delivery systems) to send unsolicited bulk messages indiscriminately.

Chapter 8
Music is the Key:
Using our Enduring Memory for Songs to Help Users Log On

Marcia Gibson
Institute for Research in Applicable Computing, University of Bedfordshire, UK

Karen Renaud
University of Glasgow, UK

Marc Conrad
Institute for Research in Applicable Computing, University of Bedfordshire, UK

Carsten Maple
Institute for Research in Applicable Computing, University of Bedfordshire, UK

ABSTRACT

Devising access control systems to support needs and capabilities of users, as well as the security requirements of organisations, is a key challenge faced in many of today's business environments. If users are to behave securely, they must not be overburdened with unworkable authentication policies and methods. Yet the prevailing alphanumeric password can be a double-edged sword: secure passwords are inherently difficult to recall and vice-versa. Consequentially, a growing number of alternatives are emerging. In this chapter, the authors describe one novel scheme - a musical password. Musipass was designed with the user in mind and is tailored toward the task of authentication on the Web, where biometric and token-based systems have proved unsuccessful in replacing the flawed, yet prevalent traditional password. This chapter, which includes discussion on current thinking in the field of authentication, will be of interest to information managers, security practitioners, and HCI professionals.

DOI: 10.4018/978-1-4666-0197-0.ch008

INTRODUCTION

The most widely employed method of establishing an individual's eligibility to access an online file, site or service is to test their knowledge of a secret key: the familiar alphanumeric password. The level of security passwords offer against brute-force and dictionary attacks theoretically depends upon the degree of informational *entropy* (Shannon, 1948) they contain. However, it is widely acknowledged that passwords constructed of random letters, digits, and special characters are difficult to recall (Yan, Blackwell, Anderson, and Grant, 2004). For this reason, naïvely selected passwords are often derived from meaningful objects (Brostoff and Sasse, 2000), or will contain predictable patterns. These passwords offer reduced entropy, although they assist imprinting (Paivio, 1983) the password to memory.

Organizations often impose password construction policies. This seems a fitting strategy given that the rationale for password use is usually to protect assets. However, these policies usually revert a password to its prior arbitrary and unmemorable format. When faced with onerous password policies, users cope by writing passwords down or sharing one password over numerous accounts; therefore a policy intended to enhance security will often weaken it in practice (Inglesant and Sasse, 2010).

These issues become exacerbated on the web. This may emerge from the absence of security cultures which could be fostered in other settings (Johnson and Goetz, 2007), large numbers of sites requiring registration for trivial purposes (Renaud and De Angeli, 2009), user's perceptions of the economic costs involved in adhering to policy as greater than the costs of not following it (Herley, 2009), difficulties in visualizing online threats (Gaw and Felten, 2006) and because many websites are accessed infrequently; whereas the neural pathways through which memories are accessed deteriorate without frequent use (Sapolsky, 2005).

The objective of this chapter is to provide a summarized and updated follow-up to research originally published as (Gibson, Renaud, Conrad and Maple, 2009). We will discuss recent advances in the field of authentication research and in particular detail a novel approach: the *musical* password, which aims to address the weaknesses of the alphanumeric scheme while remaining suitable for inclusion in online environments. A prototype system, "*Musipass*" will be presented and a summary of results from user testing presented. Later in the chapter implementation issues are explored and opportunities for future research identified.

BACKGROUND

There are two reasons that we forget; either the information no longer exists ("*trace-dependent forgetting*"); or it exists, but cannot be retrieved ("*cue-dependent forgetting*") (Tulving, 1974). Trace-dependent forgetting happens when an item is not imprinted strongly enough, if the item has not been successfully consolidated or has become corrupted by other memory items ("*interference*"). Cue-dependent forgetting occurs when a retrieval trigger ("*cue*") is not associated with the item.

It is difficult to generate a cue for a random password and cues cannot be provided to the user during authentication (i.e. it requires "*free-recall*"), as it cannot be ascertained whether the user is a friend or a foe. When John in accounts creates the password "Fluffy" based on his pet's name or writes passwords down, what he is really trying to do is provide himself with a cue as insurance against forgetting. So what happens when John has three pets, Fluffy, Lois and Ruff? In this case interference may be experienced, where John is able to recall numerous passwords, but not the precise one to access the system in question. When an individual reuses a password over numerous accounts he or she is effectually limiting the effort required to generate and memorize the password, as well as the possibility interference will occur.

Passwords must be recalled precisely and entered correctly without feedback (i.e. they are obfuscated to shield against observation). This makes passwords more difficult to enter, especially for users with cognitive, physical or other impairments who often experience usability issues on the web more severely than others (Petrie and Keir, 2007). A wide range of factors can impact an individual's ability to use passwords: Dyslexic users often spell words unpredictably, dyspraxic users experience difficulties sequencing, users may have developmental or language difficulties (Schmidt, Kölbl, Wagner, and Strassmeier, 2004), elderly users often have difficulties retaining newly learned information (Small, Stern, Tang, and Mayeux, 1999) and some have poor reading skills (Schmidt, et al., 2004) or are unfamiliar with the designated alphabet script (Mendori, Kubouchi, Okada and Shimizu, 2002).

Mnemonic passwords have been proposed as a possible solution. These are constructed by transforming an obscure but easily remembered phrase, replacing some letters with numbers or symbols to increase entropy. Yan et al (2004) found these superior in terms of memorability and security, to weak passwords. A standard password cracking dictionary was used in the experiment and it has been noted that in reality an attacker may opt to use a specialized mnemonic dictionary, bringing the practical applicability of the findings into question. Kuo, Romanosky and Cranor, (2006) found many of the phrases were well-known, suggesting the construction of a mnemonic dictionary might be trivial.

The ease of use mnemonic passwords offer is unclear. Forget et al. (2007) found that six of sixteen subjects misunderstood how to create one. Participants in Yan et al's study may have understood what was required to use the mnemonic technique; however this may not always be the case in a real-world setting. Mnemonic passwords do not solve the problem of interference, as multiple mnemonics must be memorized. They also do not increase accessibility, because they must be entered correctly while obfuscated.

EXISTING ALTERNATIVES

Hardware-based solutions: This category includes biometrics and tokens. However the outlay cost (Florencio and Herley, 2007) and lack of installation and operating knowledge (Coventry, De Angeli and Johnson, 2003) can be prohibitive, especially in online environments.

Visual passwords: Where the usual alphanumeric alphabet is replaced with images. Depending upon implementation, while forming a password the user will:

- Select images from a larger challenge set ("Image-based").
- Select coordinates within an image ("Location-based").
- Draw a picture or create a path of actions in a visual environment ("Path-based").

The idea is based on the "Picture superiority effect" (De Angeli, Coventry, Johnson and Renaud, 2005) which describes our tendency to be able to remember images more accurately than semantic or syntactic memories, although alphabets must be chosen carefully to avoid predictable passwords being selected (Davis, Monrose, and Reiter, 2004; Thorpe and van Oorschot, 2007). They can be prone to observation (Wiedenbeck, Waters, Sobrado, and Birget, 2006) and reliance on the visual channel alone reduces accessibility.

MUSICAL PASSWORDS

Sound could potentially form the basis for a very large password alphabet. People enjoy listening to music (Renflow and Gosling 2003) and perhaps uniquely of the proposed modalities it has a physio-emotional effect upon many; who report feeling intense chills when an especially pleasurable composition is heard (Nusbaum and Silvia, 2010). We are naturally predisposed to process music and this is triggered during everyday exposures (Bigand and Poulin-Charronnat, 2006).

Scherer and Zentner (2001) point out music often accompanies emotionally charged events, such as weddings and funerals. If this is correct, musical pieces could act as very efficacious cues. Secondly, music is processed at a lower level of the brain than other semantic memories, increasing resistance to interference (LeDoux, 1992).

Observability is less problematic because earphones can be used to shield sounds from being overheard. We set about designing a prototype, "Musipass" to see whether we could leverage these attributes to create a secure and memorable authentication scheme.

Designing Musipass

Interaction Style

When enrolling, we decided users would listen to a number of clips, and select a subset to form a password. At authentication they would be presented with "their" password clips, along with a set of distractors and asked to identify those contained in their password to authenticate.

Password Length and Number of Distractors

Musical passwords are a new technology, we did not know prior to our investigation how users would react to them. We decided to ask users to select a short sequence of four clips from a relatively small set of 32 distractors, with all clips played back to the user separately. This should minimise frustration resulting from a too time-consuming authentication.

Number of Attempts

In our prototype, once a user had entered an incorrect password sequence, they would be offered the option to retry or to quit to a questionnaire. For experimental purposes, we did not limit the number of retries.

Triggering Playback

Each musical clip is represented as an icon, with playback triggered when an icon is moused over (sighted individuals) or tabbed into focus (non-sighted individuals). To select a password clip, the user presses "Enter" or clicks the icon.

Password Letter Repetition

Allowing repetition enhances security in traditional passwords as it increases the overall password space. In Musipass, allowing repetition increases the risk users will opt to reduce the effort required by memorizing only one or two secret clips. This would be predictable and negatively impact security, therefore repetition is not supported.

Sequential or Non-Sequential Password

If multiple password letters (clips) are selected in sequence from a single group of distractors, the user must recognize the clips *and* free-recall the order in which they were selected. This adds an additional level of complexity and may cause difficulties for some users. We removed the burden by breaking the alphabet the user selects from into small subgroups, with one password symbol per group and presenting *these* in sequence.

Alphabet Design

- **Push or pull:** People are often open about their musical preferences and some are fairly predictable (Hirsch, 2007; Jackson, 2005). It is infeasible to allow users to upload their own sound clips: we will use a fixed set of clips and ask users to choose from these.

- **Musical style:** We used familiar melodies - so called *"old-familiar"* tunes. Smith (1932) argues that we gain pleasure from familiar things, and this lies behind our inertia for change. Lazarsfeld and Field (1946) found that 76% liked to listen to music and, of those, 16% favored familiar music. Lower percentages preferred other music types. People are likely to have been exposed to well-known tunes, aiding autobiographical cue creation (Rentflow and Gosling, 2003).
- **Duration:** Bella, Peretz and Aronoff (2003) found familiarity for a melody could be experienced after 3 to 6 notes and recognition after a further 2 notes were heard. We used musical excerpts which are short enough in duration to minimize authentication time while remaining lengthy enough to enable recognition.
- **Rhythm:** Wells, Burnett and Moriarty (1989) found that rhythmic music enhances memorability. Mélen and Deliége (1995) found that recognition was better for rhythmic transformations of musical pieces. We exploited this, offering clips with easily-recognized rhythms.
- **Vocal or instrumental:** We used clips containing lyrics and melody. Vocal music is more memorable than instrumental music (Sewell and Sarel, 1986). The words and tune are processed independently (Besson,Faïta, Bonnel and Requin, 2002) but there are strong connections between the areas of the brain processing them (Peretz, Radeau, and Arguin, 2004). Crowder and Serafine (1986) showed that the lyrics and melody of a song could cue one another, especially when the music is familiar.
- **Hooks:** Monaco and Riordan (1980) define a hook as: "*a musical or lyrical phrase that stands out and is easily remembered*" (p178). A hook is a series of notes that endures in memory. We chose approximately five second vocal hooks originating from songs predominantly from the 1920s-1970s. Examples are, "I got it bad" by Ella Fitzgerald and "I can't control myself" by The Troggs.

Underlying Architecture

Research into improving the security of recognition-based authentication (Gibson, Conrad and Maple, 2010), considers the number of alphabet letters available for use in visual and sound-based schemes as being *virtually infinite*, only bounded by the processing capabilities of the system on which the alphabet is generated. Although some letters will be indistinguishable, the virtual infinity of the alphabet means a suitably abundant number of distinguishable letters should still be available. Examples of virtually infinite alphabets are the set of unique images indexed in Google or all top selling singles in a country and time frame.

To mitigate the risk posed by the limited number of letters that can be presented before the effort required in searching becomes problematic and to overcome practical issues of storage and transmission, this model proposes the alphabet be distributed over the systems requiring it and that a unique child set of these (also unique) per-system subsets be presented to each user during authentication. Research into the security of conventional passwords finds that reducing password popularity is key to securing internet-scale systems (Schechter, Herley and Mitzenmacher, 2010), this sits well with the infinite alphabet password (IAP) model, where the uniqueness of each user's alphabet ultimately forces the selection of unique passwords. More formally, in IAP:

The set of letters that can be combined to formulate passwords, $A = \{a_1, a_2, ...\} \cong \mathrm{N}$ is modeled to be infinite. For illustrative purposes we assume a user wants to authenticate to a server, S via a client node over an network, with the password itself stored as a database entry on the server. As a consequence of the infinity of A, we let different servers carry different alphabets such that Σ denotes a system of servers with $S \in \Sigma$ and $A_S \subseteq A$ denotes an alphabet for use in authentication onto $S \in \Sigma$ then $A_S \cap A_T = \varnothing$ for any $T \in \Sigma$ with $S \neq T$. Since $\mathrm{N} \times \mathrm{N} \cong \mathrm{N}$, this is possible if $\Sigma \cong \mathrm{N}$ is modeled as an infinite set of servers.

The enrolment process is accomplished by the user supplying to the system a unique identifier, u. Formats for u can be biometric data, hardware token, PIN or a username. u is the then stored via a one-way hash function as a record on $S \in \Sigma$. The server S on receipt of the user id u generates randomly a finite subset, $A_{S,u} \subseteq A_s$ which becomes that user's password alphabet. This is sent to the client device for presentation, where the user selects from $A_{S,u}$ a predefined number of elements to form a password. This password is transmitted to S where it is also associated with u concluding the enrollment process.

To ensure that symbols do not appear in more than one presentation set $A_{S,u}$ (i), thus removing the requirement that the user memorizes sequence as well as the identity of their password members, it can optionally be required that the password sequence is injective, by specifying that $A_{S,u}(i) \cap A_{S,u}(j) = \varnothing$ for any $i \neq j$. In a conventional alphabet this would reduce security, because the average search space for a brute force attack is considerably reduced. However, as the alphabet itself is modeled as infinite, so too is the resulting theoretical search space.

An added benefit of the IAP model is that error feedback and recovery can be provided to the authentic user without inadvertently providing the same for an attacker. Here we assume (for example) that the user selects two password elements from each presented set of letters. The user's password is $(a_{t(1)}...a_{t(n)})$ with n even and $a_{t(2m-1)}, a_{t(2m)} \in A_{S,u}(m)$ for $1 \leq m \leq n/2$. When the password letter selection (b,c) from m is correct i.e. $(b,c) - (a_{t(2m-1)}, a_{t(2m)})$ the user is presented with set $A_{S,u}(m+1)$ unless $2m=n$ in which case access is granted. When the selection is incorrect however, the user is exposed to a different unrelated set also randomized in placement, $B_{S,u}(m,b,c) \subseteq A$ with all sets $A_{S,u}(m)$ and $B_{S,u}(m,b,c)$ being disjuct to prevent the possibility of an intersecti on attack. On presentation of $B_{S,u}(m,b,c)$ the authentic user may notice that the presented set is unfamiliar and different from the expected set $A_{S,u}(m)$ and opt to restart the authentication attempt from beginning. The user who does not recognize the disjunctive nature of $A_{S,u}(m)$ may be identified as a potential intruder and be implicitly excluded from the system due to the inability to select the password element s which are not contained in decoy set $B_{S,u}(m,b,c)$.

We decided to design our prototype system so that it appears to be identical to the IAP scheme for the end-user, although we only used one server and to gather information on the popularity of musical passwords selected we opted for a small A_S set of 201 sounds and selected at random 36 of these to populate each user's $A_{S,u}$ set. Hence we weakened the condition that $A_{S,u}$ is completely disjunct for any two users.

Therefore, in Musipass (assuming the attacker knows the username), an online brute force attack would achieve a positive result on average in 6561/2 attempts and in an offline attack, 1,583,960,400/2 attempts. The latter is roughly equivalent to a 5 character *randomly selected* traditional password over an alphabet of 62 letters (i.e. a-z, A-Z and 0-9). In a "real-world" implementation we assume a lock-out mechanism would be used after a number of failed attempts to mitigate the online threat and that *As* would be larger than the 201 clips we used, strengthening against the offline threat. For example, if we used 2,000 clips on the server, the average offline attack would yield a result in around $1.595 \times 10^{13}/2$ attempts, equivalently closer to a 7 or 8 character randomly selected conventional password, yet there is no reduction is usability as the user is never exposed to this alphabet in its entirety. Even with a lock-out mechanism, there is a risk of low and slow attacks. Here options for mitigation include intrusion monitoring techniques or adoption of longer password sequences (a possibility we plan to address in future). Finally, by generating individualized user alphabets, the authentication in effect becomes two-way. Not only does the user authenticate himself to the server, but the server authenticates itself to the user due to the absence of his personal alphabet on a masquerading server. IAP is therefore particularly useful for deployment in systems where users are at high risk of phishing and spoofing attacks.

Testing Musipass

Musipass was implemented in Flash and embedded in a PHP web page, this allowed rapid development. A database was used to collect data about interactions and user's reactions were collected via questionnaires. Participants were invited to visit the site and test Musipass. Links to the experiment were provided via email, Facebook, to personal contacts and via groups and mailing lists specifically selected for their international participation, or interests in music, accessibility or security (see Figure 1).

Visitors were provided with a description of the experiment and where they opted to participate, were asked to:

1. Provide an email address (as username and means for communication).
2. Create a traditional password that had not been used previously and that they felt would be secure.
3. Re-enter the password.
4. Authenticate using the new password.

Once the user had authenticated (or gave up their attempt), the Musipass interface was loaded. We then asked participants to:

5. Select a song clip from a choice of nine over each of four screens.

Figure 1. Musipass setup and training screens

6. Enter a short description for each chosen clip (to strengthen the memory trace – akin to asking users to re-type their password).
7. Authenticate with the new musical password.
8. Fill out a questionnaire to express their opinion.

A week later, emails were sent inviting them to return and attempt a second authentication with their traditional and Musipass passwords. Any user returning before the end of the seven days was prohibited from accessing the test. Participants were then given the opportunity to complete a final post-evaluation questionnaire.

RESULTS

The experiment ran for 52 days. 133 people carried out the initial enrollment and authentication, "*phase one*", 94 returned to carry out a second authentication, "*phase two*".

Demographics

- **Age:** During both phases the majority of users were aged between 26 and 35 (39.8% overall during phase one and 39.3% in phase two). Participation of older users was minimal, with only 2.2% (three users) in the 56-65 age group and 1.5% (two users) in the over 65 category at phase one. During phase two, two users returned to participate from each of the 56-65 and over 65 groups.
- **Country:** We looked up the location of page requests based upon IP addresses, most came from the US (60%) and the UK (19%). A further 14% originated in Europe, including Germany, France, Ireland, Austria, Sweden, Norway, Italy and Spain. Just over 1% of requests were from Australia. Countries making up less than 1% each of page requests were Canada, Jordan, the Russian Federation, Mexico and Japan. A further 1% of requests could not be resolved. This suggests our results are mainly relevant to Western audiences. Particularly as those from outside this area may not have had exposure to the clips we deemed as being "old-familiar".
- **Impairments:** Almost all phase one respondents had full hearing, with exceptions being one with mild hearing loss, and one whose hearing is corrected to normal with an aid. One of the two returned for phase two. Four phase one participants (3%) had suffered a 20% loss of vision, all others had normal or corrected to normal vision. All four returned to participate in phase two. Four participants had a disability, one a color vision deficiency, one dyslexia, and one attention deficit hyperactivity disorder. One participant opted not to disclose the nature of their disability. Three of the four returned for phase two.
- **Musical experience:** Musical experience might affect performance. We asked participants to categorize their experience as, "None", "Listen Frequently", "Play instrument", "Professional Musician" or "Other". Nineteen gave their experience as "Other", but on closer inspection could be mapped to one of the four categories. For example, one participant described their experience as *"married to a pianist and composer" and* was reclassified as, "Listen frequently". Another said: *"degree in e-music; musical performer since age 5 - some pro; improvisor"* and was recategorized as "Professional musician". In phase one, the number of participants with no experience was 18 (13.5%), those who listen frequently was 49 (36.8%), those playing an instrument was 44 (33%) finally, 22 (16.5%) of the sample were profes-

Table 1. Phase one results (p = 0.4982)

	Successful	Failed	Quit	% Success rate
Traditional	133	0	N/A	100
Musipass	131	0	2	98.4

sional musicians. In phase two, these were, "None" 11 (11.7%), "Listen frequently" 33 (35.1%), Play instrument (35.1%), Professional musician (18%).

- **Connection speed:** Connections typically ranged between 300 and 10,000 Kbps. The lowest recorded download speed was 198 Kbps, this user was able to authenticate successfully in both phases. Our results however, might not be relevant for those with slower connections.

Memorability of Passwords and Reactions to Musipass during Phase One

We coded the result from each Musipass authentication attempt as:

- **Successful:** The participant successfully logged in.
- **Failed:** The participant had failed to recognize and recover from instances of decoy clip set presentation, and who on reaching the final log in screen subsequently selected a non-password element, and
- **Quit:** The participant realized decoy clips were offered, but when given the choice of re-attempting or quitting to the questionnaire, opted to quit.

Traditional passwords were more memorable than musical passwords after initial enrollment (Table 1). However the difference was statistically *insignificant* (Fisher's $p > 0{:}05$).

Phase One Questionnaire

We asked how long it took to recognize the password clips, offering four options: "Almost immediately", "After 2-3 seconds", "Only after a full clip" or, "I needed to listen more than once". Most participants (74.4%), recognized their clips almost immediately, whilst 19.5% recognized their clips after 2-3 seconds. The remaining 6% said that they had to listen in full, or needed to listen more than once.

When asked to rate how much they liked Musipass on a scale of 1 *(disliked very much) to* 5, *(liked very much)*, the mode average response was four - most users liked the system, but not to any extreme.

We asked how easy it was to remember their clips on a scale of 1 (*very difficult*) to 5 (*very easy*). The mode average response was five, "*very easy".* We asked users how satisfied they were after Musipass setup and training was complete with the amount of time it took to carry out the log in on a scale from 1 (*Very dissatisfied*) to 5 (*Very satisfied*). The mode response was two, overall participants were unsatisfied with the time taken. When asked how easy it was to go through the process of choosing their clips on a scale from 1 (*Very difficult*) to 5 (*Very easy*) the mode response was four, suggesting most users found this easy to do. Participants rated how time consuming it was to choose password clips from 1 (*Not time consuming*) to 5 (*Very time consuming*). The mode average response was four, users felt it took too long to enroll. We asked how much mental effort was involved in choosing the sounds on a scale of 1 (*Very little effort*) to 5 (*A great deal of effort*), the average response was two. When asked if they thought someone who knew them well would be able to guess the clips they chose, on a scale of 1(*Yes*) to 5 (*No*). The mode average response was two, indicating most people thought their musical passwords could be guessed.

Clip Popularity

Dictionary attacks utilize non-standard frequencies in the distribution of passwords over the available space. For this attack to be successful, non-standard frequencies must exist in the passwords selected (i.e. there are common passwords). The strength of a musical password against this attack is a result of relative clip popularity. If a small group of clips are more popular, it is likely they would be included in passwords more often, increasing the likelihood that common passwords will be created. We tested clip popularity based upon each clip's number of appearances during enrollment and the number of times it was selected as part of a password. The hypotheses tested are as follows:

Alternative hypothesis, $H_A \equiv$ Sound is popular
True null, $H_T \equiv$ Sound is unpopular
Effective null hypothesis, $H_0 \equiv$ Sound is not popular or unpopular

We then applied the following in statistical hypothesis testing with 0.05 the threshold for acceptance:

H_0: μpopularity = μbinomial
H_T: μpopularity $\leq \mu$bionomial

Overall, 62% of the alphabet was found neither popular or unpopular. 15% were popular and 21% unpopular. In practice traditional passwords tend to utilize a smaller subset of the space they theoretically provide, although this alphabet is available to all users, all the time. When we scale our figures over the 36 sounds a single user would be exposed to during enrollment in Musipass, we expect, on average to see around five popular sounds included. To form the sounds into a password, at least one must appear per selection screen, the chance of this is 27% (104,976 of 376,992 permutations). This seems why, after comparing passwords created in Musipass we observe that none were identical. We also note that had IAP been implemented fully, it would (regardless of clip popularity) not be possible to create an off-the-shelf dictionary, as each alphabet is individual to each user.

Memorability and Reactions during Phase Two

Participants found it easier to remember musical passwords than traditional passwords during the second phase, with a 91% success rate in Musipass compared to 62% for traditional passwords (Table 2). Many participants returned after a period of disuse that was longer than seven days (mode=7, mean=9) with one user successfully authenticating with Musipass after 36 days away from the system.

Full details of success rates grouped by number of days passing between the phases are given in Figure 2.

A high success rate (88-100%) was achieved up until the eleventh day, after which time the

Table 2. Phase two results (p = 0.4982)

	Successful	Failed	Quit	% Success rate
Traditional	58	36	N/A	62
Musipass	86	5	3	91

Figure 2. Success rates by days passing

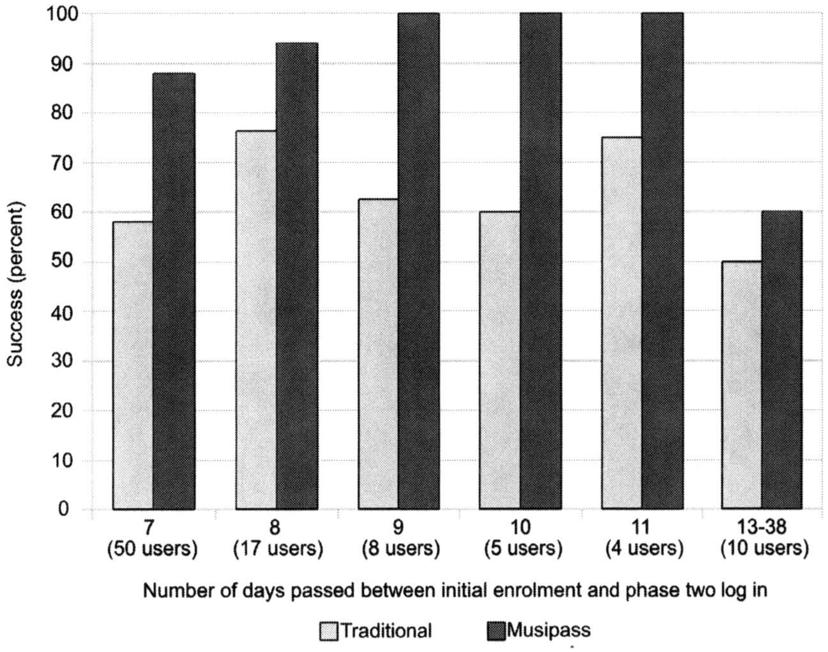

dataset became sparse and we began to observe less of a marked difference between the two methods.

Effect of Demographic Variables

The number of days passing between the initial enrollment and authentication during phase two was identified as a confounding variable. This was removed by isolating results gathered from participants returning on the seventh day. We re-ordered this data by age and musical experience (Figures 3 and 4). Here, we did not find a positive correlation between age and ability to authenticate with either password type up to the 46-55 age group (we were unable to carry out the analysis for older users, as the sample for this group was too small). This led us to conclude that at least up to the age of 55, age did not affect success rate.

Professional musicians and non-musicians tested similarly for traditional password authentication success rates, but there was a higher success rate in Musipass from professional musicians then there was from the non-musical group. However, only four non-musical participants returned on the seventh day and without more data we still could not be sure about the existence of a relationship between level of musical experience and the ability to log in with Musipass.

Data from participants in the "Listen frequently", "Play instrument" and "Professional musician" categories was more abundant. We observed a positive correlation for traditional password memorability within data from these groups – the more experienced people were, the better they remembered their password strings. Since ability to recall text strings is not usually associated with musical ability, we conclude that musical experience most likely affects memory in general, possibly due to the way musicians are trained to recall complicated patterns whilst performing; strengthening memory as a whole.

Figure 3. Traditional password success rate by musical experience and age

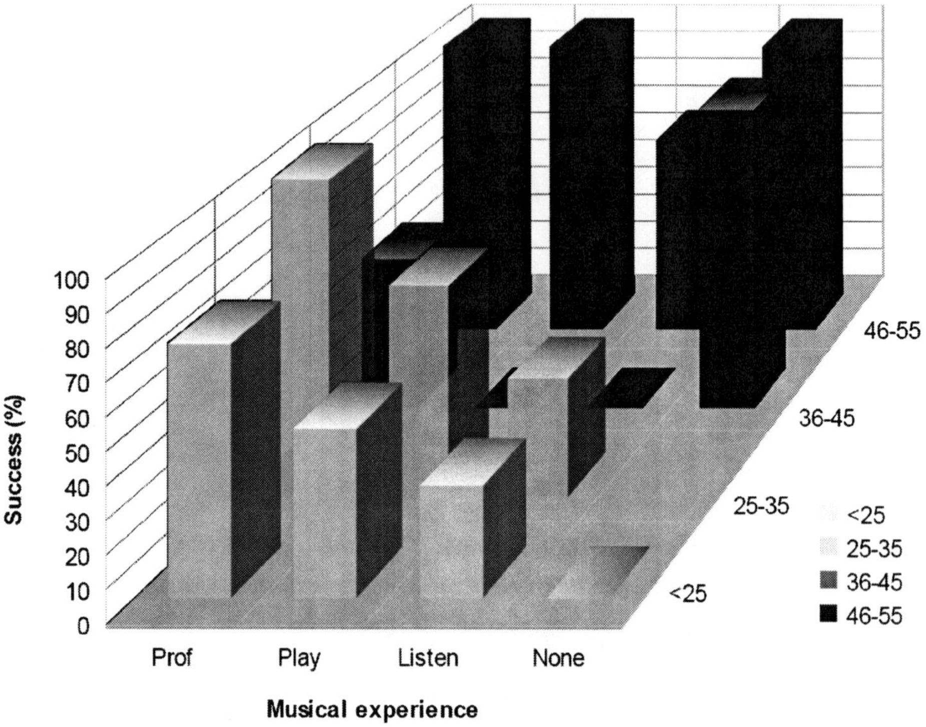

Phase Two Questionnaire

The overall response from phase two participants was very positive. When asked how much mental effort was involved logging in with Musipass on a scale of 1 (*very little mental effort*) to 5, (*too much mental effort*). The mode response was 1: *very little mental effort*. Likewise, most participants found recognizing their clips very easy, rating this as 1, on a scale from 1 (*very easy*) to 5 (*very difficult*).

Below we include some typical comments regarding memorability:

"I thought it worked very well and found it very easy, without cheating! Though I did recognize some of the other songs in each group I knew instinctively that they were not the right ones. When I came across my choice I immediately knew it and moved on without listening to the others. Million times more easy to recall using the songs, I couldn't remember my text password having a random word"

"...i'm also amazed on how easy it was to identify the selected clips (believe it was by emotional connections but also by negative relationships with the other clips; btw i still can't remember my textual password!)"

"After trying unsuccessfully to log in with my alphanumeric password, the usefulness of Musipass became clear. I wouldn't want to have to use it for things I log in to often, such as online banking or email, but for lesser used passwords, this would be a better option than guessing, trying to retrieve it from a note or document, or waiting to have it emailed to me..."

Figure 4. Musipass success rate by experience and age

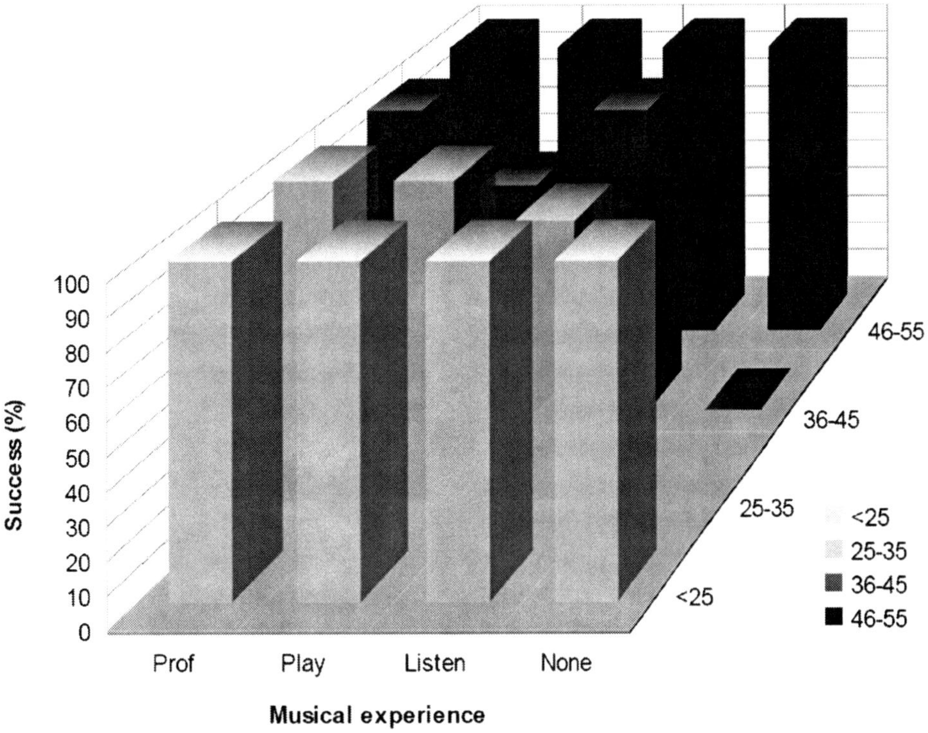

Although most users were able to authenticate successfully with Musipass, a few expressed concerns about interference:

"well, I couldn't remember my text password either, so it's a wash! :) it was particularly confusing when there were two or more songs on the same screen that i'm fond of or familiar with; it was hard to find a reason to choose one over the other during password selection, and hard to remember which I'd picked when I returned."

"If several other sites were using Musipass and, potentially, using similar songs I'm not sure it will work.

I recognized "the songs I liked" and I would need to be persuaded that I could successfully disambiguate different selections of songs. I hope you'll pursue it."

We asked users how long it took them to recognize their clips: "Almost immediately", "After 2-3 seconds", "Only after I had listened to the full clip" or, "I had to listen to the options more than once". The figures had not changed much from the phase one responses, with 50% able to recognize their clips almost immediately and 40.4% recognizing them after 2-3 seconds. The remaining 9.5% listened in full or multiple times. One participant made an interesting point, again related to interference:

"I was pleasantly surprised by the immediacy of my recognition of the music clips. Perhaps this is because my mind is less clogged with musical passwords than with text-based passwords?"

We asked how frustrated participants felt during authentication on a scale of 1 (*Not frustrated at all*) to 5, (*Very frustrated*), the average response was 1 (*Not frustrated at all*). When asked how they felt about the time involved in logging in to Musipass on a scale from 1 (*It was very quick*) to 5 (*it took too much time*), the average response was four. Even though participants enjoyed using the system, they did not think the time required was practical. Typical feedback was:

"I remebered the music login easily, though had forgotten the text one. Probably if i had to log in more often than the one week gap I prob would have remembered it. Also if I was trying to log in for something specific that I really needed to know then the time required for loggin in may get annoying. However in the scenario given, ie leasurly login with no urgency, it was pretty much the most fun login I've ever done:D".

"I think it was really fun, but I am not sure how I would like it if I had to play so many clips just to login to my email, or something like that, which I want to do quickly."

Finally, we asked participants how much they liked Musipass overall on a scale of 1 (*Disliked very much*) to 5, (*Liked very much*), the average response was four, most users liked the system. A few participants expressed concerns about observation and password strength (we didn't want to complicate instructions, so did not explain that alphabets would differ between users, extending the range of possibilities, or that the placement of icons was shuffled). We feel it is important to consider these viewpoints, as perception of functionality is often indicative of technology acceptance. Typical comments were:

"even though it sometimes takes me several attempts to remember which of 5 passwords I have used for a site, this still felt longer, and i was also conscious that if it wen't wrong I was potentially going to have to do it again which would definately be longer. I also am always using my computer in public space and would not want to long into anything confidential in an audible way that others could overhear"

"it's an interesting concept but I'm not sure how it would work in practice while making the paranoid nerd types like myself feel secure in our password selections. (nothing like random strings to make you sleep better at night!)"

"Doesn't seem very secure, and takes a while to log in. Reusing an easy-to-remember text password would be faster."

Discussion

Musipass is highly memorable. Users authenticated successfully after a full week away from the system. They appeared to like the system, enjoying the experience of choosing the sound clips and returning to attempt to remember them a week later. They found Musipass easy to use and were not at all frustrated during enrollment or authentication.

Participants had concerns about the guessability of choices. Our analysis suggests that the prevalence of easy to guess passwords (particularly if IAP is implemented) is lower than in traditional passwords, which are all too often easy to guess. However the question remains whether this is also the case when the attacker is a friend or a family member, or who is able to research preferences perhaps via social networking websites. Guessability may be worsened if we allow users to upload their own choices into the system, this could also lead to copyright problems. If our user's perceptions are correct and passwords in Musipass *are* easy to guess, this does not necessarily make Musipass superfluous in the world of authentication. Many systems ask users to authenticate themselves more for convenience than to achieve any measure of protection. In these systems, where authentication is required to deliver a measure of customization or support attribution, or when users are at high risk of phishing or spoofing attacks we could feasibly make use of a system like Musipass.

Techniques for hardening Musipass against guessing might include issuing the clips rather than allowing freedom of choice. This option may however, impact negatively on memorability. Another option is to populate the system with many musical genres and to vary these between users. It is then less likely that choices will be predictable. We could also personalize alphabets further, for example populating one with songs by Elvis Presley for an Elvis Presley fan. Here, guessability would be reduced and enjoyment enhanced - although interference might occur due to the similarity of the tracks. On the other hand a user who listens to them regularly, knowing them well and having built strong biographical associations might experience *enhanced* distinguishability and memorability.

Even though people complain about traditional passwords, the fact is they are very convenient (Morris and Thompson, 1979). Although participants indicated liking Musipass, their comments show that they were exasperated due to its time-consuming nature. If users anticipate having to authenticate with a time-consuming mechanism a number of times a day, one can readily anticipate their dismay. Liddell, Renaud and De Angeli (2003) experienced this reluctance when they asked users to listen to music and then choose an associated picture, users concentrated on the pictures alone, considering the listening phase to be too time-consuming. Liddell et al. used students as participants most of which are young with few memory difficulties. On the contrary, older users are plagued by memory problems and more willing to accept some inconvenience in return for increased memorability. Renaud (2006) found that older users were not concerned about the time-consuming nature of a visual scheme they tested, their memory difficulties made the memorability of the mechanism far more important than how long it took to authenticate.

In its current form, perhaps the future of Musipass lies within the context of low risk systems, which are used infrequently, by users who are more concerned about forgetting than convenience. As Musipass provides long-term memorability, it may also prove useful as a recovery mechanism once a conventional password is forgotten. Here Musipass might be offered as an alternative to security questions, which are prone to interference and tend to be based on personal (hence *researchable*) information or attributes.

CONCLUSION

We reported on the development and web-based trials of a scheme called "Musipass". Musipass used musical clips as an alphabet and utilized the IAP model as its architecture. IAP allows many of the criticisms commonly aimed at recognition-based authentication, in particular with regard to vulnerability to brute force and dictionary attacks to be mitigated. Sound-based passwords can be designed to rely on recognition or cued-recall for authentication and music especially, is pleasant to experience for a large proportion of users and is highly memorable. Musipass offers some of the memorability of image-based schemes to which it is well suited as counterpart; catering to the needs of users unable to gain access via the visual channel. When used with earphones, musical passwords are less prone to eavesdropping than image-based or conventional passwords. Attacks using specialized hardware, such as directional microphones cannot be categorically ruled out and further research is required into the possibility and success rates of these. It should be noted that the additional equipment required would make this attack more difficult to achieve than simply glancing over while an alphanumeric password is entered.

We tested Musipass and traditional passwords for memorability after a period of disuse. Overall, Musipass offered better performance, with

48% more successful authentication attempts than with traditional naively selected passwords. Participants returned for the second phase of the experiment from seven to thirty-eight days from the date of initial set up. We found that when we isolated data from participants returning on the seventh day, there was no identifiable correlation between age and password memorability. We did identify a correlation between musical experience and ability to authenticate using a traditional password; suggesting music performance strengthens the memory as a whole. The overall reaction to Musipass was positive, with the majority of participants liking it and finding it easy to use. Like other recognition-based schemes, one drawback is the amount of time required during the process.

FUTURE WORK

We hope to encourage further research into the efficacy and feasibility of alternate modality authentication systems. In addition to questions already raised, areas for future investigation include, whether users might persevere with previously unfamiliar tunes long enough for them to become familiar. If this turns out to be the case, the possibilities for alphabet inclusion are increased. We might for example, use creative-commons music. Ours was a research prototype and in US and UK copyright law would be treated as "fair use" (UK Copyright Service, n.d.; US Copyright Office, n.d.). In a non-research system, even if non-profit making, this may not be the case and the clips will need to be paid for. If we are to remain faithful to our originally intended purpose, ensuring inclusivity for groups who find conventional approaches difficult, it seems unfair to ask them to pay for the service, or to view advertisements only to be given the same opportunity to authenticate that others take for granted. Perhaps record companies could submit password clips, in return for showcasing the work of artists. As people have a preference for the familiar, this could positively affect sales.

Another question is how many musical passwords people can remember. Research suggests that music memories are less prone to interference than other types, though it seems advisable to test this in the context of authentication. If multiple musical passwords are difficult to remember, implementation as single-sign-on may provide a viable alternative. The majority of participants said they didn't have to listen to all clips presented, selecting "theirs" as soon as they heard them and moving on. This serves as anecdotal evidence that people do not find the distractors becoming as familiar to them as their password clips. Our study involved a lengthy delay between enrollment and authentication. Trials involving regular use, perhaps on a daily basis, might be better placed to confirm this as fact.

Reporting task times from our online study would have been misleading. It cannot be guaranteed that participants did not stop during the experiment to do other things (at least one told us they *did* do this). Although the authentication was too time consuming, the question remains as to exactly how long it took. We are currently in the process of repeating the experiment in the lab to gather data on this.

Finally, our design should be considered as one possible implementation for a sound-based password. The choices made for the alphabet and password selection procedure were based on research into enhancing memorability and security. The literature on the subject is vast, and it may prove useful to populate sound-based systems and interaction therewith differently, enhancing efficacy.

REFERENCES

Bella, S. D., Peretz, I., & Aronoff, N. (2003). Time course of melody recognition: A gating paradigm study. *Perception & Psychophysics*, *65*(7), 1019–1028. doi:10.3758/BF03194831

Besson, M., Faïta, F., Bonnel, A.-M., & Requin, J. (2002). Singing in the brain: Independence of music and tunes. *Psychological Science*, *9*(6), 494–498. doi:10.1111/1467-9280.00091

Bigand, E., & Poulin-Charronnat, B. (2006). Are we "experienced listeners"? A review of the musical capacities that do not depend on formal musical training. *Cognition*, *100*, 100–130. doi:10.1016/j.cognition.2005.11.007

Brostoff, S., & Sasse, M. A. (2000). Are passfaces more usable than passwords? A field trial investigation. In S. McDonald, (Ed.), *People and Computers XIV - Usability or Else! Proceedings of HCI 2000,* (pp. 405-424). Springer.

Coventry, L., De Angeli, A., & Johnson, G. (2003). Usability and biometric verification at the ATM interface. In *CHI '03: Proceedings of the SIGCHI Conference on Human Factors in Computing Systems* (pp. 153-160). New York, NY: ACM Press.

Crowder, R. G., & Serafine, M. L. (1986). Physical interaction and association by contiguity in memory for the words and melodies of songs. *Memory & Cognition*, *18*(5), 469–476. doi:10.3758/BF03198480

Davis, D., Monrose, F., & Reiter, M. K. (2004). On user choice in graphical password schemes. In *SSYM'04: Proceedings of the 13th Conference on USENIX Security Symposium*, (p. 11). Berkeley, CA: USENIX Association.

De Angeli, A., Coventry, L., Johnson, G., & Renaud, K. (2005). Is a picture really worth a thousand words? Exploring the feasibility of graphical authentication systems. *International Journal of Human-Computer Studies*, *63*, 128–152. doi:10.1016/j.ijhcs.2005.04.020

Florencio, D., & Herley, C. (2007). A large-scale study of web password habits. *In WWW'07: Proceedings of the 16th International Conference on World Wide Web*. (pp. 657-666). New York, NY: ACM.

Forget, A., Chiasson, S., & Biddle, R. (2007). Helping users create better passwords: Is this the right approach? In *SOUPS '07: Proceedings of the Third Symposium on Usable Privacy and Security* (pp. 151-152). New York, NY: ACM.

Gaw, S., & Felten, E. W. (2006). Password management strategies for online accounts. In *SOUPS'06:* Proceedings of the Second Symposium on Usable Privacy and Security (pp. 44-55). New York, NY: ACM.

Gibson, M., Conrad, M., & Maple, C. (2010). Infinite alphabet passwords: A unified model for a class of authentication systems. In S. K. Katsikas & P. Samarati (Eds.), *SECRYPT*, (pp. 94-99). SciTePress.

Gibson, M., Renaud, K., Conrad, M., & Maple, C. (2009). Musipass: Authenticating me softly with "my" song. In *NSPW '09: New Security Paradigms Workshop* (pp. 85-100). New York, NY: ACM.

Herley, C. (2009) So long and no thanks for the externalities: The rational rejection of security advice by users. *In NSPW '09: New Security Paradigms Workshop* (pp. 133-144). New York, NY: ACM.

Hirsch, L. E. (2007). Weaponizing classical music: Crime prevention and symbolic power in the age of repetition. *Journal of Popular Music Studies*, *19*(4), 342–358. doi:10.1111/j.1533-1598.2007.00132.x

Inglesant, P. G., & Sasse, M. A. (2010). The true cost of unusable password policies: password use in the wild. *Proceedings of the 28th International Conference on Human Factors in Computing Systems* (CHI '10), (pp. 383-392). New York, NY: ACM.

Jackson, M. (2005, 10 January). Music to deter yobs by. *BBC News Magazine*. Retrieved December 12, 2010 from http://news.bbc.co.uk/1/hi/magazine/4154711.stm

Johnson, M. E., & Goetz, E. (2007). *Embedding information security into the organization. IEEE Security and Privacy* (pp. 16–24). May/June.

Kuo, C., Romanosky, S., & Cranor, L. F. (2006). Human selection of mnemonic phrase-based passwords. In *SOUPS '06: Proceedings of the Second Symposium on Usable Privacy and Security* (pp. 67–78). New York, NY: ACM.

Lazarsfeld, P., & Field, H. (1946). *The people look at radio*. Chapel Hill, NC: University of North Carolina Press.

LeDoux, J. E. (1992). Emotion as memory: Anatomical systems underlying indelible neural traces. In Christianson, S. (Ed.), *Handbook of emotion and memory: Theory and research* (pp. 269–288). Hillsdale, NJ: Erlbaum.

Liddell, J., Renaud, K. V., & De Angeli, A. (2003). *Authenticating users using a combination of sound and images. Short paper presented at British Computer Society, HCI 2003*. UK: Bath.

Mélen, M., & Deliége, I. (1995). Extraction of cues or underlying harmonic structure: Which guides recognition of familiar melodies? *The European Journal of Cognitive Psychology*, *7*(1), 81–106. doi:10.1080/09541449508520159

Mendori, T., Kubouchi, M., Okada, M., & Shimizu, A. (2002). Password input interface for primary school children. In *Proceedings of the International Conference on Computers in Education (ICCE02)*. Auckland, New Zealand: IEEE Computer Society.

Monaco, B., & Riordan, J. (1987). *The platinum rainbow... How to make it big in the music business*. Sherman Oaks, CA: Omnibus Books.

Morris, R., & Thomson, K. (1979). Password security: A case history. *Communications of the ACM*, *22*(11), 594–597. doi:10.1145/359168.359172

Nusbaum, E. C., & Silvia, P. J. (2010). Shivers and timbres: Personality and the experience of chills from music. *Social Psychological and Personality Science*, October.

Paivio, A. (1983). The empirical case for dual coding. In Yuille, J. (Ed.), *Imagery, memory and cognition: Essays in honour of Allan Paivio* (pp. 307–322). Hillsdale, NJ: Erlbaum.

Peretz, I., Radeau, M., & Arguin, M. (2004). Two-way interactions between music and language: Evidence from priming recognition of tune and lyrics in familiar songs. *Memory & Cognition*, *32*(1), 142–152. doi:10.3758/BF03195827

Petrie, H., & Kheir, O. (2007). The relationship between accessibility and usability of websites. In *CHI '07: Proceedings of the SIGCHI Conference on Human Factors in Computing Systems* (pp. 397-406). New York, NY: ACM.

Renaud, K. (2006). A visuo-biometric authenticaton mechanism for older users. In McEwan, T., Gulliksen, J., & Benyon, D. (Eds.), *People and Computers XIX — The Bigger Picture* (pp. 167–182). London, UK: Springer. doi:10.1007/1-84628-249-7_11

Renaud, K., & De Angeli, A. (2009). Visual passwords: Cure-all or snake-oil? *Communications of the ACM*, *52*(12), 135–140. doi:10.1145/1610252.1610287

Rentfrow, P. J., & Gosling, S. D. (2003). The do re mi's of everyday life: The structure and personality correlates of music preferences. *Journal of Personality and Social Psychology*, *84*(6), 1236–1256. doi:10.1037/0022-3514.84.6.1236

Sapolsky, R. (2005). Stressed out memories. *Scientific American Mind*, *14*(5), 28.

Schechter, S., Herley, C., & Mitzenmacher, M. (2010). Popularity is everything: A new approach to protecting passwords from statistical guessing attacks. In *HotSec'10: Proceedings of the 5th USENIX Workshop on Hot Topics in Security*. USENIX Association.

Scherer, K. R., & Zentner, M. R. (2001). Emotional effects of music: Production rules. In Juslin, P. N., & Sloboda, J. A. (Eds.), *Music and emotion: Theory and research* (pp. 361–392). Oxford, UK: Oxford University Press.

Schmidt, A., Kölbl, T., Wagner, S., & Strassmeier, W. (2004). Enabling access to computers for people with poor reading skills. In C. Stary & C. Stephanidis (Eds.), *8th ERCIM Workshop on User Interfaces for All, Lecture Notes in Computer Science (LNCS), vol. 3196* (pp. 96–115). Vienna, Austria: Springer.

Sewall, M. A., & Sarel, D. (1986). Characteristics of radio commercials and their recall effectiveness. *Journal of Marketing, 50*(1), 52–60. doi:10.2307/1251278

Shannon, C. (1948). A mathematical theory of communication. *The Bell System Technical Journal, 27*, 379–423.

Small, A., Stern, Y., Tang, M., & Mayeux, R. (1999). Selective decline in memory function among healthy elderly. *Neurology, 52*, 1392–1396.

Smith, A. B. (1932). The pleasures of recognition. *Music & Letters, 13*(1), 80–84. doi:10.1093/ml/13.1.80

Thorpe, J., & van Oorschot, P. C. (2007). Human-seeded attacks and exploiting hot-spots in graphical passwords. *In SS'07: Proceedings of the 16th Conference on USENIX Security Symposium* (Article 8), Berkeley, CA: USENIX Association.

Tulving, E. (1974). Cue-dependent forgetting. *American Scientist, 62*, 74–82.

UK Copyright Service. (n.d.). *Factsheet P-01: UK copyright law*. Retrieved December 12, 2010m from http://www.copyrightservice.co.uk/copyright/p01_uk_copyright_law

US Copyright Office. (n.d.). *Fair use*. Retrieved December 12, 2010, from http://www.copyright.gov/fls/fl102.html

Wells, W. D., Burnett, J., & Moriarty, S. (1989). *Advertising: Principles and practice*. Prentice Hall.

Wiedenbeck, S., Waters, J., Sobrado, L., & Birget, J.-C. (2006). Design and evaluation of a shoulder-surfing resistant graphical password scheme. In *AVI'06: Proceedings of the Working Conference on Advanced Visual Interfaces* (pp. 177-184). New York, NY: ACM.

Yan, J., Blackwell, A., Anderson, R., & Grant, A. (2004). Password memorability and security: Empirical results. *IEEE Security and Privacy, 2*(5), 25–31. doi:10.1109/MSP.2004.81

ADDITIONAL READING

Adams, A., & Sasse, M. A. (1999). Users are not the enemy. *Communications of the ACM, 42*(12), 40–46. doi:10.1145/322796.322806

Barton, B. F., & Barton, M. S. (1984). User-friendly password methods for computer-mediated information systems. *Computers & Security, 3*(3), 186–195. doi:10.1016/0167-4048(84)90040-3

Blood, A. J., & Zatorre, R. J. (2001). Intensely pleasurable responses to music correlate with activity in brain regions implicated in reward and emotion. *Proceedings of the National Academy of Sciences of the United States of America, 98*(11), 818–823.

Conrad, M., French, T., & Gibson, M. (2006). A pragmatic and musically pleasing production system for sonic events. *In IV'06: Proceedings of Tenth International Conference on Information Visualization,* (pp 630–635). IEEE Computer Society.

Dhamija, R., & Perrig, A. (2000). Déjà vu: A user study using images for authentication. In *Proceedings of USENIX Security Symposium, (*pp 45–58), Denver, Colorado, USA. USENIX Association.

Dunphy, P., Heiner, A. P., & Asokan, N. (2010). A closer look at recognition-based graphical passwords on mobile devices. In *SOUPS'10: Proceedings of the Sixth Symposium on Usable Privacy and Security*. (Article 3). ACM: New York, NY, USA.

Eschrich, S., Munte, T. F., & Altenmüller, E. O. (2008). Unforgettable film music: the role of emotion in episodic long-term memory for music. *BMC Neuroscience*, *9*, 48. doi:10.1186/1471-2202-9-48

Franklin, K. M., & Roberts, J. C. (2004). A path based model for sonification. In *IV'04: Proceedings of Eighth International Conference on Information Visualization*, (pp. 865–870). IEEE Computer Society.

Gallace, A., & Spence, C. (2008). The cognitive and neural correlates of "tactile consciousness": A multisensory perspective. *Consciousness and Cognition*, *17*, 370–407. doi:10.1016/j.concog.2007.01.005

Gibson, M., Conrad, M., Maple, C., & Renaud, K. (2010). Accessible and Secure? Design Constraints on Image and Sound Based Passwords, In *i-Society'10: Proceedings of International Conference on Information Society*. IEEE Computer Society.

Herley, C., Oorschot, P. C., & Patrick, A. S. (2009). Passwords: If We're So Smart, Why Are We Still Using Them? In *Dingledine, R. Golle, P. (Eds.) Financial Cryptography and Data Security. Lecture Notes In Computer Science, Vol. 5628*. pp.230-237. Springer-Verlag, Berlin, Heidelberg

Kaufman, E., Lord, M., Reese, T., & Volkman, J. (1949). The discrimination of visual number. *The American Journal of Psychology*, *62*, 498–525. doi:10.2307/1418556

Kuber, R., & Yu, W. (2006). Authentication using tactile feedback. Paper presented at *British Computer Society, HCI Engage 2006, Interactive experiences*. London, UK.

Kuber, R., & Yu, W. (2010). Feasibility study of tactile-based authentication. *International Journal of Human-Computer Studies*, *68*(3), 158–181. doi:10.1016/j.ijhcs.2009.11.001

Moncur, M., & Leplâtre, G. (2007). Pictures at the ATM: exploring the usability of multiple graphical passwords. In *CHI'07: Proceedings of the SIGCHI conference on Human factors in computing systems* (pp. 887-894). ACM, New York, NY, USA.

Nanayakkara, S., Taylor, E., Wyse, L., & Ong, S. H. (2009). An enhanced musical experience for the deaf: design and evaluation of a music display and a haptic chair. In *CHI'09: Proceedings of the 27th international conference on Human factors in computing systems*. ACM, New York, NY, USA.

Open, I. D. Foundation (n.d.). *About the Open ID foundation*. Retrieved December 12, 2010 from http://openid.net/foundation/

Renaud, K. (2009). Web authentication using Mikon images. In *CONGRESS'09: World conference on privacy, security, trust and the management of e-business*, (pp. 79-88). IEEE Computer Society.

Shay, R., Komanduri, S., Kelley, P. G., Leon, P. G., Mazurek, M. L., Bauer, L., et al. (2010). Encountering stronger password requirements: user attitudes and behaviors. In *SOUPS'10: Proceedings of the Sixth Symposium on Usable Privacy and Security.* (Article 2). ACM, New York, NY, USA.

Shibata, D. (2001) Brains of deaf people "hear" music. *International Arts-Medicine Association Newsletter,* 16,4.Retrieved December 12, 2010 from http://www.iamaonline.org/Dec01_IAMA_NL.PDF.

United Stated Access board. (2000). *Electronic and Information Technology Accessibility Standards (Section 508).* Retrieved December 12, 2010 from http://www.access-board.gov/sec508/standards.htm

Web Accessibility Initiative. (2006). *Policies Relating to Web Accessibility.* Retrieved December 12, 2010 from http://www.w3.org/WAI/Policy/

Wobbrock, J. O. (2009). TapSongs: tapping rhythm-based passwords on a single binary sensor. In *UIST'09: Proceedings of the 22nd annual ACM symposium on User interface software and technology,* (pp.93-96). ACM, New York, NY, USA.

Yan, J. J. (2001). A note on proactive password checking. In *NSPW'01: Proceedings of the 2001 workshop on New security paradigms,* (pp. 127-135). ACM, New York, NY, USA.

KEY TERMS AND DEFINITIONS

Brute Force Attack: Attacker sequentially works through all possible passwords until a valid one is obtained. Can be "offline" where attacker obtains a file containing hashed passwords, subsequently encodes possibilities and compares to file or, "online" where guesses are made directly at interface. Will find *all* passwords given sufficient time and space.

Dictionary Attack: Attacker uses a dictionary of common passwords and uses these in an attempt to gain access. Can also be implemented on or off-line. Saves *time* compared to brute force, though not guaranteed to find every password.

Entropy: In this context, the randomness or lack of predictability of a password's distribution throughout the available space.

Low and Alow Attack: Similar to a brute force attack, although attacker distributes guesses over a number of accounts to avoid detection.

Musical Password: A password which utilizes *music* as the alphabet.

Password Alphabet: The set of letters that can be included to form passwords.

Password Space: The number of unique passwords that can be created from an alphabet.

Single-Sign-On (SSO): A system which allows access to numerous accounts once authenticated to a single session – reduces the number of passwords requiring memorization.

Chapter 9
Information System Integrated Security

Milena Tvrdíková
VSB-Technical University Ostrava, Czech Republic

ABSTRACT

A comprehensive and integrated view on the security of an Information System considering all its parts (hardware, software, human factor, data, and the impact of real world) is presented in the chapter. The security of information systems cannot be solved only by management of Information Technologies, because Information Technologies constitute only a part of Information System. The design of a well-implemented information security management system is the reliable way towards the safety of information in a company or in an institution. Integrated approach to the security of an Information System is introduced, and recommendations for managing the security of the Information System are given.

INTRODUCTION

Information is an asset to the company having substantial value. Therefore it must be suitably protected. With the increasing interconnection among companies and their environs the need to protect this information is more important. With the increasing digitization, information is exposed to an increasing number of different threats and vulnerabilities.

DOI: 10.4018/978-1-4666-0197-0.ch009

Information exists in various forms. Information can be printed or written on a paper, stored electronically, sent by mail, electronically captured on film or can be mentioned in conversation.

Information security management is focused on a wide range of threats and ensures business continuity, minimizes business losses, and maximizes return on investment and of business opportunities. Defining, promoting and improving the quality of information security can be essential to maintaining competitiveness, cash flow, profitability, legal compliance, and reputation of the company.

Information systems of companies suffer by increasing number of security threats from various sources, including computer fraud, espionage, sabotage, vandalism, fires and floods. Sources of damage, such as computer viruses and hackers are becoming more common, growing in sophistication and danger. Despite all of these external threats, the greatest danger is the human factor, i.e. the employees of the company.

Many information systems were not designed to be safe. Safety of information system, which can be achieved through technical means, it is insufficient and should be accompanied by appropriate management and procedures. Therefore, safety management information system requires a comprehensive approach to the solution. It need participation the employees of the company and also owners, suppliers, third parties, customers, and other external entities. Last but not least help of specialist is needed.

Security of information system is an important part of the design and development of information system. It is important for the protection of critical infrastructure both in the private and the public sector. It would be wrong to narrow this problem only on the issue of treatment of information technology security, since information technology is only one part of information system. It is necessary to have a complex look on the safety of information system and to ensure the information system in all its parts and all its interfaces.

Information is an asset to the company having substantial value. It must therefore be suitably protected. With the increasing interconnection of environmental companies is the need to protect this information is still timely. Because of the increasing digitization of information is exposed to an increasing number of different threats and vulnerabilities.

Information exists in various forms (forms). They can be printed or written on paper, stored electronically, sent by mail or electronically captured on film or spoken in conversation.

Information security management is focused on a wide range of threats and ensures business continuity, minimize business losses and maximize return on investment and business opportunities. Defining, promoting and improving the quality of information security may be essential to maintaining competitiveness, cash flow, profitability, legal compliance and reputation of the company.

Still, companies are increasingly and their information systems to withstand security threats from various sources, including computer fraud, espionage, sabotage, vandalism, fires and floods. Sources of damage, such as computer viruses, hackers and denial of service type attacks are becoming more common, growing in sophistication and danger. Despite all of these external threats are the greatest danger is the human factor, i.e. the employees of the company.

Many information systems were not designed to be safe. Safety information system, which can be achieved through technical means, it is inadequate and should be accompanied by appropriate management and procedures. Safety management information system therefore requires a comprehensive approach to the solution, the company co-workers, co-owners, suppliers, third parties, customers and other external entities. Last but not least is the need specialist help.

Information system security is an important part of its design and development, it is important for the protection of critical infrastructure in both private and public sectors. It would be wrong to narrow this problem only on the issue of treatment of information technology security, since information technology is only one part of information systems. It is necessary to look at the safety complex and strive to ensure the organization's information system in all its parts and all its interfaces.

CURRENT THREATS TO INFORMATION SECURITY

A number of companies all around the world focus on analyzing threats to information security. McAfee, Inc. a company providing security solutions, published in 2006 a survey of foreseen trends in security threats (McAfee, 2006):

- The number of password-stealing Web sites will increase,
- The volume of spam, particularly image spam, will increase again. Previously, spam was used for unsolicited advertising e-mails. Gradually, this phenomenon spread into other types of internet communication, including discussion forums, comments or instant messaging,
- Harmful code (malware) will increase – the term malware covers computer viruses, Trojan horses, spyware and adware,
- Mobile phone attacks will become more prevalent,
- Identity theft will increase,
- The uses of computer programs that perform automated attacks (bots) will increase. Bots are automated programs that work on the Internet. Bots are often not supported, but there are several useful of bots (they automatically performs various mechanical tasks),
- The number of rootkits will increase – rootkit is a set of computer programs and technologies, which help to conceal the presence of harmful programs by hiding the files, in which they are installed, API calls, Windows registry files, processes, network connection and system services so that the presence of the harmful software could not be revealed using accessible system tools,
- Vulnerability of software will augment.

Ernst & Young published in 2007 a Global Information Security Survey, where are presented the technologies expected to will shortly be in the centre of attention in terms of security management (PSIB ČR '07, Ernst & Young, NBÚ, DSM, 2007):

- Mobile media technologies,
- Mobile information technologies (PDA, smartphones). Smartphones have similar functions and use as traditional PDAs, but benefit from ability of direct internet connectivity, without any additional device,
- Wireless applications,
- Website applications.

Server virtualization is the biggest threat from a security standpoint, for half the company (see Table 1).

One of the most interesting finding is that 40% of respondents considered the biggest security threat to portable storage devices and intend to devote more attention to this issue next year.

The amount and complexity of attacks is increasing. As the development of direct attacks by the various services and the development of particular attacks using social engineering (to gain and exploit information about the environment, the structure of enterprises and institutions, as well as information about social habits and sets of behaviour in specific situations).

User deception techniques:

- Phishing - fake or web site. Attacker tries to obtain sensitive personal information (such as credit card number, user name, password, etc.). Very often performed using a fake phishing web site, which seems credible.
- Pharming - Phishing similar - albeit much more sophisticated. Pharming is based on a false translation of the name server's IP address.

Table 1. Information security in companies and institutions research results (PSIB ČR '07, Ernst & Young, NBÚ, DSM, 2008)

	Type	No. of positive responses in % of total respondents
Most frequent security incidents	Spam	86
	Power outage	85
	Hardware error	77
	Computer virus	79
	User's error	60
Biggest threats to information security	Internet and email	58
	Internal users	51
	External attacker	32
	Non-existent, unsuitable security policy	21
Security measures	Firewall	93
	Monitoring and virus control	86
	Internet usage guidelines	55
	Penetration testing	18
	Implementation of procedures and measures controlling compliance with directives	14
	Formally defined security policy in a documented form	48

- Attacks through social engineering - convincing and influencing user in order to deceive them so that they may believe that someone else could handle them. Used fraudulent techniques:

Example: Merely half of the companies and institutions in the Czech Republic have prepared their recovery plan of information system functionality. Moreover, the recovery plan has never been tested or has not been tested frequently enough by one third of the companies. One third of companies and institutions have never performed risk analysis and only 19% of companies set aside a budget dedicated to information security.

Research also shows that nearly 70% of companies use external management company to manage their information security. In such cases it is important to co-coordinating activities with outside firms have clearly defined procedures.

Accepted standard in Europe, is ISO / IEC 17799/BS779. (Czech Standards Institute, 2006). The term "information security" comes from the British standard BS 7799, later adopted by ISO as ISO 17799 and ISO 27001 (Czech Standards Institute, 2006). The main objective of information security is the protection of information in all its forms. Basic safety principles - confidentiality, integrity and availability must be ensured. (Čermák, 2007).

Information system security is an integral part of its design and development. The importance of high quality security of information systems increases with the increasing number of threats, with their operation and with the requirements of regulatory authorities on owners and customers. It would be misleading to limit this problem to the area of information technology security. Information technology represents only one component of information systems. For vision of security,

Figure 1. IS security components source

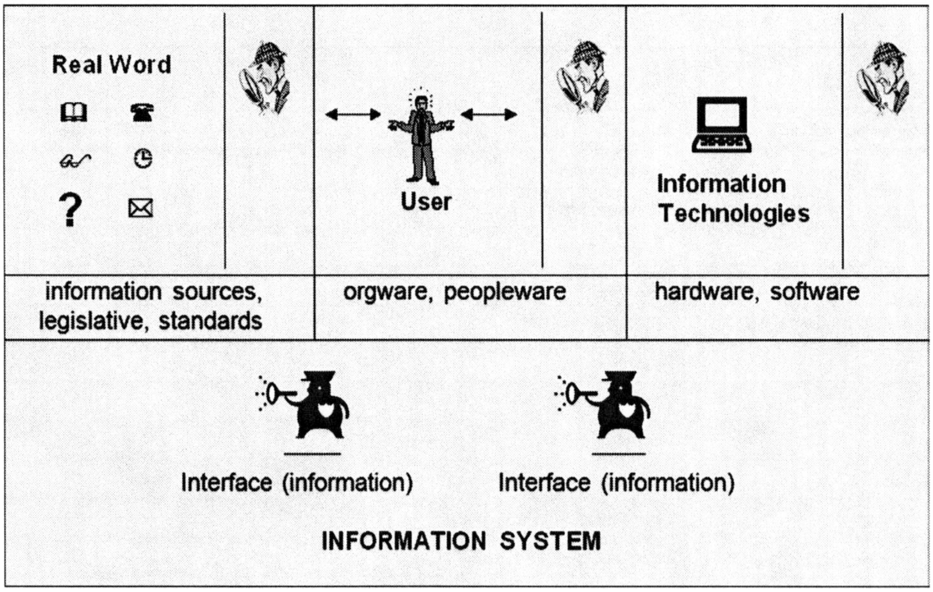

it is essential view the information system in its complexity. The aim is to ensure the information system of company in all its components and all interfaces.(Peltier, 2000).

SECURITY OF INDIVIDUAL INFORMATION SYSTEM COMPONENTS

Management of comprehensive information systems security is often underestimated, which is caused by the fact that if no security incident occurs in the information system, investment to security generates no tangible result.

Figure1 shows: that information system consists not only of information and communication technologies, but also of their users and real world around in which it exists. It is therefore necessary to deal with security of all components and with security of the real assets of IS – that is stored, transmitted, and processed information.

Attacks against Information Technologies

Information technologies consist of hardware and software. On their interface data are transmitted towards users.

Attacks against information technologies can be divided into (Tvrdíková, 2008):

- Interception or destruction – temporary or permanent inaccessibility to an IS component
- Eavesdropping – unauthorized access to an IS component
- Modification – change of an IS component
- Addition of data or function – penetration of disinformation into IS

Attacks against hardware can mostly be defeated by security systems and steadfast building protection. It concerns following attacks:

- Interception or destruction – accidents (natural disasters), damage, theft

- Eavesdropping – theft (of a device, a processor, a memory, or a part of a memory)
- Addition of function – change of regime function

Attacks against software are mostly carried by professionals and cannot be entirely prevented, though it is possible to make their efforts more difficult through the use of security measures. Attacks can be divided into:

- Interception or destruction – software erasure (deliberate or unintentional)
- Eavesdropping – copying
- Modification – change of software
- Addition of data or function – errors, viruses etc.

Key elements of data security comprise:

- Integrity – certainty that data are precise, cleaned and protected from unauthorized modification
- Confidentiality – prevention from leakage to unauthorized users at any moment of data processing
- Availability – data capacity of information system must be of such dimension so that authorized end-users are able to access data that are reliable and on time

Attacks against data are extremely dangerous as data are frequently irretrievable, and they represent inner assets of every information system. Attacks can be classified as:

- Interception or destruction – data erasure (deliberate or unintentional)
- Eavesdropping – data copying
- Modification – change of data
- Addition of value – transaction modification

User Protection

Viewed form user perspective, four main areas of computer security can be defined:

Firstly, Identity Management covers use of chip cards, accounts, passwords and associated user rights. Secondly, configuration management consists of such system set-up and maintenance, so that no unauthorized person could access it. Thirdly, Threats Management includes detection, recognition, defeat and identification of all attempts to break to the system. Finally, credential management deals with electronic signature and encryption. (Peltier, 2000).

Five elements of ideal system for identity, security and privacy of individuals in IS are often cited:

- Authentication - refers to the verification of the user in communication
- Authorization – refers to the verification that the user in communication is really granted the rights he is requesting
- Privacy – communication cannot be eavesdropped
- Integrity – content of communication cannot be modified without authorization,
- Non-repudiation – one party of a transaction can not deny having received or sent a transaction

Protecting your personal computer:

- Disc Protection – password protected operating system, management of access rights to folders and discs, password validity control, erasing RAM memory when logging off or attacked. Hardware encryption of discs, folders and files.
- Security access card managing user's access in cases where a single computer is used by a number of users (chip cards, identification cards, optical memory cards).

- Providing security of the communication channels between portable and communication technology equipment.
- Using signatures with aim to ensure non-repudiation and integrity (e.g. digital signature).

Real World's Influence on Information Systems Security

In relation to information system security, the influence of real world is reflected in information sources, legislation and standards. All those influence quality and security of information systems. It is crucial to ensure security of information systems, mainly of their quality and safety, through their careful selection, organizational security measures and internal regulations and norms that will precisely define legal sources of information for a defined information system. (Mandia & Prosise, 2002).

Legislation in this field is constantly developing in connection with our lives becoming increasingly digitalized. Following is the essential legislation on information systems security:

- Personal Data Protection Act
- Protection of Classified Information Act
- Regulation on the Security of Information and Communication Systems and other Electronic Devices Handling Classified Information
- Regulation on the Electronic signature and the Certification of Shielded Chambers

Major support to security system implementation is provided through security standards. Two essential standards are:

- International Standard ISO/IEC 17799:2000, divided into 11 parts and 39 security areas. It offers guidelines and voluntary directions for information security management. This widely recognized standard is meant to provide a high level, general description of the areas considered important when initiating, implementing or maintaining information security in an organization. It covers topics such as: IT Security Policy and Models, IT Security Planning and Management, IT Security Techniques, Selection of Security Requirements, Security Requirements for External Connections.
- ISO/IEC 27001:2005 specifies the requirements for information security management. It supports process orientated security management through definition of methodology designed to ensure the selection of adequate security controls, recommended by ISO/IEC 17799:2005 standard, based on a risk analysis. ISO/IEC 17799:2005 standard is used in companies and institutions for ISMS certification.
- Another important standard is ISO 27002, which contains over 5,000 security measures that can be used when initiating an information security management system, helping to monitor and improve the system (see Figure 2).

Apart from above listed standards, other standards are used for specific areas.

When using the above described process as explained in standard, the focus is on:

- Understanding information security requirements in an organization, and need for information security policy and targets
- Implementing and using information security management measures in the context of overall organization's risk management
- Monitoring and re-evaluating ISMS performance and effectiveness
- Continuous improvement (modifications) based on objective assessment

Figure 2. (Plan-Do-Check-Act) initiating a security management system in accordance with ISO/IEC 27001 standard (Chlup, 2008)

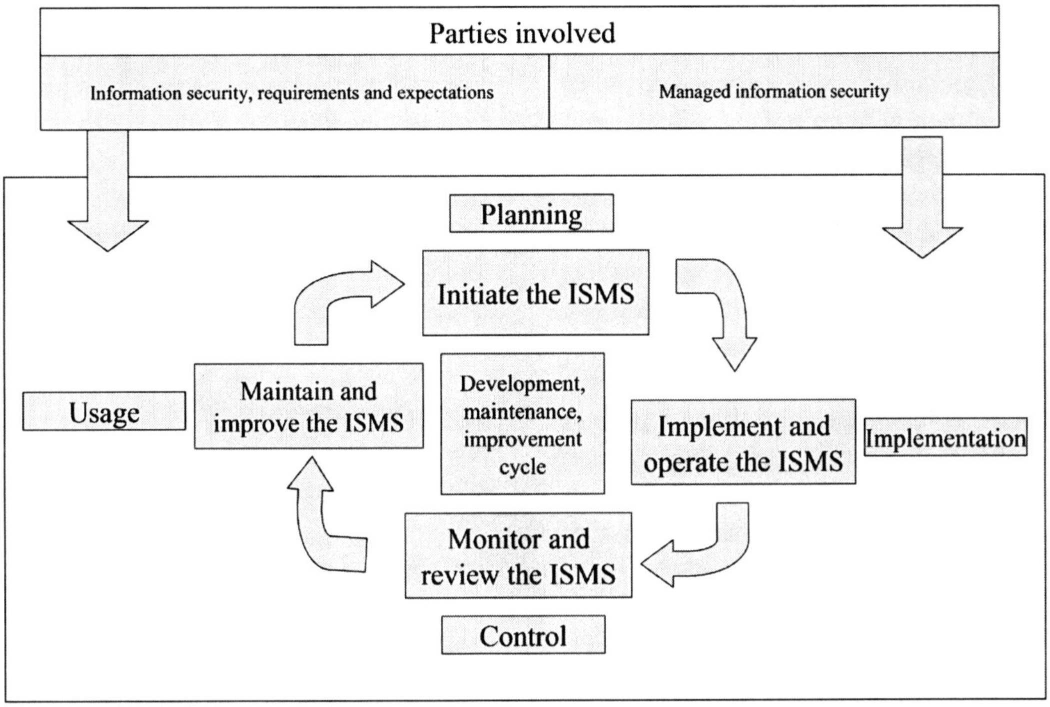

Security Evaluation Criteria

The most renowned set of security evaluation criteria is the American TCSEC (Trusted Computer System Evaluation Criteria) standard that assesses the effectiveness in three fields of computer security:

- Policy – access control management, confidentiality levels
- Accountability – recognition of user's identity, monitoring of their activities
- Assurance – independent evaluation requirements, ongoing execution of security functions

Divisions differ according to which requirements are fulfilled: beginning with D (Minimal protection), then classes C1, C2 (Discretionary protection), B1, B2, B3 (Mandatory protection) to A class (Verified protection).

European criteria have several classes, ranging from class E0 where no specific requirements are defined to class E6, which requires all measures to defined and documented.

The Canadian criteria, called CTCPEC, have 4 classes each subdivided into several levels.

The above mention criteria provided foundation for common criteria (CC) – which were approved as ISO/IEC 15408 standard with Evaluation Assurance Levels EAL 1 to EAL 7.

Security Policy

Security policy is a set of measures covering formal and normative frame of information security in a company or an institution. It also describes implementation process of technical and administrative measures for daily operations of a company or an institution.

First step in creation of IS security policy of an organization is an elaboration of information security study, which describes current status of information security in a specific organization.

Subsequently, a risk analysis is to be performed. It is a time consuming task and it should be carried out in close co-operation with the IS supplier and closely co-operating companies and organizations. People who are well familiar with company's environment should be involved in the risk analysis study. Specialized software, tools and methods can be used in risk analysis, as well as services of specialized companies who have ample experience in this field. Information obtained by risk analysis are fundamental for company's information security, therefore, it must be kept confidential and accessible to strictly defined audience only.

Based on the result of the risk analysis, security policy is created. It consists of two parts:

- General security policy, which covers: description of the organization and its processes, security policy objectives, security infrastructure (roles, functions), identification of assets, confidential data and general threats, description of present status, description of security measures and contingency plans.
- System security policy that defines implementation of security policy in a specific system of a company or an institution. System security policy is a set of rules and principles for protection of information system. Significant part of the document is devoted to description of roles, responsibilities and rights, dealing with incidents and security testing.

The security policy should be reviewed after any significant change in the information system in order to avoid uncontrolled patching of unreliable areas in the system.

Typically, the security policy is divided into physical, personal, IT, administration and process security.

With security mechanisms based on security policy being in place, it is essential to monitor their constant functionality. With relation to increasingly sophisticated attacks on information systems and their ever increasing pace of development, it is recommended to outsource monitoring to external companies specialized in such tasks and holding special knowledge in this field.

RECOMMENDED APPROACH TO INFORMATION SYSTEM SECURITY MANAGEMENT

In the first step, it is fundamental to define areas with potential risks and consider what and to which extend is threatened by such risks. Based on those assumptions boundaries should be defined and rules of information system security management should be set.

Following system of security management is recommended:

- Develop information technology security policy,
- Identify roles and responsibilities in an organization,
- Manage configuration of information systems,
- Manage changes,
- Make all employees aware of information system security,
- Select and implement appropriate security measures,
- Prepare contingency plans and system and data recovery after accidents,
- Manage risks, including identification and assessment of:
    - assets that need to be protected,

  - threats,
  - vulnerabilities,
  - impacts,
  - security measures,
  - residual risks,
  - limitations,
- Including:
  - maintenance,
  - security audit,
  - monitoring,
  - revision.

Having covered this area, it is possible to work on objectives, strategy and security policy of information system.

One of the key factors in analyzing and considering security solutions is a comprehensive view of individual issues. The selected solutions are not always well balanced and integrated, and it happens that they do not correspond with real needs and demands. Imbalance can be caused by excessive focus on technical security aspects, which seem to be more straightforward rather than focusing on security in connection to the human factor. It is frequently not fully recognized that human factor is equally important and together with technical devices it constitutes an integral part of the information system security. In other words, if the state-of-the-art hardware is used together with sophisticated measures against external attacks to protect information system, issues of internal attacks should be solved in detail at the same time. The success or failure of security protection will ultimately depend not only on the technical solution itself, but on strict application of organization rules. Such rules should be dealt with in relation to the security system life cycle.

Overall, the security management system can be divided into two parts:

- Awareness of all employees of information system security

In order for security measures to be effective, it is essential to stick to the basic policies when using computer systems. It means that users do not share access names, passwords and access codes. Obviously, not even in written form, with the exception of sealed envelopes stored in a safe that are opened in case of exceptional situations of crisis. Moreover, when choosing a password or a code, it is important to select such system that will not allow the password or the code to be broken easily. Extreme precaution must be taken, when working through the Internet.

In addition, it is crucial to abide by the rules concerning sending and receiving of prohibited attachment types, downloading of any unknown application or self-extracting files, visiting prohibited or risky web sites etc. Correct setting of firewall and proxy server rules can significantly limit undesirable behavior of users, but it can never eliminate it totally. It is necessary that the users abide by the basic security rules.

- Selection and implementation of suitable technical measures

This term covers areas such as: implementation of access cards, limited access to data according to real needs of users and level of data importance, right set-up of users communicating through Internet, antivirus control of all communication coming from and into internal network and the like. Technical part of system security can be achieved through correct firewalls settings, selection of suitable internal architecture and in numerous other ways.

When assessing the security, it is fundamental to consider that every system is as strong, as strong is its weakest link. In case of information system security, it is definitely the user who represents the weakest link.

Example case: As an example case we can describe a situation where a company selected an appropriate security system, and set up identification, authorization, control, record keeping and user rights systems. However, people working in this system evade the rules and settings by changing names of e-mail attachments so that the names are approved during security check and prohibited attachments are not revealed. After reception to their station attachment is re-named again to its original name and the problem is caused. An application "smuggled" in such way can be extremely harmful and the damage may result in massive complication for company's operations.

CONCLUSION

Information Security Management System is the term being used for a system of management concerned with information security. ISMS must be part of overall company management system. It is based on risk analyses and it offers integrated mechanism of continuous analysis, implementation, control, maintenance and improvement of information security system aiming to prevent systematically incidents occurrence. ISMS should contain reliable mechanisms of internal control and enforceable rules and obligations for all parties concerned. Key requirement of ISMS implementation is top management support and active participation in security policy. (Mandia & Prosise, 2002).

No organization using information and communication technologies as part of their information system can do without security measures. In any case, it is advisable to approach all information system security issues in a comprehensive manner with regard to all individual elements. It is by far not enough simply to create security policy – it is vital to make all employees well aware of its existence so that safe behavior becomes standard.

Information security combines technical and organization measures. No information system is and never will be absolutely secure. However, every information system can be secure enough with regards to the purpose, for which it is used.

REFERENCES

Čermák, I. (2007). *Security threats and information systems security status at Czech public universities. Security Policy* (pp. 12–17). Plzeň, Czech Republic: The University of West Bohemia in Pilsen.

Chlup, M. (2008, August). *The introduction of safety management system - ISMS, PDCA model.* Protect your data. Retrieved November 2010, from http://www.chrantesidata.cz/cs/art/1148-dil-2

Czech Standards Institute. (2006, September). *Code of practice for information security management.* ČSN ISO/IEC 17799 (369790) Information technology - Security techniques. Retrieved January 2011, from http://shop.normy.biz/d.php?k=75901

Mandia, K., & Prosise, C. (2002). *Computer attack: Detection, defense and immediate rectification.* Prague, Czech Republic: Computer Press.

McAfee. (2006, August). *Global security threats and trends.* McAfee: Proven Security - Security Spotlight. Retrieved January 2011, from https://mcafee.imiinc.com/nai7588/aug06/article3.jsp

Peltier, T. R. (2000). *Information security policies, procedures and standards.* Auerbach Publication.

PSIB ČR '07, Ernst & Young, NBÚ, DSM. (2007, December). *Information security survey in the Czech Republic 2007.* PSIB ČR '07, Ernst & Young, NBÚ, DSM – Data security management. Retrieved November 2010, from www.dsm.tate.cz/cz/psib-cr-2007

PSIB ČR '07, Ernst & Young, NBÚ, DSM. (2008, December). *Information security survey in Slovakia 2008.* PSIB ČR '07, Ernst & Young, NBÚ, DSM – Data security management. Retrieved January 2011, from www.dsm.tate.cz/cz/psib-cr-2008

Tvrdíková, M. (2008). Information System integrated security. In 7th *International Computer Information Systems and Industrial Management Applications Conference* (pp. 153-154). Los Alamitos, CA, USA.

ADDITIONAL READING

Dobda, D. (1998). *Protection of data in information systems*. Prague, Czech Republic: Grada. (In Czech)

Hrabalová, M., & Fišer, O. (2005). *Security and development of information systems Software development 2005* (pp. 47–52). Ostrava, Czech Republic: Tanger. (In Czech)

Kovacich, G. L. (2003). *The information system security officer's guide*. Burlington, USA: Elsevier Science

Negroponte, N. (1995). *Being Digital*. New York, USA: Alfred and Knopf, Inc.

Smejkal, V. (2007). *Information systems security in public services System integration 2007* (pp. 102–118). Prague, Czech Republic: CSSI OECONOMICA. (In Czech)

Tvrdíková, M. (2007). Overall IS security. In J. Rychlík (Ed.), *Security policy IS* (pp. 61-66), Pilsen, Czech Republic: The university of West Bohemia in Pilsen. (In Czech)

Tvrdíková, M. (2010). *Information Security Management System and Security Policy in Company Transfer of knowledge and European funds to the economical sector of countries of the European Union* (pp. 309–316). Poznan, Poland: Higher School of Banking.

KEY TERMS AND DEFINITIONS

Attacks against Information Technologies: These are attacks against hardware and software - interception or destruction, eavesdropping, addition of function and modification.

Components of Information System: Information technologies (software, hardware), users (organizational rules, human factors), real world (information resources, legislative, standards) and interfaces between them.

Information Security Management System: Information Security Management System is the term being used for a system of management information security. Information Security Management System must be part of overall company management system. It is based on risk analyses and it offers integrated mechanism of continuous analysis, implementation, of control, maintenance and occurrence improvement of information security system aiming to prevent systematically the incidents.

Real World: In relation to information system security, the influence of real world is reflected in information sources, legislation and standards.

Security of Information System: Security of information system is an essential part of its conception, development and reliability. This part of the system cannot be completely separated from the other and must be consistent with other.

Security Policy: Security policy is a set of measures covering formal and normative frame of information security in a company or an institution.

User Protection: Five elements of ideal system for identity, security and privacy of individuals in IS are often cited authentication, authorization, privacy, integrity and non-repudiation.

Chapter 10
Surveillance Communities of Practice:
Supporting Aspects of Information Assurance for Safeguards and Compliance Monitoring

Peter Goldschmidt
The University of Western Australia, Australia

ABSTRACT

This discussion focuses primarily on supporting communities of practice tasked with compliance monitoring in complex environments. Here, the decision makers, as members of the surveillance community of practice, may be confronted with rapidly changing information, and the solution or solutions may be required rapidly at a low cost. In these cases, fully automated monitoring or surveillance systems are limited in their utility because of dynamic contexts and temporal and spatial variations. Managing these limitations typically requires human judgement to assess the results of these monitoring systems. Other reasons for requiring human judgement include a need for the surveillance results to be verified and assured with substantiating evidence, and the delegation of control and responsibility when actioning remedial responses to generated alerts and alarms. Surveillance Information Systems performance depends on reducing the decision time for remedial action by verifying alarms and generating actionable indicators, in context. This chapter discusses support and assurance of surveillance monitoring and compliance verification knowledge management of surveillance results. The aim is to support information assurance real time alarm identification and verification, assurance and management decision making by tracking the parameters monitored by the existing information assurance monitoring infrastructure and operating work systems, and using that data/knowledge to create useful and actionable information. The goal is to reduce the (information assurance remedial action) time to decision to enable accurate and rapid operational execution.

DOI: 10.4018/978-1-4666-0197-0.ch010

INTRODUCTION

Work systems (Alter 2006) supporting communities of practice tasked with assessing the results of surveillance operations typically use a matching process by which some predetermined conditions are compared with observed events or event related information. If an unacceptable variance is detected this is usually followed by the generation of an alert or alarm highlighting the variance. The alarm is presented to an evaluating agent in order to determine the alarm context and validity and to recommend one or more remedial actions to reduce the variance. For surveillance in complex environment such as defence, the financial markets, national security, medical and public health monitoring and critical industrial processes, the evaluating agent need to be human. The goal is to be, as practically as possible, informed as to what is happening as opposed to knowing what has happened.

BACKGROUND

Typical monitoring operations align with (Boyd 1976) the Observe, Orient, Decide, Act (OODA) construct. The primary monitoring process, the matching component, fulfils the Observe function and in some cases may also include the Orient function, whereby the context in which the variance occurred is also taken into account. If not, then the human agent fulfils this function when assessing the variance. There may also be a temporal issue when assessing the context, as this may change over time for any given variance. Based on this assessment, a Decision is then made to Act in order to remedy the observed variance. The aim of a surveillance operations decision support work system is to reduce the time between the Decide and Act components, with assurance that the underlying evidence supporting the variance is sound.

Broadly, five problem areas drive this necessity to assure and verify the alarm:

1. The quality of the data/information being monitored and the quality of the primary monitoring process;
2. The potential biases inherent in the evaluating agent's analysis of the variance and the supporting or refuting evidence;
3. The combination of the alarm and contextual or environmental evidence;
4. The accountability and transparency of the verification and assurance process, and
5. The accuracy and efficacy of the remedial action.

Current Issues Relating to Surveillance Monitoring

Ubiquitous intelligence and pervasive computing (combined with the new management paradigm described by Gabriel (2003), where the old iron cage of management command and control has now been replaced by a flexible glass cage of transparency, accountability, flexibility and the continuous monitoring of human activities, often in real-time) calls for a need to further research electronic data monitoring and practice, including monitoring of societies. These may be the workplace society, the society in general or the surveillance communities of practice who are tasked with this activity. These societies are generally interlinked and cannot readily be seen as mutually exclusive as they may all, at some point, be monitored, assessed and be subject to remedial actions. Gabriel points out that this glass cage work environment has led to a degree of employee alienation and distrust of the accompanying monitoring. Combined with Bohn's et al. (2004), observations that the "new monitoring techniques extend far beyond credit-card checks, call-logs and postings. Not only will the spatial scope of such monitoring activities be significantly extended in ambient-intelligence landscapes, but their temporal coverage will also greatly increase, starting from pre-natal diagnostic data stored on babies hospital smart-cards, to activity patterns in kindergarten and schools, to workplace monitoring and senior citizen's health monitoring... such comprehensive monitoring techniques create opportunities to cross personal privacy borders which form the basis for perceived privacy violations."

A current dilemma exhibited is a tendency of citizens (this author included) to question the lack of governance oversight and due diligence following the occurrence of an adverse event, whilst simultaneously questioning the need for surveillance monitoring because of real or perceived breaches in personal privacy. Whilst we also encounter millions of individuals sharing intimate personal details on social media such as Facebook, Twitter and the like.

Given that surveillance and related monitoring activities are now, for better or for worse, part of our social and professional environment, it is timely to focus on supporting the surveillance monitoring communities of practice in order to ensure the efficacy of their activities.

Issues Relating to the Surveillance Process

The electronic monitoring of data related to individuals and groups of individuals is described as "dataveillance" by Clarke (1988). He highlights the inherent dangers of drawing conclusions from this data, and points out that a major problem in "dataveillance" is the high noise to signal ratio which may result in misleading conclusions (Davis and Ord 1990) acknowledge the problem of setting threshold levels in an ever-changing environment. "With any set of tolerance levels, deviant (even fraudulently motivated) behaviour may escape detection. Tightening tolerance levels limits increases the likelihood that exception conditions will trigger an alert but also increases false positive alerts since the number of instances that fall outside the tolerance increase. The cost for the analyst (the decision-maker) to review the additional non-exception condition alerts must be assessed in relation to the imputed value of identifying the additional true exceptions detected by more stringent limits."

Subsequent advances made in improving the quality of this data have, in general, reduced the problem of misleading results produced by "noisy data". These advances include improvements in data processing and the increased use of sophisticated computational techniques such as statistical, knowledge-based and artificial neural computational methods.

These systems are centred on the events being monitored and the events' source agents. Their results, however, may still require human judgment to determine their validity.

Research in monitoring has focused on improving the initial identification of anomalous events e.g. (Green and Swets 1966 and Abdi 2007), including a discussion on Signal Detection Theory where a signal is present but missed by the detection artefact or decision maker. This has led to the introduction of various techniques that have, in general, been an improvement on preceding ones. The improvements have been partly motivated by a desire to improve the accuracy of the results generated by these primary monitoring systems; to reduce the costs associated with surveillance and increase its reliability, consistency, productivity and effectiveness; to free up resources so that they can be redirected to activities with greater payoffs; and to improve overall risk management in general, in an increasingly complex and competitive global environment.

Currently, with the increased proliferation of sensors and other primary monitoring technologies, the resulting information overload and the cost to the evaluating agents, as described by Davis and Ord, have been exacerbated. These evaluating agents are also subject to biases and limitations.

In general, decision support is required because decisions are based on input from various cooperating agents, each with different criteria, and may invoke selectivity, which involves using only a portion of the information available. Another reason is that human analysts typically make poor decisions when they must take into account several attributes simultaneously, and psychological studies have shown that individuals cannot simultaneously keep in mind more than 7 +/- 2 elements (Kahneman 1973) In addition, the problem model may be difficult to understand and to build, and the data may be partially unknown. The problem domain may be complex (with the decision maker confronted with rapidly changing information), and the solution may be required rapidly at a low cost. There is tendency not to stray from the initial judgment even when confronted with conflicting evidence: this is termed anchoring. Inconsistency is observed when alternatives are presented repeatedly to a subject for evaluation, especially when successive presentations are well separated by other choices. For these reasons there may be a need for the decision-making process to be supported, to ensure consistent, reliable decisions.

Freedman and Mathai (1995) point out that "Difficulties arise because in general, (1) the unusual subjects are not known – they must be discovered or inferred from the data; (2) the definition of 'unusual pattern of behaviour' is subjective and possibly changes with every analysis and over time; and (3) the quantity of the data in an analysis is overwhelming".

Friedman and Stuzin (1991) discussing the computational approaches used by primary monitoring systems, note that the problems encountered with analytical models used or proposed for surveillance monitoring, including models for predicting behaviour as well as models used for compliance monitoring, include incomplete model theories – models often contain incomplete theories as well as incomplete data; incomplete model inputs – even the best models occasionally produce decisions much worse than a human analyst would, because they do not include some important factors; and incomplete model outputs – the analyst's risk preference in dealing with uncertain outcomes might differ from that of the model. Conversely, the analyst's role is trivialised if the model makes all the decisions; and incomplete explanations arise if models provide precision at the expense of intuition and common sense.

These analytical, predictive and compliance models are often rejected by decision makers. Consequently, to compensate for these limitations, some analysts "tune" results by making heuristic adjustments to the analytical model. This tuning produces a model forecast that is consistent with intuitive expectations, and maintains the detail and structure of the analytical model. However, as Pindyck and Rubinfeld (1976); Freedman and Stuzin (1991) show, tuned forecasts can easily be misused, as reported by (William et al. 2007) Alternatively, a cognitive model of an analyst, implemented as static expert system, might perform better at predictive tasks than an analytical model. However, static cognitive models fail in domains where there is too much reliance on judgment. In these domains, judgments are dynamic and their representation is difficult to quantify and verify.

The Primary Monitoring and Alarm Verification Environment

The context or environment in which the variance occurs can be classified along the simple to complex continuum.

The primary monitoring and alarm verification environment can be classified by levels of complexity, characterised by their place on the simple or complex environmental continuum in which they operate and the decisions required to determine instances of non-compliance.

Constraints may take the form of an organisation's predetermined policies and procedures, needed to ensure data and event integrity, contractual agreements, and statutory requirements. These constraints are not mutually exclusive and can be seen as bounds or threshold levels. The parameters used to construct these levels may change with modifications to threshold requirements such as evolutionary changes in constraints and changes in data and event requirements. A simple environment is so-called because: 1) the threshold levels either seldom change or only change over the longer term; 2) the identification of the variance fulfils the conditions of necessary and sufficient evidence to determine an instance of non-compliance; and 3) the decisions, needed to determine if events comply, lie on the structured to highly structured portion of the decision-making continuum. The degree to which the bounds of the threshold levels are set, very narrow to very broad, determines the type of decision required. Under a simple environment the bounds or threshold limits are narrow, characteristic of structured decisions such as data input integrity and customer credit checks. Decision-making in this environment is ex-ante, made of a single step, and the constraints are all predetermined.

In a complex environment, decision-making is ex-post, complex and may require multiple steps. Initial monitoring uses a priori thresholds broader than in a simple environment, i.e. more granular, and produces exceptions that identify suspected non-compliant events (SNCEs). Once these exceptions have been produced, the decision-maker must substantiate true positive exceptions. This task must be broken down into smaller components and sub-goals must be developed (Simon 1973), to identify, categorise and discard any false positive exceptions. False negatives do not generate an exception, and allow possible suspect events to slip through the surveillance sieve. If the threshold limits are stringent enough, marginal false negatives could be subsumed and later considered. Nevertheless, this would not necessarily reduce the occurrences of true false negatives, as their characteristics may not be known. True positives are those exceptions that the decision-maker has determined are indeed anomalous. Evidence for this decision uses the results of the initial monitoring as well as important information related to the event, characterised a need for judgmental expertise.

Addressing These Issues for Complex Environments

A framework developed by Goldschmidt (2007) starts to address the issues of assuring and verifying true positive alarms and managing the false positive alarms in complex environments. The framework includes methods to support assurance of surveillance monitoring and compliance verification knowledge management.

Based on this framework, a proof of concept prototype, Alert Coding (ALCOD), was developed. The prototype was successfully tested at the Surveillance division of the Australian Stock Exchange, where quantitative and qualitative information plus surveillance analysts' judgment are required to verify surveillance results in a highly complex environment. The object of the Surveillance division is to ensure the health of trading on this market. The stock exchange was chosen as it represents one of the most complex and dynamic environments in which to test the construct. Current research is now being conducted in domains such as compliance and safeguards verification of asset management and machine condition monitoring in the oil, gas and waste water industries; and the verification of results generated by continuous audit. These applications, now termed Adaptive Real-time Alarm Management (AR-TAM) constructs are based on an adaptation of ALCOD, the financial auditing construct.

The assurance of compliance monitoring requires decision support and appropriate domain knowledge, relevant to the level of the user, to manage the results of the surveillance monitoring. This is required in order to identify the necessary and sufficient evidence verifying or refuting the generated alerts. This secondary monitoring is based on supporting the human evaluation of the exceptions or variances produced by the primary monitoring system, to determine if a generated exception is feasible. This is similar to an analytical review (AR) conducted by auditors, characterised as a diagnostic-inference process. Koonce (1993) defines AR as the diagnostic process of identifying and determining the cause of unexpected fluctuations in account balances and other financial relationships. Similarly, second tier monitoring problem solving identifies and determines the causes of unexpected variances resulting from the primary monitoring facility. Analytical review (AR) typically follows four distinct diagnostic inference components: accumulation and evaluation of relevant information; initial recognition of unusual fluctuations; subsequent hypothesis generation; and information search and hypothesis evaluation (Blocher and Cooper 1988).

Evidence accumulation and evaluation is guided by the results of the primary monitoring constructs. Subsequently a hypothesis of the potential causes of the observed variance is generated. A diagnostic approach is employed which takes the form of defeasible logic, which means that any inference made may only be tentative, as the inference may require revision if new information is presented. The decision-maker must evaluate all possible legitimate reasons for the occurrence of the variant. If none is found, the hypothesis of non-compliance is strengthened.

PROBLEM STRUCTURE

Structuredness of the complex problem is two-fold (Sol 1982): the variance identification is the structured component, and the accumulation of evidence supporting or refuting the noncompliant event (NCE) hypothesis is the ill-structured component. The variance is typically the product of some algorithm indicating a possible occurrence of NCEs, but in order to substantiate a true NCE the required accumulation of evidence requires judgment of agent behaviour. These include the source of the event, the identification of the source agent's possible motivations, the environment in which the source agent is operating and the impact this event may have on the environment.

Coordination: The Review Process to Facilitate Truth Maintenance

Coordination refers to the managing of interactions between multiple agents cooperating in some collective task. Optimal organisational design depends on the task environment and with an audit team or group this is hierarchical (Pete et al. 1993). The objective is to reduce the problems discussed by Freedman and Klein ibid. and Friedman and Stuzin ibid) to reduce any potentially redundant activities conducted by the evaluating agents, and to increase efficiency and effectiveness. The agent or agents may be human or machine based. Machine based or independent software agents function as repositories of human opinions related to the event under scrutiny. These machine agents can be kept current using case-based or machine learning techniques, however human judgement is usually still required before remedial action is approved.

The process of review for evaluating judgments when auditing financial data and information is well established in the auditing literature (Koonce1993, p559]. To facilitate coordination, evaluating agents should communicate their findings via a communication protocol. Communication protocol establishes the means and modes of communication between agents. Information exchange can be either via an implicit communication mechanism such as a common memory or blackboard, or via explicit communication mechanisms such as message sending. Using the blackboard approach, the SNCE's details plus the evaluating agents' assumptions and results are posted. This facilitates more senior agents' imposing their criteria on lesser agents' results, as well as using their task specific criteria to further refine the classifications.

AR-TAM Implementation

The technology used to develop the AR-TAM model uses a novel combination of existing proven object oriented, fuzzy expert systems using prototypical templates and database technologies. The components of the system include the databases, the graphic user interfaces (GUIs) for human agents, expert systems technologies, and communication and coordination protocols. Application domains currently being researched include monitoring (surveillance) systems such as surveillance telemetry, machine performance monitoring, targeting, broad area surveillance, sensor outputs and fraud monitoring. The primary monitoring systems produce alarms, some true alarms and some false. These alerts must be verified and substantiated in order to reduce the analyst's workload and allocate resources judiciously. In order to verify the true alarms, the false alarms need to be identified. AR-TAM analyses all alarms produced by the monitoring systems and identifies, verifies, substantiates and categorises these alarms, generating prioritised actionable codes indicating what further actions need to be taken. It also records audit trails of the alarm details and their identification, verification, substantiation and categorisation. This information is encapsulated and associated with the original alarm and its source.

Applying the AR-TAM technology to existing monitoring infrastructure requires application specific middleware to retrieve monitoring system output and access to reference databases; input interfaces; alarm categories and types; information used to verify the alarm; classifications of alerts and actions to be taken; knowledge acquisition (i.e. analysts' check lists and procedure manuals) of verification procedures (i.e. threat matrix verification); user interfaces; communication and coordination procedures applied to protocol; output specifications and interfaces; and cost functions if required.

Human analysts are used by AR-TAM as evaluating agents; however, if human judgment has been previously recorded (as in policy guidelines, check lists, meta rules, past cases or human judgment recorded in a distributed environment by on-the-spot human intel), then humans may be replaced by machine agents.

General Description of the Model Behaviour

The compliance analyst's primary goal is to evaluate all possible information that can repudiate the hypothesis of non-compliance. AR-TAM operationalises this goal by developing a set of appropriate environmental and alarm specific propositions derived from the premise set associated with the SNCE case under review, the analyst's default assumptions (the Relevance Measures - RMs) and the analyst's environmental and event specific assumptions (the Linguistic Variables – LV associated with a positive response to the cues).

The first step is the retrieval of the SNCE hypothesis. Control rules on the blackboard retrieve this hypothesis from the output of the primary monitoring system. Based on the alarm type, the blackboard meta rules then select the Boolean cues appropriate to this alarm type. The hypothesis is screened for plausibility by using the positive Boolean responses attached to these metrics and associated linguistic variables. The linguistic variables metrics are elicited from the analysts at run time and used to adjust the relevance measures to produce the adjusted evidence at the atomic level. These evidence measures are then combined to form evidence chunks which are further combined to produce a feasible alarm classification. The classification's evidence values are then ranked, and the results summarised. The outcome is the alarm classification plus supporting evidence. This outcome and the updated coordination knowledge are then posted on the blackboard to facilitate review.

The goal of the AR-TAM system is to:

- Identify false alarm sets
- Verify true alarm landscapes and context
- Generate prioritised actionable indicators, and
- Provide an audit trail

AR-TAM Objectives

The AR-TAM model supports the surveillance decision makers, by augmenting the functionality of the monitoring system architecture in order to facilitate:

1. Operator, analyst and supervisor judgment – when necessary.
2. Fulfilling the necessary and sufficient conditions verifying true positive alerts and identifying and verifying the false alerts.
3. Management of alert knowledge by encapsulating and recording the alerts with all their associated details. This includes the initial as well as 'in-process' details relating to the alert and its analysis.
4. Inheritance of operating environment, regulatory, supervisory and business rules as well as computational methods, knowledge and data from the control blackboard at the local level or higher in the organisation, to allow for assumption based truth maintenance. This ensures all decisions comply with management constraints and assumptions (keeping everyone on the same page).
5. A double weighting technique allowing for a relevance measure relating to the degree of relevance associated with each atomic condition (piece of data or information, in context). This measure is then weighted by a 'level of importance': i.e. how important this data/information is in relation to the observed condition at the atomic level. This second weight is part of the operators, analysts, and supervisor judgment component.
6. Use of prototypical templates updatable directly or via inheritance.
7. Use of previous alert classification knowledge (from knowledge repository to minimise alert reporting (time and context sensitive) and therefore reducing 'alert information overload'.
8. Speeding up the assessment process, therefore reducing the risk exposure time
9. Assessment of both the alert specific details as well as relevant operating environment details i.e. the environment in which the alert occurred.

CONCLUSION

AR-TAM operates in highly complex environments. Domains where the threshold granularity is high and the decision-making time factor is short may benefit from the decision support discussed. It is essential for accountability that organisations in these domains ensure transactions identified as suspected NCE are scrutinised and substantiated. This assists in minimising false positive conclusions that may result from the speed, volume and increased complexity of transactions, and from the information used to analyse them. AR-TAM also addresses the danger of drawing misleading conclusions from that electronic monitoring of data related to individuals and groups of individuals. Assurance and compliance monitoring team infrastructure support includes aspects of information systems, cognitive sciences, decision support and auditing judgment. Fuzzy set theory is advocated in decision environments where there may be a high degree of uncertainty and ambiguity, catering for qualitative and quantitative evidence validating and assuring the assertion of non-compliance.

The AR-TAM system technology verifies the necessary and sufficient conditions supporting or refuting positive alarms and optimises the actionable response – in context with the generated alarms and their environment. This is accomplished using business rules and a template-based, multi-agent tool that assists operators, analysts and supervisors to manage the large volumes of data generated within the existing monitoring infrastructure. The system accumulates alarm specific and alarm environmental information appropriate to the generated alarm, generates prioritised actionable indicators, and supports supervising analysts in assessing the actionable priorities when assessing these alarms. The technology also provides for the analyst's judgment when assessing alarms; a horizontal team decision support environment; and an audit trail of decisions; and it supports a drill down for vertical (hierarchical) review facility.

Current research efforts in monitoring and assurance systems, for example, still concentrate on improving the efficiency and accuracy of primary monitoring systems. Whilst this is necessary, further research opportunities exist in addressing and improving the utility and effectiveness of supporting the community of practice responsible for evaluating and responding to the results of these primary systems and ensuring their accountability, transparency, reliability, and accuracy. Motivations for this research includes improving overall surveillance operations, reducing the time to remedial action, and to reduce some of the misgivings about monitoring systems noted by Bohn et al. and Gabriel.

REFERENCES

Abdi, H. (2007). Signal detection theory. In Salkind, N. J. (Ed.), *Encyclopaedia of measurements and statistics*. Thousand Oaks, CA: Sage.

Alter, S. (2006). *The work system method: Connecting people, processes, and IT for business*. Larkspur, CA: Work System Press.

Bohn, J., Coroama, V., Langheinrich, M., Mattern, M., & Rohs, M. (2004) Social, economic, and ethical implications of ambient intelligence and ubiquitous computing. In E. Aarts, W. Weber & J. Rabaey (Eds.), *Ambient intelligence*. Springer-Verlag.

Boyd, J. R. (1976). An organic design for command and control. In Boyd, J. R. (Ed.), *A discourse on winning and losing. Unpublished lecture notes*.

Clarke, R. (1988). Information Technology and dataveillance. *Communications of the ACM, 31*(5), 498–512. doi:10.1145/42411.42413

Davis, S., & Ord, K. (1990). Improving and measuring the performance of a security industry surveillance system. *Interfaces, 20*(5), 31–42. doi:10.1287/inte.20.5.31

Freedman, R., & Mathai, J. (1995). Market analysis for risk management and regulation: An artificial intelligence approach. In Freedman, R., Klein, R., & Lederman, J. (Eds.), *Artificial intelligence in the capital market* (pp. 315–326). Chicago, IL: Probus Publishing.

Freedman, R., & Stuzin, G. J. (1991). Knowledge-based methodology for tuning analytical models. *IEEE Transactions on Systems, Man, and Cybernetics, 21*(2), 347–358. doi:10.1109/21.87083

Gabriel, Y. (2003). Glass palaces and glass cages. *Ephemera: Theory & Politics in Organization, 3*(3), 166-184. Retrieved from http://www.ephemeraweb.org/journal/3-3/3-3gabriel.pdf

Goldschmidt, P. (2007). Managing the false alarms: A framework for assurance and verification of surveillance monitoring. *Information Systems Frontiers: A Journal of Research and Innovation. Special Issue on Secure Knowledge Management, 9*(5), 541–556.

Green, D. M., & Swets, J. A. (1966). *Signal detection theory and Pscyhophysics*. New York, NY: Wiley.

Kahneman, D. (1973). *Attention and effort*. Englewood Cliffs, NJ: Prentice Hall.

Koonce, L. (1993). A cognitive characterisation of audit analytical review. *Auditing: A Journal of Practice and Theory*, 12(supplement), 57–76.

Libby, R. (1985). Availability and the generation of hypotheses in analytical review. *Journal of Accounting Research*, *23*(2), 648–667. doi:10.2307/2490831

Libby, R., & Trotman, K. (1993). The review process as a control for differential recall of evidence in auditor judgments. *Accounting, Organizations and Society*, *18*(6), 559–574. doi:10.1016/0361-3682(93)90003-O

Marx, G. (2002). What's new about the 'new surveillance'? Classifying for change and continuity. *Surveillance & Society*, *1*(1), 8–29.

Pete, A., Kleinman, D., & Pattipati, K. (1993). Tasks and organisational signal detection model of organisational decision making. *Intelligent Systems in Accounting. Financial Management*, *2*(4), 289–303.

Pindyck, R., & Rubinfeld, D. L. (1976). *Econometric models and economic forecasts*. Ne York, NY: McGraw-Hill.

Pope, K. S., & Serger, J. L. (1978). *The stream of consciousness: Scientific investigations into the flow of human experience*. New York, NY: Plenum Press.

Simon, H. (1973). The structure of ill structured problems. *Artificial Intelligence*, *4*(3–4), 181–201. doi:10.1016/0004-3702(73)90011-8

Sol, H. (1982). *Simulation in Information Systems development*. PhD dissertation, University of Groningen, The Netherlands.

Surveillance Studies Network. (2011). *Surveillance & Society*. ISSN 1477-7487

William, H., Starbuck, F., & Milliken, J. (1998). Challenger: Fine-tuning the odds until something breaks. *Journal of Management Studies*, *25*(4), 319–340.

ADDITIONAL READING

Busby, J., & Strutt, J. (2001). *What Limits the Ability of Design Organizations to Predict Failure?* Proceedings of the Institution of Mechanical Engineers (215) Part B: 1471-4. Clarke, R. http://www.rogerclarke.com/DV/

Chang, A., Bailey, A. Jr, & Whinston, A. (1993). Multi-auditor Cooperation: A Model of Distributed Reasoning. *IEEE Transactions on Engineering Management*, *20*(4), 346–359. doi:10.1109/17.257727

de Kleer, J. (1986). An assumption based truth maintenance system. *Artificial Intelligence*, *28*(2), 127–162. doi:10.1016/0004-3702(86)90080-9

Denning, D. (2006). Dorothy Denning's Home Page. Retrieved from http://www.cs.georgetown.edu/~denning/index.html.

FBI. (1999). *Digital storm*. FBI Annual Report. Retrieved www.fbi.gov/programs/lab/labannual99.pdf.

Howorka, G. V., Anderson, L. A., Goul, K. M., & Hine, M. (1995). *A Computational Model Of Coordination for the Design of Organisational Decision Support Systems*. Intelligent Systems in Accounting. *Financial Management*, *4*(1), 43–70.

Jacob, V., & Pirkul, H. (1992). A Framework for Supporting Distributed Group Decision-Making. *Decision Support Systems*, *8*(1), 17–28. doi:10.1016/0167-9236(92)90034-M

Jin, Y., & Levitt, R. E. (1993). *i-Agents: Modeling Organisational Problem Solving in Multi-Agent Teams*. Intelligent Systems in Accounting. *Financial Management*, *2*(4), 247–270.

Pieters, R., & Zeelenberg, M. (2005). On Bad Decisions and Deciding Badly: When Intention-Behavior Inconsistency is Regrettable. *Journal of Organizational Behavior and Human Decision Processes*, *97*(1), 18–30. doi:10.1016/j.obhdp.2005.01.003

Starbuck, W., & Milliken, F. (1988). Challenger: Fine-Tuning the Odds Until Something Breaks. *Journal of Management Studies*, *25*(4), 319–340. doi:10.1111/j.1467-6486.1988.tb00040.x

Weaver, E., & Richardson, G. (2006). Threshold Setting and the Cycling of a Decision Threshold. *System Dynamics Review*, *2*(1), 1–26. doi:10.1002/sdr.327

KEY TERMS AND DEFINITIONS

Compliance Monitoring Verification: The accumulation and verification of the necessary and sufficient evidence supporting or refuting an alarm generated by monitoring activities.

Dataveillance: See http://www.rogerclarke.com/DV/.

Secondary Monitoring: The monitoring and analysis of the alarms generated by monitoring activities.

Surveillance Thresholds: The bounds (upper and lower) which triggers alarms when breached.

Uberveillance: Omnipresent 24/7 electronic surveillance. - Surveillance that is always on and always with you, referring to a surveillance technology that is embedded within the human body.

ENDNOTE

Alert-KM Pty Ltd. holds exclusive intellectual property rights to the AR-TAM and CMAD business process methods. This IP is covered full patents for Australian 758491, Singapore, 200106150-6, USA, 6,983,266, patent pending Hong Kong 02106820.1; Canada 2,366,548, EU Patent Cooperative Treaty International Application No. PCTAU00/00295(19 countries).

Chapter 11
Not Every Cloud Brings Rain:
Legal Risks on the Horizon

Sylvia Kierkegaard
International Association of IT Lawyers, Denmark

ABSTRACT

The promise of a utility-based IT service delivery model is well understood and highly desirable. Moving towards cloud-based computing is emerging and gaining acceptance as a solution to the tasks related to the processing of information. Cloud computing promises a single portal view to better manage email, archiving, and records retention. However while cloud computing certainly brings efficiencies, it is still immature and carries serious risks to business information. The questions around risk and compliance are still largely unknown and need to be ironed out. Cloud computing opens numerous legal, privacy, and security implications, such as copyright, data loss, destruction of data, identity theft, third-party contractual limitations, e-discovery, risk/insurance allocation, and jurisdictional issues. This chapter will provide an overview and discuss the associated legal risks inherent in cloud computing, in particular the international data transfer between the EU and non- EU states.

INTRODUCTION

Information is the heart and soul of many businesses. The information that companies generate and share are generating a wealth of benefits. E-mail, social media, mobile phones, drop boxes, increased internet devices and broadband connections have enabled businesses and consumers to exchange high data volumes and files everywhere and over vast networks with high speed communication.

Information is now available and shared to an extent almost unimaginable 5 years ago due to the increasing digitization and modern technology. At the same, it has caused organizations to struggle with the high volumes and diversities of information and seek solutions to manage the

DOI: 10.4018/978-1-4666-0197-0.ch011

information and to reduce cost through effective information governance.

Information Governance (Info Governance) is the specification of decision rights and an accountability framework to encourage desirable behavior in the valuation, creation, storage, usage, archiving and deletion of information. It includes the processes, roles, standards and metrics that ensure the effective and efficient use of information to enable an organization to achieve its goals. (Logan, 2009) These include the management of information securely, efficiently and effectively-*what information is retained, where and for how long, and how it is retained (e.g., protected, replicated and secured), who has access to it and how the polices are enforced.* They encompass not only suitable policies, accountability, and procedures but also the technology to create a solid governance framework. Unmanaged and inconsistently managed information increases risk and cost.

Information technology officers are looking for technologies that will help them focus more on the benefits to the organization, which can bring institutional agility, flexibility and cost saving. Moving towards cloud-based computing is emerging and gaining acceptance as a solution to the tasks related to the processing of information. Cloud promises a single portal view to better manage email, archiving, and records retention (etc). Since web 2.0, "*cloud computing*" has been the buzz word in the IT industry. Cloud advocates argue that implementing any form of IT or information governance is far easier and far more effective in a fully-virtualized private cloud model than in the traditional, physical IT world.

The promise of a utility-based IT service delivery model is well understood and highly desirable. However while cloud computing certainly brings efficiencies, it is still immature and carries serious risks to business information. The questions around risk and compliance are still largely unknown and need to be ironed out.

The European Union is addressing the challenges concerning the threat to information security specific to cloud computing through several measures. This article will provide an overview of cloud computing and discuss the current and emerging legal risks and emerging legal issues for businesses using cloud computing.

CLOUD COMPUTING: ONCE UPON A TIME

"Cloud" is a metaphor for the Internet. Thus, cloud computing is the usage of the Internet as a computing infrastructure and resource. The idea of computation being delivered in public space was proposed by computer scientist John MacCarthy who proposed the idea of computation being delivered in public space. In 2006, Eric Schmidt of Google described their approach to Software as Service (SaaS) as cloud computing at the Search Engine Strategies Conference. (Google Press Center, 2006) Amazon included the word "cloud" in EC2 (Elastic Compute Cloud) when it was launched a few weeks later.

Cloud Computing found its origin in the success of server virtualization and the possibilities to run IT more efficiently through server consolidation. Soon, visionaries came up with idea to bring virtualization to a next level by implementing some early storage and network virtualization techniques and thus making abstraction of the hardware in the entire data center. Add to this self-provisioning and auto scaling, and cloud computing was born. (Leyden, 2009) The most important contribution to cloud computing has been the emergence of "killer apps" that provided access to large bodies of map data. In 2009, as Web 2.0 hit its stride, Google and Microsoft, among others, formalized the Application Programming Interfaces (APIs). Mashups exploded and everyone sat up and took notice of the opportunities for innovation bootstrapped upon the shared capabilities of Google's code and servers, and the underlying data licensed by Google. (Miller, 2008)

The key aspect of cloud computing is that the users do not have or need to have the knowledge, control or ownership of the computer and network infrastructure. The users just simply access the software or service they require to use and pay for what they use. Therefore, "in cloud-service engagements, buyers [users] only need to care about the service [level or quality] without worrying about its implementation. (Khan, 2009) Because cloud computing services are available at all times, they solve the problem of intermittent availability of applications. Cloud computing services allow users to store their data and their applications on networked servers rather than on local computers and data centers. They do not require software that sits on a PC or laptop, other than an Internet connection and a Web browser. These companies are finding that cloud computing can provide power, low costs, functionality and flexibility. Mobility workers can access their applications and data from multiple locations, such as offices, home computers, client sites, airports, and smart phones. (Stroh, et al, 2009) Cloud computing, virtualization and mobility all entered the limelight because of the net savings they represent.

Cloud Computing Defined

With an ever-growing list of cloud computing service providers and emerging applications, there abounds so many definitions flying around that it has been a struggle to find a common definition of cloud computing. How does one define this infrastructural paradigm shift that is sweeping across the enterprise IT world?

Cloud computing is loosely defined as an Internet – based development and use of computer technology. As its name suggests, data is stored in "the clouds" and the programs that run it are in the "cloud" (or the Internet). The concept is not new - Active Server Pages (ASPs), outsourcing, Web site hosting and browser-based applications are all forms of cloud computing. A similar model, known as Software as a Service (SaaS), is already popular among large companies. What probably differ are the strata of services that cloud computing offers and that the data and the programs no longer live on the computer. The main philosophy of cloud computing is to provide every required things as a service.

Cloud Computing is a paradigm that is composed of several strata of services. These include services like Infrastructure as a Service, Storage as a Service, Platform as a Service and Software as a Service. The main goal of cloud computing is to provide ICT services with shared infrastructure and the collection of many systems. In cloud computing every facility is provided in terms of service in the cloud, which can be perceived as a layer of architecture offering numerous resources in different layers. It assumes that the hardware, software and data storage are stored in cyberspace (cloud) instead of residing on desktop or internal servers. The objective of outsourcing in the clouds is to free up company resources, and minimize costs. Companies pay only for the amount of services they use.

In cloud computing, the Internet is used to provide utility computing services and platforms, as well as a collection of computing software and services that can be accessed via the Internet. These ICT services include data storage, software applications, and email and file exchanges with shared infrastructure and the collection of many systems.

A report from the European Union on cloud computing has proposed a standard definition of the concept: A cloud, the report asserts, is an "elastic execution environment of resources involving multiple stakeholders and providing a metered service at multiple granularities for a specified level of quality (of service)." (Jeffrey et al, 2010) The Report also states that clouds do not refer to a specific technology, but to a general provisioning paradigm with enhanced capabilities.

Among the functional characteristics of a compute cloud, as identified by the report, are 'elasticity', 'reliability' and 'availability'.

The US National Institute of Standards and Technology (NIST, 2009) offers a more specific and lengthy definition. It defines cloud computing as:

Cloud computing is a model for enabling convenient, on-demand network access to a shared pool of configurable computing resources (e.g., networks, servers, storage, applications, and services) that can be rapidly provisioned and released with minimal management effort or service provider interaction. This cloud model promotes availability and is composed of five essential characteristics**,** *three* service models, *and four* deployment models.

The NIST describes the characteristics as follows:

- **Essential Characteristics:**
    - *On-demand self-service.* A consumer can unilaterally provision computing capabilities, such as server time and network storage, as needed automatically without requiring human interaction with each service's provider.
    - *Broad network access.* Capabilities are available over the network and accessed through standard mechanisms that promote use by heterogeneous thin or thick client platforms (e.g., mobile phones, laptops, and PDAs).
    - *Resource pooling.* The provider's computing resources are pooled to serve multiple consumers using a multi-tenant model, with different physical and virtual resources dynamically assigned and reassigned according to consumer demand. There is a sense of location independence in that the customer generally has no control or knowledge over the exact location of the provided resources but may be able to specify location at a higher level of abstraction (e.g., country, state, or datacenter). Examples of resources include storage, processing, memory, network bandwidth, and virtual machines.
    - *Rapid elasticity.* Capabilities can be rapidly and elastically provisioned, in some cases automatically, to quickly scale out and rapidly released to quickly scale in. To the consumer, the capabilities available for provisioning often appear to be unlimited and can be purchased in any quantity at any time.
    - *Measured Service.* Cloud systems automatically control and optimize resource use by leveraging a metering capability at some level of abstraction appropriate to the type of service (e.g., storage, processing, bandwidth, and active user accounts). Resource usage can be monitored, controlled, and reported providing transparency for both the provider and consumer of the utilized service.
- **Service Models:**
    - *Cloud Software as a Service (SaaS).* The capability provided to the consumer is to use the provider's applications running on a cloud infrastructure. The applications are accessible from various client devices through a thin client interface such as a web browser (e.g., web-based email). The consumer does not manage or control the underlying cloud infrastructure including network, servers, operating systems, storage, or even individual application capabilities, with the possible exception of limited user-specific application configuration settings.

    - *Cloud Platform as a Service (PaaS).* The capability provided to the consumer is to deploy onto the cloud infrastructure consumer-created or acquired applications created using programming languages and tools supported by the provider. The consumer does not manage or control the underlying cloud infrastructure including network, servers, operating systems, or storage, but has control over the deployed applications and possibly application hosting environment configurations.
    - *Cloud Infrastructure as a Service (IaaS).* The capability provided to the consumer is to provision processing, storage, networks, and other fundamental computing resources where the consumer is able to deploy and run arbitrary software, which can include operating systems and applications. The consumer does not manage or control the underlying cloud infrastructure but has control over operating systems, storage, deployed applications and possibly limited control of select networking components (e.g., host firewalls).
- **Deployment Models:**
    - *Private cloud.* The cloud infrastructure is operated solely for an organization. It may be managed by the organization or a third party and may exist on premise or off premise.
    - *Community cloud.* The cloud infrastructure is shared by several organizations and supports a specific community that has shared concerns (e.g., mission, security requirements, policy, and compliance considerations). It may be managed by the organizations or a third party and may exist on premise or off premise.
    - *Public cloud.* The cloud infrastructure is made available to the general public or a large industry group and is owned by an organization selling cloud services.
    - *Hybrid cloud.* The cloud infrastructure is a composition of two or more clouds (private, community, or public) that remain unique entities but are bound together by standardized or proprietary technology that enables data and application portability (e.g., cloud bursting for load-balancing between clouds).

Cloud Computing market is typically segmented according to the following:

- Public cloud (services offered over the internet) is a cloud computing environment that is open for use to the general public, whether individuals, corporations or other types of organizations. Amazon Web Services are an example of a public cloud.
- Private cloud (internal enterprise) is a cloud computing-like environment within the boundaries of an organization and typically for its exclusive usage.
- Hybrid cloud (a mix of both) is a computing environment combining both private (internal) and public (external) cloud computing environments. May either be on a continuous basis or in the form of a 'cloudburst'.

LEGAL RISKS

Cloud computing generally refers to providing access to computer software through an Internet browser, with the software and data stored at a remote location at a "data center" or "server farm," instead of residing on the computers' hard drive or on a server located on the user's premises.

Basically, the data created and managed by these services are stored offsite, in the "cloud and managed by private firms that provide remote access through web-based device. Although the cost benefits of moving from traditional IT structures to the cloud are often clear, there are issues that corporations need to consider when making the switch to the cloud model. Cloud computing opens numerous legal, privacy and security implications, such as copyright, data loss, destruction of data, identity theft, third-party contractual limitations, e-discovery, risk/insurance allocation and jurisdictional issues. For example, the data which is the subject of litigation may not be accessible by the provider, leading to spoliation of evidence. Some of the key security issues in cloud computing are:

- Who has access to facilities to data
- What happens to data in the event of a disaster and intrusion
- What happens to data if company goes bankrupt
- Insurance or liability coverage- will they handle claims of privacy breaches and hacking?
- What restrictions on cross border data transfer?
- Where will the data be stored?
- Where are the servers?
- What kind of data will be in the cloud?
- Where do the data subjects reside?
- Where will the data be stored?

Contract Issues

Cloud computing services generally provide the users a standard contract with weak obligations. Many of them are one sided contracts, which disclaim liability, offer no warranties and impose responsibility on the users for issues like data location or disaster recovery. Some of the contracts often lack contingency plans for what would happen if one or more of the companies involved suffer a disruption or data breach. The language is often ambiguous and does not define how data will be handled and encrypted. In some cloud agreements, a vendor's maximum liability is relatively small, frequently limited to fees paid in a one- or two-month subscription period or none at all. For example, the terms of service for google apps are:

GOOGLE AND PARTNERS DO NOT WARRANT THAT

(i) GOOGLE SERVICES WILL MEET YOUR REQUIREMENTS,

(ii) GOOGLE SERVICES WILL BE UNINTERRUPTED, TIMELY, SECURE, OR ERROR-FREE,

(iii) THE RESULTS THAT MAY BE OBTAINED FROM THE USE OF GOOGLE SERVICES WILL BE ACCURATE OR RELIABLE,

(iv) THEQUALITYOFANYPRODUCTS, SERVICES, INFORMATION, OR OTHER MATERIAL PURCHASED OROBTAINEDBYYOUTHROUGH GOOGLE SERVICES WILL MEET YOUR EXPECTATIONS ()

(Source: http://www.google.com/apps/intl/en/terms/user_terms.htm)

These disclaimers are actually ineffective against statutory liabilities, especially when they are not in conformity with consumer protection or product liability. Even in a business-to-business context, cloud providers may not be able to exclude all risk relating to service interruptions or data loss. Liability arises for negligence and other forms of product liability.

Under international law, specifically Article 35 of the UN Convention on International Sales of Goods (CISG)," sellers are liable for any lack of conformity of the goods with the contract." The "*as is*" warranties in the imposed standard form can be challenged under the EU Unfair Contract Terms Directive 93/13/EEC, which imposes limits in the kind of terms and conditions particularly in relations to exclusions of liability. "*As is*" warranties are services/goods provided as they are without any promise of being suitable or attaining a certain level of performance. In the US, such onerous contractual terms could be considered "unconscionable."

Aside from the default position contained in the standard form, cloud agreements fail to include terms relating to compliance with export of personal data to other countries, privacy laws, back-up schedules, vendor's disaster recovery plan and data recovery responsibilities. Other limitations include the following:

- Customer unable to decrease the number of users during a subscription term;
- Remedies for breach of a limited warranty restricted to termination and refund of prepaid unused fees;
- Supplier to delete all customer data after 30 days after termination, unless a request for such data is made within such time period by the customer.

Data Protection

In a cloud agreement, the vendor normally provides the hardware infrastructure, the operating system, the application, and the backup service. Hardware and software are no longer procured and operated by users themselves but obtained as services. Documents, e-mails and other data will be stored on-line, "in the cloud", making them accessible from any PC or mobile device. To provide these resources, providers often rely on other cloud providers for storage or computer capacity. This means that many third parties may access the data across a number of jurisdictions. In many instances, the storage location of the data is not disclosed and the consumer is not aware where the processing takes place. The co-location and virtual software segregation of resources raise serious concerns about data leakage due to misconfiguration, software failure or exploited hypervisor vulnerabilities where virtualized. (ENISA, 2010)

When users release the data in the cloud, they might "not even "own them unless it has been stipulated in the Service Agreements. The client cedes control of his documents. In many cases, the cloud provider does not provide sufficient and adequate information on their data handling practices. Cloud providers have tended to forgo strong security solutions. In cases where there are multiple transfers of data, the data protection risk is exacerbated.

The security risk is further aggravated when the provider is changed. Cloud services are frequently offered through third-party providers that may have little ability or leverage to alter the security practices of the data centers from whom they are acquiring cloud resources, and are therefore unable to offer similar protections to their customers. (Bennet, 2010)

Since data generally has to be unencrypted at the point of processing, this means that if it is processed using cloud computing, it will generally be present in unencrypted form on a machine in the service provider's or subcontractor's network. There is therefore a risk of data security breaches, data loss and destruction, as well as dangers of theft or sabotage by a rogue employee of the service provider or subcontractor. (Mowbray, 2009)

Because most cloud services on a given server are shared between multiple organizations, full or timely deletion of data may be impossible because the disk to be destroyed also store data from other clients. In some instances, extra copies of data may not be available. For users who subscribe to cloud providers without effective encryption, the security risk is higher.

Compounding the problem is the lack of harmonized data retention period in different jurisdictions. How long are certain data being kept? Countries that are part of the European Union are bound by EC Directives, but their interpretation of these rules is often inconsistent. In the European Union, the Data Retention Directive 2006/24/EC allows the member states to retain data between 6 and 24 months. Under the Directive, authorities can request access to details such as IP address and time of use of every e-mail, phone call and text message sent or received. Member States have different retention times with Italy having the shortest retention period. Legislation also imposes different retention period for different types of data - employment records, tax records, health and safety files-posing more problems for the companies.

Data located in particular jurisdictions may be subject to disclosure through extensive government surveillance. For example, US Federal District Court Judge Michael Mosman ruled on June 23, 2009 (Nos. 08-9131-MC, 08-9147-MC) that e-mail should not be afforded the same protection against unlawful searches and seizures under the Fourth Amendment. Mosman declared that people who send emails cannot expect to have the same level of privacy as when one sends a regular piece of mail through the post office. Thus, the police can serve the ISP providers with a search warrant and get the information turned over without notifying an e-mail account holder. Mosman reasoned that when we send e-mails and instant messages, they travel from computer to computer and are "stored "by ISP providers. Therefore, when the government obtains the e-mail of the account holder and reads it, it does not have to inform the user that it has done this. It has only to tell the internet service provider - that a search and seizure of the "papers and effects" has taken place. The lack of adequate data protection in many countries and the intrusion powers of government agencies threaten the confidentiality and privacy of data stored in the clouds. Cloud users do not have the confidence that as their data moves from the desktop to the cloud, it will stay private and secure.

Finally, not all cloud services are created equal. Some are more robust than the others. If a cloud vendor goes bankrupt, there is a serious possibility that the customer will lose access to the IT resources – hardware and software and copy of their data, especially when the cloud provider did not have adequate backup procedures.

Transborder Transfer in the EU

Cloud computing allows the constant flow of data between the user's computer and multiple cloud servers located around the world creating conflicting legal obligations. Most likely, personal data may be sent to multiple servers worldwide. From a legal standpoint, different legal rules will apply depending on where the data is or has been and what country has jurisdiction over these data.

The European Data Protection Directive 95/46 regulates the processing of personal data within the European Union and imposes wide ranging obligations regarding the collection, storage and use of personal information. The Directive primarily regulates data controllers. A *controller* is defined in Article 2 of the Directive as the natural or legal person or public agency that "alone or jointly with others" determines "the purposes and means of processing" personal data. A *processor* is a natural or legal person or agency that processes data on behalf of a controller. "Processing" is defined very broadly in the Directive to include collection, use, storage, manipulation, disclosure, disposal, and virtually any other action with personal data.

The Directive applies to a cloud provider established in the EU or acting as processor for a controller established in the EU, as well as a provider which uses equipment (such as servers) in an EU Member State or acting as processor for a controller using such equipment. Under Article 17 of the EU Data Protection Directive 95/46, data controllers must implement appropriate technical and organizational measures to protect personal data against(1) accidental or unlawful destruction or loss; (2) unauthorized alteration, disclosure or access (in particular where the processing involves the transmission of data over a network); and (3) all other unlawful forms of processing. The Directive applies to all personal data that fall within the scope of EU jurisdiction regardless of where the data are processed. Article 6 of the Directive requires data controllers to process personal data for purposes compatible with those for which it was initially collected. In the context of cloud computing, this should deter controllers from using information for incompatible purposes.

However, Article 3 excludes from the scope of application of the Directive data processing carried out "by natural persons in the course of a purely personal or household activity" (the 'household exception'). If the information uploaded to the cloud is not covered by the Directive because it is information of a personal nature, then the processing activities that are carried out on behalf of the individuals involved might not be covered either. Therefore cloud providing services will not be caught by the Directive if the processing service is carried out on behalf of end users acting in their personal capacity.

The Directive also imposes an obligation on companies not to transfer personal data from their operations within the European Economic Area (EEA) in the United States (and other places outside the EEA) unless the recipient in the non-EEA country provides "an adequate level of protection".

Under Article 25(1) the Directive permits the transfer of personal data outside of the EU:

The Member States shall provide that the transfer to a third country of personal data which are undergoing processing or are intended for processing after transfer may take place only if, without prejudice to compliance with the national provisions adopted pursuant to the other provisions of this Directive, the third country in question ensures an adequate level of protection.

The transfer of data to a country that is considered not adequate maybe authorized provided that the data controller obtains the consent of the data subject. However, obtaining freely given, specific and informed consent from each data subject would be burdensome. Furthermore, individuals have a fundamental right under European Union data protection law to access, block, rectify or delete their personal data. It may be difficult to effectively manage this right in a cloud computing infrastructure.

If the importing country does not ensure an adequate level of protection, the Directive contemplates further *means* by which personal data may be transferred aside from the data subject's consent. These *means* include the derogations in Article 26.

(b) the transfer is necessary for the performance of a contract between the data subject and the controller or the implementation of precontractual measures taken in response to the data subject's request; or
(c) the transfer is necessary for the conclusion or performance of a contract concluded in the interest of the data subject between the controller and a third party; or
(d) the transfer is necessary or legally required on important public interest grounds, or for the establishment, exercise or defence of legal claims; or
(e) the transfer is necessary in order to protect the vital interests of the data subject; or
(f) the transfer is made from a register which according to laws or regulations is intended to provide information to the public and which is open to consultation either by the public in general or by any person who can demonstrate legitimate interest, to the extent that the conditions laid down in law for consultation are fulfilled in the particular case.

These exceptions are mandatory.

The transfer of personal data to a third country that does not ensure an adequate level of protection requires an authorisation by the Commissioner. In order to approve the transfer, the Commissioner must at least be satisfied that the controller has provided adequate safeguards, particularly by means of appropriate contractual provisions in accordance with the proviso of Article 28(3) of the Data Protection Act.

Data controller can adduce safeguards through the following:

1. International Safe Harbor Certification
2. Binding Corporate Rules
3. Model contracts

However, the data protection authority of the German federal state of Schleswig-Holstein is of the opinion that " clouds located outside the European Union are *per se* unlawful, even if the EU Commission has issued an adequacy decision in favor of the foreign country in question (for example, Switzerland, Canada or Argentina). A Commission adequacy decision does not confer "agent" status, which normally would privilege such transfers, on entities located in the adequate jurisdiction. The recipient entities remain "third parties" which means that a transfer in the legal sense takes place and therefore a legal basis is required. The potential legal basis, for example, under German law ("fulfillment of contract" or "balancing of interests test") requires that the transfer is also "necessary." The DPA is of the opinion that there are no arguments that the use of a cloud located outside the EU is compulsory. (Press Release & Comprehensive Legal Opinion, 2008)

Safe Harbor Certification

US companies may comply either by participating in the Safe Harbor scheme administered by the US Department of Commerce. US companies that participate in the International Safe Harbor Certification, which allows data transfer from the EU to the US (but not from the EU to other countries), are considered as offering adequate data protection and data flows to those companies will continue. An EU organization can ensure that it is sending information to a U.S. organization participating in the safe harbor by viewing the public list of safe harbor organizations posted on https://www.export.gov/safehrbr/list.aspx. Claims brought by European citizens against U.S. companies will be heard in the U.S. subject to limited exceptions.

To qualify for the safe harbor, an organization can (1) join a self-regulatory privacy program that adheres to the safe harbor's requirements; or (2) develop its own self-regulatory privacy policy that conforms to the safe harbor. Organizations must comply with the seven safe harbor principles:

- **Notice:** Organizations must notify individuals about the purposes for which they collect and use information about them.
- **Choice:** Organizations must give individuals the opportunity to choose (opt out) whether their personal information will be disclosed to a third party or used for a purpose incompatible with the purpose for which it was originally collected or subsequently authorized by the individual.
- **Onward Transfer:** To disclose information to a third party, organizations must apply the notice and choice principles.
- **Access:** Individuals must have access to personal information about them that an organization holds and be able to correct, amend, or delete that information where it is inaccurate, except where the burden or expense of providing access would be disproportionate to the risks to the individual's privacy in the case in question, or where the rights of persons other than the individual would be violated.
- **Security:** Organizations must take reasonable precautions to protect personal information from loss, misuse and unauthorized access, disclosure, alteration and destruction.
- **Data integrity:** Personal information must be relevant for the purposes for which it is to be used. An organization should take

reasonable steps to ensure that data is reliable for its intended use, accurate, complete, and current.'

- **Enforcement:** In order to ensure compliance with the safe harbor principles, there must be (a) readily available and affordable independent recourse mechanisms so that each individual's complaints and disputes can be investigated and resolved and damages awarded where the applicable law or private sector initiatives so provide; (b) procedures for verifying that the commitments companies make to adhere to the safe harbor principles have been implemented; and (c) obligations to remedy problems arising out of a failure to comply with the principles.

However, the Data Protection Authority (DPA) issued a recent opinion on June18, 2010 that even self-certification to the U.S. Department of Commerce's Safe Harbor framework alone does not provide an adequate level of protection in the cloud context. Accordingly, reliance on certification to the Safe Harbor should not be used to circumvent the more strict EU legal requirements applicable to cloud computing. In addition, the DPA indicated that, because SAS 70 Type II Certificates used by some cloud providers do not contemplate the material and procedural interests of data subjects, such certifications offer only partial compliance with German legal requirements for commissioned data processing. (Ibid)

Binding Corporate Rules

Binding Corporate Rules (BCRs) are legally binding internal corporate data privacy rules that establish a corporation's practices regarding the transfer of personal information within the corporate group. Binding corporate rules are also an appropriate tool for companies seeking to implement a cloud solution. Under this route, transfers can be made where the organization demonstrates adequate safeguards with respect to the protection of personal data. The Article 29 EU Working Group document effectively endorses this route in principle, whilst also setting out guidance, both as to the content of the binding corporate rules and the procedures for organizations to adopt them. The BCRs are designed for a multinational company and therefore may not function well for cloud provider relationships. In March 2009, the Article 29 working group issued an opinion to update the standard controller-to-processor contract clauses. It identifies controllers as the entities that decide to have some personal data processed for their own purposes. It recognizes that multiple parties (such as a parent company and its affiliates or business partners) may collectively decide which data elements are needed and how they will be handled. They need not have equal voices in those decisions, and their respective responsibility and liability may be limited to their own decisions.

EU Standard Contract Clauses

Where a third country does not ensure an adequate level of protection, Directive 95/46/EC provides that the European Commission may decide that certain standard contractual clauses (SCCS) offer sufficient safeguards for transfers of personal data for the data. Model contracts or EU standard contract clauses (SCCs) allow data transfer from the EU to non-US countries. Unlike the safe harbor, data transfers under SCCs require notification to the data protection authorities in many European countries for each transfer to a country (point to point) where the legal framework is not adequate, as well as a prior approval by the local Data Protection Authorities (DPA).

In practice this is very difficult to implement in cloud computing, which entails the continuous transfer of personal data. Cloud providers are reluctant to make any contractual offer because in many cases they cannot say which countries the data will be transferred to or from. To address this problem, the EU recommends the use of Model Contracts or SCCs.

In 2002, the European Commission passed Decision 2002/87/EU which approved three sets of contractual clauses: two of these sets apply to transfers from data controllers to other data controllers, while the third set has been drafted for transfers from data controllers to recipients who act as data processors only. However, they do not always work well with multi-tiered vendor relationships.

As more and more organizations are transferring personal data to a "processor" but also to one or more "sub-processors" outside the EU/EEA, the original standard contractual clauses were no longer suitable to deal with these complex onward transfers. On 5 February 2010, the European Commission repealed the 2002 "*controller to processor*" standard contractual clauses to take account of the expansion of processing activities and new business models of companies for international processing of personal data. This was implemented on May 15, 2010 when the European Union adopted a new set of SCCs through Commission Decision 2010/87/EU of 5 February 2010 on standard contractual clauses for the transfer of personal data to processors established in third countries under Directive 95/46/EC, which deals with data transfers outside the corporate group or directly from Europe to vendors outside the United States. Under these standard contractual clauses, an EU company exporting data (controller) should instruct its processor established in a third country to treat the data with full respect to the EU data protection requirements and should guarantee that appropriate technical and security measures are in place in the destination country.

According to the newly adopted Commission Decision, where a data processor intends to subcontract any of its processing operations performed on behalf of the EU data controller, it must first obtain the prior written consent of the data controller.The written contract will impose the same obligations on the sub-processor as those imposed on the data processor under the standard contractual clauses. The subcontracting clause therefore provides that the law of the Member State in which the data controller is established also applies to contracts entered into for subcontracting services.

Where the sub-processor fails to fulfill its data protection obligations, the data processor will remain fully liable to the data controller for the performance of the sub-processor's obligations. Moreover the sub-processing shall only consist of the processing operations agreed in the initial contract entered into by the data EU controller and the data processor. The new set of standard contractual clauses only applies to subcontracting by a data processor established outside the EU/EEA of its data processing services to a sub-processor also established outside the EU/EEA. The new clauses do not apply to international sub-processing (outside the EU/EEA) by a processor established in the EU/EEA.

The subcontracting clause also includes specific liability provisions: if the sub-processor fails to fulfill its data protection obligations, the data processor remains fully liable to the data controller for the performance of the sub-processor's contractual obligations. In addition, data subjects are granted a third party beneficiary right against the EU data controller and under some circumstances, against the data processor (*e.g.*, because they have become solvent) in order to ensure the protection of their right.

The new subcontracting clause further includes the possibility for European data protection authorities to audit the full chain of sub-processing and, where appropriate, to take binding decisions on the data controller, processor and sub-processor under the applicable data protection law.

Contracts using the old model clauses can still be used where they were in force before 15 May 2010 and where the transfers and processing activities remain unchanged. However, the new model clauses must be used for any new arrangements from this date or where there are any changes to the processing.

CONCLUSION

The cloud computing model is a wonderful system when it works and a nightmare when it fails. The most worrying aspect of the dark cloud is the numerous legal, privacy and security implications. There is currently little on offer in the way of tools, procedures or standard data formats or services interfaces that could guarantee 100% data protection. It is difficult to determine whether the cloud provider is processing and storing the data lawfully, especially in the case of multiple transfers of data. Not only is there a risk of data security breaches, but cloud customers also lose control of the data processed by the cloud provider.

Regulatory bodies are grappling with the privacy and data security implications of cloud computing. Given the rapidly-evolving legal landscape, venturing into the cloud is a risky matter. The large volume of data transfers carried out on a daily basis, increased outsourcing and the emergence of new business models have opened a pandora box of security nightmares: how to facilitate easier movement of data across borders while maintaining legal protection for consumers. The European Union is trying to close security loopholes and offer best-practice solutions and guidance on governance, standards and compliance. It is trying to develop more balanced and predictable rules to enhance legal certainty. The new binding corporate rule system takes account of the expansion of processing activities and new business models for international processing of personal data, increased outsourcing and cloud computing. It is intended to provide a legitimate and efficient means to transfer personal data.

In contrast, the United States seems to take a lax approach to the principles of privacy and contractual liability. US District Court Judge Michael Mossman ruling as stated below reflects the US government's approach to privacy- the right of government law agencies to read all of the private email stored on the Internet server with only a notice to the Internet/Cloud Service Provider:

"A person uses the Internet, however, the user's actions are no longer in his or her physical home; in fact he or she is not truly acting in private space at all."

Companies seeking to implement cloud computing solutions should proceed with caution and closely monitor global developments. The challenge to companies seeking to implement cloud computing is determining what assurances should be in the contracts and how much risk and liability are being assumed when a service is moved to the 'cloud'. As the adage goes, "caveat emptor."

REFERENCES

Bennet, M. (2010). *Ruumble... Negotiating cloud computing agreements*. Law Technology News.

ENISA. (2010). *Report priorities for research on current and emerging network technologies.* Retrieved from http://www.enisa.europa.eu/act/it/library/deliverables/procent

European Commission. (2010). *Press release and comprehensive legal opinion*. Retrieved from http://ec.europa.eu/justice_home/fsj/privacy/docs/wpdocs/2010/wp169_en.pdf

Google Press Center. (2006). *Conversation with Eric Schmidt hosted by Danny Sullivan.* Search Engine Strategies Conference. Retrieved from http://www.google.com/press/podium/ses2006.html

Jefferey, K., & Neidecker-Lutz, B. (2010). *The future of Cloud Computing*. Cordis. Retrieved from http://cordis.europa.eu/fp7/ict/ssai/docs/cloud-report-final.pdf

Khan, I. (2009). Cloud Computing set to go mainstream. *Outsourcing*, *13*, 30–31.

Leyden, T. (2009). *A brief history of Cloud Computing*. Sys-Con Media. Retrieved from https://tleyden.sys-con.com/node/1150011

Logan, D. (2009). *Hype cycle for legal and regulatory information governance*. Gartner. Retrieved from http://www.gartner.com/DisplayDocument?doc_cd=208630&ref=g_rss

Mell, P., & Grance, T. (2009). *The NIST definition of Cloud Computing*. NIST.

Miller, P. (2008). *Everywhere I look I see clouds*. ZD Net. Retrieved from http://www.zdnet.com/blog/semantic-web/everywhere-i-look-i-see-clouds/179

Mowbray, M. (2009). *The fog over the Grimpen Mire: Cloud Computing and the law*. HP Laboratory.

Stroh, S., Acker, O., & Kunar, A. (2009, June 30). Why Cloud computing is gaining strength in the IT market place. *Strategy + Business*. Retrieved from http://www.strategy-business.com/article/li00131?gko=c331a

Chapter 12
Securing the Extended Enterprise:
A Method for Analyzing External Insider Threat

Virginia N. L. Franqueira
University of Twente, The Netherlands

André van Cleeff
University of Twente, The Netherlands

Pascal van Eck
University of Twente, The Netherlands

Roel Wieringa
University of Twente, The Netherlands

ABSTRACT

In extended enterprises, the traditional dichotomy between insiders and outsiders becomes blurred: consultants, freelance administrators, and employees of business partners are both inside and outside of the enterprise. As a consequence, traditional controls to mitigate insider and outsider threat do not completely apply to this group of individuals, and additional or improved solutions are required. The ISO 27002 security standard, recognizing this need, proposes third-party agreements to cover security requirements in B2B relationships as a solution, but leaves open how to realize them to counter security problems of inter-organizational collaboration. To reduce this gap, this chapter presents a method for identifying external insiders and analyzing them from two perspectives: as threats and as possible mitigation. The output of the method provides input for further engineering of third-party agreements related to non-measurable IT security agreements; the authors illustrate the method using a manufacturer-retailer example. This chapter also provides an overview of the external insider threat, consisting of a review of extended enterprises and of challenges involved with external insiders.

DOI: 10.4018/978-1-4666-0197-0.ch012

1 INTRODUCTION

Today, organizations are no longer stand-alone, loosely linked only to their customers and suppliers as in the past, but are part of networks with a variety of bilateral relationships and different levels of integration and cooperation. These networks are called *business networks*, *enterprise networks* or *extended enterprises* (Wiendahl & Lutz, 2002; Jagdev & Thoben, 2001). Relationships between organizations are facilitated by fast and reliable communication over the Internet, by outsourcing activities that traditionally would only be performed in-house, by new economic models based on managed services, and by new technologies such as virtualization. Although extended enterprises have been around for several decades, what is new is the fact that organizations are increasingly outsourcing critical business processes, packaging services from different organizations into complex service bundles, and moving IT infrastructure to other private, shared or even public networks under the custody of third parties. The number of organizations part of an extended enterprise can be significant, typically reaching hundreds in large companies. This adds-up to other factors, such as the complexity of dependencies among participants of the network, geographic dispersion, and distributed sources of risk (Thoben & Jagdev, 2001), making it difficult to have a holistic overview of security across the entire business network. Nonetheless, extended enterprises are ever more attractive because they provide competitive advantage by allowing cost savings, time and quality-related benefits, and by increasing business flexibility; each participant in an extended enterprise specializes on its core competencies and takes advantage of other organizations' expertise to deliver its business mission (Jagdev & Thoben, 2001).

In a traditional enterprise it is possible to separate the organization itself (e.g., its data, IT infrastructure and internal processes) from the outside world, in particular, from organizations part of its extended enterprise. However, organizational boundaries in an extended enterprise context become overwhelmingly fuzzy (Jericho-Forum n.d.; Thoben & Jagdev, 2001; Jagdev & Thoben, 2001); this contrast is illustrated in Figure 1. The overlap of organizations in the diagram represents "holes" that must be made in firewalls to give individuals from other organizations and insiders from a specific organization access to the data it owns, distributed along the extended enterprise. Since the organization that owns the data remains accountable for its protection, regardless of where and by whom it is handled, the extended enterprise creates a new security problem, which we define as the *external insider threat problem*. External insiders, such as freelance administrators or consultants, represent a class of individuals which do neither completely fall under the class of insiders nor of outsiders of one organization, and therefore, mitigations to insiders and outsiders do not completely solve the external insider threat problem.

1.1 Chapter Contribution and Organization

In this chapter we take the point of view of one company in an extended enterprise, which we call the *focal company* or *focal organization*, and provide an in-depth look at the external insider threat problem from the perspective of this organization, and one possible solution to the problem. Therefore, the contribution of this chapter is twofold. First, it describes (in Sections 1-4) what the external insider threat problem is and which challenges intrinsic to that problem from the perspective of the business, organizational and technical aspects arise. Second, it provides (in Sections 5-9) an overview of existing solutions, introduces a new potential solution and concludes with future directions of further solutions.

The chapter is organized as follows. Section 2 reviews the concept of trust and characteristics of outsiders and insiders, and uses this to introduce

Figure 1. Shift from traditional loosely-coupled enterprises to extended, entangled, enterprises: A) Traditional enterprise; B) Extended enterprise

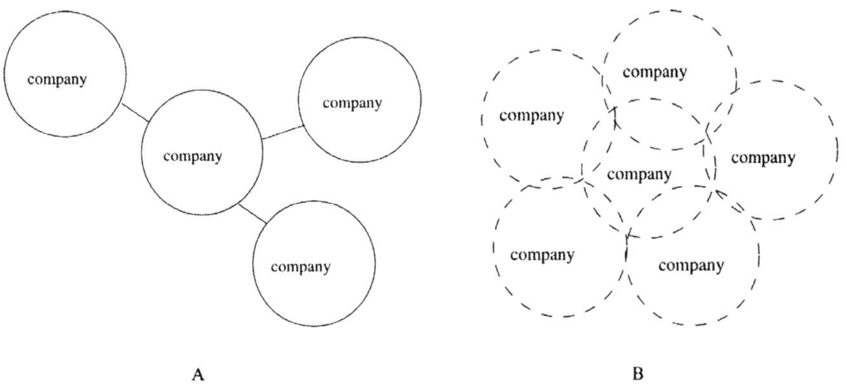

characteristics of external insiders; it also briefly introduces the modeling technique *e3value* used by the proposed method. Section 3 classifies extended enterprises, and Section 4 provides an overview of challenges involved with the external insider threat. Section 5 discusses potential solutions to counter some challenges identified, and Sections 6 and 7 present a method to help practitioners derive IT security agreements with other parties that mitigate the external insider threat problem, this way addressing another identified challenge. The chapter ends with a discussion of related work (Section 8), and of future research directions (Section 9) to address some other challenges identified in Section 5.

2 BACKGROUND

In this chapter we take the position, introduced earlier (Franqueira et al., 2010), that *external insiders* are *neither* a sub-set of insiders nor of outsiders, but rather belong to a separate set, having characteristics of both. Before we review the characteristics of outsiders, insiders and external insiders in Section 2.2, we briefly set the stage and discuss trust in extended enterprises.

2.1 Background on Trust

Trust is a core element in business-to-business (B2B) relationships (Solhaug et al., 2007; Siegrist et al., 2005; Das & Teng, 1998). Relevant in the context of extended enterprises are both B2B trust and business-to-individual trust (between focal organization, outsiders, insiders and external insiders).

Solhaug et al. (2007) discuss trust from two perspectives. From the perspective of the trustor (who is expected to trust), trust involves belief, hence, depends on the subjective probability attributed by the trustor that a trustee (who is expected to be trusted) will act as expected. From the perspective of the trustee, trust involves showing evidences of trustworthiness to allow the trustor to calculate a more objective, well-founded, probability. Because a sound measurement of trust is difficult to make and to verify, a possible alternative is to “reduce the need for trust by replacing it by assurance” (Solhaug et al., 2007). Assurance reduces the risk that an outcome will not turn out as expected by the trustor. Some authors, such as Das & Teng (1998), however, question this view that trust and control should be regarded as complementary linked (i.e. the higher the trust, the lower the need for controls, and vice versa),

Table 1. Distinction between outsiders, insiders and external insiders in respect to a focal organization

	Outsiders	Insiders	External Insiders
Trust	distrust	trust	distrust supported by B2B trust between focal organization and external insider's employer
Access	unauthorized to access private assets and authorized to access public assets	authorized to access private assets	authorized to access private assets
Control	fully subject to external controls enforced by focal organization	fully subject to internal controls enforced by focal organization	partially subject to external and/or internal controls enforced focal organization

and argue that they should rather be regarded as supplementary. Therefore, trust and control are parallel concepts which contribute to decrease risk.

For the purpose of this chapter, control refers to mechanisms that provide a certain level of security assurance to a focal organization; it can consist of policies, procedures, organizational structure and technical controls (IT Governance Institute, 2007). We distinguish between *external control*, enforced to protect private assets of a focal organization from the outside, and *internal control*, enforced to protect private assets of a focal organization from the inside. A *private asset* is regarded as an asset owned by the focal organization and that depends on its authorization to be accessed legitimately, while private assets are regarded as assets owned by the focal organization made available for the general public.

2.2 Background on Outsiders, Insiders and External Insiders

External insiders have been treated evasively in the literature. They are approached either simplistically as *insiders from trusted business partners* (Weiland et al., 2010), or generically as *partners* for statistical purposes (e.g., Verizon Data Breach Report series (Baker et al., 2008; Baker et al., 2009; Baker et al., 2010) and 7Safe Report (Bhala et al., 2010)). However, external insiders have their own characteristics and pose additional challenges, thus requiring specific mitigations, compared to insiders and outsiders. In this section we distinguish between outsider, insider and external insider considering *trust*, *access* and *control*. Table 1 summarizes the core differences between these three classes of individuals.

Outsiders

We consider, in this chapter, that outsiders have the following characteristics.

- **Trust:** Outsiders are individuals who are not trusted by the focal organization.
- **Access:** Outsiders have either unauthorized access to the private assets owned by the focal organization, or have by default authorized access to public assets owned by the focal organization.
- **Control:** Outsiders are fully subject to external controls enforced by the focal organization. For example, they are subject to rules enforced by firewalls facing the Internet in the network owned by the focal organization, are subject to policies enforced by the focal organization's public website, and by its online shop for end consumers.

Examples of outsiders are hackers, end consumers, and the general public.

Insiders

Different authors emphasize different characteristics of insiders. In this chapter, we consider that insiders have the following characteristics (Bishop, 2005; Brackney & Anderson, 2004; Hayden, 1999).

- **Trust:** Insiders are individuals who are trusted by the focal organization that employs them.
- **Access:** Insiders are granted authorized access to the private assets owned by the focal organization. Apart from authorized access, insiders also have legitimate reasons or need-to-know to perform their duties (Spitzner, 2003) which may involve sensitive tasks requiring authorizations not only the need to read, but also to write, execute and delete data. This combination of access and authorizations puts insiders in a position that can easily lead to misuse, either on purpose or by mistake. This happens when organizational assets (e.g., data, IT infrastructure and processes) are used with a different intent from what and how they were supposed to (Baker et al., 2008), causing a violation of security policies enforced by the focal organization (Bishop, 2005).
- **Control:** Insiders are fully subject to internal controls enforced by the focal organization, e.g., hierarchical controls, such as supervision and revision procedures, or access control policies, such as separation of duties and dual control enforcement.

Examples of insiders are employees, and interns (i.e. students' placement).

External Insiders

We consider in this chapter that external insider have the following characteristics.

- **Trust:** External insiders are individuals who are *not* trusted by the focal organization. However, these individuals are involved when there is a business reason for a focal organization to cooperate with another organization that it trusts to perform certain tasks. It means that the relationship between focal organization and external insiders is only established if there is a certain level of B2B trust between the business parties involved, i.e. their employer and the focal organization. This B2B cooperation may be established by means of non-contractual agreements, contractual agreements or joint ventures (Jagdev & Thoben, 2001).
- **Access:** External insiders have authorized access to the private assets owned by the focal organizational. The extent of this access and authorizations should be determined by a risk assessment process, according to security best practices, such as ISO/IEC-27001 (2005), ISO/IEC-27002 (2005). However, these guidelines recognize that it may be unfeasible to carry out risk assessment because of the lack of visibility of other companies and, instead, standard access policies can be agreed upon in B2B contracts. However, these contracts (when they exist) tend to be broad to cover a wide range of possible security breaches, and typically do not contain the level of details required that is necessary to grant and manage access to external insiders.
- **Control:** External insiders are partially subject to external and/or internal controls enforced by the focal organization. There are controls which are simply not applicable or are difficult to operationalize in the case of external insiders, and that is why they are *partially* subject to a mixture of internal and external controls. For example, we will see in Section 4 that external insiders are typically subject to social con-

trols enforced by their employers but not by the focal organization itself, there are issues involving the management of their identities by the focal organization, and many more.

Examples of external insiders are contractors, self-employed consultants, and employees of other organizations participating in the focal organization's extended enterprise who comply with the characteristics above.

2.4 Background on the e3value Technique

We review next the *e3value* modeling technique (Gordijn & Akkermans, 2003) used in the first step of the method presented in Sections 6 and 7. Figure 2 shows the e3value model of a simplified manufacturer-retailer B2B relationship.

In the e3value model, manufacturer and retailer are actors, i.e. stakeholders with an economic interest. Actors have value interfaces represented by ovals that contains "in" and "out" ports (triangles) indicating the direction that a value object can be transferred from one actor to another. Value objects can be anything with value for the stakeholders involved such as money-related objects, products, services, or more intangible objects such as legal compliance. In the figure, the manufacturer transfers end consumer product to a retailer in exchange for payment transferred back by the retailer.

Value models are used to represent which economic exchanges take place when a business need occurs; a business need is represented by a filled circle. A dashed line, called a dependency path, connects all transactions performed to satisfy the need. In general, a dependency path is an acyclic and/or graph; it ends in one or more bull's eyes (filled circle with a halo). The path merely states which transactions have to occur, but not when they must occur, and so a value model is not a coordination process model (Gordijn et al., 2000). Paths in e3value allow the estimation of economic sustainability of the business model represented. We use e3value concepts to delimit a part of the extended enterprise for analysis of external insiders in Section 7.

3 AN OVERVIEW OF THE EXTENDED ENTERPRISE

To assess the external insider threat, it is important to first have a classification of typical roles that can be played by organizations which employ them. This section presents a classification obtained through cases studies performed by the authors in different economic sectors; despite that, we do neither claim that this classification is complete nor exhaustive.

Trading Partners

Trading partners are organizations a focal organization trades with to perform the value-adding primary activities of its value chain (Porter, 1985). The main classes of trading partners are *customers* and *suppliers*. With *customers*, we refer to any

Figure 2. Value model of a simplified manufacturer-retailer relationship

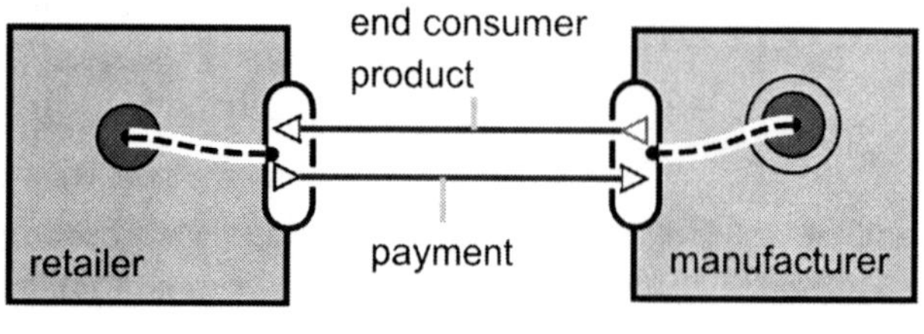

organization that directly buys products and/or services from a focal organization, either to re-sell them to their customers (e.g., retailers), or to use them as input in their own production of goods or services. With *suppliers*, we refer to organizations that directly provide a focal organization with bill-of-material goods.

Employees of trading partners who are involved in the relationship with the focal organization are all external insiders of the focal organization. Depending on their role, they pose more or less threat to the focal organization. For example, employees who manage orders may have access to price lists that often are retailer-specific, and therefore confidential.

Service Providers

We distinguish three main types of service providers in an extended enterprise, depending on whether a service provider provides a complete business process, a part of it, or is supplementary to existing business processes:

- **Business process providers:** Business process providers deliver an entire business process as a service. This business process can be a front-office or a back-office process, and can be a core or critical process on which the focal organization's business depends. Front-end processes are externally visible (to outsiders and external insiders); examples are call centers, logistics, and recruitment and selection services. Back-office processes are only visible internally (to insiders and external insiders); examples are warehousing, accounting, finance and salary administration. In both cases, however, the focal organization looses visibility of the whole business process which is outsourced to a provider.
- **Support service providers:** Support service providers deliver services involved in parts of a business process, or involved with facilities and infrastructure. These services can be related to Information Technology (IT), such as network management, data center operations, and software maintenance, or not. One special service is the provisioning of man-power to work for the focal company as a contractor; e.g., programmers, testers, and IT architects. These contractors, although external insiders, have a special characteristic: they become socially embedded into the focal organization. As a consequence, some challenges reviewed in Section 4 may not apply or apply with less intensity in this case.
- **Consultancy providers:** One specific type of service providers delivers expert advice on a particular field where specialist knowledge is needed. Such advice can be related to IT or not, e.g., consultancy to identify and/or solve technical problems and consultancy to address business needs. In both cases, consultants become external insiders of a focal organization but, like contractors, they are often socially embedded into the focal organization, minimizing some challenges discussed in Section 4.

Business Partners

Business partners are related to strategic alliances between organizations in other areas than direct trade between them. For instance, in *co-development partnerships*, a product or service is generated from the cooperation of the focal company with another company, a partnership which often remains transparent to end consumers (e.g., R&D alliances). External insiders from co-development partners have potentially access to highly sensitive information owned by the focal organization such as trade secrets, strategic information and intellectual property. *Business-complementary partners* complement the focal organization to deliver a combined solution to end consumers. A typical example is the more apparent partnership between hardware manufacturers and software vendors to deliver, e.g., laptops with operating system already installed and licensed. External insiders from such partners tend to cause less threat than the previous type of partnership, although knowledge sharing may be intense. Cooperative and consortium partners are organizations with which the focal organization shares resources, such as databases or applications (Kumar & van Dissel, 1996). For example, this occurs in the insurance and airline reservation sectors, in innovation-driven cooperatives (Thorgren et al., 2009), and in consortia for collective management of security (Gupta & Zhdanov, 2007). Employees from these other companies are also external insiders of the focal organization since they have authorized access to the shared information which is a private asset of the focal organization. They potentially share confidential information which may have, e.g., time-to-market implications, if disclosed.

Depending on the level of integration and cooperation, business partners may become joint ventures or may be merged into a single company with shared ownership (Jagdev & Thoben, 2001). In the later case, after a period of transition, external insiders from the merged company become insiders of the focal organization.

Legal Agencies

We generically call *legal agencies* the business role performed by organizations such as external audit companies, regulatory bodies, and government agencies. External auditors and regulatory bodies usually need authorized access to some of the private assets of the focal company. Individuals involved in this process are external insiders for the focal organization. They may access highly sensitive business and technical information, and may need not only access but authorization to execute tests, as in the case of SAS70 (AICPA, 2000) type 2 statements which require testing of security controls. Government agencies may be granted access to some of the focal organization's assets, e.g., for statistics purpose and to check legal compliance. Insiders of such governmental agencies are external insiders of the focal company with access to read confidential (often financial) information related to the focal organization.

4 CHALLENGES OF EXTERNAL INSIDER THREAT

After having presented an overview of extended enterprises and of external insiders in this context, we will now discuss challenges specific to this new class of individuals in terms of business, organizational and technical aspects.

4.1 Business Aspect

The aspects of trust and control give rise to several challenges related to external insider threat; they are reviewed next.

- **Trust and control:** B2B trust gives rise to at least two challenges. First, managing trust requires a clear view of risks that a trustor (who is expected to trust) is exposed to with respect to its trustees (who have to be trusted). In this respect, external insider threat is one important risk to be considered. This consideration requires an initial analysis, constant monitoring of risks between trustor and trustee, and a holistic view of dependencies which affect security. Furthermore, the trustworthiness of a trustee is difficult to estimate, to verify, and to keep up-to-date along the lifecycle of a B2B relationship. Second, there is no centralized control across an entire extended enterprise but rather distributed control mechanisms that may be spread across several organizations; therefore, organizations have to rely on B2B contracts. However, such contracts tend to be broad enough to accommodate, e.g., any breach in confidentiality, and are, therefore, not helpful to counter external insider threat.

4.2 Organizational Aspect

We review next some organizational challenges posed by external insiders, in comparison to insiders.

- **Auditing:** The focal organization tends to have full access of fine-grained logged information about insiders and auditing is at least theoretically possible. However, integration with information logged by other parties may be required for auditing activities related to external insiders and correlate them to detect misuse; these other parties may keep this information confidential.
- **Expertise to detect threat:** In the case of insiders, there is internal expertise about the technologies used by the focal organization. Likely, there are employees with know-how to detect misuse patterns and abnormal behavior. However, in extended enterprises, technology is often transferred, causing an evasion of expertise; therefore, the focal organization itself may lose the expertise to detect the threat that external insiders dealing with this technology may pose to its assets.
- **Human resources practices and behavior monitoring:** The focal organization is aware of its human resources practices. Therefore, it is aware that, e.g., employee screening is typically performed prior to employment. Additionally, typically there is a continuous social interaction with the majority of insiders, increasing the chances of detection of suspicious (internal) insider behavior. However, the focal organization does not observe human resources practices enforced by other organizations, and their subcontractors, in an extended enterprise context. This means that the focal organization does not know, e.g., whether external insiders that have access and authorizations over its assets have been screened or not. Besides, due to reduced and sporadic social interactions between insiders of the focal organization and external insiders from another organization, the chances for detection of external insiders suspect behavior are limited. Note that, as already mentioned, there are some classes of external insiders, such as certain contractors and consultants, where this problem is reduced since they are usually socially embedded into the focal organization.

4.3 Technical Aspect

Several technical challenges arise from the external insider threat. Next we provide an overview of the challenges related to IAM (Identity and Access Management), and managing the interdependencies among organizations in an extended enterprise.

- **Identity Management:** Digital identities have a lifecycle, as illustrated in Figure 3. This figure shows a physical person and several digital identities this person can assume. Each of the identities has a lifecycle comprising provisioning (when the identity is created), propagation (when the identity is disseminated to multiple systems), usage (when the physical person authenticates herself using the identity to different systems), maintenance (when attributes of the identity are updated), and deprovisioning (when the identity is deactivated).

  The problem that arises with external insiders' identities is the decoupling between who has visibility of physical persons and who has visibility of their digital identities. If the external insider is not embedded into the

Figure 3. Identity management lifecycle (adapted from Windley, 2005)

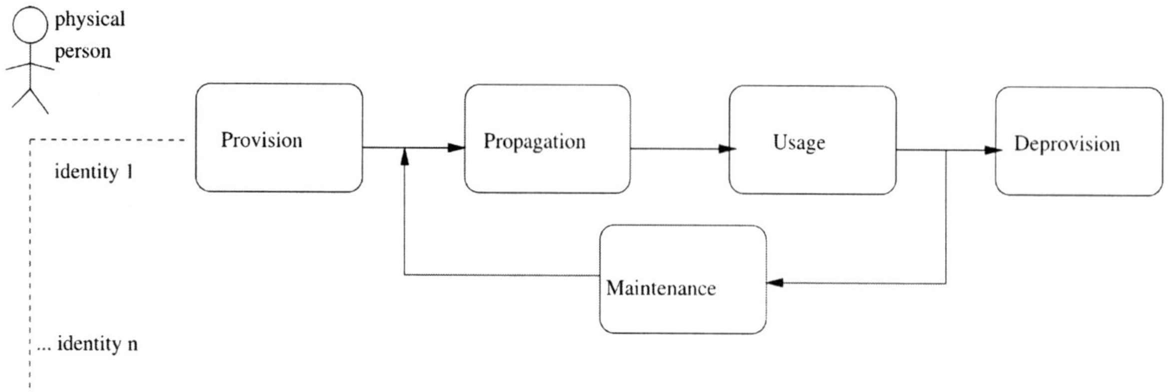

focal organization, such as in the case of certain contractors and consultants, this decoupling becomes reality. As a consequence, the focal organization has to rely on the timely and accurate communication of another organization, which has visibility of external insiders as persons, to maintain identities and authorizations of its external insiders up-to-date. For example, a single organization can have a very efficient interaction between the IT and the Human Resources (HR) departments, to assure that access and privileges of terminated insiders are revoked quickly; this routine may even be automated. But if the insider is employed by another organization, the event of termination involves the integration of the IT department of the focal organization and the HR of another organization, what makes the process more complex.

- **Access Management:** In traditional organizations, authorizations are usually granted on a need-to-know, individual basis and separation of duty policies are enforced to decrease the chance of assets misuse by internal insiders. However, in an extended enterprise setting, authorizations tend to be granted on a worst-case, partner basis (shared identities, see Baker et al., 2009), i.e. higher-than-need-to-know authorizations may be granted, and separation of duty policies may not have guaranteed enforcement across the extended enterprise. Another issue of access management relates to consensus. Reaching agreements about the semantics of roles or authorization attributes among business units of a same focal organization is hard. Reaching such agreements across different organizational domains, as is the case in extended enterprises, is even harder (Karp et al., 2010).
- **Cascading risks:** Extended enterprise may have hundreds of bilateral relationships of the types described in Section 3, forming a complex network of organizations where each organization can be seen as a node, and each relationship (which imply the notion of connectivity) as an arc (Jagdev & Thoben, 2001). Such representation allows the abstraction of extended enterprises and accommodates important characteristics of such networks: their dynamic aspect and indirect connectivity established by subcontracting (Wiendahl & Lutz, 2002). The network representation of the extended enterprise allow analysis such as the one performed by Huang et al. (2008); they identified two types of risks that can propagate in

enterprise networks: disruption (e.g., failures, malware, and misuse) and coordination risks (e.g., erroneous and poor-quality information). Their study emphasizes that a holistic view of risks is fundamental to manage interlinked risks. However, this is challenging because (i) organizations typically do not have enough information for this holistic assessment, such as regarding external insiders. Some other challenges are: (ii) the need of a minimum level of security for all nodes of the network requires agreement on standards for enforcing and monitoring security across all of them, and (iii) highly connected nodes (i.e. hubs) need extra protection; this may be challenging because it requires incentives for the necessary extra spending.

4.4 Summary of Challenges

Table 2 provides a cross-cutting overview of the discussed challenges related to the external insider threat problem.

Sections 2-4 distinguished external insiders from outsiders and insiders, presented the context in which they occur, discussed challenges intrinsic to the problem of external insider threat, and concluded with a list of ten challenges. In the next sections we switch our focus to solutions.

5 SOLUTIONS TO COUNTER THE EXTERNAL INSIDER THREAT

Organizational controls and security mechanisms that work to detect and prevent classical insider threat (e.g., user profiling and anomaly detection;

Table 2. Summary of challenges related to external insiders and the threat they pose

Challenge	Description
1	Trust and risk management are important to counter the external insider threat, but they require a holistic view of dependencies, and of threats and vulnerabilities to be effective.
2	Objective measurement of trustworthiness of other companies is fundamental for decision making, e.g., when engaging in new B2B contracts, but also towards a sounder trade-off analysis, e.g., between trust, risk and expected gain from a B2B relationship.
3	B2B contracts, when existent, are often broad and do not establish IT security agreements useful to counter the external insider threat.
4	Distribution of logging makes auditing and monitoring of external insiders hard to achieve.
5	Evasion of know-how related, e.g., to outsourced technology and IT infrastructure results in inability to detect external insider threat
6	Some internal controls that work well for insiders do not work for external outsiders, e.g., behavior monitoring.
7	Decoupling between who has visibility of external insiders as persons and who has only visibility of their identities in a B2B relationship results in mismanagement of authorizations for external insiders.
8	Higher-than-need-to-know authorizations for external insiders are difficult to detect and manage; this may be a consequence of challenges 4 and 7.
9	Consensus about semantics of roles and attributes for identity and access management across an extended enterprise requires reaching agreements that are difficult to achieve in practice; this may be aggravated by conflicting interests.
10	A minimum level of security has to be enforced across an entire extended enterprise and highly connected organizations need extra security to minimize the propagation of risks across the business network; this challenge has not only implications to security investments but also to counter external insider threat which may give rise to new cascading risks, such as the risk of knowledge sharing propagation.

see Salem et al. (2008) for a survey) may not apply completely to counter external insider threat. We review in this section three streams of research and practice proposed to deal with this problem; they partially address four of the identified challenges, namely challenges 1, 2, 7 and 8 from Table 2.

First, the Jericho-Forum (n.d.) takes the view that the increasing connectivity of organizations can be solved by data-centric security, shifting security from complete systems or infrastructure to the data itself; storing the data centrally together with the applicable policies or allowing it to flow freely on a trusted infrastructure, where the policies stick to the data. (Van Cleeff & Wieringa, 2009). However, the feasibility of data-centric security is in doubt, because it may require classification of large amounts of data at a low level of granularity; moreover, it is hard to implement in extended enterprises. Therefore, data-centric security helps to improve, e.g., challenge 8 (Table 2) but in cases where it helps, it may be prohibitively expensive.

Second, extended enterprises can opt for federated authentication architectures (Windley, 2005) to address challenge 7. In this case, each organization keeps local control of its identities, and there is a higher-level mechanism to link these identities. This way, the focal organization only deals with access management and is released from identity management regarding its external insiders. However, although federated authentication can meet several levels of assurance (Burr et al., 2006), this architecture is only an alternative when there is a high level of B2B trust regarding identity management practices enforced by the other federated organizations, agreed policies between all members of the federation, and consensus about identity attributes, such as roles. If there is no visibility over identity management of all other organizations in the extended enterprise, the focal organization cannot assess the external insider threat properly. To reduce this problem, the focal organization has to opt for expensive solutions, such as regular external auditing or even permanent internal auditing of the identity management of the other companies.

A third approach to reduce challenges 1 and 2 is to rely on the assurances provided by certifications, such as ISO/IEC-27001 (2005) and AICPA (2000), and on third party agreements made explicit in the B2B contracts. The main problem with such certifications is that their scope is limited, and outside of it no guarantees can be provided. B2B contracts are often very high-level, allowing each party to interpret the contracts in different ways, depending on the context, which does not help to understand and solve potential security issues, such as external insider threat.

We take the perspective that improving IT security agreements in B2B contracts is a step forward to deal with the external insider threat by addressing challenge 3 (Table 2), therefore, we propose a solution in this direction next. Other challenges are addressed by future directions of our solution, as discussed in Section 9.

6 PROPOSED SOLUTION TOWARDS EXTERNAL INSIDER THREAT ANALYSIS

In this section, we propose a six-step method (introduced in Franqueira & Wieringa, 2010) for analyzing the external insider threat problem. We believe that a new method – apart from existing best practices and standards – is necessary.

First, existing standards, such as ISO/IEC-27002 (2005), list a series of controls that can be put in place - but not *how* to identify external insiders in the first place. From case studies we performed, we have learned that this is a challenge in itself, and that even security-conscious organizations have problems identifying those individuals in their extended enterprise that might pose a threat. Our method shows how organizations can identify external insiders.

Rather than assessing the security of systems directly (as is often done in risk assessments) we take a top-down holistic approach for two reasons: First, we wish to understand the broader context of a system and the people involved, and avoid diving unnecessarily deep into technical details. Only when it is necessary or useful should organizations zoom into technical implementations of their systems. Second, in an extended enterprise setting, such technical details are often not available for review, because they are under the control of other organizations.

As such, our method is very distinct from the approach that one would take to identify insiders and mitigate their threat: insiders are part of the organization, are on the payroll and their responsibilities and authorizations for applications can be checked much easier.

The method's starting point (step 1) is to make a value model of the extended enterprise that cooperates to serve a particular business need. In the case presented in this chapter, we have chosen to deal with a retailer's need in respect to a typical manufacturer. As such, the value model provides a rationale to reduce the size of the network to a manageable size. Next, (step 2) we make a model of coordination activities to satisfy the need, and (step 3) of the IT architecture required to support these activities. Jointly, these three models allow us (step 4) to identify external insiders, and (step 5) data to be protected in this part of the network. Finally, using best practices security requirements, we analyze the external insider threat from the perspective of pose threat by violation of the requirement and mitigate threat by the enforcement of the requirement (step 6). The next section describes the method in more detail, where we apply it to an extended enterprise setting involving a retailer-manufacturer relationship. Table 3 shows the steps and their output.

Our motivation for the use of value models as the starting point of the proposed method derives from the fact that extended enterprises are economic networks, where each actor performs an economic role. Value models allow us to represent these roles: who provides something of value to whom, and which reciprocal value is obtained in return. From the value model, each model provides motivation for the content of the next one. For instance, the focal organization executes the processes depicted in the coordination model because they are needed to create value, as per the value model. The same way, the focal organization has the IT artifacts depicted in the IT architecture model because they are needed to support the processes depicted in the coordination model.

In the next section, the method is illustrated with a realistic retailer-manufacturer example.

Table 3. Steps in the method and their output

Step	Description	Output
1	Value modeling	limited scope, parties involved
2	Coordination modeling	high-level processes
3	Architecture modeling	relevant systems and connections
4	Identifying external insiders	external insiders
5	Identifying data to be protected	sensitive data
6	Best security practices	external insider threats
		input for IT security agreements engineering

7 METHOD APPLIED TO A RETAILER-MANUFACTURER EXAMPLE

7.1 Step 1: Value Modeling

Figure 4 shows a detailed *e3value* model of the manufacturer-retailer relationship presented earlier in a simplified form (Figure 2).

The simplified view (Figure 2) only showed the retailer need being satisfied by the manufacturer, and the economic exchange between them. The detailed view (Figure 4) shows that there are other companies involved in satisfying this basic need. For example, the manufacturer has to collect taxes (VAT) when selling products and, as a consequence, the manufacturer has an economic exchange with the tax office for legal compliance. In addition, the manufacturer itself has its needs in order to fulfill the retailer and government needs; these are fulfilled by service providers which manage the ERP system (SAP), the business transactions (EDI) and the call center, in exchange for payment. The logistics partner (warehouse & carrier) has also been modeled as an actor which fulfills the manufacturer's need to fulfill, itself, the retailer's need. This modeling choice implies that logistics are considered an indirect cost (Porter, 1985) for the purpose of this example.

Value modeling provides a rationale to set the scope of the analysis of external insiders by delimiting one part of the extended enterprise that realizes a main business interaction, in this case, between manufacturer and retailer. However, it does not provide an overview of sequencing among those parties. But, since this information is essential to identify roles and tasks that external insiders perform to satisfy the value exchanges, coordination modeling is the next step of our method.

7.2 Step 2: Coordination Modeling

We assume EDI (Electronic Data Interchange) documents are the basis upon which trading partners cooperate, and therefore coordinate, their operations. Coordination between different parties of the value chain is a key aspect for the order process fulfillment (Croxton, 2003). Figure 5 shows the main coordinated interactions between the trading parties of our example in a

Figure 4. Value model showing of a detailed manufacturer-retailer relationship (expanded from Figure 2)

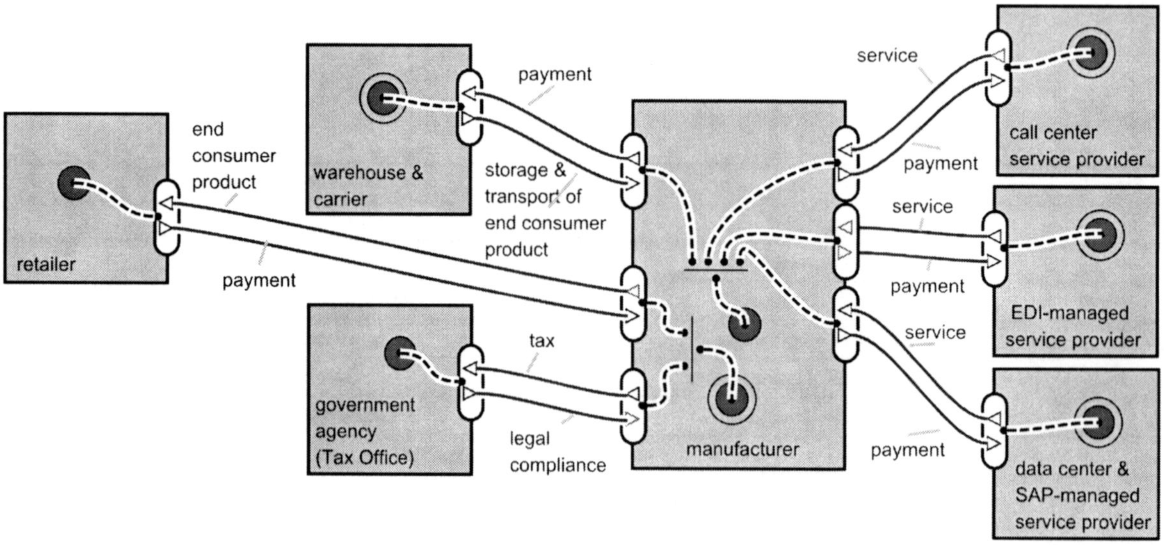

simple sequence diagram. The other three service providers not present in the diagram (call center, data center and EDI) are implicitly represented by the manufacturer, and therefore not visible, in the coordination model.

The process starts when a retailer issues an EDI-based Purchase Order (PO) to the manufacturer (item 1 in Figure 5). The order specifies which products the retailer wants to purchase and in which quantities. This triggers activities on the manufacturer side related to the approval of the PO. After approval, an EDI-based Shipment Advice is sent from the manufacturer to the warehouse (item 2). In general terms, this is an indication for the warehouse to get ready to release the products listed on the PO from stock. It triggers activities related to the replenishment of the manufacturer stock, such as those related to resource planning and purchase orders to suppliers. The manufacturer also sends an EDI-based Shipment Order (item 3) to the carrier. This document alerts the carrier to be ready to transport the products to the retailer, again triggering activities related to the manufacturer inventory management. Next, the manufacturer usually sends an EDI-based Shipment Notice to the retailer with details related to the delivery of the products (item 4), followed by an EDI-based invoice (item 5). The invoice triggers the update of accounts receivable on the manufacturer side. The next two steps involve the delivery of products (item 6) executed by the carrier that transports them from the warehouse to the retailer address, and the actual payment of the products received to the manufacturer (item 7). The last step (item 8) refers to the payment of taxes to the tax office by the manufacturer, triggering finance and accounting back-office activities.

Figure 5. Model showing the main coordination activities among the trading parties

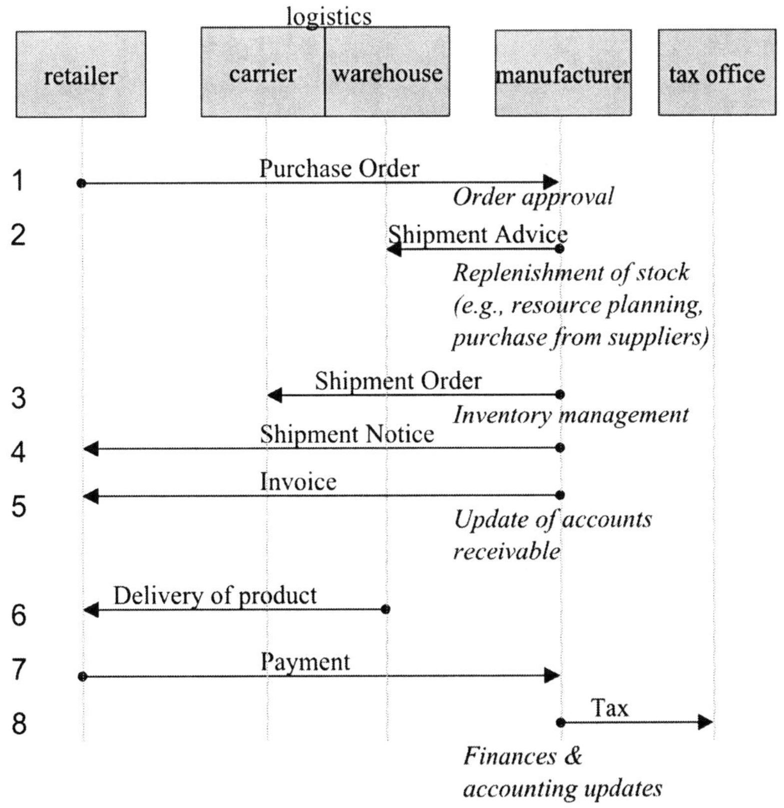

The coordination model increases understanding about the part of extended enterprise modeled but is not enough to identify the external insiders roles and to assess their capabilities to pose threat. For that, we need to model the IT architecture that supports this coordination including the activities triggered. We do this in the next step of our method.

7.3 Step 3: IT Architecture Modeling

Figure 6 shows an IT architecture used by our example manufacturer. It is consistent with both the value and the coordination models presented previously in the sense that the companies with this IT architecture can perform the coordination process described in the sequence diagram of Figure 5 and, doing so, can perform the transactions represented in the value model of Figure 4. Our method does not prescribe an architecture (or coordination process notation) and any architecture notation understandable by the stakeholders is acceptable. The diagram in Figure 6 essentially shows different parties (organizational boundaries), communication channels linking these parties (and thus crossing those boundaries), users' functionalities and IT infrastructure supporting these. The security officers and IT architects of our example company draw this kind of diagram and find them easy to use, which is one of our criteria.

One interesting aspect to notice is the fact that the trading partners and service providers represented in the value model (Figure 4) are also part of the IT architecture diagram, but not the manufacturer itself. This is because the front- and back-office activities of the coordination model (Figure 5) are performed by service providers on behalf of the manufacturer.

As indicated earlier, the starting point is a Purchase Order (PO). Employees of the retailer can place and manage POs in two ways: They can

Figure 6. Model showing an IT architecture that realizes the value and the coordination models presented in Figures 4 and 5, respectively

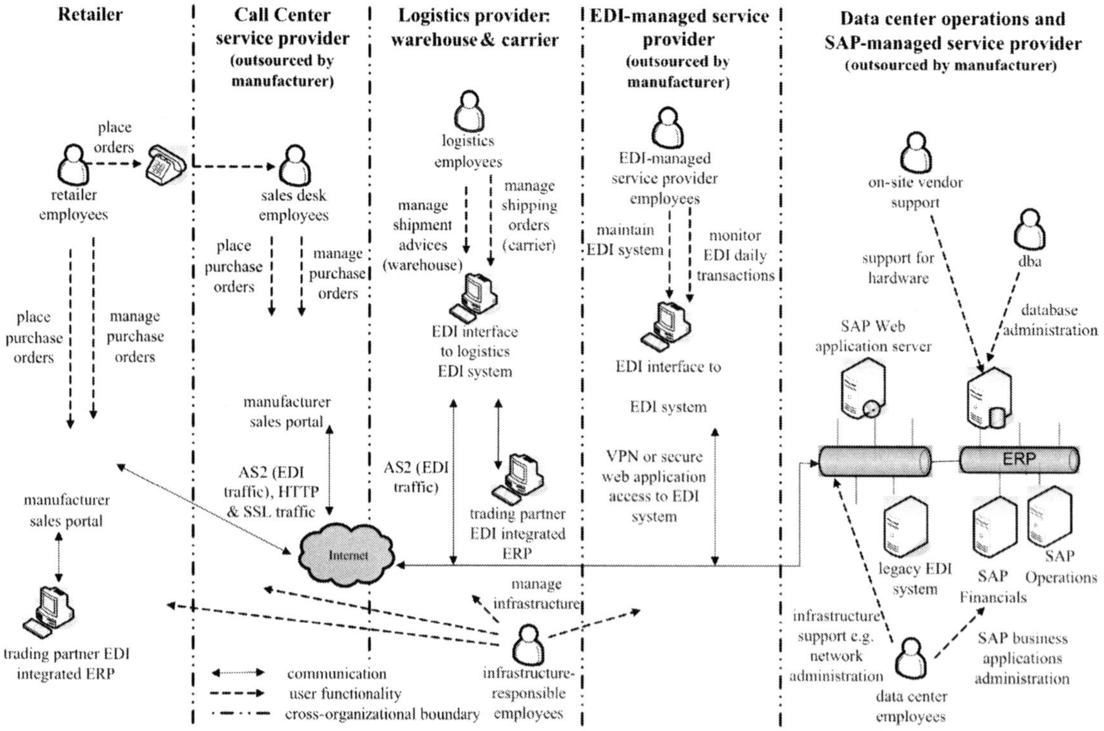

use the manufacturer sales portal; alternatively, they can use the manufacturer call center and ask a sales desk employee to place and manage their orders The EDI-based documents, such as POs, are usually transmitted via AS2 (Applicability Statement 2). AS2 is a standard which defines secure transmission over HTTP, used to send and receive EDI files over the Internet. AS2 connections require certificates issued by a Certificate Authority (Bishop, 2003) from both parties involved and use encryption for data transmission. A PO transmitted by the retailer or the sales desk employee is therefore sent via an AS2 connection to the EDI system located in the manufacturer's data center. The EDI system basically processes EDI files, and is integrated with the manufacturer's ERP (Enterprise Resource Planning) infrastructure. In our example, the manufacturer has a SAP ERP (http://www.sap.com/solutions/business-suite/erp), and this integration occurs via an interface based on SAP IDoc (Intermediate Document) technology; via this interface, documents are transferred from the EDI system to ERP systems and vice versa.

After a PO is approved, several exchanges of EDI-based files occur between the ERP infrastructure of the retailer, warehouse/carrier and the manufacturer, as shown in Figure 5. For example, employees from the logistics partner, i.e. the warehouse and carrier employees will have an EDI interface to access their logistics EDI system, used to manage shipping advices and orders, respectively. The activities triggered at each step of the whole process are performed by different business applications part of the manufacturer ERP infrastructure. For example, item 5 in Figure 5 involves SAP Financials to issue the invoice and send it automatically to the retailer, and to update the receivable accounts.

The manufacturer's legacy EDI system (located in its data center) is managed remotely by a service provider, as often happens in practice and illustrated in the diagram in Figure 6. Employees at the EDI-managed service provider perform tasks related to: (i) maintenance of the EDI system and (ii) monitoring of EDI daily transactions (AS2 n.d.). The manufacturer's ERP (platform and applications), including databases (data) and the sales portal (SAP web application and web server), as well as the IT infrastructure, are all managed, in our example, by the data center provider. Next, we identify the external insiders that support the tasks described in this section.

7.4 Step 4: Identifying External Insiders

All the roles represented in the IT architecture diagram in Figure 6 refer to *external insiders* with respect to the focal company, i.e. the manufacturer. Therefore, this diagram provides a list of external insiders in the manufacturer-retailer example.

1. Retailer employees who place and manage purchase orders
2. Aales desk employees that also place and manage purchase orders on the behalf of the retailer
3. Logistics employees who manage shipment advices and orders involved with the delivery of products for the retailer
4. EDI-managed service provider employees who maintain the manufacturer EDI system, and monitor EDI daily transactions
5. Infrastructure-responsible employees from the retailer, call center, logistics, and EDI-managed service providers
6. Data center employees who perform two types of activities: network administration and SAP business applications administration
7. Database administrators who manage the database for the data center provider
8. On-site vendor support individuals who manage data center specific hardware

Interesting to observe is the fact that external insiders, on the one hand, pose security threats to the manufacturer but, on the other hand, they can also be in a position to enforce mitigations on behalf of the manufacturer. For example, the manufacturer cannot know whether call center employees who have left their job have had their digital identity and access revoked or not, and how quickly. This represents a threat for the outsourcing provider, as well as the manufacturer, because a detected incident can have consequences for both companies involved. An illustration is the Citibank fraud revealed in Ribeiro (2005); investigations raised questions not only about identity and access management, but also about the rate of turnover and screening procedures at outsourced call center providers. On the other hand, there are employees at all of these parties that are, e.g., responsible for IT infrastructure and for their security; hence they mitigate the external insider threat but can, nevertheless, also be a source of threat.

We look at sensitive data involved in the scenario and the threat analysis process in the next two sections.

7.5 Step 5: Identifying Data to be Protected

We take a data-centric approach for the analysis of threats and mitigations, and classify the threats according to the data states recognized by the Health Insurance Portability and Accountability Act (HIPAA, 1996), that applies to organizations handling health data. According to HIPAA, there are the four data states: (i) data in motion, i.e. data in transit through a network, (ii) data at rest, i.e. data stored, (iii) data in use, i.e. data in process of being created, retrieved, updated or deleted, and (iv) data disposed, i.e. data discarded or recycled. Protecting sensitive data in each of these states becomes security goals, and this is our starting point for identifying threats.

Next, we identify sensitive data using the IT architecture shown in Figure 6; a non-exhaustive list of sensitive types of data is:

1. Customer-specific price lists for manufacturer products
2. Trading EDI-based documents
3. Customer personal data
4. Credentials such as certificates to transmit EDI documents
5. Decryption keys
6. Passwords to log on the sales manufacturer portal and for VPN connection
7. Administrative passwords to manage infrastructure and business applications (e.g. ERP environment, database, legacy EDI system) at the data center

7.6 Step 6: Reverse Engineering of Security Best Practices

In order to analyze external insider threat, we follow a backward reasoning process from best practice mitigations that represent security requirements to be fulfilled. In this case, we will use the PCI DSS (Payment Card Industry Security Standards Council, 2008, p. 8) standard, which defines 12 broad categories of security requirements for payments. Each PCI requirement is a possible mitigation to be included in an IT security agreement, and we analyze whether external insiders listed in the previous section would pose threat, and which external insiders would be responsible to mitigate that threat; results are shown in Table 4 in Appendix A.

The outcome of Table 4, output of the method, is twofold. First, it lists possible mitigations (R1-R12 in Table 4) against external insider threat, useful for negotiating IT security agreements in B2B contracts, as mandated by the ISO/IEC-27002 (2005). Second, it lists not only the external insiders who pose these threats, but also the external insiders who must implement mitigations. This provides additional support for negotiation of mitigation measures in IT security agreements as addendum to B2B contracts.

Note that the proposed method defines a rationale for the identification of external insiders and for the reasoning about external insider threat. Unlikely full risk assessment however, its coarse grained result provides a list of threat agents (i.e. external insiders' roles), a list of threats and corresponding best practice mitigations, rather than a list of risks.

8 RELATED WORK

Modeling organizations, inter-organizational relations and IT architectures can be done using several modeling techniques, each focusing on specific aspects. Well-known modeling frameworks include UML and Archimate (The Open Group, 2009). In this chapter we use three perspectives, namely value, coordination and IT architecture, to identify classes of external insiders. These have been proposed by Gordijn & Akkermans (2003) and Wieringa et al. (2008), and cover most relevant issues in detecting external insider threat, but we assume that other frameworks can be used as well, depending on the techniques used in enterprises and their preferences.

For extended enterprises, IT security agreements are prescribed as best practice by the ISO/IEC-27002 (2005, Section 6.2), however, this standard does not provide guidelines for their specification, and the method fills this gap. Another important difference between our approach and ISO 27002, is that we focus on threats rather than risks because in extended enterprises it is difficult to get information to assess risks, because it involves knowledge of existing vulnerabilities.

Enterprise governance frameworks are also related to our work. For example, the Control Objectives for Information and related Technology (COBIT) (IT Governance Institute, 2007) contains controls for IT management. It contains a process under the domain of "Delivery and Support" that covers *Manage Third-party Services*. Again, the processes described there are too broad and aim at monitoring of service delivery, rather than on security, which is essential for mitigating external insider threat. The COSO framework (COSO, 1994) focuses on management in more general terms, related to financial reporting. Here too our method can be used to satisfy these requirements.

Several data-centric security standards exist, divided by market sector and type of data. The best practices, e.g., from the Health Insurance Portability and Accountability Act (HIPAA, 1996) and PCI DCS (Payment Card Industry Security Standards Council, 2008) are the basis for our focused analysis of the external insider threat, input for IT security agreements to counter external insiders threats taking mitigations as a starting point.

Our method is not a full risk assessment methodology such as the ones proposed in frameworks like the CRAMM (Walton-on-Thames: Insight Consulting, 2005), OCTAVE (Alberts & Dorofee, 2002), and CORAS (den Braber et al., 2007). A full risk assessment is very expensive to perform in an extended enterprise context because of incomplete information available from other organizations. We do use a model-based approach, as it is used in CORAS, with the difference that CORAS' models are used to assist in risk assessment; e.g., they use threat diagrams to analyze causal relationships between threat, vulnerability, risk, unwanted incident (consequence), and asset potentially affected. We use models that have a different purpose and represent other types of relations. Our models are useful to (i) zoom-in on the relevant part of the extended enterprise from a value perspective, help to understand (ii) the B2B coordination involved and (iii) the supporting IT architecture, with an ultimate purpose: identify external insiders that play a role in a restricted part by either causing threat or countering threat. Therefore, the proposed method complements, but do not replace, a CORAS risk assessment and vice versa.

Our work is also related to the specification of Service Level Agreements (SLAs). However,

SLAs address the delivery of services in terms of measurable indicators that guarantee the quality of services (QoS) delivered. While some attributes of security can be specified and above all - measured - via SLAs (e.g., availability), others cannot not (e.g., confidentiality and integrity). Confidentiality requirements must be specified in the form of mitigation measures in IT security agreements that can be appended to SLAs (see e.g., Morali & Wieringa, 2010).

9 FUTURE RESEARCH DIRECTIONS

This section suggests three directions for future research (Sections 9.1 to 9.3). Table 5 maps these directions, as well as solutions identified in Section 5 and the proposed method described in Section 6 to the challenges summarized in Table 2. Potential solutions to challenges 4 and 5 were not addressed in this chapter.

9.1 New Access Control Paradigms

One research direction to overcome the identity and access management challenge mentioned in Section 4 is the use of an alternative access control model which avoids the inherent problems of centralized and federated identity architectures. One step forward in this direction is the authoriZation Based Access Control (ZBAC) model proposed by Karp et al. (2010). It shifts the paradigm of access control from authentication-based (such as in Role Based Access Control), where access decisions are made *after* the authentication of the requester, at request time, this way determining the authorizations she has, to authorization-based, where access decisions are made *before* the request is made based on authentication of the requester; authorization tokens are submitted along with the access request.

ZBAC has three features of interest: (i) it allows distributed access control where identity and access management are locally controlled, (ii) it allows accountability of responsibility for the access granting process, and (iii) it allows delegation of a sub-set of authorizations that a user has, decreasing the need for password sharing.

9.2 Extended Enterprise from a Network Perspective

One research direction towards better dealing with cascading risks in extended enterprise is to increase understanding of business networks from a network perspective. This calls for studies of real cases to gain insights in their structure, size, connectivity and other characteristics related to the external insider threat. Results may potentially push development on the conceptual front, allowing more accurate modeling and automatic reasoning about business networks. Results may also allow the confirmation of some hypothesis, such as that business networks are scale free (Huang et al., 2008), triggering further research to answer in which circumstances they are scale free or not, and whether scale-free network properties (Barabási, 2002) apply to them.

9.3 Holistic View of Security Risks

Several challenges related to the external insider threat (Section 4) have their cause grounded in the lack of a holistic view of security risks. However, because the spectrum of threat posed by external insiders is so large, one way forward is to scale down on one very specific aspect of this threat while still aiming for its holistic view across the extended enterprise. For example, Aljafari & Sarnikar (2009) proposes a method to assess knowledge sharing risks in inter-organizational networks. Our method can also help in this direction by providing a rationale for the analysis of, e.g., external insider threat specifically derived from administrative access to assets owned by a focal organization. Such methods, combined with the network perspective of extended enterprises (discussed above), represent an interesting

Table 5. Mapping between challenges summarized in Table 2 and solution directions

Challenge	Solution and Research direction
1	Present: Certifications (Section 5) Future: Holistic View of Security Risks
2	Present: Certifications (Section 5)
3	Present: Proposed method for identifying external insider threat (Section 6)
4	No solution direction identified in this chapter
5	No solution direction identified in this chapter
6	Holistic View of Security Risks
7	Present: Federated Authentication Architecture (Section 5) Future: New Access Control Paradigms
8	Present: Data Centric Security (Section 5) Future: New Access Control Paradigms
9	New Access Control Paradigms
10	Extended Enterprise from a Network Perspective

research direction which could be expanded to draw conclusions about the expected propagation of confidentiality and integrity-related risks.

10 CONCLUSION

This chapter sought to contribute to the governance of information security by providing an overview of the external insider threat problem and by proposing a solution to this problem. We positioned external insiders as a third set of people, distinct from insiders and outsiders, and reviewed (i) extended enterprises from this perspective, and (ii) challenges to counter the external insider threat. The proposed solution, i.e., the method presented in this chapter, provides a rationale to systematically delimit a part of the extended enterprise, to identify external insiders in that part and to analyze the external insider threat. Its output, in the form of best practice mitigations, list of external insiders, and list of threats, represents input for IT security agreements.

While we believe our method is promising, we recognize it has to be further validated in practice. Currently, we are undertaking a case study on a multinational IT service provider as a first step to validate the method. It will give us the opportunity to review the method, before at least two or three more rounds of validation with further case studies.

ACKNOWLEDGMENT

First two authors are supported by the research program Sentinels (www.sentinels.nl).

Sentinels is being financed by Technology Foundation STW, the Netherlands Organization for Scientific Research (NWO), and the Dutch Ministry of Economic Affairs.

REFERENCES

AS2. (n.d.). *AS2 processing for EDI.* Retrieved March 2010, from http://www.dcs-is-edi.com/AS2.html

AICPA. (2000). *Statement on auditing standards No. 70: Service organizations. Professional standards* (*Vol. 1*). American Institute of Certified Public Accountants Auditing Standards Board.

Alberts, C., & Dorofee, A. (2002). *Managing information security risks: The OCTAVE approach* (1st ed.). Boston, MA: Addison-Wesley.

Aljafari, R., & Sarnikar, S. (2009). A framework for assessing knowledge sharing risks in interorganizational networks. In *Proceedings of the AIS Americas Conference on Information Systems (AMCIS 2009)*. AIS Electronic Library (AISeL).

Baker, W., Goudie, M., Hutton, A., Hylender, C. D., Niemantsverdriet, J., Novak, C., et al. (2010). *2010 data breach investigations report*. Verizon Business Security Solutions. Retrieved October 2010, from http://www.verizonbusiness.com/resources/reports/rp_2010-data-breach-report_en_xg.pdf

Baker, W. H., Hutton, A., Hylender, C. D., Novak, C., Porter, C., Sartin, B., et al. (2009). *2009 data breach investigations report*. Verizon Business Security Solutions. Retrieved September 2009, from http://www.verizonbusiness.com/resources/security/reports/2009_databreach_rp.pdf

Baker, W. H., Hylender, C. D., & Valentine, J. A. (2008). *Data breach investigations report*. Verizon Business Security Solutions. Retrieved September 20008, from www.verizonbusiness.com/resources/security/databreachreport.pdf

Barabási, A.-L. (2002). *Linked: How everything is connected to everything else and what it means for business and everyday life*. Cambridge, MA: Perseus Publishing.

Bhala, S., Christodoulides, M., Cornwell, L., Jones, R., & Morris, B. (2010). *UK security breach investigation report - An analysis of data compromise cases*. 7Safe Limited. Retrieved March 2010, from http://7safe.com/breach_report/Breach_report_2010.pdf

Bishop, M. (2003). *Computer security: Art and science*. Boston, MA: Addison-Wesley.

Bishop, M. (2005). Position: Insider is relative. In *NSPW'05: Proceedings of the 2005 New Security Paradigms Workshop* (pp. 77–78). ACM Press.

Brackney, R. C., & Anderson, R. H. (2004). *Understanding the insider threat: Proceedings of a March 2004 Workshop*. Retrieved March 2010, from www.rand.org/pubs/conf_proceedings/2005/RAND_CF196.pdf

Burr, W. E., Dodson, D. F., & Polk, W. T. (2006). *NIST special publication 800-63: Information security, version 1.0.2*. National Institute of Standards and Technology.

COSO. (1994). *Internal control - Integrated framework by Committee on Sponsoring Organizations of the Treadway Commission.*

Croxton, K. L. (2003). The order fulfillment process. *The International Journal of Logistics Management, 14*(1), 19–32. doi:10.1108/09574090310806512

Das, T., & Teng, B.-S. (1998). Between trust and control: Developing confidence in partner cooperation in alliances. *Academy of Management Review, 23*(3), 491–512.

den Braber, F., Hogganvik, I., Lund, M. S., Stølen, K., & Vraalsen, F. (2007). Model-based security analysis in seven steps - A guided tour to the CORAS method. *BT Technology Journal, 25*(1), 101–117. doi:10.1007/s10550-007-0013-9

Franqueira, V. N. L., van Cleeff, A., van Eck, P. A. T., & Wieringa, R. J. (2010). External insider threat: a Real security challenge in enterprise value webs. In *ARES'2010: Proceedings of the Fifth International Conference on Availability, Reliability and Security* (pp. 446–453). IEEE Press.

Franqueira, V. N. L., & Wieringa, R. J. (2010). *Value-driven security agreements in extended enterprises.* Technical Report TR-CTIT-10-17. Enschede, The Netherlands: Centre for Telematics and Information Technology University of Twente. ISSN 1381-3625

Gordijn, J., Akkermanns, J. M., & van Vliet, J. C. (2000). Business modelling is not process modelling. In *Conceptual Modeling for e-Business and the Web, LNCS 1921* (pp. 40–51). Springer Press.

Gordijn, J., & Akkermans, J. (2003). Value-based requirements engineering: Exploring innovative e-commerce ideas. *Requirements Engineering Journal, 8*, 114–134. doi:10.1007/s00766-003-0169-x

Gupta, A., & Zhdanov, D. (2007). *Growth and sustainability of managed security services networks: An economic perspective*. In WEIS'07: 7th Workshop on the Economics of Information Security. Retrieved March 2010, from http://weis07.infosecon.net/papers/65.pdf

Hayden, M. V. (1999). *The insider threat to U.S. government information systems*. Advisory Memoranda NSTISSAM INFOSEC 1-99.

HIPAA. (1996). *Health Insurance Portability and Accountability Act.* Senate and House of Representatives of the United States of America. Retrieved March 2010, from http://www.legalarchiver.org/hipaa.htm

Huang, C. D., Behara, R. S., & Hu, Q. (2008). Managing risk propagation in extended enterprise networks. *IT Professional, 10*, 14–19. doi:10.1109/MITP.2008.90

ISO/IEC-27001. (2005). *Information technology. Security techniques. Information security management systems.* Requirements.

ISO/IEC-27002. (2005). *Information technology. Security techniques. Code of practice for information security management.*

IT Governance Institute. (2007). *CobiT 4.1 - Control objectives for information and related technology.*

Jagdev, H. S., & Thoben, K. D. (2001). Anatomy of enterprise collaborations. *Production Planning and Control, 12*(5), 437–451. doi:10.1080/09537280110042675

Jericho-Forum. (n.d.). *The what and why of deperimeterization.* Retrieved from http://www.opengroup.org/jericho/deperim.htm

Karp, A. H., Haury, H., & Davis, M. H. (2010). From ABAC to ZBAC: The evolution of access control models. *ISSA (Information Systems Security Association). Journal, 8*(4), 22–30.

Kumar, K., & van Dissel, H. G. (1996). Sustainable collaboration: Managing conflict and cooperation in interorganizational systems. *MIS Quartely, 20*, 279–300. doi:10.2307/249657

Morali, A., & Wieringa, R. J. (2010). Risk-based confidentiality requirements specification for outsourced IT systems. In *RE'10: Proceedings of the 18th IEEE Int. Requirements Engineering Conference*. IEEE Press.

Payment Card Industry Security Standards Council. (2008). *PCI quick reference guide to the payment card industry (PCI) data security standard (DSS)*, version 1.2. Retrieved June 2010, from https://www.pcisecuritystandards.org/documents/pci_ssc_quick_guide.pdf

Porter, M. E. (1985). *Competitive advantage: Creating and sustaining superior performance* (1st ed.). New York, NY: Free Press.

Ribeiro, J. (2005). *Twelve arrested, including three ex-employees of outsourcing company*. Computer World. Retrieved from http://www.computerworld.com/s/article/100900/Indian_call_center_workers_charged_with_Citibank_fraud

Salem, M. B., Hershkop, S., & Stolfo, S. J. (2008). A survey of insider attack detection research. In *Advances in Information Security: Vol. 39. Insider Attack and Cyber Security* (pp. 69–90). Springer Press.

Siegrist, M., Gutscher, H., & Earle, T. (2005). Perception of risk: The influence of general trust, and general confidence. *Journal of Risk Research, 8*(2), 145–156. doi:10.1080/1366987032000105315

Solhaug, B., Elgesem, D., & Stolen, K. (2007). Why trust is not proportional to risk. In *ARES'07: Proceedings of the Second International Conference on Availability, Reliability and Security* (pp. 11–18). IEEE Press.

Spitzner, L. (2003). Honeypots: Catching the insider threat. In *ACSAC'03: Proceedings of the 19th Annual Computer Security Applications Conference*, (pp. 170–179). IEEE Press.

Thoben, K. D., & Jagdev, H. S. (2001). Typological issues in enterprise networks. *Production Planning and Control, 12*(5), 421–436. doi:10.1080/09537280110042666

Thorgren, S., Wincent, J., & Örtqvist, D. (2009). Designing interorganizational networks for innovation: An empirical examination of network configuration, formation and governance. *Journal of Engineering and Technology Management, 26*, 148–166. doi:10.1016/j.jengtecman.2009.06.006

van Cleeff, A., & Wieringa, R. J. (2009). Rethinking de-perimeterisation: Problem analysis and solutions. In *Proceedings of the IADIS International Conference on Information Systems 2009* (pp. 105–112). IADIS Press.

Walton-on-Thames: Insight Consulting. (2005). *CRAMM user guide. Risk analysis and management method*, version 5.1.

Weiland, R. M., Moore, A. P., Cappelli, D. M., Trzeciak, R. F., & Spooner, D. (2010). *Spotlight on: Insider threat from trusted business partners*. Carnegie Mellon University: Software Engineering Institute. Retrieved June 2010, from http://www.cert.org/archive/pdf/TrustedBusinessPartners0210.pdf

Wiendahl, H.-P., & Lutz, S. (2002). Production in networks. *CIRP Annals - Manufacturing Technology, 51*(2), 573–586.

Wieringa, R., Pijpers, V., Bodenstaff, L., & Gordijn, J. (2008). Value-driven coordination process design using physical delivery models. In *Proceedings of the 27th International Conference on Conceptual Modeling* (pp. 216–231). Springer Verlag.

Windley, P. J. (2005). *Digital identity* (1st ed.). Sebastopol, CA: O'Reilly Media, Inc.

ADDITIONAL READING

Angelov, S., & Grefen, P. (2001). *B2B eContract Handling - A Survey of Projects, Papers and Standards*. CTIT Technical Report series 01-21. Enschede: Centre for Telematics and Information Technology University of Twente.

CSC Office of Innovation. (2008). *Transparency and Assurance: Putting a Measure on Digital Trust*. Technical report. Leading Edge Forum. Retrieved June 2010, from http://assets1.csc.com/features/downloads/12388_2.pdf.

Davis, E. W., & Spekman, R. E. (2003). *The Extended Enterprise: Gaining Competitive Advantage through Collaborative Supply Chains*. Financial Times Prentice Hall.

Dynes, S., Eric, H. B., & Johnson, M. E. (2005). Information Security in the Extended Enterprise: Some Initial Results From a Field Study of an Industrial Firm. In *Proceedings of International Workshop on the Economics of Information Security*. Retrieved June 2010, from http://infosecon.net/workshop/pdf/51.pdf.

Dynes, S., Kolbe, L. M., & Schierholz, R. (2007). Information Security in the Extended Enterprise: A Research Agenda. In *AMCIS'2007: Proceedings of the 13th Americas Conference on Information Systems* (pp. 1–12).

Evans, P. B., & Wurster, T. S. (1999). Strategy and the New Economics of Information. In *Creating value in the network economy* (pp. 13–34). Boston, MA, USA: Harvard Business School Press.

Farahmand, F., & Spafford, E. (2010). Understanding insiders: An analysis of risk-taking behavior. *Information Systems Frontiers*, 1–11.

Goodchild, A., Herring, C., & Milosevic, Z. (2000). Business Contracts for B2B. In *Proceedings of the CAISE00 Workshop on Infrastructure for Dynamic Business-to-Business Service Outsourcing* (pp. 63–74). CEUR-WS.org: CEUR Workshop Proceedings.

Greitzer, F. L., Moore, A. P., Cappelli, D. M., Andrews, D. H., Carroll, L. A., & Hull, T. D. (2008). Combating the Insider Cyber Threat. *IEEE Security and Privacy*, *6*, 61–64. doi:10.1109/MSP.2008.8

Gulati, R. (1995). Does Familiarity Breed Trust? The Implications of Repeated Ties for Contractual Choice in Alliances. *Academy of Management Journal*, *38*(1), 85–112. doi:10.2307/256729

Karp, A. H., Haury, H., & Davis, M. H. (2009). *From ABAC to ZBAC: The Evolution of Access Control Models*. Technical Report HPL-2009-30. HP Laboratories.

Kort, C., & Gordijn, J. (2007). Modeling Strategic Partnerships using the E3value Ontology - A Field Study in the Banking Industry. In Rittgen, P. (Ed.), *Handbook of Ontologies for Business Interaction* (pp. 310–325). Hershey, PA: IGI Global. doi:10.4018/978-1-59904-660-0.ch018

Kuhn, D. R., Coyne, E. J., & Weil, T. R. (2010). Adding Attributes to Role-Based Access Control. *Computer*, *43*, 79–81. doi:10.1109/MC.2010.155

Lund, M. S., Solhaug, B., & Stolen, K. (2010). Evolution in Relation to Risk and Trust Management. *Computer*, *43*, 49–55. doi:10.1109/MC.2010.134

Probst, C. W., Hunker, J., Gollmann, D., & Bishop, M. (2010). Aspects of Insider Threats. *Insider Threats in Cyber Security*, *49*, 1–15. doi:10.1007/978-1-4419-7133-3_1

Rossebø, J. E. Y., Hansen, K., McGrath, K., & Houmb, S. H. (2010). Towards a Framework for Evaluating Risk when Customer Premises Networks are Integrated in the Smart Grid. In *ISSRE 2010 Supplemental Proceedings: International Workshop on Risk and Trust in Extended Enterprises (RTEE'10)*.

Sharma, A. K., & Lamba, C. S. (2010). Survey on Federated Identity Management Systems. In *Recent Trends in Networks and Communications: Vol. 90. Communications in Computer and Information Science* (pp. 509–517). Berlin Heidelberg: Springer.

Smith, S., & Holmes, S. (1997). The Role of Trust in SME Business Network Relationships. In *USASBE 1997 Proceedings*. United States Association for Small Business and Entrepreneurship.

Sutton, S. G. (2006). Extended-enterprise systems' impact on enterprise risk management. *Journal of Enterprise Information Management*, *19*(1), 97–114. doi:10.1108/17410390610636904

Thomas, R. C. (2009). Total Cost of Security: A Method for Managing Risks and Incentives Across the Extended Enterprise. In *CSIIRW'09: Proceedings of the 5th Annual Workshop on Cyber Security and Information Intelligence Research Workshop* (pp. 1–14).

Zhang, Z., Zhang, X., & Sandhu, R. (2009). Towards a Scalable Role and Organization Based Access Control Model with Decentralized Security Administration. In *Handbook of Research on Social and Organizational Liabilities in Information Security* (pp. 94–117). Hershey, PA: IGI Global. doi:10.4018/9781605661322.ch006

KEY TERMS AND DEFINITIONS

Access: Is the legitimate right, or not, to physically or digitally access assets owned by a focal organization.

Asset: Is something of value for stakeholders; we distinguish between *public asset*, an asset owned by a focal organization which is available for the general public, and *private asset*, an asset owned by a focal organization which depends on its authorization to be accessed legitimately.

Control: Is a mechanism that provides a certain level of assurance to a focal organization; we distinguish between *external control*, enforced to protect private assets of a focal organization from the outside, and *internal control*, enforced to protect private assets of a focal organization from the inside.

Extended Enterprise: Is a network of organizations established by means of bilateral B2B relationships, forming a network of direct and indirect dependencies between organizations.

External Insider: Is an individual who (i) is distrusted by the focal organization but is employed by an organization which is trusted by the focal organization, (ii) has authorized access to private assets owned by the focal organization, and (iii) is partially subjected to external and/or internal controls enforced by the focal organization.

Insider: Is an individual who (i) is trusted by the focal organization, (ii) has authorized access to private assets owned by the focal organization, and (iii) is fully subjected to internal controls enforced by the focal organization.

IT Security Agreement: Is a norm to be fulfilled by a trustee to secure the assets of a trustor; it is negotiable and represents an addendum to B2B contracts.

Outsider: Is an individual who (i) is distrusted by the focal organization, (ii) does not have authorized access to private assets or, by default, authorized access to public assets owned by the focal organization, and (iii) is fully subjected to external controls enforced by the focal organization.

Trust: Or, symmetrically, distrust, is the subjective probability by which one party (the trustor) expects that another party (the trustee) performs a given action on which its welfare depends (Solhaug et al., 2007).

Trustworthiness: Is the objective probability by which the trustee performs a given action on which the welfare of the trustor depends (Solhaug et al., 2007).

APPENDIX A

Table 4 contains the output of the method performed in step 6 (Section 7.6).

Table 4. Analysis of external insiders from security best practices (R1-R12 fromPayment Card Industry Security Standards Council, 2008)

Security Goal	No.	Best practice	External Insiders as threats	External Insiders as mitigations
Protect sensitive data in motion	R1	Firewalls should be installed and maintained to filter traffic of sensitive data; this involves management of inbound & outbound traffic of network firewalls, personal firewalls, and virtual machines firewalls (when the data center uses a shared hosting environment)	Unmanaged firewalls at one or more of the parties involved (i.e. retailer, call center, logistics, EDI-managed provider and data center) at the level of network, desktop or virtual machine are a source of threat	Infrastructure-responsible employees at data center and at each party should be hold accountable for configuring and managing such firewalls
	R2	Encrypt transmission of sensitive data traveling over open, public networks	Use of communication channels such as unencrypted email, peer-to-peer or wireless connections for intentional or unintentional transmission of sensitive data	Infrastructure-responsible employees at each party need to restrict the availability of unsafe connections, e.g. for sales desk employees
	R3	Logs should be collected and analyzed not only at the OS and network levels but also at the level of application, anti-virus, database; analysis may involve correlation of information from different logs	Logs collected but not managed is a common practice; logs not analyzed at different parties cause threat of undetected unauthorized access and misuse of sensitive data	Infrastructure- and application-responsible employees at the data center and infrastructure-responsible employees at each other party should be held responsible for that
Protect sensitive data at rest	R4	Sensitive data should be stored in an unreadable way, i.e. encrypted and decryption keys should be locked in a safe, not logically nearby location	Certificates for EDI transmission and decryption keys stored at the retailer, call center and logistics organizations could be source of threat; passwords to sales portal and VPN kept unsafe by employees involved in their manipulation at every party including by the data center employees is also source of threat	Strict policies should be enforced at each party; external insider responsible should be appointed at contracted parties
	R5	Up-to-date anti-virus should be present and regularly updated not only on client desktops but also on servers hosting applications	Anti-virus are usually installed at users desktops/laptops but often not installed at servers for performance reasons; threat may come from every party involved	Infrastructure-responsible employees at data center and at each party need to manage it
	R6	Vulnerability patches and software updates should be managed	Vulnerable desktops used by retailer, call center, logistics & EDI-managed employees can be source of malware that exposes sensitive data; EDI system is a special threat because legacy systems are known to be difficult to patch	Infrastructure-responsible employees at data center and at each party need to manage it
Protect sensitive data in use	R7	Vendor-supplied defaults for system passwords and other security parameters should be changed; such passwords and security parameters span across the infrastructure level and the business application level	Weak passwords are a source of threat from data center employees, retailer, call center, logistics and EDI-managed employees	Strict policies should be enforced at each party; external insider responsible should be appointed at contracted parties. Peer review could help to make sure infrastructure- and applications-responsible employees at the data center enforce it

continued on following page

Table 4. Continued

Security Goal	No.	Best practice	External Insiders as threats	External Insiders as mitigations
	R8	Individuals should only have the authorizations they need to perform their duties (need-to-know security principle)	A same sales desk employee handling the same tasks for different customers; and separation-of-duty conflicts between tasks handled by a same employee, e.g. retailer employee that places purchase orders and approves payment of invoices represent threats	Requires supervision and review of access control lists; external insider responsible should be appointed at contracted parties
	R9	Every individual should be hold accountable to her actions; this means that actions should be traceable	The use of functional logins (same user ID) or shared password (same password for different ID) often happens in practice; retailer, logistics and call center employees may cause this threat	Requires supervision and review of access control lists; external insider responsible should be appointed at contracted parties
	R10	Physical access to sensitive data should be restricted; this also involves protecting distribution of data, e.g., via email, hardcopy, portable devices	Retailer and logistics employees that handle EDI-based documents and call center employees that handle customer personal data or customer-specific data often print and archive information, and this is a source of threat; vendor support employees with physical access to hardware parts are also threats	Requires supervision at each party; external insider responsible should be appointed at contracted parties
	R11	A policy that addresses information security, security awareness and training should be enforced, as well as strict selection and recruitment procedures	Poor security culture among employees, low level of security training, deficient screening practices; employees from retailer, call center and logistics are potential source of threat	Requires auditing at each party
Protect sensitive data disposed	R12	Data disposed should be rendered unusable, unreadable or undecipherable; this involves physical or electronic data that should either be destroyed or disposed encrypted	Retailer, logistics and call center employees may dispose hardcopy of sensitive data; vendor support employees that replaces hardware parts are also a source of threat	Requires supervision at each party; external insider responsible should be appointed at contracted parties

Chapter 13
Information Security Management Systems Cybernetics

Wolfgang Boehmer
Technische Universität Darmstadt, Germany

ABSTRACT

With the widespread dissemination of Information Technology in enterprises and households in the mid-90s, discussions began on how to manage it. Meanwhile, in the area of enterprise security management systems worldwide, enforced use of the Deming cycle initially worked against the implementation of policies. Standard management systems include ISMS (Information Security Management System) as specified in ISO 27001, BCM (Business Continuity Management System) as specified in BS 25999, and ITSM (Information Technology Service Management System) as specified in ISO 20000. In contrast to policies, these best-practice management systems continue to operate today with no formal method. Management systems have, however, some advantages that policies do not have. In this chapter, the authors present possible uses of policies with respect to management systems and identify potential applications. Furthermore, the authors present a field study, cited here, which highlights the advantages of management systems in practice. Moreover, this chapter shows how a formal description of an information security management system can be created by means of discrete-event systems theory and how an objective function for management systems can be defined.

INTRODUCTION

With the spread of information technology (IT) over the past 15–20 years, a discussion quickly began on how best to protect them. Initially, technical approaches were favored. As policies for enterprise security protection were widely adopted, however, their limits of applicability quickly became apparent. These developments took place over the decade from 1998 to 2008. For application in entire companies, however, management systems are more suitable than policies, as current trends suggest.

DOI: 10.4018/978-1-4666-0197-0.ch013

The first management system that was organized as a continuous improvement process and brought economic considerations into the field of corporate security was the British Standard, BS 7799-2, in 1998. Meanwhile, in the area of corporate security (enterprise security), management systems based on the Deming cycle became established worldwide, including ISMS (Information Security Management System) as described in ISO 27001, BCM (Business Continuity Management System) as described in BS 25999, and ITSM (Information Technology Service Management System) as described in ISO 20000. In the case of ISMS, a clear trend over time can be identified, representing an increase of approximately 1,000 certificates per year since the standard was published[1] in November 2005.

After this first phase of development in the last decade, the following questions about management services, among others, are still being discussed, with a focus on corporate security (enterprise security):

1. How to distinguish between the formulation and implementation of policies and management systems
2. How to measure the performance of management systems
3. Whether and how management systems can be linked
4. Whether and how a target function can be formulated for a management system
5. How to embed management systems in a business and a business infrastructure.
6. How to implement management systems in an agile manner

Numbers 1 to 5 of these issues will be addressed in this chapter; the remaining issue, number 6, is still an open research topic.

This chapter is organized as follows. The next section provides an overview of policies and management systems and the differences between them. The distinction is made by means of the theory of open, closed, and isolated systems. Then the following section highlights the link between systems theory and management systems, and a formal description of a management system is developed using ISO 27001 as an example. The question of modeling the controlled system is discussed in subsequent chapters with reference to various examples and to a qualitative and quantitative description of the plant. Then a field study is presented in which the preventive mitigation of risks is discussed using a risk-oriented management system based on ISO 27001. The results suggest that in addition to the ISO 27001 standard, the BS 25999 standard is also of great importance in this context and that a purely qualitative analysis of emergency processes is not sufficient. For these reasons, a method for quantifying a Business Continuity Plan (BCP) is also discussed in this section.

Finally, the question of a target function for the information security of management systems will be addressed. This discussion is necessary because, in contrast to purely economics-oriented management systems, a tradeoff exists in management systems for corporate security. This tradeoff can be resolved in various ways, for example iteratively, because it is an NP-hard problem.

OVERVIEW OF MANAGEMENT SYSTEMS AND POLICIES

The development of management systems with a focus on IT security and information security began in the late 90's and continues today. In information technology, policies have had a far-reaching significance and have been the object of many research projects. A basic description of policies can be found in (Bishop, 2003, p. 3–11 and p. 95 ff). Today, policies are successfully used in firewall configuration, authentication, and network-based factory management, to name just a few areas. A policy must initially be static in nature to encourage allowed states and discourage not-allowed states in a system, process, or object.

After some time, it was recognized that static policies do not fulfill the requirements of companies and their electronic communication infrastructures. Therefore, dynamic policies, which are flexible with respect to a temporal component, a substantive component, or both, were developed. Detailed designs for such policies can be found for example, in (Pucella and Weismann, 2004). The basic principles have been developed by van der Meyden (1996). This flexibility better meets the requirements of companies, and dynamic policies have been used in a wide range of applications.

In the book by Anderson (2006), a different policy perspective in relation to enterprise security has been discussed and extended to the *Security Engineering* field. Figure 1 in (Anderson, 2006) also reflects this view. *Policies* are initiated by *incentives,* which in turn lead to implementation mechanisms. The result of the mechanisms is that policies can be technically, organizationally, or legally implemented. Mechanisms can therefore be secure, precise, or vague. After implementation of the mechanisms, there is some degree of security *assurance*.

A significant disadvantage of policies becomes apparent if they alone are used to secure the value chain of a company. This disadvantage is that the policies do not provide feedback about their effects. Especially in an open system such as a company, this lack of response has proved to be a disadvantage.

To assess the overall security of a company, it is invaluable to obtain feedback on security status, for only then can an adequate response be generated if necessary. As a suitable method for complete protection of a company, standardized management systems based on systems theory have become the established practice. Based on the desire for complete security, for example in terms of the value chain, a universal framework for a risk-oriented management system can be outlined.

The framework is illustrated in Figure 2 based on the concept of systems theory. It is dominated by adjustments in response to perturbations (deviations) and shows policies and procedures as the dependent variables of the control loop. A disturbance will, in most cases, affect the value chain of the company. This point of view is aligned with overall enterprise security rather than with individual components.

Security is seen to be one facet of Quality of Service (QoS) and to include classical security goals such as confidentiality, availability, and

Figure 1. Security engineering framework based on policies (Anderson, 2006)

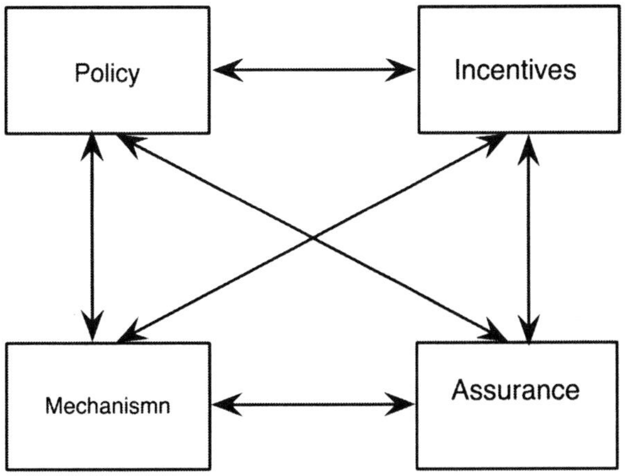

Figure 2. Security engineering system framework (Boehmer, 2011)

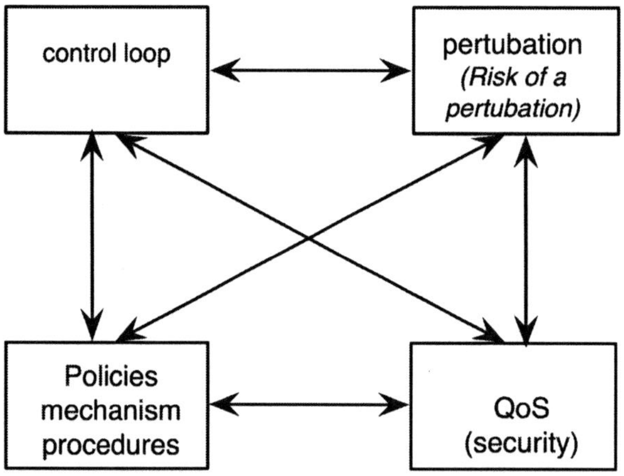

integrity. All components of the framework are in constant interaction with each other. The aim of the management system as implemented is to adjust for deviations proactively; this is a typical case for an Information Security Management System (ISMS). However, if the risk decision for a specific deviation is to act reactively after the occurrence of the deviation, this is a typical task for a Business Continuity Management System (BCMS) (Boehmer, 2009b).

The previously addressed question of the distinction between the definition of policies and management systems with regard to their application leads to the discussion and definition of open, closed, and isolated systems. Originally, this systems concept was defined in thermodynamics, but it has now been transferred to information technologies and to companies. By analogy, the various types of systems can be described as follows:

- An example of an isolated system could be a single computer that is not networked and that does not communicate with its environment, e.g., with a user. Typical examples are embedded systems which are implemented as autonomous systems.
- A closed system could be represented by a connected computer and its network of exchanges of data and information with its environment (a second party).
- An open system can be exemplified by a company, which exchanges matter (people, computers, materials) with its environment and is also linked with this environment. Companies are often described in the literature as open systems because they do not act independently, but are in many ways integrated into their environment and are therefore exposed to pressures and conditions that from the system viewpoint must be regarded as nonmodifiable (Leimer, 1990, p. 22). Moreover, Capra (Capra, 1996) argued that organizations could be described as open systems from the point of view of systems theory.

The recognition that policies are well suited to secure isolated and closed systems has become prevalent over the last decade. However, in the case of open systems, such as companies, policies are not the ideal method. It has been shown that open systems such as companies can be better protected by a risk-based management system with a control loop than by policies. Control loops can be well described using discrete-event systems theory (DES), and many of the characteristics of control loops can be transferred directly to management systems. Control loops are widely used in engineering technology for purely technical systems. For socio-technical systems such as a value chain, the features and knowledge of control loops have been used only rarely.

In the following section, the relationship between management systems and systems theory is explained in more detail.

MANAGEMENT SYSTEMS AND THE DEMING CYCLE

From the perspective of the overall security of an enterprise, the two types of policy, static and dynamic, have the same disadvantage in that they do not provide any feedback about their effect. This makes higher-level control by corporate management impossible, but such control is essential to enterprise security. Furthermore, economic issues play a wide-ranging role in company security.

Boehmer (2010) has shown that the theory of control loops for technical systems can also be applied to socio-technical systems such as the information security management systems mentioned earlier. The above-mentioned three best-practice management systems (ISMS, BCMS, and ITSM), which are based on the Deming cycle, involve a four-phase cycle, Plan-Do-Check-Act (PDCA). The PDCA cycle is based on the imperfection of socio-technical systems and the consequent need for feedback (Deming, 1986).

Historically (since 1939), management systems, or rather the PDCA cycle for quality assurance and statistical evaluation, were discussed for the first time by Shewhart (Shewhart, reprint 1980 (1939) and Shewhart, 1986). The idea was popularized by Deming, from whom the cycle gets its name (Deming, 1986). The necessity of information security for management systems has been identified by Elo and Elo (2003), and an implementation has been presented by Salehl et al. (2007). The close relationship between information security and business processes has been discussed by Solms and Solms (2005).

If the four phases are interpreted as states, the PDCA cycle can be shown to generate a standard automaton. Figure 3 sketches the Deming cycle as a state transition diagram. The four phases are presented as states $Z = \{z_1,z_2,z_3,z_4\}$, and the state transitions are presented as events $\Sigma = \{\sigma_1, \sigma_2, \sigma_3, \sigma_4\}$. $\sigma 0$ indicates the initial event in Figure 3. The final state Z_F is provided for the standard state automaton, but may not exist as a single state because the system undergoes a continuous improvement process which is represented as a cycle (loop).

To compare the Deming cycle with a control loop, it is necessary to describe both methods as standard automatons. Then the behavior of two standard automatons can be compared by the bisimulation technique. The Deming cycle D can be expressed as a quintuple:

Equation 1. Quintuple representing the Deming cycle:

$$D = \{Z, \Sigma, \delta, z_0, Z_{F\}}.$$

The transitions δ allow the system to change state, for example $z_n \xrightarrow{\sigma_n} z_{n+1}$, with the successor state determined by the transition function $z' = \delta,(z, \sigma)$. Then the Deming cycle can be described by a standard automaton D as presented in Equation 1.

A further improvement can be achieved if $Z_F = 1' \neq 1$, so that $z_1 \neq z'_1$ in the Deming cycle. This improvement criterion, applied over n cycles, yields a final stable state. As discussed by Boehmer (2009a), this condition produces a balance in the system that can be interpreted as an equilibrium state, or in other words, one in which the state of the system no longer changes. The Deming cycle is then balanced. For this case, $Z_F = 1$. The Check (check for improvements) and

Figure 3. PDCA cycle as a standard automaton according to Deming

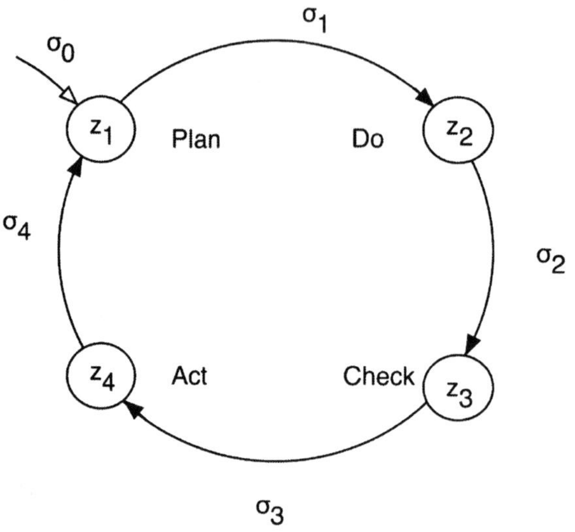

Act (perform improvements) functions are responsible for attaining the equilibrium state. In an ideal case, the system reaches equilibrium after a certain period of time.

Figure 3 sketches the Deming cycle as a state transition diagram. By analogy to the quintuple representing the Deming cycle, a control loop can also be described by a standard automaton $\hat{A}$.

Equation 2. Standard automaton:

$$\hat{A} = \left\{\hat{Z}, \hat{\Sigma}, \hat{\delta}, \hat{z}_0 \hat{Z}_F\right\}$$

The elements needed to understand the quintuple representing the standard automaton $\hat{A}$ are analogous to the states and events of the quintuple of the Deming cycle (see Equation 1). The states can be described as $\hat{Z} = \left\{\hat{z}_1, \hat{z}_2, \hat{z}_3, \hat{z}_4\right\}$ and the events as $\hat{\Sigma} = \left\{\hat{\sigma}_1, \hat{\sigma}_2, \hat{\sigma}_3, \hat{\sigma}_4\right\}$. The transition function is given by $\hat{\delta}$ and indicates a transition from one state to another, for example $\hat{z}_n \xrightarrow{\hat{\sigma}_n} \hat{z}_{n+1}$.

The two machines can be compared based on the similarity and equivalence of their response behavior. Here, similarity is determined only by the input and output values of the automaton. This type of similarity is called interface equivalence. This topic will not be discussed further here in order to pay more attention to the bisimulation. According to Milner's axiom, two states are considered equal if they cannot be distinguished by (a combination of) observations (Milner, 2006). A bisimulation between two objects is therefore a transition system that reproduces an observed behavior that is identical for two objects. If a relation exists between the states of a Deming quintuple D and a standard automaton $\hat{A}$ then the bisimulation $S_{\hat{A}D}$ applies, such that

Equation 3. Bisimulation:

$$S_{\hat{A}D} \subset \hat{A} \times D,$$

where Z_D and $\hat{Z}_{\hat{A}}$ indicate the state sets of the two automata D and $\hat{A}$. Equation 3 shows the relation between the automata $\hat{A}$ and D. The simulation relation $S_{\hat{A}D}$ maps the states of the automaton $D|z_1$ and $\hat{A}|z_1$ in the sense that the second element of the pair, e.g., $(z_1, \hat{z}_1) \in S$, is simulated by the first, and therefore $z_1 \sim \hat{z}_1$ applies. The number of states may be different in the two machines, but this does not present a contradiction within the relation S. If $D|z_k$ and $\hat{A}|z_k$ are equivalent for all input sequences k, they are called k-equivalent. In the Deming cycle, k = 4 (see Figure 3). The k -equivalent states are also l-equivalent for all $l \leq k$. Nonequivalent states are called *distinguishable*. All states that are distinguishable by input sequences of length k are k-distinct.

The preceding paragraph has shown that a Deming cycle may be expressed as a quintuple (see Equation 1) and that this behavior may be compared with any other automaton, such as $\hat{A}$ (see Equation 2) using the bisimulation function S (see Equation 3). The following paragraph describes the conversion of the control loops of a management system (ISMS) into a standard automaton $\hat{A}_{ISMS}$ and subsequently the equivalence of this automaton to the Deming standard automaton D.

Policies with feedback have, in general, been underappreciated in computer science research. In contrast, control systems engineering regularly implements control loops with built-in feedback capabilities to monitor technical systems, and these loops can be modeled in the framework of discrete-event systems (DES) theory. In general, control systems engineering is a discipline that mathematically models diverse systems in nature by analyzing their dynamic behavior. Control theory is used to create a controller mechanism that can shift the system behavior in a desired manner. Control loops have gained far-reaching significance because they are not purely technical models; they define general organizing principles that incorporate various concepts of self-regulation observed in biology, sociology, psychology, and general systems theory. An extensive body of literature discusses control loops; the reader is referred, for example, to (Miller, 1989). In the realm of control systems engineering, the task of a control loop can be defined as follows:

Definition 1: A control loop maintains the time-dependent parameters of a process within a predetermined range of values, particularly in response to disturbances.

The management systems defined in the ISO 27001, BS 25999, and ISO 20000 standards can be interpreted as socio-technical systems. Socio-technical systems differ from purely technical systems in that a subject is part of these systems. This chapter focuses only on these socio-technical management systems and in particular on their discrete-time behavior. A socio-technical system must have a controller, sensor, and actuator which must be customized for each company because the value chain differs from one company to another.

In essence, an ISMS follows a PDCA cycle, as shown in Figure 3. However, if the elements of an ISMS are transformed into the elements of a control loop, the control loop shown in Figure 4 is obtained. This representation illustrates the four elements of a Deming-cycle management system and the four elements of a control loop. Figure 4 illustrates a reference signal (setpoint) $v(k)$ within a loop that maintains the requirements for confidentiality, integrity, and availability (CIA) at predefined levels. The current security level $w(k)$ is generated by the disturbance (d) acting on the plant (the controlled system). The sensor(s) measure the current security level, denoted by $w(k)_S$. The controller is then adjusted by means of the reference signal $v(k)$ to restore the previously defined security level. As a corrective action, the signal $u(k) = v(k) - e(k)$ is created. This signal reflects the updating of the current security policy. The controller, sensor, and actuator specify, measure, and implement procedures and working instructions in the plant. The quantity $u(k)_A$ represents this signal, which acts on the plant to eliminate the perturbation (d).

The equivalence between the standard Deming cycle automaton D and the standard closed-loop automaton $\hat{A}_{ISMS}$, as expressed by Equation 4, will now be investigated. During conversion of the control loop into a standard automaton $\hat{A}_{ISMS}$, four states were defined: $\hat{z}_1$ = controller, $\hat{z}_2$ = actuator, $\hat{z}_3$ = plant (controlled system), and $\hat{z}_4$ = sensor (see Figure 4). The four states of $\hat{A}_{ISMS}$ can be compared with those of the standard Deming cycle automaton using Equation 4:

Equation 4. Comparison of states between D and $\hat{A}_{ISMS}$

$$(z_1, \hat{z}_1) =\in S = z_1 \sim \hat{z}_1$$
$$(z_2, \hat{z}_2) =\in S = z_2 \sim \hat{z}_2$$
$$(z_3, \hat{z}_4) =\in S = z_3 \sim \hat{z}_4$$
$$(z_4, \hat{z}_2) =\in S = z_4 \sim \hat{z}_2$$

Clearly, Equation 4 can be interpreted from the perspective of the standard automaton D as follows:

State 1: Plan → risk analysis according to ISO 27005, statement of applicability → Controller

State 2: Do → implement measurements (e.g., according to ISO 27002) → Actuator

State 4: Check → Check phase → Sensor

State 2: Act → Action phase, corrective action → Actuator

It is evident from Equation 4 and the states in the above list that a bisimulation does not exist for all k states of the Deming cycle (k = 4). For instance, no bisimulation exists for state $\hat{z}_3$. This indicates that the plant cannot be directly represented by the Deming cycle. The plant is defined only implicitly by the scope of the standard. The scope of an ISMS, as defined by ISO 27001, describes the value chain of a company, which is the plant (the controlled system). In contrast with control system engineering, here the controlled system (the plant) is part of the standard automaton. Consequently, an l-equivalence exists only because the state $\hat{z}_{k=3}$ is distinguishable. From the viewpoint of Discrete Event System theory, these four phases comprise a control loop, as shown in Figure 4.

Figure 4. Control loop for an ISMS as defined by ISO 27001

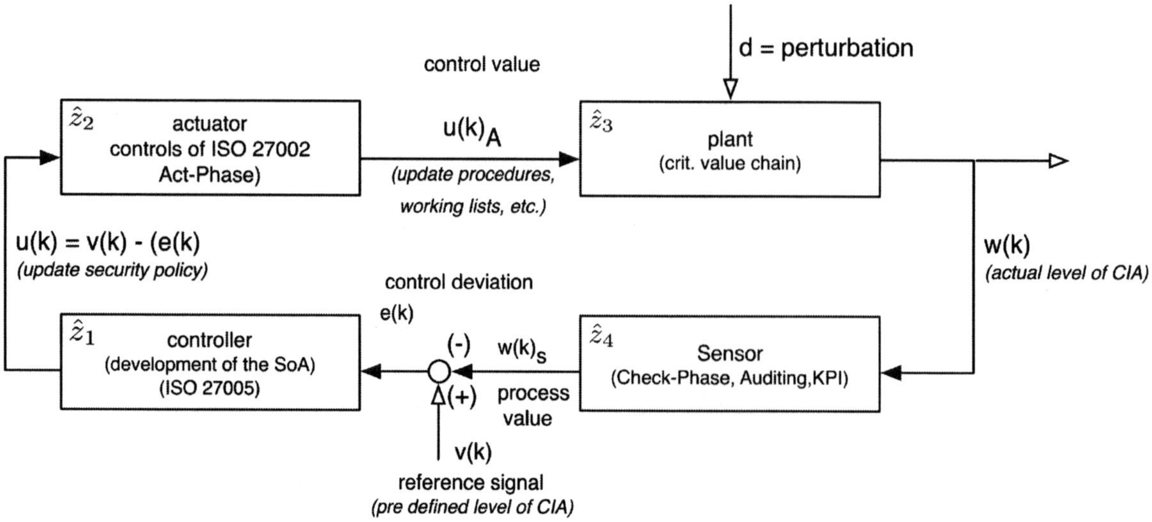

This section has discussed the elements of a control loop and of management systems and has shown their equivalence to a standard automaton with a feedback function. It has also been shown that the bisimulation (see Equation 4) between the standard automatons of the PDCA cycle using the elements of a standard loop can be expressed by the standard ISO 27001 automaton. Boehmer has performed further investigations of management systems defined by the BS 25999 and ISO 20000 standards (Boehmer, 2010b). The question also arises of whether management systems can occur only in isolation in a company, or whether multiple management systems can exist in parallel. This question has been investigated by Boehmer (2010b). From these investigations, it is clear that the three management systems can frequently be found coupled together in companies. It can be shown that ISO 20000 management systems are closely linked with ISO 27001 management systems, but only a loose link can be established between an ISO 27001 (ISMS) management system and a BS 25999 (BCMS) management system.

MODELING OF THE PLANT

The previous section showed that the controlled system in the Deming-cycle automaton could not be represented by a control loop. In a control loop, the controlled system and the disturbances acting on the controlled system play a decisive role. This section will therefore consider some aspects of quantitative modeling and discuss the controlled system.

A control system or the value chain of a company can be modeled qualitatively or quantitatively. Methods for the qualitative modeling of business processes (the value chain) include the Pi-Calculus, developed by Milner (1992), which formed the basis for the Business Process Management Notation (BPMN) and has become widespread in many areas of industry. Examples of tools based on this notation include ARIS-Designer, developed by A.W. Scheer of the University of Saarland (Scheer, 2001) and ADONIS from the University of Vienna (Kühn, 1996). These studies describe BPMN implementations of business processes using a qualitative representation. This qualitative approach is of great importance if the descriptions of business processes, definitions of interfaces, and assigned roles and resources need to be modeled. Use of a qualitative method can make business processes more transparent and improve the generation of working instructions.

A Business Continuity Experiment

On the other hand, if quantification of business processes is desired, formal methods and their implementation in tools are more appropriate. The interest in quantification may arise, for example, when determining the level of functionality needed to achieve compliance with the security criteria of a Business Continuity Plan (BCP). So far, in practice, only elaborate field experiments have been carried out. Boehmer et al. (2009c) published theoretical estimates based on the MCRL2 tool and related to formal methods. Especially in the case of a BCP, such an analysis is considered rare and has been previously verified only by a field study. The quantitative assessment of a BCP is of vital importance for a company because a BCP, in the event of a disaster, takes over responsibility for the objectives of the controlled system for a period of time. The need to establish a Business Continuity Management System (BCMS) incorporating several BCPs in case of catastrophic events in a company has been, since the Oxford study by Knight and Pretty (1996), assumed as a matter of course.

In a study by Boehmer et al. (2009c), it has been shown that formal methods can be used with process algebra, modal logic, and mu-calculus to examine BCP-based emergency processes for their performance (throughput) and their compliance with security requirements (the four-eyes principle). For these analyses, the MCRL2 tool from the *TU/e* toolkit was used. The field study involved a business process (value chain) — that is, a controlled system — and an existing emergency process (BCP), with MCRL2 used to test their performance and their level of compliance with security policies.

In this investigation, the whole state space was analyzed. From this test, non-intuitive results were obtained and are presented here. It was recognized that with the required capabilities of the previously defined emergency process (BCP), the viability of the system was not sufficient. A modification of the emergency process (BCP) was then performed, which showed that the required capabilities (throughput) and level of compliance with security policy (the four-eyes principle) could be achieved (Boehmer et al., 2009c). Use of a quantification method can make business processes more transparent and improve the generation of working instructions.

An E-Commerce Experiment

Further experiments are underway which consider a plant as an open system and study the interaction of management systems and their behavior with policies and formal methods (Brandt and Boehmer, 2011). The plant is the value chain of an e-commerce system that must respond to various load situations around the clock. For the e-business owner, one risk is that an inquiry may not be accommodated by the order-processing capacity of the e-commerce technology, and therefore sales may be lost. On the other hand, overdimensioning the technical capacity entails a reduction in revenue because the maintenance and operation costs of the oversized technical system bring in no additional sales revenue. Therefore, the objective is to find an optimal dynamic load-dependent (scalable) delivery level of technical components, which is controlled depending on time and events. Optimizing the objective function will minimize both the risk of financial loss due to lost sales and that of income reduction due to an oversized system.

To generate quantitative estimates, the business processes are modeled using formal methods. The model used is a hybrid model in which the system of levels of IT objects is modeled as a set of differential equations and the discrete system behavior by constraint automata (CA), according to the ideas expressed by Arbab et al. (2007). In practical application, this approach to estimating the capacity of IT objects is also an interesting topic for the evolving cloud computing technology.

In the two experiments described above, the preventive management of operational risk (OpRisk) was carried out essentially as a precaution so that certain risks could not occur. The next section takes up this aspect of the research and discusses decision-making for risk management and how to handle risk in controlled systems.

PREVENTIVE ADJUSTMENT OF RISKS WITH MANAGEMENT SYSTEMS

In terms of operational risks (OpRisk), the question is to define the potential loss (damage) that may arise in business operations and how it can be corrected proactively. In contrast to the market or the credit sector, no industry standard has emerged for identifying, quantifying, and managing operational risk, as noted by Boos and Schulte-Mattler (2001). An important consideration for operational risk analysis of the interaction between threats and vulnerabilities on an asset in a business process is that this analysis can retroactively affect the business process. The terms *asset*, *threat*, and *vulnerability* in this chapter are as defined in the ISO 27000 standard, sections 2.3, 2.45, and 2.46.

Unlike stock exchanges, which function under operational risks—according to Basel II, internal causes are considered in the foreground—the analysis of the possible exploitation of vulnerabilities must consider all appropriate threats. Furthermore, reliability theory plays a major role in the case of technical components.

Figure 5. Risk scenario with three different outcomes

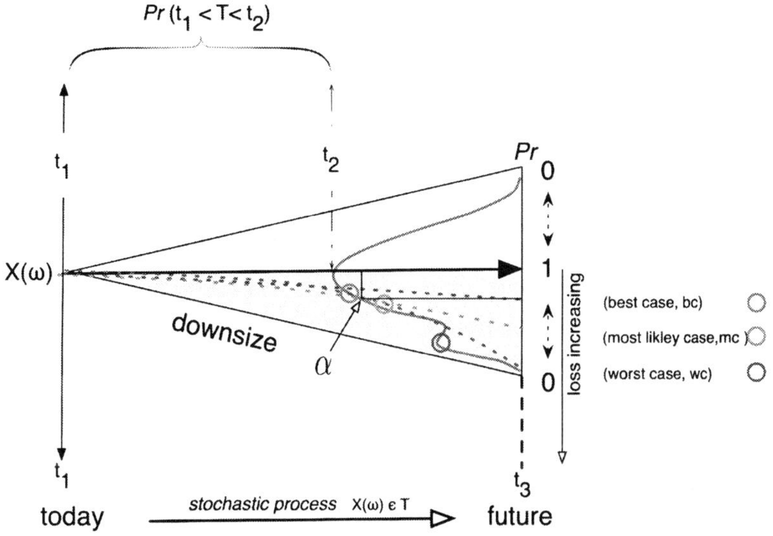

Although the approaches used in the market and financial sector are very different from those used in the field of operational risk, a desire exists, argues Leipold (2003), to obtain a single uniform measure to assess risk in the areas of market, finance, and operations. The risk measure can be expressed as a non-empty set G of measurable random variables associated with a σ-algebra A and a probability P.

Equation 5. Risk measure:

$\rho: G \rightarrow \Upsilon$.

The random variable $X(\omega)$ (see Figure 5) describes for the actual finite probability space (Ω, A, P) the potential harm over the time interval $(t \in T)$. The measure of risk interprets as necessary capital (risk capital) the amount that is necessary to drive to zero the possible loss incurred to forestall risk. The risk measure can be expected to have a number of properties (translation invariance, subadditivity, positive homogeneity, and monotonicity), as required in the pioneering work of Artzner et al. (2001) for a coherent risk measure. The corresponding measure space is determined by (Ω, A, ρ).

In the area of market and financial risks, the Value at Risk (VaR) measure is favored, or even more so, its coherent version, the Conditional Value at Risk. This measure describes the value at risk as the risk of the expected loss for a given confidence level (confidence interval α), which in a specific time interval $(t \in T)$ will not be exceeded. The CVaR describes the expected loss in the case that the VaR is exceeded. It can also be interpreted as the average worst-case loss if α (the confidence level of the VaR) is exceeded.

The operational value at risk (OpVaR) has been discussed in the literature, but there is a wide gap between theory and practice. In practice, a simple ordinal scale is still predominantly used, as proposed in the Basel Accord (2001). Also according to the Basel Accord, a textual description of risks by dividing them into classes relating to expected probability (P-robability) and severity of impact (I-mpact) is commonly used. Such methods are known as semi-quantitative methods. Through the use of two ordinal values, the risk values are entered as cell values in a P × I risk matrix, from which the risk level can then be read. If this *ad hoc* approach is used for all the risks in a value chain, a dot pattern is created in the P × I risk matrix. This risk matrix is often used to define three risk levels: low, medium, and high.

The semi-quantitative method for deriving risk level very quickly encounters its limits when several semi-quantitatively described risks need to be aggregated. The question has been raised whether the overall risks in a value chain need to be compared to the yield of the value chain. To study quantitative risk assessment in a value chain in which a management system was used for preventive mitigation of risks, a field study was performed from 2007 to 2010 in an energy company in Germany. In the following section, this field study and its findings will be presented.

Field Studies (2007–2010) at 26 Power Stations and 3 Surface Mining Operations

In a three-year field study, a leading energy company in Germany implemented an ISMS as defined by ISO 27001 at 29 locations with SCADA systems (Boehmer, 2011). Previously, the SCADA systems had been secured on the basis of security policies, but it had been increasingly recognized in recent years that the security policies were ineffective. Based on further analysis, it became clear that this company constituted an open system, and therefore an information security management system (ISMS) was implemented in accordance with ISO 27001.

The value-added processes were first extensively (qualitative) described (using ARIS-Designer) to provide as much detail as possible to the experts on the ground and to obtain a reliable description of the risk scenarios (possible undesirable changes of state of a process). It became apparent during the field study that it was easier for experts to think within a scenario and then assign different outcomes for this scenario (best case, most likely case, worst case, as shown in Figure 4) than to determine a single value of a probability density function. Similar experience with three-point estimation in the field of project management has been reported, for example in (Palmer, 1996).

The BetaPERT distribution or the underlying three-point estimate (best case, most likely case, worst case) is ideal for the determination of expert opinion and is often used for assessment of project risks. However, the BetaPERT distribution has until now not been mentioned in the literature for assessment of operational risks. It is clear, however, that if the quality of the input data is inferior, then the processed data (output data) in a distribution cannot be better; in short, garbage in, garbage out.

In this respect, the field study (the investigation of 29 power plants) placed particular emphasis on the input values for the risk scenario analysis. A risk scenario is understood to be a stochastic event described as follows:

Definition 2: A risk scenario is understood to be a model of a possible (stochastic) event (incident), contained in a set of events Ω that could happen in the future, and caused by violation of the protection objectives (confidentiality, availability, integrity) by the interaction of one or more threats representing a vulnerability.

Generally, a scenario is a possible, conceivable (stochastic) event, as expressed formally in Equation 6. It assigns a particular value to a random variable. In this context, a stochastic event can be seen as a risk event (Rsz). It will be estimated by a three-point risk estimate which assigns different loss probabilities (Pr) to a risk event (best case (bc), most likely case (mc), worst case (wc), as shown in Figure 5.

Equation 6 defines a risk scenario (Rsz) with $\varsigma = \{bc, mc, wc\}$ as the possible outcomes of this random variable $X(\omega)$ interpreted as a risk event (see Exhibit 1).

Exhibit 1. Equation 6. Different risk outcomes for one random variable

$$X(\omega) = Rsz_{\varsigma} := \begin{cases} if\varsigma = bc \mid \left(x_{bc} \ll x_{mc}\right) \wedge \Pr\left[X(\omega) = x_{bc}\right] \rightarrow best\ case \\ if\varsigma = mc \mid \left(x_{mc} > x_{bc}\right) \wedge \Pr\left[X(\omega) = x_{mc}\right] \rightarrow most\ likely\ case \\ if\varsigma = wc \mid \left(x_{wc} \gg x_{bc} \wedge x_{mc}\right) \wedge \Pr\left[X(\omega) = x_{wc}\right] \rightarrow worst\ case \end{cases}$$

The possible types of outcomes (Rszς) of risk events were estimated in workshops by local experts. An illustration of the stochastic process described by Equation 6 can be found in Figure 5. Furthermore, a distribution (the red line) of the three points representing the estimates was defined; this line shows the distribution of possible losses to absorb. In this case, the certain event (Pr = 1) is no longer a random event.

In terms of operational risks, only the grey shaded area of interest is normally referred to as a downside risk measure with X (ω) = {0, - ∞}. Assuming a time interval (t1, t3) in the probability space (Pr), the expected loss (VaR) can be determined for a confidence interval (α) by means of Equation 7, which provides a lower bound.

Equation 7. Value at Risk (VaR):

$$VaR_{\alpha} := \min\left\{x \mid \left(\Pr\left[X \leq x\right] > \alpha\right)\right\}.$$

As mentioned previously, the VaR is not a coherent risk measure, as demonstrated by Artzner (2001), because the VaR is based on a normal distribution. Figure 5 illustrates the distribution function, which was determined by the three-point risk estimation procedure. The drawback of the VaR is clearly illustrated by the reddish-brown line, which illustrates the confidence interval α. It can be clearly seen in Figure 5 that the worst-case scenario is not covered by the approximation of a purely normal distribution. Therefore, to assess single risks, the conditional VaR (CVaR) was used. The CVaR is the average loss of the worst cases.

Equation 8. Conditional Value at Risk (CVaR):

$$CVaR := \left\{x \mid \left(\Pr\left[X \leq x\right] < \alpha\right)\right\}.$$

In this context, only certain losses of interest are considered, those that are based on the intersection of assets, threats, and vulnerabilities with critical business processes.

As mentioned previously, special attention has been paid to the estimation of input variables using the three-point estimate (best case, most likely case, worst case). In addition, in the favorable consideration of the expert scenarios, an interval estimate was preferred instead of a point estimate, because probability theory is characterized by point estimation, which has so far been prevalent in risk analysis. However, it is often difficult in practice to estimate exactly the probability of an impact (best case, most likely case, worst case), as has been shown in practice in the field studies at the 29 locations. It was much easier for the surveyed experts to indicate a probability range (from - to), which is essentially a tolerance range.

Consequently, as a *precise estimate*, the information from expert opinion was incomplete, being only an indication of the lower (Lo) and upper limits (Up) between which a possible event can occur in a distribution function (see Figure 5). Therefore, each event (scenario ς = {bc, mc, wc}) was mapped into a closed interval (0,1) as a probability component. According to Weichselberger (2001), the interval probability (IP) for the closed interval Z_0 (0,1) can be defined with an σ-algebra *A* as follows.

Equation 9. Interval probability:

$$IP = A \rightarrow Z_0\left[0,1\right]$$
$$\varsigma \mapsto IP(\varsigma)\left[L_o(\varsigma),U_p(\varsigma)\right].$$

Equation 9 describes the uncertainty (error tolerance) of the expert opinions $\varsigma \mapsto IP(\varsigma)$ to the precise scenario estimates (ς) for the best case, most likely case, and worst case. Especially for the worst-case scenarios, it has been shown that the uncertainty in the estimate (the expert opinion) increases with increasing extent of damage and decreasing probability of occurrence. At this point, the limit of measurability is achieved. However, rare but high-impact risk events are of great importance in determining the value.

The three-year field study was carried out in various power plants, surface mines, gas-fired plants, coal-fired power plants, and hydroelectric plants. The goal of all power-plant processes is to produce energy (electricity) and thus to realize added value.

Energy is produced by burning fuel and operating a turbine. In addition, there are waste materials that must be disposed of. Figure 6 shows a section of the core processes, which operate in all power plants in a similar manner. To operate the main process plant (KP-0), the following key processes must occur sequentially: provide assistance and supplies (P-1), produce steam and electricity (P-2), and dispose of waste (P-3).

As an example, considering a detailed view only of the core process (P-2), it essentially consists of the parallel processes of process engineering (P-2V), control (P-2L), PDV (P-2P), and electrical (P-2E controlled). In other words, the operation of P-2 depends on the operation of subprocesses P-2V, P-2L, P-2P, and P-2E. If one of the subprocesses is not working properly, then the core process P-2 will be disrupted, and the power plant may even shut down.

On the detailed subprocess level, considering here P-2P (as shown in Figure 6), it is possible for the experts to estimate risk scenarios (best case, most likely case, worst case) and their potential effects (see Figure 5) for the process of steam and power generation. In a minority of cases, the impact can be understood by comparing the performance to the basic schedule and identifying episodes of non-fulfillment of the basic plan. The term *damage* means in this example that no energy is output from the power plant for an accounting unit of 15 minutes, thus creating a loss for the power plant owner. The core processes (P-1, P-2, P-3) must run sequentially, but in the case of P-2 only, if P-2P is operating (works). Figure 7 illustrates the process elements.

In the scenarios examined, conditions that could occur with a nonzero probability (control operations) do not follow a regular pattern. For frequent (k) repetitions of the state sequence (or control), it has been shown that the state described by Equation 10 is a very common condition (trend). Here, the common condition of the random variable $X(\omega)$ is determined as:

Equation 10. Probability of state (trend):

$$\Pr\left[X\left(\omega\right) = x_a\right] \approx 1.$$

This means that the deviation x_a in energy production, to a tolerance of + / - 5 MW, is higher than in the initial schedule, and therefore no loss occurred in the discrete time step (k). The other scenarios are described by Equation 6 and illustrated in Figure 5. The results of the risk scenarios are shown in Figure 8. The risk scenarios have been evaluated using the extended three-point estimate, represented by the blue lines or indicated by the color-coded stripes. The two arrows indicate the reduction of the loss by the implementation of the two management systems with repeated risk

Figure 6. Core processes of a power plant

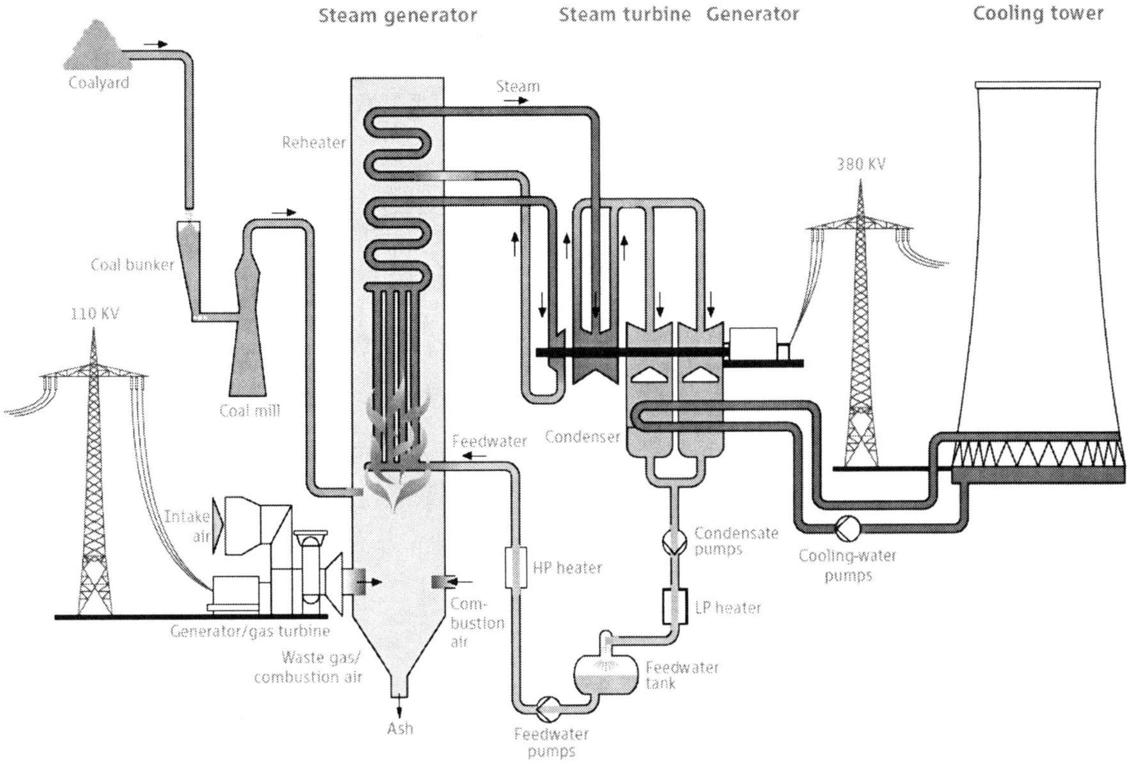

analysis. Boehmer (2011) has pointed out in his paper that Figure 8 provides a compressed representation (aggregation of single risks by means of a convolution of the density distribution) across all sites and all SCADA processes.

As a result, it can be stated that the greater the uncertainty in the approximation, the greater will be the loss and the less often it will occur (Figure 8). The lower (beige) dashed line represents the potential loss distribution after implementation of the two management systems (ISMS and BCMS). Therefore, the beige line also describes the remaining risks that are accepted by the locations. Boehmer (2009) showed that an ISMS designed to respond proactively to risks and a reactive BCMS which activates emergency processes are aligned. Decision theory has resolved the issues of which management system should be implemented for which risk scenarios and which context should be preferred to provide protection that is effective, economically efficient, or both. The following paragraph discusses further this conflict in management systems.

The reductions in expected loss which were achieved by the implementation of management systems (ISMS, BCMS) are remarkable. Although both management systems contribute to a reduction in possible losses (see the vertical arrows in Figure 8), the remaining loss expectation for rare but serious damage incidents is higher than for small but frequent losses. This is a non-intuitive result and shows the importance of developing a Business Continuity Management System and associated Business Continuity Plan (BCP). Quantifying various aspects of a Business Continuity Plan was discussed in the previous section (see the BCP experiment). Finally, it should be noted that prior assessment and reduction of operational risk, which could lead to a significant reduction in the required risk capital through the use of

Figure 7. Process element P-2P modeled with ARIS

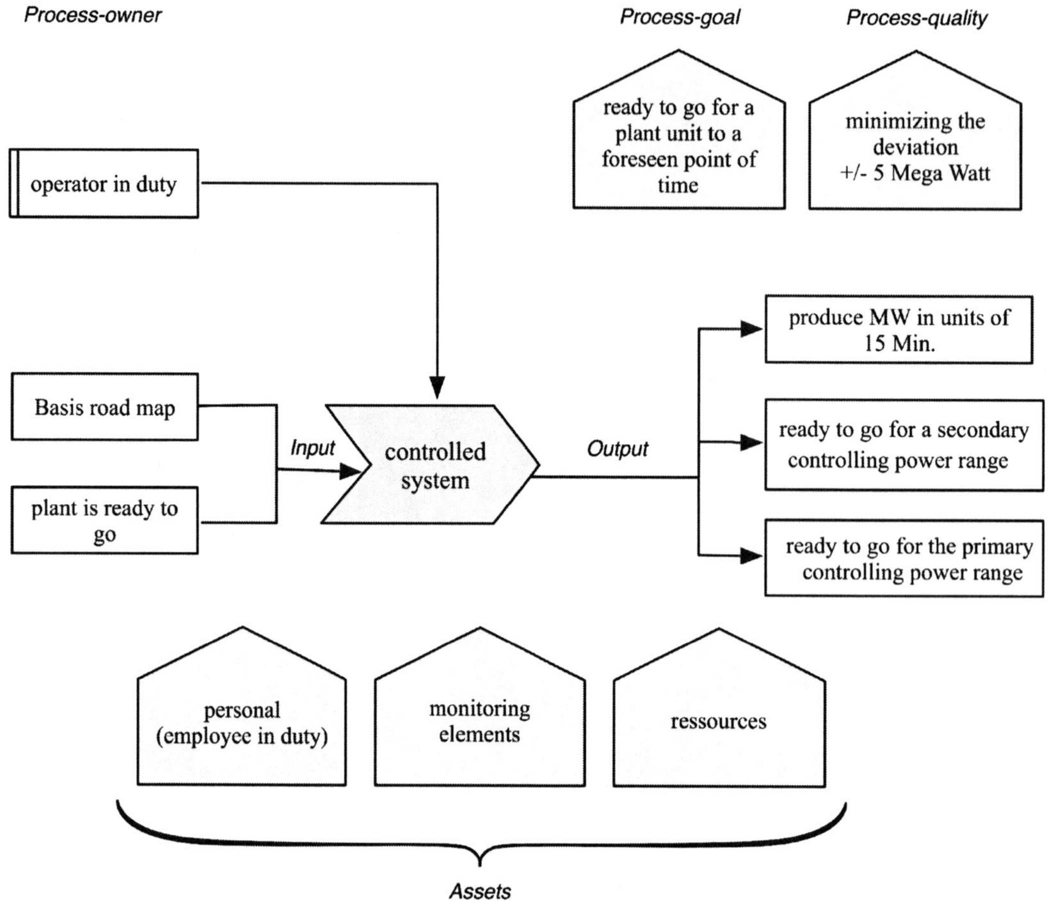

management systems, has not yet been discussed in the literature.

The following section will address the different objectives of economic efficiency and effectiveness of protection for the controlled system in a socio-technical loop and how to handle them in an information security management system.

TARGET FUNCTIONS AND MANAGEMENT SYSTEMS

This section addresses the measurement of management systems. From the literature, two methods are known to be suitable in principle for the measurement of management processes. The first is the maturity model, developed at Carnegie Mellon University. This concept, known by the acronym CMMI, is today used not only for its original purpose of measuring software development processes, but also now for measuring the maturity of information security management systems such as an ISMS. The second method is the indicator or metrics method, also known as the Key Performance Indicator (KPI) method.

Both methods have their strengths and weaknesses, but a company needs to be able to evaluate the effectiveness and efficiency of its management system, which is impossible with the maturity model. Therefore, the indicator method and the derivation of an objective function for an infor-

Figure 8. Reduction of the expected loss distribution by security management systems

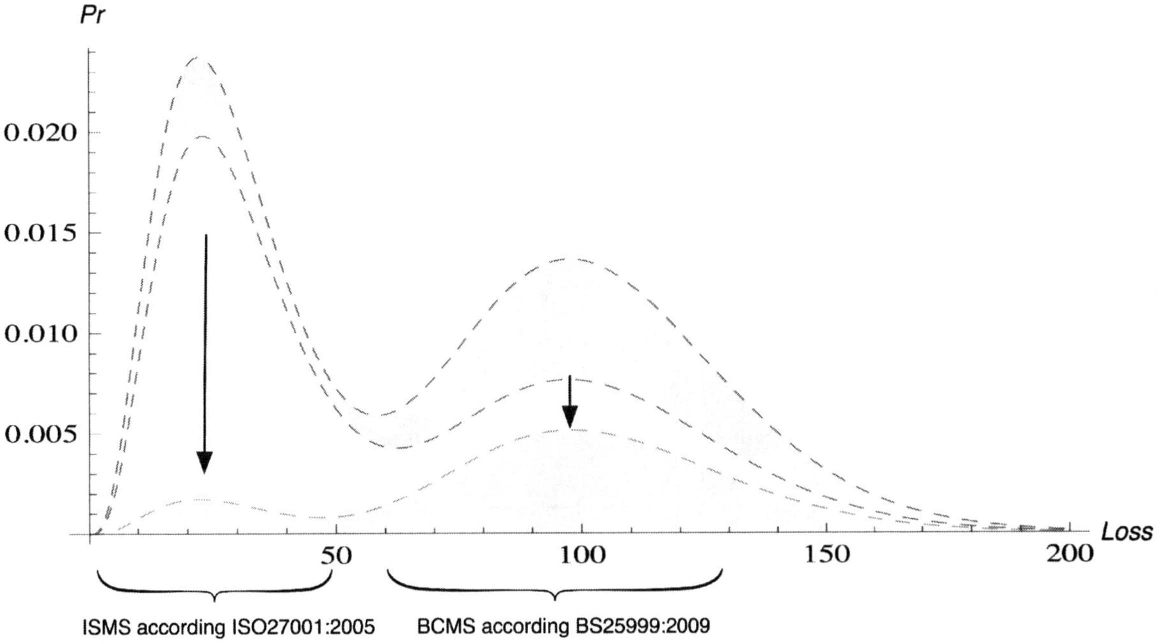

mation security management system will now be discussed.

In purely economically oriented management systems, the company is essentially set up to pursue profit objectives only (Chamberlain, 1962). This purely economically oriented management system is not suitable as a model for an information security management system.

A number of previous studies by Boehmer (2008, 2009b, 2009c) have clarified the role of the effectiveness and efficiency of a management system. However, no target function can be derived from these considerations. Therefore, a target function must be derived from the characteristics of effectiveness and economic efficiency to define a requirement for management systems of second order.

The opposing system characteristics of effectiveness and efficiency can be formulated as an optimization problem, in which the levels of effectiveness and economic efficiency are normalized to 1 and vary over an interval (0,1) to define the hypotenuse and leg of a right triangle. Figure 9 illustrates this situation. The effectiveness values, (Efk = a, a', a" | Efk $\in$ R), and the efficiency values, (Efz = b, b', b" | Efz $\in$ R), in the interval (0,1) transform this optimization problem into a graphic optimization problem. To illustrate this principle, Figure 9 shows four rectangles. The first rectangle is delimited by the values (a, b) and is marked by vertical hatching. The second rectangle is delimited by the values (a', b') and is transparent. The third rectangle is delimited by the values (a", b"). The optimization problem is solved by maximizing the area spanned by the rectangle embedded in the triangle (see Figure 9). The sides of the rectangle are denoted by a_0 and b_0. Given Efz = b" and Efk = a" and letting *f* represent the area of the rectangle, the target function can then be defined as the product of the lengths of each side:

Equation 11. Objective function:

$$f(a'',b'') = a'' \times b''.$$

Figure 9. Defining the governing objective function for a management system

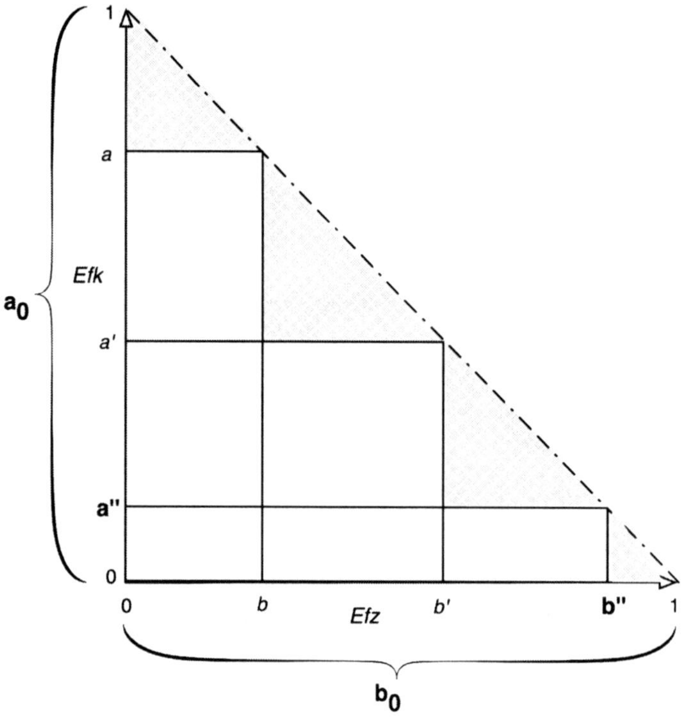

Maximizing the area of the rectangle delimited by a'' and b'' (see Figure 9) yields the following triangle relationship if b'' is given:

Equation 12. Triangle relationship:

$$\frac{a_0}{b_0} = \frac{a''}{b_0 - b''} \rightarrow a'' = \frac{a_0}{b_0} \times (b_0 - b'').$$

Maximizing the area by substituting the right side of Eq. 12 into Eq. 11 yields:

Equation 13. Second derivative:

$$f(b'') = \frac{a_0}{b_0} \times b''(b_0 - b'').$$

The question then arises of determining the point at which the function *f* has a global maximum. Because *f* is differentiable as a polynomial function, it follows that:

Equation 14. Polynomial function:

$$f(b'') = \frac{a_0}{b_0} \times (b_0 - 2b'').$$

Any solution to this equation is also a root of the function f (b''). A solution that also gives f (b'') = 0 and b'' = 0 is a useful solution. However, the best solution is given by Efk = a' and Efz = b'. This discussion concludes with a summary of the importance of the target function for operation of the control loop (see Figure 4) in the management systems discussed previously, which were designed in accordance with the ISO 27001 standard.

From the equation for a linear control loop in an ISMS as proposed by Boehmer (2010a), it can be shown that a perturbation can be compensated for in different ways, depending on how the controller and actuator are defined. From the manner in which the actions of the controller and actuator are adjusted, management systems can be divided into two classes, as discussed in (Boehmer, 2010a).

Definition 3: A first-order management system describes the compensation behavior after a disturbance in a socio-technical system.

Definition 4: A second-order management system meets the conditions of a first-order management system and also satisfies other requirements. Compensation after the disruption is also described by economic criteria. The controller operates under an overall objective function that affects the effectiveness and the economic efficiency of each compensation action.

The management system defined according to ISO 27001 satisfied the requirements of a control loop, but the standard addresses only the effectiveness of the management system (see ISO 27001, page 6, section 4.2.3.c). However, economic efficiency is not explicitly required, so the system meets the requirements for a second-order management system. Boehmer (2010a) has stated that in the ISO 27001 standard for the Check and Act phases, as well as for the Statement of Applicability (SoA), the target function must be supplemented to address effectiveness and economic efficiency. The reason is that, for management systems that influence the value chain through controller actions, it would be absurd if the risk compensation procedure did not take account of economic conditions.

SOLUTIONS AND RECOMMENDATIONS

In this chapter, it has been shown formally by equations and experimentally by a field study that information security management systems are preferable to security policies as a way to achieve enterprise security. The reason for this is the ability of management systems to compensate for disturbances in open systems. Policies are ideal, however, if the objective is to protect closed and isolated systems.

For the practical application of management systems, this means that whether a system is to be considered as an open, closed, or even an isolated system must be determined in advance. Only then can the next steps be addressed by the appropriate type of security method. If the decision is to implement a management system[2] to protect the information in a company, attention must be paid, not only to the ISO 27001 standard, but also to the ISO 27003 standard (Implementation Guide) as well as ISO 27004 (Measurement of the Management System) and ISO 27005 (Risk Management). The management system is implemented in the Check phase and continuously improved in the Act phase. However, this iterative continuous improvement process results in a state of balance or equilibrium state if the effectiveness and economic efficiency of the measures taken are carefully balanced to achieve risk prevention. This is an approach to obtaining an optimal operating condition for a company.

FUTURE RESEARCH DIRECTIONS

In spite of recent advances in management systems research, a number of interesting questions remain open, such as whether decision-making about risks is a matter for decision theory falls into the realm of game theory.

In this discussion, decision-making about risks will be addressed using decision theory. There is assumed to be a single agent, facing five alternatives with two different goals, and acting in a given environmental situation. The five alternatives for dealing with risks can be identified as *reducing*, *avoiding*, *transferring*, *accepting*, and *elimination*. The two objectives can be characterized as effective safeguarding versus protection of economic efficiency. However, certain cases could also be described as involving a technical expert to achieve optimal safeguarding and the owner of the plant (budget owner) who would prefer protection of economic efficiency. With this interpretation, the case would fall into the realm of game theory, which could identify other solutions. These aspects are currently the object of a follow-up project involving the same field study analyzed in this chapter.

CONCLUSION

The properties of static and dynamic policies are often explored in computer science. There are a number of situations in which policies play a significant role, and consideration of the theoretical treatment of these policies is useful. In this chapter, it has been shown that the implementation of current policies is not necessarily adequate for meeting the requirements of today's enterprises. In particular, the field of information security often requires feedback on the effectiveness of a set of policies. A lack of feedback creates difficulties for both the classical static policies and the newer dynamic policies. This chapter has shown that dynamic policies can be expressed using system theory with feedback control loops. It has been demonstrated that control loops in the system theory of technical systems can be used to describe the behavior of socio-technical systems. These are known as management systems, and their behavior is equivalent to the behavior of technical control loops. As examples for analysis, one standard and one management system (ISO 27001) and the behaviors of a PDCA cycle and a loop were studied. It was demonstrated that this standard can be described using system theory for the control loops. In addition, an objective classification scheme for management systems was developed. Management systems that address a dysfunction using only one controller are defined as first-order management systems. Second-order management systems use a higher-level target function as the controller.

In contrast to purely economic management systems, where the target function can be defined by a single variable (revenue), the target function of a management system for enterprise security is determined by two variables that are subject to a tradeoff. The solution to this conflict leads to an optimization problem, which can only be solved iteratively. A practical implementation was derived for one example.

REFERENCES

Anderson, R. (2006). *Security engineering: A guide to building dependable distributed systems* (2nd ed.). Cambridge, UK: Wiley.

Arbab, F., Chothia, T., Meng, S., & Moon, Y.-J. (2007). Component connectors with QoS guarantees. In Murphy, A. L., & Vitek, J. (Eds.), *Coordination 2007, LNCS 4467* (pp. 286–304). Berlin, Germany: Springer-Verlag.

Artzner, P., Delbaen, F., Eber, J. M., & Heath, D. (2001). Coherent measures of risk. *Mathematical Finance, 9*(3), 203–228. doi:10.1111/1467-9965.00068

Basel Committee. (2001). *Operational risk.* Supporting Document to the New Basel Capital Accord on Banking Supervision (May 31, 2001).

Boehmer, W. (2008). Appraisal of the effectiveness and efficiency of an information security management system based on ISO 27001. *Proceedings, Second International Conference on Emerging Security Information, Systems and Technologies (SECUWARE 2008)*, Cap Esterel, France, August 25–31, 2008, (pp. 1–8). IEEE Computer Society.

Boehmer, W. (2009a). *Cost-benefit trade-off analysis of an ISMS based on ISO 27001.* ARES Conference: The International Dependability Conference, March 16—19, 2009, Fukuoka Institute of Technology (FIT), Fukuoka, Japan, IEEE Computer Society.

Boehmer, W. (2009b). Survivability and business continuity management system according to BS 25999. *Proceedings, Third International Conference on Emerging Security Information, Systems and Technologies (SECUWARE '09)*, June 18–23, 2009, Athens/Glyfada, Greece, (pp. 142–147). IEEE Computer Society.

Boehmer, W. (2009c). Performance, survivability and cost aspects of business continuity processes according to BS25999. *International Journal on Advances in Security, 2*(4). ISSN 1942–2636

Boehmer, W. (2010a). Toward an objective function for an information security management system. *Proceedings, Third IEEE International Symposium on Trust, Security and Privacy for Emerging Applications (TSP-2010)*, Bradford, UK, 29 June–1 July, 2010, IEEE Computer Society.

Boehmer, W. (2010b). Analysis of strongly and weakly coupled management systems in information security. *Proceedings, Fourth International Conference on Emerging Security Information, Systems, and Technologies (SECURWARE 2010)*, July 18–25, 2010, Venice/Mestre, Italy, IEEE Computer Society.

Boehmer, W. (2010c). *Theorie und Anwendung diskreter ereignisorientierter und rückgekoppelter Systeme in der Informationssicherheit.* Habilitation thesis (in preparation), Technische Universität Darmstadt, Germany.

Boehmer, W. (2011). Field study to examine a possible reduction of risk capital in the case of operational risk-based control loop by security management systems. *Proceedings, Fifth International Conference on Emerging Security Information, Systems, and Technologies (SECURWARE 2011)*, August 21–27, 2011, France (in preparation).

Boos, K. H., & Schulte-Mattler, H. (2001). Basel II: Methoden zur Quantifizierung operationeller Risiken. *Die Bank, 8*, 549–553.

Capra, F. (1996). *The web of life: A new scientific understanding of living systems*. Anchor Books/Doubleday.

Deming, W. E. (1986). *Out of the crisis*. Cambridge, MA: MIT Press.

Elo, J. H. P., & Elo, M. (2003). Information security management: A new paradigm. *Proceedings, 2003 Annual Research Conference of the South African Institute of Computer Scientists and Information Technologists on Enablement through Technology (SAICSIT '03)*, Johannesburg, 130–136, South African Institute for Computer Scientists and Information Technologists, 2003.

Jaques, P. A., & Viccari, R. M. (2006). Considering students' emotions in computer-mediated learning environments. In Ma, Z. (Ed.), *Web-based intelligent e-learning systems: Technologies and applications* (pp. 122–138). Hershey, PA: Information Science Publishing.

Knight, R., & Pretty, D. (1996). *The impact of catastrophes on shareholder value. Oxford Executive Research Briefings*. Oxford, UK: Templeton College, Oxford University.

Kühn, H., Karagiannis, D., & Junginger, S. (1996). *Metamodellierung in dem BPMS-Analysewerkzeug ADONIS, Konferenz Informatik '96, Schwerpunktthema, Softwaretechnik und Standards*, 25-27 September 1996, Uni Klagenfurt.

Leippold, M., & Vanini, P. (2003). *The quantification of operational risk*. Retrieved from http://ssrn.com/abstract=481742 or doi:10.2139/ssrn.481742

Miller, R. M. (1988). Market automation: Self-regulation in a distributed environment. *ACM SIGGROUP Bulletin, 9*(2–3), 299–308. doi:10.1145/966861.45443

Milner, R. (2006). Pure bigraphs: Structure and dynamics. *Information and Computation, 204*(1), 60–122. doi:10.1016/j.ic.2005.07.003

Milner, R. (1992). Calculus of mobile processes. *Information and Computation, 100*(1), 1–40. doi:10.1016/0890-5401(92)90008-4

Pucella, R., & Weissman, V. (2004). *Foundations of software science and computation structures. Reasoning about Dynamic Policies, LNCS 2987/2004* (pp. 453–467). Berlin, Germany: Springer.

Salehl, M. S., Alrabiah, A., & Bakry, S. H. (2007). Using ISO 17799: 2005 information security management: A stope view with six sigma approach. *International Journal of Network Management, 7*, 85–97. doi:10.1002/nem.616

Scheer, A.-W. (2001). *ARIS-Modellierungs-Methoden, Metamodelle, Anwendungen*. Berlin, Germany: Springer.

Shewhart, W. A. (1939, reprint 1986). *Statistical method from the viewpoint of quality control*. Dover Publications. ISBN-13: 978-0486652320

Shewhart, W. A. (1980). Economic control of quality of manufactured product. *American Society for Quality Control., ISBN-13*, 9780873890762.

Solms, B., & Solms, R. (2005). From information security to... business security? *Computers & Security, 24*, 271–273. doi:10.1016/j.cose.2005.04.004

van der Meyden, R. (1996). The dynamic logic of permission. *Journal of Logical Computing, 6*(3), 465–479. doi:10.1093/logcom/6.3.465

Von Groote, J. F., et al. (2010). *MCRL2: Analyzing system behavior*. TU-Eindhoven. Retrieved from http://www.mcrl2.org/mcrl2/wiki/index.php/Home

Weichselberger, K. (2001). *Elementare Grundbegriffe einer allgemeineren Wahrscheinlichkeitsrechnung I*. Heidelberg, Germany: Physica-Verlag. doi:10.1007/978-3-642-57583-9

KEY TERMS AND DEFINITIONS

Control System: A control system maintains the time-dependent parameters of a process within a predetermined range of values, particularly in response to disturbances.

Cost/Benefit Analysis: Done to determine how well, or how poorly, a planned action will turn out.

Management Systems: Describes the tasks of linking management and methods to sharing management duties goals, manage and control to manage successfully.

Security policy[3]: Is a statement of what is, and what is not, allowed.

Systems Theory: Used to refer specifically to self-regulating systems that are self-correcting through feedback.

Target Function: The (unknown) function which the learning problem attempts to approximate.

Tradeoff: A situation that involves losing one aspect of something in return for gaining another aspect.

ENDNOTES

1. cfg. http://www.iso27001security.com/html/27001.html, last accessed November 2010.
2. Cfg. http://www.iso27001security.com/index.html, last accessed November 2010.
3. Cfg. Bishop, M.: Computer Security, Art and Science, p. 9, Addison-Wesley, 2005.

Chapter 14
Fraud and Identity Theft Issues

Ranaganayakulu Dhanalakshmi
Anna University, India

Chenniappan Chellappan
Anna University, India

ABSTRACT

Identity theft and identity fraud are terms used to refer to all types of crime in which someone wrongfully obtains and uses another person's personal data in some way that involves fraud or deception, typically for economic gain. In spite of the different possible attacks discussed in later chapters, this chapter can focus on phishing attacks – a form of indirect attacks– such as an act of sending an e-mail to a user falsely claiming to be an established legitimate enterprise in an attempt to scam the user into surrendering private information that will be used for identity theft. The e-mail directs the user to visit a Web site where they are asked to update personal information, such as passwords and credit card, social security, and bank account numbers, that the legitimate organization already has. Phishing attacks use 'spoofed' e-mails and fraudulent websites designed to fool recipients into divulging personal financial data such as credit card numbers, account usernames and passwords, social security numbers, et cetera. The vulnerabilities on various phishing methods such as domain name spoofing, URL obfuscation, susceptive e-mails, spoofed DNS and IP addresses, and cross site scripting are analyzed, and the chapter concludes that an integrated approach is required to mitigate phishing attacks.

1. INTRODUCTION

Identity theft is one of the major upcoming threats in cybercrime which defines as an unlawful activity where the identity of an existing person is used as a target without that person's consent. It is a specific form of identity fraud. Identity fraud is a fraud committed with identity as a target. Identity Theft and Identity Fraud can be brought under the terminology of "Identity related crime' which concerns all punishable activities that have identity as a target or a principal tool. Identity

DOI: 10.4018/978-1-4666-0197-0.ch014

theft/fraud in the financial system affects four main kinds of victims, essentially governments, private companies detaining large amounts of data, financial services providers and customers (whether businesses or natural persons) and the consequences for them vary. There are obviously direct financial losses, e.g. the amounts directly extracted by criminals from the accounts etc, but also indirect costs for businesses, governments and consumers in spoiling their names.

A person's identity is very essential, concrete, and valid in a real world and is supported by legal documents. In the online world, however, a person's identity is less tangible. Some digital data, such as passwords, account names, and logins, may not be considered elements of a person's legal identity. Such data can be made valid in identifying and providing access to other private data.

The Fair and Accurate Credit Transactions Act of 2003 (FACTA) defines Identity theft as

"A fraud committed using the identifying information of another person, subject to such further definition as the FTC [Federal Trade Commission] may prescribe, by regulation." Pursuant to FACTA, the FTC has recently proposed a more specific definition of identity theft that describes what is meant by "identifying information":

1. *The term 'identity theft' means a fraud committed or attempted using the identifying information of another person without lawful authority. Identifying information may be*
    a. *Name, SSN (Social Security Number), DOB (date of birth), Government-issued driver's license or identification number, Passport number, PAN number (Tax Payer identification number).*
    b. *Unique biometric data, such as fingerprint, voice print, retina or iris image representation*

Top-Ten IT Issues, 2010. As per a recent survey by EDUCASE, the top ten IT issues identified are:

1. Funding IT
2. Administrative/ERP/Information Systems
3. Security
4. Teaching and Learning with Technology
5. Identity/Access Management
6. a)DisasterRecovery/BusinessContinuity(tie)
7. b) Governance, Organization, and Leadership(tie)
8. Agility, Adaptability, and Responsiveness
9. Learning Management Systems
10. Strategic Planning
11. Infrastructure/Cyber infrastructure

Hence identity and access management is very crucial in this fast evolving world which finds more importance.

2. METHODS OF IDENTITY THEFT

The following overview gives the most important techniques used to obtain identity-related information. Methods of Identity theft can be classified as follows (see also Table 1).

2.1 Traditional Physical Methods

- Direct Access to information - By persons who gain trust over the individuals.
- Dumpster Diving – obtaining information from trash bins
- Theft of physical objects like purse/wallet, cell phones, computers having high source of information
- Shoulder surfing – Persons who obtain the identity data when accessing ATMs.
- Mail theft – obtaining from mail boxes
- Skimming – Magnetic strip duplication

Table 1. Taxonomy of phishing attacks

Medium of Attack	Setup	Type of attack	Target Activity
Email	a. Embedded Forms b. Attachments c. URLs	a. Phisher uses credentials b. Money Laundering	1. Login credentials 2. Banking credentials 3. Credit card details 4. Address information 5. Personal information 6. Confidential documents 7. Attack propagation 8. Botnets
Message Boards	a. URLs	a. Malware requests/sends credentials	
Advertisements/ Pop-ups	a. URLs	a. Urges to enter personal identity details b. Cross-Site scripting attacks	
Instant chat	a. URL b. Prerecorded message	a. Man-in –the middle attacks	

2.2 Technology-Based Identity Theft Techniques

- **Hacking, unauthorized access to systems, and database theft:** Hackers gain unauthorized access to users data, exploits the obtained data.
- **Phishing:** A new and fast growing online scam, a technique which masquerades as a trustworthy organization in an e-mail message. The e-mail message is used to lure victims into providing account and other personal information.
- **Pharming:** The term "pharming" is derived from the term "phishing" which is also known as "domain spoofing".
- **DNS Cache poisoning:** This technique resembles Pharming, where the users are directed to a fake website that resembles as legitimate site. The main difference is that the tampering of the DNS record is done locally on the computer used to access a website, instead of in a DNS server.
- **Spyware, Malware and viruses:** Spyware is known for causing system slowdowns or crashes as well as unwanted advertising and interminable pop-up messages which may obtain identity information.'

3. OCCURRENCES OF IDENTITY THEFT/FRAUD

3.1. Direct Attack between the Person and the Authentication Data

- **Worms – ega key logger**. Authentication data is directly taken from a person by manipulation of his input device (in most cases local computer). This attack is directed non selectively to many input devices (1: n attack); the person is not addressed directly.
- **Social engineering**. Using communication for example via telephone authentication data is directly taken from the user by giving him a seemingly plausible reason for disclosing the requested data e.g. for testing purposes by administrative personal of the enterprise's IT department. This type of attack is directed to a specific person.
- **Trojan Horses / Key logging** etc. sent via e-mail attachment. In the first step a spam mail containing malicious code in an attachment is not specifically sent to various users (1: n attack). By opening the attachment for example a key logger is installed that starts obtaining the authentication data in a second step.

3.2 Indirect Attack on Reference Data or via Other Links

- **Obtain the related identifiers & authorizations** – From the centrally stored reference data and related additional identifiers. This attack can either be 1: n or specific data records 1: 1.
- **Manipulating the reference Data**
- **Phishing**
    - Attacker sends a spam mail that seems to originate from a trusted brand name (e.g. a ban to many recipients (1: n attack).
    - Urges the recipients to click on an embedded link that leads them to a manipulated web site.
    - On this site the user is duped to enter authentication data.
- **"Man in the middle" attacks** - communication between user and system is intercepted. This type of attacks is potentially very powerful among others.
- **ReplayAttacks**. An IP-packet containing authentication data is manipulated concerning the sender address and resent to the receiving system. This type of attack is directed to a user of a specific input device (direct attack on link 1, 1: 1 attack).
- **Identity theft by redirecting the communication to a manipulated web site** e.g. by using DNS-spoofing, manipulated proxies or manipulation of rooting tables. On the manipulated web site the user is duped to enter authentication data. This type of attack is concerning some steps similar to phishing (2 steps, indirect attack on link 3, 1: n attack).

4. IMPACT OF IDENTITY THEFT AND FRAUD

Once they have your personal information, identity thieves go about their business in a variety of ways (see Figure 1).

Figure 1. Outcomes of identity theft

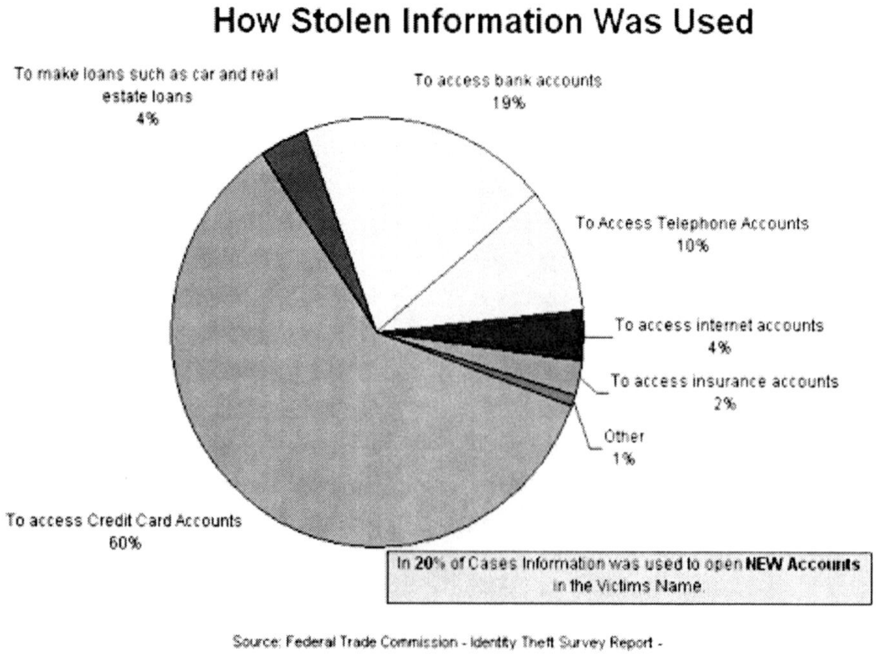

Credit card fraud:

1. Open new credit card accounts in your name.
2. May use the existing cards and don't pay the bills
3. May change the billing address on your credit card so that you no longer receive bills, and then run up charges on your account.

Bank/finance fraud:

1. Open a bank account in your name and write bad checks.
2. Authorize electronic transfers in your name from your accounts, and drain your savings.

Government documents fraud:

1. May get a driver's license or official ID card issued in your name but with their picture.
2. May file a fraudulent tax return using your information.

5. INTERNET AND ON-LINE RELATED IDENTITY THEFT: PHISHING

The objective is identity or data theft.The term "phishing" emerged in 1996 when thieves stole America Online (AOL) accounts using email as a fishing "hook" to steal passwords from AOL users. Microsoft defines it as "*Phishing is a type of deception designed to steal your identity. In Phishing scams, scam artists try to get you to disclose valuable personal data—like credit card numbers, passwords, account data, or other information—by convincing you to provide it under false pretenses. Phishing schemes can be carried out in person or over the phone, and are delivered online through spam e-mail or pop-up windows.* "(Microsoft, 2005a).

Phishing is not restricted to email and user account credentials. Attackers also use instant messaging (IM), exploited websites, peer-to-peer (P2P) networks, and search engines to download and run key logging malcode or direct victims to websites which are fraudulent or may contain malcode. The goal is no longer restricted to only username and password access to bank accounts. Social Security numbers, credit cards, passwords, logins and other confidential information are also being stolen.

- Phishing targets businesses.
- Phishing targets individuals accessing personal information.
- Phishing targets government agencies.
- Phishes link to malicious websites.

6. ANATOMY OF A PHISHING EMAIL

"Phishing" is the term for an e-mail scam also called as "Spear Phishing" that spoofs legitimate companies in an attempt to defraud people of personal information such as logins, passwords, credit card numbers, bank account information and social security numbers. For example, an e-mail may appear to come from PayPal claiming that the recipient's account information must be verified because it may have been compromised by a third party. However, when the recipient provides the account information for verification, the information is really sent to a phisher, who is then able to access the person's account.

The simplified flow of information in a phishing attack is illustrated in Figure 2 and is as follows

1. A deceptive message is sent from the phisher to the user.
2. A user provides confidential information to a phishing server
3. The phisher obtains the confidential information from the server.
4. The confidential information is used to impersonate the user.

Figure 2. E-mail based phishing attack

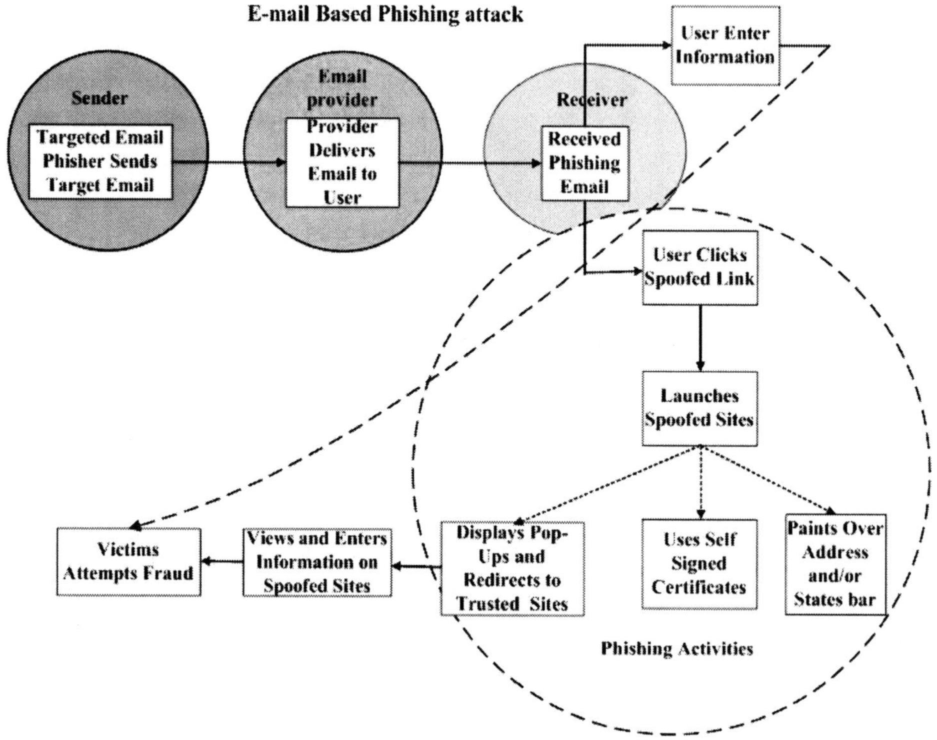

5. The phisher obtains illegitimate gain promoting online fraud and the victim attempts fraud.

Figure 3 shows an example of phishing e-mail.

The e-mail may claim that the recipient's account information is outdated, a credit card is expired, or the account has been randomly selected for verification. The request is framed in an urgent situation requiring a quick response. To collect this information, the phishing e-mail generally provides a link to a phishing Web site.

Here are ways to identify Phishing email.

Generic Greeting - Phishing emails are generalized such as "Dear User" or Dear Customer".

Fake Links – Most phishing emails use valid looking links which are called as URL obfuscation or leading to fake websites to steal the identity.

- Use of the legitimate company's image, logo, icon and similar font schemes
- Links to the legitimate websites/services
- Spoofing headers to provide a look-a-like appearance of reputable companies such as @eBay.com, @paypal.com etc.

Sense of urgency – Phishing emails generally express a sense of urgency and offering valuable proposition forcing the customers to take action immediately failing leads to serious results. For e.g. If you don't respond within 24 hours after receiving this email your account will be deactivated and removed from the server.

Legitimate looking Sender's Email id – Phishers make use of spoofed identity to act as legitimate senders.Claimed senders identity defers from the reply address email.

Figure 3. Sample phishing e-mail

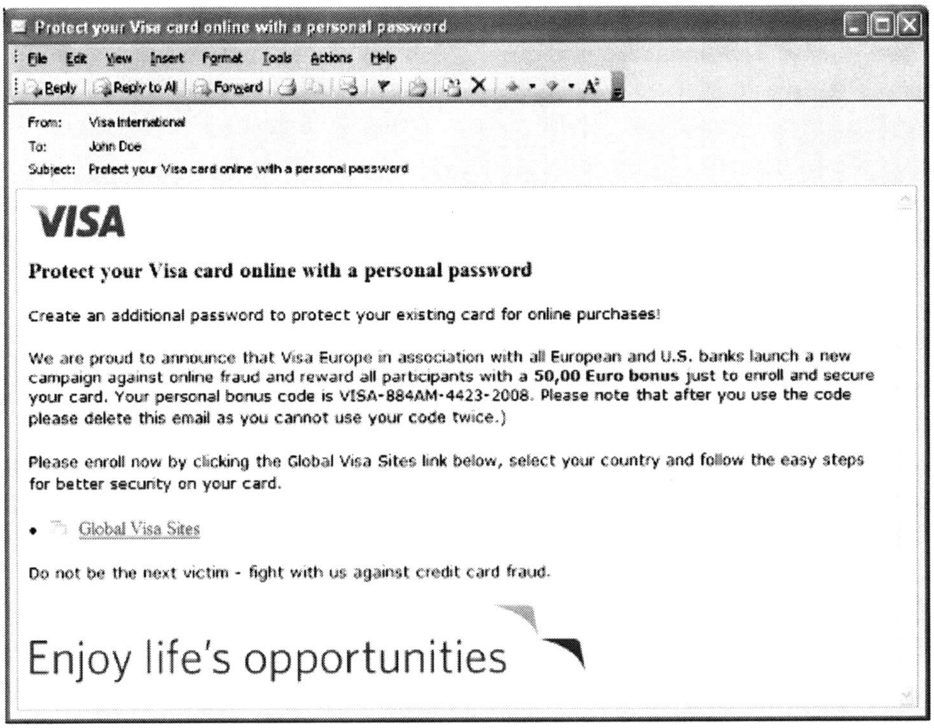

*For e.*g. From: PayPal
Reply To: Paypal21@rocketmail.com. Different reply address and claimed sender found in a phishing sample.

Attachments – Sometimes phishing emails send attachment in the email to install virus or spyware on the computer.

Assurance of Secure Transaction - Phishers try to gain the trust of recipients by assuring that the transaction is secure. Fraudulent Emails may use TRUSTe symbol to spoof users and Phishers may use Secure Socket Layer (SSL) by using the https protocol.

Code Script Checking - One of the ways to mitigate phishing attacks may be identifying or alerting or avoiding malicious JavaScript are mostly a preferable one in creating popup windows to changing the status bar of a web browser or email client. It can appear directly in the body of an email or it can be embedded in a link. Phishers can use JavaScript to hide information from the user, and potentially launch sophisticated attacks.

Use of HTML Forms in the Email - Phishers have also used HTML forms in the body of the email message to collect information from the recipients.

Mismatch between the Link Specified in the Text in the Email and the Actual Link Destination - In phishing emails, the link seen in the email is usually different from the actual link destination. In the example below, the email that appears to send the user to http://google.com instead takes the user to http://newdata.com.

Using JavaScript Event Handlers to Display False Information - Phishers use the JavaScript event handler "OnMouseOver" to show a false URL in the status bar of the user's email application.

URL Obfuscation Using an IP Address or Hexadecimal Character Codes - Phishers try to hide the destination web site by obscuring the

URL. They also use IP addresses in decimal, octal, hexadecimal format to obscure the URL or they use hexadecimal character codes to represent the numbers in the IP address.

Using an @ Symbol -Suspicious URLs to Confuse Recipients - If a page's URL contains an "at" (@) or a dash (-) in the domain name. An @ symbol in a URL causes the string to the left to be disregarded, with the string on the right treated as the actual URL for retrieving the page (Neil Chou, 2004).The link http://www.paypal.com@phish.net/ might deceive a casual observer into believing that it will open a example section of an account creation page at PayPal, whereas it actually directs the browser to a page on phish.net, using a username of the www.paypal.com page opens normally, regardless of the username supplied.

Forms -If a page contains any HTML text entry forms asking for personal data from people, such as password and credit card number. We scan the HTML for <input> tags that accept text and are accompanied by labels such as "credit card" and "password". Most phishing pages contain such forms asking for personal data, otherwise the criminals risk not getting the personal information they want.

7. DEFENSE MECHANISMS: COUNTERMEASURES AGAINST PHISHING

A variety of countermeasures against phishing have been proposed. They have been broadly classified as

- E-Mail Data analysis methods
  1. Machine Learning-statistical filtering techniques
  2. Content based filtering methods
- E-Mail Envelope analysis methods
  3. White lists/black lists/Grey lists
- Authorization and access control mechanisms
  4. Sender Policy Framework
  5. Sender ID Framework
  6. Identified internet Mail
  7. Domain Keys

7.1 Content Based Filtering Methods - Statistical Phishing Filters

Statistical phishing filters are a way to assess the relative importance of features. The feature weights are modified in such a way that on a set of emails labeled as ham, spam or phishing – the *training set* – the filter performance becomes optimal with respect to some quality criterion. However, the weighted addition of features is not the only way to combine features. If features have interactions, which indicate the existence of a phishing mail only if a specific combination of features occurs, then more complex non-linear feature combinations have to be utilized. In statistics and data mining a large number of *classifier models* have been developed which are adequate in these situations

Content-Based Filtering for Emails

An alternative way to identify phishing scams is the filtering of the email content. Content based identification of spam and phishing emails are quite different. A spam message inform the user about some product while the phisher has to deliver a message that has an unsuspicious look and pretends to come from some reputable institution. Therefore, many techniques are specific for phishing emails and some of the features include

Features for phishing email classification:

1. A number of style marker features for emails (e.g., the total number of words divided by the number of characters)
2. Structural attributes (e.g., the structure of the greeting provided in the email body)

3. The frequency distribution of selected function words (e.g., "update","Click").

Phishing filter evaluates more than 100,000 attributes of an email and uses a learning algorithm based on Bayesian statistics. A team of experts constantly tunes the filter and adapts it to the latest spamming and phishing techniques. In a comparison of Windows phishing filters the Internet Explorer filter scored best with a recall of 89% with no false positives. Fette et al. follow a similar approach, but use a larger publicly available corpus of about 7000 legitimate (ham) emails and 860 phishing emails. They propose ten different features to identify phishing scams. Nine of these features can be extracted from the email itself, while the tenth feature – the age of linked-to domain names – has to be obtained by a WHOIS query at the time the email is received. Among the remaining features is the score of a publicly available spam filter, the Spam Assassin.

Bayesian spam filtering which are best suitable for spam detection finds a vital role in identifying phishing mails also. Phishing emails are designed to look like legitimate transactional correspondence and almost always work to disguise their true source. To accurately catch phishing emails, Bayesian filters must be specifically designed for that purpose. Naïve Bayesian is a text classifier algorithm that analyzes textual features of an email to identify it as a ham or spam or phish email based on probabilistic scoring of its textual attributes. The algorithm is implemented in the Figure 4.

The Naïve Bayesian approach consists of two phases – training phase and the classification phase. The Naïve Bayes filter examines a set of known spam emails and a set of emails known to be legitimate. This filter is based on the Bayes theorem. Applied to spam, it states that the probability of an email being spam is equal to the probability of finding the same words in this email and spam, times the probability that any email is spam, divided by the probability of finding those words in an arbitrary email. The same approach can be used for phishing email detection also. Expressed in a conditional probability formula:

$$\Pr(A \mid B) = \frac{\Pr(B \mid A) \times \Pr(A)}{\Pr(B)}$$

- Pr(A|B) is the probability that a message is spam/phishing should it contain the word B.
- Pr(B|A) is the probability of the word B in spam/phishing. This value is computable from the training collection.
- Pr(A) is the probability that the email is spam/phishing (i.e. the number of spam / phishing messages divided by the number of all emails in the training collection).
- Pr(B) is the probability of word B in the collection.
- Each word in the email contributes to the e-mail's spam probability.

Training Phase

The training phase scans an existing corpus of spam and ham and phish emails. It involves

- **Parsing** - An email is parsed to identify different sections such as headers, body, to, from, subject, etc. Based on different filters different parsing techniques are used.
- **Tokenization** - Tokenization consists of creating tokens from different sections of email. These tokens will be later used to classify emails. Tokenization process is different for different filters. But it is one of the computation intensive functions of Naïve Bayesian filters.

Classification Phase

In classification phase an incoming email is classified as a spam or ham or phish. An incoming email is first tokenized to get individual tokens.

Figure 4. Naïve Bayes classifier for phishing emails

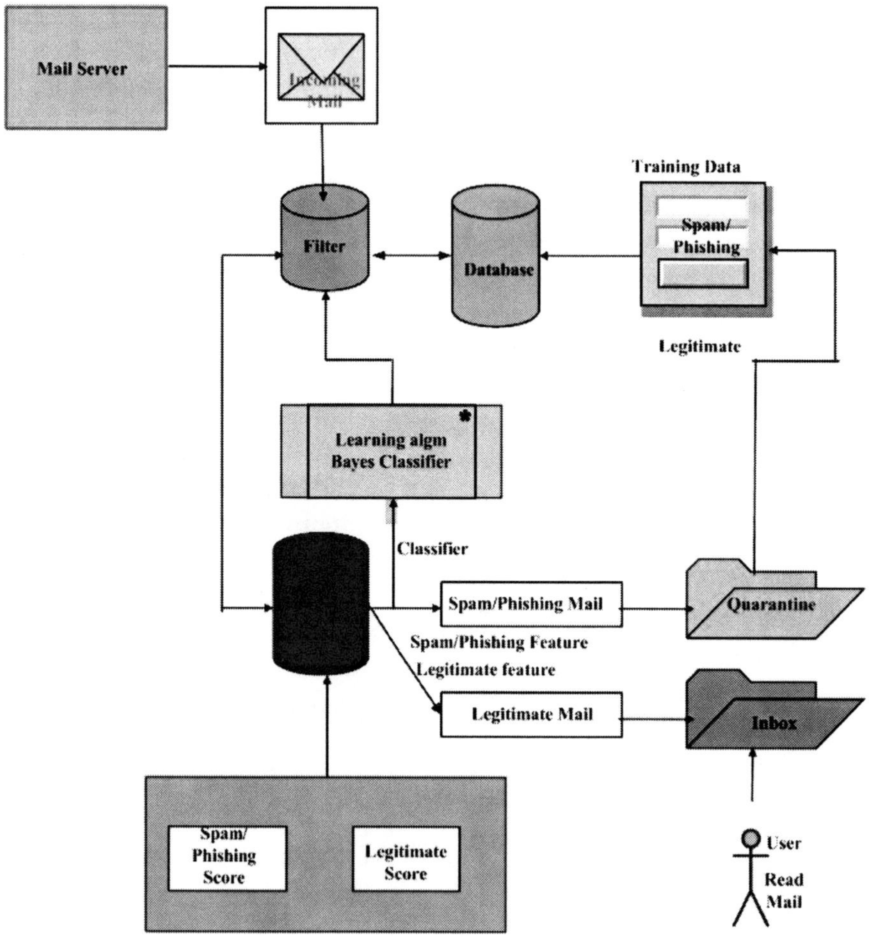

The corresponding probabilities for each token are retrieved. Naïve Bayesian formula is used to classify this email as ham or spam using these probabilities.

7.2 E-Mail Envelope Analysis Methods

7.2.1 White Lists/Black Lists/Grey Lists

One approach of phishing prevention concentrates on checking web addresses when a page is rendered in a web browser. In the Mozilla Firefox browser, for instance, each web page requested by a user is checked against a *blacklist* of known phishing sites. The average time for phishing sites to be online is only 3 days; many sites disappear within hours. It takes some time until a new phishing site is reported and added to the blacklist. Therefore the effectiveness of blacklisting is limited. An additional problem is caused by distributed phishing attacks where the links in a phishing email point to a large number of different servers are hosted on a botnet.

7.3 Authorization and Access Control Mechanisms

7.3.1 Sender Policy Framework

Sender policy frame work SPF, formerly known as "sender permitted from," can be considered as an extension to SMTP standard. Here, the envelope sender address in the "MAIL FROM:" SMTP command is verified for forgery. SPF utilizes mail exchanger (MX) records for filtering spam. Mail exchange record is a type of resource record present in the DNS, specifying the route information of an e-mail. SPF publishes the reverse MX records identifying the mail servers authorized to send e-mails from that domain. The recipient upon receiving an e-mail can verify these records to make sure that the e-mails were sent by trusted senders having SPF records.

7.3.2 Sender ID Framework (SIDF)

Sender ID framework is based on the caller ID proposal and SPF (Sender Policy Framework). This protocol is proposed to tackle the problem of spoofing the e-mail header and phishing e-mails. When the recipient's in-bound mail server receives new e-mails, it invokes the sender ID frame work, which checks the addresses of the e-mail sources against a registered list of servers that domain has authorized to send the e-mails, that is, it checks the SPF records. Once this verification has been done, the result can be used in conjunction with past behaviors, traffic patterns, sender's reputation information, and so forth. It can also be used with conventional content-based spam filters in making the final judgment, whether to deliver the e-mail to the recipient. Despite verifying the authorization and authentication information, SPF and SIDF alone are not effective in restricting spam and phishing e-mails.

7.3.3 Digitally Signed E-Mail

It is possible to use Public Key cryptography systems to digitally sign an e-mail. This signing can be used to verify the integrity of the messages content – thereby identifying whether the message content has been altered during transit. A signed message can be attributed to a specific users (or organizational) public key. Almost all popular e-mail client applications support the signing and verification of signed e-mail messages. It is recommended that users:

- Create a personal public/private key pair
- Upload their public key to respected key management servers so that other people who may receive their e-mails can verify the message's integrity
- Enable, by default, the automatic signing of e-mails
- Verify all signatures on received e-mails and be careful of unsigned or invalid signed messages – ideally verifying the true source of the e-mail. A message signature is essentially a sophisticated one-way hash value that uses aspects of the sender's private key, message length, date and time. The e-mail recipient uses the public key associated with the e-mail sender's address to verify this hash value. The contents of the e-mail should not be altered by any intermediary mail servers. It is important to note that, in general, there are no restrictions on creating a public/private key pair for any e-mail address a person may choose and consequently uploading the public key to an Internet key management server. Therefore, it is still possible for a phisher to send forth an e-mail with a spoofed address and digitally sign it with a key that they own.

7.3.4 Two-Factor Authentication

One of the more promising technologies to thwart phishing schemes involves two factors authentication. This method uses a layered approach to validate a user's credentials by using two separate methods to verify a user. A two-factor authentication technique currently being offered uses one-time passwords that expire after a single use. These passwords are generated using a shared electronic key between the user and a bank. A login is authenticated by not only the user's credentials (username/one-time password), but also the key that generates the password. If a password does happen to get stolen, it will not matter since it expires after a single use.

7.3.5 Identified Internet Mail (IIM)

IIM verifies the integrity of an e-mail using digital signatures and public key cryptography. It also validates the senders' e-mail addresses by verifying the authenticity of the associated public key. The digital signature is a hash of the e-mail content signed with the private key. An e-mail is sent along with its digital signature by the sender. When the e-mail reaches the recipient the signature is verified with the corresponding public key. The recipient's machine computes the hash of the message separately using a pre agreed hashing algorithm. An exact match between these two hashes indicates that the message has not been modified during the transit.

7.3.6 Domain Keys (DK)

It uses public keys advertised in the DNS for e-mail authentication. The objective of domain keys is to verify the integrity of the received e-mail and authenticity of the e-mail source. Domain Keys achieves this by using digital signatures, public key cryptography and DNS. A domain key is completely transparent to the existing e-mail systems with no DK support and is implemented using the optional headers and DNS records. IIM is integrated with DK to form DKIM standard.

7.3.7 Firewalls

There are e-mail firewall products that implement rules to block spam and phishing scams at the perimeter. These products offer "heuristic" rules that are updated as new phishing schemes are found. They not only block the spam, they verify the IP numbers and web addresses of the e-mail source and compare them to known phishing sites. For larger organizations, this can be an effective defense against spam and phishing.

7.3.8 Anti-Virus Technology

Though phishing scams are usually not considered a "viral" problem, if a user is infected with a worm that, in turn, installs a Trojan horse that can capture personal data, then anti-virus technologies are effective. Security best-practices direct that all users should implement an anti-virus product regardless of whether they are concerned about phishing or online fraud.

7.3.9 Browser Capabilities

The common web browser may be used as a defense against phishing attacks – if it is configured securely. Similar to the problems with e-mail applications, web browsers also offer extended functionality that may be abused (often to a higher degree than e-mail clients). For most users, their web browser is probably the most technically sophisticated application they use.

The most popular web browsers offer such a fantastic array of functionality – catering to all users in all environments – that they unintentionally provide gaping security flaws that expose the integrity of the host system to attack (it is almost a weekly occurrence that a new vulnerability is discovered that may be exploited remotely through a popular web browser). Much of the sophistication is devoted to being a "jack of all trades", and no single user can be expected to require the use of all this functionality. Customers and businesses must make a move to use a web browser that is appropriate for the task at hand. In particular, if the purpose of the web browser is to only browse Internet web services, a sophisticated web browser is not required. To help prevent many phishing attack vectors, web browser users should:

- Disable all pop-up window functionality
- Disable Java runtime support
- Disable ActiveX support
- Disable all multimedia and auto-play/auto-execute extensions
- Prevent the storage of non-secure cookies
- Ensure that any downloads cannot be automatically run from the browser, and must instead be downloaded into a directory for antivirus inspection

8. PREVENTIVE MEASURES

- **Guard your financial information.**
- **Keep Social security number confidential.** Examine the Social Security Personal Earnings and Benefits Estimate Statement for possible fraud. Provide your Social Security number only when it is required by a government agency, employer, or financial institution. Never use it for identification. Don't carry your number or card in your purse or wallet.
- **Keep passwords and PIN numbers Safe:** Put strong passwords on your credit card, bank, and other accounts. Avoid using easily remembered numbers or available information like mother's maiden name, date of birth, phone number, or the last four digits of your Social Security number. Passwords should be more than eight characters in length, and contain both capital letters and at least one numeric character. Use different passwords for banking, e-commerce, e-mail, and other accounts. Memorize your passwords. Don't carry them in your purse or wallet.
- **Keep your mail safe.** It contains account numbers and other personal information.
- **Lock it up.** Keep your personal information locked up at home, at work, at school, in your car, and other places where you might keep it so others won't have easy access to it.
- **Stay safe online – To avoid Phishing Scams.** Don't send sensitive information such as credit card numbers by email, since it's not secure.
- **Check your credit reports regularly & ask for free copies of your credit reports in certain situations.** Cancel accounts you don't use or need. Carry only the cards and identification you need when you go out.

9. CONCLUSION

Identity theft, the taking of a person's identity for the purpose of committing a criminal act, is a serious concern as it violates the individual victim and wreaks huge financial losses on the commercial victim. Phishing has become a serious threat to global security and economy. Because of the fast rate of emergence of new phishing websites and because of distributed phishing attacks it is difficult to curb them using a specific approach. Hence an integrated approach combining the various methodologies has been proposed to mitigate phishing – Online identity and fraud a form of cybercrime. Criminals use various techniques to acquire and use personal information. The acquisition techniques used reflect their level of expertise and commitment. The techniques used also vary depending on their motive, which is usually either financial gain or concealment. The techniques used by identity thieves cover a wide spectrum of sophistication. Some of them are elaborate schemes, conducted online, which require specialized knowledge of the inner workings of the internet. Some techniques involve tricking unsuspecting and trusting information custodians into releasing personal information. At the other end of the spectrum, identity theft can be as simple as sifting through an organization's or an individual's trash to find discarded documents containing valuable personal information.

An important aspect of identity theft techniques is that they almost always provide anonymity to the thief. That is one of the main reasons why the crime is so popular and often so rewarding to the perpetrator. Identity thieves are always discovering new techniques... Identity thieves have been quick to realize the benefits of operating in this fashion. This creates further exposure for individuals and a real challenge for law enforcement officials and legislators.

10. FUTURE RESEARCH DIRECTIONS

Fake identities and identity theft are considered one of the most important issues for the citizen - but in fact are equally important to organizations, such as banks, given the current prevalence of so-called "phishing". Phishing poses a significant threat for organizations. They are the targets of spear phishing and other identity theft based vulnerabilities. Threats and vulnerabilities have to be identified and should be addressed based on level of security needed and user/application profile in an auto configuration mode, so that users get more trust in the network and applications. Such functionality will raise the trust among the users...In the information society of the future, the breakthrough regarding these issues for transactions and electronic processes will be two-fold: there will be some services that can be used anonymously in community-based or information-retrieval scenarios where there are only loose virtual trust relationships and there are no valuable goods involved.

ACKNOWLEDGMENT

This work is supported by the NTRO, Government of India. NTRO provides the fund for collaborative project "Smart and Secure Environment" and this paper is modeled for this project. Authors would like to thanks the project coordinators and the NTRO members.

REFERENCES

Abu-Nimeh, S., Nappa, D., Wang, X., & Nair, S. (2007). A comparison of machine learning techniques for phishing detection. In *Proceedings of the eCrime Researchers Summit*, 2007.

Adida, B., Hohenberger, S., & Rivest, R. (2005). *Lightweight encryption for email*. USENIX Steps to Reducing Unwanted Traffic on the Internet Workshop (SRUTI), 2005.

Anti-Phishing Working Group. (2006). *Phishing activity trends report*, June 2006. Retrieved from http://antiphishing.org/reports/apwg report june 2006.pdf

Anti-Phishing Working Group. (n.d.). *Phishing archive*. Retrieved from http://www.antiphishing.org/phishing archive.html

Bergholz, J.-H., Chang, G. H., Paaß, G., Reichartz, F., & Strobel, S. (2008). Improved phishing detection using model-based features. In *Proceedings of the Conference on Email and Anti-Spam* (CEAS), 2008.

Birk, D., Dornseif, M., & Gajek, S. & Grobert. F. (2006). *Phishing phishers—Tracing identity thieves and money launderers*. Horst Gortz Institute for IT Security, Ruhr University Bochum, Tech. Rep. TR-HGI-01-2006.

Chou, N., Ledesma, R., Teraguchi, Y., Boneh, D., & Mitchell, J. (2004). *Client-side defense against Web-based identity theft*. In 11th Annual Network and Distributed System Security Symposium (NDSS '04), San Diego, 2004.

Chuan, Y., & Wang, H. (2009). BogusBiter: A transparent protection against phishing attacks. *ACM Transactions on Internet Technology*, *10*(2), 1–30.

Cranor, L., Egelman, S., Hong, J., & Zhang, Y. (2006). *Phinding phish: An evaluation of anti-phishing toolbars.* Technical report, Carnegie Mellon University, Nov. 2006.

Emigh, A. (2005). *Online identity theft: Technology, chokepoints and countermeasures.* Report of the Department of Homeland Security – SRI International Identity Theft Technology Council, October 3, 2005.

Fette, N., Sadeh, S., & Tomasic, A. (2007). Learning to detect phishing emails. In *Proceedings of the International World Wide Web Conference (WWW)*, Banff, Alberta, Canada, May 2007.

Garera, S., Provos, N., Rubin, A. D., & Chew, M. A. (2007). Framework for detection and measurement of phishing attacks. In *Proceedings of the 2007 ACM Workshop on Recurring Malcode*, (pp. 1-8).

Jacobsson, M., & Myers, S. (2007). *Phishing and countermeasures - Understand the increasing problem of electronic identity theft.* New Jersey: Wiley.

Kirda, E., & Kruegel, C. (2005). Protecting users against phishing attacks. *Proceedings of the 29th Annual International Computer Software and Applications Conference (COMPSAC'05)*, Edinburgh, UK, 2006, (pp. 517-524).

Ma, J., Saul, L. K., Savage, S., & Voelker, S. M. (2009). Identifying suspicious URLs: An application of large-scale online learning. In *ICML '09: Proceedings of the 26th Annual International Conference on Machine Learning*, (pp. 681–688).

Mathew, A. R., Al Hajj, A., & Al Ruqeishi, K. (2010). *Cyber crimes: Threats and protection.* 2010 International Conference on Networking and Information Technology.

Parno, B., Kuo, C., & Perrig, A. (2006). *Phoolproof phishing prevention.* In Financial Cryptography and Data Security (FC'06), 2006.

Sheng, S., Wardman, B., Warner, G., Cranor, L. F., Hong, J., & Zhang, C. (2009). *An empirical analysis of phishing blacklists.* In CEAS 2009: Sixth Conference on Email and Anti-Spam, July 2009.

Wu, M. (2006). *Fighting phishing at the user interface.* PhD Thesis, MIT.

Xiang, G., & Hong, J. (2009). A hybrid phish detection approach by identity discovery and keywords retrieval. In *Proceedings of the 18th International Conference on World Wide Web (WWW'09,* (pp. 571-580).

Yue, Z., Egelman, S., Cranor, L. F., & Hong, J. (2007). Phinding phish: Evaluating anti-phishing tools. *Proceedings of the 14th Annual Network and Distributed System Security Symposium* (NDSS 2007). Carnegie Mellon University.

Zhang, Y., Hong, J., & Cranor, L. (2007). Cantina: A content-based approach to detecting phishing websites. In *Proceedings of the 16th International Conference on World Wide Web*, (pp. 639 – 648).

KEY TERMS AND DEFINITIONS

Bayesian Filter: A program that uses Bayesian logic to evaluate the header and content of an incoming e-mail message and determine the probability that it constitutes spam and phishing Emails.

E-Mail Spoofing: The forgery of an e-mail header so that the message appears to have originated from a legitimate or trustworthy source.

E-Mail Authentication: Ensuring a valid identity on an email to prove and protect email sender identity.

Identity Theft: The criminal act of stealing personal information in which an impostor uses the name, social security number, and/or other identifying information of a victim to open credit accounts, use existing credit accounts, or otherwise acquire benefits using the victim's identity.

Phishing: The criminally fraudulent process of attempting to acquire sensitive information such as usernames, passwords and credit card details by masquerading as a trustworthy entity in an electronic communication.

Sender Policy Framework (SPF): Checks the "envelope sender" of an email message—the domain name of the initiating SMTP server. Sender path authentication that helps recipients identifies the authorized mail servers for a particular domain, and validate that emails they received did in fact originate from these authorized sources.

Spear Phishing: An e-mail spoofing fraud attempt that targets a specific organization, seeking unauthorized access to confidential data.

Chapter 15
Information Security Governance and Standard Based Management Systems

Margareth Stoll
University of Innsbruck, Austria

Ruth Breu
University of Innsbruck, Austria

ABSTRACT

The importance of information and Information Systems for modern organizations as a key differentiator is increasingly recognized. Sharpened legal and regulatory requirements have further promoted to see information security governance as part of corporate governance. More than 1.37 million organizations worldwide are implementing a standards based management system, such as ISO9001 or others. To implement information security governance and compliance in an effective, efficient, and sustainable way, the authors integrate these standard based management systems with different information security governance frameworks and the requirements of the international ISO/IEC 27001 information security management standard to a holistic information security governance model. In that way information security is part of all strategic, tactical, and operational business processes promotes corporate governance and living information security. The implementation of this innovative holistic model in several organizations and the case studies results are described.

INTRODUCTION

Due to globalization and increasing competition, information and supporting technology have become key asset and differentiators for modern organizations. Organizations and their information and information systems are faced with security threats from a wide range of sources, including computer-assisted fraud, espionage, sabotage, vandalism, fire or flood. 92% of large enterprises had a security incident in the last year with an average cost of 280.000-690.000 £ for the worst incident (PricewaterhouseCoopers, 2010). Mobile

DOI: 10.4018/978-1-4666-0197-0.ch015

and cloud computing, off-shoring, social networks and the increasingly interconnected, flexible and virtualized business complexity and dependencies are still great challenges for existing information security governance.

In the last years, the legal and regulatory requirements in this area have been sharpened. Most modern corporate governance guidelines, and always more laws, make the board and specifically the CEO responsible for the well-being of the organization. Lack of security compliance may result in loss of confidence of customers, partners and shareholders, as well as severe civil and criminal penalties for board members (Saint-Germain, 2005; Clinch, 2009). More and more organizations are reducing their business risks by seeking assurance that their supplier and partners are properly protecting information assets and ensuring business continuity (Saint-Germain, 2005). In this respect the availability of all essential assets, confidentiality, data integrity and legal and regulatory compliance are central for organizations' success and integral part of good IT and corporate governance (Da Veiga & Eloff, 2007; Solms & Solms, 2009; Sowa, Tsinas & Gabriel, 2009). This poses great challenges for small and medium sized organizations. They need a very efficient and functional approach, which can be smoothly integrated in their daily business.

Several international best practices for information security management have been developed to provide guidance and ensure comprehensiveness. Some of the most commonly used include Control Objectives for Information and related Technology (COBIT), Information Technology Infrastructure Library (ITIL) and national guidelines, such as NIST SP 800 series in the US or IT Security Guidelines from the Federal Office for Information Security in Germany. More than 12.934 organizations worldwide have just implemented an information security management system in accordance to ISO/IEC 27001 (International Standard Organization [ISO], 2010). This international standard provides a model for establishing, operating, monitoring, maintaining and improving an information security management system to meet the specific security and business objectives of the organization. Thereby the organization's overall business strategy, objectives and requirements, the legal, statutory or regulatory requirements and the contractual security obligations, as well as the organization's business risks, processes and procedures are taken into account (ISO, 2005a; 2005b).

More than 1.37 million organizations of different sizes and scopes have implemented management systems based on international standards (e.g. quality ISO 9001, or environment ISO 14001, IT service management ISO 22000 and others) (ISO, 2010). All these management systems require common principles: the establishment and communication of organization objectives and strategies, the management of business processes, an adequate resource management and the continual improvement of the organization (ISO, 2008). The management system must be documented, communicated, implemented and continuously improved. These systems are implemented more frequently in a holistic way. According with the organizational purpose and objectives different aspects, like quality, environment, hygiene, social, occupational health and safety or others are integrated.

To meet optimally all information security requirements and compliance we have developed an efficient, effective and sustainable information security governance model. The innovation of this information security governance model is the integration of different information security governance frameworks with the ISO 9001 standard for quality management systems or other international standards for management systems, as well as with the international standard for information security management IEC/ISO 27001 and best-practice methods (COBIT, ITIL) (IT Governance Institute, 2007; Office of Government Commerce [OGC], 2007). This holistic approach integrates information security governance into all strategic, tactical and operational business processes and promotes thereby corporate governance and living information security.

The next subsection explains the common requirements of ISO 9001 quality management systems or other international standards for management systems, the main requirements for information security management in accordance to the IEC/ISO 2700x family and analyzes some information security governance frameworks and best-practice methods in order to construct our holistic information security governance model (subsection 3). After the implementation of that model (subsection 4) we report and discuss our case studies experiences (subsection 5). At the end we give an outlook with proposals for further research directions (subsection 6) and our conclusions (subsection 7).

RESEARCH FRAMEWORK

Main Requirements of Standard Based Management Systems

The ISO 9001 standard for quality management systems and other standards for management systems require common principles (ISO, 2008):

- The vision, policy, objectives and strategies of the organization must be established and communicated to fulfill the requirements of all interested parties (stakeholders) (see top of Figure 1).
- All business processes for service or product realization including the management process, support processes, resource processes and optimization processes must be defined to meet the organizations' objectives under the focus of the respective standard (see the graphic under the top of Figure 1: starting from customers' requirement and ending with customer satisfaction ☺).

Figure 1. Main requirements of standard based management systems

- Objective and process oriented resource management must be promoted including human resource development and the management of necessary technology, infrastructures, tools and instruments (see bottom of Figure 1).
- The whole organization, their objectives and strategies, services/products and processes must be continually measured, analyzed and improved according to established processes in sense of a PDCA cycle (plan, do, check, act) (see the circle around in Figure 1).

The established management system must be documented, structured and communicated systematically. All collaborators must continually implement and improve the whole management system.

These standard based management systems are implemented more frequently in a holistic way. In accordance with the organizational purpose and objectives the management system eventually integrates environmental, hygienic, social, occupational health and safety aspects, as well as knowledge management, service management, communication management, information management, IT–management, facility management, maintenance management, controlling or others.

Main Requirements of Information Security Management Systems

We present the requirements of ISO/IEC 27001 (ISO, 2005a) and ISO/IEC 27002 (ISO, 2005b):

- An information security policy must be defined and approved by the management.
- A risk assessment must be conducted to establish a risk treatment plan to reduce risks to acceptable levels of risk. For the identified remaining risks a business continuity plan must be developed, implemented, maintained, tested and updated regularly.
- The needed resources must be determined and provided. All collaborators must be competent to perform their tasks and be aware of the relevance and importance of their information security activities. Each collaborator must contribute to the achievement of the established information security objectives.
- The effectiveness and adequacy of the information security management system must be continually improved by measuring, analyzing, auditing, reviewing and applying corrective and preventive actions in the sense of a PDCA cycle (plan, do, check / study, act).

Also this management system must be documented, structured and communicated systematically, as well as continually implemented and improved.

Information Security Governance Oriented Frameworks

To achieve effectiveness and sustainability in today's complex, interconnected world, information security must be addressed at the highest levels of the organization. It must be an integral part of corporate governance (Solms & Solms, 2009; Da Veiga & Eloff, 2007; Sowa, Tsinas & Gabriel, 2009; IT Governance Institute, 2007; OGC, 2007; ISO, 2005a, 2005b).

The board and executive management should (Organization for Economic Co-operation and Development [OECD], 2004; IT Governance Institute, 2006):

- Provide and review the strategic direction, major plans of action, risk policy, and the annual budgets and business plans;
- Set performance objectives;
- Monitor implementation and corporate performance; and

- Oversee major capital expenditures, acquisitions and divestitures.

The corporate information security policy is part of or aligned with the corporate policy. It provides direction for short and long-term business security requirements to deliver enhanced business value to all stakeholders. Business and relevant legal and regulatory requirements must be taken into account. The board indicates how important the protection of the assets is to the organization (Solms & Solms, 2009). They decide the criteria for accepting risks and the acceptable levels of risk in the context of the organization's overall business risks (ISO, 2005a). From these strategic directives a set of relevant policies, standards and procedures are deduced for the middle management (tactical layer). These are the inputs for the operational procedures and guidelines (Solms & Solms, 2009; Sowa, Tsinas & Gabriel, 2009; Da Veiga & Eloff, 2007; IT Governance Institute, 2007; OGC, 2007).

All documents produced during the top down 'direct' part must be formulated in such a way that the compliance to the specific document can be measured (Solms & Solms, 2009). To conclude the direct-execute-control cycle measurement data are extracted on the operational level. They are compiled and integrated to perform measurement and monitoring against the requirements on the tactical level. For the board and executive management strategic level reports are produced. They reflect the actual risk situation, as well as compliance and conformance to relevant directives (Solms & Solms, 2009; Sowa, Tsinas & Gabriel, 2009; Da Veiga & Eloff, 2007; IT Governance Institute, 2007). By linking transparently operational, tactical and strategic information to security objectives and to business objectives the board and executive management is supported to find and define cost benefit balanced investment strategies (Sowa, Tsinas & Gabriel, 2009), programs, projects and resource decisions.

HOLISTIC INFORMATION SECURITY GOVERNANCE MODEL

In consolidation of the different frameworks discussed above, best-practice methods (COBIT, ITIL) and based on our practical experiences we developed a holistic, integrated information security governance and quality management model (Figure 2):

- The corporate vision and policy are established by regarding the requirements of all stakeholders, as well as legal and regulatory requirements. Objectives and strategies are deduced from corporate vision and policy. Relevant information security aspects are integrated (see top of Figure 2).
- A risk assessment is conducted to establish a risk treatment plan to reduce security risks to an acceptable level of risk. For the identified remaining risks a business continuity plan is developed, implemented, maintained, tested and updated regularly (see the graphic under the top of Figure 2).
- Business process objectives are deduced from the corporate objectives by regarding the specific business, contractual, legal and regulatory requirements for the single processes. In accordance to these, we analyze and optimize all business processes in a strategically aligned way (see middle of Figure 2: the main business processes start from the first contact with the customer and his requirements and end with the delivery of the product/service and the satisfaction of the customer). In that way stakeholder requirements together with information security are improved. Information security measures and controls, identified in the risk assessment and business continuity planning, are suitably integrated into the operational processes. Thus, they are implemented, maintained, tested and updated regularly to ensure effectiveness.

Figure 2. The holistic information security governance model

The process description establishes for all process steps the associated responsible and accountable function and relevant information security requirements. Clear and traceable information security roles and responsibilities are assigned.

- The resource management (see bottom of Figure 2) specifies necessary resources, technologies and infrastructures to obtain and continually improve adequate information security. Competence objectives are deduced for all functions from the process models in alignment to corporate objectives. Appropriate trainings and awareness for all collaborators and involved partners are promoted. Their effectiveness is evaluated.
- The effectiveness, performance, compliance and adequacy of the established holistic information security governance system are continually measured, analyzed and reported using suitable methods for monitoring and measurement. Based on the actual risk situation, compliance and the achievement of established objectives necessary measures to maintain and improve corporate governance are elaborated and implemented proactively. In that way the whole system is continually improved accordingly to corporate governance objectives and strategies (see the measurement, analysis and improvement circle around Figure 2).

IMPLEMENTATION

In this section we describe in detail the implementation of our holistic information security governance model with applied methods and examples. We focus overall on governance elements (direction, process integration, controlling) and describe the methods, process and applied tools to combine ISO 9001 with the ISO/IEC 2700x family, information security governance frameworks and best-practice methods.

To implement our holistic information security governance model we execute following steps:

1. We elaborate the policy, deduce objectives and elaborate adequate strategies (see Policy and Objectives).
2. The risk assessment, risk treatment and business continuity planning are conducted intermeshed with the process analysis and process improvement (see corresponding subsections). Firstly we deduce business process objectives from corporate objectives. In the next step we analyze the processes, define relevant assets and deduce for these information security objectives from process objectives. Based on this we conduct the risk assessment and elaborate risk treatments and business continuity plans. At the end we optimize the business processes in accordance to established process objectives and integrate suitable identified information security measures, risk treatments and business continuity activities into all processes.
3. From the optimized business processes we deduce the organizational structure with function profiles and competence objectives and assign roles and responsibilities (see Resource Management). To fulfill established objectives we determine and provide necessary human, financial and technical resources accordingly to optimized resource processes (part of business processes, see step 2).
4. The whole *system documentation* must be documented, reviewed, approved, communicated, trained and implemented (see System Documentation). It is composed by directives, policies, standards, procedures, guidelines, controls, legal and regulatory interpretations, templates, checklists and other relevant documents (further *regulations*), as well as policy, objectives, strategies, process models, risk assessment, business continuity plans, the organizational structure, function profiles, role and responsibility assignment matrix and others. Its adequacy and effectiveness is periodically evaluated and optimized.
5. The whole information security governance system must be measured, analyzed, adjusted to changing requirements and continually improved to promote sustainable information security (see Continually Measurement, Analysis and Improvement). In that way it may be also necessary to restart from an earlier step, for example to change the policy. After that we must perform all successive steps again.

Policy and Objectives

We elaborate the corporate policy. Based on Quality Function Deployment (Akao, 1990) we:

1. Identify and prioritize all relevant stakeholders,
2. Determine the requirements of all stakeholders, the relevant legal and regulatory requirements for all locations and markets, all contractual and statutory obligations and the characteristics of the business and market and define the capabilities, assets and technology, and the physical environment of the organization.
3. From the focus of the single stakeholders, weighted by their priority, we prioritize all requirements and obligations. Thereby we take into account the characteristics of the business and markets and the organizational strengths and weakness.
4. We establish the corporate policy accordingly to the prioritized requirements.

Information security aspects are integrated within the holistic corporate policy. In that way the quality and information security policy, as well as scope and boundaries of the holistic management system are defined.

From the corporate policy we deduce corporate objectives together with information security objectives, such as availability, confidentiality and integrity. To each objective we assign long-term, medium-term and annual goals with appropriate metrics, targets and measurement methods to monitor their achievement and to evaluate compliance. To fulfill the established information security objectives we elaborate adequate information security strategies. Thus the entire organization is focused to accomplish the stakeholder's requirements inclusive information security, as well as legal, regulatory and standard compliance and conformance. Information security becomes an integral part of corporate governance.

Risk Assessment, Risk Treatment and Business Continuity Plan

A risk assessment is conducted for establishing a risk treatment plan to reduce risks on acceptable levels of risk in collaboration with all collaborators and partners concerned.

We deduce business process objectives from corporate objectives and analyze the processes (see Process Analysis and Process Improvement). Thereby we determine relevant assets and deduce from process objectives their required information security objectives, e.g., confidentiality, integrity and availability. This is elaborated with the executive management and approved by the board. In that way the risk assessment is aligned with strategic objectives and corporate governance. Further a good understanding of the board and executives for potential security impacts and necessary changes, projects and investments is promoted.

Regarding the corporate risk management, the enterprise context and all relevant legal, regulatory, contractual and business requirements we identify threats to those assets. The likelihood of the threats occurrence and the impacts that losses of security requirements may have on the assets are estimated by regarding currently implemented controls. For the higher risks adequate risk treatment plans (controls) are elaborated. To each control or group of controls appropriate control objectives and measurement methods are formulated in such a way that the compliance can be controlled. The board decides the criteria for accepting risks and whether the remaining levels of risk are acceptable in the context of the organization's overall business risks or further risk treatments must be developed and implemented.

The ISO/IEC 27002 and ISO/IEC 27005, national guidelines, such as NIST SP 800 series in the US or IT Security Guidelines from the Federal Office for Information Security in Germany provide helpful information for the threat analysis and risk assessment.

The risk treatment plan is integrated into the operational processes (see Process Analysis and Process Improvement). In that way the risk treatments and the existing standard based management system are integrated.

For the identified remaining risks a business continuity plan is developed and integrated into the operational processes. Thus it is implemented, maintained, tested and updated regularly to ensure that it is effective to maintain or restore operations and ensure availability at the required level and in the required time scale following interruption to, or failure of, critical business processes.

Process Analysis and Process Improvement

Standard based management systems require the analysis and improvement of all business processes to achieve established corporate objectives and to regard all requirements of the relevant standard and relevant business, legal and regulatory obligations.

We deduce in accordance to the requirements of ISO 9001, COBIT and ITIL for all business processes process objectives from corporate objectives by taking into account business, contractual, legal and regulatory requirements for each single process. In that way the process objec-

Figure 3. Process modeling method

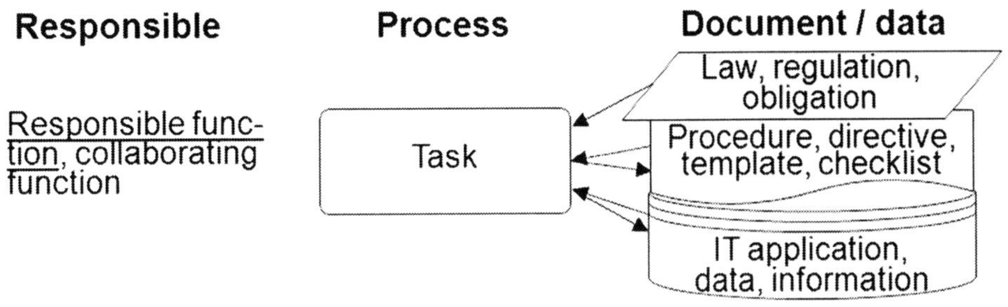

tives are aligned with strategic corporate security objectives. To propagate corporate objectives to business process objectives Quality Function Deployment (Akao, 1990) and balanced scorecard (Kaplan, 1996) provide helpful approaches.

In the next step we analyze all business processes bottom up by interviewing the collaborators involved. Beginning from the management process, we examine all production or service processes, as well as all supporting processes, resources processes and improvement processes. In that way we study also the development of new products or services.

For process modeling we use a simple structured flow-charts (see Figure 3) with three or four columns (4th for annotations, conditions, and terms), limited to one page. In that way the processes are sufficiently deeply structured. For time critical descriptions we use also Gantt charts.

The process models (see Figure 3) establish for all activities:

- Involved functions,
- Relevant laws, regulations and obligations,
- Procedures and directives, which must be regarded,
- Applied templates, documents, checklists, forms, IT applications, processed and exchanged data and information.

These process models define for all documents and data the accountable, responsible and involved functions over the whole document lifecycle (creation, review, approval, signature, release, distribution, retrieval, modification, archive and disposal). External information sources or receivers are also documented. Thus the whole document and data logistic is described. The European and most national data protection laws require for example that the data subject has the right to receive among others the information about the recipients and data processors of his data. By integrating information security governance and standard based management systems this legal requirement can be deduced efficiently from established process models.

In accordance to relevant legal and regulative security requirements we establish for each document and data class the data protection class and required protection methods for the whole data lifecycle. Examples for such information security policies are:

- Necessary and licit access rights,
- Segregation of duties,
- Data encryption,
- Signature policies with signature rights and signature procedures,
- Archiving methods and duration for current, intermediate and historical archives,
- Destruction or disposal procedures and methods.

After all business processes are harmonized and optimized together with the concerned collaborators by taking into account deduced information security objectives, as well as quality, efficiency, effectiveness and all other corporate, business, legal and regulatory requirements. In accordance to the corporate objectives we consider and integrate all relevant aspects (e.g., environment, human resource development, resource management, information management, communication management, controlling, knowledge management or others). Entire documents and data are examined for necessity and lawfulness. The general manager of a public organization, for example, appreciated overall the performance improvement by eliminating all indispensable data.

By optimizing the processes the identified controls (risk countermeasures) and business continuity tasks and tests are integrated, implemented and maintained by appropriate IT systems and workflows, if possible. Many organizations for example implement the user registration and de-registration as a sub-process, which is initiated by the human resource management application. In that way all information security aspects, which are identified in the risk assessment, are regarded and best integrated. Based on our case studies experiences it is essential to integrate all information security tasks into the daily work of the collaborators in a suitable and efficient way (see Case Studies Results and Experiences).

Other information security controls and tasks, which cannot be supported by IT in business processes are integrated in existing directives, code of conducts, process models, policies, standards, procedures, guidelines, controls, legal and regulatory interpretations, or others (further *regulations*). For each control an appropriate compliance clause specifying in which way compliance will be evaluated is defined. By the process analysis we recognize these process steps, in which experiences and interpretations of laws or regulations (lessons learned) are developed. These should be documented for later use. Thus data collection and information processing are planned and implemented systematically and structured in accordance to relevant legal and regulative requirements.

To harmonize processes and data over the whole organization we define firstly the main services or products with their corresponding processes and analyze these with the involved departments. Afterwards we harmonize and integrate common process segments, law interpretations, regulations, checklists and forms. Thus we establish a reduced number of common main processes (ca. one until five) with harmonized documents, regulations and law interpretations. Templates are developed for all necessary documents and forms (e.g., contract forms for standardized products or services). They are examined only once by specialized experts and jurisprudents. Afterwards every collaborator can fill them easily with the personal data of the customer and the required product/service. The specialized knowledge of experts is integrated also into all checklists. In that way implicit knowledge is externalized. Knowledge and information management is also improved (Davenport, 2005; Stoll, 2007a).

Resource Management

Standard based management systems require that the organization determines and provides necessary resources to obtain established objectives and to continually improve the effectiveness. Thus collaborators with adequate competences and optimal technologies, infrastructures, tools and instruments are promoted. This supports also information security:

- We deduce the organizational structure with function profiles from the assigned roles to each function at the single process steps. The function profiles consist at least of objectives, main tasks, responsibilities and required competences. Regarding the different roles of each collaborator we assign him functional objectives, responsibilities, main tasks and required competences. In that way a suitable human resource development is planned and implemented accordingly to defined, optimized processes (human resource development is a part of business processes, see step 2). The effectiveness is evaluated. The competences of all collaborators with assigned information security responsibilities are also promoted systematically, structured and sustainable. All collaborators are aware of the relevance and importance of their activities and contribute to the achievement of the established objectives.

- An optimal infrastructure and appropriate maintenance and facility management processes promote overall physical and environmental security and the availability and reliability of supporting utilities, such as power, telecommunication or air condition supply.
- Adequate technology and IT system management are essential for communications, network, operations and application security. The strong strategic alignment of all necessary information security changes, projects and investments promotes the understanding for potential security impacts of the board and executives and an appropriate funding.

System Documentation

After the establishment the whole system documentation (see Implementation step 4) must be reviewed, approved and communicated. Every collaborator must be trained on the relevant regulations for him. The collaborators and particularly the managers must implement continually the established processes and regulations. The documentation must be always actual. Laws, regulations and standards require a traceable communication and adequate training for the collaborators concerned.

Commonly the system documentation is now distributed electronically through web-based intranets, document management platforms or as pdf. New collaborators are trained on the whole documentation at their start. After periodical trainings communicate changes and promote awareness. In that way the collaborators get often too much information at once and forget it until they need it.

To provide need-oriented, operations integrated learning we elaborate the regulations regarding media-pedagogical, motivation-psychological and didactical principles (Rosenberg, 2001; Reinmann-Rothmeier, 2002). According to these principles and the analyzed expectations of the collaborators, the way for accessing the single modules should be as short as possible, clear structured and practice oriented. The documentation should be written:

- Clearly understandable and compact,
- Simply and motivating worded,
- Adjusted to the skills of the readers,
- Using expressive terms applied in the organization,
- Corresponding with organizational objectives and values,
- Offering concrete instructions and templates,
- Including a lot of examples of everyday practice and
- An extensive index.

We divide the system documentation in small modules and structure these in accordance to our holistic governance model. Further we offer different start assistances depending on the competences and needs of the users (e.g., for new collaborators, department oriented, management oriented, topics referred, based on the standard and others). In that way the documentation is comprehensive in the whole and compact for the single collaborator (see Figure 4).

Changes and improvements are commonly isolated from the documentation and cannot be discussed in a context-sensitive way. The documentation is primarily used to fulfill legal, regulative and standard requirements and changed only prior to external audits. Thus the documentation frequently is not corresponding to lived processes. Changes or improvements are quite frequently developed as hidden systems. In some organizations of our case studies we stored the system documentation on an organizational learning and knowledge system (Stoll, 2008). This system offers context sensitive, collaborative discussions and improvements. It promotes the actuality, practice-orientation, comprehensiveness, usability and efficiency of the documentation, as well as operations integrated, need-oriented learning, employee involvement and collaborative information security improvement (Stoll, 2008).

Continual Measurement, Analysis and Improvement

An increasingly faster changing environment (market, customer, technology, law or regulations) requires continual adaption of objectives, processes, risk assessment, regulations, technology and collaborators. It is a widely accepted principle that an activity cannot be managed and overall not improved continually if it cannot be measured. Thus the effectiveness and performance of the information security management system and the actual risk and compliance situation has to be ongoing evaluated and improved. Effectively implemented security measurements demonstrate the value of information security to top management, face informed decision making, demonstrate compliance, improve security confidence and enable stakeholders to continually improve information security. This is a critical success factor for sustainable information security (ISO, 2005b).

From established corporate objectives we deduced business process objectives and control objectives according to regulatory, legal and contractual requirements (see Process Analysis and Process Improvement). Due to our integrated approach we elaborate in that way also information security objectives. Appropriate measurement methods are defined to control the achievement of planned results and the effectiveness of the selected controls, as well as to improve the information security governance system. In accordance to NIST SP 800-55 (National Institute of Standards and Technology [NIST], 2008) and ISO/IEC 27004 (ISO, 2009) the relevant stakeholders are involved in each step of information security measures development to ensure commitment and promote a sense of ownership for information security compliance and performance.

Figure 4. The didactical preparation of the system documentation

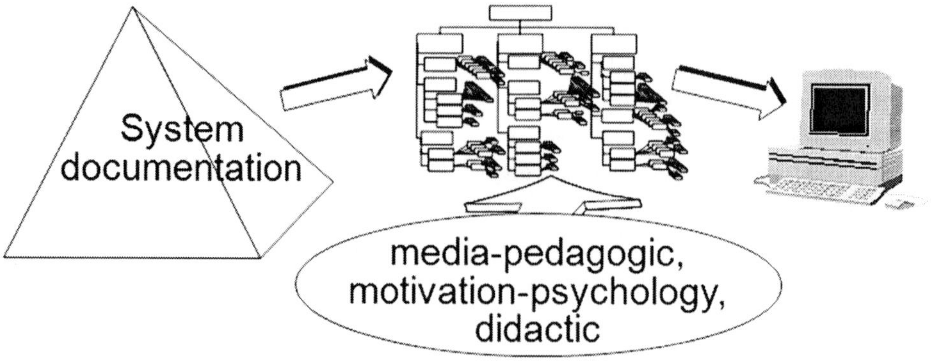

We extract measurement data at the operational level and analyze them. These data are aggregated and integrated with audit, review, assessment and test results, the feedback from different stakeholders (e.g., customers, collaborators, suppliers, partners), as well as environment observations (e.g., changed business conditions, legal and/or regulative requirements, surveys and technical reports). They are reported to all relevant stakeholders of the tactical and strategic level (Stoll & Breu, in press).

Based on our holistic information security governance approach we integrate information security evaluation with corporate controlling. Thus information security measurement and compliance information are part of the corporate business cockpit and corporate management. Based on the achievement of established objectives, and the actual risk and compliance situation necessary measures to maintain and improve corporate governance are elaborated and implemented proactively and on time. The directives are assisted in identifying and evaluating noncompliant and ineffective security processes and controls, as well as in prioritizing and deciding actions for improving or changing strategies, processes and/or controls.

Information security management requires a systemic and holistic approach. For example, if a new customer or law requires stronger confidentiality for certain data, a risk assessment over the whole data lifecycle (from receipt to disposal) must be conducted. The adequacy of the implemented regulations and the applied technical and physical security protection for all treatments and locations must be checked and eventually improved. The affected parts of the system documentation must be appropriately changed, approved, trained, implemented and evaluated in accordance to defined processes. In compliance to legal, regulatory and business requirements tracks of all changes and their communication must be maintained traceably.

At the operational level information security metrics support the identification of previously undetected or unknown information security issues, the identification of attempted security breaches and incidents, and the detection of security events. If planned results are not achieved or security issues or breaches occur, appropriate corrective and eventually preventive actions are taken accordingly to defined optimized processes (see Process Analysis and Process Improvement).

Organizational knowledge is changed and so new individual and organizational learning becomes possible (Takeuchi & Nonaka, 2004; Senge, 2003). Thus the knowledge and learning spiral, as well as the information security lifecycle are constantly pushed again (Takeuchi & Nonaka, 2004). Information security governance is sustainable maintained and improved.

CASE STUDIES RESULTS AND EXPERIENCES

This holistic information security model was implemented over several years within diverse process oriented standard based management systems in different small and medium sized organizations of distinct sectors and countries. The following case studies results were collected by established process and system measurement methods and interviewing managers and collaborators:

- **Applicability and evaluation:** The participants of the case studies passed over the years all external compliance audits. They received and maintained the international recognized ISO/IEC 27001 certificate and other management system certificates.
- **Understandable:** This model reduces complexity and is based on the model of international recognized management system standards, such as ISO 9001. More than 1.37 million organizations worldwide are

implementing such standard based management systems (ISO, 2010). The main structure of this model is well known in all these organizations. For organizations with implemented quality management systems the risk assessment and business continuity are new parts. Other management systems, such as environmental or hygienic or health and safety, have implemented also these elements, but from a different technical perspective. In our case studies, for example in a technical organization and in technical departments the collaborators regard information security aspects more helpfully for their daily work than others. In that way the existing standard based management system benefits from the integration. The collaborators consider the integration more than an extension and enriching.

- **Adaptable to specific requirements:** This model provides a generic and systemic approach, which can be best adapted to the specific requirements of each organization. For example, the same business process of an organization requires in different departments in accordance to legal requirements and the type of treated data classes (personal in one and high sensitive health data in the other) on one hand a very high confidentiality and on the other hand low or medium confidentiality. These different requirements are integrated into one single management system (including requirement analysis, risk assessment, measurement, analysis and improvement and all other elements).
- **Easy to use:** This model was simple to use for all organizations involved. The lead time to integrate information security governance varies in our case studies from three months to two years. It is depending on the complexity and diversity of an organization, their information security requirements, the degree of organization, the management commitment and overall the time invested by the collaborators involved.
- **Efficiency and cost reduction:** By integrating information security completely into a standard based management system the information security management system uses synergies, such as the existing policy, objectives, strategies, the management process, system thinking, the systematic process oriented approach, the training and improvement processes, and others. In that way the effort and costs for the introduction could be reduced in our case studies about 10-20%. The advantages are still higher during the implementation, where only the audit is extended, and the risk assessment and business continuity planning must be maintained.
- **Effectiveness:** The tight integration of information security objectives with corporate objectives, the strategic alignment of all information security projects and measures, the employee involvement and continual information security controlling promote the fulfillment of established objectives. The studied organizations achieve their planned objectives in average more than 92%.
- **Sustainability:** The first organization of the case studies obtained the certificate in 2003 and maintained it over all the years. Different chief information security officers state a tight alignment of information security with corporate objectives and strategies, a suitable integration with all business processes, and the continual measurement, analysis and improvement as great challenges, but crucial success factor for effective and ongoing information security.
- **Compliance:** Legal, regulatory, standard and business information security requirements are analyzed, implemented and

maintained by defined controlling and improvement processes. In that way legal, regulatory and standard compliance and conformance are sustainable implemented. This is specially appreciated by board members and CEOs. During the period of the case studies different legal requirements, for example, were changed. They could be integrated easily and efficiently in the established security system. Based on our holistic and preventive approach most of the requirements were already implemented. The structured and systematic approach was appreciated by the chief information security officer as helpful tool for an efficient risk assessment, the establishment of new or change of existing regulations or processes and their communication and implementation.

Success Factors and Discussion

Here we present and discuss some case studies experiences, challenges and success factors of our case studies.

Introducing information security into holistic standard based management systems requires a business-focused and suitable management system for the specific requirements of the organization. This certainly cannot be achieved by using a purchased generic manual, which does not correspond with lived processes and is not aligned with corporate objectives and strategies. The standard based management system must be evidently committed by the board and directives and implemented ongoing and effectively. If information security is integrated with a management system, which is only an alibi to certificate, information security governance cannot be supported. This may be valued as weakness of our model. It may be much better to start from zero. In that way the new information security system offers a new chance to relaunch a management system. If it is successful, it can be integrated with the "old" management system after and promote this one.

It seems obviously that information security governance must be business-focused and suitable for the specific organization. Many organizations want to implement information security with the minimalist possible effort. They require, for example generic risk assessments and information security regulations. If an organization uses such tools not only as framework or guidelines, they implement some common information security aspects, but never information security governance. Information security governance per definition must be part of corporate governance to sustain and extend organization's strategies and objectives for sustainable organizations' success (IT Governance Institute, 2006).

To deduce transparently measureable information security objectives from corporate objectives to all business processes and organizational units was a great challenge for each organization. Information security for long time was seen fundamentally as an only technical job and integral part of the information technology department. A lot of technical information security objectives, such as system availability, network security or secure authentication with appropriate controls and metrics were developed and implemented. Information security problems persisted and increased. Information security is complex and requires a collaborative and holistic approach by regarding all business processes and organizational units. For one organization, for example, the confidential treatment of all internal information and customer related information is essential. We assigned to each document and group of data the data protection class accordingly to legal requirements. How helpful would be only data encryption, if on the other side, for example, the collaborators speak very open about this data outside the organization. Practice-oriented regulations for the data treatment over the whole data lifecycle and continual security awareness by all collaborators were most important.

Based on such case studies experiences it is crucial to implement and improve information security in accordance to business and legal requirements in all business processes over the whole value network to archive sustainable information security. We invested a lot of effort in each organization to link information security requirements for each business process with corporate objectives and legal and regulatory requirements.

Information security metrics and measurement were also a great challenge for all organizations and can be still improved. Information security controlling is in most of these organizations integrated with corporate controlling. In that way information security is a topic of each board meeting and management review. It was much easier to implement information security controlling for IT service provider than for other organizations, where overall legal compliance and confidentiality for example are main information security objectives. These require more human related controls than technical controls. They are difficult to measure and must be overall audited and assessed.

Based on the case study the best way to implement sustainable information security was to integrate identified controls suitable and optimal IT supported into the everyday practice of all collaborators. To harmonize and balance the single process requirements to each other was a challenge. These discussions were excellent trainings to improve information security awareness by all collaborators involved.

Clear assigned roles and responsibilities promoted also security awareness. In that way all collaborators feel information security as part of their work and not as an add-on and take ownership for information security. We received, for example, in all organizations of the case studies suggestions for potential security breaches and improvement proposal from the collaborators. It was evident that security awareness is directly influenced by the way how actively executives take ownership for information security: they practice established directives itself, they incorporate security by all their decisions and actions and they enable and control collaborators in following these principles.

To integrate information security ongoing into the everyday business practice it is further essential to check all programs, projects and events for potential security and compliance risks and requirements. Information security governance must be an integral part of program/project management, product/system development, incident management and change management. We have implemented this aspect in all organizations with a first approach. The great influence for the most organizations was recognized over a longer period and will be further improved.

The collaborators appreciate an effectively accessible, reader friendly, clear understandably and practice-oriented documentation. An efficient and effective search function and a clear structured management system are most important for them. The invested effort to prepare the documentation regarding didactical principals was fully honoured by the collaborators. They accessed the documentation more frequently in these organizations, which regarded more didactical principals than in others.

To maintain ongoing information security governance we must improve our system dynamically and flexibly to all internal and external changes. The information security life-cycle must be pushed constantly. This requires continual organizational and technical development, which can be supported by organizational and technical tools so far as this is admitted by corporate culture. In an organization with an open, confident based, participative corporate learning culture the security awareness was much more appreciated by the same external auditors than in other organizations with a more hierarchical culture.

OUTLOOK

Based on our case studies experiences in several organizations with different management systems we can clearly state that a key success factor for information security governance is the tightly integration with other standard based management systems, such as ISO 9001 for quality management. In that way information security governance is introduced and improved in an effective, efficient and sustainable way, provided that the standard based management system is suitable for the organization and implemented at an adequate maturity level.

In this chapter we presented our approach with a governance focus by underlining strategic and controlling aspects. Further publications and research will integrate in this model technical and architecture oriented security models, as well as socio-organizational and cultural approaches.

Most different future research streams are suggested by main success factors and challenges, such as:

- **Information security controlling:** Objective deployment, metrics and stakeholder oriented reporting, as well as the integration of information security controlling, reporting and escalation with corporate controlling, performance and information management are ongoing main research streams. The strategic and corporate management dimension of information security research should be still promoted.
- **Holistic, integrated information security:** The integration of information security into all business processes over the whole value network and specially the integration with program/project management, product/system development, incident management and change management offer a wide range of research questions. An adequate assessment and treatment of information security risks, for example must be tightly integrated with project or change management or product/system development.
- **Sustainable information security:** An important future research avenue is ongoing information security. It requires an interdisciplinary approach of most different disciplines, such as corporate management, information technology, engineering, information and knowledge management, organizational development, communication science, service management, facility management, civil protection, sociology, psychology, and others.

CONCLUSION

We presented a holistic information security governance model to meet information security requirements, as well as legal, regulatory and standard compliance and conformance requirements. The innovation of this information security governance model is the integration of different information security governance frameworks with the ISO 9001 standard for quality management systems or other international standards for management systems, as well as with the international standard for information security management IEC/ISO 27001 and best-practice methods (COBIT, ITIL).

A main success factor for this holistic governance approach is a suitable integration of information security into all strategic, tactical and operational business processes:

- Information security objectives are deduced coherently from corporate objectives for all business processes, assets and organizational functions,
- An adequate and strategically aligned risk assessment is conducted,
- All business processes are optimized for information security and the established risk treatments and business continuity plans are integrated with the daily work of all collaborators,
- The effectiveness, compliance and adequacy of the implementation are continually measured, analyzed and improved.

In that way information security governance is fully integrated with corporate governance.

Based on our practical experiences over several years in distinct small and medium sized organizations this holistic information security governance model can be introduced in standard based management systems efficiently and smoothly. It supports sustainable information security governance effectively.

The confidence of customers, partners and shareholders, the availability of essential assets and data integrity, as well as legal and regulatory compliance are promoted. The price is the development, implementation and maintenance of this model.

Due to the importance of information and information systems for modern organizations as key differentiator and the sharpened governance requirements, information security must be recognized as valuable contribution to strategies and organizations' success. It must become integral part of all strategic, tactical and operational business processes and activities. This requires a practice-oriented, holistic, interdisciplinary approach for information security and information security research. Further research must be done in the direction of information security controlling, holistic integrated information security and sustainable, living information security.

REFERENCES

Akao, Y. (1990). *Quality function deployment, integrating customer requirements into product design*. Cambridge, MA: Productivity Press.

Clinch, J. (2009). *ITIL V3 and information security.* Retrieved November 3, 2010, from www.best-management-practice.com/gempdf/ITILV3_and_Information_Security_White_Paper_May09.pdf

Da Veiga, A., & Eloff, J. H. P. (2007). An information security governance framework. *Information Systems Management, 24*(4), 361–372. doi:10.1080/10580530701586136

Davenport, T. H. (2005). *Thinking for a living, how to get better performance and results from knowledge workers*. Boston, MA: Harvard Business School Press.

Great Britain. Office of Government Commerce (OGC). (2007). *Service design (SD): ITIL*. London, UK: TSO The Stationery Office.

International Standard Organization (ISO). (2005). *ISO/IEC 27001:2005, Information Technology, security techniques, information security management systems requirements*. Geneva, Switzerland: ISO.

International Standard Organization (ISO). (2005). *ISO/IEC 27002:2005, Information Technology, security techniques, code of practice for information security management*. Geneva, Switzerland: ISO.

International Standard Organization (ISO). (2008). *Quality management systems – Requirements. ISO, 9001*, 2008.

International Standard Organization (ISO). (2009). *ISO/IEC 27004:2009, Information technology, security techniques, information security management measurement*. Geneva, Switzerland: ISO.

International Standard Organization (ISO). (2010). *ISO survey of certifications 2009*. Retrieved November 23, 2010, from http://www.iso.org/iso/survey2009.pdf

IT Governance Institute. (2006). *Information security governance: Guidance for boards of directors and executive management*. Rolling Meadows, IL: IT Governance Institute.

IT Governance Institute. (2007). *COBIT® 4.1: Framework, control objectives, management guidelines, maturity models*. Rolling Meadows, IL: IT Governance Institute.

Kaplan, R. S., & Norton, D. P. (1996). *The balanced scorecard: Translating strategy into action* (reprinted ed.). Boston, MA: Harvard Business School Press.

National Institute of Standards and Technology (NIST). (2008). *Performance measurement guide for information security.* NIST Special Publication 800-55 Revision 1. Retrieved January 28, 2010, from http://csrc.nist.gov/publications/nistpubs/800-55-Rev1/SP800-55-rev1.pdf

Organization for Economic Co-operation and Development (OECD). (2004). *Principles of corporate governance*. Retrieved November 3, 2010, from http://www.oecd.org/dataoecd/32/18/31557724.pdf

PricewaterhouseCoopers LLP. (2010). *Information security breaches survey 2010.* Technical Report. Retrieved July 13, 2010, from http://www.pwc.co.uk/pdf/isbs_survey_2010_technical_report.pdf

Reinmann-Rothmeier, G. (2002). Mediendidaktik und Wissensmanagement. *MedienPädagogik, 2*(2), 1-27. Retrieved August 18, 2006 from www.medienpaed.com/02-2/reinmann1.pdf

Rosenberg, M. J. (2001). *E-learning: Strategies for delivering knowledge in the digital age*. New York, NY: McGraw-Hill.

Saint-Germain, R. (2005). Information security management best practice based on ISO/IEC 17799. *Information Management Journal, 39*(4), 60–66.

Senge, P. (2003). Taking personal change seriously: The impact of organizational learning on management practice. *The Academy of Management Executive, 17*(2), 47–50. doi:10.5465/AME.2003.10025191

Sowa, S., Tsinas, L., & Gabriel, R. (2009). BOR information security - Business ORiented management of information security. In Johnson, M. E. (Ed.), *Managing information risk and the economics of security* (pp. 81–97). New York, NY: Springer. doi:10.1007/978-0-387-09762-6_4

Stoll, M. (2007). Managementsysteme und Prozessorientiertes Wissensmanagement. In N. Gronau (Ed.), *Proceedings of the 4th Conference on Professional Knowledge Management – Experiences and Visions*: Vol. 1. (pp. 433-434). Berlin, Germany: Gito Verlag.

Stoll, M. (2008). E-learning promotes information security. In M. Iskander (Ed.), *Innovative Techniques in Instruction Technology, E-learning, E-assessment, and Education: Proceedings of the 2007 IEEE International Conference on Engineering Education, Instructional Technology, Assessment, and E-learning (EIAE 07)*. Dordrecht, The Netherlands: Springer. doi: 10.1007/978-1-4020-8739-4_54

Stoll, M., & Breu, R. (in press). Information security measurement roles and responsibilities. *Proceedings of the 2010 IEEE International Conference Telecommunication and Networking (TENE2010).*

Takeuchi, H., & Nonaka, I. (2004). *Hitotsubashi on knowledge management*. Singapore: John Wiley & Sons.

von Solms, S. H., & Solms, R. v. (2009). *Information security governance*. New York, NY: Springer. doi:10.1007/978-0-387-79984-1

ADDITIONAL READING

Anderson, C. L., & Agarwal, R. (2010). Practicing safe computing: A multimethod empirical examination of home computer user security behavioral intentions. *Management Information Systems Quarterly, 34*(3), 613–A15.

Argyris, C., & Schön, D. A. (1978; 1996). *Organizational learning*. Reading, Mass u.a.: Addison-Wesley Pub. Co.

Arnason, S. T. (2007). *How to achieve 27001 certification: An example of applied compliance management*. Abingdon: Taylor & Francis Group.

Bernard, R. (2007). Information lifecycle security risk assessment: A tool for closing security gaps. *Computers & Security*, *26*(1), 26–30. doi:10.1016/j.cose.2006.12.005

Bleicher, K. (2004). *Das konzept integriertes management: Visionen, missionen, programme*. Frankfurt: Campus-Verlag.

Brotby, K. (2009). *Information security governance: A practical development and implementation approach*. Chichester: John Wiley & Sons, Limited.

Bulgurcu, B., Cavusoglu, H., & Benbasat, I. (2010). Information security policy compliance: An empirical study of rationality-based beliefs and information security awareness. *Management Information Systems Quarterly*, *34*(3), 523–A7.

Deming, W. E. (1986). *Out of the crisis: Quality, productivity and competitive position*. Cambridge: Cambridge Univ. Press.

Dhillon, G., & Backhouse, J. (2001). Current directions in IS security research: towards socio-organizational perspectives. *Information Systems Journal*, *11*(2), 127–153. doi:10.1046/j.1365-2575.2001.00099.x

Dhillon, G., & Torkzadeh, G. (2006). Value-focused assessment of information system security in organizations. *Information Systems Journal*, *16*(3), 293–314. doi:10.1111/j.1365-2575.2006.00219.x

Ezingeard, J., & Bowen-Schrire, M. (2007). Triggers of change in information security management practices. *Journal of General Management*, *32*(4), 53–72.

Federal Office for Information Security. (2007). *IT Security Guidelines*. Retrieved January 28, 2010 from www.bsi.bund.de/cae/servlet/contentblob/475854/publicationFile/28012/guidelines_pdf.pdf

Federal Office for Information Security. (2008). *BSI Standard 100-1 Information Security Management Systems (ISMS)*. Retrieved January 28, 2010 from https://www.bsi.bund.de/SharedDocs/Downloads/EN/BSI/Publications/BSIStandards/standard_100-1_e_pdf.pdf?__blob=publicationFile

Federal Office for Information Security. (2009). *BSI-Standard 100-4: Business Continuity Management*. Retrieved January 28, 2010 from https://www.bsi.bund.de/SharedDocs/Downloads/EN/BSI/Publications/BSIStandards/standard_100-4_e_pdf.pdf?__blob=publicationFile

Gordon, L. A., Loeb, M. P., & Sohail, T. (2010). Market value of voluntary disclosures concerning information security. *Management Information Systems Quarterly*, *34*(3), 567–A2.

Hayden, L. (2010). *IT security metrics: A practical framework for measuring security & protecting data. New York u.a.* McGraw Hill.

Humphreys, E. (2007). *Implementing the ISO/IEC 27001 information security management standard*. Boston: Artech House.

Imai, M. (1986). *Kaizen (ky'zen): The key to japan's competitive success*. New York, NY: Random House.

International Standard Organization. (2008). *ISO/IEC 21827, Information technology, Security techniques, Systems Security Engineering, Capability Maturity Model® (SSE-CMM®)*. Geneva, Switzerland: ISO.

International Standard Organization. (2008). *ISO/IEC 27005:2008 Information technology, Security techniques, Information security risk management.* Geneva, Switzerland: ISO.

International Standard Organization. (2010). *ISO/IEC 27003:2010, Information technology, Security techniques, Information security management system implementation guidance.* Geneva, Switzerland: ISO.

Jaquith, A. (2008). *Security metrics: Replacing fear, uncertainty, and doubt* (4 print ed.). Upper Saddle River, NJ u.a.: Addison-Wesley.

Johnston, A. C., & Warkentin, M. (2010). Fear appeals and information security behaviors: An empirical study. *Management Information Systems Quarterly, 34*(3), 549–A4.

Juran, J. M. (1951). *Quality-control handbook.* New York: McGraw-Hill.

Kankanhalli, A., Teo, H., Tan, B. C. Y., & Wei, K. (2003). An integrative study of information systems security effectiveness. *International Journal of Information Management, 23*(2), 139. doi:10.1016/S0268-4012(02)00105-6

Savola, R. (2007). Towards a security metrics taxonomy for the information and communication technology industry. Paper presented at the *International Conference on Software Engineering Advances, 2007. ICSEA 2007.* 60-66. http://doi.ieeecomputersociety.org/10.1109/ICSEA.2007.79

Siponen, M., & Vance, A. (2010). Neutralization: New insights into the problem of employee information systems security policy violations. *Management Information Systems Quarterly, 34*(3), 487–A12.

Siponen, M. T. (2001). An analysis of the recent IS security development approaches: descriptive and prescriptive implications. In Dhillon, G. (Ed.), *Information security management: Global challenges in the new millennium.* Hershey, Pa: Idea Group Pub.doi:10.4018/978-1-878289-78-0.ch008

Smith, S., Winchester, D., Bunker, D., & Jamieson, R. (2010). Circuits of power: A study of mandated compliance to an information systems security de jure standard in a government organization. *Management Information Systems Quarterly, 34*(3), 463–486.

Spears, J. L., & Barki, H. (2010). User participation in information systems security risk management. *Management Information Systems Quarterly, 34*(3), 503–A5.

Stewart, J. M., Tittel, E., & Chapple, M. (2008). *CISSP: Certified information systems security professional study guide. Serious skills.* Indianapolis, Ind: Wiley Pub.

Stoll, M., Felderer, M., & Breu, R. (in press). Information Management for Collaborative Information Security. P*roceedings of the2010IEEE international conference systems, computing sciences and software engineering (SCSS2010).*

Tiemeyer, E., & Bachmann, W. (2009). *Handbuch IT-management: Konzepte, methoden, lösungen und arbeitshilfen für die praxis* (3, überarb u erw Aufl ed.). München: Hanser.

Trcek, D. (2003). An integral framework for information systems security management. *Computers & Security, 22*(4), 337–360. doi:10.1016/S0167-4048(03)00413-9

Weill, P., & Ross, J. W. (2004). *IT governance: How top performers manage IT decision rights for superior results.* Boston, Mass.: Harvard Business School Press.

Wood, C. (2003). *Information Security Roles & Responsibilities Made Easy*. Houston: Information Shield.

KEY TERMS AND DEFINITIONS

Business Process: A business process is a set of interrelated or interacting activities which transforms inputs into outputs to meet defined objectives by respecting constraints and requiring resources.

Information Security Governance: Information security governance is an integral part of corporate governance. It provides the strategic direction for information security, ensures that objectives are achieved, and ascertains that risks are managed appropriately and responsibly. In that way information security sustains and extends organizations strategies, objectives and controlling for sustainable organizations' success.

Information Security: Information security is the preservation of confidentiality, integrity and availability of information. In accordance to corporate objectives and strategies, as well as stakeholder's, legal, regulatory, business and standard requirements other properties, such as authenticity, accountability, non-repudiation and reliability can also be involved.

Information Security Management System: An information security management system is part of the overall management system (see Management System). It is based on a business risk approach, to establish, implement, operate, monitor, review, maintain and improve information security accordingly to stakeholder, business, standard, legal and regulatory requirements.

Management System: A management system identifies, understands and manages interrelated or interacting processes and activities to establish the organizations' objectives accordingly to stakeholders', legal, regulatory and standard requirements and to achieve those objectives sustainable. It consists of a corporate policy, objectives, planning activities, responsibilities, organizational structure, policies, practices, procedures, processes and resources. Due to external and internal changes it must be continually adjusted and improved.

Policy: The policy provides the overall intention, direction, principles and values of an organization in accordance to stakeholders', legal, regulatory and standard requirements and the characteristics of the business, the organization, its location, assets and resources. It is a framework for setting objectives and measuring their achievement.

Quality Management System: A quality management system is a management system (see "Management system") to direct and control an organization to fulfill stakeholder requirements. It includes the establishment of the quality policy and objectives, as well as quality planning, quality control, quality assurance and quality improvement.

Risk Assessment: A risk assessment is a systematic use of information to identify sources of risk, to estimate the risk and to compare the estimated risk against given risk criteria to determine the significance of the risk.

Chapter 16
A Construct Grid Approach to Security Classification and Analysis

Michael Van Hilst
Florida Atlantic University, USA

Eduardo B. Fernandez
Florida Atlantic University, USA

ABSTRACT

This chapter presents a method of mapping solution elements to regions of the problem space. Security requires complete, effective, and comprehensive coverage. Existing methodologies can enumerate known weaknesses and common solution elements. But not every solution is right for every situation. Moreover, any weakness in any component, phase, or activity can compromise the entire system. The method presented here helps map solutions to problems, and also brings attention to what might be missing. The approach, called a construct grid, divides the conceptual problem space along multiple dimensions. The space along each dimension is defined as a continuum with identifiable regions of concern. The chapter provides examples of several dimensions and the types of concerns used to define the regions of concern.

INTRODUCTION

Security must be comprehensive. A system can be compromised by any weakness in any place at any time. To assure the security of a product or system, security must be addressed for all aspects of all components in all activities, and in every phase of the product or system lifecycle. Security must be managed top-to-bottom and beginning-to-end. However, the individual practices and mechanisms that make up a system's security are limited in scope. Large numbers of solutions must be managed in combination to assure even basic levels of security.

DOI: 10.4018/978-1-4666-0197-0.ch016

The security challenge is compounded by the way real world systems are built. Consider the issues of component source in software development. Components can come from new code, open-source, runtime script, model transformation, wizard code generation, legacy application, reuse library, outsourced development, commercial-off-the-shelf, and remote web service. It is a rare and inefficient project that doesn't leverage more than a couple of these sources.

In this chapter we present a method of surveying and analyzing coverage of the problem space. When elements of security are described in terms of the solution (encryption, authorization, authentication, etc.) it is difficult to assess the overall level and extent of protection. The solutions themselves often assume a single perspective or level of architecture, and are applied in a particular level of the organization and stage of the lifecycle. Checklists can help. But in a list, the relationships between and among the items are not expressed. In our approach, the emphasis starts with the problem as a whole. The situation is viewed from a variety of perspectives, and supports many kinds of analysis, including an analysis of gaps.

At Florida Atlantic University, our group develops security methodologies based on the use of patterns. Patterns are well known solutions to common problems in given contexts. They present both the problem and the solution in a stylized, concise and easy to read form. Patterns make it possible for practitioners looking at a specific problem or task to benefit from the experience of others in a conveniently packaged form. Patterns are collected in books, posted on the Web, and discussed in conferences. By now there are hundreds, if not thousands of patterns. Patterns are best known for their use in the field of software development. But they can be used for anything. Patterns are beginning to appear in other fields such as business management and education. Our group, in collaboration with others around the world, produces security patterns that cover a range of concerns, including semantic and domain analysis (Delessy, & Fernandez, 2005)(Fernandez, VanHilst, & Pelaez, 2007)(Fernandez, & Yuan, 2000), protection mechanisms (Fernandez, Pernul, & Larrondo-Petrie, 2008), attacks and forensics (Palaez, Fernandez, Larrondo-Petrie, & Wieser, 2007)(Palaez, & Fernandez, 2006), and security architectures (Fernandez, Fonoage, VanHilst, & Marta, 2008).

In developing a methodology around the use of patterns, we faced the challenge of creating an awareness of the total security landscape and finding solutions to cover everything. While there are many solutions in the field of security, any given solution only covers a piece of the bigger problem. Given that there now exists a large and growing collection of solution patterns, how do we find an appropriate solution to a given problem, and how can we know what is covered and what is not?

In our work, we have come to the conclusion that a single end-to-end methodology, by itself, cannot realistically address all the security concerns in every situation and variation that a developer is likely to face. The variety is too great for a one-size-fits-all approach. While a systematic approach is essential, it must be augmented by the delivery of focused elements of security knowledge when and where they are needed. Patterns have proven effective for delivering focused knowledge. But choosing the right knowledge, and knowing what might still be missing, requires a broad, reflective view of the overall security situation.

The target users of this work cover a range of security stake holders. In addition to software developers, we also consider the needs and perspectives of information security managers, patterns writers, and students. Information security managers have more of a systems perspective, and an organizational perspective. Patterns writers often are looking for gaps to fill and a broader context within which to view their patterns. Students are looking to broaden their understanding of a range of security issues and perspectives.

In the following sections we describe the use of construct theory to divide the problem space into smaller, focused regions in an n-dimensional view of problem space, called a construct grid. Then we give examples of the common dimensions that we have found useful in describing a construct grid for security concerns. Regions in the problem space bear a relationship to existing work on facets and faceted search, which is discussed in section 4. Section 5 describes a way to display views of the grid using matrix diagrams from operations research. Section 6 defines additional axis types. Section 7 describes an example of our own use of the construct grid. Section 8 describes related work. Section 9 contains the conclusion.

CONSTRUCT GRID

The approach we have taken to defining the security space is top-down. We start with a complete problem space, and then carve it into different concerns along different dimensions. The idea of dividing up psychological space can be found in Euclid's elements. Its use here builds on the ideas of the psychologist, George Kelly (Kelly, 1955).

In Kelly's personal construct theory, a construct is a reference axis of two opposing poles. Wealth, for example is an axis of rich and poor. The space between the poles defines a "range of convenience" which gains further relevance with additional "planes" of distinction. "A construct is a dichotomous reference axis. It defines a family of planes orthogonal to it that divide the space." (Shaw & Gaines, 1992). Kelly described an n-dimensional grid of concepts that embodies a person's intentions and shapes their response. He called it a "role repertory grid." Each dimension (or construct) embodies an aspect of one's intentions and understanding. Conceptual space is formed by the combination of many construct dimensions. A more formal treatment of drawing distinctions in the division of psychological space can also be found in G. S. Brown's "Laws of Form" (Brown, 1971).

In our case, we are not as interested in the planes of distinction, which create the separations. Rather, our interest lies with spaces between two planes, which we call a region. Regions provide the convenience of classification, to which we attach a label. For example, consider the lifecycle of a software application. We can define the application lifecycle as a continuum from pre-project preparation to final disposal (of all artifacts). We then define lifecycle stages as regions along this continuum. From a development intent, we define regions for domain analysis, requirements, architectural analysis, design, implementation, and deployment. From an operations intent we define stages for installation, configuration, operation, maintenance, and disposal.

Regions defined on a continuum are not defined relative to each other, but, rather, in terms of their position on the continuum. Thus, regions can overlap without loss of meaning. The region for deployment, defined from the development intent, overlaps with installation, configuration, and possibly some of operation, as defined from the operation intent. This view of classification contrasts sharply with the more traditional hierarchical approach to classification, such as used, for example, to classify plants and animals. In hierarchical classification each classification must be distinct. Here, if deployment and configuration cover parts of the same space, elements in that space should be classified as both.

By using a continuum, we can relate the distinctions from different intents, and determine if any regions along the continuum have not been addressed. Developers, for example, don't often consider issues of disposal. The National Security Administration's guidelines for information systems management requires the entire lifecycle continuum to be covered. The narrower lifecycle views common in either development or operations are not sufficient when it comes to security.

The construct grid collects any number of orthogonal dimensions to form a combined multidimensional division of the space. Elements are identifiable by the combination of their classifications along multiple axes. The element's region in a multidimensional space is the intersection of the regions it occupies on each axis. In the past, we have referred to the grid as an n-dimensional matrix. In a matrix, each cell is identifiable by the indexes in each of its dimension. The use of the term matrix can, however, be misleading in that cells in a matrix are, by definition, disjoint.

At any time regions can be added along existing dimensions, or new dimensions added entirely. Extending the grid does not obsolete earlier grids – they just don't include as many distinctions.

COMMON AXES FOR SECURITY

In our work, we use these axes to classify patterns for different solution elements, and then later, to select the elements of an integrated solution. A pattern is mapped to a given region if it addresses concerns specific to that region. The axes we use include system lifecycle, attack lifecycle, architectural level, constraint level, and code source. The axis for application or system lifecycle was described above.

We classify types of security response along a continuum of the attack lifecycle, from intent to attack to the attack aftermath. The regions for defense along this continuum include avoidance, deterrence, prevention, detection, mitigation, recovery, and investigation (or forensics). Corresponding regions, reflecting the attacker's perspective, could also be defined along the same continuum.

Architectural level forms another axis. In today's systems-of-systems view of applications, many development projects address a single system or level within a larger stack of infrastructure and components. Threats, strategies, and mechanisms are different at different levels of this architecture. We define a dimension for the level of system architecture to address these differences. Because there are several different views of the system stack, depending on the domain and application, this dimension has a number of overlapping partitions. The continuum of this dimension is defined between the lowest physical level of abstraction – the wire, and the highest semantic level of abstraction – the business task. We chose the following classifications: network, transport, distribution (including gateways and brokers), platform and operating system, data, business logic, and client. A simpler notion called application spans the last three. Network, transport, and distribution may also be grouped as communication. Distribution and operating system overlap since gateways and brokers often sit on top of, and depend upon, the operating system. Since patterns can be placed in more than one cell, there is no real need for exact or disjoint classification.

Level of constraint is also an axis. Leveson's studies of safety failures at NASA (Leveson, 2004) show that accidents can follow failures of constraints at higher levels than just mechanisms and developers. Accidents are prevented by constraints at many levels of organization, from low level mechanisms, up through operators, managers, organizational policy and practices, regulators, governmental regulation and policy, and ultimately international treaties and standards. Failures can often be traced to factors at many levels. Policy and enforcement failures, for example, played a significant role in the BP Gulf of Mexico oil well disaster.

We incorporated Leveson's insight and defined another dimension for level of constraint. This dimension defines a continuum from simple device mechanisms to societal (national and international) levels of regulation and oversight. Following the levels identified in Leveson's work, we partition the axis for level of constraint into mechanism, operator, developer, organizational, and regulatory. The National Training Standard for Information Systems Security Professionals (INFOSEC) (National Security Agency, 1994) is mostly concerned with practices, policies, and regulations. The Common Criteria has functional requirements that apply at the level of mechanisms (Common Criteria Sponsoring Organization, 2007). But it also has assurance requirements that concern organizational processes to document actions taken. The development of a configuration management plan is a Common Criteria assurance requirement that applies at the organizational level, and also in the system lifecycle stage of domain analysis. The Common Criteria and other standards such as Sarbanes-Oxley (One Hundred Seventh Congress, 2002) and the Systems Security Engineering Capability Maturity Model (International Systems Security, 2003) themselves belong at the regulatory level.

We introduced a list of component source types in the introduction. The list of component source types can be mapped to a continuum based on the control of details, from full control of details to no control. We defined regions along this continuum for new code, open-source, runtime script, model transformation, wizard code generation, legacy application, reuse library, outsourced development, commercial-off-the-shelf, and remote cloud or web service. Common security practices often assume the development is always new code. But each of these regions pose different security issues.

FACETS

Region labels correspond to facets as used in component reuse. A facet is a simple label, like those used in Google Mail. In component reuse, facets generally identify different properties of the component. Classification for component reuse has a long history. Prieto-Diaz made a strong case for faceted classification over hierarchical classification (Prieto-Diaz, 1991). He provided seven criteria for a classification scheme:

1. It must accommodate continually expanding collections,
2. It must support finding components that are similar, not just exact matches,
3. It must support finding functionally equivalent components across domains,
4. It must be very precise and have high descriptive power.
5. It must be easy to maintain, that is, add, delete, and update the class structure and vocabulary without need to reclassify.
6. It must be easily usable by both the librarian and end user, and
7. It must be amenable to automation.

Our use of regions in a construct grid is equivalent to facets and satisfies the first six criteria. In our case, it is not clear how automation would apply. Prieto-Diaz's earlier component work concerned only finding a close match, classified largely by aspects of the solution. Our construct grid emphasizes properties of the problem. It also serves an educational purpose for navigating the problem space (described below), and for identifying gaps. In the Prieto-Diaz solution, support for navigation was limited. It said nothing about what was missing.

Practitioners using the grid can identify their current focus or concern by choosing the applicable region, or range of regions, along each dimension, and then look for patterns that fall into the intersection of all. In this sense, it is no different than labeling patterns with facets and using the facets to search. But there are several important distinctions. First, by defining regions along continua in an n-dimensional space, the practitioner can navigate to adjoining, and thus related, regions of the space for added context and deeper understanding. Second, by looking at the number of regions a pattern covers, and the size of region they represent, developers gain insight into not only the degree of generality, but also the type of generality the pattern entails. Third, by looking at regions or space where solutions are missing, solution developers can identify gaps that have yet to be addressed.

The use of a construct grid for problem concerns is not limited to a particular methodology. Practitioners using any method can use construct grids to better identify tasks and concerns and to locate patterns relevant to each concern. A chosen method dictates the sequence and timing of tasks to be perform, while the grid provides guidance to more specific knowledge or ideas for how to perform the tasks. This approach is consistent with, for example, McGraw's notion of security "touch points" (McGraw, 2006).

DISPLAY

Operations research provides 7 management tools to visually organize non-quantitative information and ideas (Mizuno, 1988). These tools are: relationship diagrams, affinity diagrams, tree diagrams, matrix diagrams, prioritization matrices, arrow diagrams, and process decision program charts. In organizing collections of patterns, the patterns community already uses three of these tools: relationship diagrams, affinity diagrams, and tree diagrams. Here, we propose to use a fourth tool, the matrix diagram. We find the use of matrix diagrams to be a convenient way to improve the quality and usability of pattern collections for the consumers of patterns.

Figure 1 shows a grid that maps patterns with a single dimension of the problem space. For a single mapping, we use an L-Shaped matrix diagram. The dimension for type of protection partitions the problem space of an attack into stages along the continuum from its initial conception to the aftermath of its having happened. Each category identifies the type of response appropriate to the corresponding stage of attack. From this matrix it is easy to see which stages of attack are not addressed.

Figure 2 shows a mapping of patterns on three dimensions of the problem space. Because it is not critical to visualize relationships between the different dimensions, we can present this view as a T-shaped matrix diagram. By extension, the vertical axis can be stacked with any number of additional dimensions.

In both Figures 1 and 2, the diagrams can capture slices and projections of the other axes. In the case of a slice, data is taken from only one region of an orthogonal axis. In the case of a projection, the contents of multiple regions, and commonly all regions, of the orthogonal axis are combined.

Figure 1. An L-shaped matrix diagram of relationships between patterns and protection type

Security pattern vs. Type of protection	**Check-pointed System**	**Protected System**	**Stateful Firewall**	**WiMax Security**
Avoidance				
Deterrence				
Prevention		X	X	X
Detection			X	
Mitigation	X			
Recovery	X			
Forensics			X	

Figure 2. An extended T-shaped matrix with patterns and three dimensions of the problem space

Protection Type	**Avoidance**				X
	Deterrence				X
	Prevention		X	X	X
	Detection			X	
	Mitigation	X			X
	Recovery	X			X
	Forensics			X	
	Security Pattern	**Check-pointed System**	**Protected System**	**Stateful Firewall**	**Virtual Machine**
Lifecycle Stage	**Domain Analysis**				
	Requirements				
	Analysis	X		X	X
	Design	X	X	X	X
	Implementation	X			X
	Integration				X
	Deployment				X
	Operation				X
	Maintenance				X
	Disposal				X
Architecture Layer	**Network**				
	Transport			X	X
	Operating System	X	X	X	X
	Distribution			X	X
	Data	X	X		X
	Business Logic	X	X		X
	Client/Application	X	X		X

OTHER TYPES OF AXES

Some groups of concerns are defined by distinctions that cannot easily be arranged on a bipolar continuum. An example of such distinctions occurs when defining the application domain. There are different concerns for business systems, portable or embedded devices, the military, and infrastructure control. It would be hard to arrange all these domains on some sort of continuum. There are also distinctions that are only meaningful in a local situation and not generally applicable. An example of the latter might be the division of roles in a particular domain or organization. In both cases, even though we can't meaningfully arrange them on a bi-polar continuum, the distinctions involved can still be of value for analysis and classification. Some properties of the construct grid can still apply. For example, domain regions can overlap, and names for domain regions can be sufficiently common to use as facets.

Since the addition of new axes does not reduce the value of existing axes, we allow the use of arbitrary axes, even when they do not meet ideal criteria. We call such axes, "secondary" or "auxiliary" axes.

Many classifications of patterns (such as those described in 8), and the original facet classification of components (described in section 4), use properties of the solution, or solution type, rather than from the problem. Such classifications are useful when comparing one solution to another, or when a specific solution is needed to fit a framework or specification. We were able to map the types of defense to stages in an attack. But solution concerns like authorization, authentication, access control, privacy, integrity, and non-repudiation are not so easily arranged. We use such classifications without providing a meaningful order.

Collections of security practices often include a list of security principles, like the principle of least privilege. Viega and McGraw (Viega & McGraw, 2001), for example, use a list of 10 security principles, while in Steel, Nagappan, and Lai (Steel, Nagappan, & Lai, 2005) there are 12. OWASP (Open Web Security, 2004) lists 15 principles, as well as 10 secure coding principles, 20 weaknesses or vulnerabilities and 12 countermeasures. Such lists do not really divide up the problem space. But they could provide an auxiliary dimension to rank solution patterns, based on how many and which principles they apply or address.

In carving up the problem space, a security team could include an auxiliary dimension to indicate the level or type of assurance available or achieved. For example, the assurance could be a continuum from none to fully documented. Or it could simply indicate a list of options such as spot check, policy, active monitor, or formal proof.

A danger in composing point solutions occurs at the interface between components of the solution. For example, in a heterogeneous system, some parts may be.NET while others are J2EE. New code may interface to a legacy system or use interchangeable web services. On a different dimension, subsystems may be formed by combining outsourced with legacy code. Unique security issues may occur at the interface between different types of components, where the two interact or coexist. The grid can be used to isolate and document interface issues by replicating an axis, orthogonal to itself. The resulting 2-dimensional slice is analogous to a mileage chart, with lists of cities on both axes. In this chart, elements represent interfaces between corresponding components: outsource to legacy, legacy to web service,.NET to J2EE, etc.

USAGE

We are currently applying our construct grid to a classification of security patterns for Service Oriented Architecture. Here, we discuss our efforts to use the grid for classification and give an example of how the classifications could be used.

Patterns are mapped in the same way they would be tagged. Each dimension is considered separately. Patterns are identified at the point in each dimension, and thus the matrix, where their content affects decisions that will be made. If the distinctions of a dimension are not relevant, for example, if the pattern is not specific to any domain but applicable to all, then its classification on that dimension is "any" or "all." As an example, the anti-patterns in Kis (Kis, 2002) apply at the developer level of constraint in the requirements phase. Some patterns refer to legacy components, while component source is not relevant to others. In a test conducted by our team, collaborators from Florida, Brazil, and Japan independently classified the same 6 patterns from the Open Group, and Anwar, Yurcik, Johnson, Hafiz, and Campbell (Anwar, Yurcik, Johnson, Hafiz, & Campbell, 2006). The matrix views made it easy to check off the relevant boxes. The results of the experiment showed only minor differences in five of the six axes used. Domain was the exception, where it proved harder to assign ranges of applicability. The fact that the domain axis does not have a defined bipolar continuum, as discussed in Section 6, may have contributed to the differences on this axis.

Figure 3 shows the classifications of the XACML Access Control Evaluator pattern. The pattern describes a mechanism that is applied in the design stage of development when using the XACML protocol. The type of response is prevention since the attack happens and is turned away. The control is used in the distribution level of the system architecture. Component source is not relevant as it is applicable to all classifications along this axis. We use the designation of "all" to indicates that we can either ignore this dimension, or count this pattern as relevant to every region of this dimension. For the domain classification, the pattern is specific to the domains of e-commerce and Service Oriented Architecture, as these are the domains where XACML is used. As it describes a component of the solution architecture, a classification on an additional axis for solution concern is also useful.

Figure 4 illustrates a mapping of design patterns in 2 lifecycle phases and at different levels of architecture. Only a small sample of patterns is shown. While all of the patterns in the figure are applicable to Service Oriented Architecture, some apply more generally to other domains, as well. We grouped the patterns within Design along a secondary dimension with Filtering, Access Control and Authentication. In the figure, we show patterns from the Domain Analysis phase, where the developer would find patterns that explain the domain standards and technologies later used in the design phase. A developer might also navigate to adjoining Analysis phase cells (not shown) to look for general patterns on Filtering, Access Control and Authentication. While the patterns are found in these locations in the matrix, understanding their role in a system, and how they relate to one another, still requires a pattern language diagram and other tools and methods for pattern application.

RELATED WORK

Lists are often used in security. DoD and NIST maintain lists of checklists for securely configuring various software applications, while CERT and NIST list 24,000+ known software exploits. The Common Criteria (Common Criteria Sponsoring Organization, 2007) and SSE-CMM (ISO/IEC 21827) (International Systems Security, 2003) both include lists of assurance areas that must be documented to satisfy certification. Hoglund and McGraw list 49 types of software attacks (Hogland, & McGraw, 2004). Microsoft has produced lists of flaws and attack trees, for use in a secure development process (Howard, & LeBlanc, 2003)(Howard, & Lipner, 2006)(Lipner, & Howard, 2005). In contrast to these long lists of heterogeneous concerns, each dimension of our matrix covers a more cohesive and concise range of concepts identified with generally recognizable partitions.

Figure 3. Classifications of the XACML access control evaluator

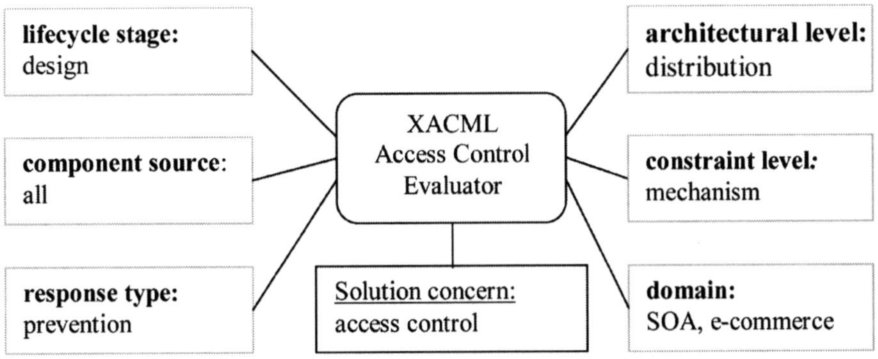

Figure 4. A sample of patterns in a focused and flattened (2.5D) snippet of the matrix

	Domain Analysis	**Design**		
		Filtering	Access Control	Authentication
Application		Application Firewall	Reference Monitor	Authenticator
Operating System			OS Ref. Monitor	OS Authenticator
Distribution	SAML XACML	XML Firewall	XACML Access Control Evaluator	SAML Authenticator
Transport	TLS	Proxy Firewall		Remote Authenticator
Network	IPsec	Packet Filter Firewall		

Schumacher et al. have defined a methodology for secure systems design using security patterns (Schumacher, Achermann, & Steinmetz, 2000) (Schumacher, Fernandez, Hybertson, Buschmann, & Sommerlad, 2006). Like us, they propose applying security at all stages of the software lifecycle. They propose using a vulnerability database to keep track of possible attacks and countermeasures. But they do not provide details on how to apply security to all the development stages, nor how to verify coverage of concerns.

Trowbridge et al. (Trowbridge, Cunningham, Evans, & Brader, 2004) describe an "organizing table" to organize patterns and identify gaps, and include a discussion of identifying relationships by exploring adjacent cells. But they limit their classification to two heterogeneous dimensions for viewpoints and interrogatives. Their 5 viewpoints are business, integration, application, operation, and development, each of which is then subdivided into architect, designer, and developer. The 110 patterns classified fall into only two categories: integration and application, and three concerns: data, function, and network.

Hafiz et al. (Hafiz, Adamczyk, & Johnson, 2007) identify four potential classification dimensions: protection type, application context, threat, and Trowbridge's viewpoints. In the end they proposed a hierarchy based on application context followed by threat. They took more the perspective of a collector than that of the user. They make an effort to place each pattern in a unique position in the hierarchy, and express the concern that too many patterns fell in too few cells. In the paper, they state, "Any organization effort must begin by collecting the items to be organized." We address the need to also identify the items that are missing, and thus begin with the space to be covered.

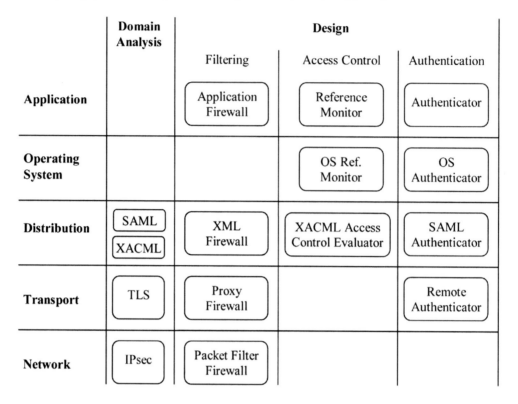

Fernandez et al. classify patterns based on architectural levels and concerns (Fernandez, Washizaki, Yoshioka, Kubo, & Fukazawa, 2008). For example, access control can be defined in the application and reflected to the database and to the operating system. Architecture levels and security concerns are two possible dimensions in the proposed matrix.

It should be noted that a multidimensional space can be aligned with cell divisions in Trowbridge et al, (Trowbridge, Cunningham, Evans, & Brader, 2004) or Hafiz et al. (Hafiz, Adamczyk, & Johnson, 2007) without hierarchical grouping. From the users' perspective, reducing orthogonal classifications to a single hierarchy achieves little and hinders the exploration of relationships along different dimensions. Moreover, if patterns are meaningful in multiple places, then they should be found in multiple places.

Many of the patterns we have looked at appear also in Steel et al. (Steel, Nagappan, & Lai, 2005). Steel et al. grouped their patterns only according to the layers in a 4-tier architecture, while we, applied more distinctions. A number of differences can be observed. By forcing each pattern to occupy only one cell, important information was lost or distorted. For example, in Steel et al. Yoder and Barcalow's Checkpoint was identified as a Client (Web) pattern, and merged with the Open Group's Checkpointed System pattern as one of a group of checkpoint patterns in the same cell. In our classification, Checkpoint is an analysis phase pattern applicable to all three application layers and addresses a general approach to prevention, while Checkpointed System is a design phase pattern applicable to the client layer and addresses a mechanism for recovery. The two patterns are quite different.

CONCLUSION

The method of classifying concerns presented here addresses security from the perspective of the problem. It takes a holistic view, dividing the original space along multiple dimensions and describing narrower concerns in terms of overlapping regions in that space. Unlike point solutions and methods based on descriptions of the solution, our approach provides a comprehensive view of security from multiple perspectives, and identifies gaps. The method supports a variety of analysis methods and is consistent with common security standards and practices.

For creators or collectors of patterns, the method supports a faceted approach to classification that is both systematic and intuitive to use. In our own experience, the classifications created by several different individuals showed a reasonable level of consistency, indicating that the classifications have value as a means of communication.

For users of patterns, and solution providers in general, the method is not a methodology in its own right. Rather, it is a tool for analysis and documentation to map solution elements to regions of the problem space. The approach presented here should be used to augment proven practices already in place.

REFERENCES

Anwar, Z., Yurcik, W., Johnson, R., Hafiz, M., & Campbell, R. H. (2006). Multiple design patterns for Voice over IP (VoIP) security. *Proceedings of the 25th IEEE International Performance, Computing, and Communications Conference*. doi: 10.1109/.2006.1629443.

Brown, G. S. (1971). *Laws of form*. George Allen and Unwin.

Common Criteria Sponsoring Organization. (2007). *Common criteria for information technology security evaluation part 2: Security functional components,* version 3.1 rev 2. Retrieved from http://www.commoncriteriaportal.org/files/ccfiles/CCPART2V3.1R2.pdf

Delessy, N., & Fernandez, E. B. (2005). Patterns for the extensible access control markup language. *Proceedings of the 12th Pattern Languages of Programs Conference (PLOP2005)*. Retrieved from http://hillside.net/plop/2005/proceedings/

Fernandez, E. B., Fonoage, M., VanHilst, M., & Marta, M. (2008). The secure three-tier architecture pattern. *Proceedings of the 2008 International Conference on Complex, Intelligent and Software Intensive Systems* (pp. 555-560). IEEE Computer Society. doi: 10.1109/CISIS.2008.51

Fernandez, E. B., Pernul, G., & Larrondo-Petrie, M. M. (2008). Patterns and pattern diagrams for access control. *Proceedings of the 5th International Conference on Trust, Privacy, and Security in Digital Systems (TRUSTBUS'08), LNCS 5185* (pp. 38-47). Springer.

Fernandez, E. B., VanHilst, M., & Pelaez, J. C. (2007). Patterns for WiMax security. *Proceedings of the European Conference on Pattern Languages of Programming.*

Fernandez, E. B., Washizaki, H., Yoshioka, N., Kubo, A., & Fukazawa, Y. (2008). Classifying security patterns. *Proceedings of the 10th Asia-Pacific Web Conference (APweb'08), LNCS 4976* (pp. 342-347). Springer. Retrieved from http://www.neu.edu.cn/apweb08/

Fernandez, E. B., & Yuan, X. (2000). Semantic analysis patterns. *Proceedings of the 19th International Conference on Conceptual Modeling (ER2000),* (pp. 183-195).

Hafiz, M., Adamczyk, P., & Johnson, R. E. (2007, July/August). Organizing security patterns. *IEEE Software, 24*(4), 52–60. doi:10.1109/MS.2007.114

Hogland, G., & McGraw, G. (2004). *Exploiting software: How to break code*. Addison-Wesley.

Howard, M., & LeBlanc, D. (2003). *Writing secure code* (2nd ed.). Microsoft Press.

Howard, M., & Lipner, S. (2006). *The security development lifecycle*. Microsoft Press.

International Systems Security Engineering Association. (2003). *Systems security engineering - Capability maturity model* (ISO/IEC 21827). Retrieved from http://www.sse-cmm.org/docs/sse-cmm.pdf

Kis, M. (2002). Information security antipatterns in software requirements engineering. *Proceedings of the 9th Pattern Languages of Programs Conference (PLoP2002)*. Retrieved from http://hillside.net/plop/plop2002/final/mkis_plop_2002.pdf

Leveson, N. (2004). A new accident model for engineering safer systems. *Safety Science, 42*(4), 237–270. doi:10.1016/S0925-7535(03)00047-X

Lipner, S., & Howard, M. (2005). *The trustworthy computing development lifecycle*. Retrieved from http://msdn2.microsoft.com/en-us/library/ms995349.aspx

McGraw, G. (2006). *Software security: Building security in*. Addison-Wesley.

Mizuno, S. (1988). *Management for quality improvement: The seven new QC tools*. Productivity Press.

National Security Agency. (1994). *National training standard for information systems security professionals* (NSTISSI-4011). Retrieved from http://www.nsa.gov/ia/academia/cnsstesstandards.cfm

One Hundred Seventh Congress of the United States of America. (2002). *Sarbanes-Oxley act*. Retrieved from http://news.findlaw.com/hdocs/docs/gwbush/sarbanesoxley072302.pdf

Open Web Security Application Project. (2004). *The OWASP testing project*. Retrieved from http://www.modsecurity.org/archive/OWASPTesting_PhaseOne.pdf

Palaez, J., & Fernandez, E. B. (2006). Network forensics in wireless VOIP networks. *Proceedings of the 4th Latin American and Caribbean Conference for Engineering and Technology (LACCEI 2006).*

Palaez, J., Fernandez, E. B., Larrondo-Petrie, M. M., & Wieser, C. (2007). Attack patterns in VOIP. *Proceedings of the 14th pattern languages of programs conference (PLoP2007)* Retrieved from http://hillside.net/plop/2007/papers/PLoP2007_PelaezEtAl.pdf

Prieto-Diaz, R. (1991). Implementing faceted classification for software reuse. *Communications of the ACM, 34*(5), 88–97. doi:10.1145/103167.103176

Schumacher, M., Achermann, R., & Steinmetz, R. (2000). Towards security at all stages of a system's life cycle. *Proceedings of the International Conference on Software, Telecommunications, and Computer Networks (Softcom)*. Retrieved from http://www.ito.tu-darmstadt.de/publs

Schumacher, R., Fernandez, E. B., Hybertson, D., Buschmann, F., & Sommerlad, P. (2006). *Security patterns: Integrating security and systems engineering*. Wiley.

Shaw, M. L. G., & Gaines, B. R. (1992, October). Kelly's "geometry of psychological space" and its significance for cognitive modeling. *The New Psychologist*, October, 23-31. Retrieved from http://pages.cpsc.ucalgary.ca/~gaines/reports/PSYCH/NewPsych92/index.html

Steel, C., Nagappan, R., & Lai, R. (2005). *Core security patterns: Best practices and strategies for J2EE, web services and identity management*. Prentice Hall.

Trowbridge, D., Cunningham, W., Evans, M., & Brader, L. (2004). *Describing the enterprise architecture space*. Retrieved from http://msdn2.microsoft.com/en-us/library/ms978655.aspx

Viega, J., & McGraw, G. (2001). *Building secure software: How to avoid security problems the right way*. Addison-Wesley.

KEY TERMS AND DEFINITIONS

Checklist: A list of items, tasks, or concerns to be addressed, usually in an exhaustive manner. Checklists serve as an aid to overcome the failings of human memory and attention.

Facet: A word or phrase that describes a shared aspect, property, or characteristic of a subset of items within a larger group. Facets are used to organize large collections and are used as search terms to find subsets of interest, for example, within a large collection of email messages.

Grid: A mesh that covers a spatial area, dividing it into cells that can be assigned identifiers and used for spatial indexing. Grids usually involve tessellation with no gaps or overlaps. For lack of a better term, we remain consistent with the spirit, but in this work we allow overlaps.

Matrix: A mathematical convenience for organizing values into orthogonal rows and columns. Cells in a row or column are contiguous and enumerated for reference.

Methodology: A coordinated framework of processes and sub-processes, that work in combination to complete a complex task. Each process is iteself an orderly and systematic process for attaining a goal or part of a goal.

National Training Standard for Information Systems Security Professionals: A set of standards created by the United States National Security Administration that define a minimum set of issues to be addressed in the training of information systems security professionals.

Pattern: A stylized method of capturing and expressing a general reusable solution to a commonly occurring problem. Patterns are nuggets of knowledge, usually validated by experts, that can be used ala carte.

Chapter 17
Towards an Organizational Culture Framework for Information Security Practices

Joo Soon Lim
The University of Melbourne, Australia

Shanton Chang
The University of Melbourne, Australia

Atif Ahmad
The University of Melbourne, Australia & SECAU – Security Research Centre, Edith Cowan University, Australia

Sean Maynard
The University of Melbourne, Australia

ABSTRACT

In organizations, employee behaviour has a considerable impact on information security. The organizational culture (OC) that shapes acceptable employee behaviours is therefore significant. A large body of literature exists that calls for the cultivation of security culture to positively influence information security related behaviour of employees. However, there is little research examining OC that enables the implementation of information security. The authors address the unsubstantiated claim that there is an important relationship between OC and the ability to successfully implement information security. Findings suggest that security practices can be successfully implemented within eight organizational culture characteristics. Investigation of these organizational culture characteristics from a security perspective is an important step toward future empirical research aimed at understanding the relationship between OC and the implementation of systematic improvement of security practices. The research and practical implications of these findings are discussed, and future research areas are explored.

DOI: 10.4018/978-1-4666-0197-0.ch017

INTRODUCTION

Security threats from insiders in an organization are recognized as a major concern in the implementation of information security practices (Straub, 1986; Workman, Bommer, & Straub, 2008). According to the annual CSI Computer Crime and Security Survey (2007), insider threat was cited by 59 percent of respondents, overtaking virus attacks as the most reported security incident (Richardson, 2007). Recent studies support this new trend (Furnell & Thompson, 2009). This indicates the need to look at human behavior within organizations. In addition, research shows that within organizations, it is OC that has an impact on employees' behaviors. OC has this impact because it is a set of shared values, beliefs, and practices that shape and direct the attitudes and behaviors (Schein, 1992). Therefore several researchers have suggested that the impact of OC in influencing the security behavior of employees must be considered (Dhillon, 1997; Von Solms, B., 2000). Subsequently, the importance of OC in information security has stimulated in-depth research in the hope that findings will assist in influencing the security behavior of employees.

Over the past decade, information security culture (ISC) remains among the top ranked concerns of information security researchers and industries practitioners (Lim, Chang, Maynard, & Ahmad, 2009; Lim, Ahmad, Chang, & Maynard, 2010). Many academic researchers argue that ISC is vital in protecting organizational information and that security behavior should be inculcated in the routine activities of each employee as a way forward in addressing information security problems (Von Solms, B., 2000; Schlienger & Teufel, 2002, 2003). As for industry practitioners, the Organization for Economic Co-operation and Development (OECD) Council and SANS has specially drawn the guidelines for moving toward a culture of information security (OECD, 2002, 2005; SANS, 2005) for the same purpose.

However, although many organizations acknowledge the importance of OC in information security behavior, many researchers have found that the OC in these organizations had not provided adequate support to security practices. For example, Knapp et al (2006) found that security training is not an integral part of most organizations and Helokunnas & Kuusisto (2003) found that none of the small to medium sized enterprises in their study had fully cultivated an ISC. These findings indicate that further empirical work is needed to investigate the cultural characteristics that provide support to security practices.

Broadly speaking, ISC has been studied in the light of various concepts and models of organizational theory. It has been researched from the perspective of Schein's (1992) three layered model (Schlienger & Teufel, 2002, 2003; Zakaria & Gani, 2003); Habermas's theory (Kuusisto, Nyberg, & Virtanen, 2004); organizational behaviors (Martins & Eloff, 2002; Veiga & Eloff, 2009); Detert Schroeder, & Mauriel's (2000) model (Chia, Maynard, & Ruighaver, 2002; Ruighaver, Maynard, & Chang, 2007); and conceptual frameworks (Lim et al., 2009; Lim et al., 2010). While such concepts and models are valuable and provide further understanding of ISC, we conclude from our review that little work has looked at cultural characteristics that enable the implementation of information security practices in organizations.

The above discussion leads to the following research question: *what are the prevailing cultural characteristics that are conducive to information security practices in organizations?* Given the limited literature on this topic, we attempt to explore this question using a case study methodology. The rest of the chapter is divided into four sections. First, we review previous relevant research on OC and ISC, highlighting the gap in existing advances. Second, we justify the methods used to research this gap. Third, we discuss the results of the case studies. Fourth, we provide a culture framework for information security practices. In the final section, we discuss the contributions, and conclude by discussing further research direction in the area.

BACKGROUND

This section presents an overview of the relevant literature including a summary of OC, ISC, the issues of ISC, and adaptation of Ruighaver et al's (2007) model as an analytical framework.

Organizational Culture

Organizational culture has been referred to as the system of shared beliefs and values that guides the behaviors of its members to maintain suitable patterns of social systems to survive in the dynamic environment (Schein, 1992). Several researchers have referred to OC as "the way we do things around here" (Deal & Kennedy, 1982). Although there are a plethora of definitions of OC, there is a common view that OC consists of some combination of artifacts or practices, values and beliefs, and underlying assumptions that organizational members share about appropriate behaviors (Schein, 1992; Hofstede & Hofstede, 2005).

Organizational culture has a significant impact on the behavior of organizations and employees. According to Robbins (1989), OC has a number of functions within organizations including a boundary setting role that differentiates organizations. OC helps to generate the commitment of employees to organizations and it maintains and enhances social system stability. OC also acts as a sense-making and control mechanism that shapes attitudes and behaviors of employees. Research on OC, beliefs and values therefore suggests actions of an organization's members are consistently influenced (both knowingly and unknowingly on the member's part) by the organization's prevailing cultural characteristics.

However, a thorough search of the literature showed that majority of studies tends to focus on particular aspects of OC without providing a comprehensive framework addressing the definition and measurement of OC other than Detert et al's (2000) framework, which is comprehensive and providing a holistic view to measure OC.

Information Security Culture

Information security culture has been defined as the totality of human attributes such as behaviors, attitudes, and values that protect all kinds of organizational of information (Dhillon, 1997; Martins & Eloff, 2002). Others have suggested that ISC should support all activities in a way that information security becomes a natural aspect in daily activities of every employee (Von Solms, B., 2000; Schlienger & Teufel, 2002, 2003; Thomson, von Solms, & Louw, 2006). ISC exists when every organization member is aware of the relevant risks and preventive measures, to improve the information security (OECD, 2002). While ISC has been defined from different perspectives, there seems to be a consensus that organizations need ISC to protect information.

Explorations into the relationship between OC and security practices tend to be adaptations of Schein's (1992) three-layered cultural model, assessing underlying assumptions, espoused values, and artifacts (Schlienger & Teufel, 2002, 2003; Zakaria & Gani, 2003; Vroom & von Solms, 2004; Van Niekerk & Von Solms, 2006); adaptation of Denison's (1990) and Cameron & Freeman's (1991) OC studies, to examine the relationship between OC and information security management (Chang & Lin, 2007); and adaptation of Detert et al., (2000)'s framework, to explore the security culture (Ruighaver et al., 2007).

Studies utilizing Schein's (1992) model, Denison (1990), Cameron & Freeman (1991), and Detert et al's (2000) model provide a better understanding of the relationship between OC and security practices, however, none of these studies provide a clear articulation of the sort of cultural characteristics that enable or inhibit various information security practices, and therefore it is here we focus our own investigations.

THE ISSUES OF INFORMATION SECURITY CULTURE

Ruigahver et al's (2007) adopted Detert et al's (2000) OC model and mapped the cultural characteristics underlying information security to its cultural dimensions. We aim to progress this avenue of research by looking at the cultural characteristics underlying information security and then relating it to security practices to see the extent and nature of the relationship between them.

Ruighaver et al. (2007) as an Analytical Framework

We utilized Ruighaver et al's (2007) conceptual framework to ensure a structured and systematic approach to the interpretation of our data. The conceptual framework is synthesized from a series of case studies (Chia et al., 2002; Chia, Maynard, & Ruighaver, 2003; Tan, Ruighaver, & Ahmad, 2003; Koh, Ruighaver, Maynard, & Ahmad, 2005; Maynard & Ruighaver, 2006). Ruighaver et al's (2007) framework consists of eight cultural characteristics underlying information security as follow:

- *The basis of truth and rationality in the organization* - This value is typically called "management by fact" and is central value in total quality management (TQM). In security literature, these beliefs will be the recognition of the importance of security and how the adequacy and effectiveness of security is measured (Chia et al., 2002). However, many organizations are found to believe that their security is good, but do not really make any attempt to measure its success, except anecdotally (Ruighaver et al., 2007). Thus, we propose that top management should make decision on information security based on facts and the beliefs that security is important.
- *Nature of time and horizon* - In the TQM, there is a premium placed on long term commitment to enhance quality in the long run. Although little work can be found in the security literature regarding long term security enhancement strategies, however, Ruighaver et al (2007) argued that organizations with high security culture should place emphasis on long term commitment and strategic management. Thus, we propose that long term commitment is necessary to improve information security.
- *Motivation* - In the TQM, the sources of problems should be searched for in processes rather than employees. Similarly, Ruighaver et al., (2007) suggested that organizations with a good security culture need to have appropriate processes in place to motivate employees in relation to security. Therefore, we propose that appropriate processes are important to motivate employees in adhering to security policy.
- *Stability versus change/ innovation/personal growth* - Change or continuous improvement is one of the fundamental dimensions of the TQM philosophy. In security, change is often seen as bad as it can result in the introduction of new risks (Ruighaver et al., 2007). However, security can never be guaranteed 100% and organizations need to check that their security posture is not static, but to improve continually to improve organizational security (Chia et al., 2002). As such, we propose that continuous improvement is important to improve information security.
- *Orientation to work, task, and co-workers* - A fundamental TQM belief is that it is

important to involve all employees in decision making. Employees should be made to feel responsible for security by involving them in security education. However, their sense of ownership will be influenced by the amount of social participation they have in security activities (Ruighaver et al., 2007). For this reason, we propose that employees' involvement in security activities is important in improving information security.

- *Isolation versus collaboration/ cooperation* - TQM focuses on the importance of cooperation instead of isolation for achieving maximum effectiveness. It is important that security policy should be created collaboratively from various facets of the organization to ensure its comprehensiveness and acceptance (Clark-Dickson, 2001). The lack of collaboration with the stakeholders in security decision making may often lead to a dangerously narrow focus of security (Ruighaver et al., 2007). Therefore, we propose that collaboration with departments and employees is important to improve information security.
- *Control, coordination, and responsibility* – In the TQM, a shared vision and shared goals among employees and management are critical for organizational success (Deming, 1986; Detert et al., 2000). Along the same line, Ruighaver et al., (2007) postulate that members of a high security culture organizations hold shared organizational vision and goals about organizational security. As such, we argue that a shared security visions and goals are important to improve organizational security.
- *Orientation and focus-internal and/or external* – TQM focuses on customer and external stakeholders and their success ought to be judged against external benchmarks (Detert et al., 2000). Ruighaver et al (2007) argue that the focus of an organization's security depends on the environment in which the organization operates. However, they found that those that tend to have medium to high levels of security, have a focus that is both inward and outward looking. Similarly, we argue that the balance of external and internal focus is important to improve organization's security.

We have reviewed Ruighaver et al's (2007) eight cultural dimensions and we intend to determine if these cultural characteristics are actually associated to security practices as claimed, through empirical testing. To this end we consider some companies with high security profile and associated security practices to see if the cultural characteristics are present.

Research Methodology

Multiple case study methodology (Yin, 1994; Walsham, 1995) is adopted in this study to uncover the research questions that look into the cultures characteristics influencing the implementation of security practices. The case study approach is particularly appropriate as it captures the organizational dynamics of the phenomenon (Klein & Myers, 1999). In addition, it is more appropriate to examine the inherent complexity of the phenomenon by interpreting the shared understanding of the stakeholders (Klein & Myers, 1999).

Altogether, 18 semi-structured interviews were conducted with 14 interviewees including staff from a bank and a security print company as shown in Table 1. The interviews focused on the involvement of the interviewees during the implementation of security practices. On average each of these interviews lasted for an hour. Additional sources of data, including on-site observation and documentation also provided useful insight into the implementation processes.

Table 1. Demographic of case organizations

	Bank	Security Print Company
Number of employees	5,500	90
Number of Interviewees	8	6
Number of Interviews	10	8
Job Titles	Chief Information Officer (CIO), IT Security Manager, IT Development Manager, HR Manager, Head of Learning and Development (LDV), Security and Financial Crime Manager, Business Information Risks Officer (BIRO), Administration Clerk.	Managing Director (MD), Security & Audit Manager, IT Manager, Human resource (HR) Executive, Production & Sales Coordinator, and Receptionist.
Expected Organization Security Awareness Level	High	High

Data analysis was performed in parallel with data collection. The analysis was conducted iteratively - cycling between empirical data, the theoretical framework, and the related literature as proposed by (Eisenhardt, 1989). Based on the collected data, the interview transcripts were used to prepare a detailed case description, containing a summary of the OC characteristics that support the implementation of security practices. Data was validated with several individuals who are familiar with the OC as well as with the security practices and the entire data analysis process was repeated multiple times to case study development (Yin, 1994; Klein & Myers, 1999).

CASE DESCRIPTION

Background of the Bank

The Bank is one of the largest banking and financial services organizations in the world, with offices in many countries and territories. It was the first institution in Malaysia to offer a dual security log-into Internet Banking via its security device. Currently the bank has a network of 40 branches nationwide and employs more than 5,000 people in Malaysia.

Security Practices at the Bank

Top Management Support for Security Practices

The Bank's Board of Directors (BOD) and senior management readily convey their concerns about security risks and the potential for impact on the reputation of the organization. The security policy implemented in this branch of the organization has been cascaded from the principle headquarters. There is evidence that top management participate in key security decisions and security activities. Moreover, top management takes security awareness and security training modules thereby leading by example.

Formal Security Structure and Security Strategy

The BOD has appointed a steering committee headed by the Chief Risk Officer (CRO) to oversee risk in general and information security risk in particular. The organizational structure features a Business Information Risks Officer (BIRO) responsible for implementing and enforcing security policies and procedures. Other appointments include the Chief Operating Officer (COO) as Chief Information Security Officer (CISO). The

BIRO reports directly to the CISO. Under this structure, the BIRO is required to appoint Deputy BIRO (DBIRO) across departments to assist in enforcing security policies.

Assignment of Security Responsibilities

The BIRO enforces security policies by making a random check to see whether desks are cleared from sensitive information with the assistance of DBIROs across the organization. The HR department performs integrity screening on potential employees before offering them a letter of employment. It includes a police check, a bankruptcy check, and character references. The department of IT is responsible for issuing users ids, passwords, disabling of USB ports, and email filtering. Overall risks are the responsibility of the compliance and audit department. The security banking and investigation department handles cases of frauds.

Security Awareness and Training

Security awareness and training is mandatory for every employee. The bank implements Electronic Learning Module Systems (ELMS) that enable all employees to take electronic modules in information security across the country. Modules are offered on money laundering, information risks, and reputation risks which are mandatory for all employees including the Chief Executive Officer (CEO). Passing assessment is mandatory and progress can be monitored. Results are recorded on employees' key performance index and may indirectly affect promotion opportunities.

Security Controls and Monitoring

The bank implements various security controls and monitoring tools. All employees are required to sign the non-disclosure agreement. Physical security measures include CCTV cameras installed all over the building and security guards stationed at strategic points. Employees are issued with access cards that only allow access to their office floor. Access to computer systems is monitored centrally by the IT security department. Moreover, the use of USB ports have been disabled and all notebooks are installed with safe boot with encrypted hard disks by desktop department.

Communications and Reporting Mechanism

Employees have to read through the pop up screen (security reminder) before they proceed to access organization's information systems. Security policies are made available to all employees via the intranet. In addition, the latest security threats are broadcasted via intranet to update employees. There are also feedback mechanisms in place for employees to make suggestions or reporting security errors.

Response to External and Internal Requirement

The Bank is regulated by regulatory bodies and auditors and is expected to comply with the central bank's requirement to protect customers' privacy. Internally, the bank takes measures to protect organizational information and customer information in an effort to gain customer confidence and trust. Ongoing awareness programs, training, and enforcement exist to improve information security.

Background of the Security Print Company

Security Print was incorporated in Malaysia in 1983 as a privately owned company. It is one of the first certified security printers in the world with High Security Management System awarded by INTERGRAF (The International Confederation for Printing & Allied Industries) for delivering high quality, and customer-focused solutions largely to banks and financial institutions.

Security Practices at Security Print

Top Management Support for Security Practices

Security Print prints highly sensitive and confidential documents for its customers. Senior management plays an active role in implementing security practices to protect organizational information. Senior management understands the importance of fulfilling customers' requirements and needs especially in protecting customers' privacy. Senior management translates their beliefs and values into security policy and practices.

Security Certification

Security Print was working towards obtaining Information Security Management System (ISMS), ISO 27001 at the time of data collection. The driving force behind the information security certification is to increase customer confidence and trust.

Assignment of Security Responsibilities

Security Print adopted documented security policy. The company understands the importance of assignment of security responsibilities. The HR department is responsible for the induction program, which includes IT security and awareness. New employees are required to undergo the induction program within two weeks of joining the company. The Audit and Compliance departments along with HR are responsible for the ongoing enforcement of security policies and procedures.

Security Awareness and Training

During the induction program, new employees are briefed on the importance of security and the consequences of violating security policies. However, there is no ongoing security awareness or security training program for employees. Existing employees only attend the yearly information sharing conducted by the IT department or experts from outside. However, employees are reminded of the importance of information security through department briefings and meetings from time to time.

Security Controls and Monitoring

Visitors are required to sign-in at the guard house by filling in a form that is subsequently signed by the employee who the visitor meets with. Guards perform security checks on the boot of employee cars when they leave the building. The HR department performs police checks on potential employees before issuing them with a letter of employment. All employees require a user id and password to log in to computer systems. USB ports are disabled as a matter of policy and employees are not allowed to bring in USB devices. Moreover, cameras and electronic devices are banned within Security Print and mobile phones are banned in production offices.

Communications and Reporting Mechanism

Security Print has no intranet, however, the importance of security is communicated through security posters, briefings and meetings. Every head of department must remind their employees of the importance of security during the briefing or meetings. In addition, compliance and audit managers are expected to brief employees during random checks.

Response to External and Internal Requirement

Since the customer base of Security Print is largely from the financial sector, senior management have taken measures to ensure adequate response to external requirements as well as internal imperatives. Internally, security controls and monitoring must be in place to protect customer information. Legal requirements must be complied with. It has to be audited by its customers twice yearly.

Past researchers have accepted that information security is complex, and has multiple dimensions (Von Solms, Basie, 2001). The security practices at the Bank and the Security Print Company above are not necessarily complete, because the dynamic nature of information security prevents any such fixed boundaries. Von Solms (2001) postulates that multiple dimensions of the discipline is not the most important factor, but rather that the dimensions must come together to create a security environment. While these security practices help the Bank and the Security Print Company to protect organizational information, however, we still do not know what the various organizational culture characteristics that enable these security practices to be cultivated in these organizations are.

Findings

The following Table 2 shows the organizational culture characteristics that are present in both cases. It is argued that these organizational culture characteristics might be important for the security practices mentioned above to be present at the Bank and Security Print.

DISCUSSION

Security Decision Making Should Rely on Facts and Rationality

Although both The Bank and Security Print believe in the importance of information security, their beliefs stem from different concerns and perspectives. The Bank's beliefs are rooted in the need to prevent security incidents, whereas, the Security Print Company perceives a constant threat from its competitors. To improve information security the Bank has appointed a steering committee to oversee the compliance of risk in general and information risk in particular. As for the Security Print Company, it believes, as a matter of priority, that providing a secure environment is critical in gaining customer trust. Consequently, it was working towards accreditation of ISMS, ISO 27001 to prove to customers that it is capable of protecting the sensitive information and privacy of its customers.

The belief that facts and data should form the backbone of decision making has long been supported in OC literature. What is seen as rational and true enables employees to make decisions (Saphier & King, 1985; Reynolds, 1986). The underlying idea behind this value is that any system based on cause and effect requires measurement and data to make improvements. In organizations, this could take the form of security penetration test, external and internal audit, which indicates the security measures that would improve the protection of organizational information.

We argue that no matter what kind of beliefs or concerns that organizations hold, organizations should make security decisions based on facts and scientific findings. While different companies have different beliefs and concerns, however, achieving optimal security for that organization's particular situation will still be important (Ruighaver et al., 2007). Security managers must educate senior management about information security as their beliefs about the importance of security are often more important than the beliefs of end-users (Shedden, Ahmad, & Ruighaver, 2006).

Proposition 1: There is a relationship between decision making based on the notion that security is important and security practices

Long-Term Commitment to Improve Security

As security incidents happened in the group, the Bank's top management decided to introduce a long term strategy by adopting BIRO's structure, which appoints the COO as CISO to oversee the

Table 2. The key organizational culture characteristics identified at the Bank and the Security Print Company

Organization culture characteristics underlying information security	Exemplar evidence of security practices at Bank	Exemplar evidence of security practices at Security Print
Security decision making should rely on facts and rationality that security is important.	*"We actually have set up[a] risk committee and function that actually look after IT security, and physical security all come into play. We evolve because we have security incidents. We have been fined for losing data in transit by our insurance company "* (source: CIO)	*"So far for my managing director (MD) is actually planning to go for ISMS as well because this is actually security printer, we already certified by CSWA security printer, now the next step is ISMS, to prove to people that we are actually having ISMS standard to secure users' data.* (source IT Manager)
Improving information security requires a long-term commitment	*"You can see the way I put it, a formal security structure. That must be a long term goal. A short term thing you do not form a formal structure. And there are very senior people in control on them....So, therefore is definitely long term".* (source: CIO)	*"We are going for Information Security Management System (ISMS), ISO 27001. And we have been doing this for a long period but we continually want to do this for the future"* (source: IT Manager)
Proper security systems and processes motivate employee to adhere to security policies and procedures.	*"Yes I am aware of the existence of the policy. We read on the intranet. Information always issued via intranet.. So, if the bank wants to issue new policy, it is going to publish on intranet. So we have to alert, every time if we want to know about information or anything, we can read through the intranet.* (source: administration clerk)	*"When you walk in, you have to put all your belongings into lockers. That is the reminder that no hand phone (mobile) is allowed in this organization...when you walk out, your car will be checked. These are things to remind that your are being watched"* (source: MD)
Organizations must make continuous changes to improve information security.	*"Earlier I mentioned about if there is a breach, there is a report, there is an investigation. Part of the actions point is to look for how to prevent. So we can re-educate them. What are the things that we can improve so that it can go back to policy and procedures, and then we need to communicate to the rest telling them that there is an update, review, can you please practice? "* (source: CIO)	*"Each time when we have auditor, they come in, auditor will always find fault. They never give you caught free. This is where we learned from all these people [auditors]. So, this is where we learned and that is where, we educate ourselves."* (source: MD)
Employees should be involved in improving the overall organization's information security	*"Information security is the responsibility of each and every one of the manager and staff in this organization. Security structure requires BIRO to appoint his deputy(s) across departments to assist him in implementing and enforcing security policies"* (source: IT Security manager)	*"During induction, we told them data are actually confidential and you have to abide by certain rules. So, when they know about that, then they realized that information is highly confidential and they have to responsible for the information"* (source: security and audit manager)
Collaboration and cooperation are necessary for effective information security.	*"Actually, we are working very closely with the CIO and together with IT security as well, We got lots of cooperation from IT security to work out in other projects which is IT related* (source: BIRO)	*"Yes, we have a party to enforce it. We have another guy [who] calls audit and security manager. He is not under IT department. Enforce must be done by third party".* (source: IT Manager)
A shared security vision and shared security goals are critical for effective information security.	*"We make sure that clear desk policy is highly promoted, everyone got the message because we think that this is the one that will create greater awareness that information is valuable and it should be kept and protected to ensure that customers trust on us, to ensure that we are protecting customer information and bank information".* (source: BIRO)	*"We have quality policy, environmental policy, and security policy. These are the policies that you have to instill in each and every one of your staff in the sense that everywhere you go you need to have posters and reminders in different languages to tell them you are in this environment"* (source: security and audit manager)

continued on the following page

Table 2. Continued

Organization culture characteristics underlying information security	Exemplar evidence of security practices at Bank	Exemplar evidence of security practices at Security Print
Information security needs should be determined by external and internal requirements.	*"Being a bank, we are regulated by banking act, which stipulates that every member must be trained. Within a group, we are very concern about customers' privacy. We are not to divulge any customer information. This is continuously inculcating upon us.* (source: BIRO)	*"If you look at our industry, it is also a business issues because it is not only solely requirement to be a secured premise, it is also clients' requirement to have a secured premise. We have to follow certain standards, to give our clients the confidence that the products we print here is secured"* (source: MD)

"All quotes were transcribed verbatim from the audio-taped interviews"

overall risks. It also implemented an Electronic Learning Module Systems (ELMS) to enable employees to take awareness programs rolled out periodically. For Security Print, the long term strategy is to focus on customer wants and needs. Subsequently, it works towards achieving the accreditation of ISMS, ISO 27001 to gain customer confident and trust.

Ideas about long term commitment helps determine if leaders adopt long term planning and or focus on the here-and now (Denison & Mishra, 1995). As for Reynolds, the difference in time horizon for goal setting is "ad hockery versus planning" (Reynolds, 1986). In information security literature, most of the organizations found to implement on ad-hoc basis rather than long term planning to improve the security practices (Wood, 2000; Ruighaver et al., 2007). But, implementers should be cautioned that short programs, just like short term management commitment, may have little long-term impact (Straub & Welke, 1998).

We argue that organization should be driven by a long term commitment that supports the organizations' long-range security mission and goals. For example, organizations should invest in electronic learning module systems that enable every employee to undergo ongoing security awareness and training no matter where they are, rather than only focus on a small number of employees in a physical class.

Proposition 2: There is a relationship between long term plan and security practices

Proper Security Systems and Processes

The Bank recognized the importance of employees' motivation by implementing proper security systems and processes. It provides the proper reporting mechanism for employee to report security errors or unaccepted behaviors on security matters. At the same time, it also rewards employees who adhere to information security policies through employees' key performance index. As for Security Print, it adopts profit sharing with employees to retain their loyalty and also commitment to the organizations. To ensure the organization increases profit, employees need to protect customers' privacy and information to continuously gain customer confidence and businesses.

This value notes the importance of focusing on processes rather than people as the source of most errors. Employees will be intrinsically motivated to do a good job if they work in an environment without fear and have good systems in place; in contrast, they will be de-motivated by extrinsic rewards stemming from performance of processes they do not control (Deming, 1986). However, recent research has shown that when individuals are rewarded for achieving an absolute, normative, or graded level of performance, intrinsic motivation is enhanced (Cameron, J., Pierce, Banko, & Gear, 2005).

This value represents the beliefs that people want to do a good job, but are often discouraged by the systems in which they work. For example, lack of communication and reporting mechanisms can lead to many unreported errors. As a result, failures to improve that appear to be due to human error are actually due to the inadequate systems of reporting. Along the same line, Adams & Sasse (1999) postulate that it is important to challenge the view that users are never motivated to behave in a secure manner. They found that the majority of users were security conscious, as long as they perceived the need for the behaviors. Therefore, this study argues that organizations should have proper systems and processes to educate employees on the importance of safeguarding organizational information.

Proposition 3: There is a relationship between proper systems and processes and security practices

Continuous Changes to Improve Security

The Bank constantly made changes to improve security. New measures would be taken upon recommendation from the auditors or changes of technology. It would then review and update security policies and procedures based on the new measures and communicate results to employees. As for Security Print, it continues to learn from the findings and recommendation from auditors to improve the protection of information security.

This value indicates a mindset in which the state of information security is never "good enough" and is found in organizations where processes and products are continuously studied for improvement. This idea is reflected in Deming's 14 points as "improve constantly and forever, systems of production to improve quality and productivity.." (Deming, 1986). However, some individuals are open to change, whereas others are said to have a high "need for security" (Hofstede, Neuijen, Ohayv, & Sanders, 1990).

Past literature found that most organizations, which have lower security requirements have a propensity to be reactive rather than proactive, whereas, those organizations, which have a high security requirement favor stability over change (Ruighaver et al., 2007). However, the differences between organizations and the fact that their security requirements are different (Siponen & Willison, 2009) should not prevent organization from continuously improve the protection of information security. We argue that improvement of information security should be ongoing as information security is not static but dynamic and multidimensional in nature (Von Solms, Basie, 2001; Ozkana & Karabacaka, 2010).

Proposition 4: There is a relationship between continuous changes and security practices

Employees' Involvement to Improve Security

The bank involved every employee in protecting organizational information. It paid great emphasis in raising employees' security awareness; every employee from driver to CEO is required to take the assessment test. However, there is no mandatory ongoing awareness and security training at the Security Print, but only an induction course for employees upon joining the company. During the induction course all the dos and don'ts were briefed by HR department and the security and audit manager.

This idea represents the importance of involving all employees in decision making. Some individuals view work as an end in itself. For these people, work has a "task focus," and the fundamental concern is on work accomplishment and productivity (O'Reilly, Chatman, & Caldwell, 1991). In contrast, some people view social relationship as more important than productivity (Reynolds, 1986). However, it is advocated that TQM values should focus on both process improvement and results (Detert et al., 2000).

Although many organizations are often found to merely provide a brief overview of security during induction (Ruighaver et al., 2007). However, we argue that employees should be made to feel responsible by involving in security activities. Thus, it is important to involve and educate employees on their role and responsibilities in security matters. According to (LaRose, Rifon, & Enbody, 2008) when involvement is low, individuals are likely to take mental shortcuts (heuristics), and when involvement is high, or users are likely to elaborate by thinking arguments through, provided they have clear information and are not distracted from reflection.

Proposition 5: There is a relationship between long term plan and security practices

Collaboration and Cooperation to Improve Security

The Bank adopts a BIRO structure, where the BIRO is required to appoint deputy BIROs across departments to help enforcing security policies. It collaborates with all departments in protecting organizational information. For example awareness and training is conducted by the LDV department, integrity and police check is conducted by the HR department, IT is responsible for computer security, and information risk is the responsibility of the compliance and risks department. Although collaboration at Security Print is not as comprehensive as the Bank, nevertheless, there is collaboration between the HR department, and the audit and security department in performing clear desk policy and random check on employees.

Collaboration is the values that represents underlying beliefs about the nature of human relationships and how work is effectively accomplished (Schein, 1992; Denison & Mishra, 1995). For some organizations, work must be completed by individuals. In these organizations, teamwork or collaboration will be viewed as violation of individual autonomy (Detert et al., 2000). On the other hand, many organizations now face tasks that are sufficiently complex that no individual can accomplish them alone. These organizations will go after collaboration than individuals (Briggs, Kolfschoten, Gert-Jan, & Douglas, 2006).

Past literature often found that many organizations' security planning was handled by a small group of specialists and often leave it to IT department (Fitzgerald, 2007; Lim et al., 2009). These findings are not surprising as security is still seen to be highly technical and requires special expertise to deal with it. As information security is a dynamic and multidimensional discipline (Von Solms, Basie, 2001), we argue that organizations should attempt to collaborate with all departments to participate in security activities to improve the protection of organizational information.

Proposition 6: There is a relationship between collaboration and cooperation and security practices

A Shared Security Vision and Security Goals

The Bank has made the security awareness and training mandatory for all the employees. This is to ensure that employees understand the importance of security at the bank. During induction, the organization's value and ethics are inculcated into all employees as described by the HR Manager: "*I think whether security is technical or business, we look at it, it has to be built into every employee's DNA I would say*" [sic]. Although there is no shared security vision and goals for Security Print, however, employees are constantly reminded with posters and reminders that security is important in different languages all over the buildings.

This value represents the beliefs in the power of coordinated action. Underlying this value, individuals should be willing to sacrifice some autonomy for the sake of the organization (Detert et al., 2000). A shared vision and shared goals require that all staff members know and understand the organization's vision and are willing to align their action accordingly. These values are what

Deming terms "adopt a constancy purpose" in total quality management (Deming, 1986).

Senior management need to connect information security to the success or failure of the organization, helping employees understand that information leakage could close the company (Stan, 2007). This may be achieved by providing security training to raise employees' security awareness. Furthermore, senior management should discuss the security strategy and planning during the board meeting and have an annual budget for security activities (Fitzgerald, 2007) and "a goal should be to make information security a common theme in discussion around the water cooler" (Stan, 2007)

Proposition 7: There is a relationship between a shared vision and security practices

External and Internal Focus to Improve Security

Being a bank, it is required to be regulated by an external body which imposes laws and regulations from the Central Bank and auditors. Within group, it is concerned about customer privacy and personnel information. The HR department is required to perform integrity screening on all potential employees. Moreover, the use of thumb drives is banned and there is email filtering software to monitor outgoing and incoming emails. Like the bank, the Security Print is also regulated by its customers, which are mostly from financial institutions and banks. Similarly, USB ports at the company were disabled and those who need to use it are required to write to the IT manager through their department head.

The underlying value of this dimension is that organizations should focus on internal processes and external requirements to improve information security. Some organizations assume that the key to organizational success is to focus on people and processes within the organization (Detert et al., 2000). While others are focused on external constituents, customers, competitors and dynamic environment (Denison, 1990). In contrast, TQM philosophy is customer driven and actively cooperate with community, suppliers and external parties (Dean & Bowen, 1994).

Past literature shows that some organizations are forced to conform to external audit and government requirements rather than with intention to improve organization's security (Ruighaver et al., 2007). As information security is multi dimensional and dynamic, we advocate that organizations should have a balance between an internal and external focus to improve organization's security levels. The external focus should include technology change, customer requirements, and threats besides regulatory requirement, whereas, internal focus should include proper security controls, raising awareness through mandatory ongoing security training, communication and feedbacks mechanism in place.

Proposition 8: There is a relationship between balance in internal and external focus and security practices

FUTURE RESEARCH DIRECTIONS

As OC and information security is dynamic and multidimensional in nature, thus we need to identify the main organizational culture characteristics that support the security practices in organizations. We also need to understand if there is an ideal culture for all companies and industries. Furthermore, we have to examine whether we need to match a security management structure to a culture, or change a culture according to the needs of security, or any acceptable combinations. The large scale future development and validation studies of measuring approaches and instruments will be required to go on. In addition, what we also need is more longitudinal studies of culture change in relation to information security. Transverse studies can only tell us to a limited extent what is important and what is changeable. The framework and propositions provide an important step toward future empirical research aimed at understanding the relationship between OC, and the implementation of systematic improvement of information security practices.

CONCLUSION

In this study we addressed existing ambiguities in the concept of OC and its relationship to information security practices. We do so by conceptualizing through the OC, and ISC literature. We articulate Ruighaver et al (2007)'s conceptual framework of security cultural values which, we argue will facilitate the implementation of security practices in organizations. We tested it empirically through two case studies and made some interesting findings.

From a theoretical development point of view, these case studies provide much-needed empirical insight by providing a organizational culture framework for the implementation of security practices. Though previous studies have studied ISC, little is known about the organizational culture characteristics for information security. We believe that our framework has provided a better understanding of the organizational culture characteristics. This study also makes a contribution to ISC literature by extending existing knowledge based on the Ruighaver et al., (2007)'s model as an analytical framework. We believe that the framework offers a vocabulary for framing experiences and learning of ISC development.

For practitioners, this study serves the purpose of demonstrating organizational culture characteristics that are conducive to security practices. The cases illustrate the importance of the role of senior management in information security governance, especially how to develop culture of security to influence employees' behaviors and gain employees' commitment to better protect organizational information. In addition, the culture framework could assist management in identifying the technical and non-technical controls on employees' security beliefs and actions.

REFERENCES

Adams, A., & Sasse, M. A. (1999). Users are not the enemy: Why users compromise computer security mechanisms and how to take remedial measures. *Communications of the ACM*, *42*(12), 41–46.

Briggs, R., Kolfschoten, G., Gert-Jan, V., & Douglas, D. (2006). *Defining key concepts for collaboration engineering.* In Americas Conference on Information Systems, AMCIS 2006 Proceedings, Acapulco, Mexico

Cameron, J., Pierce, W. D., Banko, K. M., & Gear, A. (2005). Achievement-based rewards and intrinsic motivation: A test of cognitive mediators. *Journal of Educational Psychology*, *97*(4), 641–655. doi:10.1037/0022-0663.97.4.641

Cameron, K., & Freeman, S. (1991). Cultural congruence, strength and type: Relationships to effectiveness. *Research in Organizational Change and Development*, *5*, 23–58.

Chang, S. E., & Lin, C. S. (2007). Exploring organizational culture for information security management. *Industrial Management & Data Systems*, *107*(3), 438–458. doi:10.1108/02635570710734316

Chia, P. A., Maynard, S. B., & Ruighaver, A. B. (2002). Understanding organizational security culture. In *Proceedings of PACIS 2002*. Japan, 2002, Japan.

Deal, T. E., & Kennedy, A. A. (1982). *Corporate culture*. Reading, MA: Addison-Wesley.

Dean, J. W., & Bowen, D. E. (1994). Management theory and total quality: Improving research and practice through theory development. *Academy of Management Review, 19*, 392–418.

Deming, W. E. (1986). *Out of the Crisis*. Cambridge, MA: MIT Center for Advanced Engineering Study.

Denison, D. R. (1990). *Corporate Culture and Organizational Effectiveness. New York*. New York: Wiley.

Denison, D. R., & Mishra, A. (1995). Toward a theory of organizational culture and effectiveness. *Organization Science, 6*, 204–224. doi:10.1287/orsc.6.2.204

Detert, J. R., Schroeder, R. G., & Mauriel, J. J. (2000). A framework for linking culture and improvement initiatives in organisations. *Academy of Management Review, 25*(4), 850–863.

Dhillon, G. (1997). *Managing Information System security*. Houndmills, UK: Macmillan Press LTD.

Eisenhardt, K. M. (1989). Agency theory: An assessment and review. *Academy of Management Review, 14*(1), 57–74.

Fitzgerald, T. (2007). Building management commitment through security councils, or security council critical success factors. In Tipton, H. F. (Ed.), *Information security management handbook* (pp. 105–121). Hoboken, NJ: Auerbach Publications. doi:10.1201/9781439833032.ch10

Furnell, S., & Thompson, K. L. (2009). From culture to disobedience: Recognising the varying user acceptance of IT security. *Computer Fraud & Security, 2*, 5–10. doi:10.1016/S1361-3723(09)70019-3

Helokunnas, T., & Kuusisto, R. (2003). *Information security culture in a value net.* In Engineering Management Conference, 2003. IEMC'03. Managing Technologically Driven Organizations: The Human Side of Innovation and Change.

Hofstede, G., & Hofstede, G. N. (2005). *Cultures and organisations: Software of the mind.* New York, NY: McGraw-Hill.

Hofstede, G., Neuijen, B., Ohayv, D. D., & Sanders, G. (1990). Measuring organizational cultures: A qualitative and quantitative study across twenty cases. *Administrative Science Quarterly, 35*(2), 286–316. doi:10.2307/2393392

Klein, H. K., & Myers, M. D. (1999). A set of principles for conducting and evaluating interpretative field studies in Information Systems. *Management Information Systems Quarterly, 23*(1), 67–94. doi:10.2307/249410

Knapp, K. J., Marshall, T. E., Rainer, R. K., & Ford, F. N. (2006). Information security: Management's effect on culture and policy. *Information and Computer Security, 14*(1), 24–36. doi:10.1108/09685220610648355

Koh, K., Ruighaver, A. B., Maynard, S. B., & Ahmad, A. (2005). Security governance: Its impact on security culture. In *Proceedings of the 3rd Australian Information Security Management Conference*, Perth.

Kuusisto, R., Nyberg, K., & Virtanen, T. (2004). Unite security culture: May a unified security culture be plausible. In *Proceedings of the 3rd European Conference on Information Warfare and Security*, Royal Holloway, University of London, UK.

LaRose, R., Rifon, N. J., & Enbody, R. (2008). Promoting personal responsibility for Internet safety. *Communications of the ACM, 51*(3), 71–76. doi:10.1145/1325555.1325569

Lim, J. S., Ahmad, A., Chang, S., & Maynard, S. B. (2010). *Embedding information security culture - emerging concerns and challenges*. 14th Pacific Asia Conference on Information Systems. Taipei, Taiwan.

Lim, J. S., Chang, S., Maynard, S. B., & Ahmad, A. (2009). *Exploring the relationship between organizational culture and information security culture.* In 7th Australian Information Security Management Conference, SECAU Security Congress 2009, Perth, Western Australia.

Martins, A., & Eloff, J. (2002). *Information security culture.* In IFIP TC11 International Conference on Information Security, Cairo, Egypt

Maynard, S. B., & Ruighaver, A. B. (2006). What makes a good information security policy: A preliminary framework for evaluating security policy quality. In *Proceedings of the Fifth Annual Security Conference,* Las Vegas, Nevada USA.

O'Reilly, C. A., Chatman, J. R., & Caldwell, D. F. (1991). People and organizational culture: A profile comparison approach to assessing person-organization fit. *Academy of Management Journal, 34*(3), 487–516. doi:10.2307/256404

OECD. (2002). *OECD guidelines for the security of information systems and networks: Towards a culture of security.* Recommendation of the OECD Council, 1037th Session on 25 July 2002.

OECD. (2005). *The promotion of a culture of security for Information Systems and networks in OECD countries (16-December-2005).* Retrieved 9 March 2009, from www.oecd.org/document/42/0,2340,en_2649_34255_15582250_1_1_1_1,00.html

Ozkana, S., & Karabacaka, B. (2010). Collaborative risk method for information security management practices: A case context within Turkey. *International Journal of Information Management, 30,* 567–572. doi:10.1016/j.ijinfomgt.2010.08.007

Reynolds, P. D. (1986). Organizational culture as related to industry, position, and performance: A preminary report. *Journal of Management Studies, 23*(3), 333–345. doi:10.1111/j.1467-6486.1986.tb00958.x

Richardson, R. (2007). *2007 CSI computer crime & security survey.* Retrieved 9 March, 2009, from http://i.cmpnet.com/v2.gocsi.com/pdf/CSISurvey2007.pdf

Robbins, S. P. (1989). *Organizational behavior: Concepts, controversies, and applications* (4th ed.). New Jersey: Prentice Hall.

Ruighaver, A. B., Maynard, S. B., & Chang, S. (2007). Organisational security culture: Extending the end-user perspective. *Computers & Security, 26*(1), 56–62. doi:10.1016/j.cose.2006.10.008

SANS. (2005). *Developing a security-awareness culture. Improving security decision making,* (pp. 1-22).

Saphier, J., & King, M. (1985). Good seeds grow in strong cultures. *Educational Leadership, 43*(6), 67–74.

Schein, E. H. (1992). *Organizational culture and leadership.* San Francisco, CA: Jossey-Bass.

Schlienger, T., & Teufel, S. (2002). *Information security culture - The social-cultural dimension in information security management.* In IFIP TC11 International Conference on Information Security, Cairo, Egypt.

Schlienger, T., & Teufel, S. (2003). *Information security culture - From analysis to change.*

Shedden, P., Ahmad, A., & Ruighaver, A. B. (2006). Risk management standard-The perception of ease of use. In *Proceedings of the Fifth Annual Security Conference,* Las Vegas, Nevada, USA.

Siponen, M., & Willison, R. (2009). Information security management standards: Problems and solutions. *Information & Management, 46,* 267–270. doi:10.1016/j.im.2008.12.007

Stan, S. (2007). Beyond information security awareness training: It is time to change the culture. In Tipton, H. F. (Ed.), *Information security management handbook* (pp. 555–565). Hoboken, NJ: Auerbach Publications.

Straub, D. W. (1986). *Deterring computer abuse: The effectiveness of deterrent countermeasures in the computer security environment*. Bloomington, IN: Indiana University School of Business.

Straub, D. W., & Welke, R. J. (1998). Coping with systems risk: Security planning models for management decision making. *Management Information Systems Quarterly, 22*(4), 441–469. doi:10.2307/249551

Tan, T. C., Ruighaver, A. B., & Ahmad, A. (2003). *Incident handling: Where the need for planning is often not recognised.*

Thomson, K., von Solms, R., & Louw, L. (2006). Cultivating an organizational information security culture. *Computer Fraud & Security*, (10): 7–11. doi:10.1016/S1361-3723(06)70430-4

Van Niekerk, J., & Von Solms, R. (2006). *Understanding information security culture: A conceptual framework. Information Security South Africa*. Johannesburg, South Africa: ISSA.

Veiga, A. D., & Eloff, J. H. P. (2009). A framework and assessment instrument for information security culture. *Computers & Security, 29*, 196–207. doi:10.1016/j.cose.2009.09.002

Von Solms, B. (2000). Information security -- The third wave? *Computers & Security, 19*(7), 615–620. doi:10.1016/S0167-4048(00)07021-8

Von Solms, B. (2001). Information Security -- A multidimensional discipline. *Computers & Security, 20*(6), 504–508. doi:10.1016/S0167-4048(01)00608-3

Vroom, C., & von Solms, R. (2004). Towards information security behavioural compliance. *Computers & Security, 23*(3), 191–198. doi:10.1016/j.cose.2004.01.012

Walsham, G. (1995). Interpretive case studies in IS research: Nature and method. *European Journal of Information Systems, 4*, 74–81. doi:10.1057/ejis.1995.9

Wood, C. C. (2000). Integrated approach includes information security. *Security: For Buyers of Products. Systems & Services, 37*(2), 43–44.

Workman, M., Bommer, W., & Straub, D. (2008). Security lapses and the omission of information security measures: A threat control model and empirical test. *Computers in Human Behavior.*

Yin, R. K. (1994). *Case study research: Design and methods* (2nd ed.). Thousand Oaks, CA: Sage Publications.

Zakaria, O., & Gani, A. (2003). *A conceptual checklist of information security culture.* In 2nd European Conference on Information Warfare and Security, Reading, UK.

ADDITIONAL READING

Alfawaz, S., Nelson, K., & Mohannak, K. (2010). Information Security Culture: A Behaviour Compliance Conceptual Framework, *Australasian Information Security Conference (AISC), 2010* (pp. 1-10). Brisbane, Australia.

Baskerville, R., & Siponen, M. (2002). An Information Security Meta-Policy for Emergent Organisations. *Logistics Information Management, 15*(5/6), 337–346. doi:10.1108/09576050210447019

Cameron, K. S., & Quinn, R. E. (1999). *Diagnosing and Changing Organizational Culture*. Reading: Addison-Wesley.

D'Arcy, J., Hovav, A., & Galletta, D. (2008). User Awareness of Security Countermeasures and Its Impact on Information Systems Misuse: A Deterrence Approach. *Information Systems Research*, isre.1070.0160.

Detert, J. R., Schroeder, R. G., & Cudeck, R. (2003). The Measurement of Quality Management Culture in Schools: Development and Validation of the Sqmcs. *Journal of Operations Management*, *21*(3), 307–328. doi:10.1016/S0272-6963(02)00130-4

Dhillon, G. (2007). *Principles of Information Systems Security: Text and Cases. River Street*. Hoboken, NJ: John Wiley & Sons, Inc.

Doherty, N. F., & Fulford, H. (2006). Aligning the Information Security Policy with the Strategic Information Systems Plan. *Computers & Security*, *25*(1), 55–63. doi:10.1016/j.cose.2005.09.009

Doherty, N. F., & Perry, I. (2001). The Cultural Impact of Workflow Management Systems in the Financial Services Sector. *The Service Industries Journal*, *21*, 147–166. doi:10.1080/714005046

Dorothy, E. L., & Timothy, K. (2006). A Review of Culture in Information Systems Research: Toward a Theory of Information Technology Culture Conflict. *Management Information Systems Quarterly*, *30*(2), 357–399.

Fulford, H., & Doherty, N. F. (2003). The Application of Information Security Policies in Large Uk-Based Organisations: An Exploratory Investigation. *Information Management & Computer Security*, *11*(3), 106–114. doi:10.1108/09685220310480381

Hofstede, G. (1980). Motivation, Leadership, and Organization: Do American Theories Apply Abroad. *Organizational dynamics [0090-2616] Hofstede yr*, *75*(1), 42-63.

Knapp, K. J., Franklin, M. R., Marshall, T. E., & Byrd, T. A. (2009). Information Security Policy: An Organizational-Level Process Model. *Computers & Security*, *28*(7), 493–508. doi:10.1016/j.cose.2009.07.001

Knapp, K. J., Marshall, T. E., Rainer, R. K., & Morrow, D. W. (2004). Top Ranked Information Security Issues. In *The 2004 International Information Systems Security Certification Consortium (ISC)2 Survey Results*. Alabama: Auburn University.

Lee, Y., & Larsen, K. R. (2009). Threat or Coping Appraisal: Determinants of Smb Executives' Decision to Adopt Anti-Malware Software. *European Journal of Information Systems*, *18*, 177–187. doi:10.1057/ejis.2009.11

Pettigrew, A. M., Woodman, R. W., & Cameron, K. S. (2001). Studying Organizational Change and Development: Challenges for Future Research. *Academy of Management Journal*, *44*(4), 697–713. doi:10.2307/3069411

Pierce, W. D., Cameron, J., Banko, K. M., & So, S. (2003). Positive Effects of Rewards and Performance Standards on Intrinsic Motivation. *The Psychological Record*, *53*, 561–579.

Whitman, M. E. (2003). Enemy at the Gate: Threats to Information Security. *Communications of the ACM*, *46*(8), 91–95. doi:10.1145/859670.859675

Whitman, M. E. (2004). In Defense of the Realm: Understanding the Threats to Information Security. *International Journal of Information Management*, *24*(1), 43–57. doi:10.1016/j.ijinfomgt.2003.12.003

Whitman, M. E. (2008). *Security Policy: From Design to Maintenance*. (Vol. 11): Armonk, N.Y.

KEY TERMS AND DEFINITIONS

Enforcement of Security Policy: Activities conduct to make employees comply or adhere to security policy and actions taken against organization members that violate the security policy to deter others from doing the same.

Information Security: Concerns about information security measures to protect information assets from disclosure, integrity violation and denial of service.

Information Security Culture: A shared security beliefs, values, and behaviors that hold by organization members to maintain and protect organizational information to survive in the dynamic environment.

Information Security Policy: One of the most important controls (document) that reflects management beliefs and values towards the implementation of security practices to protect information assets.

Information Security Practices: Organizations actions and processes in place to protect organizational information.

Organizational Culture: A shared beliefs, values and behaviors that hold by organizations members to maintain internal stability in order to survive in the dynamic environment.

Security Training and Awareness: Training designed to raise users' awareness on the appropriate use, protection and security of information, and individual user responsibilities to protect the confidentiality, integrity, and availability of information assets and systems from unauthorized access, use, misuse, disclosure, destruction, modification, or disruption.

Chapter 18
Establishment of Enterprise Secured Information Architecture

Shyh-Chang Liu
I-Shou University, Taiwan

Tsang- Hung Wu
I-Shou University, Taiwan

ABSTRACT

Due to the fast progressing of the Information Technology, the issues of the information security became more important for the industry recently. Since the scopes of the information security are so broad, it hardly can be absolutely safety, not to mention only the limited resources are provided. The possible solution to enhance the security of present IT environment is to plan the safe and sound information flow (includes the strategy flow, risk management flow, and logistic flow) by integrated planning, based on the company integrated operation modes.

INTRODUCTION

IT system plays more and more important roles for the industry during the informatization process. It has to be designed from the view of company operation to make the IT technique integrates business activities successfully so that the competition ability can be enhanced. In order to sustain the daily operation, companies establish different kinds of flows to reach both the milestone and long term operation goals. That makes the needs of IT technique increased day by day, so that the ratio of IT investment also increased more. Due to the performance can not be incarnated, either the higher management or the other departments agreed that the IT department is a kind of money wasting unit because the company could not make more profit after investing huge money. Since lacking of good communications and methods, IT department can not reward the appreciations from

DOI: 10.4018/978-1-4666-0197-0.ch018

Figure 1. Enterprise information plan

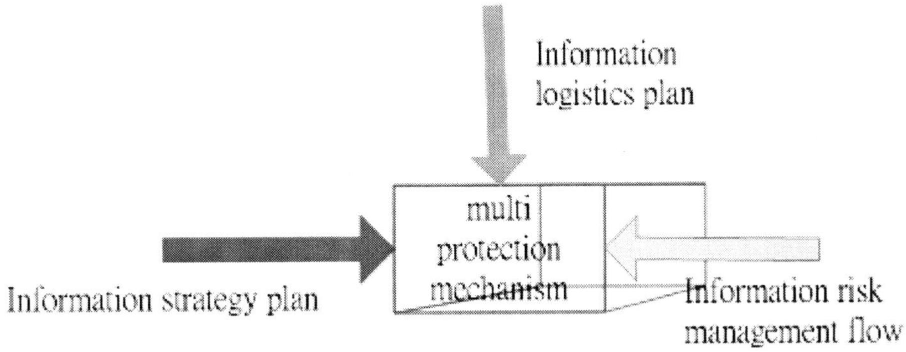

other departments but complains after spending in time and efforts to help the users to solve the problems in daily activities. Thus some conflicts happened. How to use the limited manpower to achieve the user's high expectation as well as reduce the budget of IT department becomes the current IT departments' challenge. Most present companies' IT security sole depends on security tech instead of the appropriate management code that face the possible destroys such as illegal authentications, computer virus and these destroys may influent over the expectation such as the lost of confident or key operation information. It not only affects the competition ability of the company but also the images. IT security should be established to fit three IT security principals of company that are Confidentiality, Integrity, and Availability. The Confidence is to ensure that each information process as well as the possible tapping (without authorized) places are security examined. The Integrity means the judgment of the information content is original not modified. The Availability is to prevent the crash of service and the operation ability. The information strategy plan will be introduced in the first that information strategy represents the information plan based on the company operation strategy. The information risk management will be illustrated later in this chapter. The recommendation of the logistics flow improvement includes employee's education/ training, information infrastructure adjustment as well as information risk management like Figure 1.

Information Strategy Plan

Since the IT tech can help the company to save human power, lower cost, and promote efficiency, it attracts company's close attention. The benefit that can be reward comes from the planning based on the needs of the company regardless of the fast IT tech progressing. Contrary to the endless of IT tech innovation, the company resource is limited. Thus the planning of IT strategy must be fitted with the future goal of the company. The bottleneck and needs can be found by examine the past development and present operation situation. The merits comes from finding a success operation mold, planning corresponding support measure, developing needs of core IT tech and establish the mechanism of integrated operation and evaluation mechanism. (Alonso, Verdun, & Caro, 2008) (Abdi & Dominic, 2010) (Nogueira & Reinhard, 2000) There are six ways provided to enhance the efficient and profit for information strategy planes and illustrated at the Figure 2:

- **Information technique management strategy:** How to efficiently manage it to achieve the optimal operating among the huge IT facility becomes an important issue. It needs to understand the business

Figure 2. Six ways provided to enhance the efficient and profit for information strategy planes

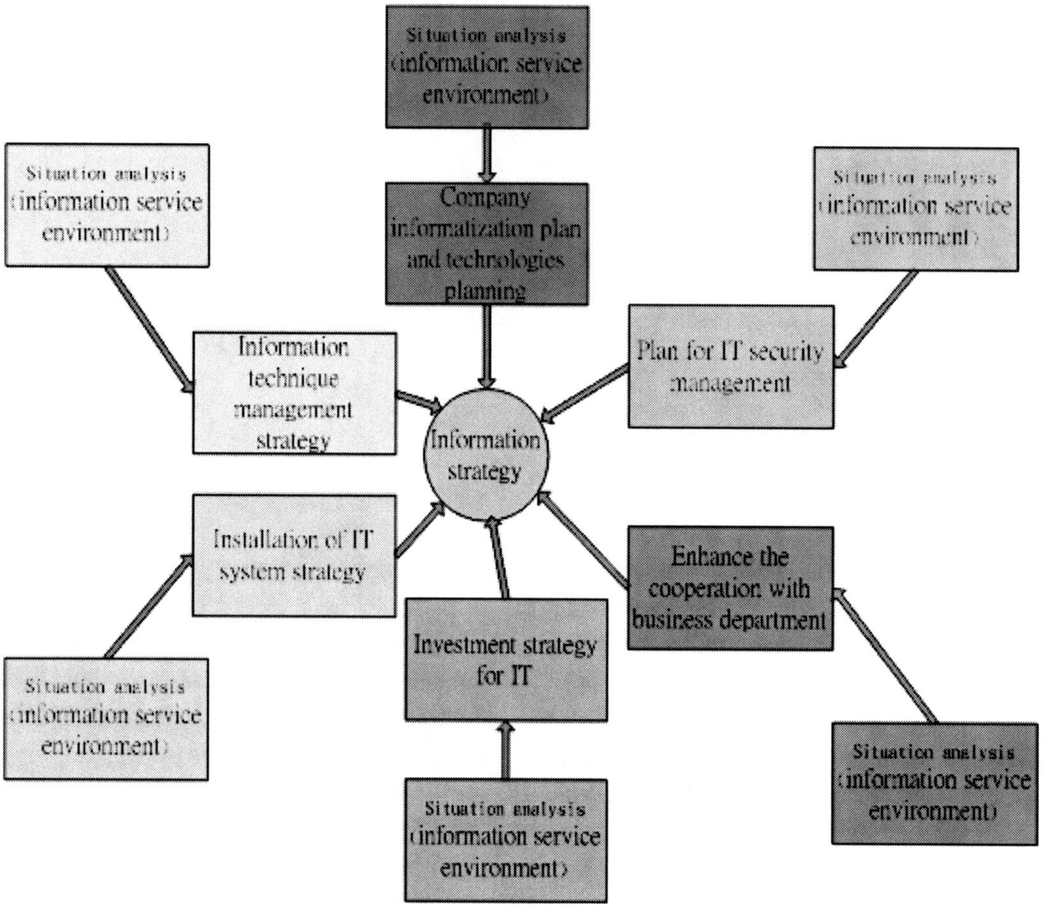

that the company is engaged in. Appropriate policies, procedures and technologies are needed to achieve its goal.

- **Installation of IT system strategy:** Because of the variety of installation and the complexity of the procedures that are required to set up the IT information system. The following types of deployments should be considered: Greenfield deployment, Legacy deployment and Installed base. Besides, plane and establish the IT systems and components, software/hardware and data, to conform the company vision as well as the operation strategy also become very important.
- **Investment strategy for IT:** Begin by looking at company's business strategy over next five to ten years and determine in which areas are planned to grow, change or improved. It will be easier to identify technologies that can help company's business if there is a clear picture of where to head and what steps must take to get there. Of course, the opponent's investment strategy and complementary assets are also considered in the planning.
- **Company informatization plan and technologies planning:** How to adjust the strategy of company informatization under the outer fast varying environment to achieve the optimal strategy and direction

becomes very important. A detailed IT plan and road map are necessary to lower IT costs and ongoing operation costs. Assess current business software applications is one important issue in the plan.

- **Plan for IT security management:** Establish the IT security management strategy based on the balance of smooth business operation and IT security. There are lots of valuable issues in the related professional journals, the company can use them to plan what the company needs.
- **Enhance the cooperation with business department:** Since long time lacking the correct communication that makes the effort spend by the IT department can not meet the requirements of business units, not mention that each side has a tendency to exclude each other. As a result, the gap tends to widen, rather than narrow. This situation can be solved by the company specification, system, meeting, and training to promote the company competition ability. Definitely the attitude of the management is also important.

The main goal of the IT strategy plan is to enhance the role of IT department in the company. Instead of being regarded as the role of money spending and strategy implementation, IT department should be converted as the leader of strategy design and innovation.

Information Risk Management Flow

The reasons of information break are plenty that includes natural disasters, human errors, and system failure. So that the appropriate risk management is a necessary, such as ISO 27001 can help company to establish the mechanism and flow of information risk management that comprises (a) Security policy: It establishes guidelines and standards for accessing the organizations information and application systems. An information security policy facilitates the communication of security procedures to users and makes them more aware of potential security threats and associated business risks. Once the information security policy has been developed it needs to be put in place within the organization and the security policy will be needed to be enforced. (b) Organization security: It manages the company's information security, maintains the information processing system, and the security of the access from the third party. It also comprises the maintenance of the security of the out resourcing. (c) Asset classification and control: It identifies the assets, who is accountable for the assets, and prepares a scheme for information classification. Executing appropriate protection action is included. (d) Personnel security: It prevents from misusing information processing facilities and protects information processing facilities by reducing risk of human errors, theft, and fraud. How well personnel comply with contractual provisions is also monitored. (e) Physical and environmental security: The objective of this category is to prevent unauthorized physical access, damage or interference to the organization's premises and infrastructure, using controls appropriates to the identified risks and the value of the assets protected. (f) Communications and operations management: The objective is to ensure the correct and secure operation of information processing facilities. It also reduces the risk of system failure and maintains the integrity and utilization of information processing and communication services. (g) Access control: The objective of access control is to control access to information, information processing facilities, and business processes. An access control policy should be established and periodically reviewed, based on the business needs and external requirements. (h) System development and maintenance: Identify the security requirements that an information system, infrastructure and business appliance meets before start the system development process. Prevent the loss, misuse and modification of user data in application system. (i) Business continuity management: Develop a business continuity management process to protect critical business processes during business disruptions, security failure, and disasters. Make sure that business continuity management process is used to prevent and recover from business disruptions, security failure, and disasters. Analyze the impact that disasters, security failures, and loss of service could have on critical business processes, and (j) Compliance: It audits and evaluates an information security management system from different axes, such as security policy, asset management, human resources security an incident management. The sustained and effect risk management be proceeded by following PDCA mode (Plan-Do-Check-Act Model) as Figure 3. Plan represents to establish the IT security management system which includes the establishment of IT security strategy, risk management and the policy of procedure and goal of related management system of security improvement system. Its goal is to produce the consistent results of company integral policy and goal. The practical implement IT security management policy, procedure and process can be regarded as Do. Check means based on the policy of IT security management, goal, practical experience, evaluation and performance during the testing process that replays the result to the management level to evaluate. Based on the internal audit of IT security management and the inspect results of management level combined with the redress and the prevent process to reach sustained improvement of IT security management system that belongs to Action. (Nogueira & Reinhard, 2000) (Boehmer, 2008)

Only the risk management is not enough, the best effect comes from the cooperation with the promotion of the information service management. The information service management can be proceeded via ITIL (IT Infrastructure Library) to raise the efficiency of service management, and ITIL covers:

(a) **Service level management:** Service level management is the process that forms the link between the IT organization and customer. The goal for service level management is to maintain and improve service quality through a constant cycle of agreeing, monitoring, reporting and improving the current levels of service. It is focused on the business and maintaining the alignment between the business and IT.
(b) **Financial management for IT services:** It determines the costs of services and provides financial accounting support to ensure expenditures fall within approved plans and that funds are well-spent. Financial management activities include: providing oversight of all IT expenditures, ensuring funds are available for planned events, providing detailed financial information for proposed initiatives, influencing the use of IT assets to maximize the return on IT investments through chargeback systems, and tracking current expenditures against the budget.
(c) **Capacity management:** Capacity management is the discipline that ensures IT infrastructure is provided at the right time in the right volume at the right price, and ensuring that IT is used in the most efficient manner.

Figure 3. ISMS cycle

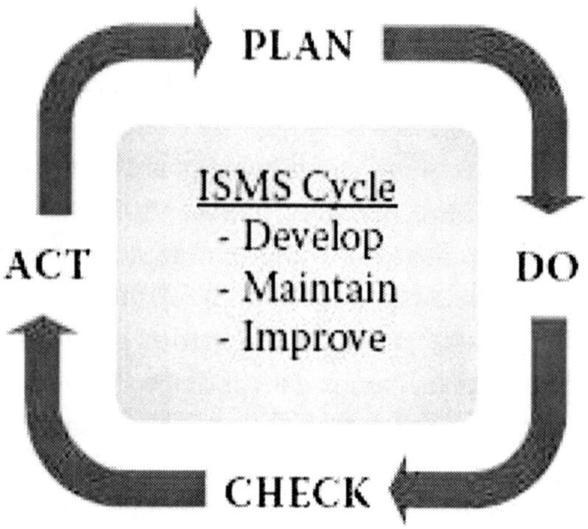

Generally, capacity management is made up of three subprocesses: business capacity management, service capacity management, and resource capacity management.

(d) **Availability management:** Availability is usual calculate based on a model involving the availability ratio and techniques such as fault tree analysis, and includes the following elements, such as seriveability, reliability, recoverability, maintainability, resilience and security.

(e) **IT service continuity management:** Continuity management is the process by which plans are put in place and managed to ensure that IT services can recover and continue after a serious incident happened. It is regarded as the recovery of the IT infrastructure used to deliver IT services, but many business these days practice the much further reading process of business continuity planning, to ensure that the whole end-to-end business process can be continued after an incidence.

(f) **Service desk:** The service desk is a single point of contact for end users who need anything from it. It handles day-to-day customer issues, end-user calls, and release service issues. The service desk is not just a call center or expended help desk, it offers a broader range of services through a more global approach to IT. It can provide an interface for other activities such as customer change requests, billing and availability management.

(g) **Incident management:** An incident is any event which is not part of the standard operation of the service and which causes, or may cause, an interruption or a reduction of the quality of the service. The object of incident management is to restore normal operations as quickly as possible with the least possible impact on either the business or the user, at a cost-effective price. Activities of the incident management comprise incident detection, classification and initial support, investigation and diagnosis, resolution and recovery, incident closure, and incident ownership, monitoring, tracking and communication.

(h) **Problem management:** A problem is the unknown cause of one or more incidents, often identified as a result of multiple similar incidents. A known error is an identified root caused of a problem. The objective of problem management is to minimize the impact of problems on the organization. Problem management plays an important role in the detection and providing solutions to problems (known errors) and prevents their recurrence.

(i) **Configuration management:** The role of configuration management is to deal with all configuration items within organization. They identify these configuration items are, control them, maintain them in the format that they are currently and then verify them. Because quality is important, configuration management should provide quality data within this database to ensure the effectiveness of the entire operation. There are a series of activities that configuration management deals with. These activities are planning, identification, configuration control, status accounting and verification and audit.

(j) **Change management:** The prime goals of change management are to:

(1) effectively response to customer's changing business needs while maximizing value, minimizing incidents, disruption and re-work and

(2) respond to the business and IT requests for change that will align the services with the business needs. The change management process ensures that the standardized methodologies are in action for efficient and effective implementation of change order or change requests in IT technology with

minimum adverse impacts upon service availability and quality.

(k) **Release management:** Release management is about monitoring how changes flow into the IT infrastructure. Whenever an item is updated, the result is referred to as a release. A release can be a major release, a minor release or an emergency release. Additionally, a release can also be classified as a delta release, full release or a packet release. The aim of release management is that it enables you to take a comprehensive view on change in the IT sector. It is needed whenever there is a major hardware installation or when new software has to be installed. Without it there would be no efficient coordination between providers and suppliers involved in the release process. The ITIL is shown as Figure 4.

The objective of IT security management is to strength the information service and to keep users safe and it needs the coordinate of the other information management systems. ITSM is one of the well known information services standard, and ISO2000 defines it as a set of information service application and audit standard. Both ITSM and ISMS combine to an information management system. Not only to avoid the information security event happened, the client satisfaction service can also be supplied only by the security information system. How to establish a reliable and maintain a matured information service environment should be considered from a broader point of view. (ISO, 2005) (Boehmer, 2010)

Information Logistics Plan

The continuity of the company cannot be suspend only by the management of strategy, risk or flow, the cooperation of logistics management is a necessary to get good results. The logistics management comprises information person's training, routine information maintenance, management and adjustment of infrastructure, and management of application programs. It is expected that the goal of company integral information planning can be sounder by appropriate logistics management. The logistics items mentioned above are illustrated here:

- **Information personnel training:** The most valuable asset of the company isn't the money, neither the equipments, that is staff. It is not easy to train professional IT persons. They need to be guided to comprehend the long term relationship to company via precise employee evaluation mechanism, well organized training and the experience inheritance. They should access, understand, and use information to increase their productivity and maximize their contributions to the success of the business.
- **Routine information environment maintenance:** After the IT strategy plans are developed, organizations cannot afford to neglect the fact that systems maintenance is the longest and costliest phase of the systems life cycle. The implication of the maintenance workload upon the IT strategy plans for an organization is a subject that deserves special attention. The organization structure needs flexibility to support the maintenance of existing system concurrently with the implementation of new technologies. This job can be completed by technical method (environment monitoring, complete testing and transaction management) and flowing method (transaction flow standard, testing flow standard).
- **Management and adjustment of infrastructure:** Infrastructure management is the management of essential operation components, such as policies, procedures, equipment, and data, for overall effectiveness. Appropriate SOP (standard operation

Figure 4. Information risk management flow

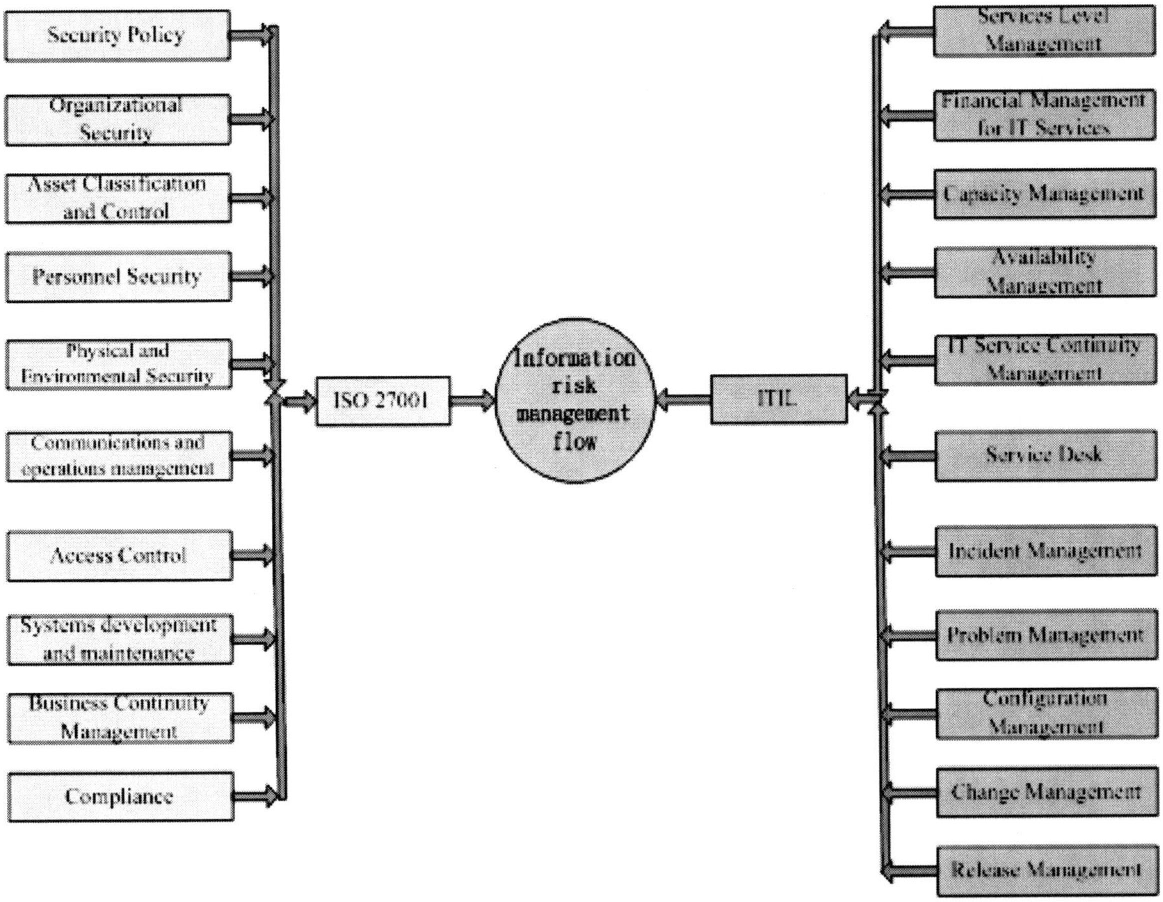

procedure) is needed when processing the adjustment.

- **Management of application programs:** An application consists of many application-specific elements, including user interface (UI), business logic, data access logic, controls, and data. These elements typically differ from one application to the next. However, all applications tend to share a common set of functionality that facilitates application implementation and management. The users are secured protected by appropriate program test, on-line management and security testing.
- IT department should comprehend which part of information business is unrelated to the core of the company after implementing the above planes. Those non-core IT business should be outsourcing. Not only the IT department can pay more attention to related core works but also more profit comes from the creative concept and methods along with the innovation brought by the outsourcing. Thus the IT department can become one source of the profit via multiple views to plan the internal information environment.
- **Physical security:** Physical security is the protection of personnel, hardware, programs, networks, and data from physical circumstances and events that could cause serious losses or damage to an enterprise,

agency, or institution. This includes protection from fire, natural disasters, burglary, theft, vandalism, and terrorism. It can be as simple as a locked door or as elaborate as multiple layers of armed security guards and guardhouse placement. The key factor is the technology used for physical security has changed over time. Access control is a kind of familiar method that can be achieved either by the security persons or access control system. The attendance such as a card has been used for a long time, and nowadays the biometric access control such as finger print becomes booming.

- **Natural disasters and protection:** Natural disasters happen everywhere. Generally, the damage brought by peoples is partial (such as a serve), but the natural disasters are more broad. For example, the most fire come from human error or arson. The chance of firing can be reduced by the daily routine procedures. Buildings must be constructed in accordance with the version of the building code that is in effect when an application for a building permit is made. Building inspectors check on compliance of a building under construction with the building code. It should use integral, fire-resistance rated wall and floor assemblies that are used to form fire compartments intended to limit the spread of fire, or occupancy separations, or firewalls, to keep fires, high temperatures and flue gases within the fire compartment of origin, thus enabling firefighting and evacuation. The computer center should not installed in the basement to prevent flooding. The sound information backup mechanism is the optimal solution to natural disasters, such as to install a remote backup center at least 30 km away from the main information center as well as not at seismeic belt. The UPS system is also a necessary for power break or abnormal.
- **Backup mechanism:** A backup or the process of backing up refers to making copies of data so that these additional copies may be used to restore the original after a data loss event. However robust the application may be, there should always be provision for a reliable disaster recovery mechanism. The medium used for backup are tapes, CD, or HD. There are two common backup modes:
  a. **Full Backup:** it means to copy data files from one location to another in full with no regard to file changes that may take place in-between backups. It is bigger in size, takes longer to perform, but easier to recover than incremental backup.
  b. **Incremental Backup:** It copies only the new and changed files of the selected data. When full backup is done, the backup software copies the new and changed files that have accumulated in-backups. However, incremental backup does not copy the files that have changed earlier than previous backup. Because increments are not overwritten, each increment is responsible for copying changes within a certain period of time.

CONCLUSION

Nowadays, the structure of industry has to be adjusted to promote the competition ability, and informatization becomes a kind of important tool to achieve it. The utilization of technique does not contribute too much effort, on the contrary the planning based on integrated flowing and management along with the organization information strategy are more important. The manager could not make effective investment, manage the information resources, effectively develop system, provide valuable information and knowledge to support company operation, neither enhances the competition superiority unless knowing the compact, the influence, and the opportunity created to the company by the essence of the IT technique. Even worse that the company may be died out since it can not produce the ascendant by using IT technique and make the lagging of electronicalizing or mobilizing.

REFERENCES

Abdi, M., & Dominic, P. D. D. (2010). Strategic IT alignment with business strategy: Service oriented architecture approach. *2010 International Symposium in Information Technology* (ITSim), vol. 3 (pp. 1473-1478).

Alonso, I. A., Verdun, J. C., & Caro, E. T. (2008). The importance of IT strategic demand management in achieving the objectives of the strategic business planning. *2008 International Conference on Computer Science and Software Engineering*, vol. 2 (pp. 235-238).

Boehmer, W. (2008). Appraisal of the effectiveness and efficiency of an information security management system based on ISO 27001. *SECURWARE '08: Second International Conference on Emerging Security Information, Systems and Technologies,* (pp. 224-231).

Boehmer, W. (2010). Toward a target function of an information security management system. *2010 IEEE 10th International Conference on Computer and Information Technology* (CIT), (pp. 809-816).

ISO. (2005). *ISO/IEC 27001 Information Technology- Security techniques- Information security management systems- Requirements.* Retrieved June 9, 2009, from http://www.iso.org/iso/catalogue_detail?csnumber=42103

Nogueira, A. R. R., & Reinhard, N. (2000). Strategic IT management in Brazilian banks. *Proceedings of the 33rd Annual Hawaii International Conference on System Sciences*, 2000.

ADDITIONAL READING

de Sousa Pereira, R. F., & da Silva, M. M. (2010). A Maturity Model for Implementing ITIL v3, Services (SERVICES-1), 2010 6th World Congress. (pp. 399-406).

The ITIL & ITSM Directory. Retrieved June 7, 2009, from http://www.itil-itsm-world.com/

Chapter 19
Information Security Management Based on Adaptive Security Policy Using User Behavior Analysis

Ines Brosso
Mackenzie Presbyterian University, Brazil

Alessandro La Neve
Centro Universitário da FEI, Brasil

ABSTRACT

This chapter presents a system for information security management based on adaptative security policy using user's behavior analysis in Information Technology. This system must be able to acquire information about the environment, space, time, equipment, hardware, and software. This information is used in the user behavior analysis. This work proposes that, based on the evidence of the user behavior, it is possible to trust or not trust the user. Levels of trust are released according to the user behavior and the rules that were previously established for the parameters, which help to establish the evidences of behavioral trust, interacting with the environment information, so as to keep trust levels updated in a more accurate and faithful way.

INTRODUCTION

Management of information security is a complex task. In general, organizations implement the management of information security deploying security policies which are based on a set of rules, laws, controls, processes (business rules, government laws, internal and access controls, authentication processes), and audit governance records in the attempt to achieve a complex generalization of security policies, so that they may be applicable to all types of users. In some organizations, security policies definitely ignore

DOI: 10.4018/978-1-4666-0197-0.ch019

aspects related to the user's privacy, and they do not even let the users know, at least, that they will be monitored whenever they access the system. Since corporate security is related to people, it should be implemented considering the environment context and the user behavior.

In this context, a system for information security management based on adaptative security policy, using user's behavior analysis is here presented.

At present, security policy, to be effective, is primarily focused on people, being very rigid at this, and only later it watches for security attack attempts. The security policy does not need to be rigid: rather it should be adaptable to the user behavior. Analysis of human behavior, therefore, is the basis for an adaptive security policy. The behavior analysis of a person can be verified by a set of rules, which consider the variables that can influence human behavior, based on the information acquired about the environment, the space, the time, the equipments, hardware and software. This information is used to analyze behavioral evidences about people, and establishes if it is possible to believe or not in the user.

Therefore, according to the user behavior, levels of trust are released, which are based on the rules that were previously established for the parameters that are necessary to establish the evidences of behavioral trust, in its different degrees.

The adaptive security policy based on user behavior analysis is the basis for the information security management, when it comes to understanding the needs of users. However, to achieve the whole security target in computing, and related technologies, it is necessary not only to have the most updated core technologies or security policies, but also to have the capacity to perform the analyses of the user behavior and the security environment.

The technological environment is growing faster than ever, getting more and more sophisticated, both in hardware and software, and it offers a diversity of options, including devices and applications. Mobile, ubiquitous, cloud, network computing and communication applications have stimulated interest in security issues, and have proposed pivotal challenges to deal with, such as integrity verification, authentication, access control, and attack prevention, among others.

In order to integrate information security management, based on adaptive security policy, with user behavior analysis, a deep understanding of Behavioral Theory, with historical, social and psychological aspects are necessary. At the same time, it also important to have full expertise in mathematical methods for handling information about people behavior, context-aware computing and self-aware computing systems, which can be the basis for an adaptive security policy based on user behavioral analysis.

This work, in the context of computer security, uses the operant and conditioning behavior defined by Skinner (1991), which rewards a response of an individual until he is conditioned to associate the need for action. In operant behavior, the environment is modified and produces consequences that are working on it again, changing the likelihood of a future similar occurrence. Operant conditioning is a mechanism for learning a new behavior. When the organism answers to an environmental stimulation, and the consequences of its reply are rewarded, this makes the probability of similar answers increase; when the consequences are punitive, such probability diminishes. People associate experiences they have gone through to similar ones they may find in life: in this case they adopt the same behavior and repeat their actions. Therefore the Skinner Theory may be very interesting to be used in Information Security Management Systems.

BACKGROUND

The methodology for the preparation of this book chapter consisted of literature review, researches on the Behavioral Theory, historical, social and psychological aspects, and the development of a Continuous Authentication System. Studies and research on mathematical methods for handling trust information,

Information security management, biometrics, context-aware computing and adaptive security policies, were also necessary. This work was based on a doctoral thesis (Brosso, 2006), relevant research work and user cases in financial applications.

INFORMATION SECURITY MANAGEMENT

Security is always a keyword in projects of Information Technology. Linked to the confidential data of organizations, there are aspects that are intangibles, such as brand, reputation and people. Therefore the increase in security systems must be efficient and able to generate alert signals, at the slightest suspicious movement, to surveillance teams. This type of procedure becomes even more necessary considering that the majority of attacks and frauds come from inside the organizations, or from persons who are authorized to have access to the system. The information security management should be based on the capture of information, and on the monitoring of safety information in an organization. In order to assure the effective management of information security, it is necessary that organizations have systems that can record everything that happens on the information technology, and corporate information security, platforms, so that they may be helpful in preventive actions against all possible attacks and frauds. This allows for a quick view of possible attacks on the network, with comprehensive and detailed reports of user actions, considering the specificity of each business activity.

The monitoring of information security is the most critical part of managing information security. Monitoring should be continuous, in full time operations, with specific agents hired to analyze user behavior, for each type of device, such as desktop, firewall, servers, operating systems, applications, network equipment, and storage platforms. Event systems and physical access controls should also be monitored, to correlate an event access with a person's location in the company. Monitoring must analyze the infrastructure, the user, the environment and the user and devices interaction.

In other words, the information management, which is hierarchically organized as shown in Figure 1, should highlight the various aspects of security that cover, among others, the different fields of applications, with mobility and transparency.

Different Aspects of Information Management Security

Organizational Security

Security is a challenge, but it is intrinsic to the security issues found in any type of network, and consists of prevention mechanisms that enable point vulnerabilities, minimize risks and weaknesses to prevent unauthorized access, attacks and destruction. The information security management should highlight the various aspects of Organizational Security Monitoring Design for security, with distributed Intrusion Detection Systems & Countermeasures, which define single and multi-source intrusion detection and response.

Vulnerability

The vulnerability of the security mechanisms is a major risk, and may have its origin either in an unintentional failure, or in malicious actions performed by members of the network. It should therefore be handled by encryption schemes, because there are threats against applications, ranging from the capture on mobile device to different levels of application, where the routing is more critical. In this system, vulnerability was

Figure 1. The hierarchy of various aspects of security

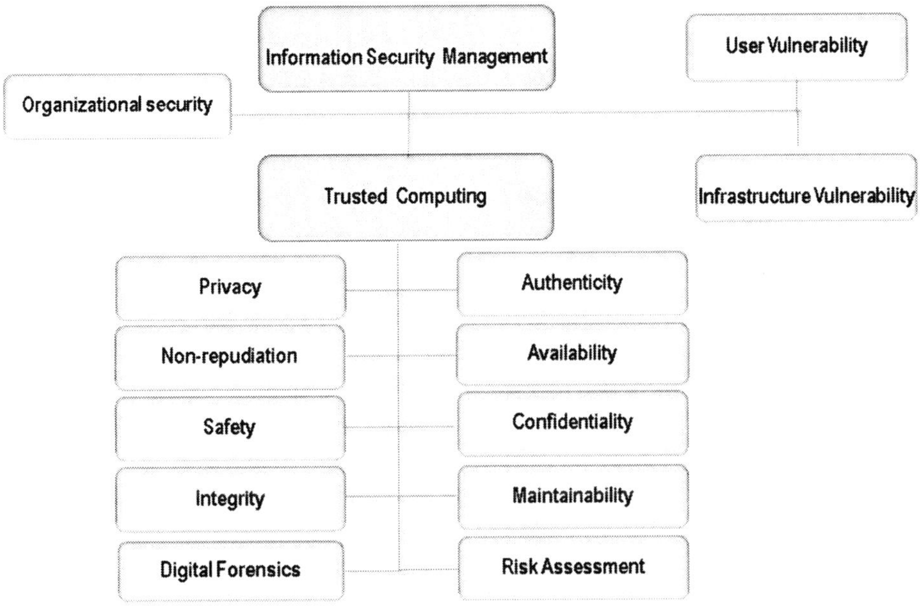

divided in two parts, namely infrastructure and user vulnerability.

Infrastructure Vulnerability

Infrastructure vulnerabilities occur both in networks and in mobile devices, such as mobile phone, PDA, notebook, palm, etc., and they can either allow access to unauthorized persons or deny access to authorized persons. In a wireless network, only the user is within range of local communications, so he can enter the network. In this case, the vulnerability of the system becomes much more serious and additional care should be taken, so that no negative interference may intervene in the application.

In a wired network, users are first identified and authenticated in order to participate in any interaction or transaction that involves exchanging of information. Since it is a private environment, the user must first be physically connected to the network, before undergoing the process of identification and authentication.

User Vulnerability

Use vulnerability, in security mechanisms, is based on images, reputation and behavior, and therefore is a very delicate and sensitive matter. The development of society and technology bring forth a new concept of image, different from the initially protected one. The image is a set of physical characteristics of a person. The image emerges as a concept of "social image" with a set of social characteristics of the individual. Protecting the image of a person has become a major concern for jurists, due to the recent technological developments, both with regard to image capture, and to reproduction.

Personality rights are those that try to defend the innate values in man, both in him and in society, in their projections. It is a very broad field of study, encompassing physical rights, regarding body integrity, rights to life, limb, body, image and voice; mental rights, relating to themselves and interior components of human personality, the freedom rights, privacy, mental integrity and confidentiality. In addition to moral rights, related to value attributes of the individual in society, the rights to identity, honor, respect and intellectual creations should also be analyzed.

The image rights have reached a relevant position within the personality rights, thanks to the extraordinary progress of communications and the importance that the image has acquired in the advertising context. The right to self-image is an essential right of humans. This fundamental characteristic of the image rights involves a series of legal consequences, because when using the image of others, either without the consent of the person who is involved, or when the use goes beyond what was authorized, there is a violation of image rights.

Personality rights are inherent to man subjectivity, therefore they are absolute, unavailable, inalienable, non-transferable indispensable and attached. However, there are limitations that restrict the exertion of the right to one's own image. These restrictions are based on the prevalence of social interest, and therefore the collective right supersedes the individual right. These limitations make use of the image that is not illegal, even without the consent of the portrayed, because they allow the violation of the image, placing it outside the legal protection. One can conclude, then, that with the exception of these possibilities, any use of images of others, without permission of the owner, constitutes a violation of image rights.

There are three types of violations:

1. **Consent:** the individual has its own image used without having given any consent to do so;
2. **Use:** the consent is given, but the use made of the image is beyond the limits of the authorization;
3. **Lack of goals that justify the exception:** the case of photographs of public interest, or famous people, the use of which leads to the lack of purpose that is required to limit the right of the image. It happens when the use of these images is not cultural or informative.

All these forms of violation of the rights to one's own image are liable to indemnification. With the violation of the right to image, the body and its functions do not change physically, but the individual is morally affected. Legal protection of the image, and consequently the images generated by technologies, is crucial because it preserves the person, while the defense of key components of their personality and their heritage, preserves the economic value they represent. Images can reflect a human behavior and the environment. The information security management should highlight the various vulnerability aspects with exploitation tools, virus/worm analysis and preserving data and images of persons and users.

Trusted Computing

With Trusted Computing, the computer system will consistently behave in expected ways, and those behaviors will be enforced by hardware and software. In practice, Trusted Computing uses cryptography to help enforce a selected behavior and to allow someone else to verify that only authorized codes run on a system. The information security management should privilege the various aspects of trusted computing, with Trust models and Trust establishment; Applications of Cryptography and Cryptanalysis in communications security; Cryptographic Hardware and Embedded Systems; Light-weight cryptography; Quantum Cryptography and Information hiding and watermarking.

Privacy

Privacy refers to the exchange of messages between users and systems with regard to confidentiality.

The user must know that he is being monitored and that his privacy is preserved. The invasion of privacy is characterized by the acquisition and dissemination of information without authorization. The information security management should highlight the various aspects of privacy, verifying rules of privacy; secure naming and addressing (privacy and anonymity), and contract agreements.

Authenticity

Authenticity means verifying the identity of the user, or process, that wants to communicate with the protected system. It must ensure that users and network systems confirm the identity of its communication peer. At first, it is necessary to identify the user and then proceed to the authentication.

At the Initial Authentication, the user informs the access code and password with which it has access to software applications in the system. Continuous Authentication, on the other hand, guarantees the authenticity of a person during the communication and the use of the application software. The system queries the database periodically, with no need for further authentication requests for confirmation. Everything is done ubiquitously: an authentication continuum that extends over the time interval in which the user interacts with the software application.

The information security management should consider the various aspects of Authenticity using rules of Access Control; Identity management; Authentication protocols and services authorization, and Biometric security technologies.

Non-Repudiation

Non-repudiation is the ability of the system to identify the origin of information received from another person, and to ensure that the information actually came from the alleged sender. The sender may not be able to deny (repudiate) sending the information that he really did. Different aspects, such as non-repudiation controlling Web, e-mail, m-commerce, e-business and e-commerce security, should be taken in consideration.

Availability

The terms anywhere and anytime serve both to allow exchange of, or access to, information and availability of services and resources of a system whenever and/or wherever they are needed.

Safety

The concept of system safety is useful in demonstrating adequacy of technologies when difficulties are faced with probabilistic risk analysis. The safety concept calls for a risk management strategy based on identification, analysis of hazards and application of remedial controls using a systems-based approach, which rely on control of conditions and causes of an accident. The information security management requires the integration of various aspects of safety providing Security management; Mobile code security; Secure Routing and upper layer protocols; Secure Cross layer design; Security modeling and protocol design and secure hardware;

Confidentiality

Confidentiality of information should only be available to authorized people. Besides the assurance of the transmitted information confidentiality, it should be considered the treatment of specific information that is stored in portable devices. For this, the various aspects of Confidentiality, defining Data and system confidentiality should be included.

Integrity

Integrity is necessary to ensure that the information is not modified or altered without consent, while moving across the computer network, and it also ensures that the system is correct. Integrity preserves data, so that they remain intact, and exchanges of information will neither be intercepted nor altered.

Crucial topics, necessary to the system, are the definition of a data and system integrity; definition of deployment and management of computer/network security policies; use of Traffic filtering and Firewalling, Virtual Private Networks (VPNs), Revocation of malicious parties, Prevention, Detection and Reaction Design, Distributed Denial-of-Service (DDoS); use of attacks and countermeasures and Testbeds, performance evaluation and formal specification methods.

Maintainability

The maintainability item of security, based upon the tasks needed to repair the system, provides an integrated environment for predicting the expected number of hours that a system, or a device, will be inoperative, or "down", while it undergoes maintenance. The information security management should highlight the various aspects of maintainability, defining a Network performance evaluation.

Digital Forensics

Digital forensics is a branch of forensic science and it is divided into several sub-branches, such as computer, network, database and mobile device forensics, with the goal of encompassing the recovery and investigation of material found in digital devices, often in relation with crime. Investigations of evidence, in specific suspects, confirm alibis or statements, determine intent, identify sources or authenticate documents. Therefore it is necessary to know the legal aspects and laws of the civil code to define corporate systems for security, using digital forensics.

The information security management should highlight the various aspects of Digital Forensics providing Investigation of material found in digital devices and Investigations about recovered evidence to support or oppose a hypothesis before a criminal court.

Risk Assessment

Risk assessment is an important activity in the area of Information Security, in order to assess risk related to information security in various products or services of the Organization. The information security management should highlight the various aspects of Risk assessment using Matrix of Risks and vulnerabilities, which must necessarily be part of the system.

SECURITY ENVIRONMENT

The information security management must consider the various aspects of the user and computing environment. The environment is distributed and this raises new technical challenges and concerns with this environment, such as security, vulnerabilities, attacks, unauthorized access, retrieval of information, privacy security, trusted authentication, reliability of software applications, energy storage capacity, need for constant battery charging devices and care about distributed devices and storage systems.

Over the last decades Internet has undergone massive transformations, migrating from a relatively focused scientific research network to a ubiquitous and pervasive communications medium for masses. This has brought changes and progress in all layers of the network hierarchy, in service-aware networking protocols and hardware, bringing about new research challenges and business opportunities.

In order to better understand the purpose of this study it is important to consider the evolution of computing and context aware technology, and its influence in the user behavior analysis, and consequently in the adaptive security policy. The Security environment, in fact, is strictly connected with context aware computing.

The Context Aware Computing

Context Aware Computing exploits the interactions of humans with devices and computing equipments to take advantage of contextual information present in communications. Information can be collected and analyzed, and serves as support for adaptation of services, according to the needs of users and hardware features and devices for interaction. The various scenarios of context-aware computing define the best practices for security in this environment, and should be able to give a safe operation, ranging from the transmission of data up to its storage, regardless of restrictions, such as resource scarcity, low memory, low processing power and limited battery life.

One of the paradigms of context-aware computing is the ability to interact with the environment and people, and to react when there are changes, both in people and in the environment, in order to continue getting information about people's location, physical condition, emotional state, and historical behavioral, among others. Works in the area emphasize the need to understand and assist the daily practices of individuals and the system; and the environment, through the provision of heterogeneous devices, offering different forms of interaction. Tracking of people is proposed using special badges and sensors around the environment. Physical-world objects are used to activate electronic devices, creating the concept of tangible interfaces that communicate with the environment.

Context Aware Environment enables the collection and use of information acquired in the context of computing devices in the environment. Context information is any information that can be used to characterize the situation of an entity, that entity being a person, place or object that is considered relevant to the interaction between a user and an application; possible information can be location, persons, objects identification, places and times. Computing and Context Aware technology are changing the concept of privacy, offering new opportunities to interact and share information. Exchange of information may happen anywhere at any time, but in this dynamic activity, loss of confidentiality may arise both during the transition of data and at the place where it will be stored. There is much privacy vulnerability in context aware computing, such that it can be considered invasion of privacy due to malicious actions, and to customization in tracking user preferences, while browsing the Internet, with the purpose of offering new products and services targeted to his needs.

Some issues of concern regarding security and privacy of users, using context-aware systems, are the increasingly common activities performed by mobile electronic devices to collect information on behavior and preferences of users, reducing privacy, and gaps and vulnerabilities that may legalize spying.

The definition of context and semantic dimensions help to decide what information is relevant to a system, however it is necessary to analyze the requirements and to model the necessary information that each dimension can provide. Schilit and Theimer (1994) define context as the location and the identification of people and objects around it, social situations and environmental conditions such as lighting and noise. The authors point out three important aspects of context: *where* the user is, *with whom* the user is and *what* resources are coming from the user.

Brosso (2010) also defines the static context as information that remains stationary during the lifetime of the entity, and identifies four sets to be used in context-aware applications, classified as *infrastructure, system, domain and environment*:

1. **Context of infrastructure** is the communication between the software application and the device used by the user to access the application. It provides subsidies to report changes of status due to failures, adding or removing a device in the environment.

2. **Context of system** is formed by the user's context, the current state of devices and services that were used, and must contain information that allow the extent to which a device is aware of other devices in its vicinity, and the extent to which an application is aware of the proximity of another one to provide services.
3. **Context of domain** refers to information about the semantics of the application domain, considering the relationships between devices and users.
4. **Context of environment** contains the information about the address and the location of a given entity.

In general, all context types require care in relation to invasion of privacy and spying, since all captured information is vulnerable and can be released to others. It is necessary to consider all the security aspects of design, implementation, deployment, architectures and modeling of heterogeneous wired and wireless computer networks, of the virtualization technology, and the pervasive computer applications as well. Context-aware applications must be able to acquire context information automatically, making them available in a computing environment at runtime. A context-aware system is such that uses contextual information to provide relevant information and / or services to the user, where relevancy depends on the user action. However, a context aware system is not limited to mobility, for there is a larger context that encompasses all systems, both in wired and wireless networks, such as systems based on biometrics and self-aware pervasive systems.

The Self-Aware Pervasive System

Nowadays the information security management uses the Self-aware pervasive systems that combine cyber-technical systems, sensors, decision element, people, and possible mobile resources and assets, together with networks, to carry out real-time monitoring and action. Such systems observe their internal behavior, as well as the external ones, with systems they interact with, in order to modify their own behavior. This is done in order to adaptively achieve their objectives, such as discovering services for their users, improving their own efficiency or Quality of Service (QoS), reducing their energy consumption, compensating for components which fail or malfunction, detecting and reacting to intrusions, and defending themselves against external attacks (Marcus, 2004).

A Self-aware pervasive system creates a distributed internal representation of its past and present experience, based on sensing and measurement, with proactive sensing, as one of the concurrent activities that it undertakes, including performance and condition monitoring (Mass, 2001).The importance of the distributed environment, across a network, where the user interacts with software applications and devices in a self-aware pervasive system, is the basis of user behavior analysis.

ADAPTATIVE SECURITY POLICY

One of the more challenging questions in security is how to specify an adaptative security policy.

The security policy does not need to be rigid, but it should adaptable to the user behavior. In this context, this work exploits security aspects, user behavior analysis, trust in behavior, and biometric technologies to be the base of an adaptative security policy. The goal for specifying adaptive security is twofold: to provide an umbrella guide to decide which future events, actions, or responses are permitted in the current policy; and to allow new security goals to be stated, in order to initiate system responses to enforce that policy, if necessary.

The security policies for computing resources must match the security policies of the organizations that use them; therefore, computer security policies must be adaptable to meet the changing security environment of their user-base. The term "adaptive security" is intended to indicate that security policies and mechanisms can change in some automated or semi-automated way in response to events.

Much work is currently being focused on specific aspects of the fields related to intrusion detection, sensor networks, architectures, and security policies. Much less effort is devoted to the integration of these aspects, so as to put them to work properly. Apparently there is not yet a reliable and widely accepted method which gives confidence that the mechanisms to be employed will work together to deliver what, and only what, is needed.

USER BEHAVIOR ANALYSIS

The user behavior analysis helps to define an adaptative security policy to the information security management. Human behavior is based on contextual information, which is retrieved by behavioral history, history of behavior reinforcement and conduct of the person to interact with the environment immediately (Witter, 2005).The scientific analysis of human behavior starts with the knowledge of the environment and isolation of the parts of an event to determine the characteristics and the dimensions of the occasion where the behavior occurs, and to define the changes that were produced in response to the environment, space, time and opportunities.

Thus, it can be said that the environment and both the virtual and physical space establish the conditions for a certain behavior. According to the user behavior, levels of trust are released, based on the rules that were previously established for the parameters which help to establish the evidences of behavioral trust, in its different degrees. It is necessary, therefore, to define some entities, used in behavior analysis, as shown below:

- **User** - User is a person who has been approved in an authentication process to have access to software applications in a specific area of computer networks and wireless.
- **Context** - Any information that can be used to characterize the situation of the environment and the user.
- **Environment** - Environmental technology: the infrastructure needed in a specific area of computer networks, wired and wireless. Technological environment: local capture information, from behavior of users that interact with software and hardware applications.
- **Time interval** - The interval of time that elapses from the initial instant the user makes his identification on a software application access to the moment he exits the application, often called the session.
- **Behavior** - The behavior is the set of actions and responses that enable the intent of a person and the technological environment; or actions that a user performs when interacting with the software applications and the technological environment.
- **Trust** - Concept assigned to the user, which may vary according to the behavioral analysis of it. Based on the evidence of user behavior it is possible to determine the level of trust to give to him. Trust is an abstract concept that expresses the belief that one has in the sincerity / authenticity of another person. The trust level of the person user is according to the analysis of his behavior. The concept of trust is a characteristic common to human beings, and is directly related to the perception, knowledge and reputation of a person about another (Platzer, 2004).
- **Trust Restriction** -It refers to the behavior of the user that runs off the expected normality. A restriction may due to be a sequence of not recommended transactions, values or places different from usual, or

others. The restriction of trust can be used in user adaptive security policy.

The focus of Behavior Analysis, as proposed by Skinner (1991), is currently applied in this work, for effective analysis of user behavior, to fulfill the requirements of user behavior analysis, according to the following steps:

Step 1: Target of the Behavior – define the target of the behavior to be analyzed, to measure the frequency with which it occurs, or capture the variable and compare with what the restrictions and historical behavior databases.

Step 2: Observe the behavior – Observe the behavior, the response and what will happen, or wait for the action of the user interaction in a given period of time, capturing the information received and waiting for the application to send a stimulus to the user to develop his behavior.

Step 3: Observe the behavior in terms of triple contingency – Observe the behavior in terms of triple contingency, which is the expression used to say that it will see the context, the response and what will happen; or wait for the action of the user interaction with application software in a given period of time, capture the information received and wait for the application to send the user a stimulus to develop a certain behavior.

Step 4: Behavior frequency – Record the rate of occurrence of the behavior (frequency) in order to measure the behavior occurred throughout the process, and store it in the user behavior database.

Step 5: Introduce the experimental variable – Where appropriate, introduce the experimental variable. It is applied to introduce a new tool for the user, such as a new code of access or a new field of application.

Step 6: Compare the frequency of behavior – Compare the frequency of behavior before and after the experimental variable or the occurrence of response. Currently, restrictions are compared to the user's past behavior. Thus, it can be said that the environment and both the virtual and physical space establish the conditions for a certain behavior.

Behavioral analysis is based on evidence of user behavior and comparison with information stored in databases of the same behavioral history. The behavioral analysis is carried out in two phases: the first is to compare the information obtained at the time the user interacts with the historical behavioral information. The second phase is to verify the existence, or absence, of behavioral constraints that can collaborate with the analysis, to convey or not to the user authentication. The capture of user behavioral information in the environment is done from the time the user is identified and accesses a software application, to the time he closes it.

The user behavior is a combination of n dimensions. The user behavior analysis uses the context variables of the environment and the trust, the concept that we human beings have regarding a person, and it is based on behavior and reputation of a person. In this way, the environmental variables model the user's behavior, in a conditioning process. This system defines a set of context variables *{who, where, when, what, why, how, rest}*, that is, the evidence of the user behavior, as follows:

- **Who** – Identification. It identifies the user in an application software session. It helps User-behavior analysis, in classifying users according to their access patterns. This is useful for personalization, targeted advertising, priority, and capacity planning.
- **Where** – Space Locality. It identifies either the location where the user is, or the device address that the user is accessing. It is of user interest, determining whether

users in the same geographical region tend to receive/request similar notification and browsing content. For analysis, it should be defined a notification message to be locally shared, if at least two users in the same cluster receive the notification.

- **When** – Time. It identifies the current time that the user is in a software application session.
- **What** – Qualification. It identifies what the user is doing in a software application session.
- **Why** – Intention. It means the action of the user to the stimulus received.
- **How** – Method. It justifies the user repetitive activities in a software application session.
- **Rest** – Restrictions. It identifies either the user behavior or the software application restrictions.

The set of context variables *{who, where, when, what, why, how, rest}* helps to decide what information is relevant to a system. However it is necessary to analyze the requirements and model the necessary information that each dimension can provide, since, in general, there is a tendency to develop a context model in which the user overrides associated problems, and this is a generalization to classify the context in temporal aspects, both static and dynamic.

To capture the behavior means to store the information of the behavioral variables *who, where, when, what, why, how and rest,* in a data structure represented by the matrix of user behavior. Given the uncertainty and doubt, it is often necessary to take decisions based on evidences, which are not always accurate. In these cases, trust should be used, which is a staff metric criterion adopted to evaluate evidence. The concept of trust is a characteristic common to humans, and is directly related to perception, knowledge and reputation that a person has about the other.

Trust in User Behavior

Trust is an abstract concept, and it reveals a belief in the sincerity / authenticity of one person in relation to another. The trust, that is the concept that we human beings have regarding a person, is based on the behavior and reputation of a person. This concept is not a unique and indivisible attribute that can be given to someone, and it is not the dichotomy of trust or not trust: on the contrary, it can be graded, and therefore it is dimensional and measurable.

Trust levels may be stipulated based on the user behavioral analysis and on trust restrictions generated by the user. The trust level of the user is given according to the analysis of his behavior. According to the user behavior, trust levels are released, to let the user have access to the application software. These levels, however, are not determined by clear and cut rules, that reflect a classification that can easily and universally be applied to human actions, but rather they must reflect the shady, undefined, and yet evident, characteristics of human behavior.

With the increase of behavior information, a more efficient support for behavior evidences analysis is generated, and the system continues performing the evidences analysis of the behavior and adjusting the trust in the user. The trust can change depending on the user, the localization, the time and the trust restrictions. With trust based on behavioral information and in the environment context information, it is possible to infer a minimum value for the initial trust, and, along the time, based on the behavior analysis and in the trust restrictions, the system will change the levels of trust. The heuristics adopted to define the initial trust can be defined according to the user activity at a particular moment, its location, the time that the behavior currently occurs, and his historical behavior.

The attribution of the subsequent levels of trust is processed in two stages.

Figure 2. The start of trust increase

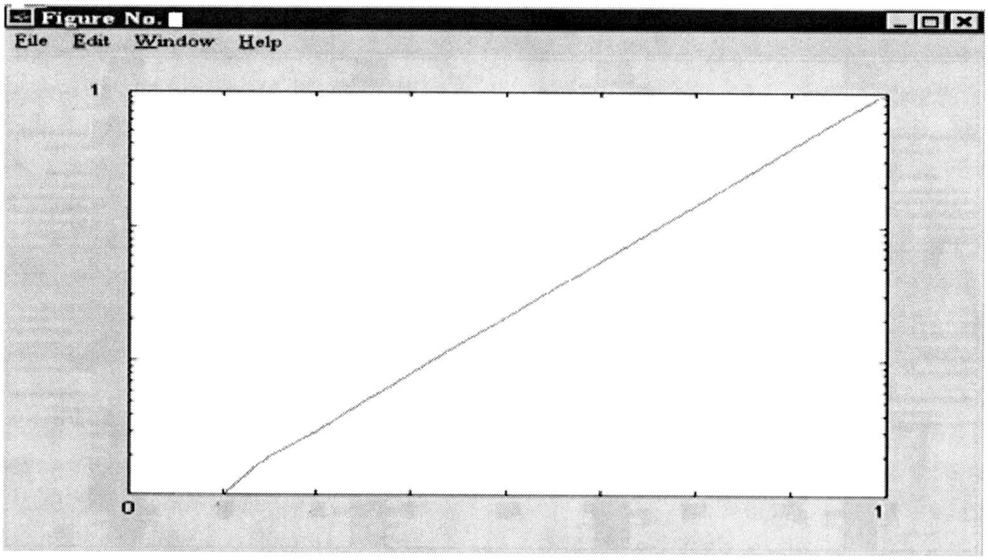

1st stage – Since there is not enough behavior information, it is attributed a minimum level of trust and, at the end, it accounts and stores the captured information.

2nd stage – In the subsequent accesses, when the user interaction increases, a verification is done, at first, in the trust restrictions database: if there are no restrictions, it compares the current behavior with the behavior information database, but if there are any changes in behavior, the alarm is triggered, the new behavior is stored, trust is re-calculated and security mechanisms are trigged.

According to Dempster (1967) and Shaffer (1976), a measure of confidence, in a universe set X that represents the total amount of confidence in the evidence of a particular set of circumstances, which varies between 0 and 1, is given by the function:

$$Cf\,(x){:}\ P\,(X) \leftarrow [0, 1]$$

Based on the evidences of the behavior, the application software establishes if it trusts the user with values in the interval (mC, mD), where mC is the initial minimum trust and mD is the initial minimum diffidence (see Figures 2-4). The confidence (Cf), the diffidence (Df) and the uncertainty (If) express all the possibilities of trust attribution to a user, in this form:

$$Cf + Df + If = 1, \text{ such that, } \{Cf, Df, If\} \quad (1)$$

The uncertainty If is defined as:

$$(If) = 1 - (Cf + Df) \quad (2)$$

If Bj is a user behavior, the System based on the evidences of the behavior, establishes if it trusts the user with values in the interval (mC, mD), where mC is the initial minimum trust and mD is the initial minimum diffidence.

The system checks the uncertainty of confidence, which is given by:

$$If\,(Bj) = 1 - (mC + mD) \quad (3)$$

If the behavior Bj is considered normal, confidence is assigned to the user, linearly and slowly.

Figure 3. The trust increase

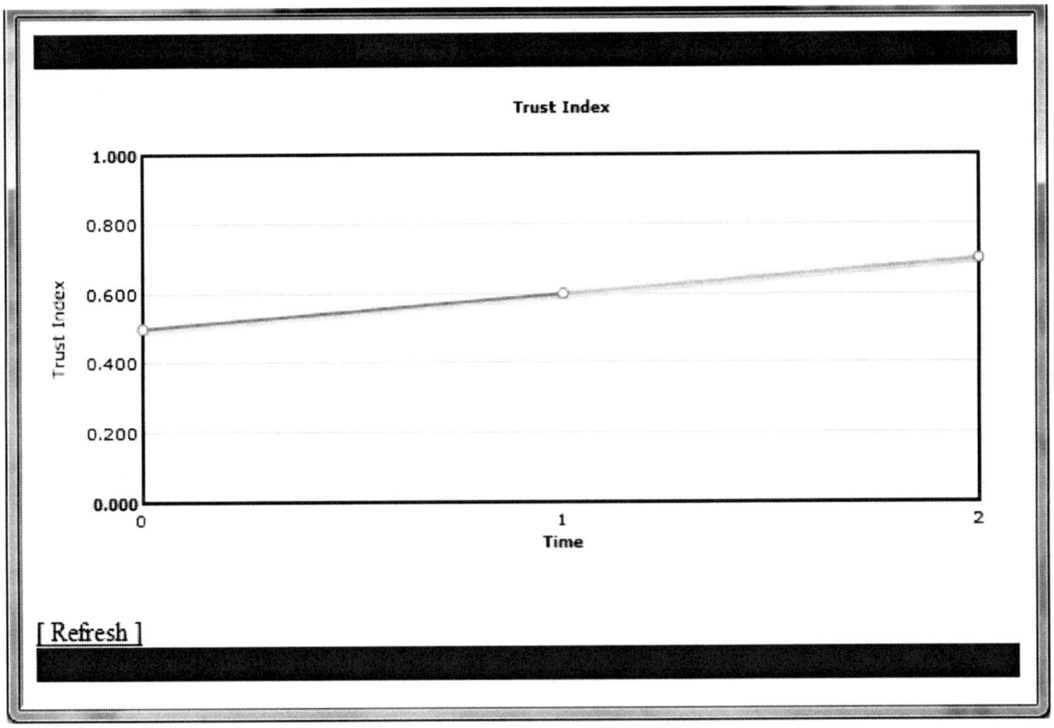

The loss of confidence is fast, and it grows exponentially.

$$Cf(x) = e^{-1x} \text{ for all } x \in (0, \infty[\qquad (4)$$

Figure 5 shows the decrease of trust in user behavior. If there is uncertainty, safety mechanisms, like sensors that capture the user information, can be triggered and compare it with the existing one in databases. If there is an unusual behavior, behavioral constraints are generated, decreasing the confidence and increasing distrust. If there are any differences, confidence in the user will be decreased, and even access and continuity of operation are liable to be blocked. In case of indications of changes, in the user's behavior, if there are uncertainties and divergences, security mechanisms and alert signals are triggered.

There is an uncertainty in the allocation of trust, however, because not always the complement of the expressed trust is distrust. Trust is a dimensional, or multidimensional, variable, because it is possible to trust, not trust or have no evidence to attribute trust over an interval of time. The user behavior analysis will be also concentrated on understanding how we can trust the user. Along the time and in accordance with the behavior analysis, the user trust level can be subject to variations, and thus, it is necessary to interact with the user, with biometric technology, to determine evidences so as to increase or to decrease trust in the user.

The client of a bank, for example, during a cash dispenser operation in a ATM Bank, can have his behavior analyzed with context variables (*who, where, when, what, why, how, rest*), which help to establish the evidences of behavioral trust, in its different degrees, based on past behaviors, actual behavior and restrictions of user behavior. The variables of context and the user behavior analysis will define the trust in the user behavior.

Figure 4. The uncertainty

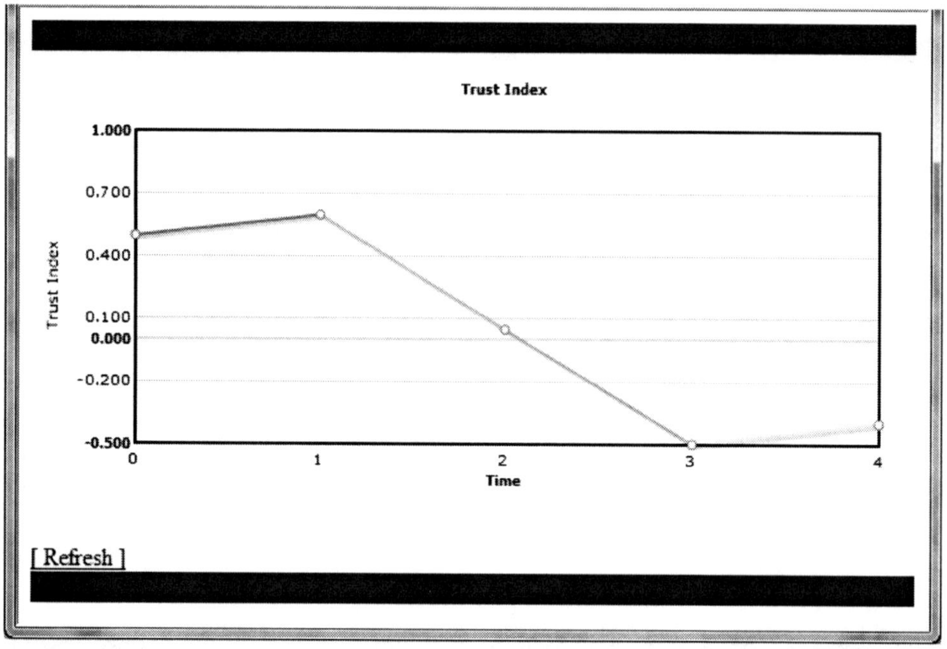

Figure 5. The trust decrease

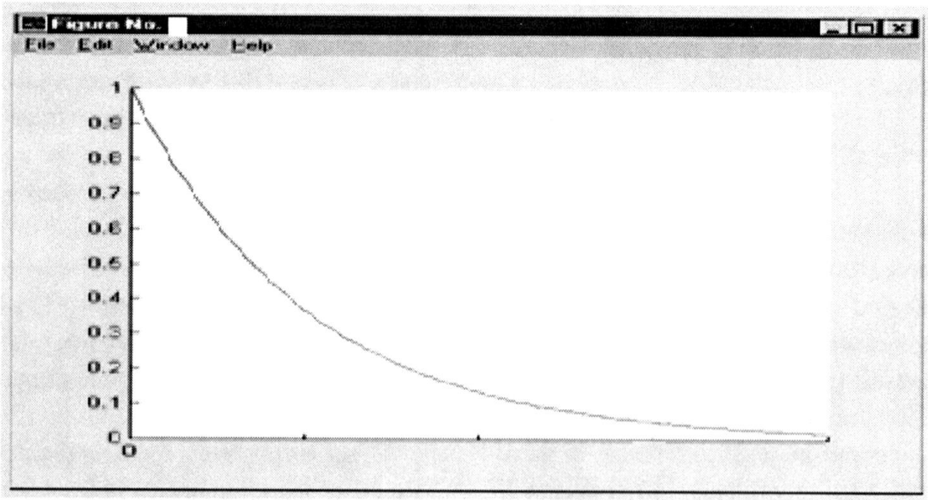

Biometrics Applied to User Behavior Uncertainty

In order to complement the trust in the user behavior analysis, the biometric technology is applied to capture behavior evidences and it collaborates with an adaptative security policy to the user. In case of indications of changes, in the user's behavior, if there are uncertainties and divergences, biometrics can help to identify and authenticate the user.

Biometrics (ancient Greek: bios ="life", metron ="measure") is the system of automated methods for uniquely recognizing humans, based upon one or more intrinsic physical or behavioral traits. Biometric technologies are pattern recognition systems that use image acquisition devices, such as scanners, cameras, sound or movement acquisition devices, such as microphones or platens in the case of voice recognition, or signature recognition technologies, to collect the biometric patterns or characteristics.

There are various types of biometric technology available in the market today and many successful applications of biometric technology.

Examples of physical characteristics include fingerprints, eye retinas and irises, facial patterns and hand measurements, while examples of mostly behavioral characteristics include signature, gaiting and typing patterns. Voice is considered a mix of both physical and behavioral characteristics (Kumar, 2003).

Multimodal is the use of multiple biometrics technology in a single application as combining, for example, face, voice, signature and fingerprint biometrics.

A biometric system deployment encompasses several functions, including identity registration, storage, assurance, protection, issuance, life cycle management, and system management, which all must be taken into account and integrated for the best results. Biometric technologies require very little cooperation or participation from the users. On the other hand, the capture of biometric characteristics that do not require the user participation, or that can be captured without the knowledge of the user, are actions that may be perceived as a threat to privacy by many individuals.

Thus, many projects aim at investigating more user friendly behavior interface techniques, handwriting and gesture recognition, interaction with pens, voice techniques and computational perception, interaction with sensors and electronic manipulation of artifacts (Kagal, 2001). Additional information about a person can be delivered through facial expressions, such as joy, sadness, surprise or anger, and this allows human beings to establish social relationships, to identify psychological profiles, to recognize the caller, to adjust and allow interaction with other people (Baer et al., 1968).

Human beings, to communicate, express much of their emotional state in facial expressions, and this information can be used computationally to interact with applications. Techniques for recognition of facial expressions that produce and influence relationships are discussed in Lee et al. (1996).Noticeable changes in facial expressions can also be perceived by recognition technologies through the movement of lips, even without sound and voice recognition (Beymer, Poggio, 1995). Physical and psychological aspects influence the human brain in the identification process. Not just the face, height, body shape and face are used in recognition, but also facial expressions, body language, and the context in which the face or the person is classified, denote the person's style, and are observed to achieve an effective recognition (Birnbrauer, 1979).

The issue of privacy becomes more serious with biometric-based recognition systems, because biometric characteristics may provide additional information about the background of an individual. The physical and behavioral characteristics of humans can be differentiated, compared, stored and converted into code to automate the authentication methods for identifying people.

Any human biological or behavioral characteristics can become a biometric identifier, provided the following properties are respected (Dhir et al., 2010):

- **Universality** - Every person should have the biometric characteristics.
- **Distinctiveness** - Two people should not have identical biometric characteristics.
- **Permanence** - The characteristics should not vary or change with time.

- **Collect Ability** - Obtaining and measuring the biometric feature(s) should be easy, non-intrusive, reliable, and robust, as well as cost effective for the application.

Biometric applications can operate in two modes, which are verification and identification. Verification is the process of comparing a presented biometric template with stored biometric reference(s) that are associated only with that specific user. Verification applications are often referred to as one-to-one matching (or 1:1). Identification is also referred to as one-to-many matching (or 1:N) to make sure that the person is not yet enrolled in the system and receiving benefits under another name or identity. In contrast with probably every other method of authentication, biometric authentication aims at being completely non-transferable. From this approach it is possible to define an adaptive security policy, based on behavioral analysis of user and biometrics to insure the effective information security management.

USER BEHAVIOR ANALYSIS WITH ADAPTATIVE SECURITY POLICY

The adaptative security policy based on user behavior analysis is the basis of the information security management, when it comes to understanding the needs of users providing unbiased, high-quality and managing user relationships effectively. However, to achieve the whole security target in Computing and related technologies, it is necessary to have more than the current core technologies or security policies, for it will also be necessary to analyze the user behavior and the security environment.

According to Skinner (1991), a person will associate the situations he has experienced with similar ones, will generalize this learning process, and will expand it to a larger context in life. A person tends to repeat the behavior in situations that are repeated. In an analogous way, during a software application session, the user behavior is conditioned when interacting with electro-electronic devices and software applications: his actions tend to be repetitive and predictable. Therefore, based on the user behavior analysis, it is possible to know the user profile and his way of acting. This information can be fundamental to create an adaptive security policy, reflecting the user interaction with the system more faithfully.

FUTURE RESEARCH DIRECTIONS

For future directions an intelligent system for information security management should therefore be prepared not to anticipate every possible action that may be taken in the future, but to be flexible enough to adapt itself more easily to the changes that will certainly come, identifying technological trends and knowing more about human behavior, which will always be the crucial aspect of security. It would be most helpful to adopt neuro-fuzzy systems, because of their capacity to use past experiences and learn new ones. Weights can be attributed in the fuzzyfication process, according to the rules that were previously established for the variables *(who, where, when, what, why, how, rest)*, which help to establish the evidences of behavioral trust, in its different degrees. A neuro-fuzzy system can feed the user behavioral database continuously, interacting with the fuzzyfication mechanism, so as to keep trust levels updated according to the user behavior, in a more accurate and faithful way, and to give more robustness to the system based on user behavior.

CONCLUSION

The steady and fast evolution of Information Technology and Communications, in its manifold aspects, has reached such a state of complexity and sophistication, that it is necessary to think of a Security Management System that is not only robust enough to correspond to our current needs, but it may also be intelligent and prepared for the future, so as to guarantee that society be really benefitted by the use of Information Technology, and be not trapped in by it.

Generally speaking, all legal electronic transactions over the net, wired or not, need full protection from malicious attacks, and every kind of malware that may be perpetrated viciously and criminally to get hold of them. Finance, economy, commerce, industry, education, services, entertainment, just to mention a few, are some examples of well known activities in our society that have been strongly benefitted by these new technologies. However, they have also become extremely vulnerable to electronic frauds and attacks, which cost billions of dollars every year, invading one's own privacy and having access to privileged data information.

No system is ever safe, and it should always be in an alert state, so as to be easily responsive and adaptive to upcoming changes. These are caused both by technology and human behavior, which occur over the time systematically. New technologies make former techniques and security procedures obsolete, and they require revision and updating. Human behavior also changes over the time, influenced both by cultural aspects and by the new technologies themselves, so that human beings establish new habits and develop new attitudes.

A modern and intelligent system for information security management should therefore be prepared not to anticipate every possible action that may be taken in the future, but to be flexible enough to adapt itself more easily to the changes that will certainly come, identifying technological trends and knowing more about human behavior, which will always be the crucial aspect of security. The knowledge of human behavior is fundamental to guarantee adaptability to a security policy, which may sustain a system to manage security information, in the dynamics of a fast changing technological environment and society. A robust security management information system, therefore, will not only guarantee individual privacy, but it also will bring benefits and promote welfare to all society.

REFERENCES

Baer, D. M., Wolf, M. M., & Risley, T. R. (1968). Some current dimensions of applied behavior analysis. *Journal of Applied Behavior Analysis*, *1*, 91–97. doi:10.1901/jaba.1968.1-91

Beymer, D., & Poggio, T. (1995). *Face recognition from one example view*. A.I. Memo 1536, Massachusetts Institute of Technology, September.

Birnbrauer, J. S. (1979). Applied behavior analysis, service and the acquisition of knowledge. *The Behavior Analyst*, *2*, 15–21.

Brosso, I. (2006) *Users continuous authentication in computers networks*. Doctoral Thesis in Digital Systems at Polytechnic School of Sao Paulo University, Brazil. Retrieved from http://www.teses.usp.br/teses/disponiveis/3/3141/tde-08122006-170242/en.php

Brosso, I., La Neve, A., Bressan, G., & Ruggiero, W. V. (2010). A continuous authentication system based on user behavior analysis. *International Conference on Availability, Reliability and Security, International Conference*, (pp. 380-385). Krakow, Poland, February 15-February 18. ISBN: 978-0-7695-3965-2

Dempster, A. P. (1967). Upper and lower probabilities induced by a multi-valued mapping. *Annals of Mathematical Statistics*, *38*, 325–339. doi:10.1214/aoms/1177698950

Dhir, V., Acet, A. S., Kumar, R., & Singh, G. (2010). Biometric recognition: A modern era for security. *International Journal of Engineering Science and Technology*, *2*(8), 3364-3380. ISSN: 0975-5462

Kagal, L., Undercoffer, A. J., & Vigil, T. (2001). *Enforcing security in ubiquitous environments*. Tech. Report, University of Maryland, Baltimore County.

Kumar, A., Wong, D. C., Shen, H. C., & Jain, A. K. (2003). *Personal verification using palmprint and hand geometry biometric*. 4th International Conference on Audio- and Video-based Biometric Person Authentication, Guildford, UK, June 9-11.

Lee, C. H., Kim, J. S., & Park, K. H. (1996). Automatic face location in a complex background using motion and color information. *Pattern Recognition*, *29*(11), 1877–1889. doi:10.1016/0031-3203(96)00036-2

Marcus, L. (2004). *Introduction to logical foundations of an adaptive security infrastructure*. Workshop on Logical Foundations of an Adaptive Security Infrastructure (WOLFASI), A subworkshop of the LICS Foundations of Computer Security (FCS'04) Workshop, LICS '04, July 12-13, Turku, Finland.

Mass, Y. (2001). *Distributed trust in open multi-agent systems. Lecture Notes in Artificial Intelligence, 2246*. Springer-Verlag.

Platzer, C. (2004) *Trust-based security in Web services*. Master's Thesis – Technical University of Vienna, May.

Schilit, B., & Theimer, M. (1994). Disseminating active map information to mobile hosts. *IEEE Network*, *8*(5), 22–32. doi:10.1109/65.313011

Shaffer, G. (1976). *A Mathematical theory of evidence*. Princeton, NJ: Princeton University Press.

Skinner, B. F. (1991). *The behavior of organisms* (p. 473). Copley Pub Group.

Todorov, J. C. (1990). The K&S in Brazil. *Journal of the Experimental Analysis of Behavior*, *54*, 151–152. doi:10.1901/jeab.1990.54-151

Witter, G. P. (2005). *Metaciência e psicologia*. São Paulo, Brazil: ALINEA. (in Portuguese)

ADDITIONAL READING

Azzini, A., Marrara, S., Sassi, R., & Scotti, F. (2007) A fuzzy approach to multimodal biometric authentication. In *Proceedings of the 11th International Conference on Knowledge-Based and Intelligent Information & Engineering Systems, KES'07*, Vietri sul Mare (SA), Italy, September.

Bauer, L., Ligatti, J., & Walker, D. (2002) *A calculus for composing security policies* - Technical Report TR-655-02, Princeton University. retrieved 9 December 2010 from http://citeseer.ist.psu.edu/bauer02calculus.html

Bidan, C., & Issarny, V. (1998) Dealing with multi-policy security in large open distributed systems, *Proceedings of 5th European Symposium on Research in Computer Security*, pages 51–66, September

Brosso, I., Bressan, G., & Ruggiero, W. V. (2010) Known User Continuous Authentication System for Consumer Application Software - *Proceedings of 2010 7th IEEE Consumer Communications and Networking Conference (CCNC)*, 9-12 Jan. 2010, On page(s): 1 – 2, Location: Las Vegas, NV, Print ISBN: 978-1-4244-5175-3

Burns,j.; Cheng, A. ; Gurung, P.; Rajagopalan, S.; Rao,P.; Rosenbluth,D.; Surendran,A.;Martin, D. (2001) Automatic management of network security policy *DARPA Information Survivability Conference and Exposition (DISCEX II)*. Volume II. Pages 12-26. Anaheim, CA. June 2001. Pub. IEEE Computer Society Press, Los Alamitos, California. ISBN: 0769512127

Corin, R; Durante,A.; Etalle,S.; Hartel,P. (2003) A trace logic for local security properties, *InternationalWorkshop on Software Verification and Validation (SVV)*, Mumbai, India, December.

Halpern, J. Y. (2003). *Reasoning about uncertainty*. Cambridge, Mass: MIT Press.

Hansmann, U. (2003). *Pervasive Computing: The Mobile World*. Springer.

Jain, A. K., Ross, A., & Sharath Pankanti, S. (2006). *Biometrics: A tool for information security*. IEEE Transactions On Information Forensics and Security.

Keromytis, A. Parekh,j.; Gross,p.; Kaiser,G.; Misra,V.; Nieh,J.;Rubenstein,D.; Stolfo,S. (2003) A holistic approach to secure survivability, *ACM Workshop on Survivable and Self-Regenerative Systems (SRS), held in conjunction with the 10th ACM International Conference on Computer and Communications Security (CCS)*. October, Fairfax, VA.

Marcus, L. (2003) Local and global requirements in an adaptive security infrastructure, *International Workshop on Requirements for High Assurance Systems (RHAS 2003)*, September.

Pankanti Prabhakar, S., & Jain, A. K. (2003). *Biometric recognition: security & privacy concerns*. IEEE Security & Privacy Magazine.

Pavlovic, D. (2000) *Towards semantics of self-adaptive software,* In P. Robertson, R. L., and Shrobe, H., eds., Self-Adaptive Software. Springer-Verlag. 2000, pp: 50-64

Poslad, S. (2009) *Ubiquitous Computing Smart Devices, Smart Environments and Smart Interaction*. Wiley. ISBN 978-0-470-03560-3, Retrieved 9 December 2010 from http://www.elec.qmul.ac.uk/people/stefan/ubicom/index.html.

Skinner, B. F. (1938). *The behavior of organisms*. New York: Appleton-Century-Crofts.

Skinner, B. F. (1953). *Science and Human Behavior*.

Stajano, F. (2002). *Security for Ubiquitous Computing* (1st ed.). John Wiley & Sons. doi:10.1002/0470848693

Teoh, A. (2004). Nearest Neighbourhood Classifiers in a Bimodal Biometric Verification System Fusion Decision Scheme, Journal of Research and Practice in Information. *Technology (Elmsford, N.Y.)*, *36*(1).

Todorov, J. C. (1990). The K&S in Brazil. *Journal of the Experimental Analysis of Behavior*, *54*, 151–152. doi:10.1901/jeab.1990.54-151

Truong, K. N., Abowd, G. D., & Brotherton, J. A. (2001) *Who, What, When, Where, How:* Design Issues of Capture & Access Applications. Georgia Institute of Technology Technical Report GIT-GVU-01-02. January.

Weiser; M.; Gold, R.; & Brown, J. S. (1999) *Ubiquitous computing* - Retrieved 9 December 2010 from http://www.research.ibm.com/journal/sj/384/weiser.html.

Whitman, M. E. (2003). Enemy at the Gate: Threats to Information Security. *Communications of the ACM*, *46*(8), 91–95. doi:10.1145/859670.859675

York, J., & Pendharkar, P. C. (2004). *Human–computer interaction issues for mobile computing in a variable work context*, Int. *J. Human-Computer Studies*, *60*, 771–797. doi:10.1016/j.ijhcs.2003.07.004

Zhu, F. Mutka. M.W. (2006) The master key: A private authentication approach for pervasive computing environments *In Fourth IEEE International Conference on Pervasive Computing and Communications (PerCom'06)*.

Chapter 20
Detecting Credit Fraud in E-Business System:
An Information Security Perspective on the Banking Sector in UK

Md Delwar Hussain Mahdi
Applied Research Centre for Business and Information Technology (ARCBIT), UK

Karim Mohammed Rezaul
Centre for Applied Internet Research (CAIR), Glyndŵr University, UK

ABSTRACT

Credit fraud (also known as credit card fraud) in e-business is a growing concern, especially in the banking sector. E-business has been established mainly on the platform of Internet system. With the evolution of electronic technologies, a faster e-transaction has been made possible by the Internet. It has been noticed that Internet fraud or e-business fraud is increasing with the increase of e-transaction. A few sorts of card (debit or credit) fraud are decreasing by the banks and the government providing detection and prevention systems. But Card-not-Present fraud losses are increasing at higher rate. In online transactions, it is obvious that there is no chance to use Chip and Pin, and also no chance to use card face-to-face. Card-not-Present fraud losses are growing in an unprotected and undetected way. This chapter seeks to investigate the current debate regarding the credit fraud and vulnerabilities in online banking and to study some possible remedial actions to detect and prevent credit fraud. A comprehensive study of online banking and e-business has been undertaken with a special focus on credit fraud detection. This research reveals a lot of channels of credit fraud that are increasing day by day. These kinds of fraud are the main barrier of promoting e-business in the banking sector.

DOI: 10.4018/978-1-4666-0197-0.ch020

INTRODUCTION

E-commerce or e-business is the important application of Internet. Internet is the main tool for e-business and banks have changed their business model with the help of Internet. Banks have extended their facilities via online. E-transaction has increased rapidly in the banking sector. The growth of online transaction gives a tremendous opportunity to banks and consumers. But credit fraud detection and prevention in the banking sector is still remained unsecure. In spite of risk, the main reason for Internet's popularity is as a marketing tool and with low cost of an online presence (Kling 1994; Cronin 1996; Boyle & Alwitt 1999). So in regard of Internet, main important issue is security (Gonca and Faruk 2009).

Statement of the Problems

Credit Fraud through Internet is continuously giving serious concern in the Information Technology arena. The tendency of credit fraud is rising with the development of Information and communication Technology. Internet has created a global market place. Internet aids e-fraudsters to spread their activities in the banking sector. E-fraudsters use Internet as a best weapon to reach to the consumer in order to steal their bank money. Banks should protect all the sensitive data providing strong detection system by using Internet Technology and also adopting fraud awareness programme.

Aims and Objectives

Aim of this research is to find out the way of credit fraud happened and, detection and prevention system in e-business in the banking sector. It also critically analyses data and findings from the research. This could be:

- Outlining the different channels of Credit Fraud in e-business in the Banking sector in UK.
- Investigating the specific reason that helps to increase credit fraud in the banking sector.
- Justifying the rule of banks and government towards fraud prevention and detection that will help save consumer.
- And try to find out some possible solutions for the future.

This research will also analyse the most vulnerable route that e-fraudsters use to make fraud to the consumers'. How banks are fighting against Credit Fraud. And what should be done to stop internal (employee) credit fraud.

Significance of the Research

It is very crucial to understand the risk of credit fraud in online transactions such as banking and shopping. Making fraud has become easy with the help of Internet and the development of ICT. In the age of globalisation, e-business is increasing rapidly and e-transaction spreading all walks of life that makes faster the lifestyle and richer to individual. E-business totally depends on two things; Internet & ICT. This is good news for bad guy also. With the help of technology, Social Hackers, e-retailer (false retailer), bank's employee and e-fraudster all are trying to convince consumers by malicious spam e-mail and website, telephone and fax to reveal their personal identity, card details and bank information. They spread their activities in online and offline (social work) as well. The possibility of fraud (Neuman 1991) is increasing though the government launched new rules and regulations to protect and detect their activities, and also all the new technologies try to control fraudulent activities in e-business. But e-fraudsters are still working well with their network and credit fraud remains the same or in some instance it is increasing.

Overview of this Research

This research has been organised as follows. The following section describes the literature review of the existing literatures relevant to this research. The subsequent section introduces the methodology of this research that explains how the research is done. We then investigate the research findings from the data collected from primary and secondary sources. The later section depicts analysis results and makes discussions on that. Finally we draw the conclusions, recommendations and further research of the existing research.

LITERATURE REVIEW

The emphasis of this chapter is to show the overview on the topics that how online transactions (banking and shopping) make consumer vulnerable and increase the risk of credit fraud in the future. In order to have a better understanding of the whole process of Credit Fraud and fraud Detection in the Banking sector, we carried out a comprehensive review of the principal themes in the literatures (Bologna 1984, Brian 1995, Hewer and Howcroft 1999, Williams and Kikalas 2005, Phillip et al. 2004, Heike and Thomas 2006, Okenyi and Owens 2007, Couto et al. 2008 and Gonca and Faruk 2009). Taking these works as references, we can define the concept of credit fraud (CF) in online, as the process of creating and making a clever & elicit understanding between buyers (consumer) and sellers (false e-retailer), e-fraudsters and clients through online activities that exchange a false ideas and offer a big winner that make client to fraud.

Credit Fraud

According to shorter Oxford English Dictionary (2002), Fraud is "The use of false representations to gain unjust advantage ; criminal deception; the quality of being deceitful insincerity; a state of delusion; an act or instance of deception; a dishonest artifice or trick". One might easily think that credit fraud refers simply to the use of others credit card money without authorisation. Actually, it comes in too many shapes and sizes, for example- theft, market manipulation, insider dealing check and mortgage fund, firm fraud, advance fee, overdraft, misinterpretations, conspiracy to defraud and host of other scams (Brian 1995).

Advantages of Internet

Since the introduction of Internet, banks are expanding their activities through Internet. Technology (Internet & phone) creates new channels for interaction with customer (Hewer and Howcroft 1999). Internet facilitates new distribution channels in retail banking (Tim 2003). Internet helps to access banking systems from remote area (kelden and Scott 2005). Consumers get more facilities in shopping, paying bills and money transfer etc. The advantages of Internet have also been studied by other authors, such as Hanson 2000; Turban et al. 2002; Turban et al. 2004 and Chaffey 2004. It creates a global market place for a business organisation and individuals. It makes easy to advertise products or services in online to the consumers and buy (goods or services) from virtual shop. It gives us convenient banking and quick information about variety of facilities. Thus Internet creates a vast opportunities for business (NFIC 2009). Internet is a great place to find gifts, compare price, and avoid the crush in stores during the holiday season. It invites us for shopping in the online shopping malls in future (John and Robyn 2002). Many legitimate companies sell their products or services through the Internet. Charities use the Internet to ask for donations.

Information Security

Information for all business organisations are an asset. So it is important and worthy of protection. For Information Security (IS) we need to comply with laws and regulations, reducing falsification of data and unauthorised access to information for minimising fraud risk. Authentication in the banking system has a significant contribution to provide all these services. It is done through password system that is not a top level of security measure. Information Security (IS) measure is an urgent need in the banking sector. No techniques or procedures can provide all the security services. Crackers always create risk in our daily life. To meet the challenge (from crackers) for IT specialists need to keep one step ahead of crackers. IT personnel need to know about the sort of attacking style and methods. To protect Information Security there are lots of technologies available for encryption of network intrusion. But at present no system is completely secure.

Virtual Banking or E-Banking or Internet Banking

A computer-controlled Web based banking services system that does not involve the usual bank branch is called virtual banking. The traditional banking system is replaced by an electronic paradigm through virtual banking. This is an innovative banking system. Costless advertisement, consumers demand, business motivation and technological improvement are the key drivers of virtual banking. The adoption of changing marketing environment (style and system) and the development of Information & Communication Technology (ICT) are causing revolution in the virtual banking system. Consumers pushing and competition in banks are two vehicles to drive in the virtualization. So, we need to consider few factors in the virtual banking: Computerization (reduce cost and time), automated teller machine (ATM) (facilitate to consumers that boost to virtual banking) and credit or debit cards helps both consumers and retailers keeping far away from cash handling.

Importance of Internet Banking

Internet banking (IB) reduces cost and time, provide convenience banking to the consumers and control over finance. Online banking operate transactions faster and easier with 24/7 self-service applications. It makes the institution more valuable to the customers and also reduces the operational costs. A physical transaction cost for bank is considerably higher than an online transaction. IB also reduces costs and time by minimising queue traffic, consumers' phone calls and printing transactions statement for mail. IB referred to as "green banking" that develop a paperless statements and billing. IB has become more forward since first introduced. Before, it allows customers to view their statements online, balance transfer between accounts and pay bills to the respective business (telephone companies or financial institutions). Over time, IB has fulfilled more demand from their online banking system. IB provides instant access to information. Consumers are looking for more facilities and added functionality in multiple areas. Easy access into online statements enables consumers to understand transaction history and helps manage their account more sustainable. Paperless statement is also a key cost benefit for the banks.

Credit Fraud and Economy

E-Banking (IB) creates lots of harms for economy through Credit fraud. Internet worm or virus spread instantly over computer systems and damage the systems. Williams and Kikalas (2005) made an examination in 2003 and showed that 82% of surveyed companies are attacked by virus or worm. Credit fraud has a great impact on economy to make it worse. The spike in fraudulent activities hit strongly with the start of the credit crunch (Victoria 2009). Plastic card transactions were 6.9 billion in 2007, whereas Fraud losses on plastic cards were £535 million in 2007 (BBA 2008). Credit Crunch increase fraudulent activities (AFP 2009, Ordnance 2008). According to the UK Association of chief Police Officers (ACPO), fraud now is estimated at costing the UK £13.9 billion a year (Ordnance 2008). The sufferers of credit fraud are the large group of consumers, shareholders, stakeholders, banks industries and government. Credit fraud (CF) has become a great threat to the consumers and it works against expanding e-business, and also fraud creates a challenge to the banks. Most of the CF are organised which is regarded as economically motivated offending involving more than two people (Chris et al. 2009) that is related to money laundering, murder, drug trafficking, hijacking, auditing, and financing.

Online CF is one kind of "cyber fraud", "e-fraud" or "e-crime" (SOCA 2009) that is merely happened to involve information and communication technology (ICT) (Douglas and Brian 2000). The purpose of exploration of stolen credit card information is to illegal access into information for financial gain (Douglas and Brian 2000). They interprets that Internet enhances cyber crime which is conducted through global electronic networks.

Credit Fraud: As an Internet Crime or E-Crime

The global rise of Internet has produced corresponding increases of credit fraud in e-business. With the rising of e-transaction in banking sector, credit fraud is rising rapidly. E-criminals are very smart in Internet technology. They can crook consumers' valuable information, identity, bank details, social-security number, national insurance number etc. from online shopping or banking transactions. Sometimes it is very difficult to recognise who are the reputable online sellers or criminals use Internet to rob people (NFIC 2009 and NCL 2009). Various Internet fraud complaints include auction fraud, credit and debit card fraud, non-delivery of goods or services (Futurist 2009). Internet has done faster and increases the volume of size of credit fraud. So, the main objectives of all cyber crimes are to obtain money by anyhow and with that relate e-criminals and dishonest employees.

Credit Fraud through Scams

We are all vulnerable to illegal scams via Internet. Online Credit Fraud includes auction fraud, credit and debit card fraud, bank details fraud, social security number fraud, valuable personal information and identity fraud through fake scams. For example - phishing, fake check scams, General Merchandise, Money Offers, Lottery Clubs, Advance fee Loan, Prizes or Sweepstakes, Friendship and Sweetheart Swindles, work-at-home plan, Information and adult services, Cramming, Bogus Invoices, prize promotions, Internet access services, charitable Solicitations and so on (NFIC & IFW 2009). Thus Internet creates some major new challenges for consumers and organisations (Phillip et al. 2004). Phishing attack is performed due to vulnerability of consumers' and Phisher creates bogus websites and looks like lawful seller one (Ankobia 2004).

Detection in the Banking Sector

In spite of providing all the security measures and control, banks and consumers are still at risk for having their information stolen. To protect and detect fraud, banks need to have very strong IT Security Policy and procedure, good network and password standards. Also they can adopt awareness programme and training for employees about e-crime that will reduce employees' vulnerability (Okenyi and Owens 2007). Process redesign may reduce credit fraud. UK Banks indicated that around one in five of their call centre staffs were involved in fraudulent activities (Victoria 2009). E-business security can be solved, if the entire Internet companies take part in the worldwide Internet Security System (Gonca and Faruk 2009). Anti-viruses and anti-spyware programmes, firewalls and so on, are doing many things about security but all of these solutions proved to be still insufficient (Gonca and Faruk 2009). As the growth of electronic payments fraud, Banks need to be extra vigilant to make sure they are not victimized. So, Banks should adapt various business processes to block or minimise fraud losses. Card Watch (2009) is the Banking industries' body in UK that work with police, retailers and other organisations to fight against plastic card fraud (BIS 2009). Also as a consumer, you need to know about e-crime, do research around you how scam can victimise you. Beware of unsolicited communication where you are asked to supply credit card or bank details, user names and password, Internet account, think twice before giving information to unknown parties.

METHODOLOGY

This section explains the overall overview of the research methodology which is accomplished by the authors. Valuable information has been gathered in this research to enable the justification of the reliability and validity of findings. We collect data from the people who are using online for banking and shopping. This is a quantitative research based on the field survey and we follow the experimental investigation provided in the literature (Bryman 2004). Primary data collection from the field survey was the main method of data collection. To make a better understanding and a worthwhile research, we collected all the related secondary data from reliable sources.

Data Collection Methods

In this research, authors used survey methods as the main data collection method because it is easy to get response by interview. This research distributes questionnaires to the customers, college and university students, and the people who are related to the banks. A total of 1600 questionnaires were distributed for both e-mail and field survey. 800 questionnaires were sent through e-mail and another 800 questionnaire were distributed for the field survey. Total 744 feedbacks were received in which 268 responses came from online survey and 476 came from field survey. The response rate was 48% and 89 questionnaires were not fill in completely and excluded from this study. So, the remaining 655 feedbacks were used to analysis.

The prime concern of the questionnaire was to explore the consumers' attitude, their behaviour, activities & Internet usability and decision making tendency when they use online banking. E-mail addresses were collected from yahoo group and facebook. The secondary data were collected from books, journals, online books, online journals, conferences papers, reliable website, government and financial organisations publications, computer security publications etc.

Ethical Consideration

During the data collection, we were very careful and made sure that respondent's privacy would keep secret strictly and confidentially. Also in the questionnaire we did not include any question that can make respondents vulnerable to risk.

RESEARCH FINDINGS

This section represents the responses and feedbacks from the participants as we have explained in the previous section (methodology). The research questionnaires were distributed among the customers regardless of their online banking credit fraud.

Online Banking Fraud

In 2008, losses for online banking fraud from scams such as phishing and spyware have increased 132% from the previous year (Fraud 2009). Due to increase in phishing incidents,

Figure 1. Graphical representation of online banking fraud losses (Fraud 2009)

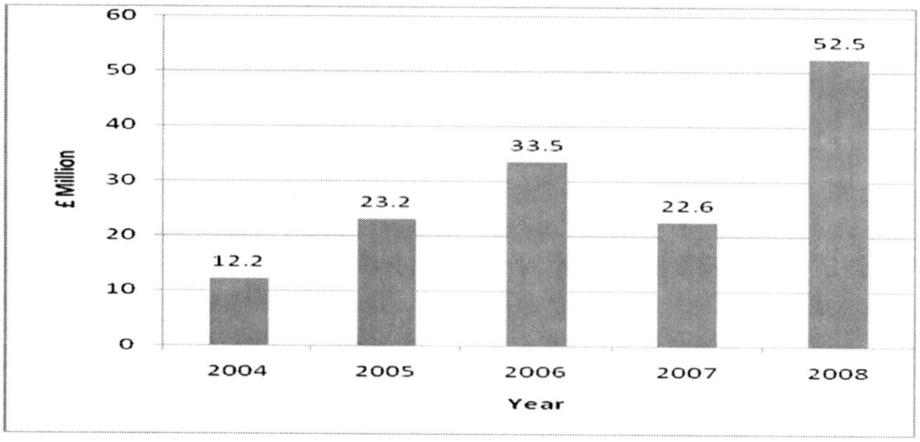

online banking customers are increasingly being targeted by malware attacks. And over 10.5 billion transactions were made on UK cards in 2008, a total value of £603 billion (Fraud 2009). Card spending on Internet has risen over the last five years. Card-not-present fraud losses were rising up 13% in 2008 by Phone, Internet and mail order (Fraud 2009). It was the largest type of card fraud in the UK. From 2000 to 2008 Card-not-present fraud losses rose by 350%; over the same time period, the total value of online shopping alone was increased by 1,077% up (Fraud 2009). Figure 1 shows year-on-year fraud losses in online banking from 2004 to 2008 and all figures are in millions.

Plastic Cards

According to the UK Card Association and APACS (2009), there were 148.9 million payment cards in issue in the UK at the end of 2008, which included 76.3 million Debit cards, 72.5 million credit and charge cards. Over 10.5 billion transactions were made on UK cards in 2008, to a total value of £603 billion. The average number of cards per person in 2008 was 3.4. Spending on plastic cards in the UK amounted to £397 billion last year, which comprised £247 billion on Debit cards and £150 billion on credit & charge cards. Internet card spending has risen nearly fourfold over the last five years to £41.2 billion in 2008. Figure 2 explains year-on-year annual fraud losses on plastic card in UK and how it is growing up from 2000 to 2008.

Card-Not-Present Fraud Losses in UK

According to the UK Card association and APACS (2009), Phone, Internet and mail order (card-not-present or CNP) fraud was £328.4 million in 2008 (up 13%). This is the largest type of card fraud in the UK. From 2000 to 2008 Card-not-present fraud losses rose by 350%; over the same time period, the total value of online shopping alone increased by 1,077% (up from £3.5 billion in 2000 to £41.2 billion in 2008) (Fraud 2009). Figure 3 shows clearly how Card-not-Present fraud losses were increasing year-on-year in UK from 2000 to 2008.

Card Fraud Losses Spilt by Type (as Percentage of Total Losses)

Where card usage and transaction volume continue to increase, plastic card fraud losses against total turnover at 0.124% are still significantly less than in 2001 (before the introduction of Chip and PIN), when fraud to turnover was 0.183% (Fraud

Figure 2. Annual losses on plastic card in UK (Fraud 2009)

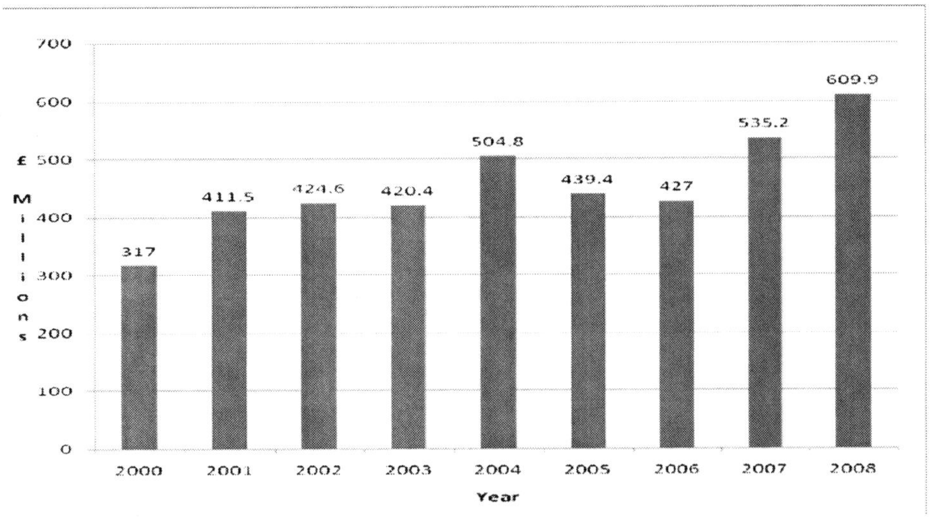

Figure 3. Card-not-present fraud losses in UK (Fraud 2009)

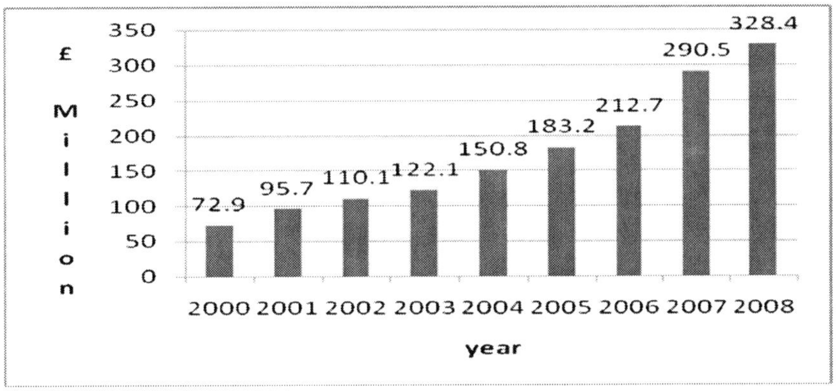

2009). Figure 4 (a & b) show that how card fraud is getting changed over time and how fraudsters are changing their technique and style with the help of technology. In Figure 4(a) shows that 1998 Card-not-present fraud was only 10%, with the increase of e-transaction this kind of fraud was growing up at 54% at Figure 4(b).

UK Retailer (Face-to-Face) Fraud

According to the UK card association and APACS (2009), UK retailer (face-to-face) fraud was £98.5m in 2008 (up 35%), where in the UK high street have declined by 55% since peaking at £218.8m in 2004. Face-to-face total card fraud losses year-on-year was decrising though it was increasing in 2008. It has been possible to minimise the retailer fraud with the help of Chip and PIN and password authentication. Figure 5 shows year-on-year changes of face-to-face card fraud amount in UK from 2004 to 2008.

Internet or E-Commerce Fraud on Cards

Internet or E-commerce fraud on cards is estimated at £181.7 million in 2008, an increase of 2% since 2007 when e-commerce fraud losses

Figure 4. Card fraud losses spilt by type (as percentage of total losses) (Fraud 2009)

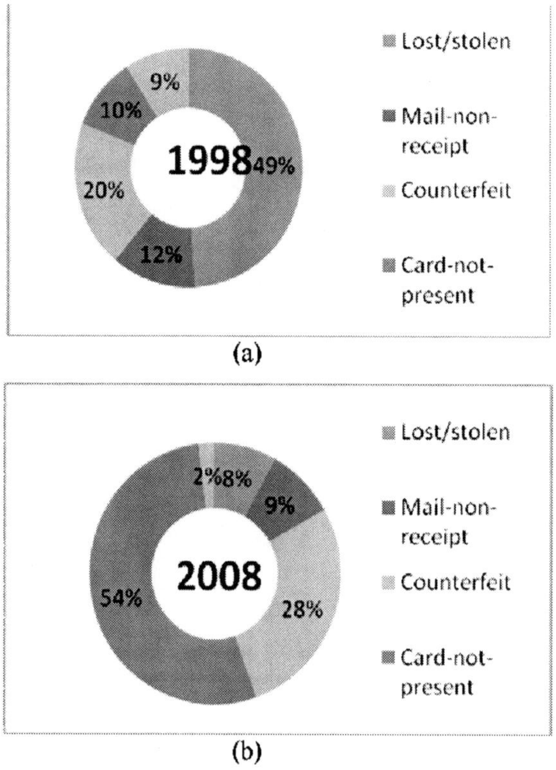

Figure 5. UK retailer (face-to-face) fraud (in million) (Fraud 2009)

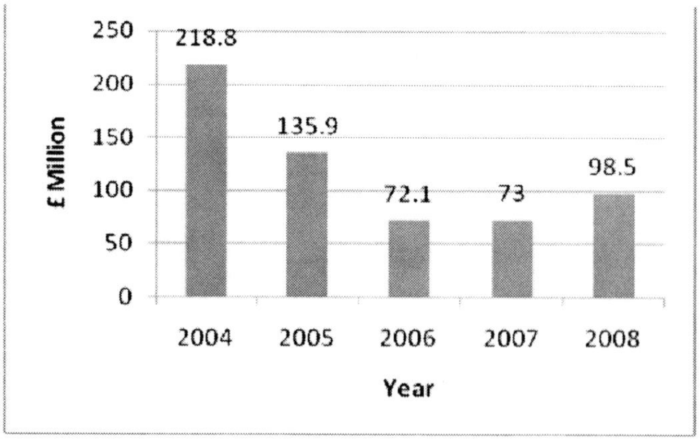

were £178.3m. Internet fraud now accounts for 55% of card-not-present losses down from 61% in 2007. The fall in losses may be an indication that fraud is migrating away from the Internet to other card-not-present channels (Fraud 2009). Internet or e-commerce fraud is increasing outside the UK at higher rate than UK (domestic) by using UK issued card. Figure 6 shows total e-commerce fraud in UK and outside the UK by UK issued card.

Figure 6. Internet or E-commerce fraud on cards (Fraud 2009)

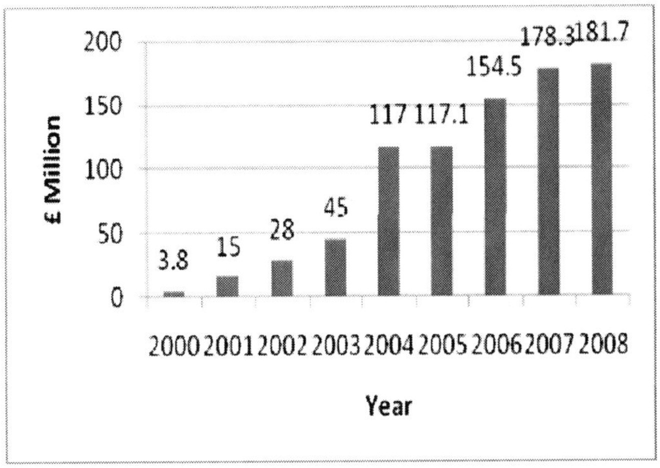

Phishing

Phishers set up a website that is a fake version of genuine bank website, and then send out thousands or even millions of spam emails trying to convince people to click on a link that will send them to the fake website. There were 43,991 phishing websites targeted against UK banks and building societies in 2008, up from 25,797, which was in turn an increase of 14,156 in 2006 (Fraud 2009).

Malware

Although the rising number of phishing incidents has undoubtedly helped to raise online banking fraud losses, we also know that online banking customers are increasingly being targeted by malware attacks. Malware (malicious software) includes computer viruses that can install on a computer without the user's knowledge.

Spyware

Spyware is a type of computer virus that can be installed on someone's computer without his/her realisation. Spyware is sometimes capable of acting as a 'keystroke logger', capturing all of the keystrokes entered into a computer keyboard. The e-mails are normally related to Internet banking and try to dupe people into visiting or clicking on the link to the malicious website using a variety of excuses.

Money Mules

Most of the fraudsters behind online banking scams are locked overseas, and they need an accomplice with a UK bank account to act as a ''money mule" or money transfer agent, to launder the funds obtained as a result of online scams. There were 1,623 money mule recruitment advertisements recorded in 2008, compared with 1,462 in 2007 (Fraud 2009). Figure 7 shows how money mule recruitment was increasing in online from 2005 to 2008.

Internet Usability

This survey found that (Figure 8) a large number of respondents, i.e. 67% (from Internet using people) use Internet for banking and shopping at home, 17% respondents use Internet at home and library both, 12% people use only library for Internet and 4% people use cafe for banking and shopping via Internet in the UK.

Figure 7. Number of mule recruitment adverts in 2005-2008 (Fraud 2009)

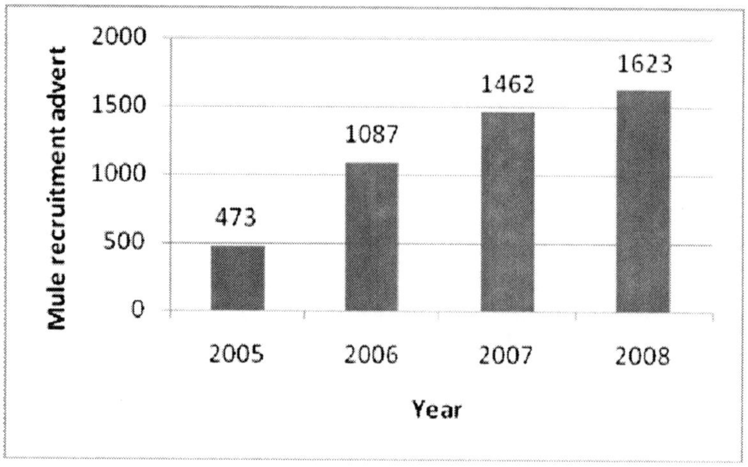

Figure 8. Graphical representation of Internet usability

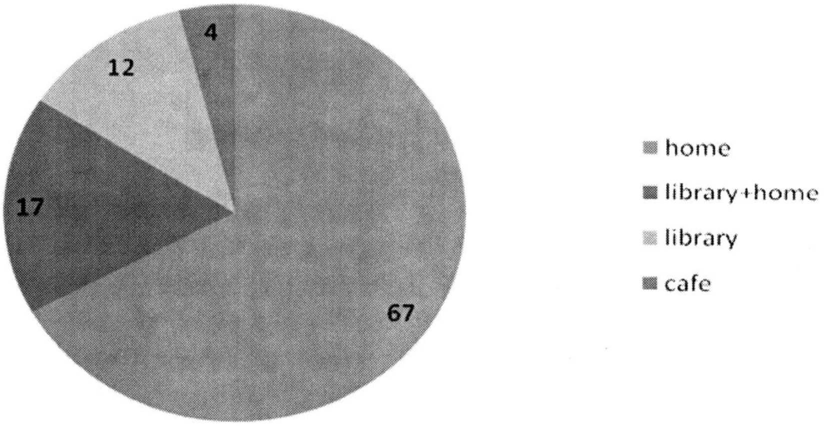

Spam (Scam) E-Mail

This research (Figure 9) explores how many spam e-mails are received by the people every day. E-fraudsters use scam or phishing e-mail to make fraud to consumer in online banking. 5% people receive 1-19 spam email, 54% people receive 20-24 spam e-mail, 9% people receive 25-29 spam e-mail, 4% people receive 30-34 spam email, 6% people receive 35-39 spam e-mail, 4% people receive 40-44 spam e-mail and 3% people receive more than 45 spam e-mail every day.

Different Type of Phishing or Scam E-Mail

Survey shows (Table 1) that 23.21% respondents receive 'lottery prize winner' as a highest scam e-mail, 14.05% respondents receive 'work-at-home plan' scam e-mail, 12.98% respondents receive 'summer holyday booking' scam e-mail, 8.70% respondents receive 'Advance fee for loan' scam e-mail, 4.27% respondents receive 'Nigerian money offer' scam e-mail, 13.28% respondents receive all of the above scam e-mail and 23.51% respondents (Internet users) do not know about

Figure 9. Spam (scam) or phishing e-mail received everyday

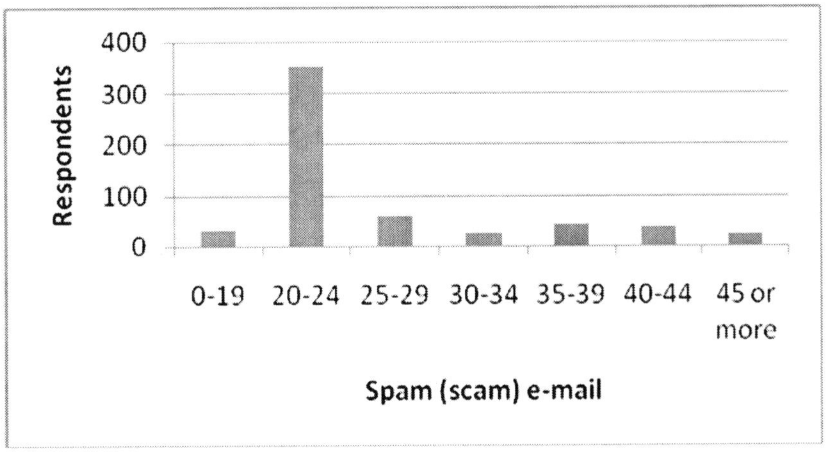

scam or phishing e-mail. The authors conducted this research by distributing questionnaire and have taken short interview simultaneously to the respondents about the answer that focus on the research topics.

Attacked by Phishing or Scam E-Mail in Life

As stated earlier (Table 1), the survey shows that 23.51% of respondents do not know what phishing or scam e-mail is and how they are affected by the scams. 27% respondents are two times attacked in their life and more than five times attacked in life is the lowest one. Here, none means respondents never attacked in their whole life by phishing or scam e-mail because they do not use online banking or shopping (see Table 2).

Table 1. Different types of phishing or scam e-mail received

Category	Value	Percentage
Lottery prize winner	152	23.21%
Work-at-home plan	92	14.05%
Summer holyday booking	85	12.98%
Advance for loan	57	8.70%
Nigerian money offer	28	4.27%
All of them	87	13.28%
Do not know	154	23.51%

Victim of Debit or Credit Card or Bank Money Fraud

The survey shows that 20% of respondents fall into card (debit or credit) fraud victim one time in their entire life, and also 14%, 8%, 1% and 1% of respondents fall into card (debit or credit) fraud victim two times, three times, four times or more respectively in their life. None means that

Table 2. Attacked by phishing or scam e-mail in life

Category	Value	Percentage
One time	92	14%
Two times	176	27%
Three times	129	19%
Four times	44	7%
Five times	31	5%
More than Five	24	4%
None	159	24%

Figure 10. Victim of debit or credit card or bank money fraud

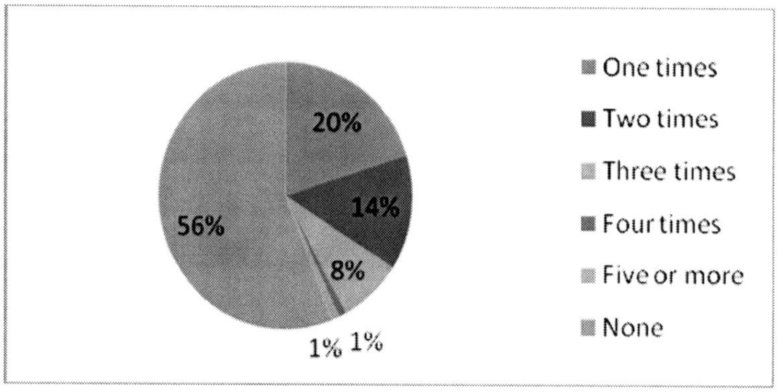

respondents did not get victimised in life because they did not use online banking or shopping. They occupied 56%. See the Table 3 and Figure 10.

Online Banking Activities

The survey investigate that 27% of respondents use online banking to check bank statements and account balance, 13% considered to pay bill (money), 4% said to transfer account balance, 2% respondents use online banking to organise their bank accounts, 41% said they use online banking for doing all of the four activities and 13% (none) respondents said that they are not involved with the above activities. See the Table 4.

Length of Time in Using Online Banking

Respondents were asked about the length of time that they were using online banking. 20.62% respondents said that they have been using online banking for last 6 months. The users of online banking for one year occupied 36.02% and 15.27% respondents using for two years. Three years and four years users are respectively 14.35% and 7.33%. Five years or more users are 6.41% (see Table 5).

Victimised by Paying Bill over the Phone

The survey explores that 67% of respondents were never victimised in their entire life. Because

Table 3. Victim of debit or credit card or bank money fraud

Category	Value	Percentage
One time	131	20%
Two times	91	14%
Three times	53	8%
Four times	6	1%
Five or more	6	1%
None	368	56%

Table 4. Online banking activities

Category	Value	Percentage
Check bank statements and account balance	178	27%
Paying bill	82	13%
Balance transfer	27	4%
Organise account	14	2%
All of them	268	41%
None	86	13%

Table 5. Length of using online banking

Category	Value	Percentage
6 month	135	20.62%
1 Year	236	36.02%
2 Year	100	15.27%
3 Year	94	14.35%
4 Year	48	7.33%
5 Year or more	42	6.41%

one of the main reasons is either they did not use online banking or they are more sensitive about using online banking. 20% user's got victimised for one time, 10% respondents were for two times and 3% of users got victimised for three times by paying bill over the telephone communication (see Figure 11).

Losing Money Online

This research reports that 44.89% of respondents lose money when they use online for shopping, 10.08% of respondents lose money when they use online banking, 14.65% of respondents lose money (credit) when they use online for paying bill and also use phone, 15.73% of respondents lose money (credit) when they use online for taking part in auction. 14.65% of respondents said that they did not lose money (credit) in online; either they did not use online shopping and banking or they are more conscious about their identity (see Figure 12).

Characteristics of Online Transaction

In this research, the authors asked the respondents about the main characteristics in online transaction (banking and shopping). 84% of respondents said that online transaction is easy, cheaper and less time consuming, 9% respondents said that it is expensive but safer and 7% respondents found it securer than making transaction physically (see Table 6).

Who are Involved with Credit Fraud

According to the present survey, 34% of respondents interprets that e-fraudsters are liable to make credit fraud in online transactions, 24% respondents pointed out the social hacker, 18% of respondents think that some employees have a relationship with e-fraudsters that contributes towards increasing customer vulnerability to fraud, 10% respondents thought that e-retailers also have an impact to make credit fraud and 14% respondents said that all of them are also liable for credit fraud in online transactions (see Table 7).

Figure 11. Victimised by paying bill over the phone

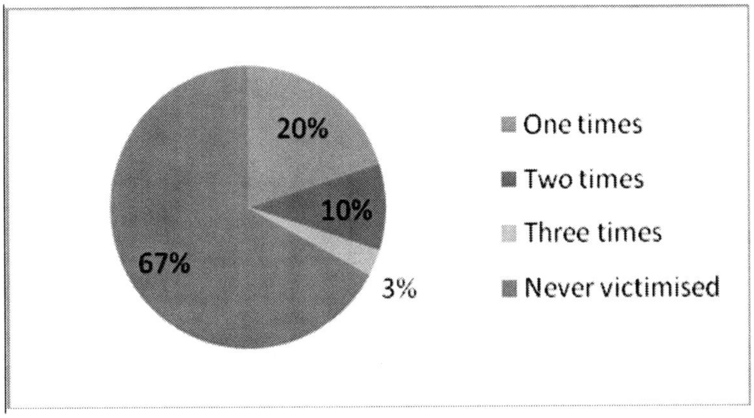

Figure 12. Losing money online

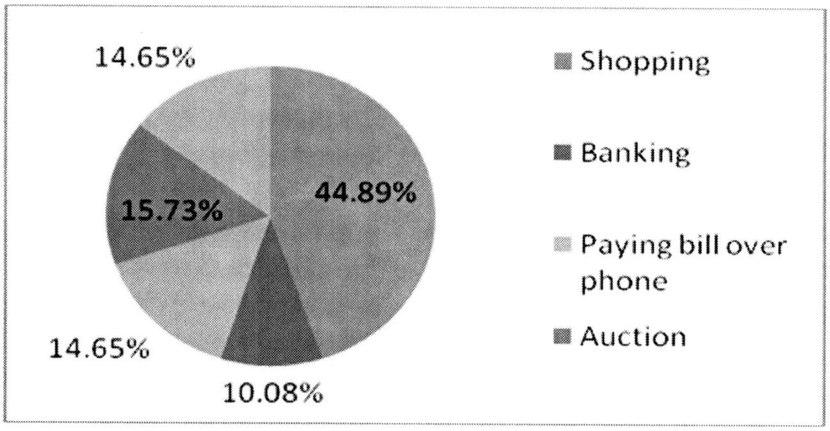

Main Responsible Body to Stop Credit Fraud

Participants were asked about who is the main responsible body to stop credit fraud in online. In response to this question, 6% thought consumers' have a responsibility to stop credit fraud in online transaction, 6% said police, 10% said Card Company, 12% said government has a responsibility and 17% said banks have responsibility to stop credit fraud in online. And also 49% thought all of the above bodies are responsible to stop credit fraud in online transaction (see Table 8 and Figure 13).

How to Minimise Credit Fraud

Consumers' were asked that "do you think banks' need to provide more security protection (for consumer) to stop credit fraud in online?" In response to the question, 9% of respondents straightway said "No", 43% said "Yes", which means that banks need to provide more security protection than existing one. Also 48% said "Yes" but banks need to provide more security protection to save consumer and simultaneously need to increase more security awareness programme (see Figure 14).

DATA ANALYSIS AND DISCUSSION

The explanation of collected data may include data interpretation, some statistical measurements and summarisation. The most important things to know about the data are that it has to be interpreted. Data collection and analysis take place in close conjunction and feeding into each other.

Table 6. Main characteristic of on line transaction

Category	Value	Percentage
Easy, cheaper & time consume	550	84%
Expensive but safer	61	9%
Secure than physically	44	7%

Table 7. Involvement with credit fraud

Category	Value	Percentage
E-fraudster	220	34%
Social hacker	159	24%
Employee	117	18%
E-retailer	64	10%
All of them	95	14%

Table 8. Main responsible body to stop credit fraud

Category	Value	Percentage
Consumer	39	6%
Police	42	6%
Card company	66	10%
Government	78	12%
Bank	108	17%
All of them	322	49%

Figure 13. Main responsible body to stop credit fraud

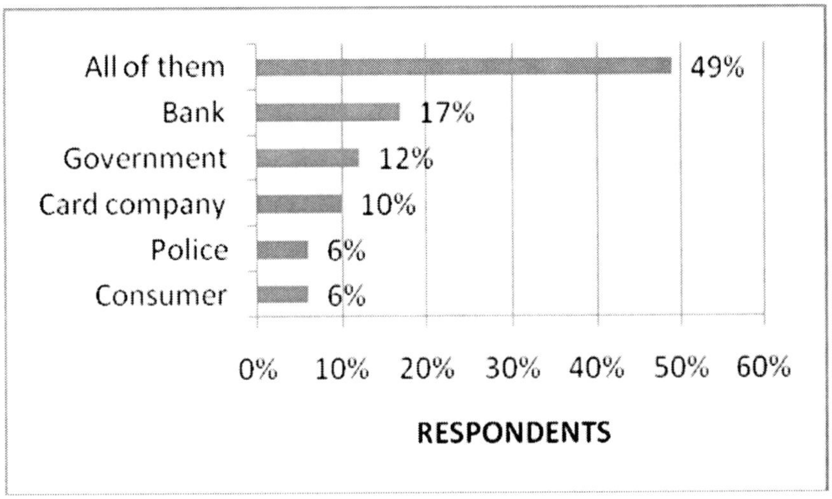

Figure 14. Responses on how credit fraud can minimise

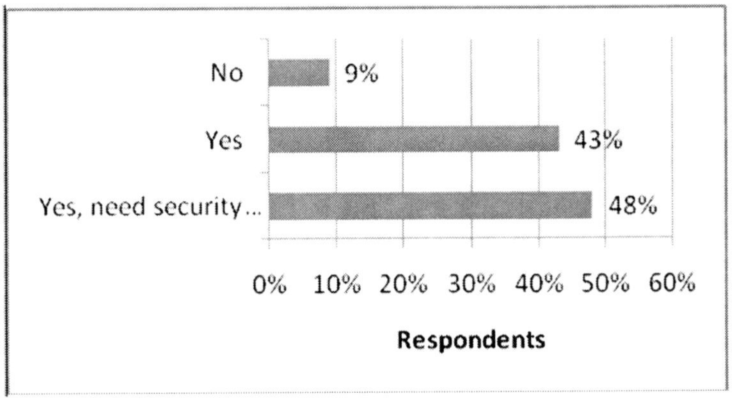

Hypothesis Formation

It is crucial to emphasise the fact that credit fraud in E-business in the banking sector in UK is rising with the help of ICT. And also the development of Internet technology and increasing demand of online shopping and banking. This is increasing the vulnerability of consumers. Based on all of the above facts and the research objectives the following hypotheses have been formulated:

Hypothesis-1: Credit Fraud in e-business especially in the banking sector is increasing with the help of Internet and the development of Information and Communication Technology (ICT).

Hypothesis-2: Social Hacker, e-retailer (false e-retailer), e-fraudsters and banks' Employees (dishonest employee) contribute to increasing Credit Fraud in the banking sector.

Hypothesis-3: Online banking popularity is increasing in the young generation.

Hypothesis-4: Credit Fraud Detection in e-business in the banking sector could not meet the challenges that come from Hackers.

Hypothesis Analysis and Justification

Hypothesis-1: Credit Fraud in e-business especially in the banking sector is increasing with the help of Internet and the development of Information and Communication Technology (ICT).

The study found that 23 million adults banked online in 2008, 55% of Internet users do banking online, use is highest among 24 to 35 year olds, where over two-thirds of Internet users access at least one account online and 94% of online bankers access their main current account (Fraud 2009). Almost all types of card fraud losses is decreasing but Card-Not-Present (CNP) fraud losses is increasing from 2000 to 2008 (fraud 2009). According to the UK Card Association and APACS (2009), in UK total card-not-present fraud losses were 10% in 1998 and grew up 54% in 2008 (see Figure 4).

Hypothesis-2: Social Hacker, e-retailer (false e-retailer), e-fraudster and banks' employees contribute to increasing Credit Fraud in the banking sector in online.

Internet or E-commerce fraud losses on cards are estimated at £181.7 million in 2008 and increase of 2% since 2007 when e-commerce fraud losses were £178.3m and Internet fraud now accounts for 55% (Fraud 2009). 43,991 phishing websites targeted against UK banks and building societies in 2008, up from 25,797, which was in turn an increase of 14,156 in 2006 (Fraud 2009). The rising number of phishing incidents has undoubtedly helped raise online banking fraud losses. We also know that online banking customers are increasingly being targeted by malware (malicious software) attacks which is done by social hacker, e-retailer (false e-retailer), e-fraudster. Spyware e-mails are normally related to Internet banking and try to dupe people into visiting or clicking on the link to the malicious website using a variety of excuses.

Hypothesis-3: Online banking popularity is increasing in young generation.

This research found that 23 million adults banked online in 2008, 55% of Internet user's do banking online, use is highest among 24 to 35 year olds (Fraud 2009). The increase in credit fraud should be seen through alongside growing use of these shopping channels, as well as increasing numbers of business accepting cards remotely. The total value of online shopping alone increased by 1,077% increased up from £3.5 billion in 2000 to £41.2 billion in 2008 (Fraud 2009).

Hypothesis-4: Credit Fraud Detection in online banking could not meet the challenges (from Hackers) to the customers.

This study explores that providing security protection (from the government and banks) is not enough to save consumers in online banking and shopping. That is why consumers are still at risk which is explained in the literature review. From 2000 to 2008 card-not-present fraud losses rose by 350%, counterfeit card fraud increases 19% in 2008, annual plastic card fraud increase 14% in 2008 (Fraud 2009). Consumers' were asked if they think banks' need to provide more security protection (for consumer) to stop credit fraud in online. In response to the question, 48% of respondents said "Yes" but banks need to provide more security protection to save consumer and increase more security awareness programme simultaneously (see Figure 14).

Discussion

With the increase of e-transaction Internet fraud or e-business fraud is increasing. A few sort of card (debit or credit) fraud is decreasing by providing detection and prevention system. But Card-not-present fraud losses (fraud by phone, mail order, online shopping and banking) are increasing at higher rate. It is because there is no possibility to use Chip and PIN, where card is not used face-to-face (see Figures 1, 2, 3, 4, 5 and 6). Though Chip and PIN based password authentication is a top security measure it cannot detect and protect fraud in online transaction as there is no option to enter password. As a result Card-not-present fraud losses are growing up an unprotected and undetected way in e-business system.

Counterfeit Card Fraud Prevention

Counterfeit card fraud is a huge card crime in the UK. The responsibility is not only for retailer but also for everyone. It is essential that we should be vigilance in spotting and stopping counterfeit card fraud.

According to Card Watch (2009), there are some key steps that will help to show if a card is a counterfeit.

1. Check the first four digits on MasterCard and Visa cards.
2. Check for the 'MC' on MasterCard and 'flying V' on Visa Card.
3. Check that the card has a special mark when held under a UV (ultra violet) light.
4. Check that the card number on the card matches the number on the till print-out.

APACS (2009) also provides some tips to protect consumers and provides useful advice on how to better protect people from fraud.

Look after your cards and card details at all times. Ensure you are the only person that knows your PIN. Never write it down or record it. Put your personal safety first. If someone is crowding or watching you, cancel the transaction and go to another machine. Do not share personal information unless you are entirely confident.

Online Fraud Prevention

- **Banking safely online:** Make sure your computer has up-to-date ant-viruses software and a firewall installed. Before you bank online ensure that the locked padlock or unbroken key symbol is showing in your browser. Be wary of unsolicited e-mails, known as phishing emails and requesting personal information. Ensure your browser is set to the highest level of security notification and monitoring. Always access Internet banking sites by typing the bank's address into your web browser. If you are a victim of online banking fraud you have protection through the banking code, which states that unless you have acted fraudulently or without reasonable care you will not be liable for losses caused by someone else.
- **Shopping safely online:** Sign up to verify by Visa or MasterCard Secure Code whenever you are given the option whilst shopping online. Only shop on secure sites, before submitting card details ensure the locked padlock or unbroken key symbol

is showing in your browser. The retailer's Internet address will change from 'http' to 'https' when a connection is secure. Print out your order and keep copies of the retailer's terms and conditions, return policy, delivery conditions, postal address (not a post office box) and phone number (not a mobile number).

Industry Measures to Prevent Online Banking Fraud

According to APACS (2009), the banking industry works alongside a number of online partners to tackle this type of fraud, such as the Serious Organised Crime Agency, overseas law enforcement agencies, technology companies, anti-virus firms and Internet Services Providers. A number of initiatives are already in place: Monitoring of the Internet at industry and bank level to detect and close down phishing-related websites. Two-way communication with online partner's security intelligence can be shared and used effectively. Development and use of clear and consistent advice for consumers. One of the initiatives introduced by some banks to provide a higher level of the online banking security is the roll-out of hand held Chip and PIN card reading devices. These devices work via a customer inserting their Chip and PIN card into a hand-held card reader and entering their PIN. On confirming the PIN entered, the card reader generates a unique, onetime only pass code, which the card holder provides, when prompted during a transaction, for authentication with their online bank. This solution helps to ensure that the person conducting business online is the genuine customer and will make these types of transaction even safer. The industry has also created www.banksafeonline.org.uk to help customers to stay safe while banking online. The site details types of online banking scams, how to spot them and how to protect yourself from falling victim.

- **Using cards overseas:** Before you go overseas, only take cards with you that you intend to use; leave others in a secure place at home. Make sure you have your card company's 24-hour contact phone number. Make sure your card company has up-to-date contact details for you. If your cards are registered with a card protection agency, ensure you have their contact number and your policy number with you.
- **When you are overseas:** Take the same precautions as you would in the UK; look after your cards and card details, and shield your PIN with your free hand when typing it into a keypad in a shop or at a cash machine. Consider wearing a concealed money belt to keep your cards, cash and traveller's cheques safe.
- **When you get back:** Check your card statements carefully for unfamiliar transactions. If there are any, report them to your card company as soon as possible.
- **If you become a victim of card fraud:** Report lost or stolen cards or suspected fraudulent use of your card to your card company immediately. If you are the victim of plastic card or online banking fraud you should only report the offence to the relevant bank or Card Company.

Best Practice for Successful Solution

Choosing an optimal Internet banking solution is the first step in achieving new levels of success with online bankers. Choosing providers that can minimise the impact of the conversion process is the second. Banks are considering a conversion to reduce cost and enhance efficiencies while building a competitive edge through Internet banking. Banks must first determine if the conversion is financially feasible. Then, the institution should develop a detailed plan with strategies for a successful conversion. We can take few combined steps for Network Security measure.

1. All components need to be secure.
2. All end users need to be educated about Network Security.
3. All Networks are actively monitored that have any weakness and breaches.

CONCLUSION, RECOMMENDATIONS AND FURTHER RESEARCH

Conclusion

In the age of globalisation, world is getting closer and smaller by eliminating constraints of time and distance by the help of Internet (Kothari and Kothari 2001) and ICT. Banks and retailers are spreading their activities in online to facilitate consumer. Customer can shop in online shopping mall from remote area. They can operate banking activities from wheelchair. Online banking and shopping is much easier than doing physically (in branch or store) but risk of credit fraud is greater in online than branch or store. One of the main applications of Internet is e-commerce. Though credit fraud is increasing continuously, at the same time e-transaction is increasing at a high rate in retail business (for shopping) and in the banking sector. So many ways (phishing, spyware, malware, money mule recruitment, lost or stolen card, mail-non-receipt, counterfeit card, card-not-present, card ID theft, cash machine) and bodies (e-retailers) are involved in Credit fraud in e-business in the banking sector. Employees' fraud currently still be going unprotected and unreported that is the key danger sign for banking sector. National Fraud Reporting Centre (NFRC) is the main authority for monitoring banking fraud and report to the police (BBA 2008). And also several public organisations: Serious Fraud Office (SFO), National Crime Squad (NCS), Serious Organised Crime Agency (SOCA), National Hi-Tech Crime Unit (NHTCU), National Criminal Intelligence Service (NCIS) are working against credit fraud. British Bankers' Association (BBA) is working with cooperation all of the above institutions to detect and prevent Credit Fraud (BBA 2008, SFO 2009, SOCA 2009). 'The Get Safe' Online campaign was the first Internet security awareness campaign, organised by the government along with SOCA, BT, eBay, HSBC, Microsoft and secure Trading (Coaker 2009).

Recommendations

Considering this quantitative research, the authors are willing to provide some recommendations from the light of the findings and results of the study.

- Banks need to do fraud awareness programmes (for customer and staff) and staff training programmes that will help remove staff vulnerability to fraud.
- E-business will be successful when all the e-retailers, e-marketers, banks and financial institutions will come in a one platform to detect and prevent fraud.
- In the light of this research, banks and government need to pay more attention to control Card-not-present fraud losses in e-business. Because these kinds of fraud losses are increasing rapidly in online transaction (see Figure 3).

Further Research

This research shows the different channels of credit fraud in E-business especially in the banking sector. It has done much work on credit fraud but fraud detection and prevention has not been discussed in details. Also it could not find out the internal fraud (employee fraud) that may relate with e-fraudster. Further research can be conducted on the field of employee fraud and how it could be minimised. Further research is also required to justify the findings of this study and find out the specific reason of credit fraud and the best way to prevent the fraud in e-business in the banking sector.

REFERENCES

AFP. (2009). Payments fraud a growing concern. Bancography, June. Retrieved June 17, 2009, from www.bancography.com

Ankobia, R. (2004). *Vulnerabilities in Web applications, painful lessons*. Advice (Un) Heeded, 8th World Multi-Conference on Systemic, Cybernetic and Informatics USA, July 18-21, 2004, Orlando, Florida.

APACS. (2009). *Spot & stop counterfeit card fraud*. Association for Payment Clearing Services. Retrieved July 22, 2009, from www.apacs.org.uk/

BBA. (2008). British Bankers' Association Annual Report 2007/08. Retrieved June 29, 2009, from www.bba.org.uk/

BIS. (2009). *Fraud and scams*. Department for Business Innovation & Skills. Retrieved June 24, 2009, from http://search.berr.gov.uk/

Bologna, J. (1984). Corporate fraud: The basics of prevention and detection, (pp. 1, 15). Butterworth Publishers.

Boyle, B., & Alwitt, L. (1999). Internet use within the U.S plastics industry. *Industrial Marketing Management*, *28*, 327–341. doi:10.1016/S0019-8501(98)00012-1

Brian, W. (1995). *Introduction page*. Serious Fraud Office, Little, Brown and Company.

Bryman, A. (2004). *Quantity and quality in social research*, (pp. 11-44). Routledge, Taylor and & Francis Group.

Card Watch. (2009). *Fraud: The facts 2009*. Retrieved July 22, 2009, from www.cardwatch.org.uk

Card Watch. (2009). Stop and stop card fraud retailer training pack. Retrieved July 22, 2009, from www.cardwatch.org.uk

Chaffey, D. (2004). *E-business and e-commerce management* (2nd ed.). London, UK: Prentice Hall.

Chris, H., Keith, H., Azrini, W., & Emma, W. (2009). In Tombs, S. (Ed.), *Criminology* (2nd ed., p. 342). Oxford University Press.

Coaker. (2009). *Internet crime: House of Commons Hansard written answers*. Retrieved June 29, 2009, from http://www.publications.parliament.uk/

Couto, P. J., Tiago, B. F., Tiagi, B. T., & Vieira, C. J. (2008). The utilization of Internet by European companies. *The Journal of Business*, *5*(6), 41. Retrieved June 25, 2009 from www.journalofe-business.org.

Cronin, M. (1996). *The Internet strategy handbook: Lesson from the new frontier of business*. Boston, MA: Harvard Business School Press.

Douglas, T., & Brian, D. L. (2000). *Cybercrime, law enforcement, security and surveillance in the information age,* (p. 3, 7). Routledge, Taylor & Francis Group.

Fraud. (2009). *Fraud: The facts 2009*. Retrieved August 22, 2009, from www.apacs.org.uk/

Futurist. (2009). Internet fraud on the rise. *The Futurist, 43*(4), 15. Retrieved June 20, 2009, from http://web.ebscohost.com/

Gonca, T. Y., & Faruk, K. (2009). User rating system for the Internet (URSI) and central authority for internet security (CAIS). *The Journal of Business*, *5*(6), 1. Retrieved June 25, 2009 from from http://www.journalofe-business.org/

Hanson, W. (2000). *Principal of Internet marketing*. Cincinnati, OH: South- Western College Publishing.

Heike, N., & Thomas, S. (2006). Digital coins: Fairness implemented by observer. *Journal of Theoretical and Applied Electronic Commerce Research*, 1(1). Retrieved June 14, 2009, from http://www.jtaer.com/

Hewer, P., & Howcroft, B. (1999). Consumers' channel adoption and usage in the financial services industry: A review of existing approaches. *Journal of Financial Markets*, *3*(4), 344–358.

Hughes, T. (2003). Marketing challenges in e-banking: Standalone or integrated? *Journal of Marketing Management*, *19*, 1067–1085. doi:10.1362/026725703770558321

John, V. B., & Robyn, W. (2002). Barriers to purchasing on the Internet. *The Journal of Business*, *2*(1), 27. Retrieved June 27, 2009 from from http://www.journalofe-business.org

Keldon, B., & Scott, E. H. (2005). The effect of heterogeneous risk on the early adoption of Internet banking technologies. *Journal of E-Banking*, *10*. Retrieved June 25, 2009, from http://papers.ssrn.com/

Kling, R. (1994). Reading all about computerization: How genre conventions shape social analyses. *The Information Society*, 147–172. doi:10.1080/01972243.1994.9960166

Kothari, V., & Kothari, M. P. (2001). E-business: What have we learned. *The Journal of Business*, *1*(2), 5. Retrieved June 27, 2009 from from http://www.journalofe-business.org/

NCL. (2009). *National Consumers Leagues*. Retrieved June 17, 2009, from http://www.nclnet.org/news/2007

Neuman, R. (1991). *The future of the mass audience*. Cambridge, MA: Cambridge University Press.

NFIC & IFW. (2009). *National Fraud Information Centre and Internet Fraud Watch*. Retrieved June 17, 2009, from http://www.fraud.org/Internet

Okenyi, P. O., & Owens, T. J. (2007). On the anatomy of human hacking: A global prospective. *Information Security Journal, 16*(6). Retrieved June 20, 2009, from http://bura.brunel.ac.uk/

Ordnance Survey. (2008). BBA's 6th Annual Financial Crime Conference, 25 -26 November. Retrieved June 24, 2009, from http://www.bba.org.uk/

Pennington, V. (2009). Fighting fraud, op risk & compliance. *ProQuest, 10*(5), 36-39. Retrieved June 17, 2009, from http://proquest.umi.com/pqdlink/

Phillip, B., Blaise, J. B., & Charles, R. V. (2004). Internet fraud: A global perspective. *Journal of E-Business,* 4(1). Retrieved June 18, 2009, from http://www.journalofe-business.org/

SFO. (2009). *Serious Fraud Office*. Retrieved June 29, 2009, from https://www.sfo.gov.uk/

SOCA. (2009). *Serious Organised Crime Agency*. Retrieved June 29, 2009, from http://www.soca.gov.uk/

Sorter Oxford English Dictionary. (2002). In Trumble, W. R., & Stevenson, A. (Eds.), *On historical principles* (5th ed., *Vol. 1*, p. 1028). Oxford University Press.

The UK Card Association. (2009). *Fraud: The facts 2009*. Retrieved July 22, 2009, from www.theukcardsassociation.org.uk

Turban, E., King, D., Lee, J., & Viehland, D. (2004). *Electronic commerce: A managerial perspective*. Prentice Hall International Inc.

Turban, E., Lee, J., King, D., & Chung, H. (2002). *Electronic commerce: A managerial perspective*. Prentice Hall International Inc.

Williams, G., & Kikalas, T. (2005). *Operating systems – Worm targets. IGGeS submission*. Journal.

KEY TERMS AND DEFINITIONS

Credit Fraud: Is an extensive term used to distinguish theft and fraud committed using a credit card or any similar payment mechanism as a fraudulent source of funds in a transaction. The purpose may be to obtain goods without paying, or to obtain unauthorised funds from an account. Credit card fraud is also an adjunct to identity theft.

E-Business: The buying and selling of products and services by businesses and consumers through an electronic medium especially over the Internet. However any transaction that is completed solely through electronic measures can be considered e-business. Note that e-commerce is a subset of an overall e-business strategy.

Hacking: Is an act of gaining unauthorised access to computer systems and network resources to acquire knowledge about the system and how it works.

Information Security: Means protecting information and information systems from unauthorized access, use, disclosure, disruption, modification, perusal, inspection, recording or destruction.

Malware: Online banking customers are increasingly being targeted by malware attacks. Malware (i.e. malicious software) includes computer viruses that can install on a computer without the user's knowledge.

Phishing: Is an e-mail fraud scam conducted for the purposes of information or identity theft.

Spam or Scam Email: Sending a message indiscriminately to multiple mailing lists, individuals, or newsgroups.

Virtual Banking/e-Banking/Internet Banking/Online Banking: A computer-controlled Web based banking services system that does not involve the usual bank branch is called virtual banking. Automated Teller Machine (ATM) is an example of virtual banking which is also known as e-banking. Internet banking or online banking is a system which allows individuals to perform banking activities at home via the Internet. Internet banking reduces cost and time, provide convenience banking to the consumers and control over finance.

Chapter 21
Safeguarding Australia from Cyber-Terrorism: A SCADA Risk Framework

Christopher Beggs
Security Infrastructure Solutions, Australia

Matthew Warren
Deakin University, Australia

ABSTRACT

Terrorist groups are currently using information and communication technologies (ICTs) to orchestrate their conventional attacks. More recently, terrorists have been developing a new form of capability within the cyber-arena to coordinate cyber-based attacks. This chapter identifies that cyber-terrorism capabilities are an integral, imperative, yet under-researched component in establishing, and enhancing cyber-terrorism risk assessment models for SCADA systems. This chapter examines a cyber-terrorism SCADA risk framework that has been adopted and validated by SCADA industry practitioners. The chapter proposes a high level managerial framework, which is designed to measure and protect SCADA systems from the threat of cyber-terrorism within Australia. The findings and results of an industry focus group are presented in support of the developed framework for SCADA industry acceptance.

INTRODUCTION

Cyber-terrorism is "non-state actors' use of ICTs to attack and control critical information systems with political motivation and the intent to cause harm and spread fear to people or at least with the anticipation of changing domestic, national or international events" (Beggs, 2005). For example, an individual who has political motive and penetrates a Supervisory Control and Data Acquisition (SCADA) system controlling gas pressure in a gas plant by manipulating the pipeline and causing an explosion would be classified as cyber-terrorism,

DOI: 10.4018/978-1-4666-0197-0.ch021

because bystanders and civilians would be harmed and motivation to effect political change would have occurred.

SCADA systems have evolved since the 1960s from stand alone systems to networked architectures that communicate across large distances. Their implementation has migrated from custom hardware and software to standard hardware and software platforms (Krutz, 2005). SCADA systems form part of Australia's critical infrastructure. They are used to remotely monitor and control the delivery of essential services and products, such as electricity, gas, water, waste treatment and transport systems (TISN, 2008) The need for security measures within these systems was not anticipated in the early development stages as they were designed to be closed systems and not open systems such as the Internet. The increasingly networked and linked infrastructure of modern SCADA systems has changed those early security plans. Utilities in the industrial control sector have integrated these SCADA networks with their business networks which unfortunately has exposed them to a series of vulnerabilities and risks (Internet Security Systems, 2005).

Currently, organisations within Australia that are controlling critical infrastructure systems such as SCADA are now vulnerable to cyber-terrorism. Attacks and cases in recent years such as the Polish Tram System 2008, Estonia 2007, SQL Slammer 2003, Queensland 2000 and Gazprom 1999, as well as many others, highlight the vulnerability in critical infrastructures and serve to highlight the possibility of cyber-terrorism occurring. These cases and attacks have prompted further research and investigation into the cyber-terrorism threat as research gaps have been recognised by the authors when conducting a literature review on the topic and by interviewing experts in the field. Some of the major gaps identified were the elements of SCADA security risk assessment, terrorist groups' cyber-capability and SCADA critical infrastructure protection including SCADA system vulnerabilities.

For non state actors (Cyber-terrorism group) to be a threat against a SCADA system requires a terrorist or group to have a high level of malicious intent and a high level of knowledge of SCADA systems and ICTs. This paper presents a framework that has been developed to measure and protect SCADA systems from the threat of cyber-terrorism within Australia. The paper also examines the findings and results of a SCADA industry focus group that has been conducted in order to validate the cyber-terrorism SCADA risk framework for industry adoption and acceptance. The framework is made up of the following stages:

CYBER-TERRORISM SCADA RISK ASSESSMENT

This cyber-terrorism SCADA risk assessment subset represents the first stage processes in measuring and protecting SCADA systems from the threat of cyber-terrorism within Australia. The subset discusses the various steps that should be used to conduct a risk assessment on a SCADA system. These steps have been adopted and aligned with the procedures documented in the AS/NZS ISO 31000:2009 risk management standard. Some of the procedures and steps for conducting a risk assessment have been customised to fit a generic SCADA risk assessment and some stages within the process have been modified to suit the SCADA environment. This stage only provides a baseline security risk assessment process that is applicable for SCADA systems. Organisations can use this subset and modify it to suit their SCADA configuration and their organisation requirements and needs.

The purpose of this stage is to provide a generic method for conducting a security risk assessment within a SCADA environment. This subset is the first stage within the cyber-terrorism SCADA risk framework. The subset is based on the AS/NZS ISO 31000:2009 risk management standard which is used by many organisations to conduct risk assessment. This standard has provided the basis for the development of this subset and is referred throughout the document (Based upon Standards Australia, 2009). The cyber-terrorism SCADA risk assessment subset provides the generic stages, steps and recommendations to conduct a risk assessment on a SCADA system, which will assist in identifying vulnerabilities and threats to an organisation's SCADA environment.

SCADA Risk Management Process Overview

This section of the subset gives a brief overview of the risk management process for a SCADA system. The main elements of the risk management processes for a SCADA system are:

- Communicate and consult SCADA;
- Establish the context for SCADA;
- Identify risks of SCADA;
- Analyse risks of SCADA;
- Evaluate risks of SCADA;
- Treat risks for SCADA;
- Monitor and review SCADA.

Stage 1.1 Communicate and Consultation

Communication and consultation are important considerations at each step of the risk management process for a SCADA system. It is important to develop a SCADA communication plan that addresses issues relating to SCADA risks and the process to manage SCADA for both internal and external stakeholders. This should be developed at the earliest stage of the risk management process. Stakeholders are likely to make judgements about SCADA risks based on their perceptions. Since the views of the stakeholders can have a significant impact on the decisions made, its important that their perceptions of risk be identified and recorded and integrated into the decision making process. A team of consultants is useful to help identify risks and bring together expertise to analyses SCADA risks and for ensuring different views are appropriately considered in evaluating risks and for change management during SCADA risk treatment. Below is a summary of the steps needed within stage 1.1 of the SCADA risk assessment:

- Develop a SCADA communication plan;
- Record risk perceptions of SCADA;
- Integrate risk perceptions into the decision making process for SCADA;
- Develop a consultative team to define the SCADA context and the ownership of SCADA risks.

Stage 2.1 Establish the Context for SCADA

Establishing the SCADA context defines the basic parameters within which SCADA risks must be managed and sets the scope for the rest of the SCADA risk management process. The context includes the organisation's external and internal environment and the purpose of the SCADA risk management activity. Stage 2.1 has been aligned with the AS/NZS ISO 31000:2009 risk management standard.

- *Stage 2.1.1 Establish the Context*
    - Establish the external context for SCADA operation
    - Establish regulation and guidelines for SCADA;
    - Establish competitive threats towards SCADA and the organisation;
    - Assess financial implications of the external environment for SCADA;
    - Establish the organisation's strengths, weaknesses, opportunities and threats for SCADA operation;
    - Establish external stakeholders for SCADA i.e. outsourced expertise such as SCADA consultants and SCADA engineers;

    - Establish communication channels and policies for external stakeholders of SCADA.
- *Stage 2.1.2 Establish the internal context for SCADA*
    - Assess the culture of the organisation in relation to SCADA operations;
    - Establish the internal stakeholders such as SCADA users, SCADA engineers and IT personnel;
    - Establish the internal structure for SCADA operation;
    - Establish specific levels of capability for SCADA users/employees and SCADA systems and processes within the SCADA environment;
    - Establish specific goals, objectives and strategies for the internal context for SCADA.
- *Stage 2.1.3 Establish the risk management context for SCADA*
    - Define and establish SCADA goals, objectives, strategies, scope and parameters of the SCADA environment;
    - Balance and identify cost benefits and opportunities for the SCADA environment;
    - Specify the nature of the decisions that have to be made within the SCADA environment;
    - Define the extent of SCADA activity in terms of time and location;
    - Identify any scoping or framing studies needed for SCADA and their objectives and resources required;
    - Define the depth of the risk management activities that need to be carried out for the SCADA environment;
    - Define specific roles and responsibilities of stakeholders who are participating the SCADA risk management process;
    - Define the relationships between the SCADA risk management process and other processes within other sectors of the organisation.
- *Stage 2.1.4 Develop risk criteria for SCADA*
    - Develop criteria against which SCADA risks is to be evaluated;
    - Decisions on risk treatment for SCADA are based on factors such as operational, technical, financial, legal, social, safety environmental or other criteria;
    - The criteria should reflect the context defined above;
    - The risk criteria for SCADA must correspond to the type of risks and they way in which risk levels are expressed.
- *Stage 2.1.5 Define the structure for the rest of the process for SCADA*
    - Define structure of SCADA into elements and steps in order to provide logical framework to ensure that significant SCADA risks are not overlooked.

Stage 3.1 Identify Risk of SCADA

This stage of the process identifies the risks that need to be managed for the SCADA environment. Developing a structured systematic process is critical to identify SCADA risks because a risk not identified at this stage may be excluded from further analysis. Identification should include SCADA risks whether or not they are under the control of the organisation.

- *Stage 3.1.1 List SCADA risks, what can happen, where and when to the SCADA environment.*
    - Establish a comprehensive list of SCADA risks that might impact the SCADA environment.
- *Stage 3.1.2 Why and how it can happen*
    - Identify possible causes and scenarios of SCADA risks.

- *Stage 3.1.3 Tools and techniques*
  - Approaches that can be used to identify SCADA risks are checklists, judgements based on experience and records, flow charts, brainstorming, system analysis, scenario analysis and systems engineering techniques.

Stage 4.1 SCADA Risk Analysis

SCADA risk analysis is concerned with developing an understanding of the risks. It provides an input to decisions on whether risks need to be treated and the most appropriate and cost effective risk treatment strategies. SCADA risk analysis involves consideration of the sources of risk both positive and negative consequences and the likelihood that those consequences may occur. SCADA risk is analysed by combining consequences with their likelihood and in most circumstances existing controls are taken into consideration.

- *Stage 4.1.1 Evaluate existing controls of SCADA*
  - Identify the existing SCADA processes, devices or practices that act to minimise negative risks or enhance positive risks and assess their strengths and weaknesses. Controls may arise as outcomes of previous risk treatment (See Stage 3 of cyber-terrorism SCADA risk framework SCADA controls subset).
- *Stage 4.1.2 Consequences and likelihood*
  - The magnitude of the consequences of an event, should it occur and the likelihood of the event and its associated consequences, are assessed in the context of the effectiveness of the existing strategies and controls that are been applied to SCADA. Consequences and likelihood may be estimated using statistical analysis and calculations either quantitative or qualitative. The most significant information sources and techniques should be used when analysing consequences and likelihood which are listed below:
  - Past records of SCADA;
  - Relevant experience of SCADA;
  - Relevant published literature of SCADA;
  - Market research of SCADA;
  - Results of public consultation of SCADA;
  - SCADA experiments and prototypes;
  - Economic, engineering or other models;
  - Specialists and expert judgements.

Some techniques will use include:

- Specialists and expert judgements;
- Interviews with SCADA experts and engineers;
- Focus Groups- SCADA experts;
- Questionaries for SCADA;
- Models and Simulations of SCADA;
- Assumptions made in the analysis should be clearly stated.

- *Stage 4.1.3 Types of analysis*
  - Quantitative analysis uses numerical values for the consequences and likelihood using data from a variety of SCADA sources. Consequences may be determined by modelling the outcomes of an event or set of events or by extrapolation from experimental studies or past data. This type of analysis is recommended to be used depending on the organisations SCADA environment.
  - Qualitative analysis uses words to describe the magnitude of the potential consequences and the likelihood that those consequences will occur. These

scales can be adapted or adjusted to suit the circumstances and different descriptions maybe be used for different risks.
  - Qualitative analysis is recommended to be used:
    - As an initial screening activity to identify SCADA risks which require more detailed analysis;
    - Where the kind of analysis is appropriate for decisions or;
    - Where the numerical data or resources are inadequate for a quantitative analysis.
  - Semi-quantitative analysis uses qualitative scales such as those described above. The objective is to produce a more expanded ranking scale than is usually achieved in qualitative analysis, not to suggest realistic values for risk such as is attempted in quantitative analysis. Semi-quantitative analysis may not differentiate properly between risks particularly when either consequences of likelihood are extreme. Depending on the SCADA configuration and environment this method or analysis maybe applicable.
- *Stage 4.1.4 Sensitive analysis*
  - Some estimates with the SCADA risk analysis maybe imprecise, a sensitivity analysis should be carried out to test the effect of uncertainty in assumptions and data. Sensitivity analysis also is a way of testing the appropriate controls for risk treatment.

Stage 5.1 Evaluate Risk of SCADA

SCADA risk evaluation involves comparing the level of risk found during the analysis process with SCADA risk criteria established when the context was considered. The purpose of the risk evaluation is to make decisions based on the outcome of risk analysis, about which risks need treatment and treatment priorities.

Stage 6.1 Treat Risk for SCADA

SCADA risk treatment involves identifying the range of options for treating risks, assessing these options and the preparation and implementation of treatment plans.

Stage 6.1.2 Identifying Options for the Treatment of SCADA Risks with Positive Outcomes

Treatment options for SCADA risks having positive outcomes which are not necessarily mutually exclusive or appropriate include:

- Actively seeking an opportunity by deciding to start or continue with an activity likely to create or maintain it where this is feasible for SCADA and the organisation;
- Changing the likelihood of the opportunity, to enhance the likelihood of beneficial outcomes for SCADA;
- Changing the consequences to increase extent of the gains for SCADA;
- Sharing the opportunity between parties of SCADA;
  - Contracts
  - Partnership
  - Joint ventures
  - Sharing costs
- Retaining the residual opportunity for SCADA.

Stage 6.1.3 Identifying Options for Treating Risks with Negative Outcomes for SCADA

Treatment options for risk having negative outcomes are similar in concept to those for treating risks with positive outcomes, although the implications are different. Some options include:

- Avoiding the risk by deciding not to start or continue with the activity that gives rise to the SCADA risk. However inappropriate risk avoidance may increase other risks which could lead to the loss of opportunities for gain.
- Changing the likelihood of the risk, to reduce the likelihood of the negative outcomes of SCADA
- Changing the consequences, to reduce the extent of the losses. This includes pre-event measures such as reduction in inventory or protective devices for SCADA and post event responses such as continuity plans.
- Sharing the risk between parties for SCADA
    - Contracts;
    - Insurance;
    - Partnership;
    - Joint ventures;
    - Sharing cost.
- Retaining the risk for SCADA

Stage 6.1.4 Assessing Risk Treatment Options for SCADA

Selecting the most appropriate option involves balancing the costs of implementing each option against the benefits derived from it. The cost of managing SCADA risks need to be equal with the benefits obtained. It is important to consider all direct and indirect costs of SCADA and benefits whether tangible or intangible. A number of options may be considered and applied either individually or in combination including:

- Sensitive Analysis;
- Contracts and risk treatment supporting insurance and other risk financing;
- Legal and social responsibility requirements for SCADA may override financial costs and benefit analysis of SCADA.

Risk treatment options should consider the values and perceptions of stakeholders and the most appropriate ways to communicate with them. It is important to compare the full costs of not taking action against the budgetary saving. SCADA risk treatment may introduce new SCADA risks which need to be identified, assessed, treated and monitored. If, after treatment, there is residual risk, a decision should be taken about whether to retain this risk or repeat the risk treatment process for SCADA.

Stage 6.1.5 Preparing and Implementing Treatment Plans for SCADA

The purpose of treatment plans for SCADA is to document how the chosen options will be implemented. The treatment plans for SCADA should include:

- SCADA proposed actions;
- SCADA resource requirements;
- SCADA responsibilities;
- SCADA timing;
- SCADA performance measures and
- SCADA reporting and monitoring requirements.
- SCADA treatment plans should be integrated with the management and budgetary processes of the organisation.

Stage 7.1 Monitor and Review SCADA

Ongoing review is essential to ensure that the SCADA management plan remains relevant. Factors that may affect the likelihood and consequences of an outcome may change as many the factors that affect the suitability or cost of the treatment options. It is therefore necessary to repeat the risk management process cycle regularly. Monitoring and review involves learning lessons from the risk management process by reviewing events, the treatment plans and their outcomes.

Stage 8.1 Record the Risk Management Process for SCADA

Each stage of the risk management process should be recorded appropriately. Assumptions, methods, data sources, analyses, results and reasons for decisions should be all recorded. Decisions concerning the making and capture of records include:

- The legal and business needs for SCADA records;
- The cost of creating and maintaining SCADA records;
- The benefits of re-using SCADA information.

Stage 9.1 Establishing Effective Risk Management for SCADA

An organisation should develop a risk management policy and plan for SCADA and support arrangements. This will enable risk management to be implemented effectively throughout the organisation.

Stage 9.1.1 Evaluate Existing Practices and Needs for SCADA

Before starting the risk management process the organisation should review its existing risk management process and should critically analyse and review those elements of the risk management process that are already in place. The review should structure:

- The maturity, characteristics and effectiveness of existing business and risk management culture and SCADA systems;
- The degree of integration and consistency of risk management across the organisation and across different types of risks;
- The SCADA processes and SCADA systems that should be modified or extended;
- SCADA constraints that might limit the introduction of systematic risk management;
- Legislative or compliance requirements for SCADA;
- Resource constraints for SCADA.

Stage 9.1.2 SCADA Risk Management and Planning

Risk management plan should define how risk management for SCADA is to be conducted throughout the organisation. The risk management plan for SCADA should be embedded into policy development, business and strategic planning and change management processes.

Stage 9.1.3 Ensure the Support of Senior Management for SCADA

An awareness and commitment to SCADA risk management at senior management levels is important when conducting SCADA risk management. This can be achieved through ongoing support of senior leaders and senior executives for risk management and for the development and implementation of the risk management policy and plan.

Stage 9.1.4 Develop and Communicate the SCADA Risk Management Policy

The organisation's senior managers should define and document its SCADA policy for managing risk, including its objectives and commitment to SCADA risk management. The SCADA policy may include:

- The objective for managing SCADA risk;
- The links between the SCADA policy and the organisation strategic plan;
- The extent and types of risk the organisation will take;
- The process used to manage SCADA risk;
- Accountabilities for managing particular SCADA risks;
- Details of management support for SCADA;
- A statement on how SCADA risk management will be measured and reported;
- A commitment to the periodic review of the SCADA risk management system and to the SCADA policy.

It is important to establish a team to communicate and increase the awareness of the SCADA risk management policy document.

Stage 9.1.5 Establish Accountability and Authority for SCADA

The senior managers are responsible for managing risks in the organisation. All personnel are responsible for managing risks in their areas of controls such as SCADA. This can be facilitated by:

- Specifying those accountable for the management of SCADA risk;
- Establishing performance measurement and reporting processes for SCADA;
- Ensuring the appropriate levels of recognition, reward, approval and sanction.

Stage 9.1.6 Customise the SCADA Risk Management Process

The SCADA risk management process should be customised for the organisation policies and procedures and its environment.

Stage 9.1.7 Ensure Adequate Resources for SCADA Risk Management

The organisation should identify resource requirements for risk management. This should include:

- People and skills;
- Documented process and procedures;
- Information systems and database and money for specific risk treatment.

The risk management plan should specify how the risk management skills of managers and staff will be developed and maintained. The risk management information systems may possess the capability to:

- Record details of SCADA risks, controls and priorities and show any changes in them;
- Record risk treatments and associated resource requirements;
- Record details of incidents and loss events and the lessons learned;
- Track accountability for risks, controls and treatments;
- Track progress and record the completion of risk treatment actions;
- Allow progress against the risk management plan to be measured;
- Trigger monitoring and assurance activity.

INDUSTRY ADOPTION AND ACCEPTANCE FOCUS GROUP VALIDATION AND EXAMINATION

The framework presented has been validated by a SCADA industry focus group. The results and findings from the focus group are discussed below providing further data in order to validate the frameworks' importance and significance within an industry based context (*SeeBeggs and Warren 2007 for further focus group validation and results).*

Industry Focus Group Aims and Purposes

The focus group involved 5 participants from a SCADA "Tier 1 Top 5" engineering consulting company who contributed to the focus group in order to provide feedback and data on how widely the framework could be used within in industry and how the consulting company could use the framework to assist their clients who are owners and operators of SCADA systems within critical infrastructures.

Participant "A" was a certified security risk practitioner who had several years experience within the security industry. This participant had worked on various security projects within the critical infrastructure arena and has specialised certifications, accreditation and qualifications of risk standards. Participant "A" had extensive experience in conducting risk assessments and security audits as well as implementing and developing security policy. Participant "B" was a SCADA control systems engineer who had previous experience working with SCADA systems including SCADA system design, SCADA architecture and SCADA implementation across many different industry sectors. This participant was a senior SCADA expert in the field who had been involved in various SCADA projects in recent years within Australia and overseas. Participant "C" was another senior SCADA engineer who had worked previously for various SCADA vendors developing SCADA software and hardware. This participant had advanced knowledge of SCADA equipment and applications and had been designing and implementing SCADA systems for several years. Participant "D" was another senior SCADA control systems engineer who had worked on numerous SCADA projects within multiple critical infrastructure sectors. This participant had over 20 years experience with industrial control systems including SCADA and Programmable Logic Controllers (PLC's) and Distributed Control Systems (DCS) systems. Participant "E" was a junior control systems engineer who has experience in designing SCADA HMI screens and SCADA applications for industrial controls systems. This participant had a very high level knowledge of engineering coding and programming skills for customised SCADA applications for many different SCADA sectors.

Focus Group Study Theme

The focus group involved an experienced facilitator who assisted in moderating the discussion between all participants. The focus group presented a cyber-terrorism SCADA attack scenario which established the significance as well as the usability of the framework and its overall contribution to the research area. The focus group's aim was to collect data based around these discussion questions:

- Does the framework follow a process that organisations could easily adopt to measure and protect against the threat of cyber-terrorism to SCADA?
- How widely would SCADA asset owners, SCADA engineers or industry practitioners use the framework presented?
- If you are a SCADA asset owner or SCADA engineer and you needed to evaluate the likelihood of cyber-terrorism occurring against your SCADA system. How widely would you use the Cyber-terrorism SCADA Capability Assessment Model (Stage 2) of framework to measure this likelihood?

- Would there be any industry implications when using or adopting the framework?

Industry Focus Groups Findings and Results

The discussion and findings is based on how widely industry would adopt the cyber-terrorism SCADA risk framework. Participant "B" suggested that the "framework follows a process that addresses vulnerability". This participant believed that the proposed framework provides a "formal approach at identifying risks against SCADA." Participant "B" argued "that there is a need for a framework for SCADA engineers and consultants when identifying SCADA risks" such as cyber-terrorism. Such comments suggest that the framework has a valid purpose and can be of value to the SCADA community. Participant "B" argued that in the "past SCADA consultants have not followed a comprehensive approach in assessing these types of threats." Participant "B" claimed that with "previous risk assessments workshops" the participant had been involved in that "no formal approach was being used for SCADA." This participant gave an example regarding "regular password changes when employees leave the utility who are SCADA users." The participants claimed that "these types of processes were not readily adopted at plant sites that he had been involved in." Participant "B" suggested that the framework "provides a process that would encourage SCADA consultants to be more security aware and would enable them to perform a comprehensive and detailed risk assessment on SCADA systems." Participant "B" suggested "that industry and consultants require a framework to assess SCADA security risks." Also, the participant suggested that they had "not seen a framework that specifically addressed SCADA security risks." The comments from participant "B" once again reinforce the frameworks' originality, significance and overall contribution to knowledge and the SCADA community.

Participant "B" also argued that an "issue faced in using this framework may be the creditability of assessing outside organisations' ability to measure the cyber-capability of terrorist groups." However the participant agreed that if TISN or a trusted government security agency could be used to assess the cyber-capability of terrorist groups that "this would contribute to the overall creditability." The present authors explained that this was included as a suggested procedure and guideline in the model and that creditability could be overcome by a trusted source such as TISN or ASIO. This once again reiterates the significance of having a cyber-terrorism steering group in order to assess and estimate scores within the cyber-terrorism SCADA capability assessment model.

Likewise, Participant "C" claimed that there may "be implications when implementing the framework on rather large installations when selecting hardware and equipment that may not be installed until three years." This participant suggested that capability of the "hardware may not be able to be updated in order to meet the growing threat level." The present authors suggest that technology will constantly being changing and that updating and reviewing of the entire model at least every 6 months or accordingly to each organisation's needs and requirement levels would assist in overcoming such problems. This suggests that the framework is adaptable to ongoing change and refinement and also demonstrates the model's flexibility with each individual organisation, providing even further validation and acceptance.

Also, Participant "D" suggested that there would be a "great deal of confidence in adopting the framework as there is no framework that exists" that addresses cyber-terrorism and SCADA risks. This participant believed that "educating users about the framework would be beneficial in the adoption process." The present authors agree with the participant's comments and suggests that the framework could be adopted relatively easily by educating SCADA engineers on the cyber-terrorism and SCADA risk process. Participant

"D's" comments once again demonstrate that the framework is useful and significant for SCADA engineers and SCADA asset owners. This overall adds value to the framework's purpose, but more importantly to the overall research contribution.

Furthermore, Participant "A" argued that the framework provides an "original process" and "that there is no framework that deals with this type of threat." The participant claimed that the "framework demonstrated a "suggested process to mitigate risk." Participant "A" argued that once a "framework is launched then obviously through experience it builds." This participant suggested that the framework was "brilliant" and that adopting the framework "looks at a process that could be put into place." Participant "A" said that a "framework in place such as this had not been done before." Participant "A" argued that it's "on the tips, tongues, minds and heart of the corporate world and government security agencies all over the world." This participant believed that there was "a lot of merit" in the framework and its contribution. Also, the participant argued that it "provided a starting point that could be vertically integrated" into organisations. Likewise, "keeping it simple" was another suggested comment by Participant "A" who claimed that "government agencies are trying to get their head around the cyber-terrorism threat." The present authors strongly agree with such comments made by Participant "A" and believes that the framework provides a systematic and fluid process that could be simply used and adopted by industry and government. Participant "A" said that the framework gives "SCADA engineers an understanding of what risk assessment processes there are for SCADA." This ultimately again adds strong value to the overall validity, purpose and adoption phase of the framework within industry. Participant "A" also claimed that the framework is very useful as it gives "suggestion and view points" and if the framework "could be rated out of 100 I would give it 500 as there is definitely merit in it." The participant's comments, reinforces the framework's validity and significance within the SCADA community.

Similarly, Participant "E" suggested that on "previous projects regarding SCADA security risk assessments they had never used a formal approach or framework in identify threats against SCADA." After adopting and using the framework proposed this participant believed "that it was of great benefit as it identified gaps and security issues that were not previously recognised" in assessing SCADA threats such as cyber-terrorism. This participant firmly agreed that the "framework was of great value and benefit." This highlights that the framework has subsequently been adopted on various projects within the SCADA "Tier 1 Top 5" engineering consulting company. This once again demonstrates the framework's overall significance and purpose, and also reinforces the framework's validity and industry acceptance and adoption.

Likewise, Participant "C" reinforced the use and acceptance of the framework and said "that in terms of assets owners, they would use the framework in order to determine the risks they face from threats including cyber-terrorism." Participant "A" said that "SCADA asset owners would use the framework because the threat of cyber-terrorism is evolving." However the participant claimed that many SCADA asset owners are "not aware of the framework for cyber-terrorism because the concept is so new." Participant "A" suggested that most "SCADA asset owners don't even know what cyber-terrorism means" and that "they have not ventured into this area." However, the participant suggested that "some major utilities companies are aware of this issue and would use the framework." The participant argued "that it's an education and culture process and that there would be some people screaming down the door for this type of thing." Participant "A" said that the framework would "need to be engaged with SCADA engineers and that education would be required." The present authors would like to acknowledge that the framework is actively being presented throughout industry which is providing the opportunity to educate SCADA engineers and SCADA asset owners of the threat of cyber-terrorism against SCADA systems. It also is encouraging SCADA asset owners to adopt the framework in order to assess security threats such as cyber-terrorism. Participant "A" also suggested that there was definitely a need for such a framework within corporate Australia." The present authors agree with the comments suggested by Participant "A" indicate that the framework provides a major contribution to all SCADA engineers and consultants. He has also encouraged all members of the SCADA community to embrace and acknowledge the real dangers faced from cyber-terrorism and other associated security risks, when adopting the framework.

On the other hand, there were some industry implications that were discussed within the focus group. Participant "D" claimed that "small organisations may not adopt the framework because it may be too costly to implement." This participant suggested that "certain types of industries that use SCADA systems may not see any benefit." For example, the participant suggested that organisations that "make plastic bottles using SCADA systems may not see any value any adopting the framework." Participant "D" agreed that these types of organisations may not be a subjected to a terrorist attack such as cyber-terrorism." Participant "C" also supported this comment by suggesting "that in some industries down time on SCADA systems and PLC's is not as critical as in other sectors." The present authors agree with both participants and suggests that the framework would be more suitable and appropriate for large organisations controlling critical infrastructure such as power, gas and water, etc. The present authors also agree that cost would be an implication for smaller organisations as they may not have the funding to carry out the SCADA risk process and the cyber-terrorism capability assessment model by funding and organising the cyber-terrorism steering group. These issues and implications would only be applicable to certain types of organisations. As the majority of SCADA systems are controlled by very large critical infrastructure organisations and therefore the framework should be targeted towards these types of infrastructures.

This is supported by Participant "B" who suggested that the "framework would be used in major process industries such as power, water oil and gas where any type of shut down is hugely costly." This participant also suggested "that the framework would be useful at the board level as they would be interested in risks that would shut down processes within the plant." The participant claimed that the framework "would support this as high risks could be identified" such as cyber-terrorism. Also, Participant "B" suggested the use of the "cyber-terrorism steering group" would be adopted if the organisations had the budget. This participant provided an example that "if cyber-terrorism was their number one risk", that "his organisation would definitely go ahead with acquiring the resources through TISN, and ASIO in order to make an assessment for the cyber-terrorism SCADA capability model." This once again demonstrates enormous value and significance for organisations to adopt the cyber-terrorism SCADA risk framework.

The main implications identified from participants within the focus group in regards to industry adoption included:

- Cost of implementing the framework;
- Education and cultural issues need to be considered when implementing the framework;
- Small organisations may not adopt the framework as it may not be suitable to their industry;
- The framework needs to be industry specific and targeted to larger organisations.

These implications would only be applicable to certain organisations and would not affect the overall purpose of the frameworks functionality usability and adoption within an industry based context.

Lastly, the industry focus group provided positive feedback on how widely the framework would be adopted by industry SCADA professionals. The results and findings have demonstrated how organisations and SCADA practitioners would use the framework and also how important a framework such as the one presented is needed within industry.

In summary, the main findings and results regarding the industry adoption phase of the model within industry has been identified by the third focus group in order to provide further validation of the cyber-terrorism SCADA risk framework. Below is a summary of the results and findings:

- There is no framework readily available that address cyber-terrorism and SCADA;
- There is a great need within industry for a framework that deals with SCADA security threats such as cyber-terrorism;
- The framework would be most suitable for large process control organisations that depend on criticality for their operations;
- The framework maybe costly to implement for smaller organisations;
- The framework has merit and is of great value and significance within the SCADA industry;
- The framework would be widely accepted and used by many organisations that use SCADA systems.

FUTURE RESEARCH

The future direction of the research will be the continued development and refinement of the SCADA risk framework. The research will focus upon implementing the framework with a number of industrial contexts and determine common themes and issues in relation to the framework.

CONCLUSION

This chapter has presented a framework to measure and protect SCADA systems from the threat of cyber-terrorism within Australia which various experts from various industrial sectors have tested and validated as an effective means to identify Australian SCADA systems' vulnerabilities, terrorist' capabilities and the means to control factors to reduce terrorists' possibilities for conducting successful attacks against these infrastructure assets.

The industry focus group findings demonstrated how widely the framework would be used within industry and has suggested how significant and important the framework is needed within industry. The overall acceptance by industry once again provides the present authors and the research community with a framework that is highly regarded and valuable to all SCADA practitioners. These results and outcomes have assisted in addressing how to measure and protect SCADA systems from cyber-terrorist threats. The research developed is of great significance and value to the SCADA security community and to organisations that are controlling SCADA systems within Australia. The research has provided organisations with a methodology to measure and to protect against the threat of cyber-terrorism, but more importantly, has demonstrated the need for new counter-terrorism security models to assist with assessing new cyber security threats such as cyber-terrorism.

REFERENCES

Australia, S. (2009). *Risk management.* (AS/NZS ISO 31000:2009). Retrieved March 1, 2010, from http://www.standards.com.au

Beggs, C. (2005). Cyber-terrorism a threat to Australia? In Khosrow-Pour, M. (Ed.), *Managing modern organisation with Information Technology* (pp. 472–475). Hershey, PA: Information Resources Management Association.

Beggs, C., & Warren, M. (2007). Safeguarding Australia from cyber-terrorism: A proposed cyber-terrorism SCADA risk framework for Australia. *The Journal of Information Warfare*, 7(1), 24–35.

Denning, D. (2000). *Cyber-terrorism testimony before the Special Panel on Terrorism Committee on Armed Services US House of Representatives.* Georgetown University. Retrieved September 29, 2009, from http://www.cs.georgetown.edu/~denning/infosec/cyberterror.html

Internet Security Systems. (2005). *Assessment and remediation of vulnerabilities in the SCADA and process control systems of utilities*. Retrieved October 27, 2009, from http://documents.iss.net/whitepapers/SCADA.pdf

Krutz, R. (2005). *Securing SCADA systems*. Indianapolis, IN: Wiley Technology.

Times, N. Y. (2007, June 2). A cyber-blockade in Estonia. *The New York Times*. Retrieved July 23, 2009, from http://www.nytimes.com/2007/06/02/opinion/02sat3.html

Trusted Information Sharing Network (TISN). (2008). *What is SCADA?* Retrieved October 2, 2009, from http://www.tisn.gov.au/www/tisn/tisn.nsf/Page/e-Security#_What_is_SCADA?

ADDITIONAL READING

Beggs, C. (2010). *Safeguarding Infrastructure Assets from Cyber-terrorism: Measuring and Protecting SCADA systems from Cyber-terrorists in Australia*. Germany: LAP Lambert Academic Publishing.

Beggs, C., & Warren, M. (2007). "Safeguarding Australia from Cyber-terrorism: A Proposed Cyber-terrorism SCADA Risk Framework for Australia," *The Journal of Information Warfare. ECU Perth, Australia*, 7(Issue 1), 24–35.

Clarke, R., & Kanke, R. (2010). *Cyber War: The Next Threat to National Security and What to Do About It*. USA: ECCO Press.

Colarik, A. (2006). *Cyber Terrorism: Political and Economic Implications*. USA: Idea Group. doi:10.4018/978-1-59904-021-9

Denning, D. (1998). *Information Warfare and Security*. Addison-Wesley.

Igure, V. (2008). *Security Assessment of Scada Protocols: A Taxonomy Based Methodology for the Identification of Security Vulnerabilities in Scada Protocols*. Germany: LAP Lambert Academic Publishing.

Krutz, R. (2005). *Securing SCADA Systems*. USA: Wiley Publishers.

Slay, J., & Koronios, A. (2006), Information Technology Security & Risk Management, John Wiley & Sons, Milton, Qld.

Verton, D. (2003) Black Ice: The Invisible Threat of Cyber-terrorism. Osborne/McGraw-Hill, USA. ISBN 0072227877.

Weiss, J. (2010). *Protecting Industrial Control Systems from Electronic Threats*. New York: Momentum Press.

Wiles, J. (2008). *Techno Security's Guide to Securing SCADA: A Comprehensive Handbook On Protecting The Critical Infrastructure*. USA: Syngress Publishers.

KEY TERMS AND DEFINITIONS

Critical Infrastructure Protection: Protection of key critical systems. These key critical systems relate to national critical systems such as power, water, electricity, banking, etc.

Cyber Terrorism: the use of ICTs to attack and control critical information systems with political motivation and the intent to cause harm and spread fear to people.

Information Security: With regards to this chapter refers to the security of the information systems that are used and the data that is processed.

Risk: Protecting information systems from unauthorised access, disclosure, modification, or destruction of information.

Safeguards: (also known as countermeasures) are technologies, physical security devices, organisational procedures and policies that avoid, counteract or minimise security risks.

SCADA: This is known as *S*upervisory *C*ontrol *a*nd *D*ata *A*cquisition. In the USA these systems are referred to as industrial control systems.

SCADA Security: The use of security technologies to protect SCADA systems.

Chapter 22
Detecting Compliance Failures in Unmanaged Processes

Yurdaer N. Doganata
IBM T.J. Watson Research, USA

ABSTRACT

The importance and the challenges of detecting compliance failures in unmanaged business processes is discussed, and the process of creating and verifying internal controls as a requirement of enterprise risk management framework is explained. The effect of using automated auditing tools to detect compliance failures against internal control points in unmanaged business processes is investigated. Risk exposure of a business process due to compliance failures is analyzed, and the factors that affect the risk exposure of a business process are evaluated.

INTRODUCTION

Detecting compliance failures help organizations better control their operations and remain competitive. The quality of product and services can not be ensured in a business if the processes do not conform to design goals and comply with the rules and regulations. Moreover, organizations may be subject to serious financial penalty as well as civil and penal consequences if they failed to comply with established guidelines, rules and regulations.

DOI: 10.4018/978-1-4666-0197-0.ch022

Hence, the impact of non-compliance may have severe consequences that need to be managed either by reducing or eliminating the associated risk. Companies invest significantly on detecting compliance failures to ensure governance and manage risk. The cost of reducing the risk of being non-compliant could run into millions of dollars (Greengard, 2005). AMR Research survey reveals that the spending of companies on governance and risk management and compliance expected to grow to $29.8 billion in 2010, up nearly %4 over the $28.7 billion spent in 2009 (AMR Research, 2010).

Compliance can be managed relatively easy when the set of interrelated and interacting activities to achieve business goals are coordinated by business process management systems. This is the case where processes are well structured and documented. When the activities in a business process are structured enough, the transitions from one activity to another are automated by software systems. In a fully automated structured business process real time information about the status of various activities can be collected by business activity monitoring software (McCoy, 2002). Hence, compliance of processes against rules and regulations can be checked automatically. In such automated environments, the trace of the business operations is completely visible and it possible to know who did what and when.

In reality, business activities span multiple systems and organizations across modern enterprises, integrating legacy and newly developed software applications. There exists no single system or organization that controls the process end to end. Operations often depend on activities that rely heavily on human interaction without predefined control structures. Human actors decide what to do to achieve business goals. Since the transitions between human activities can not be fully automated or monitored by software systems, the visibility of end to end business operations is reduced. The processes that consist of such activities are called *unmanaged processes*. In the absence of business process management software with business activity monitoring that registers various aspects of the business operations, compliance check is usually performed manually by auditors, hence it is costly, time consuming.

There are primarily two challenges in ensuring compliance of unmanaged or partially managed processes. The first challenge is to increase the traceability of end to end operations. This requires tracking, capturing and correlating relevant aspects of the business operations. Once the visibility of the operations is increased, the second challenge is to create internal controls without depending on in depth knowledge of IT system and business application code. Creating and deploying new internal controls should be done without incurring additional IT cost. If the operations are tractable and the relevant business artifacts can be gathered, automated auditing systems and tools can detect compliance failures continuously and reduce the cost of employing auditors significantly.

In the absence of process automation software that can control and record who did what and when, the compliance check is a costly and time consuming task performed manually by auditors (AMR Research, 2010). Automated continuous auditing systems, on the other hand, provide for an almost cost-free auditing opportunity if the initial cost of building such a system is excluded. Such a system can run continuously and performs evaluation for all process instances without adding to the cost of auditing. While continuous auditing systems eliminate or reduce the dependency on audit professionals, they are not infallible. The tools that are built to realize automated continuous auditing rely on information extraction from process events and information, including e-mail transactions between the people within the organizations. The extracted information about the processes may contain errors and due to these errors the decision on the compliance may be faulty. Moreover, the testing of a compliance condition may require a level of text analysis that is not yet available in automated systems. Hence, the automated systems can perform fast and extensive auditing of the internal control points at the cost of making mistakes. As a result, some compliance failures may be missed while some other cases that are compliant may be declared non-compliant.

The focus of this chapter is to discuss the factors that impact the effectiveness of continuous assurance with automated audit tools. The subject is important for organizations which need to determine how much they should invest to remain compliant. The chapter helps understanding the characteristics of the operational environment that affects the efficiency of automated tools and the conditions that necessitate hiring experts for manual auditing to avoid compliance failures. Ultimately, the companies expect to reduce the risk exposure at least as much as they spend for compliance assurance. Therefore, they need to know how they can optimize the return on their investment.

BACKGROUND

Businesses describe their operations in terms of activities that are performed to realize the defined business goals. These activities, their interrelations and interactions constitute the building blocks of the business processes of organizations. Traditionally business processes are enacted manually and guided by the knowledge of the people who established the business goals and the associated activities around the business goal. Manual enactment of business processes, however, are costly, time consuming and error prone since they are human centric.

Advances in computing technologies have led to the development of software systems that are used to automate the execution of some of these processes. These are called *Business Process Management Systems (BPMS)* (Weske, 2007). While BPMS have been providing many benefits for coordinating activities within the enterprise and help improving the productivity and efficiency, a full automation of all activities in a modern enterprise does not seem realistic. This is mainly because today's enterprise applications span cross systems and organizations where newly developed software applications are integrated with legacy system. In addition, often business processes rely on human activities that cannot always be predicted and the information exchange is based on e-mail or attachments where the content is unstructured. In such environments, the next activity in a sequence of activities is not always determined by rules executed by automation software, but by the human decision. Before the advancements of computers, the business interactions were always between people. Today, the transactions are between various resources that include both people and automated systems.

When all the transactions between activities and parties are fully controlled by automation software based pre-defined rules or process definitions, the associated process is called a "managed" process. In managed processes whenever an activity ends, the next activity is determined by the automation software. This implies that if human intervention is necessary to start or end a task, then the process cannot be fully automated, hence it cannot be called "managed". A process which cannot be fully automated is called an "unmanaged" process. An important characteristic of unmanaged processes is that some of the transitions between its activities are non-deterministic. This means that when an activity ends, there is uncertainty about the next activity. This may cause integrity lapses in complex business environment since actual operations may differ from what they are originally designed for. In such an environment, the compliance of business processes to pre-established rules and regulation cannot be ensured.

In order to manage the risk associated with compliance failures and for the continuous assurance of business goals, organizations use Enterprise Risk Management framework such as COSO ERM (COSO, 2004, 2009, 2010). ERM framework provides for a systematic way of creating internal control points as part of audit and compliance activities. Internal controls can provide a reasonable assurance that the goal of an organization is met and for some organizations they are required by law (Sarbanes-Oxley Act, 2002).

INTERNAL CONTROLS

Internal controls are primarily created to manage the execution of an activity or set of activities for the purpose of preventing business risk

Figure 1. "Opening a new job" process model

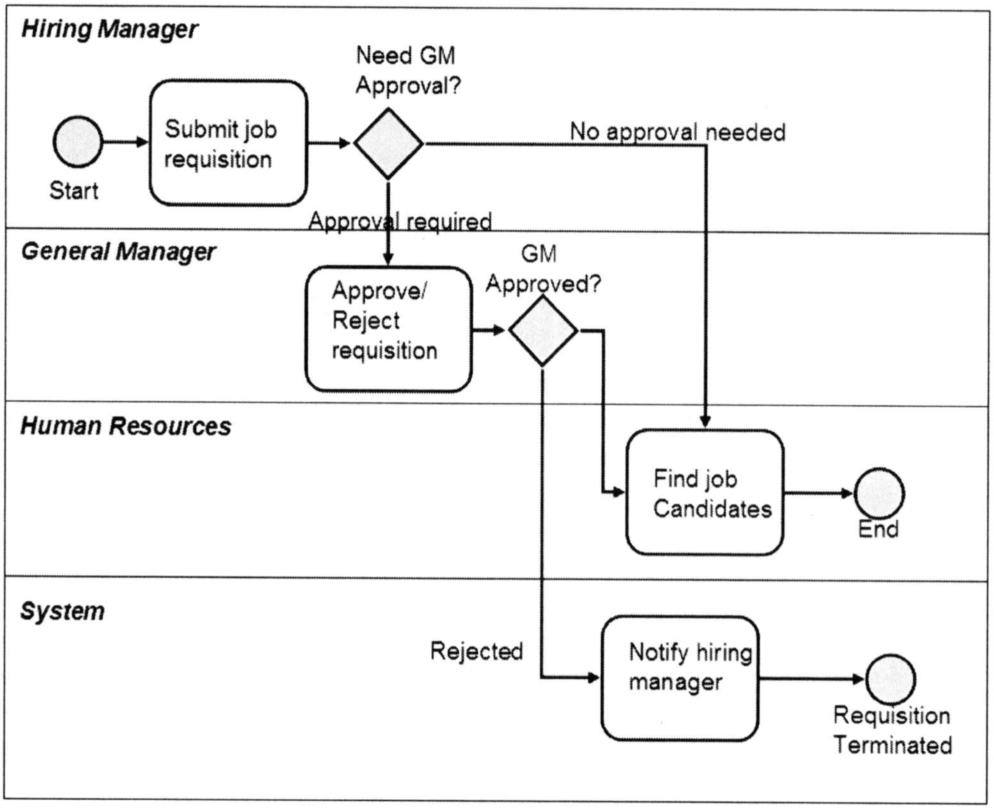

from occurring (COSO, 2010). The steps of the process of creating internal controls can be outlined as identifying business process and the associated goal, assessing the risk of achieving the business goal, determining the control points to check to prevent business risk from occurring and testing if the internal controls are working as intended. A new position open process shown in Figure 1 is used to explain the steps of creating internal controls. The example can be found in IBM Websphere Lombardi manual (n.d.). In the example process shown in Figure 1, the hiring manager submits a job requisition for a position. If this is for a new job position, the requisition is routed to the general manager for approval. If this is for an existing position, the requisition is routed directly to human resources. The general manager evaluates the submitted requisition for a new position and either approved it or rejects it. This is represented by "Approve/reject requisition" task. If approved, the requisition is routed to human resources. Otherwise, it is terminated and the hiring manager is notified

The business goal is to introduce an effective hiring process which requires the oversight of general manager who makes the planning for new job positions while bypassing the approval process for existing positions which have already been approved. Hence, the compliance goal associated with this business goal can be stated as: "Ensure that general manager approves every 'new' job positions opened". According to the process definition, before human resources start searching for candidates for a new position, they must have the approval of the general manager. This is not necessary for existing positions. When the 'Find job candidates" task is not automated by a process management system, i.e., enacted manually, and it is controlled by human, there may be errors. In a fully automated system, approvals are kept in a content management system and the" Find job candidates" activity may not be initialized until a notification is received from the content management system about the approval of the general manager. In contrast to fully automated systems, there is a risk of non-compliance in human centric systems where finding a candidate is a human action and the person who is responsible for this task may overlook the type of position and may ignore the rejection from general manager. Once the risk is identified, then the control point is determined to eliminate it. A potential internal control provides for a reasonable assurance for potential risk and hence, can be stated as: "There must be an evidence of general manager approval, before candidates are searched for the 'new' job opening".

If the internal controls are represented in terms of the artifacts that can be captured during the execution of the business process, then automated tools can be used to check the compliance. In this example, if the approval or the rejection of general manager is linked to the job requisition id and stored, then it is possible to check if the task 'Find job candidates' is executed with proper approval or not. Automation of compliance checking enables continuous assurance of compliance, which requires capturing relevant aspects of the process around a control point from execution traces.

Traditional organizations use manual auditing for compliance assurance. Manual auditing involves the use of subject matter experts, but typically covers only a small set process instances because of time and cost constraints. The cost of improving the status of compliance and reduce the risk of being non-compliant by using experts could run into millions of dollars for many organizations (Greengard, 2005). In many cases, audits are performed in a quarterly or yearly basis, and cases are selected through statistical sampling. There is thus a trade of between the cost of sampling sufficient number of cases and the possibility of poor auditing which may cause missing opportunities for corrective action. While traditional audits are performed a few times a year, it is widely believed that compliance is an ongoing process that goes beyond testing and evaluating the internal controls of a sampled space. Thus many corporations focus on enhancing or implementing systems to ensure compliance on a continuous basis.

The COSO board recognizes the need to monitor internal controls effectively (2009). Effective monitoring of internal control point within the enterprise through internal controls requires the visibility of end to end operations. In a fully automated systems all the executions steps of the business processes are visible and execution steps are traceable. Pre-defined conditions that determine transactions between activities are embedded in the automation software and can be traced to control risk and compliance. In case of unmanaged processes, however, techniques are needed to increase the visibility of end to end operations based on the actual execution traces such as business provenance tracking.

Software systems that track the provenance is particularly important in case of unmanaged processes, since majority of compliance spending goes to manual labor of auditors and consultants who spend a lot of time to track the lineage of business tasks and items. Advances in data management, processing and analysis systems have led to development of tools which can automate auditing process. Automated auditing took is based in business provenance technology explained that is developed to increase the traceability of end to end operations in a flexible and cost effective way.

A number of works (Ruopeng, Sadiq, & Governatori, 2008; Goedertier & Vanthienen, 2006) advocate addressing control objectives early in design time and propose supporting mechanism for business process designers. A method is proposed in (Ruopeng, Sadiq, & Governatori, 2008) to help the process designers to measure the compliance degree of a given process model against the set of objection. A language is introduced in (Goedertier

& Vanthienen, 2006) to express temporal rules about the obligations and permissions in order to help the designers at the process modeling time to validate and verify business contracts. In many traditional systems, however, the control objectives were not known at the time of process design. They are added to the risk management system later and the audit tools are customized based on the control objectives over existing business operations. In this chapter, in measuring the effectiveness of compliance tools, the control objectives are not assumed to be known at the time of process design.

The method presented in this chapter to measure the effectiveness of automated audit tools does not depend on a particular process tracking technology or control point representation. There has been an extensive research on developing business rules approach to control and influence the behavior of business processes (IBM, n.d.; Business Rule Group, 2000) and attempts to formally represent internal control points (Christopher, Muller, & Pfitzmann, 2006). These studies are left outside the scope of this chapter since the chapter focuses on detecting compliance failures directly from process instances without making any prior assumptions about the structure of the business process.

The effectiveness of the tool is measured by its capacity to detect compliance failures during the execution of an unmanaged business process. This is accomplished by identifying an internal control point and comparing the number of non-compliance instances detected in the presence and in the absence of auditing tool. As a result of this comparison, how much the traditional auditing process performed by auditors under a budget constraint can be improved by employing auditing tool is quantified. The approach is based on inferring the prevalence of non-compliance and the performance of the automated auditing tool from a set of sample test results.

In the next section, the building blocks of an automated audit tool are described.

AUTOMATED AUDIT TOOLS

An automated auditing tool is a software system that captures information relevant to the internal control points of a business process, puts them into context and computes the compliance status for each control point. Auditing tools rely on correlating the data extracted from the underlying IT system to the relevant aspects of business control points effectively. Hence, relating the business goals to IT level data constitutes the core of this technology as described in (Curbera et al., 2008). Figure 2 outlines the step of building such a system which starts with converting business rules and regulations into compliance goals (Step 1). Compliance goals are identified by examining the business rules and deciding what action steps are needed. In other words, from the business rules expressed in the language of business people, compliance goals are identified. In the sample 'new position open' process above, the compliance goals is stated as "Ensure that general manager approves every 'new' job positions opened" (Step 1). This lays the ground work for setting up IT rules for compliance. Once the compliance goals are identified; tasks, activities, resources, artifacts and their relations that are relevant to the identified goal are determined and mapped onto a data model. As an example, the associated activities and artifacts related to the goal defined above are 'Approve/Reject requisition' task, approval or rejection messages and the type of job requisition (Step 2). Recording probes collect event data and the associated business artifacts related to the compliance goal from the underlying information system and map them onto provenance data (Step 3 and 4). In the example above, the event data related to opening a job requisition, sending the approval/rejection to content management system, activities of human resource constitute the relevant data related to the process. A "provenance graph" is then formed with the data objects constituting the nodes and the relations among the data objects the edges. The

Figure 2. Steps for compliance checking

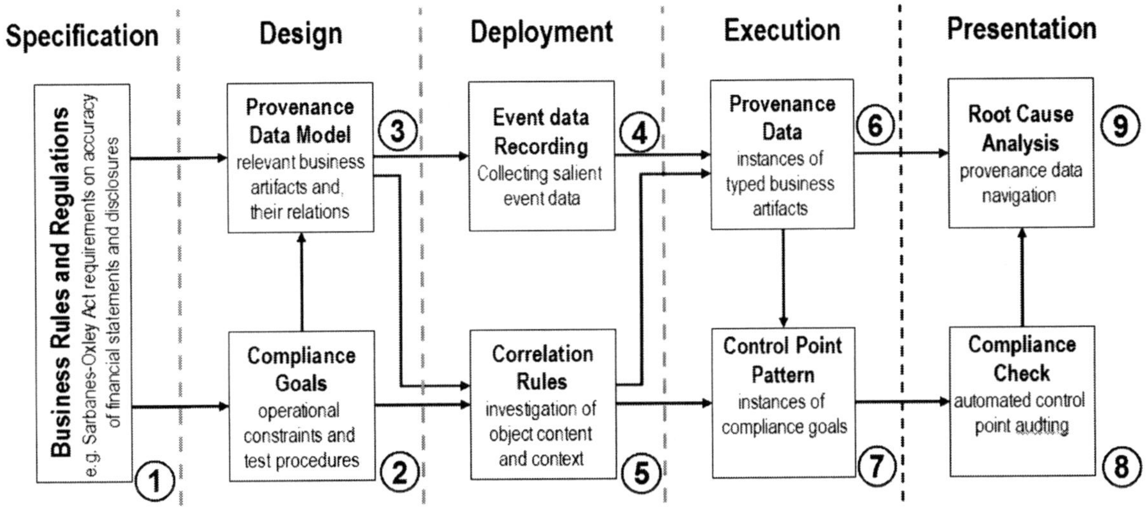

data objects are correlated by using the compliance goals and the underlying data model (Step 5). Business control points are then expressed in terms of data entities extracted from the process execution trace as graph patterns (Step 6). Hence, control points provide a bridge between various components of the business operations and the actual data that could be consumed the IT system. A business control point that can be expressed in terms of the data produced and consumed by the IT system can be computed to check compliance in step 7. Root cause analysis of compliance failures can be done by querying the provenance graph in step 9. Provenance graph is formed by running correlation rules over the provenance data object. Root cause analysis is performed by querying the provenance data.

MEASURING EFFECTIVENESS OF AUDITING TOOLS

The problem of using automated audit tools to determine compliance failures is equivalent to determining the prevalence of a condition through screening the population by using test which is fallible. The tests that are not %100 accurate have been used extensively in health services to estimate the prevalence of a medical condition or a disease. Similarly, it is possible to determine the prevalence of non-conformance in process execution traces by using automated auditing tools. In partially managed processes, where transactions are not fully controlled and are based on human centric activities, automatic auditing may not be perfect. As an example, in the "new position open' process, the internal control requires that the evidence of general manager's approval must exist for every new job opening. If the general manager sends her approval to the human resources via e-mail, and the e-mail is stored as an evidence of approval then the text analysis of the e-mail is necessary to confirm that the message is indeed for the approval of a specific job opening. The text analysis, on the other hand, is not error free. Hence, the automated auditing tools are fallible in making classification for compliance.

The problem of identifying non-compliant instances of business processes is a binary classification problem where the process traces are grouped into two based on if certain internal controls are satisfied or not. There is always a trade

Figure 3. Comparison of manual and automated audit in terms of cost, speed and accuracy

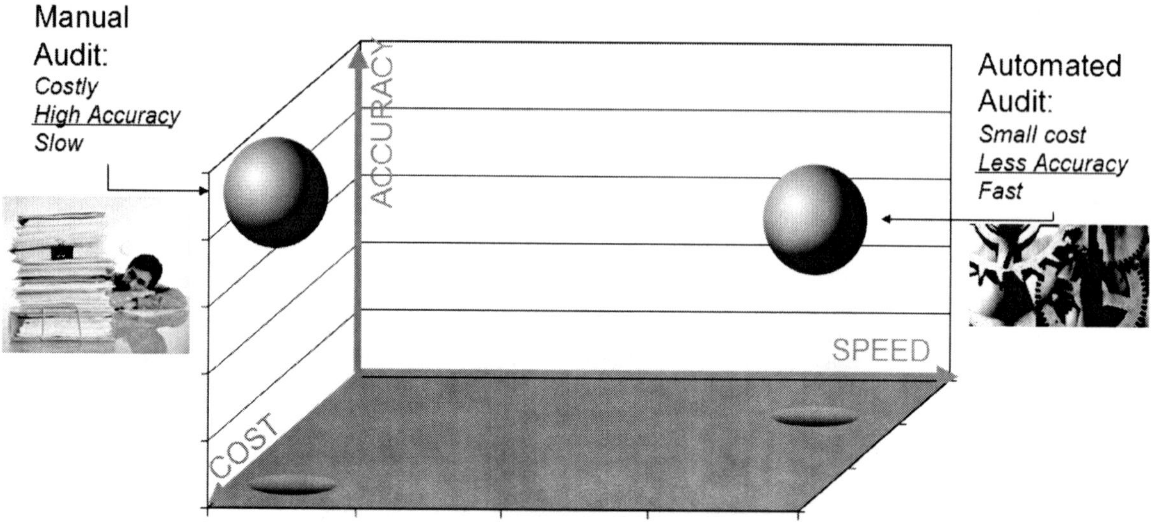

off between the quality of classification and the cost. Audits performed by expert can be assumed always correct, provided that human errors in auditing are negligible. On the other hand, there is a significant cost associated with the manual auditing. Hence, the number of process instances that can be audited manually is limited by the budget constraints. In contrast to manual auditing, the cost of auditing by automated tools can be assumed negligible allowing all process instances to be audited without incurring extra cost. The result of such automated classification, however, is fallible. Figure 3 illustrates the comparison of manual auditing with automated auditing based on speed, accuracy and cost. As depicted in Figure 3, automated auditing is less costly, fast but less accurate at the same time.

The compliance officer with a limited budget has to find an optimum way of detecting compliance failures. If he decides to spend his entire budget to hire expert for audit, then it may not be possible to cover all process instances. If he decides to save money and run the automated tool, on the other hand, he may cover all process instances but there may be a significant number of false negatives which may expose the risk of non-compliance. The optimum solution lies between utilizing automated tools along with hiring some experts. Regardless, effectiveness of the automated tool needs to be measured.

In order to measure the effectiveness of the automated audit tool, a methodology is considered that enables detecting the largest number of non-compliant instances within a budget constraint. The methodology is based on evaluating all process instances by using the automated audit machine and asking experts randomly re-evaluate some of the instances marked as compliant and noncompliant by the automated machine. The approach is modeled below.

The performance of such an auditing tool is measured by its *sensitivity* and *specificity,* since the tools is basically used for binary classification of process instances as compliant and non-compliant. Sensitivity measures the proportions of actual positives (that is non-compliant cases) which are correctly identified, while specificity measures the proportions of negatives (compli-

Figure 4. Depiction of regions labeled as compliant and non-compliant by the tool

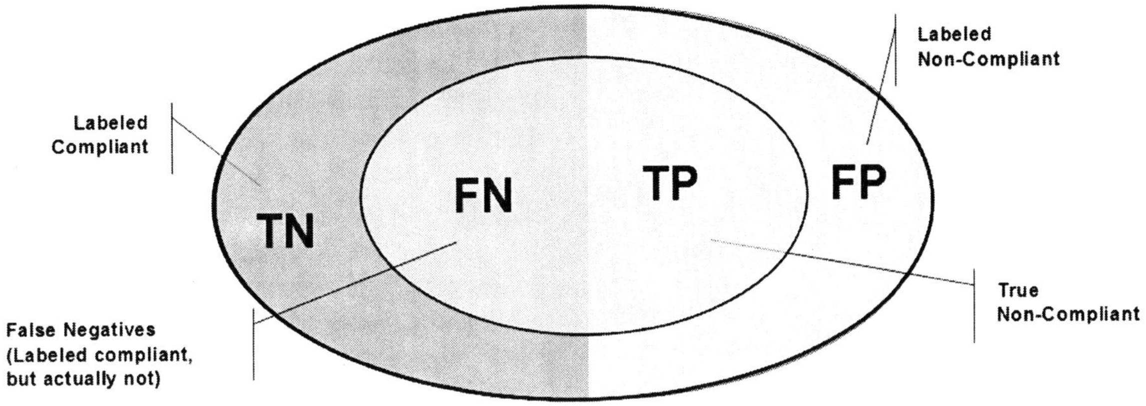

ant cases) which are correctly identified. The probability that a randomly selected instance is actually compliant is defined as *Pr (I = 0)*, the probability that a fallible auditing tool labels an instance compliant is defined as *Pr (F = 0)* and non-compliant as *Pr (F = 1)*. Hence,

η, Sensitivity: $TP/(TP + FN) = Pr(F=1/I=1)$ (1)

θ, Specificity: $TN/(TN+FP) = Pr(F=0/I=0)$ (2)

where *TP* (True Positive) is the number of non-compliant instances labeled as non-compliant, *FN* (False Negative) is the number of non-compliant instances labeled as compliant, *TN* (True Negative) is the number of compliant instances labeled as compliant, *FP* (False Positive) is the number of compliant instances labeled as non-compliant. Figure 4 depicts the regions labeled as compliant and non-compliant and illustrates *TN, TP, FN, FP* instances.

Given a fallible auditing tool with sensitivity and specificity (η, θ), and given a fixed budget to fund the use of audit experts, the goal is to find out how much the detection of non-compliant process instances can be improved. As discussed before, poor auditing may cause missing opportunities for corrective action; hence the number of non-compliant cases detected as a result of auditing should be maximized. On one hand, budget constraint limits the number of cases that can be audited by using an expert. On the other hand, a fallible automated audit machine can be used to evaluate every process instance without incurring extra cost. The goal is to device a methodology for enabling to detect the largest number of non-compliant instances possible under these constraints. One possible methodology is to evaluate all process instances by using the automated audit machine and ask experts randomly re-evaluate M_1 cases among the ones marked as non-compliant (Region N) and M_2 among the ones marked as compliant (Region C) by the automated audit machine. This way the sample space that the experts operate is reduced. It is assumed that the budget limits the expert evaluation of only $M = M_1 + M_2$ cases. The effectiveness of the proposed methodology can be measured by comparing the expected number of non-compliant process instances detected. If the number is higher than what experts would have determined under budget constraint without using the methodology, then it can be concluded that the methodology improves the auditing process in general.

The probability that a randomly selected process instance is labeled non-compliant, *P(F=1)*, by the auditing tool is ($p_{11+}p_{01}$). Given the condition that the auditors work only on instances labeled as non-compliant by the tool (Region N, all *TP* and *FP* instances), probability that the auditors detect a non-compliant case is

$$\Pr(I = 1 / F = 1) = \frac{p_{11}}{p_{11} + p_{01}} \quad (3)$$

Similarly, the probability that an auditors detects a non-compliant cases among the ones labeled as compliant by the tool (Region C, all TN and FN instances) is

$$\Pr(I = 1 / F = 1) = \frac{p_{10}}{p_{00} + p_{10}} \quad (4)$$

Hence, the average number of non-compliant cases detected by using this method can then be found as below where the function W is called the "worth" of this method.

$$W = M_1 \frac{p_{11}}{p_{11} + p_{01}} + M_2 \frac{p_{10}}{p_{10} + p_{00}} \quad (5)$$

The worth function is maximized by making the experts work either in the region labeled as compliant (Region C) or as non-compliant (Region N) depending on the values of p_{11} /($p_{11+}p_{01}$) and p_{01} /($p_{00+}p_{01}$) provided that the budget constraint M is less than the size of both regions. This is a reasonable assumption since the size of process instances in both regions are usually much larger than M. Hence,

$$\max\{W\} = \begin{cases} M\dfrac{p_{11}}{p_{11} + p_{01}} & \dfrac{p_{01}}{p_{01} + p_{00}} \le \dfrac{p_{11}}{p_{11} + p_{01}} \\ M\dfrac{p_{10}}{p_{10} + p_{00}} & \dfrac{p_{10}}{p_{10} + p_{00}} \le \dfrac{p_{11}}{p_{11} + p_{01}} \end{cases} \quad (6)$$

In the absence of auditing tool, we would only rely on the efforts of the audit experts. The average worth of this practice would then be the product of M and the prevalence of non-compliance, p. Let W_0 be the worth of using only experts as auditors, the expected worth is then

$$W_0 = M_p \quad (7)$$

Potential improvement of using auditing tool can then be measured by the ratio of the worth functions $max\{W\}$ and $W_{0,}$ i.e., improvement, Ω, is equal to $max\{W\}/\ W_0$. From (6) and (7), the improvement function Ω is found as:

$$\Omega = \begin{cases} \dfrac{p_{11}}{(p_{11} + p_{01})p} & \dfrac{p_{01}}{p_{01} + p_{00}} \le \dfrac{p_{11}}{p_{11} + p_{01}} \\ \dfrac{p_{10}}{(p_{10} + p_{00})p} & \dfrac{p_{10}}{p_{10} + p_{00}} \succ \dfrac{p_{11}}{p_{11} + p_{01}} \end{cases} \quad (8)$$

where p is the prevalence of non-compliance among the process instances, that is the probability that a randomly selected process instance is actually non-compliant or $Pr(I = 1)$. Equation (8) shows that the improvement is the ratio the probability that a randomly selected process instance is found non-compliant by the expert and the prevalence. Depending on the region (labeled compliant or non-compliant) experts work the probability that a randomly selected process instance is found non-compliant by the expert is either $p_{11}/\ (p_{11+}p_{01})$ or $p_{10}/\ (p_{10+}p_{00})$. It is clear from the equation that there is always going to be improvement since the probability detecting non-compliant instances by employing only auditors in the specified region is greater than p. The reason for this is that the prevalence of the region labeled by auditing tool is greater than p as long as labeling is not done randomly.

Equation (8) is an expression for the improvement factor, however not useful if the probabilities are not tied to sensitivity and the specificity of the automated audit tool. In order to simplify the calculations, the joint probabilities $p_{11}, p_{01}, p_{10}, p_{00}$ are approximated with their mean values by using the sensitivity, η, and specificity, *θ,* definitions given in equations (1) and (2)

$$p_{00} = P(I=0,\ F=0) = \theta.(1-p) \quad (9)$$

$$p_{10} = P(I=1,\ F=0) = (1-\eta).p \quad (10)$$

$$p_{01} = P(I=0,\ F=1) = (1-\theta).(1-p) \quad (11)$$

$$p_{11} = P(I=1,\ F=1) = \eta.p \quad (12)$$

It is a common practice to assume that prior information is in the form of a beta density distribution for prevalence, specificity and sensitivity following the Bayesian approach in the presence of misclassification (Joseph, Gyorkos, & Coupal, 1995). The reason for selecting Beta distribution is that it is a flexible family of distribution and a wide range of density shapes can be derived by changing the associated parameters of a beta distribution (Katsis, 2005). It is also a conjugate prior distribution for the binomial likelihood which simplifies the derivation of the posterior distribution significantly. Let Beta(α,β) denote a probability density function of a beta distribution with parameters (α,β) and assume that that prevalence, sensitivity and specificity are independent beta distributions as Beta(α,β), Beta(α_1,β_1) and Beta(α_2,β_2), then the following approximations can be derived from equations (9) – (12) and the fact that mean value of a Beta(α,β) distribution function is given as $\alpha / \alpha + \beta$:

$$p_{00} \sim E(\theta.(1-p)) = \frac{\alpha_2\beta}{(\alpha_2+\beta_2)(\alpha+\beta)} \quad (13)$$

$$p_{10} \sim E((1-\eta)p) = \frac{\alpha\beta_1}{(\alpha_1+\beta_1)(\alpha+\beta)} \quad (14)$$

$$p_{01} \sim E((1-\theta).(1-p)) = \frac{\beta_2\beta}{(\alpha_2+\beta_2)(\alpha+\beta)} \quad (15)$$

$$p_{11} \sim E(\eta.p) = \frac{\alpha_1\alpha}{(\alpha_1+\beta_1)(\alpha+\beta)}. \quad (16)$$

The improvement factor is then calculated from equation (8) as a function of α and β parameters of the beta distribution functions of prevalence of non-compliance, sensitivity and specificity of the audit tool. In order to better understand the effect of sensitivity and specificity on the improvement as a function of prevalence, improvement function can be approximated as follows by using (13)-(16) as follows:

$$\Omega = \frac{1}{p(1-\Psi)+\Psi} \quad (17)$$

where

$$\Psi = \begin{cases} \dfrac{1-\theta}{\eta} & if \quad \dfrac{p_{01}}{p_{01}+p_{00}} \leq \dfrac{p_{11}}{p_{11}+p_{01}} \\ \dfrac{\theta}{1-\eta} & if \quad \dfrac{p_{01}}{p_{01}+p_{00}} \succ \dfrac{p_{11}}{p_{11}+p_{01}} \end{cases} \quad (18)$$

In Figure 5, the percentage improvement is plotted as a function of Ψ for various prevalence values changing between *0.1* and *1*. The performance of the auditing tool for each key control point is also mapped on the same figure. In general, the improvement percentage is significantly higher when both the prevalence and Ψ are small and it converges to zero as Ψ converges to 1. In order to explain this behavior, without lack of generality, let's focus on the case where experts are asked to examine only process instances labeled as non-compliant (Region N) by the automated machine. Hence, equation (20) becomes $\Psi = ((1-\theta)/\eta)$ and indicates that as the specificity and the sensitivity increases, the value of Ψ decreases. In effect, the improvement percentage increases. This is expected since as the sensitivity of an audit machine improves, the likelihood of detecting non-compliant process instances by using the tool improves as well. This is why the improvement percentage is higher for smaller Ψ values. On the other hand, as Ψ approaches to 1, i. e., the sum of the specificity and the sensitivity approaches to one, improvement disappears. The reason for this is that in this case the likelihood of detecting non-compliant process instances approaches to, p, the prevalence. This can be explained as follows: When *sensitivity* is equal to (1 – *specificity*), the likelihood of having false positives becomes equal to likelihood of having true positives. In other words, the following holds

$$\eta = \frac{TP}{TP + FN} = 1 - \theta = 1 - \frac{TN}{TN + FP} = \frac{FP}{TN + FP} \tag{19}$$

Equation (21) implies that

$$\frac{TP}{FP} = \frac{TP + FN}{TN + FP} \tag{20}$$

where *TP, TN, FP* and *FN* are the number of true positive, true negative, false positive and false negative observations respectively. Further manipulation of equation (20) yields:

$$\frac{TP}{TP + FN} = \frac{TN + FP}{TN + FP + TP + FN} = p \tag{21}$$

Here, TP, TN, FP and FN stand for the numbers of true positives, true negatives, false positives and false negatives. Note that this is also equal to the likelihood of detecting non-compliant instances in region N:

$$\frac{p_{11}}{(p_{11} + p_{01})} \approx \frac{TP}{TP + FP} = p \rightarrow \Omega = 1 \tag{22}$$

Equation (22) shows that working in region N does not give any advantage since the detecting a non-compliant process instances in this region is equivalent to the prevalence. The same argument holds for the other region without lack of generality. This means that labeling process instances with the auditing tool does not improve the rate of detecting non-compliant instances if the *sensitivity* of the automated machine is equal to 1 – *specificity*.

Using Sample Process Instances to Measure Effectiveness

As seen above, the effectiveness of automatic compliance detection depends on the prevalence of non-compliance as well as the performance of the detection tool. In order to measure the effectiveness of using automated tools to manage the risk around a particular internal control, prevalence of non-compliance for the internal control, p, and the associated sensitivity and the specificity of the automated tool need to be inferred. Inference about prevalence $p \sim Beta(\alpha,\beta)$, sensitivity $\eta \sim Beta(\alpha_1,\beta_1)$ and specificity $\theta \sim Beta(\alpha_2,\beta_2)$ can be drawn by running a test using the auditing tool and observing true positives and false negatives as depicted in Figure 6. The technique is well known in the literature as Gibbs sampler algorithm (Gelfand & Smith, 1990; Gelfand et al., 1990; Katsis, 2005; Geman & Geman, 1984). Gibbs sampler is an iterative Markov-chain Monte Carlo technique developed to approximate intractable posterior distributions. The algorithm uses the observed data to compute the posterior distributions of prevalence, specificity and sensitivity by applying Bayes' theorem and conversely computes the distributions of the observed data by using the prior distributions of prevalence,

Figure 5. Percentage of improvement as a function of $\Psi = (1-\theta)/\eta$

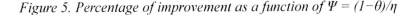

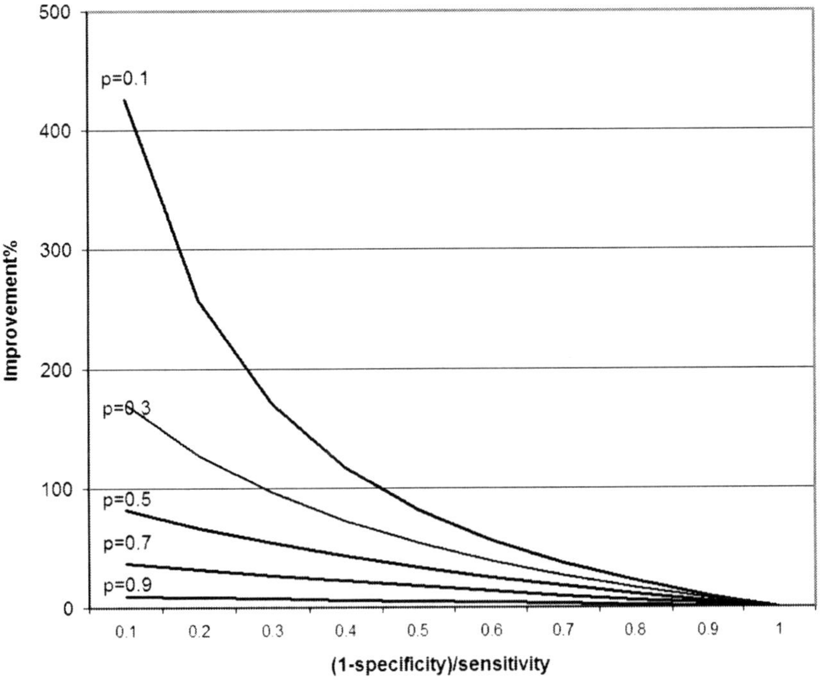

sensitivity and specificity as described in (Geman & Geman, 1984).

Let the actual status of an internal control point is known for N sample process instances and the auditing tool marks $n_{\cdot 0}= n_{10}+n_{00}$ instances as non-compliant *(F=1)* and $n_{\cdot 0}= n_{10}+n_{00}$ instances are marked as compliant *(F=0)* where n_{11}, n_{10}, n_{01} and n_{00} are the number true positives, false negatives, false positives and true negatives respectively as shown in *Figure 6*.

Gibbs sampler derives posterior probability distributions that best fit given prior distributions *Beta* (α,β), *Beta*(α_1,β_1) and *Beta*(α_2,β_2) and observed data, n_{11}, n_{10}, n_{00} and n_{01}. As described in (Joseph, Gyorkas, & Coupal, 1995), arbitrary starting values can be chosen for each parameter. Gibbs sampler converges to the true values of the posterior distributions after running tens of thousands of iterations.

The Pooled Prevalence Calculator (n.d.) provides for an on-line calculator to estimate the true prevalence based on testing of individual samples using a test with imperfect sensitivity and/ or specificity. The input values required for the calculator are illustrated in Figure 7. That is if the test results over *N* sample process instances as shown in Figure 6 are known then the input values for the calculator can be derived. These include the number of samples (process instances) tested, the number of samples labeled positive (non-compliant), α and β parameters for prior prevalence, sensitivity and specificity distributions, number of iterations to be simulated in the Gibbs sampler, number of iterations to be discarded to allow convergence of the model and initial number of true positives n_{11} and false negatives n_{10}. The initial α and β values for prior distributions are selected by using the fact that $\alpha/(\alpha+\beta)$ is the mean value of a beta distribution and by using the observed data given in Figure 6. As an example, the mean value of the prior prevalence can be approximated as $N_1/(N_1+N_0)$. Hence, the

Figure 6. Test results of N sample process instances

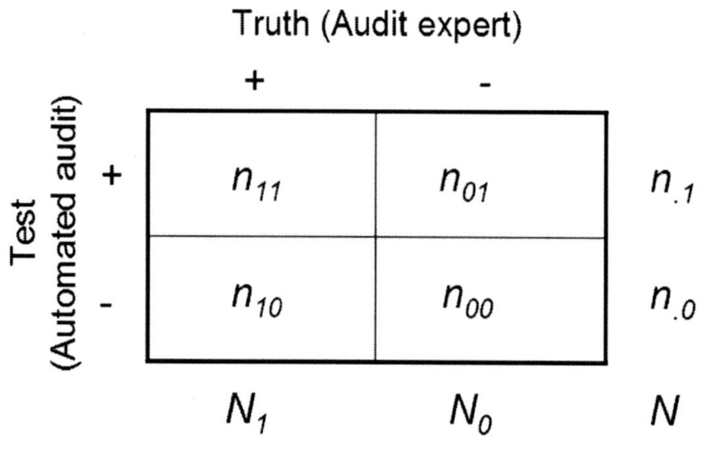

beta value for prior prevalence is approximated as N_0 and the alpha value is approximated as N_1. Similarly, the initial alpha value is n_{11}, initial beta value is $n_{10}$is for sensitivity and the initial alpha value is n_{00}, initial beta value is $n_{01}$for specificity.

For the sample internal control point described in 'new position open process' and stated as "Evidence of general manager approval must exist, before candidates are searched for the 'new' job opening", assume 135 process instances are examined and found that 8 of these instances are not compliant. The auditing tool runs over the same sample set and produces 7 true positives (n_{11}), 1 false negative (n_{01}), 8 false positives (n_{10}) and 119 true negatives (n_{00}). Hence, $N_1 = n_{11} + n_{10} = 15$; $N_0 = n_{01} + n_{00} = 120$. Once the initial values are calculated and entered into the prevalence calculator, the mean values of prevalence, sensitivity and specificity are found as

$E(p)=0.074$, $E(\eta)=0.826$ and $E(\theta)=0.934$.

From equation (17), the improvement factor, Ω, is calculated 6.75. Therefore, the percentage improvement is found as $(\Omega-1)$ x100 = 575%. This is the improvement obtained by using automated auditing tools to check the compliance of the internal control point which is stated as "Evidence of general manager approval must exist, before candidates are searched for the 'new' job opening" under budget constraint. In real life, there are thousands of process instances which cannot be audited manually under budget constraints. Here, after the automated tool labeled process instances, experts are asked to audit only those process instances marked as non-compliant (positive). For the sample set, automated audit tool marks only 15 cases as non-compliance. Hence, manual auditing cases is reduced from 135 to 15.

PRACTICAL CONSIDERATIONS

As mentioned in the introduction section, there is a cost associated with non-compliant process instances. The cost is determined by the amount of penalties that the company will pay for not complying with the rules and regulation as well as the cost of not being able to ensure quality and remain competitive. Compliance officer are responsible to determine the amount of risk exposure for being non-compliant and find ways to minimize the risk.

Risk exposure is the cost of being non-compliant for all process instances that are subject to auditing and it can be reduced by auditing internal

Figure 7. Input and corresponding output values of the prevalence calculator

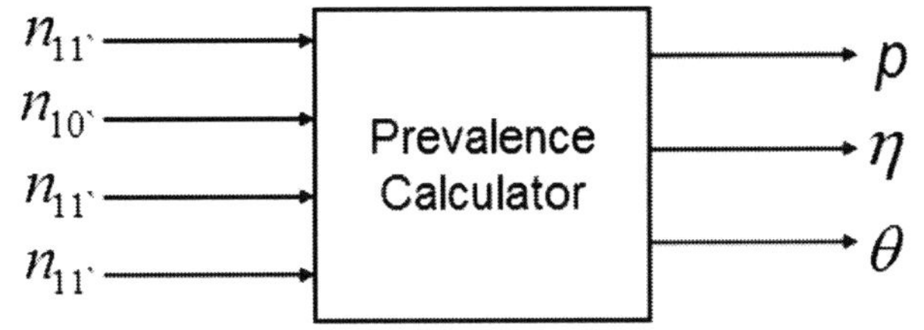

controls for every process instance, detecting and eliminating the cause of non-compliance. While risk exposure can be completely eliminated by auditing every process instance, this may not be a cost effective solution. One of the challenges in reducing the risk exposure is to decide how much budget should be allocated for auditing. Budget allocation must be sufficient enough to justify the investment by reducing the cost associated with risk exposure. Risk exposure is proportional to the number of process instances, percentage of instances covered by audit and the penalty paid for every non-compliant case. In order for the investment to make financial sense, the return of investment must be at least positive. In this case, return is the amount that risk exposure is reduced. A company is expected to reduce the risk exposure at least as much as it spends for compliance assurance.

In the previous section, it was shown that by using auditing tools and limited manual auditing the detection of non-compliance instances can be improved by a factor, Ω, as expressed in equation 17. Improvement factor depends on the prevalence of non-compliance, sensitivity and the specificity of the auditing tool. Note that this is an improvement over what can be done manually on limited set of process instances. Due to budget constraints, the set is usually much less than the total number of process instances. Hence, by using the methodology described in the previous section and the automated audit tool, the prevalence of non-compliance can be reduced by a factor of $\lambda\ \Omega\ p$ where $0<\lambda<1$ is the ratio of the process instances that can be audited manually within the budget constraint.

By detecting and fixing some of non-compliant cases within the set of all process instances, the prevalence of non-compliance is improved since there is less number of non-compliant instances after the detected non-compliant instances are fixed. As a result, the new prevalence of non-compliance is found as follows:

$$p' = p - (1 - \lambda I) = p(1 - \frac{\lambda}{p(1-\Psi)+\Psi}) \quad for \quad \lambda I \leq 1 \tag{23}$$

Since the risk exposure is proportional to the prevalence, then the percent of reduction in risk exposure, Φ, can be found as *100x* $\lambda\ \Omega$

$$\Phi = 100x(\frac{\lambda}{p(1-\Psi)+\Psi}) \quad for \quad \lambda \leq p(1-\Psi)+\Psi \tag{24}$$

In other words, if the risk exposure has to be reduced Φ % then (24) has to be satisfied. Equation (24) has practical implications. Desired reduction percentage may not be achieved due to the constraint on λ, the ratio of the process instances that can be audited manually within the budget constraint and Ψ, the performance measure of the tool for a given prevalence of non-compliance, p. This means that for a given p, it may not be possible to build a tool that could reduce the risk at a desired level. Figure 8 shows the risk exposure reduction percentage as a function of $\Psi=(1-\theta)/\eta$ which is a measure of automated audit tool performance.

Figure 8. Reduction of risk exposure as a function of Ψ for different λ values when prevalence is 0.3

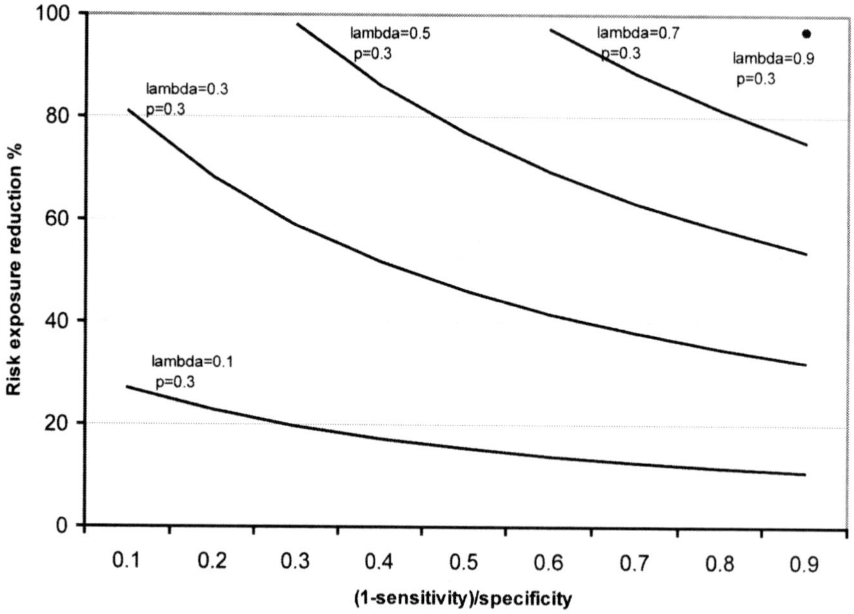

Hence, in order to reduce the risk exposure to the desired level for a given prevalence *p*, λ and Ψ values should be selected as plotted in Figure 7. The values of λ and Ψ determine the operating point where λ is controlled by the number of manually audited process instances and Ψ is related to the performance measure of the tool which is tunable. Figure 7 shows that risk exposure is reduced more with higher λ values and lower Ψ values. As an example, when the prevalence of non-compliance is, *p=0.3*, then the risk exposure can be reduced %20 provided that the operating point is λ =0.1 and Ψ =0.3. Since λ is the ratio of the process instances that can be audited manually within the budget constraint, it is directly proportional with the cost of hiring auditors for manual auditing. Ψ, on the other hand, is the ratio of *(1-sensitivity)* to *specificity* of the automated audit tool and there is a cost associated with building tools with desired performance tooling. Hence, the reduction in risk exposure must be large enough to cover the cost of hiring experts and tuning automated auditing tool for the desired performance.

Figure 8 shows that risk exposure is reduced most with higher values of λ. This is expected since λ is related to the number of process instances manually audited by experts that are labeled as non-compliant by the auditing tool. As λ increases, the number of actually non-compliant process instances in the system is reduced along with the risk. In the example depicted by Figure 8, when λ = 0.9, i.e., 90% of all process instances labeled non-compliant examined by experts, and the *(1-sensitity)/specificity* of the audit tool is 0.9, the risk exposure is almost completely eliminated. This is the case when either the sensitivity or the specificity of the tool is very high, hence almost all the process instances labeled non-compliant are actually non-compliant and they are all detected and eliminated by experts.

Figure 9, on the other hand shows the effect of prevalence of non-compliance on the risk exposure reduction when λ is constant. The designers of risk management systems need to know how the sensitivity and the specificity values of the automated tool should be tuned to reduce the ex-

Figure 9. Reduction in risk exposure as a function of Ψ for different prevalence values when λ = 0.3

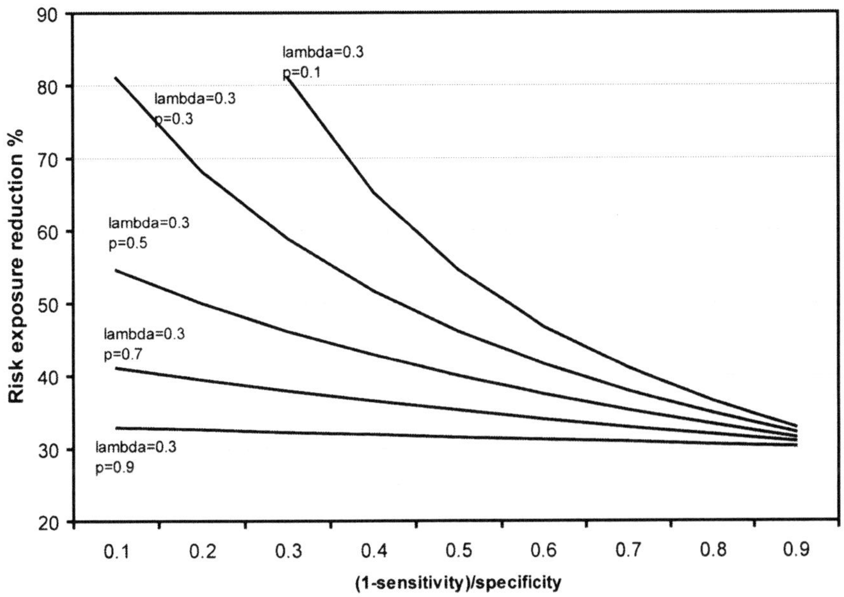

posure to the desired amount when the prevalence of non-compliance is constant.

Achieving the desired risk exposure reduction for a given prevalence of non-compliance may not be possible with an automated audit tool, if the sensitivity and the specificity measures of the tool cannot be tuned. Figure 10 demonstrates this fact for different λ and prevalence, *p*, values. As an example for λ = 0.3 and *p*=0.1, represented as the solid line in the second group of curves, the risk exposure reduction cannot be more than 60% no matter how good the auditing tool is.

On the other hand, if *p*=0.1, reduction in risk exposure can be increased to 70% by adjusting the Ψ level to 0.2. This means that even if the sensitivity of the tool is 1, i.e., the tool is capable of identifying all actual non-compliant cases, the specificity of the tool, i.e., the proportions of negatives (compliant cases) which are correctly identified must be larger than 0.8. Since Ψ≤0.2 can only be satisfied when specificity is greater than 0.8 if sensitivity is 1.

FUTURE RESEARCH DIRECTIONS

Designing effective automated auditing tools reduces the auditing cost and the risk exposure associated with the non-compliant process instances. The effectiveness of an automated audit tool, however, depends on the sensitivity and the specificity of the tool in detecting the compliance failures. The question of how to design an automated auditing system with the desired performance measures is an area that needs further investigation. This should start with defining the factors around a control point that would affect the design of an effective automated audit system. There are many factors that cannot be controlled in partially managed or unmanaged processes. These factors are mostly related to human interactions supported by collaboration software such as e-mail, calendar system, and others. In some cases, detecting compliance requires the analysis of a document or the body of an e-mail to decide if the document is sufficient to satisfy the compliance. In such cases, the performance of the auditing

Figure 10. Ψ= (1-sensitivity)/specificity as a function of desired level of risk exposure reduction

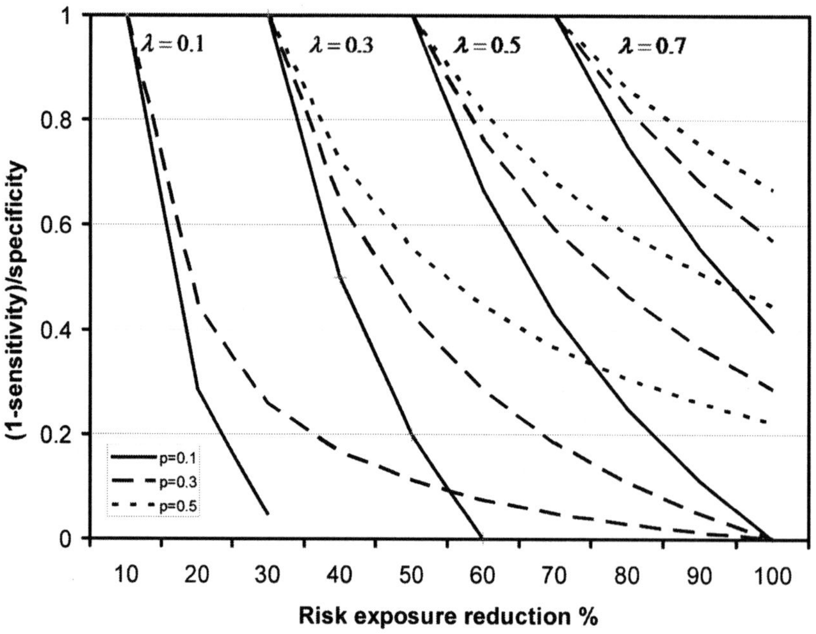

tool is directly related to the accuracy of the text analysis software. Since it is not practical to build automated audit system for every control point, it is important to know how to tune an automated system for a particular control point. If tuning is not possible to achieve the desired risk exposure reduction, then the visibility of the underlying operations may need to be increased. There are no established standards for measuring the visibility of business processes. Hence, the impact of business process visibility on designing effective automated audit tools could not be established either. If the visibility of a business process can be measured in terms of the likelihood of detecting compliance failures, then the internal controls can be set more properly and the design of the automated audit systems may be improved more.

CONCLUSION

Detecting compliance failures effectively and eliminating them is important for the health of a business and a challenge for processes that are not managed. Processes with low levels of automation, which are essentially unmanaged processes, rely on an efficient auditing procedure as the only way to prevent systemic non-compliance. In order to increase auditing efficiency for unmanaged processes, automated auditing tools can be used to complement manual auditing by subject matter experts and expand the amount of process instances that can be audited within budget constraints. The effectiveness of an automated audit tool depends on both the prevalence of non-compliant cases as well as the performance of the tool. Measuring the effectiveness of auditing procedures in reducing the risk exposure of a business process help making smarter decision on employing subject matter experts and utilize automated audit tools. Organizations need to understand how effectively they can reduce the risk exposure with the allocated auditing budget. Reader of this chapter will find enough details and analysis for the factors that impact risk exposure reduction. In particular, the chapter is expected to help compliance officer to evaluate the return of their compliance investments in terms of reduced risk exposure.

REFERENCES

Business Rule Group. (2000). *Defining business rules – What are they really?* Final report, revision 1.3. Retrieved November 26, 2010, from http://www.businessrulesgroup.org/first_paper/br01c1.htm

Christopher, G., Müller, S., & Pfitzmann, B. (2006). *From regulatory policies to event monitoring rules: Towards Model-driven compliance automation. IBM Research Report RZ 3662*. IBM Zurich Research Laboratory.

COSO. (2004). *Enterprise risk management-integrated framework*. Retrieved March 22, 2011, from http://www.coso.org/documents/COSO_ERM_ExecutiveSummary.pdf

COSO. (2009). *Guidance on monitoring internal control systems*. American Institute of Certified Public Accountants Press.

COSO. (2010). Home page. Retrieved March 22, 2010, from http://coso.org/IC.htm

Curbera, F., Doganata, Y., Martens, A., Mukhi, M., & Slominski, A. (2008). Business provenance - A technology to increase traceability of end-to-end operations. *Proceedings of OTM Conferences*, (pp. 100-119).

Gelfand, A. E., Hills, S. E., & Racine-Poon, A. (1990). Illustration of Bayesian inference in normal data using Gibbs sampling. *Journal of the American Statistical Association, 85*, 972–985. doi:10.2307/2289594

Gelfand, A. E., & Smith, A. F. M. (1990). Sampling-based approaches to calculating marginal densities. *Journal of the American Statistical Association, 85*, 348–409. doi:10.2307/2289776

Geman, S., & Geman, D. (1984). Stochastic relaxation, Gibbs distributions, and the Bayesian restoration of images. *IEEE Transactions on Pattern Analysis and Machine Intelligence, 6*, 721–741. doi:10.1109/TPAMI.1984.4767596

Goedertier, S., & Vanthienen, J. (2006). Designing compliant business processes with obligations and permission. In Eder, J., & Dustdar, S. (Eds.), *BPM Workshops 2006, LNCS 4103* (pp. 5–14). Heidelberg, Germany: Springer. doi:10.1007/11837862_2

Greengard, S. (2005). Compliance software's bonus benefits. *Business Finance Magazine*. Retrieved November 1, 2010, from http://businessfinancemag.com/article/compliance-softwares-bonus-benefits-0201

IBM. (n.d.). *Websphere, Lombardi ed., version 7.1: Quick start tutorial*. Retrieved November 26, 2010, from http://publib.boulder.ibm.com/infocenter/wle/v7r1/index.jsp?topic=/wle/common/topic/starting_ae.html

Joseph, L., Gyorkos, T. W., & Coupal, L. (1995). Bayesian estimation of disease prevalence and the parameters of diagnostic tests in the absence of a gold standard. *American Journal of Epidemiology, 141*(3).

Katsis, A. (2005). Sample size determination of binomial data with the presence of misclassification. *Metrika, 63*, 323–329. doi:10.1007/s00184-005-0411-2

McCoy, D. W. (2002). Business activity monitoring: Calm before the storm. *Gartner Research*, LE-15-9727. Retrieved March 22, 2011, from http://www.gartner.com/resources/105500/105562/105562.pdf

Pooled Prevalence Calculator. (n.d.). Retrieved from http://www.ausvet.com.au/pprev/

Research, A. M. R. (2010). *The governance, risk management, and compliance spending report.* Boston, MA: AMR Research.

Ruopeng, L., Sadiq, S., & Governatori, G. (2008). Compliance aware business process design. *BPM 2007 Workshops. LNCS, 4928*, 120–131.

Sarbanes-Oxley Act of 2002. (2002). Pub. L. 107-204. Retrieved November 26, 2010, from http://www.gpo.gov/fdsys/pkg/PLAW-107publ204/content-detail.html

Weske, M. (2007). *Business process management: Concepts, languages, architectures.* Berlin, Germany: Springer.

ADDITIONAL READING

Doganata, Y., & Curbera, F. (2009). A method of calculating the cost of reducing the risk exposure of non-compliance process instances. *Proceedings of the first ACM workshop on Information security governance.*

Tanner, M. A. (1991). *Tools for statistical inference.* New York: NY Spring-Verlag.

VonHalle, B. (1994). Back to Business Rules Basics. *Database Programming and Design.* 15-18.

KEY TERMS AND DEFINITIONS

Automated Audit Tool: A software application that evaluates the process instances to provide an assessment of internal control points.

Compliance: Confirmation that the process meets the requirements of prescribed rules and regulations.

Business Process Visibility: Ability to capture business artifacts related to business activities.

Business Provenance: Lineage of the artifacts created during business process execution that includes resources, tasks, data and their relations.

Internal Control Point: A procedure to ensure that process adheres to policies, rules or regulations.

Prevalence of Non-compliance: The ratio of non-compliant process instances in the set of all process instances.

Risk Exposure: The expected financial penalty to be paid for being non-compliant.

Unmanaged Business Processes: Business processes where the transaction between activities cannot be automated by software.

Chapter 23
Loss of Data: Reflective Case Studies

Ian Rosewall
Deakin University, Australia

Matt Warren
Deakin University, Australia

ABSTRACT

This chapter will focus upon the impact of Generation F - the Facebook Generation - and their attitudes to security. The chapter is based around discussing the loss of data, the prevention approaches and enforcement policies that are currently being investigated, and the implications that this has upon the modern, working environment. The changing landscape of work presents the issue of the Need to Know against the modern, working practises of Need to Share, a conflict that needs to be resolved as a matter of urgency. Many hold the view that it would be wrong to return to the Cold War scenario, however the modern position of Need to Share leads to a steadily rising fear of Information Insecurity. Accepting this situation means that working practises within large organisations need to be reviewed without ignoring the benefits of the new and emerging technologies and yet still be vigilant with regards to Information security.

INTRODUCTION

The chapter will include a number of real life case studies; Wikileaks, Ministry of Defence - Burton Report (UK) and Disclosure issues within the Victorian Police (Australia), these case studies will discuss the loss of data, prevention approaches, enforcement policies and 'need to know' versus 'need to share' and illustrate the Global perspective of these issues and open discussions for Information disclosure, deliberate or otherwise.

This first case study, (Case Study 1) Information Security Disclosure: A Case Study (Rosewall and Warren 2009) will focus upon the impact of Generation F - the Facebook Generation and their

DOI: 10.4018/978-1-4666-0197-0.ch023

attitudes to security. It will focus on the findings of a major UK incident and the implications that this has had. The case study identifies 51 recommendations to improve the situation of data security within the military of the UK. These recommendations will be the data for the analysis and will form an overview of the case study's point of view as regards the younger generation and data security. This discussion will suggest another interpretation of the results supplied by Burton (2008)

The second case study (Case Study 2) views similar problems as mentioned above that have been noted within the Police service in Australia in particular the state of Victoria. The Victorian police have had a chequered past and unauthorised Information disclosure has featured prominently in their recent history. The cases that will be alluded to, are not used in order to apportion blame but, rather, to illuminate certain areas of the various reports that have been cited. As far back as 2003 The Victorian Police review finds ".....inconsistent and inadequate approach to data Management" (Mc Kenzie 2009).

The final case study (Case Study 3) investigates the implications of the popularity of Wikileaks which has been obvious over the past few years. It has been described thus: *"Wikileaks is an uncensorable version of Wikipedia for untraceable mass document leaking and analysis."* This may, on first sight seem desirable but, when it is deemed as being 'uncensorable' do we take it that there can be only one view of these 'facts'? unlike its namesake Wikipedia which would allow for a balanced view perhaps this is not the site that it first portrays.

These three case studies will discuss The issues surrounding the Loss of Data, the current prevention approaches, the compliance /non compliance with enforcement policies and the dilemma facing current work practices of 'need to know' versus 'need to share'

BACKGROUND

UK Government Case Study (Case Study 1)

In November 2007 Her Majesty's Revenue and Customs (HRMC) (This department deals, amongst other things, with Child Benefit payments to families in the UK), lost 2 CD's containing (BBC 2007):

- 7.25 million claimants;
- 15.5 million children, including some who no longer qualify but whose family is claiming for a younger child;
- 2.25 million 'alternative payees' such as partners or carers;
- 3,000 'appointees' who claim the benefit under court instructions ;
- 12,500 agents who claim the benefit on behalf of a third party.

The discs contained 25 million records. These included the names, addresses, dates of birth, National Insurance numbers and, where relevant, bank and building society details.

Following this incident, the British Prime Minister Gordon Brown, commissioned a review into Data Handling procedures within government. In June 2008 the final report was published `Data Handling Procedures in Government: Final Report` with key recommendations (Cabinet Office, 2008). These measures were to be adopted by all UK Government Departments.

On the evening of 9/10th January 2008 a laptop was stolen from a Royal Naval recruitment Officers car in Birmingham, England. It contained 600,000 unencrypted personal records of potential recruits and circa 400,000 next of kin and referee records. On the 11th January the Incident was reported to Ministers of the British Government. It had not been reported that the Information was unencrypted until the 14th January. On the 24th

January the Secretary of State announced to the commons that he had Invited Sir Edmund Burton to undertake a full Investigation (BBC 2008).

The Burton Report was tasked with reviewing the MOD's protection of its personal data after the theft of a laptop in Birmingham on the 9/10 January 2008. Burton's review was carried out using the terms of reference set out by the UK Secretary of Defence (Burton, 2008) which stated:

"To establish the exact circumstances and events that led to the loss by MOD of personal data; to examine the adequacy of the steps taken to prevent any recurrence, and of MOD policy, practise and management arrangements in respect of the protection of personal data more generally; to make recommendations; and to report to MOD's permanent secretary not later than 30th April 2008".

Victorian Police Case Study (Case Study 2)

Data management, or the lack thereof, was also blamed for the Murder of Terence Hodson and his wife in May 2004. Investigations which led to the arrest of Rodney Charles Collins in June 2008 found that he had his own surveillance dossier. When questioned on the matter he claimed that he had found them at a bus stop (Gary 2008). Collins is also 'a person of interest' for the murder of the aforementioned Terence Hodson, a police informant and his wife.

Further allegations from prominent people were directed at the Surveillance unit within the Victorian Police, and their management of the Hodson files in particular, Tony Fitzgerald QC in his January 2005 report found that the system in place was "grossly inadequate"

The "Investigation into Victoria Police's Management and Law Enforcement Assistance Program (LEAP)" was highly critical of the systems in place and found there to be "chronic failings' (McKenzie, 2009). Confirmation that several of the reported leaks have been traced back to the forces Surveillance team which has been highlighted by a damning article in 'The Australian' newspaper "The force revealed yesterday that details from at least two secret dossiers on targeted criminals had been leaked to underworld figures from the force's covert surveillance unit" (Gary 2008).

Wikileaks Case Study (Case Study 3)

This case study will discuss 'need to know' versus 'need to share' in the form of Wikileaks. (http://www.wikileaks.org) Wikileaks describes itself as an *'open government group', 'anti corruption group' or a whistle blower's site'* (Aftergood, 2010). Grand ideals to be sure, but does wikileaks live up to its claims, indeed *should* it live up to its claims. (Rosewall and Warren 2010a)

'Open government' is a political belief that suggests that the business of government and any state administration should be opened to *'effective public scrutiny and oversight'*. Anti corruption groups are for those who wish to address corruption challenges at their workplace, and finally whistleblowers are for those who hold deep concerns that their organisations hold illegal or unethical practices within that workplace. (Aftergood, 2010)

Rosewall and Warren (2010a) argue that the Wikileaks case study is used to encapsulate the following dilemmas; Is Information Private? Do we have an issue with the Web2 Generation Y? Are people discerning with the information they divulge/receive? Does the format alter the content? Do we have all of the facts?

The Context (Generation Y)

Many papers have been written about Generation Y (Gen Y), about their perspective on Information and the sharing of that information. Generation Y are defined as those born between 1982 – 2000 according to McCrindle (2010).

Typically, Gen Y is your twenty-something-year-old employee who is, at this point, likely be engaged as a graduate, associate or in a support role within the workplace. This demographic is tech-savvy and engaging, and reminds other generations that workplaces can, and should, be fun. The flipside is that Gen Y has been criticised as being short on skills, demanding, impertinent and disloyal. They often appear to have a blatant disregard for, or maybe a lack of understanding of, rank and file, and tend to question tradition. Gen Y is unafraid to challenge the organisational establishment (Williams, 2010). Descriptions of Generation Y are wide and plentiful, the search to 'pigeon hole' them continues to this day, each trying to show a different perspective. For the purposes of this book chapter, Williams's depiction seems to encapsulate most people's views quite well, although not definitive it provides a wide enough view to use within the confines of this chapter.

Several academic papers suggest that Generation Y, apart from their 'Tech Savvy' approach to sharing their personal and private information through "Facebook", "Twitter" and other social networking have an Ignorance of, or a disregard for, Information security. Further to the description above comes some worrying statistics from Garretson (2007) that would appear to enhance this perception of Generation Y.

Companies that believe they have communicated their policies sufficiently might need to think again. According to a survey done by security vendor Senforce last March, 73% of the 308 respondents said they store corporate data on removable media, and 46% said they did not have — or were unaware of — corporate security policies that protect that information (Garretson, 2007).

There are over 4 million Australians in generation Y, the RSA surveyed more than 1,000 Generation Y adults about online security issues and found that *"young adults regularly engage in risky behaviors that compromise their privacy and reputation."* The concern here is that if Gen Y employees struggle to keep personal information private, can they be trusted with sensitive business data? This generation has long been accused of not having respect for security without reason. If they do not see the point of the security measure they are quite likely to ignore it. For example this generation probably sees no issue with 'outing' a sorority. On first sight this might seem to be a valid point but the issue prevails, who makes this judgment and where does it stop, a good example maybe wikileaks themselves. They portray themselves as a site that tells all except where *they* get this information. So one rule for us.....?

The following discussion will investigate (possible) relationships between what has happened in the Victorian Police Force, (Case Study 2) the emergence of a new breed of Police Officer from the era of Generation Y and the authors of the report mentioned above who, most probably, because of seniority, are unlikely to have been born in the same era. (Rosewall & Warren 2010) It will temper this with the point of view offered by Burton (case Study 1) and consider both of these within the parameters of a society that accepts, and actively encourages, websites such as Wikileaks (case Study 3).

ISSUES

This section of the chapter will discuss and analyse the findings and recommendations of the three case studies with particular focus on the categories that Burton (case Study 1) has assigned certain problems to, the findings of the Victorian Police investigation(Case Study 2) and Issues raised by Rosewall &Warren (2010a) with regards to Wikileaks (Case Study 3).

Case Study 1: UK Government Case Study

Burton (2008) offers us what he describes as "six areas of Major concern":

1. Cultural Changes (The Facebook Generation)
2. New ways of working
3. Decline in Security
4. Resourcing Security
5. Accounting for Computers and USB devices
6. 'Need to Know' versus 'Need to Share'

Case Study 2: Victorian Police Case Study

Information Security and the Victorian Police State Surveillance Unit report (OPI, 2010) offers ten areas in need of improvement, not surprisingly these ten areas seem to reflect or mirror those of their British counterpart.

1. The State Surveillance Unit of Victoria Police (the Unit) has taken steps to improve information security practices since mid 2008. However, to date, improvements lack a robust governance and risk management framework and a commitment to implementing the CLEDS Standards.
2. Until recently, Unit Instructions were prescriptive and provided inadequate practical guidance relating to effective information security systems.
3. Until recently, Victoria Police corporate information management leadership and technological support were deficient. As a result the Surveillance Unit had a 'go it alone' attitude, resulting in stand-alone systems.
4. Surveillance operatives are fundamentally sound at gathering information, but their practices in the storage, use and dissemination of that information are, at times, flawed.
5. Managers and leaders within the Unit have been focused on achieving operational outcomes and have neglected administrative and accountability processes.
6. Managers and leaders within the Unit have relied on past experience without embracing change and improving practices and information handling processes.
7. Information and intelligence provided to the Unit from investigators are not in a consistent format and Requests for Surveillance continue to contain large amounts of inappropriate material.
8. Until recently, the Unit's Intelligence Cell operated as an under-resourced information management centre rather than as a dynamic intelligence analysis unit providing support to operatives.
9. The Surveillance Unit currently uses Victoria Police's intelligence and investigation system 'Interpose' as a document management system and under-utilises its capacity to manage intelligence, analysis and information dissemination.
10. Inadequate formal attention is paid to risk management or the assessment of current practices with a view to continuous improvement.

Case Study 3

The third case study "Wikileaks: The Truth or Not" (Rosewall and Warren 2010a) examine several issues that are used to add perspective to the discussion;

- Is Information Private
- Do we have an issue with the Web2 Generation Y
- Are people discerning with the information they divulge/receive
- Does the format alter the content
- All of the facts??

Discussion of These Issues

Burton's six areas of Major concern: (Case Study 1)

1. **Cultural Changes (The Facebook Generation):** Burton accepts that there has been a significant change within the culture whereby we now live in an environment where *"the rapid and often uninhibited exchange of Information is the norm"* A situation where this, behaviour in the workplace, could be devastating. Burton suggests that this behaviour should be *"tempered by common sense and sound judgement"* he also rules out the possibility of returning to the paper systems and thinking of fifteen years ago, arguing that it cannot be considered practical in the modern working environment.
2. **New ways of working:** In order to illustrate this point the report cites the Human Resources Management System (HRMS) and explains that this system is an example of capitalising on new technologies and the shift in cultural developments. The risk management of this *"better access to personal data"* as yet, has not been recognised at 'Board' level. This highlights generic problems within the British military, in that they see this as an add on. Bishop (2003) informs us that: "*Security is not an add-on or merely an operational concept, it is a property that must be designed and built into every system.*" Perhaps we could add here "from the outset".
3. **Decline in Security:** Anecdotal evidence would suggest that these modern working practises has produced a decline in the security at department level and more disturbingly at a personal level. Burton goes on to say that *".. the younger generation of MOD staff are not inculcated with the same culture of protecting Information as their counterparts from previous generations."* Alluding of course, to the 'cold war' era, where Information security was of paramount importance.
4. **Resourcing Security:** As is the trend in governments to make themselves cost effective, cuts in staff are inevitable, thus making the resourcing of security difficult. Burton cites the need for *"accreditation, audit and compliance"* and yet the department has *"a significant shortage of accreditors who are crucial to the validation of security measures in ICT systems"* Interestingly there is no mention here of security training even though many authors highlight it's need, Michael E. Whitman (2003) suggests that "*Information security continues to be ignored by top managers, middle managers, and employees alike. The result of this neglect is that organizational systems are far less secure than they might otherwise be and that security breaches are far more frequent and damaging than is necessary*".
5. **Accounting for Computers and USB devices:** In this very brief section Burton makes us aware that the *"accounting for Laptops, PDA's and USB devices and the reporting of losses, is poor....."* He argues that this can cause ineffective management of the security of the data and the devices on which data is stored, although there is a set procedure for this (MOD 2004).
6. **'Need to Know' versus 'Need to Share':** The report addresses the issue of the MOD philosophy of "Need to Know" against the modern working practises of "Need to Share" a conflict that needs to be resolved as a matter of urgency. Burton holds the view that it would be "impractical" to return to the 'Cold War' scenario, however the modern position of "Need to Share" leads to *"unacceptable vulnerabilities"*. Accepting this situation means that working practises within the

MOD need to be reviewed without ignoring the benefits of the new emerging technologies and yet still being vigilant with regards to Information security.

In the process of forming the 51 recommendations for this report Burton identified areas of concern within the MOD which reflect the current social environment in which we live and the potential dangers that this "Facebook Generation" can inflict upon today's modern military. On closer inspection of these 51 recommendations Rosewall and Warren (2009) concentrated on the recommendations that alluded to the 'People' section and examine whether, at least some of them, could be expressed in a slightly different manner.

There seemed to be a tendency to highlight the process within the people environment as opposed to the people in the people environment. Continued use of the word 'accountability' as opposed to 'awareness', the 'stick' and little evidence of the 'carrot'. However Burton does go on to say: *"Beyond the expert community there is little evidence of awareness of the Data Protection Act or its implications for the chain of command"* and admits that there is a *"need for appropriate training."* Along with this data protection training there is also a 'need' for personal security training at all levels within the MOD, Which seems, on the surface, to have been overlooked in this report which would appear to focus more closely on the 'Personal data' as opposed to 'personal security of that data'. The foundation of any computer security education or training should provide the student with the motivation for the field, i.e. why do we worry about computer security, why is there a problem, and what are the potential consequences.

As with all Public Sector departments the perceived need to capture as much information as possible 'just in case' is prevalent in the minds of those who work within the HQ areas. It is interesting that in the glossary that accompanies the Burton report there is a definition of Information Assurance, Information Security and Information Security Management System (ISMS) but not one for Information! What exactly is being stored, what is relevant, what is data and what is Information. The similarity of two 'Public Sector' working practices on opposite sides of the world is staggering, that of the Burton report in the UK (Case Study 1) and the assessment of the "Information Security and the Victorian Police State Surveillance Unit report (OPI, 2010) (Case Study 2) by Rosewall and Warren (2010) which offers ten areas in need of improvement, not surprisingly these ten areas seem to reflect or mirror those of their British counterpart.

Information Security and the Victorian Police State Surveillance Unit Report (OPI, 2010) (Case Study 2)

1. The State Surveillance Unit of Victoria Police (the Unit) has taken steps to improve information security practices since mid 2008. However, to date, improvements lack a robust governance and risk management framework and a commitment to implementing the CLEDS Standards.

The report highlights severe cracks in the expected procedures not least, that there was only one person within the team who had formal clearance which would match the standards set out for and by Commonwealth Government. Further to this there "..was some doubt as to the validity of that vetting, particularly in relation to the Australian Government Requirements" As with most civil service departments the emphasis for the solution is more 'frameworks' and more 'governance' putting aside the fact that the current frameworks and governance procedures are not being adhered to., then why expect new frameworks and governance to be more readily acceptable.

"Anecdotal evidence would suggest that these modern working practises has produced a decline in the security at department level and more disturbingly at a personal level. Burton goes on to say that ".... the younger generation of MOD staff are not inculcated with the same culture of protecting Information as their counterparts from previous generations." Alluding of course, to the 'cold war' era, where Information security was of paramount importance" (Rosewall & Warren 2009).

Frameworks and the governance should be clearly defined and live within the confines of the task they serve to monitor. The modern Generation Y do not accept instructions per se rather, they have been taught to question everything. Whilst this is highly commendable in some aspects of Police work there are other areas that have to be written in stone. The handling of the Gen Y attitudes is nothing more difficult than to clarify why these actions must be followed. Hansen (2010) suggests that: "Generation Y workers should learn to choose battles carefully, not question every single decision made, and give employers a chance to adapt to their style of work".

2. Until recently, Unit Instructions were prescriptive and provided inadequate practical guidance relating to effective information security systems.

Again this finding highlights the 'if you just tell people, it will happen' attitude to leadership.

What is really interesting in the review, is the staff's perception of Information security and how they personally, view their interaction with it. Despite the array of severe breaches of security that have been highlighted here they (the staff) appear to be happy with the current position.

The staff survey shows for example, when asked the question "Individual SSU operatives exhibit high information security awareness at all times" a result of nearly 90% felt that they either agreed or strongly agreed that this was the case, and 93% felt that their team leader sets a positive example for the secure handling of information and SSU assets.

3. Until recently, Victoria Police corporate information management leadership and technological support were deficient. As a result the Surveillance Unit had a 'go it alone' attitude, resulting in stand-alone systems.

This finding has little to do with the staff per se but rather that the staff that were available to the unit were insufficient and undertrained. The staff involved seemed to try to 'make the best of a bad job'. These finding are not a reflection of the attempts to do the job but rather, a situation that appears to be prevalent in any not for profit organisation. The report was damning of the attitudes of staff but also accepting that the unit reflected a lack of information security awareness which could point to the lack of appropriate training and or understanding of how information security should be conducted.

4. Surveillance operatives are fundamentally sound at gathering information, but their practices in the storage, use and dissemination of that information are, at times, flawed.

This rather sweeping statement appears to be based in fact when it is set against the examples given previously of gross misconduct within the unit in regards to the amount of information that has become available to the general public by, either leaks, or poor handling abilities of the staff of the SSU. However when the question was asked in the staff survey "I clearly understand Victoria Police information security policies and procedures regarding acceptable use/handling of information" 71% were quite sure that they understood what was expected of them. What is alarming here is that 29%, nearly a third of those questioned either didn't know or actually disagreed with the statement. Yet when the question posed changed it's context to "I clearly understand my responsibilities for handling and safeguarding information" 93% of staff moved to the right of the Likert scale. This could suggest that although they clearly understand what is expected they either disregard it or believe that they were correct not to adhere to it on this occasion.

This relates to the view that "While some people refer to this cohort of people as Generation Why for a reason, it is not so much an issue of a lack of respect for authority as much as it is that this group has been raised by their parents to question everything and raise questions when they don't understand something. This generation is very independent and not afraid to challenge the status-quo. Many in Generation Y want a relationship with their boss like the ones they have with their parents. It's not that these folks have little respect for authority; on the contrary, they feel employers do not respect them" (Hanson 2010).

Perhaps, the statistics in this case may add to Hanson's perspective and extend his point of view to, that if Gen Y do not agree with something they have been told without explanation, that they will simply ignore it.

5. Managers and leaders within the Unit have been focused on achieving operational outcomes and have neglected administrative and accountability processes.

"The modern position of "Need to Share" leads to "unacceptable vulnerabilities". Accepting this situation means that working practises within the MOD need to be reviewed without ignoring the benefits of the new emerging technologies and yet still being vigilant with regards to Information security"(Rosewall & Warren 2009).

Although Rosewall and Warren are discussing the UK's Ministry of Defence (MOD) (Case Study 1) the relevance is clear. This need to focus on the outcome and not on the means, reveals 'unacceptable vulnerabilities'. In the case of the Victorian Police it is alleged that this attitude caused the death of at least one person. A key view could be "....police do not exercise legislative power; that is to say, they do not make laws. This observation may seem trite, but its implications are sometimes overlooked. Less obvious, but equally important is the need to guard against vesting in the police discretionary powers which, for practical purposes, may amount to powers to make law, or to dispense with the compliance with the law" (Gleeson 2010).

It could be argued that taking more care over administrative and accountability processes could also be of great value to the Victorian Police, in as much as following due process could provide evidence of accountability when cases of disclosure are aired.

6. Managers and leaders within the Unit have relied on past experience without embracing change and improving practices and information handling processes.

On reading the report it becomes clear that there is no line of accountability within the management structure. Job descriptions do not appear to cover these duties specifically so, once again, the onus is on each individual manager to interpret the duties that they are expected to perform. Some managers have created their own checklists to try to maintain some sense of order, although this does not appear to have been filtered down the chain of command. This became evident when a large number of sicknesses amongst the management members happened, the rest of the team were clearly not equipped to deal with the situation. As described earlier this lack of clarity allows the Gen F members of the team to find their own solutions. Technology has allowed this generation to multitask and find shortcuts in achieving tasks which may not be the most secure route. Although change can be a good thing, and should be embraced at senior management level. There is also a case for keeping the same ideology, security, but achieve it in a different way. Various accounts of unsupervised access to sensitive information and unauthorised persons obtaining this Information, is the area that needs to changed by whatever means necessary.

The example given above, absent managers, gives rise to the situation where untrained staff are required to undertake tasks that they see as boring and or unnecessary, or beyond their capabilities and without proper security training offer up the possibilities of unauthorised information disclosure on a massive scale. Although the staff that were surveyed believe that they are up to the job it has been proved that they are not. The report identifies this aspect as gross understaffing and this does appear to be the case. "This situation, since 2008 does seem to be improving, but still the 'untrained' aspect would appear to remain." OPI (2010).

7. Information and intelligence provided to the Unit from investigators are not in a consistent format and Requests for Surveillance continue to contain large amounts of inappropriate material.

The report suggests that staff that were feeding the information "..... did not know what to exclude from a surveillance request, so they included everything" this on occasions, could be upwards of 100 pages and would have countless photocopies made of them with no restrictions or audit trails conducted. This practice has now ceased to a large extent.

The report identifies that there is an inherent fault in their security management that most of the information that they hold not only lacks the robustness that we, the general public, expect but also that the information that they do hold is not classified correctly, or worse still not classified at all. This was admirably demonstrated by the reports acceptance that the unit received information gleaned from telephone intercepts which it was 'not equipped' to receive or store. The unit therefore had breached statutory obligations. Which would suggest, that they were unaware of these obligation or, they chose to ignore them. This was further compounded when the report found that they had also breached the Victorian Police corporate policies on intelligence management.

Ironically, the procedure for requesting data from the unit was, initially, by phone which is generally considered to be the least used forum by Gen and more the preferred method of Generation X. This conversation was the basis of whether or not the request was moved on to the next stage. Gen Y are far more likely to prefer the e-mail approach which would facilitate a more formal request with some detail included and a more robust audit trail. The e-mail approach is stage two for the generation X style of request, therefore perhaps, it could be suggested that the Gen Y have the upper hand in this instance. However, once the information was released it would invariably contain much more information than was requested or for that matter, should have included. This brings us back to the 'need to know' versus 'need to share' situation was has been suggested is very much the trait of the Gen Y mentality.

8. Until recently, the Unit's Intelligence Cell operated as an under-resourced information management centre rather than as a dynamic intelligence analysis unit providing support to operatives.

A review conducted in 2005 found (OPI 2010) that there was a confusing array of information flows within the unit. This prompted the author of that report to suggest that, within the unit there should exist, an intelligence cell. An ad hoc cell was created which proved to be less than expected. It was poorly resourced and was staffed with individuals that were unqualified which led to a lack of direction. In this particular case, the Gen Y members would certainly be able to contribute, as they are often described as being 'technology savvy' and have the ability to think outside of the box without the history, or baggage that the Generation X staff would bring to the party. Too often the older generations would proffer the argument that "we have always done it this way". The situation within the unit obviously needed new thinking and new ways, tempered by the experience of the Generation X staff but not restrained by them.

9. The Surveillance Unit currently uses Victoria Police's intelligence and investigation system Interpose as a document management system and under-utilises its capacity to manage intelligence, analysis and information dissemination.

On the 1st July the unit moved to using 'Interpose' a bespoke software for the correlation and dissemination of intelligence data for use by its police force. OPI (2008). The reservations that the report highlights, tend to allude to the operation of this system rather than blame being apportioned to the unit. Staff are required to manually enter data into the new document. Requests have been forwarded, asking for a template which could be used by staff making requests. However they have been advised, a solution is probably available but it will take a few years to develop! This again highlights areas that the new generation could be of a great advantage. In order to accept that this is possible we will need to rectify the situation, that is generally accepted namely that the attitudes of Gen Y staff in the workplace can lead to potential conflict between the different generations within the workplace. A survey by Lee Hecht Harrison found that "60% of employers experience tension between employees from different generations. This tension is often two-way with 70% of older employees dismissive of younger workers' abilities while 50% of younger employees are dismissive of older co-workers." If the Gen Y staff could solve the problems mentioned above, perhaps we could enjoy a more stable working relationship and alter some of the statistics that Harrison has put forward.

10. Inadequate formal attention is paid to risk management or the assessment of current practices with a view to continuous improvement.

The staff survey that was conducted, (OPI 2010) shows that the current staff are more than happy with their current state of awareness their argument lies in that they feel that the formal attention that has to be paid, 'inhibits their ability to perform their roles" and yet the survey shows that these same members of staff, or at least 89% believe that their unit fully complies with their information security responsibilities. This paradox could be the result of a poorly constructed questionnaire or, the staff's lack of what exactly is information security, which again raises the issue of understanding and training.

The OPI 2010 report concludes that there are failures in the proper authorisation processes, 'who should receive what'. The practice of operatives and investigators exchanging information without any security controls is an issue which is likely to increase when the Gen Y start to move up the promotion ladder with their perceived 'need to share' beliefs. This was highlighted by the report's findings that the culture within the unit was one that believed that 'more information is better'. The Wikileaks case study would hold that that is the case. The examination of the issues raised within this case study might put a slightly different hue on that.

Case Study 3: Wikileaks

- Is Information Private

As a working definition of the privacy of information we should expect that an individual can reasonably assume that no recording is taking place, and information which has been provided for specific purposes from one individual to another can reasonably expect will not be made public especially if that information is not in the public interest. Aftergood (2010) cites Last year, for example, " *WikiLeaks published the "secret ritual" of a college women's sorority called Alpha Sigma Tau. Now Alpha Sigma Tau (like several other sororities "exposed" by WikiLeaks) is not known to have engaged in any form of misconduct, and WikiLeaks does not allege that it has. Rather, WikiLeaks chose to publish the group's confidential ritual just because it could.* " It is just this sort of "Information Vandalism" that has besmirched the Wikileaks website.

- Do we have an issue with the Web2 Generation Y

The right to know can sometimes be taken too literally. The sharing of music and films, *pirating*, has long been an issue in modern times. WikiLeaks has engaged in this behaviour. Last year it published the full text of a book about corruption in Kenya called "It's Our Turn to Eat" by the reporter Michela Wrong without permission. This would, have course, of had a massive impact on sales. Is this just another example of feeding Generation Y with what it wants regardless of the consequences.

- Are people discerning with the information they divulge/receive

Much has been written about the *rights* of the people *to all and any information*, and in the majority of cases this is seen as laudable however, once we enter into global trade is this the right attitude? Would a worker within Microsoft making the next great windows application be justified in publishing? does this make a more fair market?, is the market fair? Microsoft can afford to do R&D to a greater extent because of its market position, if this was removed due to shared information, would it be a sound business activity?

- Does the format alter the content

On the 30th October 1938:

"Thousands of people, believing they were under attack by Martians, flooded newspaper offices and radio and police stations with calls, asking how to flee their city or how they should protect themselves from "gas raids." Scores of adults reportedly required medical treatment for shock and hysteria. The hoax worked, historians say, because the broadcast authentically simulated how radio worked in an emergency. "Audiences heard their regularly scheduled broadcast interrupted by breaking news". (Lovgen 2005).

First of all this was NOT a hoax because, it had been advertised before and during the broadcast that, it was a *dramatisation* of a H.G Wells book. So why were there cases of mass hysteria? Are we now seeing the like again? Is Julian Assange and his website, wikileaks, just another, updated Orson Wells on steroids?

- All of the facts??

The most worrying impact of including all the facts comes when we hear that after WikiLeaks published intelligence documents which would appear to list the names and villages of Afghans who have been cooperating with the American military. News reports tell us that "*it didn't take long for the Taliban to react*". A spokesman for the group quickly threatened to "punish" any Afghan listed as having "collaborated" with the U.S. and the Kabul authorities. (Aftergood 2010)

FUTURE RESEARCH

The next stage of the research will be to look at the Wikileaks case study and determine what are the key issues. The research will continue to focus upon a number of case studies relating to

Information Disclosure and determine common themes and issues. Future research will focus upon the organisational issues in relation to Information disclosure and the global context of information disclosure such as the Wikileaks example.

CONCLUSION

After close analysis of this document it was revealed that the theft that sparked this report was merely the tip of the iceberg. Several thefts within government departments led UK Ministers to question the very fabric of their data handling capabilities. The Burton report has identified several issues outside of its remit, begging the question, has the investigation gone far enough? Was the remit for this report too restrictive? Further research into these questions bares thought.

This case study has only scratched the surface of Burton's report there are several areas that need further examination an example of which is, in the glossary that accompanies this report there is a definition of Information Assurance, Information Security and Information Security Management System (ISMS) but not one for data, information or knowledge. The staggering amount of data that was stolen highlights the need to re-evaluate the way that the MOD and for that matter, other public sectors store, use and abuse data and information. There are several mentions of the 'cold war' within the main report. Which is viewed with some distain, and yet it favours this attitude to that of the 'Facebook' generation which in itself offers a whole new outlook on the work environment and could open up a plethora of problems for UK government departments which rely on the discretion of its employees.

The Victorian police have had a chequered past and unauthorised Information disclosure has featured prominently in their recent history. The cases that were highlighted, are not used in order to apportion blame but, rather to invoke discussions in this area

The case study shows the impact of organisational culture and its relation to Information Security. In regards to this case study we have focused upon the Victorian State Police in Australia and the cultural problems that they are having regards to the disclosure of Information. The study also reviews some of the key findings put forward by the Victorian Office of Police Integrity to solve these problems. There has been discussion of (possible) relationships between, what has happened in the Victorian Police Force and the emergence of a new breed of Police Officer from the era of Generation Y. The report is damning of the lack of control of information within the Victorian Police Force, in particular of the surveillance unit. In addition that they posed a "significant risk" in Information security for far too long. We have shown a possible failure to 'adhere to protocols' when the Information was on a need to know basis, moreover that it was being negligent in its classification of this information.

The key findings illustrate the modern position of "Need to Share" which can lead to "unacceptable vulnerabilities". Accepting this situation means that working practises within any organisation needs to be constantly reviewed without ignoring the benefits of the new emerging technologies "...and yet still being vigilant with regards to Information security."(Rosewall & Warren 2009)

Is there an issue with the Generation Y or is this thirst for knowledge, all knowledge, just a natural progression. 'a survival of the fittest'? Certainly many authors believe that Generation Y are responsible for many of these issues. This generation has long been accused of not having respect for security without reason, the problem lies in who decides what is reasonable. We all have rights and some believe *to all and any information,* and in the majority of cases this is seen as laudable. The major issue is should one person or a group of five people within Wikileaks have that power to disclose any information. On what ethical or moral ground does Wikileaks have the right to do this, have the right to interpret this information or the right to tell the world? You could have a situation where misinformation is being reported by Wikileaks as actually being fact, you then have a major issue, because it has then started to change people's perception based on untrue information and is the weakness of Wikileaks. *Just because something is posted on Wikileaks, "how do we know it's true, how do we know it's not disinformation"?* (Warren, 2010).

REFERENCES

ABC (Australian Broadcasting Company). (2010). *Julian Assange: WikiLeaks*. Retrieved September 1, 2010, from http://www.abc.net.au/tv/bigideas/stories/2010/06/08/2920615.htm

BBC. (2007). *UK's families put on fraud alert*. Retrieved September 10, 2009, from http://news.bbc.co.uk/2/hi/7103566.stm

BBC. (2008). *MoD Facebook generation warning*. Retrieved September 5, 2009, from http://news.bbc.co.uk/2/hi/uk_news/politics/7473818.stm

Bishop, M. (2003). What is computer security? *IEEE Security and Privacy*, *1*(1), 67–69. doi:10.1109/MSECP.2003.1176998

Burton, E. (2008). *Report into the loss of MOD personal data*. Minsitry of Defence, UK. Retrieved September 15, 2009, from http://www.mod.uk/NR/rdonlyres/3E756D20-E762-4FC1-BAB0-08C68FDC2383/0/burton_review_rpt20080430.pdf

Cabinet Office. (2008). *Data handling procedures in government: Final report*. UK Government. Retrieved September 15, 2009, from http://www.cabinetoffice.gov.uk/media/65948/dhr080625.pdf

Fisher, J., Gillespie, W., Harshman, E., & Yeager, F. (1999). *Whistleblowing on the Web*. Retrieved September 1, 2010, from http://www.bc.edu/bc_org/avp/law/st_org/iptf/commentary/content/fisher_gillespie_etal.html

Garretson, G. (2007). Balancing Generation Y preferences with security. *Network World*. Retrieved September 1, 2010, from http://www.networkworld.com/news/2007/082907-security-standard-5.html?page=2

Gary, H. (2008, 15 August). State's force still full of leaks. *The Australian*.

Gleeson, A. (2010). *Police accountability and oversight: An overview*. Retrieved September 1, 2010, from http://www.walk.com.au/pedestrian-council/Page.asp?PageID=339

Hansen, R. (2010). *Perception vs. reality: 10 truths about The Generation Y workforce*. Retrieved September 1, 2010, from http://www.quintcareers.com/Gen-Y_workforce.html

Lovgen, S. (2005). Behind the 1938 radio show panic. *National Geographic News*. Retrieved September 1, 2010, from URL:http://news.nationalgeographic.com/news/2005/06/0617_050617_warworlds.html

Mc Kenzie, N. (2009, 16 October). Watchdog's report damns police over leaked files - Systemic failure to manage data. *The Age*.

McCrindle, M. (2008). *The ABC of XYZ: Generational diversity at work*. McCrindle Research Pty Ltd. Retrieved October 20, 2009, from http://www.quayappointments.com.au/email/040213/images/generational_diversity_at_work.pdf

McCrindle, M. (2010). *Understanding Gen Y*. Retrieved September 1, 2010, from http://www.learningtolearn.sa.edu.au/Colleagues/files/links/UnderstandingGenY.pdf

Ministry of Defence. (2004). *JSP 541 - MOD information security alert warning and response policy manual, UK.*

Office of Police Integrity (OPI). (2010). *Report - Information security and the Victorian Police State surveillance unit.* Victoria, Australia.

Rosewall, I., & Warren, M. J. (2009), Information security disclosure: A case study. *Proceedings of 7thAustralian Information Security Management Conference*, (pp. 39-47). Perth, Australia: Edith Cowan University.

Rosewall, I., & Warren, M. J. (2010). Information security disclosure: A Victorian case study. *Proceedings of 8th Australian Information Security Management Conference.*

Rosewall, I., & Warren, M. J. (2010a). Wikileaks: The truth or not. *Proceedings of 8th Australian Information Security Management Conference.*

Schneier, B. (2000). *Secrets & lies: Digital security in a networked world* (1st ed.). New York, NY: John Wiley & Sons, Inc.

SmartManager. (2010). Getting workplace value from Generation Y. Retrieved September 1, 2010, from http://www.smartmanager.com.au/web/au/smartmanager/en/pages/87_workplace_value_gen_y.html

Wall Street Journal. (2009). *Gary Hamel's blog: The Facebook Generation vs. the Fortune 500.* Retrieved September 15, 2009, from http://blogs.wsj.com/management/2009/03/24/the-facebook-generation-vs-the-fortune-500

Warren, M. (2010). Changing culture paves way for more Wiki-style leaks. *Radio Australia National.* Retrieved September 1, 2010, from http://www.radioaustralia.net.au/connectasia/stories/201007/s2966371.htm

Whitman, M. E. (2003). Enemy at the gate: Threats to information security. *Communications of the ACM, 46*(8), 91–95. doi:10.1145/859670.859675

Williams, K. (2010). *Understanding Generation Y.* Retrieved September 1, 2010, from www.dynamicbusiness.com.au/.../understanding-generation-y.html

ADDITIONAL READING

Hutchinson, W., & Warren, M. (2001). *Information Warfare: Corporate Attack and.* Defence in the Digital Age, Butterworth-Heinneman.

Pye, G., & Warren, M. J. (2006a) 'Critical Infrastructure Protection, Modelling and Management: An Australian Commercial Case Study', in 5th European Conference on Information Warfare and Security, Academic Conference Limited (ACL), Helsinki, Finland, pp. 177-190.

Pye, G., & Warren, M. J. (2006b). Security Management: Modelling Critical Infrastructure. *Journal of Information Warfare, 5*(1), 46–61.

Redman, J., Warren, M., & Hutchinson, W. (2005). System Survivability: A Critical Security Problem. *Information Management & Computer Security, 13*(3), 182–188. doi:10.1108/09685220510602004

Warren, M., & Hutchinson, W. (2000). Cyber attacks against supply chain management systems: a short note. *International Journal of Physical Distribution & Logistics Management, 30*(Iss: 7/8), 710–716. doi:10.1108/09600030010346521

KEY TERMS AND DEFINITIONS

Data Management: The systematic collection, organisation and analysis of data.

Generation F, or **the Facebook generation,** or more commonly known as **Generation Y:** Generation Y are defined as those born between 1982 – 2000 according to McCrindle (2010).

Generation X: Generally accepted as being the generation following the baby boom.

Information Security: With regards to this chapter refers to the security of the information systems that are used and the data that is processed.

Information Security Disclosure: Information that has been disclosed either accidentally as in case study 1 or maliciously as in case study 3.

Ministry of Defence: The Ministry of Defence (MoD) is the British Government Department that are responsible for implementation of any government defence policy. It is also the headquarters of the British Armed Forces.

Public Sector: Industries or services provided or funded by the government as in the case of the British MOD or the Victorian Police.

Web 2: Web applications that facilitate interactive information sharing.

Compilation of References

ABC (Australian Broadcasting Company). (2010). *Julian Assange: WikiLeaks*. Retrieved September 1, 2010, from http://www.abc.net.au/tv/bigideas/stories/2010/06/08/2920615.htm

Abdi, M., & Dominic, P. D. D. (2010). Strategic IT alignment with business strategy: Service oriented architecture approach. *2010 International Symposium in Information Technology* (ITSim), vol. 3 (pp. 1473-1478).

Abdi, H. (2007). Signal detection theory. In Salkind, N. J. (Ed.), *Encyclopaedia of measurements and statistics*. Thousand Oaks, CA: Sage.

Abu-Nimeh, S., Nappa, D., Wang, X., & Nair, S. (2007). A comparison of machine learning techniques for phishing detection. In *Proceedings of the eCrime Researchers Summit*, 2007.

Ackerman, M., & Mainwaring, S. (2005). Privacy issues in human-computer interaction. In Cranor, L., & Garfinkel, S. (Eds.), *Security and usability: Designing secure systems that people can use* (pp. 381–400). Sebastopol, CA: O'Reilly.

Acquisti, A. (2004a). Privacy in electronic commerce and the economics of immediate gratification. In *Proceedings of the 5th ACM Conference on Electronic Commerce - EC '04* (p. 21). Presented at the 5th ACM Conference, New York, NY, USA. doi:10.1145/988772.988777

Acquisti, A. (2004b). Privacy and security of personal information. In L. Camp & S. Lewis (Eds.), *Economics of Information Security, Advances in Information Security* (Vol. 12, pp. 179-186). Springer US. Retrieved from http://dx.doi.org/10.1007/1-4020-8090-5_14

Acquisti, A., Dingledine, R., & Syverson, P. (2003). On the economics of anonymity. In *Financial cryptography* (pp. 84-102). Retrieved from http://www.springerlink.com/content/cbyufprgwjgubhlb

Acquisti, A. (2008). Identity management, privacy, and price discrimination. *IEEE Security & Privacy Magazine*, *6*(2), 46–50. doi:10.1109/MSP.2008.35

Acquisti, A., & Grossklags, J. (2005). Privacy and rationality in individual decision making. *Security & Privacy, IEEE*, *3*(1), 26–33. doi:10.1109/MSP.2005.22

Adams, A., & Sasse, M. A. (1999). Users are not the enemy: Why users compromise computer security mechanisms and how to take remedial measures. *Communications of the ACM*, *42*(12), 41–46.

Adida, B., Hohenberger, S., & Rivest, R. (2005). *Lightweight encryption for email*. USENIX Steps to Reducing Unwanted Traffic on the Internet Workshop (SRUTI), 2005.

AFP. (2009). Payments fraud a growing concern. Bancography, June. Retrieved June 17, 2009, from www.bancography.com

Ahn, G.-J., Ko, M., & Shehab, M. (2009). Privacy-enhanced user-centric identity management.

AICPA. (2000). *Statement on auditing standards No. 70: Service organizations. Professional standards* (*Vol. 1*). American Institute of Certified Public Accountants Auditing Standards Board.

Akao, Y. (1990). *Quality function deployment, integrating customer requirements into product design*. Cambridge, MA: Productivity Press.

Akerlof, G. A. (1970). The market for "lemons": Quality uncertainty and the market mechanism. *The Quarterly Journal of Economics*, *84*(3), 488–500. doi:10.2307/1879431

Alberts, C., & Dorofee, A. (2002). *Managing information security risks: The OCTAVE approach* (1st ed.). Boston, MA: Addison-Wesley.

Alfawaz, S., Nelson, K., & Mohannak, K. (2010). *Information security culture: A behaviour compliance conceptual framework.* Paper presented at the Australasian Information Security Conference (AISC), Brisbane, Australia.

Aljafari, R., & Sarnikar, S. (2009). A framework for assessing knowledge sharing risks in inter-organizational networks. In *Proceedings of the AIS Americas Conference on Information Systems (AMCIS 2009)*. AIS Electronic Library (AISeL).

Allen, J. (2005). *Governing for enterprise security*. Pittsburgh: Technical Note. Carnegie Mellon University.

Allen, J. H., & Westby, J. R. (2007). *Governing for enterprise security (GES)- Implementation guide, article 1: Characteristics of effective security governance*. Pittsburgh: Carnegie Mellon University.

Alonso, I. A., Verdun, J. C., & Caro, E. T. (2008). The importance of IT strategic demand management in achieving the objectives of the strategic business planning. *2008 International Conference on Computer Science and Software Engineering*, vol. 2 (pp. 235-238).

Alter, S. (2006). *The work system method: Connecting people, processes, and IT for business*. Larkspur, CA: Work System Press.

Anderson, R. (2001). Why information security is hard - An economic perspective. In *Computer Security Applications Conference* (pp. 358-365). Las Vegas.

Anderson, R. (2006). *Security engineering: A guide to building dependable distributed systems* (2nd ed.). Cambridge, UK: Wiley.

Anderson, R., Böhme, R., Clayton, R., & Moore, T. (2008). *Security economics and the internal market*. ENISA.

Ankobia, R. (2004). *Vulnerabilities in Web applications, painful lessons*. Advice (Un) Heeded, 8th World Multi-Conference on Systemic, Cybernetic and Informatics USA, July 18-21, 2004, Orlando, Florida.

Anti-Phishing Working Group. (2006). *Phishing activity trends report*, June 2006. Retrieved from http://antiphishing.org/reports/apwg report june 2006.pdf

Anwar, Z., Yurcik, W., Johnson, R., Hafiz, M., & Campbell, R. H. (2006). Multiple design patterns for Voice over IP (VoIP) security. *Proceedings of the 25th IEEE International Performance, Computing, and Communications Conference*. doi: 10.1109/.2006.1629443.

APACS. (2009). *Spot & stop counterfeit card fraud.* Association for Payment Clearing Services. Retrieved July 22, 2009, from www.apacs.org.uk/

Arbab, F., Chothia, T., Meng, S., & Moon, Y.-J. (2007). Component connectors with QoS guarantees. In Murphy, A. L., & Vitek, J. (Eds.), *Coordination 2007, LNCS 4467* (pp. 286–304). Berlin, Germany: Springer-Verlag.

Areiza, K. A., Barrientos, A. M., Rincón, R., & Lalinde-Pulido, J. G. (2005a). Hacia un modelo de madurez para la seguridad de la información. *3er Congreso Iberoamericano de seguridad Informática*, (pp. 429–442).

Artzner, P., Delbaen, F., Eber, J. M., & Heath, D. (2001). Coherent measures of risk. *Mathematical Finance*, *9*(3), 203–228. doi:10.1111/1467-9965.00068

AS2. (n.d.). *AS2 processing for EDI.* Retrieved March 2010, from http://www.dcs-is-edi.com/AS2.html

Australia, S. (2009). *Risk management*. (AS/NZS ISO 31000:2009). Retrieved March 1, 2010, from http://www.standards.com.au

Backhouse, J., Hsu, C. W., & Silva, L. (2006). Circuits of power in creating *de jure* standards: Shaping an international information systems security standard. *Management Information Systems Quarterly*, *30*, 413–438.

Baer, D. M., Wolf, M. M., & Risley, T. R. (1968). Some current dimensions of applied behavior analysis. *Journal of Applied Behavior Analysis*, *1*, 91–97. doi:10.1901/jaba.1968.1-91

Baker, W. H., Hutton, A., Hylender, C. D., Novak, C., Porter, C., Sartin, B., et al. (2009). *2009 data breach investigations report*. Verizon Business Security Solutions. Retrieved September 2009, from http://www.verizonbusiness.com/resources/security/reports/2009_databreach_rp.pdf

Baker, W. H., Hylender, C. D., & Valentine, J. A. (2008). *Data breach investigations report*. Verizon Business Security Solutions. Retrieved September 20008, from www.verizonbusiness.com/resources/security/databreachreport.pdf

Baker, W., Goudie, M., Hutton, A., Hylender, C. D., Niemantsverdriet, J., Novak, C., et al. (2010). *2010 data breach investigations report*. Verizon Business Security Solutions. Retrieved October 2010, from http://www.verizonbusiness.com/resources/reports/rp_2010-data-breach-report_en_xg.pdf

Baldwin, A., Casassa Mont, M., Beres, Y., & Shiu, S. (2010). Assurance for federated identity management. *Journal of Computer Security - Digital Identity Management (DIM 2007), 18*(4), 541-572.

Banathy, B. H. (1996). *Designing social systems in a changing world*. Springer.

Barabási, A.-L. (2002). *Linked: How everything is connected to everything else and what it means for business and everyday life*. Cambridge, MA: Perseus Publishing.

Barlette, Y., & Vladislav, V. (2008). *Exploring the suitability of IS security management standards for SMEs*. Paper presented at the Hawaii International Conference on System Sciences, Proceedings of the 41st Annual, Waikoloa, HI, USA.

Barrientos, A. M., & Areiza, K. A. (2005). *Integration of a safety management system with an information quality management system*. Universidad EAFIT.

Bartsch, S., Sohr, K., & Bormann, C. (2009). *Supporting agile development of authorization rules for SME applications*. Paper presented at the CollaborateCom 2008, LNICST 10, ICST Institute for Computer Sciences, Social-Informatics and Telecommunications Engineering 2009.

Basel Committee. (2001). *Operational risk*. Supporting Document to the New Basel Capital Accord on Banking Supervision (May 31, 2001).

Batista, J., & Figueiredo, A. (2000). SPI in very small team: A case with CMM. *Software Process Improvement and Practice*, *5*(4), 243–250. doi:10.1002/1099-1670(200012)5:4<243::AID-SPIP126>3.0.CO;2-0

BBA. (2008). British Bankers' Association Annual Report 2007/08. Retrieved June 29, 2009, from www.bba.org.uk/

BBC News Middle East. (2010, September 26). *Stuxnet worm hits Iran nuclear plant staff computers*. Retrieved from http://www.bbc.co.uk/news/world-middle-east-11414483

BBC. (2007). *UK's families put on fraud alert*. Retrieved September 10, 2009, from http://news.bbc.co.uk/2/hi/7103566.stm

BBC. (2008). *MoD Facebook generation warning*. Retrieved September 5, 2009, from http://news.bbc.co.uk/2/hi/uk_news/politics/7473818.stm

Beggs, C. (2005). Cyber-terrorism a threat to Australia? In Khosrow-Pour, M. (Ed.), *Managing modern organisation with Information Technology* (pp. 472–475). Hershey, PA: Information Resources Management Association.

Beggs, C., & Warren, M. (2007). Safeguarding Australia from cyber-terrorism: A proposed cyber-terrorism SCADA risk framework for Australia. *The Journal of Information Warfare*, *7*(1), 24–35.

Bella, S. D., Peretz, I., & Aronoff, N. (2003). Time course of melody recognition: A gating paradigm study. *Perception & Psychophysics*, *65*(7), 1019–1028. doi:10.3758/BF03194831

Bennet, M. (2010). *Ruumble... Negotiating cloud computing agreements*. Law Technology News.

Bergholz, J.-H., Chang, G. H., Paaß, G., Reichartz, F., & Strobel, S. (2008). Improved phishing detection using model-based features. In *Proceedings of the Conference on Email and Anti-Spam* (CEAS), 2008.

Berthold, O., Federrath, H., & Köpsell, S. (2001). Web MIXes: A system for anonymous and unobservable Internet access. In H. Federrath (Ed.), *Designing Privacy Enhancing Technologies, Lecture Notes in Computer Science* (Vol. 2009, pp. 115-129). Berlin, Germany: Springer. Retrieved from http://dx.doi.org/10.1007/3-540-44702-4_7

Bertino, E., Paci, F., & Shang, N. (2009). *Keynote 2: Digital identity protection - Concepts and issues.* International Conference on Availability, Reliability and Security. IEEE Computer Society.

Bertocci, V., Serack, G., & Baker, C. (2007). *Understanding Windows CardSpace: An introduction to the concepts and challenges of digital identities*. Amsterdam, The Netherlands: Addison-Wesley Longman.

Besson, M., Faïta, F., Bonnel, A.-M., & Requin, J. (2002). Singing in the brain: Independence of music and tunes. *Psychological Science*, *9*(6), 494–498. doi:10.1111/1467-9280.00091

Beymer, D., & Poggio, T. (1995). *Face recognition from one example view*. A.I. Memo 1536, Massachusetts Institute of Technology, September.

Bhala, S., Christodoulides, M., Cornwell, L., Jones, R., & Morris, B. (2010). *UK security breach investigation report - An analysis of data compromise cases*. 7Safe Limited. Retrieved March 2010, from http://7safe.com/breach_report/Breach_report_2010.pdf

Bigand, E., & Poulin-Charronnat, B. (2006). Are we "experienced listeners"? A review of the musical capacities that do not depend on formal musical training. *Cognition*, *100*, 100–130. doi:10.1016/j.cognition.2005.11.007

Birk, D., Dornseif, M., & Gajek, S. & Grobert. F. (2006). *Phishing phishers—Tracing identity thieves and money launderers*. Horst Gortz Institute for IT Security, Ruhr University Bochum, Tech. Rep. TR-HGI-01-2006.

Birnbrauer, J. S. (1979). Applied behavior analysis, service and the acquisition of knowledge. *The Behavior Analyst*, *2*, 15–21.

BIS. (2009). *Fraud and scams*. Department for Business Innovation & Skills. Retrieved June 24, 2009, from http://search.berr.gov.uk/

Bishop, M. (2005). Position: Insider is relative. In *NSPW'05: Proceedings of the 2005 New Security Paradigms Workshop* (pp. 77–78). ACM Press.

Bishop, M. (2003). *Computer security: Art and science*. Boston, MA: Addison-Wesley.

Bishop, M. (2003). What is computer security? *IEEE Security and Privacy*, *1*(1), 67–69. doi:10.1109/MSECP.2003.1176998

Boehmer, W. (2008). Appraisal of the effectiveness and efficiency of an information security management system based on ISO 27001. *SECURWARE '08: Second International Conference on Emerging Security Information, Systems and Technologies*, (pp. 224-231).

Boehmer, W. (2009a). *Cost-benefit trade-off analysis of an ISMS based on ISO 27001*. ARES Conference: The International Dependability Conference, March 16—19, 2009, Fukuoka Institute of Technology (FIT), Fukuoka, Japan, IEEE Computer Society.

Boehmer, W. (2009b). Survivability and business continuity management system according to BS 25999. *Proceedings, Third International Conference on Emerging Security Information, Systems and Technologies (SECUWARE '09)*, June 18–23, 2009, Athens/Glyfada, Greece, (pp. 142–147). IEEE Computer Society.

Boehmer, W. (2009c). Performance, survivability and cost aspects of business continuity processes according to BS25999. *International Journal on Advances in Security*, *2*(4). ISSN 1942–2636

Boehmer, W. (2010). Toward a target function of an information security management system. *2010 IEEE 10th International Conference on Computer and Information Technology* (CIT), (pp. 809-816).

Boehmer, W. (2010a). Toward an objective function for an information security management system. *Proceedings, Third IEEE International Symposium on Trust, Security and Privacy for Emerging Applications (TSP-2010)*, Bradford, UK, 29 June–1 July, 2010, IEEE Computer Society.

Boehmer, W. (2010b). Analysis of strongly and weakly coupled management systems in information security. *Proceedings, Fourth International Conference on Emerging Security Information, Systems, and Technologies (SECURWARE 2010)*, July 18–25, 2010, Venice/Mestre, Italy, IEEE Computer Society.

Boehmer, W. (2010c). *Theorie und Anwendung diskreter ereignisorientierter und rückgekoppelter Systeme in der Informationssicherheit.* Habilitation thesis (in preparation), Technische Universität Darmstadt, Germany.

Boehmer, W. (2011). Field study to examine a possible reduction of risk capital in the case of operational risk-based control loop by security management systems. *Proceedings, Fifth International Conference on Emerging Security Information, Systems, and Technologies (SECURWARE 2011)*, August 21–27, 2011, France (in preparation).

Bohn, J., Coroama, V., Langheinrich, M., Mattern, M., & Rohs, M. (2004) Social, economic, and ethical implications of ambient intelligence and ubiquitous computing. In E. Aarts, W. Weber & J. Rabaey (Eds.), *Ambient intelligence*. Springer-Verlag.

Bologna, J. (1984). Corporate fraud: The basics of prevention and detection, (pp. 1, 15). Butterworth Publishers.

Boos, K. H., & Schulte-Mattler, H. (2001). Basel II: Methoden zur Quantifizierung operationeller Risiken. *Die Bank*, *8*, 549–553.

Boyd, D., & Heer, J. (2006). *Profiles as conversation: Networked identity performance on Friendster*. In Hawaii International Conference on Systems Science (vol. 39). Kauai, HI: IEEE Computer Society.

Boyd, J. R. (1976). An organic design for command and control. In Boyd, J. R. (Ed.), *A discourse on winning and losing. Unpublished lecture notes.*

Boyle, B., & Alwitt, L. (1999). Internet use within the U.S plastics industry. *Industrial Marketing Management*, *28*, 327–341. doi:10.1016/S0019-8501(98)00012-1

Brackney, R. C., & Anderson, R. H. (2004). *Understanding the insider threat: Proceedings of a March 2004 Workshop*. Retrieved March 2010, from www.rand.org/pubs/conf_proceedings/2005/RAND_CF196.pdf

Brian, W. (1995). *Introduction page*. Serious Fraud Office, Little, Brown and Company.

Briggs, R., Kolfschoten, G., Gert-Jan, V., & Douglas, D. (2006). *Defining key concepts for collaboration engineering.* In Americas Conference on Information Systems, AMCIS 2006 Proceedings, Acapulco, Mexico

Brosso, I. (2006) *Users continuous authentication in computers networks*. Doctoral Thesis in Digital Systems at Polytechnic School of Sao Paulo University, Brazil. Retrieved from http://www.teses.usp.br/teses/disponiveis/3/3141/tde-08122006-170242/en.php

Brosso, I., La Neve, A., Bressan, G., & Ruggiero, W. V. (2010). A continuous authentication system based on user behavior analysis. *International Conference on Availability, Reliability and Security, International Conference*, (pp. 380-385). Krakow, Poland, February 15-February 18. ISBN: 978-0-7695-3965-2

Brostoff, S., & Sasse, M. A. (2000). Are passfaces more usable than passwords? A field trial investigation. In S. McDonald, (Ed.), *People and Computers XIV - Usability or Else! Proceedings of HCI2000*, (pp. 405-424). Springer.

Coventry, L., De Angeli, A., & Johnson, G. (2003). Usability and biometric verification at the ATM interface. In *CHI'03: Proceedings of the SIGCHI Conference on Human Factors in Computing Systems* (pp. 153-160). New York, NY: ACM Press.

Brown, G. S. (1971). *Laws of form*. George Allen and Unwin.

Bryman, A. (2004). *Quantity and quality in social research*, (pp. 11-44). Routledge, Taylor and & Francis Group.

Burr, W. E., Dodson, D. F., & Polk, W. T. (2006). *NIST special publication 800-63: Information security, version 1.0.2*. National Institute of Standards and Technology.

Burton, E. (2008). *Report into the loss of MOD personal data.* Minsitry of Defence, UK. Retrieved September 15, 2009, from http://www.mod.uk/NR/rdonlyres/3E756D20-E762-4FC1-BAB0-08C68FDC2383/0/burton_review_rpt20080430.pdf

Business Rule Group. (2000). *Defining business rules – What are they really?* Final report, revision 1.3. Retrieved November 26, 2010, from http://www.businessrulesgroup.org/first_paper/br01c1.htm

Cabinet Office. (2008). *Data handling procedures in government: Final report*. UK Government. Retrieved September 15, 2009, from http://www.cabinetoffice.gov.uk/media/65948/dhr080625.pdf

Calvo-Manzano, J. A., Cuevas, G., San Feliu, T., De Amescua, A., García, L., & Pérez, M. (2004). Experiences in the application of software process improvement in SMES. *Software Quality Journal*, *10*(3), 261–273. doi:10.1023/A:1021638523413

Cameron, K. (2005, 05). *Microsoft's vision for an identity metasystem*. Kim Cameron's Identity Weblog. Retrieved August, 2010, from http://www.identityblog.com/stories/2005/07/05/IdentityMetasystem.html

Cameron, K., & Jones, M. B. (2007). Design rationale behind the identity metasystem architecture. In *ISSE/SECURE 2007 Securing Electronic Business Processes* (pp. 117-129). Retrieved from http://dx.doi.org/10.1007/978-3-8348-9418-2_13

Cameron, J., Pierce, W. D., Banko, K. M., & Gear, A. (2005). Achievement-based rewards and intrinsic motivation: A test of cognitive mediators. *Journal of Educational Psychology*, *97*(4), 641–655. doi:10.1037/0022-0663.97.4.641

Cameron, K., & Freeman, S. (1991). Cultural congruence, strength and type: Relationships to effectiveness. *Research in Organizational Change and Development*, *5*, 23–58.

Cantor, S., Kemp, J., Maler, E., & Philpott, R. (2005). *Assertions and protocols for the OASIS security assertion markup language (SAML) V2.02*. OASIS.

Capra, F. (1996). *The web of life: A new scientific understanding of living systems*. Anchor Books/Doubleday.

Card Watch. (2009). *Fraud: The facts 2009*. Retrieved July 22, 2009, from www.cardwatch.org.uk

Card Watch. (2009). Stop and stop card fraud retailer training pack. Retrieved July 22, 2009, from www.cardwatch.org.uk

Carey-Smith, M. T., Nelson, K. J., & May, L. J. (2007). *Improving information security management in nonprofit organisations with action research.* Paper presented at the 5th Australian Information Security Management Conference, Perth, Western Australia.

Cavusoglu, H., Mishra, B., & Raghunathan, S. (2004). A model for evaluating IT security investments. *Communications of the ACM*, *47*(7), 87–92. doi:10.1145/1005817.1005828

Čermák, I. (2007). *Security threats and information systems security status at Czech public universities. Security Policy* (pp. 12–17). Plzeň, Czech Republic: The University of West Bohemia in Pilsen.

Chadwick, D. W., & Inman, G. (2009, May). Attribute aggregation in federated identity management. *Computer*, *42*(5), 33–40. doi:10.1109/MC.2009.143

Chaffey, D. (2004). *E-business and e-commerce management* (2nd ed.). London, UK: Prentice Hall.

Chang, S. E., & Lin, C. S. (2007). Exploring organizational culture for information security management. *Industrial Management & Data Systems*, *107*(3), 438–458. doi:10.1108/02635570710734316

Chaudhury, A., Rao, R., & Wang, J. (2005). An extreme value approach to Information Technology security investment. *ICIS 2005 Proceedings*. Retrieved from http://aisel.aisnet.org/icis2005/29

Chaum, D. L. (1981). Untraceable electronic mail, return addresses, and digital pseudonyms. *Communications of the ACM*, *24*(2), 84–90. doi:10.1145/358549.358563

Chia, P. A., Maynard, S. B., & Ruighaver, A. B. (2003). Understanding organizational security culture. In Hunter, M. G., & Dhanda, K. K. (Eds.), *Information Systems: The challenges of theory and practice* (pp. 335–365). Las Vegas, NV: Information Institute.

Chlup, M. (2008, August). *The introduction of safety management system - ISMS, PDCA model*. Protect your data. Retrieved November 2010, from http://www.chrantesidata.cz/cs/art/1148-dil-2

Chou, N., Ledesma, R., Teraguchi, Y., Boneh, D., & Mitchell, J. (2004). *Client-side defense against Web-based identity theft*. In 11th Annual Network and Distributed System Security Symposium (NDSS '04), San Diego, 2004.

Chris, H., Keith, H., Azrini, W., & Emma, W. (2009). In Tombs, S. (Ed.), *Criminology* (2nd ed., p. 342). Oxford University Press.

Christopher, G., Müller, S., & Pfitzmann, B. (2006). *From regulatory policies to event monitoring rules: Towards Model-driven compliance automation. IBM Research Report RZ 3662*. IBM Zurich Research Laboratory.

Chuan, Y., & Wang, H. (2009). BogusBiter: A transparent protection against phishing attacks. *ACM Transactions on Internet Technology*, *10*(2), 1–30.

Clark, J., van Oorschot, P. C., & Adams, C. (2007). Usability of anonymous Web browsing. In *Proceedings of the 3rd Symposium on Usable Privacy and Security - SOUPS '07* (p. 41). Presented at the 3rd symposium, Pittsburgh, Pennsylvania. doi:10.1145/1280680.1280687

Clarke, R. (1988). Information Technology and dataveillance. *Communications of the ACM, 31*(5), 498–512. doi:10.1145/42411.42413

Clauset, A., Newman, M., & Moore, C. (2004). Finding community structure in very large networks. *Physical Review E: Statistical, Nonlinear, and Soft Matter Physics, 70*, 066111. doi:10.1103/PhysRevE.70.066111

Clegg, S. R. (1989). *Frameworks of power*. London, UK: Sage.

Clinch, J. (2009). *ITIL V3 and information security.* Retrieved November 3, 2010, from www.best-management-practice.com/gempdf/ITILV3_and_Information_Security_White_Paper_May09.pdf

Coaker. (2009). *Internet crime: House of Commons Hansard written answers*. Retrieved June 29, 2009, from http://www.publications.parliament.uk/

Cobit. (2006). *Guidelines*. Information Security Audit and Control Association.

Coles-Kemp, E., & Overill, R. E. (2007, 2-3 July). *The design of information security management systems for small-to-medium size enterprises.* Paper presented at the ECIW - The 6th European Conference on Information Warfare and Security, Shrivenham, UK.

Common Criteria Sponsoring Organization. (2007). *Common criteria for information technology security evaluation part 2: Security functional components,* version 3.1 rev 2. Retrieved from http://www.commoncriteriaportal.org/files/ccfiles/CCPART2V3.1R2.pdf

Coopersmith, J. (1998). Pornography, technology and progress. *Icon, 4*, 94–125.

COSO. (1994). *Internal control - Integrated framework by Committee on Sponsoring Organizations of the Treadway Commission.*

COSO. (2004). *Enterprise risk management-integrated framework*. Retrieved March 22, 2011, from http://www.coso.org/documents/COSO_ERM_ExecutiveSummary.pdf

COSO. (2009). *Guidance on monitoring internal control systems*. American Institute of Certified Public Accountants Press.

COSO. (2010). Home page. Retrieved March 22, 2010, from http://coso.org/IC.htm

Couto, P. J., Tiago, B. F., Tiagi, B. T., & Vieira, C. J. (2008). The utilization of Internet by European companies. *The Journal of Business, 5*(6), 41. Retrieved June 25, 2009 from http://www.journalofe-business.org

Cover Pages, O. A. S. I. S. (2008, October). *Microsoft 'Geneva' framework supports SAML 2.0, WS-Federation, and WS-Trust.* Retrieved July 2010, from http://xml.coverpages.org/ni2008-10-29-a.html

Cranor, L., Egelman, S., Hong, J., & Zhang, Y. (2006). *Phinding phish: An evaluation of anti-phishing toolbars.* Technical report, Carnegie Mellon University, Nov. 2006.

Cronin, M. (1996). *The Internet strategy handbook: Lesson from the new frontier of business*. Boston, MA: Harvard Business School Press.

Crowder, R. G., & Serafine, M. L. (1986). Physical interaction and association by contiguity in memory for the words and melodies of songs. *Memory & Cognition, 18*(5), 469–476. doi:10.3758/BF03198480

Croxton, K. L. (2003). The order fulfillment process. *The International Journal of Logistics Management, 14*(1), 19–32. doi:10.1108/09574090310806512

Curbera, F., Doganata, Y., Martens, A., Mukhi, M., & Slominski, A. (2008). Business provenance - A technology to increase traceability of end-to-end operations. *Proceedings of OTM Conferences,* (pp. 100-119).

Czech Standards Institute. (2006, September). *Code of practice for information security management.* ČSN ISO/IEC 17799 (369790) Information technology - Security techniques. Retrieved January 2011, from http://shop.normy.biz/d.php?k=75901

Da Veiga, A., & Eloff, J. H. P. (2007). An information security governance framework. *Information Systems Management, 24*(4), 361–372. doi:10.1080/10580530701586136

Das, T., & Teng, B.-S. (1998). Between trust and control: Developing confidence in partner cooperation in alliances. *Academy of Management Review, 23*(3), 491–512.

Davenport, T. H. (2005). *Thinking for a living, how to get better performance and results from knowledge workers.* Boston, MA: Harvard Business School Press.

Davis, D., Monrose, F., & Reiter, M. K. (2004). On user choice in graphical password schemes. In *SSYM'04: Proceedings of the 13th Conference on USENIX Security Symposium,* (p. 11). Berkeley, CA: USENIX Association.

Davis, M., & Canny, J. Van House, N., Good, N., King, S., Nair, R., … Reid, N. (2005). MMM2: Mobile media metadata for media sharing. In *Proceedings of the 13th Annual ACM International Conference on Multimedia* (Hilton, Singapore, November 06 - 11, 2005), MULTIMEDIA '05, (pp. 267-268). New York, NY: ACM.

Davis, F. D. (1989). Perceived usefulness, perceived ease of use, and user acceptance of Information Technology. *Management Information Systems Quarterly, 13*(3), 319–340. doi:10.2307/249008

Davis, S., & Ord, K. (1990). Improving and measuring the performance of a security industry surveillance system. *Interfaces, 20*(5), 31–42. doi:10.1287/inte.20.5.31

De Angeli, A., Coventry, L., Johnson, G., & Renaud, K. (2005). Is a picture really worth a thousand words? Exploring the feasibility of graphical authentication systems. *International Journal of Human-Computer Studies, 63*, 128–152. doi:10.1016/j.ijhcs.2005.04.020

De Capitani, S., Foresti, S., & Jajodia, S. (2008, October 27, 2008). *Preserving confidentiality of security policies in data outsourcing.* Paper presented at the WPES'08, Alexandria, Virginia, USA.

De Cock, D., Wouters, K., & Preneel, B. (2004). Introduction to the Belgian EID Card. In *Public Key Infrastructure* (pp. 621-622). Retrieved from http://www.springerlink.com/content/rqm391495220px5n

Deal, T. E., & Kennedy, A. A. (1982). *Corporate culture.* Reading, MA: Addison-Wesley.

Dean, J. W., & Bowen, D. E. (1994). Management theory and total quality: Improving research and practice through theory development. *Academy of Management Review, 19*, 392–418.

Delessy, N., & Fernandez, E. B. (2005). Patterns for the extensible access control markup language. *Proceedings of the 12th Pattern Languages of Programs Conference (PLOP2005).* Retrieved from http://hillside.net/plop/2005/proceedings/

Deming, W. E. (1986). *Out of the Crisis.* Cambridge, MA: MIT Center for Advanced Engineering Study.

Dempster, A. P. (1967). Upper and lower probabilities induced by a multi-valued mapping. *Annals of Mathematical Statistics, 38*, 325–339. doi:10.1214/aoms/1177698950

den Braber, F., Hogganvik, I., Lund, M. S., Stølen, K., & Vraalsen, F. (2007). Model-based security analysis in seven steps - A guided tour to the CORAS method. *BT Technology Journal, 25*(1), 101–117. doi:10.1007/s10550-007-0013-9

Denison, D. R. (1990). *Corporate Culture and Organizational Effectiveness. New York.* New York: Wiley.

Denison, D. R., & Mishra, A. (1995). Toward a theory of organizational culture and effectiveness. *Organization Science, 6*, 204–224. doi:10.1287/orsc.6.2.204

Denning, D. (2000). *Cyber-terrorism testimony before the Special Panel on Terrorism Committee on Armed Services US House of Representatives.* Georgetown University. Retrieved September 29, 2009, from http://www.cs.georgetown.edu/~denning/infosec/cyberterror.html

Department of Defense. (2003). *Systems security engineering capability maturity model* (SSE-CMM), version 3.0.

Detert, J. R., Schroeder, R. G., & Mauriel, J. J. (2000). A framework for linking culture and improvement initiatives in organisations. *Academy of Management Review, 25*(4), 850–863.

Dhamija, R., & Dusseault, L. (2008). The seven flaws of identity management: Usability and security challenges. *IEEE Security & Privacy Magazine, 6*(2), 24–29. doi:10.1109/MSP.2008.49

Dhillon, G. (1997). *Managing Information System security.* Houndmills, UK: Macmillan Press LTD.

Dhillon, G. (1999). Managing and controlling computer misuse. *Information Management & Computer Security, 7*(4), 171–175. doi:10.1108/09685229910292664

Dhillon, G., & Backhouse, J. (2000). Information System security management in the new millennium. *Communications of the ACM, 43*(7), 125–128. doi:10.1145/341852.341877

Dhillon, G., & Backhouse, J. (2001). Current directions in IS security research: Towards socio-organizational perspectives. *Information Systems Journal, 11*(2), 127–153. doi:10.1046/j.1365-2575.2001.00099.x

Dhillon, G., & Moores, S. (2001). Computer crimes: Theorizing about the enemy within. *Computers & Security, 20*(8), 715–723. doi:10.1016/S0167-4048(01)00813-6

Dhir, V., Acet, A. S., Kumar, R., & Singh, G. (2010). Biometric recognition: A modern era for security. *International Journal of Engineering Science and Technology, 2*(8), 3364-3380. ISSN: 0975-5462

Dick, B. (2000). *Applications*. Sessions of Areol. Action research and evaluation.

DiMicco, J. M., & Millen, D. R. (2007). Identity management: Multiple presentations of self in Facebook. In *Proceedings of the 2007 International ACM Conference on Supporting Group Work* (Sanibel Island, Florida, USA, November 04 - 07, 2007), 383–386.

Dingledine, R., Freedman, M. J., & Molnar, D. (2000). Accountability measures for peer-to-peer systems. In *Peer-to-peer: Harnessing the power of disruptive technologies*. O'Reilly Publishers.

Dingledine, R., & Mathewson, N. (2005). Anonymity loves company: Usability and the network effect. In *Designing security systems that people can use*. O'Reilly Media.

Dojkovski, S., Lichtenstein, S., & Warren, M. J. (2006). *Challenges in fostering an information security culture in Australian small and medium sized enterprises*. Paper presented at the 5th European Conference on Information Warfare and Security, Helsinki, Finland.

Douglas, T., & Brian, D. L. (2000). *Cybercrime, law enforcement, security and surveillance in the information age,* (p. 3, 7). Routledge, Taylor & Francis Group.

Dumortier, J., Kelm, S., Nilsson, H., Skouma, G., & Van Eecke, P. (2003). *The legal and market aspects of electronic signatures*. Interdisciplinary Centre for Law & Information Technology, Katholieke Universiteit Leuven.

Dutta, A., & McCrohan, K. (2002). Management's role in information security in a cyber economy. *California Management Review, 45*(1), 67–87.

e-Authentication Initiative. (2007). *E-authentication guidance for federal agencies*. US.

Eisenhardt, K. M. (1989). Agency theory: An assessment and review. *Academy of Management Review, 14*(1), 57–74.

Elo, J. H. P., & Elo, M. (2003). Information security management: A new paradigm. *Proceedings, 2003 Annual Research Conference of the South African Institute of Computer Scientists and Information Technologists on Enablement through Technology (SAICSIT '03)*, Johannesburg, 130–136, South African Institute for Computer Scientists and Information Technologists, 2003.

Eloff, J., & Eloff, M. (2003). Information security management - A new paradigm. *Annual Research Conference of the South African Institute of Computer Scientists and Information Technologists on Enablement through Technology,* SAICSIT'03, (pp. 130-136).

Emigh, A. (2005). *Online identity theft: Technology, chokepoints and countermeasures.* Report of the Department of Homeland Security – SRI International Identity Theft Technology Council, October 3, 2005.

ENISA. (2010). *Report priorities for research on current and emerging network technologies.* Retrieved from http://www.enisa.europa.eu/act/it/library/deliverables/procent

Ernst & Young. (2004). *Global information security survey 2004*. Retrieved from www.ey.com/global/download.nsf/International/2004_Global_Information_Security_Survey/$file/2004_Global_Information_Security_Survey_2004.pdf

European Commission. (2010). *Press release and comprehensive legal opinion*. Retrieved from http://ec.europa.eu/justice_home/fsj/privacy/docs/wpdocs/2010/wp169_en.pdf

Farmer, R., & Glass, B. (2010). *Building Web reputation systems*. O'Reilly Media, Inc.

Federal Information Security Management Act. (2002). *Federal Information Security Management Act of 2002.*

Federrath, H., Jerichow, A., Kesdogan, D., Pfitzmann, A., & Spaniol, O. (1997). Mobilkommunikation ohne Bewegungsprofile. In Pfitzmann, A., & Mueller, G. (Eds.), *Mehrseitige Sicherheit in der Kommunikationstechnik* (pp. 169–180). Boston, MA: Addison Wesley.

Feigenbaum, J., Freedman, M. J., Sander, T., & Shostack, A. (2002). Economic barriers to the deployment of existing privacy technologies (position paper). In *Proceedings of the Workshop on Economics of Information Security.*

Fernandez, E. B., & Yuan, X. (2000). Semantic analysis patterns. *Proceedings of the 19th International Conference on Conceptual Modeling (ER2000),* (pp. 183-195).

Fernandez, E. B., Fonoage, M., VanHilst, M., & Marta, M. (2008). The secure three-tier architecture pattern. *Proceedings of the 2008 International Conference on Complex, Intelligent and Software Intensive Systems* (pp. 555-560). IEEE Computer Society. doi: 10.1109/CISIS.2008.51

Fernandez, E. B., Pernul, G., & Larrondo-Petrie, M. M. (2008). Patterns and pattern diagrams for access control. *Proceedings of the 5th International Conference on Trust, Privacy, and Security in Digital Systems (TRUSTBUS'08), LNCS 5185* (pp. 38-47). Springer.

Fernandez, E. B., VanHilst, M., & Pelaez, J. C. (2007). Patterns for WiMax security. *Proceedings of the European Conference on Pattern Languages of Programming.*

Fernandez, E. B., Washizaki, H., Yoshioka, N., Kubo, A., & Fukazawa, Y. (2008). Classifying security patterns. *Proceedings of the 10th Asia-Pacific Web Conference (APweb'08), LNCS 4976* (pp. 342-347). Springer. Retrieved from http://www.neu.edu.cn/apweb08/

Fernández-Medina, E., Jurjens, J., Trujillo, J., & Jajodia, S. (2009). Model-driven development for secure Information Systems. *Information and Software Technology Journal, 51*(5), 809–814. doi:10.1016/j.infsof.2008.05.010

Fette, N., Sadeh, S., & Tomasic, A. (2007). Learning to detect phishing emails. In *Proceedings of the International World Wide Web Conference (WWW)*, Banff, Alberta, Canada, May 2007.

Fisher, J., Gillespie, W., Harshman, E., & Yeager, F. (1999). *Whistleblowing on the Web.* Retrieved September 1, 2010, from http://www.bc.edu/bc_org/avp/law/st_org/iptf/commentary/content/fisher_gillespie_etal.html

Fitzgerald, T. (2007). Building management commitment through security councils, or security council critical success factors. In Tipton, H. F. (Ed.), *Information security management handbook* (pp. 105–121). Hoboken, NJ: Auerbach Publications. doi:10.1201/9781439833032.ch10

Florencio, D., & Herley, C. (2007). A large-scale study of web password habits. *In WWW'07: Proceedings of the 16th International Conference on World Wide Web.* (pp. 657-666). New York, NY: ACM.

Flyvbjerg, B. (2001). *Making social science matter: why social inquiry fails and how it can count again.* Cambridge, UK: Cambridge University Press.

Fontana, A., & Frey, J. (2005). The interview. In Denzin, N. L. (Ed.), *The SAGE handbook of qualitative research* (3rd ed., pp. 695–727). Thousand Oaks, CA: SAGE Publication.

Forget, A., Chiasson, S., & Biddle, R. (2007). Helping users create better passwords: Is this the right approach? In *SOUPS '07: Proceedings of the Third Symposium on Usable Privacy and Security* (pp. 151-152). New York, NY: ACM.

Franqueira, V. N. L., & Wieringa, R. J. (2010). *Value-driven security agreements in extended enterprises.* Technical Report TR-CTIT-10-17. Enschede, The Netherlands: Centre for Telematics and Information Technology University of Twente. ISSN 1381-3625

Franqueira, V. N. L., van Cleeff, A., van Eck, P. A. T., & Wieringa, R. J. (2010). External insider threat: a Real security challenge in enterprise value webs. In *ARES'2010: Proceedings of the Fifth International Conference on Availability, Reliability and Security* (pp. 446–453). IEEE Press.

Fraud. (2009). *Fraud: The facts 2009.* Retrieved August 22, 2009, from www.apacs.org.uk/

Freedman, R., & Mathai, J. (1995). Market analysis for risk management and regulation: An artificial intelligence approach. In Freedman, R., Klein, R., & Lederman, J. (Eds.), *Artificial intelligence in the capital market* (pp. 315–326). Chicago, IL: Probus Publishing.

Freedman, R., & Stuzin, G. J. (1991). Knowledge-based methodology for tuning analytical models. *IEEE Transactions on Systems, Man, and Cybernetics*, *21*(2), 347–358. doi:10.1109/21.87083

Fritsch, L., & Abie, H. (2008). Towards a research road map for the management of privacy risks in Information Systems. In *Sicherheit 2008: Sicherheit, Schutz und Zuverlässigkeit. Konferenzband der 4. Jahrestagung des Fachbereichs Sicherheit der Gesellschaft für Informatik e.V. (GI)* (pp. 1-15).

Fritsch, L., & Rossnagel, H. (2005). Die Krise des Signaturmarktes: Lösungsansätze aus betriebswirtschaftlicher Sicht. In *SICHERHEIT 2005* (pp. 315–327). GI.

Fritsch, L., Roßnagel, H., Schwenke, M., & Stadler, T. (2005). Die Pflicht zum Angebot anonym nutzbarer Dienste: Eine technische und rechtliche Zumutbarkeitsbetrachtung. *Datenschutz und Datensicherheit*, *29*(10), 592–596.

Furnell, S., & Thompson, K. L. (2009). From culture to disobedience: Recognising the varying user acceptance of IT security. *Computer Fraud & Security*, *2*, 5–10. doi:10.1016/S1361-3723(09)70019-3

Futurist. (2009). Internet fraud on the rise. *The Futurist*, *43*(4), 15. Retrieved June 20, 2009, from http://web.ebscohost.com/

Gabriel, Y. (2003). Glass palaces and glass cages. *Ephemera: Theory & Politics in Organization*, *3*(3), 166-184. Retrieved from http://www.ephemeraweb.org/journal/3-3/3-3gabriel.pdf

Galetta, D. F., Henry, R., McCoy, S., & Polak, P. (2004). Web site delays: How tolerant are users? *Journal of the Association for Information Systems*, *5*(1). Retrieved from http://aisel.aisnet.org/jais/vol5/iss1/1

Garera, S., Provos, N., Rubin, A. D., & Chew, M. A. (2007). Framework for detection and measurement of phishing attacks. In *Proceedings of the 2007 ACM Workshop on Recurring Malcode*, (pp. 1-8).

Garretson, G. (2007). Balancing Generation Y preferences with security. *Network World*. Retrieved September 1, 2010, from http://www.networkworld.com/news/2007/082907-security-standard-5.html?page=2

Gary, H. (2008, 15 August). State's force still full of leaks. *The Australian*.

Gaw, S., & Felten, E. W. (2006). Password management strategies for online accounts. In *SOUPS'06:* Proceedings of the Second Symposium on Usable Privacy and Security (pp. 44-55). New York, NY: ACM.

Gelfand, A. E., Hills, S. E., & Racine-Poon, A. (1990). Illustration of Bayesian inference in normal data using Gibbs sampling. *Journal of the American Statistical Association*, *85*, 972–985. doi:10.2307/2289594

Gelfand, A. E., & Smith, A. F. M. (1990). Sampling-based approaches to calculating marginal densities. *Journal of the American Statistical Association*, *85*, 348–409. doi:10.2307/2289776

Geman, S., & Geman, D. (1984). Stochastic relaxation, Gibbs distributions, and the Bayesian restoration of images. *IEEE Transactions on Pattern Analysis and Machine Intelligence*, *6*, 721–741. doi:10.1109/TPAMI.1984.4767596

Gibson, M., Conrad, M., & Maple, C. (2010). Infinite alphabet passwords: A unified model for a class of authentication systems. In S. K. Katsikas & P. Samarati (Eds.), *SECRYPT*, (pp. 94-99). SciTePress.

Gibson, M., Renaud, K., Conrad, M., & Maple, C. (2009). Musipass: Authenticating me softly with "my" song. In *NSPW'09: New Security Paradigms Workshop* (pp. 85-100). New York, NY: ACM.

Gilbert, E., & Karahalios, K. (2009). Predicting tie strength with social media. In *CHI '09: Proceedings of the 27th International Conference on Human Factors in Computing Systems*, New York, NY, USA, (pp. 211-220). ACM.

Gleeson, A. (2010). *Police accountability and oversight: An overview*. Retrieved September 1, 2010, from http://www.walk.com.au/pedestriancouncil/Page.asp?PageID=339

Goedertier, S., & Vanthienen, J. (2006). Designing compliant business processes with obligations and permission. In Eder, J., & Dustdar, S. (Eds.), *BPM Workshops 2006, LNCS 4103* (pp. 5–14). Heidelberg, Germany: Springer. doi:10.1007/11837862_2

Goffman, E. (1959). *The presentation of self in everyday life*. New York, NY: Doubleday.

Goldschmidt, P. (2007). Managing the false alarms: A framework for assurance and verification of surveillance monitoring. *Information Systems Frontiers: A Journal of Research and Innovation. Special Issue on Secure Knowledge Management*, *9*(5), 541–556.

Gonca, T. Y., & Faruk, K. (2009). User rating system for the Internet (URSI) and central authority for internet security (CAIS). *The Journal of Business*, *5*(6), 1. Retrieved June 25, 2009 from http://www.journalofe-business.org/

Google Press Center. (2006). *Conversation with Eric Schmidt hosted by Danny Sullivan.* Search Engine Strategies Conference. Retrieved from http://www.google.com/press/podium/ses2006.html

Gordijn, J., Akkermanns, J. M., & van Vliet, J. C. (2000). Business modelling is not process modelling. In *Conceptual Modeling for e-Business and the Web, LNCS 1921* (pp. 40–51). Springer Press.

Gordijn, J., & Akkermans, J. (2003). Value-based requirements engineering: Exploring innovative e-commerce ideas. *Requirements Engineering Journal*, *8*, 114–134. doi:10.1007/s00766-003-0169-x

Gordon, L. A., Loeb, M. P., Lucyshyn, W., & Richardson, R. (2005). CSI/FBI computer crime and security survey. *Computer Security Institute, 25.*

Gordon, L. A., & Loeb, M. P. (2002). The economics of information security investment. *ACM Transactions on Information and System Security*, *5*(4), 438–457. doi:10.1145/581271.581274

Great Britain. Office of Government Commerce (OGC). (2007). *Service design (SD): ITIL*. London, UK: TSO The Stationery Office.

Green, D. M., & Swets, J. A. (1966). *Signal detection theory and Pscyhophysics*. New York, NY: Wiley.

Greengard, S. (2005). Compliance software's bonus benefits. *Business Finance Magazine*. Retrieved November 1, 2010, from http://businessfinancemag.com/article/compliance-softwares-bonus-benefits-0201

Greenwald, S. J., Olthoff, K. G., Raskin, V., & Ruch, W. (2004). The user non-acceptance paradigm: INFOSEC's dirty little secret. In *Proceedings of the 2004 Workshop on New Security Paradigms* (pp. 35-43). Nova Scotia, Canada: ACM. doi:10.1145/1065907.1066032

Greenwood, D. J., & Levin, M. (2005). Reform of the social sciences and of universities through action research. In Denzin, N. K., & Lincoln, Y. S. (Eds.), *Handbook of qualitative research* (3rd ed., pp. 43–64). London: Sage.

Gupta, A., & Zhdanov, D. (2007). *Growth and sustainability of managed security services networks: An economic perspective*. In WEIS'07: 7th Workshop on the Economics of Information Security. Retrieved March 2010, from http://weis07.infosecon.net/papers/65.pdf

Gupta, A., & Hammond, R. (2005). Information systems security issues and decisions for small businesses. *Information Management & Computer Security*, *13*(4), 297–310. doi:10.1108/09685220510614425

Hafiz, M., Adamczyk, P., & Johnson, R. E. (2007, July/August). Organizing security patterns. *IEEE Software*, *24*(4), 52–60. doi:10.1109/MS.2007.114

Hagen, J. M., Albrechtsen, E., & Hovden, J. (2008). Implementation and effectiveness of organizational information security measures. *Information Management & Computer Security*, *16*(4), 377–397. doi:10.1108/09685220810908796

Halliday, S., Badenhorst, K., & Solms, R. V. (1996). A business approach to effective information technology risk analysis and management. *Information Management & Computer Security*, *4*(1), 19–31. doi:10.1108/09685229610114178

Hansen, R. (2010). *Perception vs. reality: 10 truths about The Generation Y workforce*. Retrieved September 1, 2010, from http://www.quintcareers.com/Gen-Y_workforce.html

Hansen, M., Berlich, P., Camenisch, J., Clauß, S., Pfitzmann, A., & Waidner, M. (2001). Privacy-enhancing identity management. *Information Security Technical Report*, *9*(1), 35–44. doi:10.1016/S1363-4127(04)00014-7

Hansen, M., Schwartz, A., & Cooper, A. (2008). Privacy and identity management. *IEEE Security & Privacy Magazine*, *6*(2), 38–45. doi:10.1109/MSP.2008.41

Hanson, W. (2000). *Principal of Internet marketing*. Cincinnati, OH: South- Western College Publishing.

Hareton, L., & Terence, Y. (2001). A process framework for small projects. *Software Process Improvement and Practice*, *6*, 67–83. doi:10.1002/spip.137

Hayden, M. V. (1999). *The insider threat to U.S. government information systems*. Advisory Memoranda NSTISSAM INFOSEC 1-99.

Health Insurance Portability and Accountability Act, 74 Federal Register 3295-3328 C.F.R. *(1996)*.

Heike, N., & Thomas, S. (2006). Digital coins: Fairness implemented by observer. *Journal of Theoretical and Applied Electronic Commerce Research*, 1(1). Retrieved June 14, 2009, from http://www.jtaer.com/

Helokunnas, T., & Kuusisto, R. (2003). *Information security culture in a value net*. In Engineering Management Conference, 2003. IEMC'03. Managing Technologically Driven Organizations: The Human Side of Innovation and Change.

Herley, C. (2009) So long and no thanks for the externalities: The rational rejection of security advice by users. *In NSPW'09: New Security Paradigms Workshop* (pp. 133-144). New York, NY: ACM.

Herzberg, F. (1968). One more time: How do you motivate employees? *Harvard Business Review*, *46*(1), 53–62.

Hevner, S., & March, J., Park, & Ram, S. (2004). Design science research in Information Systems. *Management Information Systems Quarterly*, *28*(1), 75–105.

Hewer, P., & Howcroft, B. (1999). Consumers' channel adoption and usage in the financial services industry: A review of existing approaches. *Journal of Financial Markets*, *3*(4), 344–358.

Heymann, P., Koutrika, G., & Garcia-Molina, H. (2007). Fighting Spam on social Web sites: A survey of approaches and future challenges. *IEEE Internet Computing*, *11*(6), 36–45. doi:10.1109/MIC.2007.125

HIPAA. (1996). *Health Insurance Portability and Accountability Act*. Senate and House of Representatives of the United States of America. Retrieved March 2010, from http://www.legalarchiver.org/hipaa.htm

Hirsch, L. E. (2007). Weaponizing classical music: Crime prevention and symbolic power in the age of repetition. *Journal of Popular Music Studies*, *19*(4), 342–358. doi:10.1111/j.1533-1598.2007.00132.x

Hoff, J. V., & Hoff, F. V. (2010). The Danish eID case: Twenty years of delay. *Identity in the Information Society*, *3*(1), 155–174. doi:10.1007/s12394-010-0056-9

Hofstede, G., & Hofstede, G. N. (2005). *Cultures and organisations: Software of the mind*. New York, NY: McGraw-Hill.

Hofstede, G., Neuijen, B., Ohayv, D. D., & Sanders, G. (1990). Measuring organizational cultures: A qualitative and quantitative study across twenty cases. *Administrative Science Quarterly*, *35*(2), 286–316. doi:10.2307/2393392

Hogland, G., & McGraw, G. (2004). *Exploiting software: How to break code*. Addison-Wesley.

Hoogervorst, J. A. P. (2009). *Enterprise governance and enterprise engineering*. Springer. Gantz, J. F., & Reinsel, D. (Eds.). (2010). *The expanding digital universe: A forecast of worldwide information growth through 2010*. IDC.

Howard, M., & LeBlanc, D. (2003). *Writing secure code* (2nd ed.). Microsoft Press.

Howard, M., & Lipner, S. (2006). *The security development lifecycle*. Microsoft Press.

Hsu, C., Baptista, J., Tseng, J., & Backhouse, J. (2003). The key to trust? Signalling quality in the PKI market. In *ECIS 2003 Proceedings*. Retrieved from http://aisel.aisnet.org/ecis2003/64

Huang, C. D., Behara, R. S., & Hu, Q. (2008). Managing risk propagation in extended enterprise networks. *IT Professional*, *10*, 14–19. doi:10.1109/MITP.2008.90

Hughes, T. (2003). Marketing challenges in e-banking: Standalone or integrated? *Journal of Marketing Management, 19*, 1067–1085. doi:10.1362/026725703770558321

Hühnlein, D., Roßnagel, H., & Zibuschka, J. (2010). *Diffusion of federated identity management*. In SICHERHEIT 2010. Berlin, Germany: GI.

Hvarre, J. (2004). Electronic signatures in Denmark: Free for all citizens. *E-Signature and Law Journal, 1*(1), 12–17.

IAAC. (2005). *IAAC position paper on identity assurance (IdA): Towards a policy framework for electronic identity*. Retrieved August, 2010, from http://www.iaac.org.uk

IBM. (n.d.). *Websphere, Lombardi ed., version 7.1: Quick start tutorial*. Retrieved November 26, 2010, from http://publib.boulder.ibm.com/infocenter/wle/v7r1/index.jsp?topic=/wle/common/topic/starting_ae.html

InCommon Federation. (2008). *Identity assurance assessment framework*. Retrieved August 2010, from http://www.incommonfederation.org/docs/assurance/ InC IAAF 1.0 Final.pdf

InCommon Federation. (2010). Retrieved October, 2010 from http://www.incommonfederation.org/

Information Security Forum. (2007). *The standard of good practice for information security*. Information Security Forum.

Information security management maturity model (ISM3 v.2.0). (2007).

Inglesant, P. G., & Sasse, M. A. (2010). The true cost of unusable password policies: password use in the wild. *Proceedings of the 28th International Conference on Human Factors in Computing Systems* (CHI '10), (pp. 383-392). New York, NY: ACM.

International Standard Organization (ISO). (2005). *ISO/IEC 27001:2005, Information Technology, security techniques, information security management systems requirements*. Geneva, Switzerland: ISO.

International Standard Organization (ISO). (2005). *ISO/IEC 27002:2005, Information Technology, security techniques, code of practice for information security management*. Geneva, Switzerland: ISO.

International Standard Organization (ISO). (2008). *Quality management systems – Requirements. ISO, 9001*, 2008.

International Standard Organization (ISO). (2009). *ISO/IEC 27004:2009, Information technology, security techniques, information security management measurement*. Geneva, Switzerland: ISO.

International Standard Organization (ISO). (2010). *ISO survey of certifications 2009*. Retrieved November 23, 2010, from http://www.iso.org/iso/survey2009.pdf

International Systems Security Engineering Association. (2003). *Systems security engineering - Capability maturity model* (ISO/IEC 21827). Retrieved from http://www.sse-cmm.org/docs/sse-cmm.pdf

Internet Security Systems. (2005). *Assessment and remediation of vulnerabilities in the SCADA and process control systems of utilities*. Retrieved October 27, 2009, from http://documents.iss.net/whitepapers/SCADA.pdf

Is it a Policy, a Standard or a Guideline? (2010). *SANS: Information Security Policy Templates*. Professional Orgnaization. Retrieved November 29, 2010, from http://www.sans.org/security-resources/policies/

ISO. (2005). *ISO/IEC 27001 Information Technology- Security techniques- Information security management systems- Requirements*. Retrieved June 9, 2009, from http://www.iso.org/iso/catalogue_detail?csnumber=42103

ISO/IEC 17799. (2000). *Information Technology - Security techniques - Code of practice for information security management*.

ISO/IEC 27001. (2005). *Information Technology - Security techniques information security management systems - Requirements*.

ISO/IEC 27002. (2007). *Information Technology - Security techniques - The international standard code of practice for information security management*.

ISO/IEC20000. (2005). *Service management IT*.

IT Governance Institute. (2006). *Information security governance: Guidance for boards of directors and executive management*. Rolling Meadows, IL: IT Governance Institute.

IT Governance Institute. (2007). *CobiT 4.1 - Control objectives for information and related technology*.

IT Governance Institute. (2007). *CobiT 4.1*. Isaca.

IT Governance Institute. (2007). *COBIT® 4.1: Framework, control objectives, management guidelines, maturity models*. Rolling Meadows, IL: IT Governance Institute.

Ives, B., Walsh, K. R., & Schneider, H. (2004). The domino effect of password reuse. *Communications of the ACM*, *47*(4), 75–78. doi:10.1145/975817.975820

Jackson, M. (2005, 10 January). Music to deter yobs by. *BBC News Magazine*. Retrieved December 12, 2010 from http://news.bbc.co.uk/1/hi/magazine/4154711.stm

Jacobsson, M., & Myers, S. (2007). *Phishing and countermeasures - Understand the increasing problem of electronic identity theft*. New Jersey: Wiley.

Jagdev, H. S., & Thoben, K. D. (2001). Anatomy of enterprise collaborations. *Production Planning and Control*, *12*(5), 437–451. doi:10.1080/09537280110042675

Jaques, E. (1998). *Requisite organization: A total system for effective managerial organization and managerial leadership for the 21st century* (revised 2nd edition). Baltimore, MD: Cason Hall & Co.

Jaques, P. A., & Viccari, R. M. (2006). Considering students' emotions in computer-mediated learning environments. In Ma, Z. (Ed.), *Web-based intelligent e-learning systems: Technologies and applications* (pp. 122–138). Hershey, PA: Information Science Publishing.

Jefferey, K., & Neidecker-Lutz, B. (2010). *The future of Cloud Computing*. Cordis. Retrieved from http://cordis.europa.eu/fp7/ict/ssai/docs/cloud-report-final.pdf

Jensen, M. C., & Meckling, W. H. (1976). Theory of the firm: Managerial behavior, agency costs and ownership structure. *Journal of Financial Economics*, *3*(4), 3–24. doi:10.1016/0304-405X(76)90026-X

Jensen, M. C., & Meckling, W. H. (1992). Specific and general knowledge, and organizational structure. In Werin, L., & Wijkander, H. (Eds.), *Contract economics* (pp. 251–274). Oxford, UK: Blackwell. doi:10.1111/j.1745-6622.1995.tb00283.x

Jericho-Forum. (n.d.). *The what and why of de-perimeterization*. Retrieved from http://www.opengroup.org/jericho/deperim.htm

Johnson, P. (2003, September 2). *What are policies, standards, guidelines and procedures?* MindfulSecurity.com – The Information Security Awareness Resource. Retrieved November 29, 2010, from http://mindfulsecurity.com/2009/02/03/policies-standards-and-guidelines/

Johnson, M. E., & Goetz, E. (2007). *Embedding information security into the organization. IEEE Security and Privacy* (pp. 16–24). May/June.

John, V. B., & Robyn, W. (2002). Barriers to purchasing on the Internet. *The Journal of Business*, *2*(1), 27. Retrieved June 27, 2009 from http://www.journalofe-business.org/

JonDonym. (2010). *Software downloads*. Retrieved November 30, 2010, from https://anonymous-proxy-servers.net/en/software.html

Jones, Q., Gandhi, S. A., Whittaker, S., Chivakula, K., & Terveen, L. (2004). Putting systems into place: A qualitative study of design requirements for location-aware community systems. In *Proceedings of Computer-Supported Cooperative Work* (CSCW '04), Chicago, (pp. 202-211). ACM Press.

Jones, S., & O'Neill, E. (2010). Feasibility of structural network clustering for group-based privacy control in social networks. *Proceedings of the Sixth Symposium on Usable Privacy and Security*. Redmond, Washington.

Jøsang, A., & Pope, S. (2005). User centric identity management. In A. Clark, K. Kerr, & G. Mohay (Eds.), *AusCERT Asia Pacific Information Technology Security Conference*, (p. 77).

Jøsang, A., Fabre, J., Hay, B., Dalziel, J., & Pope, S. (2005). *Trust requirements in identity management*. Newcastle: Australasian Information Security Workshop 2005.

Jøsang, A., Zomai, M. A., & Suriadi, S. (2007). Usability and privacy in identity management architectures. *Proceedings of the Fifth Australasian Symposium on ACSW Frontiers*, vol. 68, (pp. 143-152).

Jøsang, A., Ismail, R., & Boyd, C. (2007). A survey of trust and reputation systems for online service provision. *Decision Support Systems*, *43*(2). doi:10.1016/j.dss.2005.05.019

Joseph, L., Gyorkos, T. W., & Coupal, L. (1995). Bayesian estimation of disease prevalence and the parameters of diagnostic tests in the absence of a gold standard. *American Journal of Epidemiology, 141*(3).

Jürjens, J. (2002). UMLsec: Extending UML for secure systems development. In J. Jézéquel, H. Hussmann, & S. Cook (Eds.), *UML 2002 — The Unified Modeling Language, Lecture Notes in Computer Science* (vol. 2460, pp. 1-9). Berlin, Germany: Springer. Retrieved from http://dx.doi.org/10.1007/3-540-45800-X_32

Kagal, L., Undercoffer, A. J., & Vigil, T. (2001). *Enforcing security in ubiquitous environments*. Tech. Report, University of Maryland, Baltimore County.

Kahneman, D. (1973). *Attention and effort*. Englewood Cliffs, NJ: Prentice Hall.

Kantara Initiative. (2010). Retrieved August, 2010, from http://kantarainitiative.org/

Kaplan, R. S., & Norton, D. P. (1996). *The balanced scorecard: Translating strategy into action* (reprinted ed.). Boston, MA: Harvard Business School Press.

Karp, A. H., Haury, H., & Davis, M. H. (2010). From ABAC to ZBAC: The evolution of access control models. *ISSA (Information Systems Security Association). Journal, 8*(4), 22–30.

Kaspersky Lab - Virus News. (2010, September 24). *Kaspersky Lab provides its insights on Stuxnet worm.* Antivirus Company. Retrieved November 29, 2010, from http://www.kaspersky.com/news?id=207576183

Katsis, A. (2005). Sample size determination of binomial data with the presence of misclassification. *Metrika, 63*, 323–329. doi:10.1007/s00184-005-0411-2

Katz, M. L., & Shapiro, C. (1994). Systems competition and network effects. *The Journal of Economic Perspectives, 8*(2), 93–115. doi:10.1257/jep.8.2.93

Keldon, B., & Scott, E. H. (2005). The effect of heterogeneous risk on the early adoption of Internet banking technologies. *Journal of E-Banking, 10*. Retrieved June 25, 2009, from http://papers.ssrn.com/

Khan, I. (2009). Cloud Computing set to go mainstream. *Outsourcing, 13*, 30–31.

Kirda, E., & Kruegel, C. (2005). Protecting users against phishing attacks. *Proceedings of the 29th Annual International Computer Software and Applications Conference (COMPSAC '05)*, Edinburgh, UK, 2006, (pp. 517-524).

Kis, M. (2002). Information security antipatterns in software requirements engineering. *Proceedings of the 9th Pattern Languages of Programs Conference (PLoP2002)*. Retrieved from http://hillside.net/plop/plop2002/final/mkis_plop_2002.pdf

Klein, H. K., & Myers, M. D. (1999). A set of principles for conducting and evaluating interpretative field studies in Information Systems. *Management Information Systems Quarterly, 23*(1), 67–94. doi:10.2307/249410

Kling, R. (1994). Reading all about computerization: How genre conventions shape social analyses. *The Information Society*, •••, 147–172. doi:10.1080/01972243.1994.9960166

Kluge, D. (2008). *Formal information security standards in German medium enterprises*. Paper presented at the CONISAR: The Conference on Information Systems Applied Research.

Knapp, K. J., Marshall, T. E., Rainer, R. K., & Ford, F. N. (2006). Information security: Management's effect on culture and policy. *Information Management & Computer Security, 14*(1), 24–36. doi:10.1108/09685220610648355

Knight, R., & Pretty, D. (1996). *The impact of catastrophes on shareholder value. Oxford Executive Research Briefings*. Oxford, UK: Templeton College, Oxford University.

Koh, K., Ruighaver, A. B., Maynard, S. B., & Ahmad, A. (2005). Security governance: Its impact on security culture. In *Proceedings of the 3rd Australian Information Security Management Conference*, Perth.

Koonce, L. (1993). A cognitive characterisation of audit analytical review. *Auditing: A Journal of Practice and Theory*, 12(supplement), 57–76.

Koppe, V. (2005). *Die Geldkarte der deutschen Kreditwirtschaft: Aktuelle Situation und Ausblick*. Retrieved February 28, 2005, from www.geldkarte.de

Korhonen, J. J., Hiekkanen, K., & Lähteenmäki, J. (2009). EA and IT governance – A systemic approach. In J. Politis (Ed.), *Proceedings of the 5th European Conference on Management, Leadership and Governance* (pp. 66-74). Reading, UK: Academic Publishing Limited.

Korhonen, J. J., Yildiz, M., & Mykkänen, J. (2009). Governance of information security elements in service-oriented enterprise architecture. In R. Bilof (Ed.), *10th International Symposium on Pervasive Systems, Algorithms, and Networks - I-SPAN 2009* (pp. 768-773). Los Alamitos, CA: CPS, IEEE Computer Society.

Kostina, A., Miloslavskaya, N., & Tolstoy, A. (2009). *Information security incident management process.* Paper presented at the SIN'09.

Kothari, V., & Kothari, M. P. (2001). E-business: What have we learned. *The Journal of Business, 1*(2), 5. Retrieved June 27, 2009 from http://www.journalofe-business.org/

Kotulic, A. G., & Clark, J. G. (2004). Why there aren't more information security research studies. *Information & Management, 41*(5), 597–607. doi:10.1016/j.im.2003.08.001

Kramer, J. (2003). *The CISA prep guide: mastering the certified information systems auditor exam.* New Jersey: John Wiley and Sons.

Krutz, R. (2005). *Securing SCADA systems.* Indianapolis, IN: Wiley Technology.

Kühn, H., Karagiannis, D., & Junginger, S. (1996). *Metamodellierung in dem BPMS-Analysewerkzeug ADONIS, Konferenz Informatik '96, Schwerpunktthema, Softwaretechnik und Standards*, 25-27 September 1996, Uni Klagenfurt.

Kumar, A., Wong, D. C., Shen, H. C., & Jain, A. K. (2003). *Personal verification using palmprint and hand geometry biometric.* 4th International Conference on Audio- and Video-based Biometric Person Authentication, Guildford, UK, June 9-11.

Kumar, K., & van Dissel, H. G. (1996). Sustainable collaboration: Managing conflict and cooperation in interorganizational systems. *MIS Quartely, 20*, 279–300. doi:10.2307/249657

Kuo, C., Romanosky, S., & Cranor, L. F. (2006). Human selection of mnemonic phrase-based passwords. In *SOUPS '06: Proceedings of the Second Symposium on Usable Privacy and Security* (pp. 67–78). New York, NY: ACM.

Kuusisto, R., Nyberg, K., & Virtanen, T. (2004). Unite security culture: May a unified security culture be plausible? In *Proceedings of the 3rd European conference on information warfare and security,* London, United Kingdom. 2004.

Lampinen, A., Tamminen, S., & Oulasvirta, A. (2009). All my people right here, right now: Management of group copresence on a social networking site. In *Proceedings of the ACM 2009 International Conference on Supporting Group Work* (Sanibel Island, Florida, USA, May 10 - 13, 2009), 281–290.

LaRose, R., Rifon, N. J., & Enbody, R. (2008). Promoting personal responsibility for Internet safety. *Communications of the ACM, 51*(3), 71–76. doi:10.1145/1325555.1325569

Lazarsfeld, P., & Field, H. (1946). *The people look at radio.* Chapel Hill, NC: University of North Carolina Press.

Leach, J. (2003). Improving user security behaviour. *Computers & Security, 22*(8), 685–692. doi:10.1016/S0167-4048(03)00007-5

Lederer, S., Dey, A. K., & Mankoff, J. (2002). *A conceptual model and a metaphor of everyday privacy in ubiquitous computing.* Intel Research Berkeley, Tech. Rep. IRB-TR- 02- 017, 2002.

Lederer, S., Hong, J., Dey, A., & Landay, J. (2004). Personal privacy through understanding and action: Five pitfalls for designers. *Personal and Ubiquitous Computing, 8*(6), 440–454. doi:10.1007/s00779-004-0304-9

LeDoux, J. E. (1992). Emotion as memory: Anatomical systems underlying indelible neural traces. In Christianson, S. (Ed.), *Handbook of emotion and memory: Theory and research* (pp. 269–288). Hillsdale, NJ: Erlbaum.

Lee, C. H., Kim, J. S., & Park, K. H. (1996). Automatic face location in a complex background using motion and color information. *Pattern Recognition, 29*(11), 1877–1889. doi:10.1016/0031-3203(96)00036-2

Lee, D., Park, J., & Ahn, J. (2001). *On the explanation of factors affecting e-commerce adoption* (pp. 109–120).

Lee, V. C., & Shao, L. (2006). Estimating potential IT security losses: An alternative quantitative approach. *IEEE Security and Privacy*, *4*(6), 44–52. doi:10.1109/MSP.2006.151

Leidner, D., & Kayworth, T. (2006). A review of culture in information systems research: toward a theory of information technology culture conflict. *Management Information Systems Quarterly*, *30*(2), 357–399.

Leippold, M., & Vanini, P. (2003). *The quantification of operational risk*. Retrieved from http://ssrn.com/abstract=481742 or doi:10.2139/ssrn.481742

Leveson, N. (2004). A new accident model for engineering safer systems. *Safety Science*, *42*(4), 237–270. doi:10.1016/S0925-7535(03)00047-X

Lewandowski, J. O. (2005). Creating a culture of technical caution: Addressing the issues of security, privacy protection and the ethical use of technology. In *Proceedings of the 33rd Annual ACM SIGUCCS Conference on User Services*, Monterey, USA, 2005.

Leyden, T. (2009). *A brief history of Cloud Computing*. Sys-Con Media. Retrieved from https://tleyden.sys-con.com/node/1150011

Libby, R. (1985). Availability and the generation of hypotheses in analytical review. *Journal of Accounting Research*, *23*(2), 648–667. doi:10.2307/2490831

Libby, R., & Trotman, K. (1993). The review process as a control for differential recall of evidence in auditor judgments. *Accounting, Organizations and Society*, *18*(6), 559–574. doi:10.1016/0361-3682(93)90003-O

Liddell, J., Renaud, K. V., & De Angeli, A. (2003). *Authenticating users using a combination of sound and images. Short paper presented at British Computer Society, HCI 2003*. UK: Bath.

Lim, J. S., Ahmad, A., Chang, S., & Maynard, S. B. (2010). *Embedding information security culture - emerging concerns and challenges*. 14th Pacific Asia Conference on Information Systems. Taipei, Taiwan.

Lim, J. S., Chang, S., Maynard, S. B., & Ahmad, A. (2009). *Exploring the relationship between organizational culture and information security culture*. In 7th Australian Information Security Management Conference, SECAU Security Congress 2009, Perth, Western Australia.

Linares, S., & Paredes, I. (2007). *IS2ME: Information security to the medium enterprise* [Electronic Version]. Retrieved from http://www.is2me.org/introduccion-en.html

Lipner, S., & Howard, M. (2005). *The trustworthy computing development lifecycle*. Retrieved from http://msdn2.microsoft.com/en-us/library/ms995349.aspx

Lippmann, S., & Roßnagel, H. (2005). Geschäftsmodelle für signaturgesetzkonforme Trust Center. In O. K. Ferstl, E. J. Sinz, S. Eckert, & T. Isselhorst (Eds.), *Wirtschaftsinformatik 2005* (pp. 1167-1186). Physica-Verlag HD. Retrieved from http://dx.doi.org/10.1007/3-7908-1624-8_61

Litfin, T. (2000). *Adoptionsfaktoren*. Deutscher Universitäts-Verlag.

Lockhart, H., Andersen, S., Bohren, J., Sverdlov, Y., Hondo, M., Maruyama, H., et al. (2006, December). *Web services federation language* (WS-Federation), version 1.1.

Logan, D. (2009). *Hype cycle for legal and regulatory information governance*. Gartner. Retrieved from http://www.gartner.com/DisplayDocument?doc_cd=208630&ref=g_rss

Lovgen, S. (2005). Behind the 1938 radio show panic. *National Geographic News*. Retrieved September 1, 2010, from URL:http://news.nationalgeographic.com/news/2005/06/0617_050617_warworlds.html

Ma, J., Saul, L. K., Savage, S., & Voelker, S. M. (2009). Identifying suspicious URLs: An application of large-scale online learning. In *ICML '09: Proceedings of the 26th Annual International Conference on Machine Learning*, (pp. 681–688).

Madsen, P., & Itoh, H. (2009). Challenges to supporting federated assurance. *Computer*, *42*, 42–49. doi:10.1109/MC.2009.149

MageritV2. (2005). *Metodología de Análisis y Gestión de Riesgos para las Tecnologías de la Información, V2*. Ministerio de Administraciones Públicaso.

Mahler, A., & Rogers, E. M. (1999). The diffusion of interactive communication innovations and the critical mass: the adoption of telecommunications services by German banks. *Telecommunications Policy*, *23*(10-11), 719–740. doi:10.1016/S0308-5961(99)00052-X

Maler, E., Nadalin, A., Reed, D., Rundle, M., & Thibeau, D. (2010, March). *The open identity trust framework (OITF) model.*

Maler, E., & Reed, D. (2008). The Venn of identity: Options and issues in federated identity management. *IEEE Security & Privacy Magazine*, *6*(2), 16–23. doi:10.1109/MSP.2008.50

Mandia, K., & Prosise, C. (2002). *Computer attack: Detection, defense and immediate rectification*. Prague, Czech Republic: Computer Press.

Marcus, L. (2004). *Introduction to logical foundations of an adaptive security infrastructure*. Workshop on Logical Foundations of an Adaptive Security Infrastructure (WOLFASI), A sub-workshop of the LICS Foundations of Computer Security (FCS'04) Workshop, LICS '04, July 12-13, Turku, Finland.

Markines, B., Cattuto, C., & Menczer, F. (2009). Social Spam detection. In *Proceedings of the 5th International Workshop on Adversarial Information Retrieval on the Web,* AIRWeb-09.

Martin, J. (2002). *Organizational culture: mapping the terrain*. London, UK: Sage.

Martins, A., & Eloff, J. (2002). *Information security culture.* In IFIP TC11 International Conference on Information Security, Cairo, Egypt

Marx, G. (2002). What's new about the 'new surveillance'? Classifying for change and continuity. *Surveillance & Society*, *1*(1), 8–29.

Mass, Y. (2001). *Distributed trust in open multi-agent systems. Lecture Notes in Artificial Intelligence, 2246.* Springer-Verlag.

Mathew, A. R., Al Hajj, A., & Al Ruqeishi, K. (2010). *Cyber crimes: Threats and protection.* 2010 International Conference on Networking and Information Technology.

Matsuura, K. (2003). *Information security and economics in computer networks: An interdisciplinary survey and a proposal of integrated optimization of investment* (Computing in Economics and Finance 2003 No. 48). Society for Computational Economics. Retrieved from http://econpapers.repec.org/RePEc:sce:scecf3:48

May, C. (2003). Dynamic corporate culture lies at the heart of effective security strategy. *Computer Fraud & Security*, *5*, 10–13. doi:10.1016/S1361-3723(03)05011-5

Maynard, S. B., & Ruighaver, A. B. (2006). What makes a good information security policy: A preliminary framework for evaluating security policy quality. In *Proceedings of the Fifth Annual Security Conference,* Las Vegas, Nevada USA.

Mc Kenzie, N. (2009, 16 October). Watchdog's report damns police over leaked files - Systemic failure to manage data. *The Age*.

McAfee. (2006, August). *Global security threats and trends.* McAfee: Proven Security - Security Spotlight. Retrieved January 2011, from https://mcafee.imiinc.com/nai7588/aug06/article3.jsp

McCoy, D. W. (2002). Business activity monitoring: Calm before the storm. *Gartner Research*, LE-15-9727. Retrieved March 22, 2011, from http://www.gartner.com/resources/105500/105562/105562.pdf

McCoy, D., Bauer, K., Grunwald, D., Kohno, T., & Sicker, D. (2008). Shining light in dark places: Understanding the Tor Network. In N. Borisov & I. Goldberg (Eds.), *Privacy Enhancing Technologies, Lecture Notes in Computer Science* (vol. 5134, pp. 63-76). Berlin, Germany: Springer. Retrieved from http://dx.doi.org/10.1007/978-3-540-70630-4_5

McCrindle, M. (2008). *The ABC of XYZ: Generational diversity at work*. McCrindle Research Pty Ltd. Retrieved October 20, 2009, from http://www.quayappointments.com.au/email/040213/images/generational_diversity_at_work.pdf

McCrindle, M. (2010). *Understanding Gen Y.* Retrieved September 1, 2010, from http://www.learningtolearn.sa.edu.au/Colleagues/files/links/UnderstandingGenY.pdf

McGinnis, S. K., Pumphrey, L., Trimmer, K., & Wiggins, C. (2004). Sustaining and extending organization strategy via Information Technology governance. *Proceedings of the 37th Hawaii International Conference on System Sciences.*

McGraw, G. (2006). *Software security: Building security in*. Addison-Wesley.

McKnight, D. H., Choudhury, V., & Kacmar, C. (2002). Developing and validating trust measures for e-commerce: An integrative typology. *Information Systems Research*, *13*(3), 334–359. doi:10.1287/isre.13.3.334.81

Mekelburg, D. (2005). Sustaining best practices: How real-world software organizations improve quality processes. *Software Quality Professional*, *7*(3), 4–13.

Mélen, M., & Deliége, I. (1995). Extraction of cues or underlying harmonic structure: Which guides recognition of familiar melodies? *The European Journal of Cognitive Psychology*, *7*(1), 81–106. doi:10.1080/09541449508520159

Mell, P., & Grance, T. (2009). *The NIST definition of Cloud Computing*. NIST.

Mendori, T., Kubouchi, M., Okada, M., & Shimizu, A. (2002). Password input interface for primary school children. In *Proceedings of the International Conference on Computers in Education (ICCE02)*. Auckland, New Zealand: IEEE Computer Society.

Mertz, D. (2002). *Spam filtering techniques: Six approaches to eliminating unwanted e-mail*. Retrieved September 01, 2002, from http://www.ibm.com/developerworks/linux/library/l-spamf.html

Miller, P. (2008). *Everywhere I look I see clouds*. ZD Net. Retrieved from http://www.zdnet.com/blog/semantic-web/everywhere-i-look-i-see-clouds/179

Miller, R. M. (1988). Market automation: Self-regulation in a distributed environment. *ACM SIGGROUP Bulletin*, *9*(2–3), 299–308. doi:10.1145/966861.45443

Milner, R. (1992). Calculus of mobile processes. *Information and Computation*, *100*(1), 1–40. doi:10.1016/0890-5401(92)90008-4

Milner, R. (2006). Pure bigraphs: Structure and dynamics. *Information and Computation*, *204*(1), 60–122. doi:10.1016/j.ic.2005.07.003

Ministry of Defence. (2004). *JSP 541 - MOD information security alert warning and response policy manual, UK*.

Mishne, G., Carmel, D., & Lempel, R. (2005). Blocking blog spam with language model disagreement. In *AIRWeb '05: Proceedings of the 1st International Workshop on Adversarial Information Retrieval on the Web*, (pp. 1–6). New York, NY: ACM.

Mizuno, S. (1988). *Management for quality improvement: The seven new QC tools*. Productivity Press.

Monaco, B., & Riordan, J. (1987). *The platinum rainbow... How to make it big in the music business*. Sherman Oaks, CA: Omnibus Books.

Morali, A., & Wieringa, R. J. (2010). Risk-based confidentiality requirements specification for outsourced IT systems. In *RE'10: Proceedings of the 18th IEEE Int. Requirements Engineering Conference*. IEEE Press.

Morris, R., & Thomson, K. (1979). Password security: A case history. *Communications of the ACM*, *22*(11), 594–597. doi:10.1145/359168.359172

Mowbray, M. (2009). *The fog over the Grimpen Mire: Cloud Computing and the law*. HP Laboratory.

Nabi, S. I., Nabi, S. W., Tipu, S. A. A., Haqqi, B., Abid, Z., & Alghathbar, K. (2010). Data confidentiality and integrity issues and role of information security management standard, policies and practices – An empirical study of telecommunication industry in Pakistan. In *Security Technology, Disaster Recovery and Business Continuity International Conferences, SecTech and DRBC 2010, Future Generation Information Technology Conference, FGIT 2010*, Jeju Island, Korea, December 13-15, 2010, Communications in Computer and Information Science (CCIS) (vol. 122). Berlin, Germany: Springer.

Nadalin, A., Goodner, M., Gudgin, M., Barbir, A., & Granqvist, H. (2007). *WS-trust 1.3*. *Organization for the Advancement of Structured Information Standards*. OASIS.

National Institute for Standards and Technology. (2010). Retrieved August, 2010, from http://www.nist.gov

National Institute of Standards and Technology (NIST). (2008). *Performance measurement guide for information security*. NIST Special Publication 800-55 Revision 1. Retrieved January 28, 2010, from http://csrc.nist.gov/publications/nistpubs/800-55-Rev1/SP800-55-rev1.pdf

National Institute of Standards and Technology. (2006). *Electronic authentication guideline*.

National Security Agency. (1994). *National training standard for information systems security professionals* (NSTISSI-4011). Retrieved from http://www.nsa.gov/ia/academia/cnsstesstandards.cfm

NCL. (2009). *National Consumers Leagues*. Retrieved June 17, 2009, from http://www.nclnet.org/news/2007

Neumann, P. G. (1994). Risks of passwords. *Communications of the ACM*, *37*(4), 126. doi:10.1145/175276.175289

Neuman, R. (1991). *The future of the mass audience*. Cambridge, MA: Cambridge University Press.

NFIC & IFW. (2009). *National Fraud Information Centre and Internet Fraud Watch*. Retrieved June 17, 2009, from http://www.fraud.org/Internet

Ngo, L., Zhou, W., & Warren, M. (2005). Understanding transition towards information security culture change. In *Proceedings of the Third Australian Information Security Management Conference*, Perth, Australia, 30 September 2005.

Nogueira, A. R. R., & Reinhard, N. (2000). Strategic IT management in Brazilian banks. *Proceedings of the 33rd Annual Hawaii International Conference on System Sciences*, 2000.

Nosworthy, J. D. (2000). Implementing information security in the 21st century – Do you have the balancing factors? *Computers & Security*, *19*(4), 337–347. doi:10.1016/S0167-4048(00)04021-9

Nusbaum, E. C., & Silvia, P. J. (2010). Shivers and timbres: Personality and the experience of chills from music. *Social Psychological and Personality Science*, October.

O'Brien, R. (1998). *An overview of the methodological approach of action research*.

OASIS. (2009, July). *Identity metasystem interoperability*, version 1.0. OASIS Standards.

OASIS. (2010). *OASIS: Advanced open standards for the global information society*. Retrieved August, 2010 from http://www.oasis-open.org/

OECD. (2002). *OECD guidelines for the security of information systems and networks: Towards a culture of security*. Recommendation of the OECD Council, 1037th Session on 25 July 2002.

OECD. (2005). *The promotion of a culture of security for Information Systems and networks in OECD countries (16-December-2005)*. Retrieved 9 March 2009, from www.oecd.org/document/42/0,2340,en_2649_34255_15582250_1_1_1_1,00.html

Office of Police Integrity (OPI). (2010). *Report - Information security and the Victorian Police State surveillance unit*. Victoria, Australia.

Office of the e-Envoy, UK. (2002). *Registration and authentication - e-government strategy framework policy and guidelines*. Retrieved August, 2010 from http://www.cabinetoffice.gov.uk/csia/documents/pdf/ RegAndAuthentn0209v3.pdf

Ohki, E., Harada, Y., Kawaguchi, S., Shiozaki, T., & Kagaua, T. (2009). *Information security governance framework*. Paper presented at the WISG'09.

Okenyi, P. O., & Owens, T. J. (2007). On the anatomy of human hacking: A global prospective. *Information Security Journal*, *16*(6). Retrieved June 20, 2009, from http://bura.brunel.ac.uk/

Olson, J., Grudin, J., & Horvitz, E. (2005). A study of preferences for sharing and privacy. In *CHI '05 Extended Abstracts on Human Factors in Computing Systems*, Portland, OR, USA, (pp. 1985–1988).

One Hundred Seventh Congress of the United States of America. (2002). *Sarbanes-Oxley act*. Retrieved from http://news.findlaw.com/hdocs/docs/gwbush/sarbanes-oxley072302.pdf

Open Web Security Application Project. (2004). *The OWASP testing project*. Retrieved from http://www.modsecurity.org/archive/OWASPTesting_PhaseOne.pdf

Ordnance Survey. (2008). BBA's 6th Annual Financial Crime Conference, 25 -26 November. Retrieved June 24, 2009, from http://www.bba.org.uk/

O'Reilly, C. A., Chatman, J. R., & Caldwell, D. F. (1991). People and organizational culture: A profile comparison approach to assessing person-organization fit. *Academy of Management Journal*, *34*(3), 487–516. doi:10.2307/256404

Organic Law Data Personal Protection, 15/1999 C.F.R. (1999).

Organization for Economic Co-operation and Development (OECD). (2004). *Principles of corporate governance*. Retrieved November 3, 2010, from http://www.oecd.org/dataoecd/32/18/31557724.pdf

Ozkana, S., & Karabacaka, B. (2010). Collaborative risk method for information security management practices: A case context within Turkey. *International Journal of Information Management*, *30*, 567–572. doi:10.1016/j.ijinfomgt.2010.08.007

Ozment, A., & Schechter, S. E. (2006). *Bootstrapping the adoption of Internet security protocols*. In Fifth Workshop on the Economics of Information Security. Presented at the WEIS 2006, Cambridge, UK.

Paivio, A. (1983). The empirical case for dual coding. In Yuille, J. (Ed.), *Imagery, memory and cognition: Essays in honour of Allan Paivio* (pp. 307–322). Hillsdale, NJ: Erlbaum.

Palaez, J., & Fernandez, E. B. (2006). Network forensics in wireless VOIP networks. *Proceedings of the 4th Latin American and Caribbean Conference for Engineering and Technology (LACCEI 2006)*.

Palaez, J., Fernandez, E. B., Larrondo-Petrie, M. M., & Wieser, C. (2007). Attack patterns in VOIP. *Proceedings of the 14th pattern languages of programs conference (PLoP2007)* Retrieved from http://hillside.net/plop/2007/papers/PLoP2007_PelaezEtAl.pdf

Parno, B., Kuo, C., & Perrig, A. (2006). *Phoolproof phishing prevention*. In Financial Cryptography and Data Security (FC'06), 2006.

Payment Card Industry Security Standards Council. (2008). *PCI quick reference guide to the payment card industry (PCI) data security standard (DSS)*, version 1.2. Retrieved June 2010, from https://www.pcisecuritystandards.org/documents/pci_ssc_quick_guide.pdf

Peeters, J., & Dyson, P. (2007). Cost-effective security. *IEEE Security and Privacy*, *5*(3), 85–87. doi:10.1109/MSP.2007.56

Peltier, T. R. (2000). *Information security policies, procedures and standards*. Auerbach Publication.

Pennington, V. (2009). Fighting fraud, op risk & compliance. *ProQuest*, *10*(5), 36-39. Retrieved June 17, 2009, from http://proquest.umi.com/pqdlink/

Peretz, I., Radeau, M., & Arguin, M. (2004). Two-way interactions between music and language: Evidence from priming recognition of tune and lyrics in familiar songs. *Memory & Cognition*, *32*(1), 142–152. doi:10.3758/BF03195827

Pete, A., Kleinman, D., & Pattipati, K. (1993). Tasks and organisational signal detection model of organisational decision making. *Intelligent Systems in Accounting. Financial Management*, *2*(4), 289–303.

Petrie, H., & Kheir, O. (2007). The relationship between accessibility and usability of websites. In *CHI '07: Proceedings of the SIGCHI Conference on Human Factors in Computing Systems* (pp. 397-406). New York, NY: ACM.

Pfitzmann, A., & Waidner, M. (1986). Networks without user observability — Design options. In F. Pichler (Ed.), *Advances in Cryptology — EUROCRYPT' 85, Lecture Notes in Computer Science* (vol. 219, pp. 245-253). Berlin, Germany: Springer. Retrieved from http://dx.doi.org/10.1007/3-540-39805-8_29

Pfitzmann, A., Pfitzmann, B., & Waidner, M. (1991). ISDN-mixes: Untraceable communication with very small bandwidth overhead. In *Proceedings of the GI/ITG-Conference "Kommunikation in Verteilten Systemen" (Communication in Distributed Systems)* (pp. 451–463).

Phillip, B., Blaise, J. B., & Charles, R. V. (2004). Internet fraud: A global perspective. *Journal of E-Business*, 4(1). Retrieved June 18, 2009, from http://www.journalofe-business.org/

Pindyck, R., & Rubinfeld, D. L. (1976). *Econometric models and economic forecasts*. Ne York, NY: McGraw-Hill.

Platzer, C. (2004) *Trust-based security in Web services*. Master's Thesis – Technical University of Vienna, May.

Ponemon Institute. LLC. (2010). *2009 annual study: Cost of a data breach - Understanding financial impact, customer turnover, and preventive solutions*. Retrieved from http://www.ponemon.org/local/upload/fckjail/general-content/18/file/US_Ponemon_CODB_09_012209_sec.pdf

Pooled Prevalence Calculator. (n.d.). Retrieved from http://www.ausvet.com.au/pprev/

Pope, K. S., & Serger, J. L. (1978). *The stream of consciousness: Scientific investigations into the flow of human experience*. New York, NY: Plenum Press.

Porter, M. E. (1985). *Competitive advantage: Creating and sustaining superior performance* (1st ed.). New York, NY: Free Press.

PricewaterhouseCoopers LLP. (2010). *Information security breaches survey 2010*. Technical Report. Retrieved July 13, 2010, from http://www.pwc.co.uk/pdf/isbs_survey_2010_technical_report.pdf

Priedhorsky, R., Chen, J., Lam, S. K., Panciera, K., Terveen, L., & Riedl, J. (2007). Creating, destroying, and restoring value in Wikipedia. In *Proceedings of GROUP '07*.

Prieto-Diaz, R. (1991). Implementing faceted classification for software reuse. *Communications of the ACM*, *34*(5), 88–97. doi:10.1145/103167.103176

Proceedings of the2009IEEE International Conference on Communications (pp. 998-1002). Piscataway, NJ: IEEE Press.

PSIB ČR '07, Ernst & Young, NBÚ, DSM. (2007, December). *Information security survey in the Czech Republic 2007*. PSIB ČR '07, Ernst & Young, NBÚ, DSM – Data security management. Retrieved November 2010, from www.dsm.tate.cz/cz/psib-cr-2007

PSIB ČR '07, Ernst & Young, NBÚ, DSM. (2008, December). *Information security survey in Slovakia 2008*. PSIB ČR '07, Ernst & Young, NBÚ, DSM – Data security management. Retrieved January 2011, from www.dsm.tate.cz/cz/psib-cr-2008

Pucella, R., & Weissman, V. (2004). *Foundations of software science and computation structures. Reasoning about Dynamic Policies, LNCS 2987/2004* (pp. 453–467). Berlin, Germany: Springer.

Reinmann-Rothmeier, G. (2002). Mediendidaktik und Wissensmanagement. *MedienPädagogik*, *2*(2), 1-27. Retrieved August 18, 2006 from www.medienpaed.com/02-2/reinmann1.pdf

Renaud, K. (2006). A visuo-biometric authenticaton mechanism for older users. In McEwan, T., Gulliksen, J., & Benyon, D. (Eds.), *People and Computers XIX — The Bigger Picture* (pp. 167–182). London, UK: Springer. doi:10.1007/1-84628-249-7_11

Renaud, K., & De Angeli, A. (2009). Visual passwords: Cure-all or snake-oil? *Communications of the ACM*, *52*(12), 135–140. doi:10.1145/1610252.1610287

Rentfrow, P. J., & Gosling, S. D. (2003). The do re mi's of everyday life: The structure and personality correlates of music preferences. *Journal of Personality and Social Psychology*, *84*(6), 1236–1256. doi:10.1037/0022-3514.84.6.1236

Research, A. M. R. (2010). *The governance, risk management, and compliance spending report*. Boston, MA: AMR Research.

Resnick, P., Zeckhauser, R., Swanson, J., & Lockwood, K. (2006). The value of reputation on eBay: A controlled experiment. *Experimental Economics*, *9*(2), 79–101. doi:10.1007/s10683-006-4309-2

Reynolds, P. D. (1986). Organizational culture as related to industry, position, and performance: A preminary report. *Journal of Management Studies*, *23*(3), 333–345. doi:10.1111/j.1467-6486.1986.tb00958.x

Ribeiro, J. (2005). *Twelve arrested, including three ex-employees of outsourcing company*. Computer World. Retrieved from http://www.computerworld.com/s/article/100900/Indian_call_center_workers_charged_with_Citibank_fraud

Richardson, R. (2007). *2007 CSI computer crime & security survey*. Retrieved 9 March, 2009, from http://i.cmpnet.com/v2.gocsi.com/pdf/CSISurvey2007.pdf

Rieger, S. (2009). User-centric identity management in heterogeneous federations. *Proceedings of the 2009 Fourth International Conference on Internet and Web Applications and Services* (pp. 527-532). Washington, DC: IEEE Computer Society.

Robbins, S. P. (1989). *Organizational behavior: Concepts, controversies, and applications* (4th ed.). New Jersey: Prentice Hall.

Rogers, E. M. (2003). *Diffusion of Innovations* (5th ed.). Free Press.

Rosenberg, M. J. (2001). *E-learning: Strategies for delivering knowledge in the digital age*. New York, NY: McGraw-Hill.

Rosewall, I., & Warren, M. J. (2009), Information security disclosure: A case study. *Proceedings of 7th Australian Information Security Management Conference*, (pp. 39-47). Perth, Australia: Edith Cowan University.

Rosewall, I., & Warren, M. J. (2010). Information security disclosure: A Victorian case study. *Proceedings of 8th Australian Information Security Management Conference.*

Rosewall, I., & Warren, M. J. (2010a). Wikileaks: The truth or not. *Proceedings of 8th Australian Information Security Management Conference.*

Roßnagel, H. (2006). On diffusion and confusion – Why electronic signatures have failed. In *Trust and privacy in digital business* (pp. 71-80). Retrieved from http://dx.doi.org/10.1007/11824633_8

Roßnagel, H. (2010). The market failure of anonymity services. In *Information Security Theory and Practices, Security and Privacy of Pervasive Systems and Smart Devices, 4th IFIP WG 11.2 International Workshop, WISTP 2010, Passau, Germany, April 12-14, 2010. Proceedings, Lecture Notes in Computer Science* (vol. 6033, pp. 340-354).

Roßnagel, H., Zibuschka, J., Pimenides, L., & Deselaers, T. (2009). Facilitating the adoption of Tor by focusing on a promising target group. In *Identity and privacy in the Internet age* (pp. 15-27). Retrieved from http://dx.doi.org/10.1007/978-3-642-04766-4_2

Roßnagel, H. (2009). *Mobile qualifizierte elektronische Signaturen*. Gabler Verlag. doi:10.1007/978-3-8349-8182-0

Ruighaver, A. B., Maynard, S. B., & Chang, S. (2007). Organisational security culture: Extending the end-user perspective. *Computers & Security, 26*(1), 56–62. doi:10.1016/j.cose.2006.10.008

Ruopeng, L., Sadiq, S., & Governatori, G. (2008). Compliance aware business process design. *BPM 2007 Workshops. LNCS, 4928*, 120–131.

Ryan, J. J., & Ryan, D. J. (2006). Expected benefits of information security investments. *Computers & Security, 25*(8), 579–588. doi:10.1016/j.cose.2006.08.001

Saint-Germain, R. (2005). Information security management best practice based on ISO/IEC 17799. *Information Management Journal, 39*(4), 60–66.

Salehl, M. S., Alrabiah, A., & Bakry, S. H. (2007). Using ISO 17799: 2005 information security management: A stope view with six sigma approach. *International Journal of Network Management, 7*, 85–97. doi:10.1002/nem.616

Salem, M. B., Hershkop, S., & Stolfo, S. J. (2008). A survey of insider attack detection research. In *Advances in Information Security: Vol. 39. Insider Attack and Cyber Security* (pp. 69–90). Springer Press.

SANS. (2005). *Developing a security-awareness culture. Improving security decision making*, (pp. 1-22).

Saphier, J., & King, M. (1985). Good seeds grow in strong cultures. *Educational Leadership, 43*(6), 67–74.

Sapolsky, R. (2005). Stressed out memories. *Scientific American Mind, 14*(5), 28.

Sarbanes-Oxley Act of 2002. (2002). Pub. L. 107-204. Retrieved November 26, 2010, from http://www.gpo.gov/fdsys/pkg/PLAW-107publ204/content-detail.html

Schechter, S., Herley, C., & Mitzenmacher, M. (2010). Popularity is everything: A new approach to protecting passwords from statistical guessing attacks. In *HotSec'10: Proceedings of the 5th USENIX Workshop on Hot Topics in Security*. USENIX Association.

Scheer, A.-W. (2001). *ARIS-Modellierungs-Methoden, Metamodelle, Anwendungen*. Berlin, Germany: Springer.

Schein, E. (1992). *Organisational culture and leadership* (2nd ed.). San Francisco, CA: Jossey-Bass.

Scherer, K. R., & Zentner, M. R. (2001). Emotional effects of music: Production rules. In Juslin, P. N., & Sloboda, J. A. (Eds.), *Music and emotion: Theory and research* (pp. 361–392). Oxford, UK: Oxford University Press.

Schilit, B., & Theimer, M. (1994). Disseminating active map information to mobile hosts. *IEEE Network, 8*(5), 22–32. doi:10.1109/65.313011

Schlienger, T., & Teufel, S. (2002). *Information security culture - The social-cultural dimension in information security management.* In IFIPTC11 International Conference on Information Security, Cairo, Egypt.

Schlienger, T., & Teufel, S. (2003). *Information security culture - From analysis to change*.

Schlienger, T., & Teufel, S. (2003a). *Analyzing information security culture: Increased trust by an appropriate information security culture*. In 14th International Workshop on Database and Expert Systems Applications (DEXA'03), Prague, Czech Republic.

Schlienger, T., & Teufel, S. (2003b). Information security culture – From analysis to change. In *Proceedings of the 3rd Annual Information Security South Africa Conference* (ISSA 2003), Johannesburg, South Africa, 9-11 July.

Schmidt, A., Kölbl, T., Wagner, S., & Strassmeier, W. (2004). Enabling access to computers for people with poor reading skills. In C. Stary & C. Stephanidis (Eds.), *8th ERCIM Workshop on User Interfaces for All, Lecture Notes in Computer Science (LNCS), vol. 3196* (pp. 96–115). Vienna, Austria: Springer.

Schneier, B. (2000). *Secrets & lies: Digital security in a networked world* (1st ed.). New York, NY: John Wiley & Sons, Inc.

Schumacher, M., Achermann, R., & Steinmetz, R. (2000). Towards security at all stages of a system's life cycle. *Proceedings of the International Conference on Software, Telecommunications, and Computer Networks (Softcom)*. Retrieved from http://www.ito.tu-darmstadt.de/publs

Schumacher, R., Fernandez, E. B., Hybertson, D., Buschmann, F., & Sommerlad, P. (2006). *Security patterns: Integrating security and systems engineering*. Wiley.

Senge, P. (2003). Taking personal change seriously: The impact of organizational learning on management practice. *The Academy of Management Executive*, *17*(2), 47–50. doi:10.5465/AME.2003.10025191

Sewall, M. A., & Sarel, D. (1986). Characteristics of radio commercials and their recall effectiveness. *Journal of Marketing*, *50*(1), 52–60. doi:10.2307/1251278

SFO. (2009). *Serious Fraud Office*. Retrieved June 29, 2009, from https://www.sfo.gov.uk/

Shaffer, G. (1976). *A Mathematical theory of evidence*. Princeton, NJ: Princeton University Press.

Shannon, C. (1948). A mathematical theory of communication. *The Bell System Technical Journal*, *27*, 379–423.

Shapiro, C., & Varian, H. R. (1999). *Information rules: A strategic guide to the network economy*. Boston, MA: Harvard Business School Press.

Shaw, M. L. G., & Gaines, B. R. (1992, October). Kelly's "geometry of psychological space" and its significance for cognitive modeling. *The New Psychologist*, October, 23-31. Retrieved from http://pages.cpsc.ucalgary.ca/~gaines/reports/PSYCH/NewPsych92/index.html

Shedden, P., Ahmad, A., & Ruighaver, A. B. (2006). Risk management standard-The perception of ease of use. In *Proceedings of the Fifth Annual Security Conference*, Las Vegas, Nevada, USA.

Sheng, S., Wardman, B., Warner, G., Cranor, L. F., Hong, J., & Zhang, C. (2009). *An empirical analysis of phishing blacklists*. In CEAS 2009: Sixth Conference on Email and Anti-Spam, July 2009.

Shewhart, W. A. (1939, reprint 1986). *Statistical method from the viewpoint of quality control*. Dover Publications. ISBN-13: 978-0486652320

Shewhart, W. A. (1980). Economic control of quality of manufactured product. *American Society for Quality Control., ISBN-13*, 9780873890762.

Shostack, A. (2003). *People won't pay for privacy: Reconsidered*. In 2nd Annual Workshop on Economics and Information Security. Robert H. Smith School of Business.

Siegrist, M., Gutscher, H., & Earle, T. (2005). Perception of risk: The influence of general trust, and general confidence. *Journal of Risk Research*, *8*(2), 145–156. doi:10.1080/1366987032000105315

Simon, H. (1973). The structure of ill structured problems. *Artificial Intelligence*, *4*(3–4), 181–201. doi:10.1016/0004-3702(73)90011-8

Siponen, M., & Willison, R. (2009). Information security management standards: Problems and solutions. *Information & Management*, *46*(5), 267-270. doi:doi: DOI: 10.1016/j.im.2008.12.007

Siponen, M. (2006a). Information security standards: focus on the existence of process not its content. *Communications of the ACM*, *49*(8), 97–100. doi:10.1145/1145287.1145316

Siponen, M. T. (2000). A conceptual foundation for organizational information security awareness. *Information Management & Computer Security*, *8*(1), 31–41. doi:10.1108/09685220010371394

Siponen, M. T. (2005). Analysis of modern IS security development approaches: towards the next generation of social and adaptable ISS methods. *Information and Organization*, *15*(4), 339–375. doi:10.1016/j.infoandorg.2004.11.001

Siponen, M. T., & Oinas-Kukkonen, H. (2007). A review of information security issues and respective research. *Association for Computer Machinery SIGMIS Database*, *38*(1), 60–80.

Siponen, M., & Willison, R. (2009). Information security management standards: Problems and solutions. *Information & Management*, *46*, 267–270. doi:10.1016/j.im.2008.12.007

Skeels, M. M., & Grudin, J. (2009). When social networks cross boundaries: A case study of workplace use of Facebook and LinkedIn. In *Proceedings of the ACM 2009 International Conference on Supporting Group Work* (Sanibel Island, Florida, USA, May 10 - 13, 2009), 95–104.

Skinner, B. F. (1991). *The behavior of organisms* (p. 473). Copley Pub Group.

Small, A., Stern, Y., Tang, M., & Mayeux, R. (1999). Selective decline in memory function among healthy elderly. *Neurology*, *52*, 1392–1396.

SmartManager. (2010). Getting workplace value from Generation Y. Retrieved September 1, 2010, from http://www.smartmanager.com.au/web/au/smartmanager/en/pages/87_workplace_value_gen_y.html

Smith, A. B. (1932). The pleasures of recognition. *Music & Letters*, *13*(1), 80–84. doi:10.1093/ml/13.1.80

SOCA. (2009). *Serious Organised Crime Agency*. Retrieved June 29, 2009, from http://www.soca.gov.uk/

Sol, H. (1982). *Simulation in Information Systems development*. PhD dissertation, University of Groningen, The Netherlands.

Solhaug, B., Elgesem, D., & Stolen, K. (2007). Why trust is not proportional to risk. In *ARES'07: Proceedings of the Second International Conference on Availability, Reliability and Security* (pp. 11–18). IEEE Press.

Solms, B. V., & Solms, R. V. (2004). The 10 deadly sins of information security management. *Computers & Security*, *23*(5), 371–376. doi:10.1016/j.cose.2004.05.002

Solms, B., & Solms, R. (2005). From information security to... business security? *Computers & Security*, *24*, 271–273. doi:10.1016/j.cose.2005.04.004

Sorter Oxford English Dictionary. (2002). In Trumble, W. R., & Stevenson, A. (Eds.), *On historical principles* (5th ed., *Vol. 1*, p. 1028). Oxford University Press.

Sowa, S., Tsinas, L., & Gabriel, R. (2009). BOR information security - Business ORiented management of information security. In Johnson, M. E. (Ed.), *Managing information risk and the economics of security* (pp. 81–97). New York, NY: Springer. doi:10.1007/978-0-387-09762-6_4

Spears, J. L., & Barki, H. (2010). User participation in Information Systems security risk management. *Management Information Systems Quarterly*, *34*(3), 503–522.

Spitzner, L. (2003). Honeypots: Catching the insider threat. In *ACSAC'03: Proceedings of the 19th Annual Computer Security Applications Conference*, (pp. 170–179). IEEE Press.

Spurling, P. (1995). Promoting security awareness and commitment. *Information Management & Computer Security*, *3*(2), 20–26. doi:10.1108/09685229510792988

Stan, S. (2007). Beyond information security awareness training: It is time to change the culture. In Tipton, H. F. (Ed.), *Information security management handbook* (pp. 555–565). Hoboken, NJ: Auerbach Publications.

Stanton, J. M., & Stam, K. R. (2006). *The visible employee: Using workplace monitoring and surveillance to protect information assets-without compromising employee privacy or trust*. Medford, NJ: Information Today, Inc.

Steel, C., Nagappan, R., & Lai, R. (2005). *Core security patterns: Best practices and strategies for J2EE, web services and identity management*. Prentice Hall.

Stephenson, P. (2004). Forensic Análisis of Risks in Enterprise Systems. *Law, Investigation and Ethics,* Sep/Oct, 20-21.

Stoll, M. (2007). Managementsysteme und Prozessorientiertes Wissensmanagement. In N. Gronau (Ed.), *Proceedings of the 4th Conference on Professional Knowledge Management – Experiences and Visions*: Vol. 1. (pp. 433-434). Berlin, Germany: Gito Verlag.

Stoll, M. (2008). E-learning promotes information security. In M. Iskander (Ed.), *Innovative Techniques in Instruction Technology, E-learning, E-assessment, and Education: Proceedings of the 2007 IEEE International Conference on Engineering Education, Instructional Technology, Assessment, and E-learning (EIAE 07).* Dordrecht, The Netherlands: Springer. doi: 10.1007/978-1-4020-8739-4_54

Stoll, M., & Breu, R. (in press). Information security measurement roles and responsibilities. *Proceedings of the 2010 IEEE International Conference Telecommunication and Networking (TENE2010).*

Straub, D. W. (1986). *Deterring computer abuse: The effectiveness of deterrent countermeasures in the computer security environment.* Bloomington, IN: Indiana University School of Business.

Straub, D. W., & Welke, R. J. (1998). Coping with systems risk: Security planning models for management decision making. *Management Information Systems Quarterly, 22*(4), 441–469. doi:10.2307/249551

Straub, D., Loch, K., Evaristo, R., Karahanna, E., & Strite, M. (2002). Toward a theory-based measurement of culture. *Journal of Global Information Management, 10*(1), 13–23. doi:10.4018/jgim.2002010102

Stroh, S., Acker, O., & Kunar, A. (2009, June 30). Why Cloud computing is gaining strength in the IT market place. *Strategy + Business.* Retrieved from http://www.strategy-business.com/article/li00131?gko=c331a

Surveillance Studies Network. (2011). *Surveillance & Society.* ISSN 1477-7487

Takeuchi, H., & Nonaka, I. (2004). *Hitotsubashi on knowledge management.* Singapore: John Wiley & Sons.

Tan, T. C., Ruighaver, A. B., & Ahmad, A. (2003). *Incident handling: Where the need for planning is often not recognised.*

Tawileh, A., Hilton, J., & McIntosh, S. (2007). Managing information security in small and medium sized enterprises: A holistic approach. In Pohlmann, N. (Ed.), *ISSE/SECURE 2007 Securing Electronic Business Processes* (*Vol. 4*, pp. 331–339). doi:10.1007/978-3-8348-9418-2_35

The OpenId Foundation. (2007). *OpenID authentication 2.0 - Final Specification.* Retrieved 2010, from http://openid.net/specs

The UK Card Association. (2009). *Fraud: The facts 2009.* Retrieved July 22, 2009, from www.theukcardsassociation.org.uk

Thoben, K. D., & Jagdev, H. S. (2001). Typological issues in enterprise networks. *Production Planning and Control, 12*(5), 421–436. doi:10.1080/09537280110042666

Thomas, I., & Meinel, C. (2010). *An identity provider to manage reliable digital identities for SOA and the Web.* 9th Symposium on Identity and Trust on the Internet. Gaithersburg, MD: ACM.

Thomson, K., & Von Solms, R. (2005). Information security obedience: A definition. *Computers & Security, 24*(1), 69–75. doi:10.1016/j.cose.2004.10.005

Thomson, K., von Solms, R., & Louw, L. (2006). Cultivating an organizational information security culture. *Computer Fraud & Security,* (10): 7–11. doi:10.1016/S1361-3723(06)70430-4

Thorgren, S., Wincent, J., & Örtqvist, D. (2009). Designing interorganizational networks for innovation: An empirical examination of network configuration, formation and governance. *Journal of Engineering and Technology Management, 26,* 148–166. doi:10.1016/j.jengtecman.2009.06.006

Thorpe, J., & van Oorschot, P. C. (2007). Human-seeded attacks and exploiting hot-spots in graphical passwords. *In SS'07: Proceedings of the 16th Conference on USENIX Security Symposium* (Article 8), Berkeley, CA: USENIX Association.

Times, N. Y. (2007, June 2). A cyber-blockade in Estonia. *The New York Times.* Retrieved July 23, 2009, from http://www.nytimes.com/2007/06/02/opinion/02sat3.html

Todorov, J. C. (1990). The K&S in Brazil. *Journal of the Experimental Analysis of Behavior, 54,* 151–152. doi:10.1901/jeab.1990.54-151

Tor Project. (2010). *Anonymity online*. Retrieved November 30, 2010, from http://www.torproject.org/

Trompeter, C. M., & Eloff, J. H. P. (2001). A framework for the implementation of socio-ethical controls in information security. *Computers & Security*, *20*(5), 384–391. doi:10.1016/S0167-4048(01)00507-7

Trowbridge, D., Cunningham, W., Evans, M., & Brader, L. (2004). *Describing the enterprise architecture space*. Retrieved from http://msdn2.microsoft.com/en-us/library/ms978655.aspx

Trusted Information Sharing Network (TISN). (2008). *What is SCADA?* Retrieved October 2, 2009, from http://www.tisn.gov.au/www/tisn/tisn.nsf/Page/e-Security#_What_is_SCADA?

Tsiakis, T., & Stephanides, G. (2005). The economic approach of information security. *Computers & Security*, *24*(2), 105–108. doi:10.1016/j.cose.2005.02.001

Tuffley, A., & Grove, B., & G, M. (2004). SPICE for small organisations. *Software Process Improvement and Practice*, *9*, 23–31. doi:10.1002/spip.191

Tulving, E. (1974). Cue-dependent forgetting. *American Scientist*, *62*, 74–82.

Turban, E., King, D., Lee, J., & Viehland, D. (2004). *Electronic commerce: A managerial perspective*. Prentice Hall International Inc.

Tvrdíková, M. (2008). Information System integrated security. In *7th International Computer Information Systems and Industrial Management Applications Conference* (pp. 153-154). Los Alamitos, CA, USA.

UK Copyright Service. (n.d.). *Factsheet P-01: UK copyright law*. Retrieved December 12, 2010m from http://www.copyrightservice.co.uk/copyright/p01_uk_copyright_law

US Copyright Office. (n.d.). *Fair use*. Retrieved December 12, 2010, from http://www.copyright.gov/fls/fl102.html

Valdevit, T., Mayer, N., & Barafort, B. (2009). Tailoring ISO/IEC 27001 for SMEs: A guide to implement an information security management system in small settings. In O'Connor, R. V. (Eds.), *EuroSPI 2009, CCIS 42* (pp. 201–212). Berlin, Germany: Springer-Verlag. doi:10.1007/978-3-642-04133-4_17

van Aken, J. E. (2004). Management research based on the paradigm of the design sciences: The quest for field-tested and grounded technological rules. *Journal of Management Studies*, *41*, 219–246. doi:10.1111/j.1467-6486.2004.00430.x

van Aken, J. E., & Romme, A. G. L. (2009). Reinventing the future: Adding design science to the repertoire of organization and management studies. *Organization Management Journal*, *6*(1), 5–12. doi:10.1057/omj.2009.1

van Cleeff, A., & Wieringa, R. J. (2009). Rethinking de-perimeterisation: Problem analysis and solutions. In *Proceedings of the IADIS International Conference on Information Systems 2009* (pp. 105–112). IADIS Press.

van der Meyden, R. (1996). The dynamic logic of permission. *Journal of Logical Computing*, *6*(3), 465–479. doi:10.1093/logcom/6.3.465

Van Niekerk, J., & Von Solms, R. (2006). *Understanding information security culture: A conceptual framework. Information Security South Africa*. Johannesburg, South Africa: ISSA.

Veiga, A. D., & Eloff, J. H. P. (2009). A framework and assessment instrument for information security culture. *Computers & Security*, *29*, 196–207. doi:10.1016/j.cose.2009.09.002

Viega, J., & McGraw, G. (2001). *Building secure software: How to avoid security problems the right way*. Addison-Wesley.

Visser, W., Matten, D., Pohl, M., & Tolhurst, N. (2008). *The A to Z of corporate social responsibility*. New Jersey: John Wiley and Sons.

Von Groote, J. F., et al. (2010). *MCRL2: Analyzing system behavior*. TU-Eindhoven. Retrieved from http://www.mcrl2.org/mcrl2/wiki/index.php/Home

Von Solms, B. (2000). Information security -- The third wave? *Computers & Security*, *19*(7), 615–620. doi:10.1016/S0167-4048(00)07021-8

Von Solms, B. (2001). Information Security -- A multidimensional discipline. *Computers & Security*, *20*(6), 504–508. doi:10.1016/S0167-4048(01)00608-3

Von Solms, R., & Von Solms, B. (2004). From policies to culture. *Computers & Security*, *23*(4), 275–279. doi:10.1016/j.cose.2004.01.013

von Solms, R., & von Solms, S. H. (2006). Information security governance: A model based on the direct-control cycle. *Computers & Security*, *25*(6), 408–412. doi:10.1016/j.cose.2006.07.005

von Solms, S. H. (2006). Information security – The fourth wave. *Computers & Security*, *25*, 165–168. doi:10.1016/j.cose.2006.03.004

von Solms, S. H., & Solms, R. v. (2009). *Information security governance*. New York, NY: Springer. doi:10.1007/978-0-387-79984-1

von Solms, S. H., & von Solms, R. (2005). From information security to business security? *Computers & Security*, *24*, 271–273. doi:10.1016/j.cose.2005.04.004

Vries, H., Blind, K., Mangelsdorf, A., Verheul, H., & Zwan, J. (2009). *SME access to European standardization. Enabling small and medium-sized enterprises to achieve greater benefit from standards and from involvement in standardization*. Rotterdam, the Netherlands. (A. 2009 o. Document Number)

Vroom, C., & von Solms, R. (2004). Towards information security behavioural compliance. *Computers & Security*, *23*(3), 191–198. doi:10.1016/j.cose.2004.01.012

Wall Street Journal. (2009). *Gary Hamel's blog: The Facebook Generation vs. the Fortune 500*. Retrieved September 15, 2009, from http://blogs.wsj.com/management/2009/03/24/the-facebook-generation-vs-the-fortune-500

Walsham, G. (1995). Interpretive case studies in IS research: Nature and method. *European Journal of Information Systems*, *4*, 74–81. doi:10.1057/ejis.1995.9

Walton-on-Thames: Insight Consulting. (2005). *CRAMM user guide. Risk analysis and management method*, version 5.1.

Warren, M. (2010). Changing culture paves way for more Wiki-style leaks. *Radio Australia National*. Retrieved September 1, 2010, from http://www.radioaustralia.net.au/connectasia/stories/201007/s2966371.htm

Weichselberger, K. (2001). *Elementare Grundbegriffe einer allgemeineren Wahrscheinlichkeitsrechnung I*. Heidelberg, Germany: Physica-Verlag. doi:10.1007/978-3-642-57583-9

Weiland, R. M., Moore, A. P., Cappelli, D. M., Trzeciak, R. F., & Spooner, D. (2010). *Spotlight on: Insider threat from trusted business partners*. Carnegie Mellon University: Software Engineering Institute. Retrieved June 2010, from http://www.cert.org/archive/pdf/TrustedBusinessPartners0210.pdf

Wells, W. D., Burnett, J., & Moriarty, S. (1989). *Advertising: Principles and practice*. Prentice Hall.

Weske, M. (2007). *Business process management: Concepts, languages, architectures*. Berlin, Germany: Springer.

Whitman, M. E. (2003). Enemy at the gate: Threats to information security. *Communications of the ACM*, *46*(8), 91–95. doi:10.1145/859670.859675

Whitman, M. E. (2008). Security policy: From design to maintenance. In *Information Security: Policy, Processes, and Practices, Advances in Management Information Systems* (*Vol. 11*, pp. 123–151). Armonk, NY: M. E. Sharpe Inc.

Whitman, M. E., & Mattord, H. J. (2008). *Principles of information security* (3rd ed.). Delmar.

Whitten, A., & Tygar, J. D. (1999). *Why Johnny can't encrypt: A usability evaluation of PGP 5.0, 169-184.*

Wiander, T. (2008). *Implementing the ISO/IEC 17799 standard in practice – Experiences on audit phases*. Paper presented at the AISC '08: The Sixth Australasian Conference on Information security, Wollongong, Australia.

Wiander, T., & Holappa, J. (2006). *Theoretical framework of ISO 17799 compliant information security management system using novel ASD method.*

Wiedenbeck, S., Waters, J., Sobrado, L., & Birget, J.-C. (2006). Design and evaluation of a shoulder-surfing resistant graphical password scheme. In *AVI '06: Proceedings of the Working Conference on Advanced Visual Interfaces* (pp. 177-184). New York, NY: ACM.

Wiendahl, H.-P., & Lutz, S. (2002). Production in networks. *CIRP Annals - Manufacturing Technology, 51*(2), 573–586.

Wieringa, R., Pijpers, V., Bodenstaff, L., & Gordijn, J. (2008). Value-driven coordination process design using physical delivery models. In *Proceedings of the 27th International Conference on Conceptual Modeling* (pp. 216–231). Springer Verlag.

William, H., Starbuck, F., & Milliken, J. (1998). Challenger: Fine-tuning the odds until something breaks. *Journal of Management Studies, 25*(4), 319–340.

Williams, K. (2010). *Understanding Generation Y*. Retrieved September 1, 2010, from www.dynamicbusiness.com.au/.../understanding-generation-y.html

Williams, G., & Kikalas, T. (2005). *Operating systems – Worm targets. IGGeS submission*. Journal.

Windley, P. J. (2005). *Digital identity* (1st ed.). Sebastopol, CA: O'Reilly Media, Inc.

Witter, G. P. (2005). *Metaciência e psicologia*. São Paulo, Brazil: ALINEA. (in Portuguese)

Wood, C. C. (2000). Integrated approach includes information security. *Security: For Buyers of Products. Systems & Services, 37*(2), 43–44.

Wood, C. C. (2008). *Information security policies made easy* (10th ed.). Houston, TX: Information Shield.

Workman, M., Bommer, W., & Straub, D. (2008). Security lapses and the omission of information security measures: A threat control model and empirical test. *Computers in Human Behavior*.

Wu, M. (2006). *Fighting phishing at the user interface*. PhD Thesis, MIT.

Xiang, G., & Hong, J. (2009). A hybrid phish detection approach by identity discovery and keywords retrieval. In *Proceedings of the 18th International Conference on World Wide Web (WWW'09,* (pp. 571-580).

Xu, X., Yuruk, N., Feng, Z., & Schweiger, T. A. (2007). SCAN: A structural clustering algorithm for networks. In *Proceedings of the 13th ACM SIGKDD International Conference on Knowledge Discovery and Data Mining*, KDD '07, (pp. 824-833). New York, NY: ACM Press.

Yan, J., Blackwell, A., Anderson, R., & Grant, A. (2004). Password memorability and security: Empirical results. *IEEE Security and Privacy, 2*(5), 25–31. doi:10.1109/MSP.2004.81

Yin, R. K. (1994). *Case study research: Design and methods* (2nd ed.). Thousand Oaks, CA: Sage Publications.

Yue, Z., Egelman, S., Cranor, L. F., & Hong, J. (2007). Phinding phish: Evaluating anti-phishing tools. *Proceedings of the 14th Annual Network and Distributed System Security Symposium* (NDSS 2007). Carnegie Mellon University.

Zakaria, O. (2004). Understanding challenges of information security culture: A methodological issue. In *Proceedings of the Second Australian Information Security Management Conference*, Perth, Australia, 26 November 2004.

Zakaria, O. (2006). *Internalisation of information security culture amongst employees through basic security knowledge*. In IFIP TC11 International Conference on Information Security, Karlstad, Sweden, 22-24 May 2006.

Zakaria, O., & Gani, A. (2003). *A conceptual checklist of information security culture*. In 2nd European Conference on Information Warfare and Security, Reading, UK.

Zhang, Y., Hong, J., & Cranor, L. (2007). Cantina: A content-based approach to detecting phishing websites. In *Proceedings of the 16th International Conference on World Wide Web*, (pp. 639 – 648).

Zibuschka, J., Fritsch, L., Radmacher, M., Scherner, T., & Rannenberg, K. (2007). Enabling privacy of real-life LBS: A platform for flexible mobile service provisioning. In *New Approaches for Security, Privacy and Trust in Complex Environments: Proceedings of the 22nd IFIP TC-11 International Information Security Conference* (vol. 232, pp. 325-336). Sandton, South Africa.

About the Contributors

Manish Gupta received his PhD in Management Science and Systems and an MBA in Information Systems and Finance from State University of New York, Buffalo, NY, USA in 2011 and 2003, respectively. He received his undergraduate degree in Mechanical Engineering from Institute of Engineering and Technology, Lucknow, India in 1998. He has more than twelve years of experience in Information Systems, security policies, and technologies. He currently works in a Northeast US bank in information security division. He has published 4 books in the area of information security, ethics, and assurance. He has authored or co-authored more than 50 research articles in leading journals, conference proceedings, and books including *DSS, ACM Transactions, IEEE*, and *JOEUC*. His papers have received best paper awards. He serves in editorial boards of several international journals and has served in program committees of several international conferences. He holds several professional designations including CISSP, CISA, CISM, CRISC, ISSPCS, CIW Security Analyst, and PMP. He is a member of Sigma Xi, Beta Gamma Sigma, ISACA, and ISC2. He received prestigious 2008 ISC^2 information security scholarship (awarded on to only 7 researchers around the world) from ISC^2 and also received PhD Student Achievement Award from SUNY Buffalo.

John Walp has more than 17 years of Information Technology experience, more than half of which has been focused on information security challenges. He currently serves as Administrative Vice President and Corporate Information Security Officer for M&T Bank, a $70 billion financial institution headquartered in Buffalo, NY. Previously, he held the role of Vice President, Network Security Solutions Manager for M&T. His responsibilities include forming and executing the overall strategy for Information Security and Privacy at M&T Bank. This includes groups which focus on external and internal network security, which are made up of key security systems such as firewalls, intrusion detection/prevention systems, and security information management platforms. In addition, his organization supports the functions of access management, and compliance and risk management. Mr. Walp was selected as the 2009 North East Information Security Executive of the Year, an honor given by the Executive Alliance. The ISE Northeast Awards recognize information security executives and their teams who demonstrate outstanding leadership in risk management, data asset protection, regulatory compliance, privacy, and network security across the region including the states of Connecticut, Maine, Massachusetts, New Hampshire, New Jersey, New York, Rhode Island, and Vermont. John is a Certified Information Systems Security Professional (CISSP) as well as a Certified Information Security Manager (CISM). He is a graduate of the FBI Citizens Academy and serves as Executive Vice President of the FBI's Buffalo InfraGard Membership Alliance. Mr. Walp also serves on the advisory board of the Center of Excellence in Information Systems Assurance Research and Education (CEISARE) at the University of Buffalo. He is a member of the High-Tech Crime Consortium and the U.S. Secret Services Electronic Crimes Task Force. A Veteran of the United State Air Force, he served his country for 22 years which included both active and reserve service. In 2004, Mr. Walp was recalled to active duty and deployed to the Kingdom of Kuwait in support of Operation Iraqi Freedom and Operation Enduring Freedom. He was selected as part of an elite logistics cadre to aid in establishing the Central Command's Deployment and Distribution Operations Center. He holds a Bachelor of Science in Computer Information Systems from State University of New York College at Buffalo. He and his wife Laurie have four children and make their home in Amherst, NY.

Raj Sharman is an Associate Professor in the Management Science and Systems Department of the State University of New York at Buffalo. His expertise is in information assurance, disaster preparedness and response management, patient safety and health care systems, business value of Information Technology investments, technology valuation and performance, and imaging systems. He has published in national and international journals and is the recipient of several grants from university and external agencies, including the National Science Foundation.

* * *

Atif Ahmad is an information security researcher and independent security consultant based at the Department of Information Systems, University of Melbourne. He completed his Ph.D. in Digital Forensics. His research interests are in asymmetric warfare and information security risk assessments especially where knowledge artifacts are concerned. In previous years Atif has worked as a consultant for Pinkerton and WorleyParsons where he applied his expertise to Internet corporations and critical infrastructure installations. Atif is a Board Certified Protection Professional (CPP) with the American Society for Industrial Security and holds an adjunct position at the Secau Security Research Centre at Edith Cowan University.

Khaled Alghathbar, PhD, CISSP, CISM, PMP, BS7799 Lead Auditor, is an Associate Professor and the Founder and Director of the Centre of Excellence in Information Assurance in King Saud University, Riyadh, Saudi Arabia. He is a security advisor for several government agencies. His main research interest is in information security management, policies, biometrics, and design. He received his PhD in Information Technology from George Mason University, USA. He received many awarded and medals locally and internationally. He published more than 75 scientific papers in international conferences and journals. He is well known speaker in this field and participated in many national and international events. Dr. Khaled Alghathbar has one US patent and in the process of filing 9 patents in the fields of information assurance.

Ghmlas Saleh Al-Ghmlas is currently an IT Project manager and a team member in Information Center, Saudi Arabia National Guard. He is also working at the Center of Excellence in Information Assurance (CoEIA) as trainer. In 2003, he graduated from College of Computer Sciences and Information, King Saud University with a B.A. degree in Information Systems. In 2004, he completed the Military Academic Officers Training in King Khalid Military Academy. In 2006, he got a diploma in American Language CRS (ALC) from Defense Language Institute English Language Center, San Antonio, TX. In

2007, he got a diploma in Signal basic Officer Leader from United States Army Signal Center and Fort Gordon, Augusta, GA. He has MCSE and CCNA certificates and is currently pursuing Master's degree in Information Systems from King Saud University.

Ajit Balakrishnan is the Founder, Chairman, and Managing Director of the Rediff.com. He is also a director of Rediffusion Dentsu Young & Rubicam Private Limited, India Abroad Publications, Inc. India, New York, Inc., India Abroad Publications (Canada) Inc., Value Communications Corporation, and VuBites India Private Limited. Mr. Balakrishnan is also Chairman of the Board of Governors of The Indian Institute of Management Calcutta and Chairman of the Working Group of Internet Governance set up by the Government of India. Mr. Balakrishnan holds a Bachelor's degree in Physics from Kerala University and a Post Graduate Diploma in Management from the Indian Institute of Management, Kolkata. He is active in the area of collective intelligence and machine learning for last few years and has co-authored couple of research papers in these fields.

Christopher Beggs is the Director of Security Infrastructure Solutions. He holds a PhD in Cyber-terrorism and SCADA security from Monash University and is a Certified SCADA Security Architect and SANS-GIAC Security Professional. He has been conducting security assessments for critical infrastructure asset owners and operators as well as assisting them in designing, developing, and implementing SCADA security risk management programs. He is the key technical adviser for critical infrastructure security projects and assessments and has had extensive experience in providing consulting and academic services on a range of security risk management initiatives. He is also a specialist Lecturer at Deakin University in Master's of Information Security Management and has authored and co-authored numerous books, book chapters, and journal and conference papers on SCADA security and cyber-terrorism.

Wolfgang Boehmer hold an Ph.D. in Applied Physics from the University of Hamburg (Germany), and he is a Research Scientist and Lecturer in Information Security, Computer Science Department, Security Engineering Group from the Technische Universitaet Darmstadt (Germany). His research interests include security management systems, control systems, risk analysis, applied Game Theory in the field of security in large and small enterprises, business continuity management systems (BCMS), and mobile networks.

Ruth Breu has been full Professor at the University of Innsbruck since 2002 and head of the research group Quality Engineering (QE). She passed her degrees at the University of Passau and Technische Universität München and worked as freelance consultant for renowned companies for several years. QE's research topics include model-driven quality assurance, workflow management, and planning of IT landscapes. In addition, QE has achieved an internationally leading position in the areas of security engineering and security management. Since 2004, more than 20 projects were funded by third parties, among them the EU-IST projects SecureChange and PoSecCo. Moreover, Ruth Breu is head of the competence centre QE LaB, funded within the Austrian Laura Bassi Centres of Expertise initiative and four international industry partners. Ruth Breu is General Chair of the ACM SACMAT 2011 Symposium and Co-General Chair of the ACM/IEEE International Conference MODELS 2012.

Ines Brosso, PhD, has Master (2000) and Ph.D.(2006) degrees in Electrical Engineering, concentration in Digital Systems and Security, from the Polytechnic School of Engineering, University of Sao Paulo, Brazil. Dr. Brosso is an Adjunct Professor, Coordinator of Laboratory of Security and the postgraduate course in Information Security at College of Computation and Informatic at Mackenzie Presbyterian University, campus São Paulo, Brazil, and works at Banco Bradesco SA since 1990 as the Information Security Specialist. Dr. Brosso worked as a Systems Development Analyst at Asea Brown Boveri Electrical Industry (1980-1989), and has various publications in international events. Research areas of interest include: security in computer networks, context-aware computing, biometrics, and adaptative security policies.

Shanton Chang is a Senior Lecturer in Information Systems, University of Melbourne. He completed his Ph.D. in Managing Multicultural Workforces at Monash University. His current primary areas of research include the social aspects of broadband enabled technology adoption, information needs in health and education, and information security culture. He also has particular interest in the ways young people engage with online social technologies and the factors for successful uptake and adoption of social and other Web 2.0 technologies in different contexts.

C. Chellappan is a Professor and Head in the Department of Computer Science and Engineering at Anna University, Chennai, India. He received his B.Sc. in Applied Sciences and M.Sc in Applied Science–Applied Mathematics from PSG College Technology, Coimbatore under University of Madras in 1972 and 1977. He received his M.E and Ph.D in Computer Science and Engineering from Anna University in 1982 and 1987. He was the Director of Ramanujan Computing Centre (RCC) for 3 years at Anna University (2002–2005). He has published more than 60 papers in reputed international journals and conferences. His research areas are computer networks, distributed/mobile computing and soft computing, software agent, object oriented design, and network security.

Eng Chew is Professor of Business and IT Strategy at the University of Technology, Sydney (UTS), and part-time Industry Advisor. From 2005 to 2008, he held the UTS-Gartner Chair of Business and IT Strategy at UTS. He is a former Chief Information Officer of SingTel Optus, and has over 25 years of industry experience in IT and Telecommunications in Australia. His achievements include delivery of several hundreds of million Australian dollars of business value through business process re-engineering and organizational transformation. Under the Gartner Chair, he has advised many Gartner clients and produced insightful research papers for Gartner on China's ICT telecommunications industry market trends, China's ICT R&D and education institutions, and China's CIO leadership maturity. He has delivered keynote speeches on IT leadership and management practices and trends, including global IT outsourcing services.

André van Cleeff holds a MSc degree in Computer Science and a MA degree in Sociology. He has six years of experience in the software industry, designing and developing distributed systems that span multiple organizational boundaries. Currently he is PhD candidate at the University of Twente. His research focuses on security-relevant differences between physical and digital systems, a crucial element in understanding today's cloud-based and virtualized IT infrastructures.

Marc Conrad is a Senior Lecturer in Computer Science in the Faculty of Creative Arts, Technology, and Science at the University of Bedfordshire in the United Kingdom. In his role of Academic Director he ensures the quality of the teaching provision within the field of Computing of the Department of Computer Science and Technology. He received his PhD in Mathematics in 1998 from the Universität des Saarlandes, Germany, on Units in Cyclotomic Number Fields; since then he has published in a variety of areas such as algebraic number theory, modeling, programming languages, security, project management, social media, and music. Marc Conrad is a member of the British Computer Society, the Institute for Mathematics and its Application, and the Croatian Mathematical Society. His personal web site is at http://perisic.com/marc

R. Dhanalakshmi is a PhD student in the Department of Computer Science and Engineering at Anna University, Chennai, India. She received her BE Computer Science and Engineering from Bharathidasan University and M.Tech Advanced Computing from Shanmugha Arts, Science , Technology, and Research Academy, Thanjavur. She has published papers in various international journals and conferences. Her research is on Web mining and digital forensics.

Yurdaer N. Doganata is a research staff member at IBM T. J. Watson Research Center, Hawthorne, NY. He received B.S. and M.S. degrees from the Middle East Technical University, Ankara, Turkey, and a Ph.D. degree from the California Institute of Technology, Pasadena, California, all in Electrical Engineering. He joined IBM Research in 1989, and since then, he has worked and managed projects in broad research topics, including queuing theory, intelligent transportation systems, multimedia servers, Web-based collaboration, electronic services, search for technical support, and finally, unstructured information management. His current research interests include the application of information management technologies to business integrity problems, focusing on providing continuous auditing by using business provenance data. Dr. Doganata holds a number of patents, research awards, and is the author of numerous papers and book chapters.

Pascal van Eck received his MSc degree in Computer Science from Vrije Universiteit Amsterdam in 1995. From 1995 until January 2000, he worked as a research assistant at the Artificial Intelligence Department of Vrije Universiteit. In 2001, he successfully defended his PhD thesis on a formal, compositional semantic structure for the dynamics of multi-agent systems. Starting February, 2000, he works at the Information Systems Group of the Department of Computer Science, University of Twente, as an Assistant Professor. His research interests include IT governance and alignment of business and IT architectures at the enterprise level.

Eduardo B. Fernandez (Eduardo Fernandez-Buglioni) is a Professor in the Department of Computer Science and Engineering at Florida Atlantic University in Boca Raton, Florida. He has published numerous papers on authorization models, object-oriented analysis and design, and fault-tolerant systems. He has written three books on these subjects. He has lectured all over the world at both academic and industrial meetings. He has created and taught several graduate and undergraduate courses and industrial tutorials. His current interests include patterns for object-oriented design and Web services security. He holds a MS degree in Electrical Engineering from Purdue University and a Ph.D. in Computer Science from UCLA. He is a Senior Member of the IEEE, and a Member of ACM. He is an active consultant for industry, including assignments with IBM, Allied Signal, Motorola, Harris, Lucent, and others.

Eduardo Fernandez-Medina holds a PhD and an MSc. in Computer Science from the University of Sevilla. He is an Associate Professor at the Escuela Superior de Informática of the University of Castilla-La Mancha in Ciudad Real (Spain) (Computer Science Department, University of Castilla La Mancha, Ciudad Real, Spain)- his research activity being in the field of security in information systems, and particularly in security in business processes, databases, data warehouses, and Web services. Fernández-Medina is co-editor of several books and chapter books on these subjects, and has published several dozens of papers in national and international conferences (BPM, UML, ER, ESORICS, TRUSTBUS, etc.). He is author of several manuscripts in national and international journals (*Decision Support Systems, Information Systems, ACM Sigmod Record, Information Software Technology, Computers & Security, Computer Standards and Interfaces*, etc.). He leads the GSyA research group of the Department of Computer Science at the University of Castilla-La Mancha, in Ciudad Real, Spain and belongs to various professional and research associations (ATI, AEC, AENOR, IFIP WG11.3, etc.)

Virginia N. L. Franqueira currently works as a postdoc researcher at the University of Twente, The Netherlands, where she also received her Ph.D. in Computer Sciences (November 2009). She received a M.Sc. degree, also in Computer Science, from the Federal University of Espirito Santo (UFES, Brazil) in 2003. Her main research interests are multi-step attacks in computer networks, security risks in extended enterprises, security risk estimation, and security requirements. She has eleven years of experience in industry, working as a software development and System Test project leader, preparing new business proposals opportunities and gathering requirements at several engineering companies and at the Xerox Software Development Center (Vitoria, Brazil).

Marcia Gibson is a final year PhD student in the Institute for Research in Applicable Computing at the University of Bedfordshire. Her research focuses on the development and evaluation of secure authentication systems to support and enable users who find using conventional techniques problematic. She has a BSc(Hons) in Computer Science and a Master's by Research in Computer Security.

Peter Goldschmidt received a B.Sc. from California State University (Business Administration - Quantitative Methods and Computer Systems), and an M.Ec. (Applied Econometrics) and Ph.D. (Computer Science and Finance) from The University of Western Australia. He has over 25 years' experience in IS/IT and economic and quantitative analysis. He is active in academia, industry, business, government, and international organisations as a researcher, adviser, and consultant; presented to numerous international conferences, published extensively, and reviewed for international journals and conferences. His Ph.D. dissertation was awarded the 1997 International Outstanding Doctoral Dissertation Award, eligible for doctorates completed 1994 -1996, from the Information Systems section of The American Accounting Association. He is currently a Professor in Information Management at UWA Business School, working in the areas of knowledge management, decision support, agent technology, and artificial intelligence applied to business, compliance infrastructure, and asset management work flow decision support. He is a recipient of an Australian COMET grant to commercialise his PhD research. He is the Principal and

Chair of the company Alert-KM Systems, which holds the IP (100%) of the CMAD technology. Since he completed his PhD in 1997, investigating and proposing a new approach to support Compliance Monitoring for Anomaly detection (CMAD) in Complex Environments, he has extended this research from compliance monitoring of stock exchange transactions (stock market surveillance) to diverse areas such as CMAD applied to the energy and petroleum industry, asset management in engineering, aerospace, and defence.

Kari Hiekkanen is a Lecturer and Researcher at Aalto University School of Science, Department of Computer Science and Engineering. His current teaching and research areas include Enterprise Architectures, IT Governance, Cloud Computing, and other organizational aspects of IT and service innovation. Prior to current academic role, he has nearly 20 years of working experience in various large IT service providers such as WM-Data and Logica, where he has held several management and executive positions in product and service development, technology strategy, and overall IT strategy. He has participated in national and international standardization in the areas of IT governance, SOA, and distributed cloud services.

Sylvia Kierkegaard is a Visiting Professor of Law at University of Southampton; Professor – PhD supervisor at the Communications University of China (Beijing); Visiting Professor at X'ian Jiatong University, among others. Sylvia is the President of the International Association of IT Lawyers (IAITL). She is the Chairman/Principal Investigator of the EU Co-Reach Project on IPR in the New Media for the government of Germany, Netherlands, UK, Austria, and China. The task of Co-Reach is to make a comparative analysis of copyright laws and provide legislative recommendations and government policies. She is a Legal Expert at the EU and the Council of Europe. She was the EU Senior Legal Expert on Info Security for China and currently advises numerous organisations on various legal issues relating to computer law. She is the Conference Chairman of the LSPI Conference Series (www.lspi.net), Editorial Board Member of over 30 international journals and 5 national journals, keynote speaker in numerous international conferences, Scientific Adviser to the European Privacy Association and the Association Internationale de Lutte Contre la Cybercriminalité, and Chairman- program Committee member of numerous conferences. She is the Editor-in-Chief of the *International Journal of Private Law*; Editor-in-Chief of the *Journal of Intl. Commercial Law and Technology*; Managing Editor of the *Journal of Legal Technology Risk Management*; and European Editor of the *International Journal of Intercultural Information Management*. She is the author of over 2000 articles and books.

Janne J. Korhonen is a researcher at Aalto University School of Science, Department of Computer Science and Engineering. Recently, Korhonen has been involved with development of conceptual frameworks for Enterprise Architecture, EA Governance, and SOA Maturity, with a particular focus on Enterprise Architecture Governance. He has also been lecturing at the Enterprise Systems Integration and Enterprise Systems Architecture courses. Among his academic endeavors, Korhonen is an independent IT and business consultant, having over ten years of consulting experience in a variety of extensive, mission-critical, and international IT projects pertaining to enterprise and solution architectures, business process management, and enterprise application integration. He has participated in international BPM standardization and a number of global and corporate-level architecture development endeavors.

Joo Soon Lim is a PhD candidate in Information Systems at the department of Information Systems, University of Melbourne. He has M.Sc. degree in Computer Science from the University of Putra, Malaysia and an MBA (Electronic Commerce) from the Charles Sturt University, Australia. His current research focuses on successful uptake and adoption of information security policy, and behavioral and organizational aspects of information privacy and security. He is particularly interested in understanding cultural influence on users' behaviors and developing necessary tools to help them in protecting organizational information.

Shyh-Chang Liu received the B.S. from National Tsing Hua University in 1981, and M.S. degree and Ph.D. degree from Department of Electrical Eng., Clemson University, U.S.A. in 1986 and 1991. Currently, He is an Associate Professor of Department of Information Engineering I-Shou University, Taiwan, Republic of China. Besides teaching, he also cooperated with companies for projects in the areas of wireless communications and networking. His research field focused in wireless communication, network application development, and security.

Md Delwar Hussain Mahdi was awarded the Bachelor of Arts (Honours) degree in the field of Business Administration from University of East London, UK in September 2009. His thesis topic was "Credit Fraud Detection in the Banking Sector in UK: A focus on E-Business," supervised by Dr. Karim Mohammed Rezaul. He received his B.Com (Honours) degree in the area of Management in 1997 and M.Com degree in Management in 1999 from National University of Bangladesh. He was an Assistant Manager of POSOBID NGO (Non-Governmental Organisation) at Moulvibazar, Bangladesh from July 1999 to April 2005. His research interests include e-business, information security, business, and management Information Systems.

Carsten Maple is the Pro Vice Chancellor for Research & Enterprise at the University of Bedfordshire. Previously he was Head of the Computer Science and Technology Department. Carsten has an international research reputation and extensive experience of institutional strategy development and interacting with external agencies as well as substantial experience of chairing and participating in committees and boards at all levels of an HE institution. Carsten is a member of several professional societies including: Elected member of CPHC Committee, Education Advisor for TIGA, Adviser for cs4fn, Fellow of British Computer Society, Member of IEEE, and Member of IEEE Computer Society. He is also appointed a Professor at North Eastern University, China. His interests include: information security, trust and authentication in distributed systems, graph theory, and optimisation techniques.

Sean Maynard is a Lecturer in the Department of Information Systems at the University of Melbourne. He completed his Ph.D. in Evaluation of Security Policy Quality. Starting his academic career in Information Systems focusing on the use of computing technology to aid senior management (EIS) and the evaluation of decision support systems; his research over the past decade has been in the area of information systems security, in particular focusing on the evaluation of security policy quality and on the investigation of security culture within organizations. Sean also has interests in logistics and supply chain management with a focus on the simulation of the logistics supply chain. He has been involved with running computer simulations within executive programs in logistics and supply chain over the past 18 years.

Christoph Meinel is the CEO and President of the Hasso Plattner Institute for IT-Systems Engineering (HPI) and full Professor for Computer Science at the University of Potsdam since 2004. He studied Mathematics and Computer Sciences at the Humboldt-University, and received his PhD degree there in 1981. His habilitation thesis (1988) was about complexity theory. He worked in Humboldt University in Berlin, Max-Planck-Institut für Computer Science, and Paderborn University. In 1992 he was appointed a full Professor for Computer Science at the University of Trier. He is also a Professor both at the School of Computer Science of the Technical University of Beijing (China) and at the Luxembourg Institute of Advanced Studies in Information Technology. He is the author or co-author of 10 textbooks, various conference proceedings, and more than 350 peer-reviewed scientific papers. His research interests focus on in Internet technology and systems, particularly in the fields trust and security engineering, Web-University and innovation research (design thinking). He is member of various scientific boards, Chief Editor of the scientific electronic journal *Electronic Colloquium on Computational Complexity* (http://eccc.hpi-web.de), of the *IT-Gipfelblog*, (www.it-gipfelblog.de) and the *Tele-TASK archive* (http://www.tele-task.de).

Juha Mykkänen, PhD, works as a research Director in University of Eastern Finland, School of Computing, Health Information Systems Research and Development unit. He has managed and participated in various national and international projects and initiatives related to social and health information systems research and development. His research interests and areas of expertise include enterprise architectures, application integration, interoperability standardization, information systems development methods, and SOA, especially in relation to wellbeing information management. He has participated in national and international standardization of health information systems as well as various organizations and associations such as Health Level Seven, International Medical Informatics Association, IEEE, and Object Management Group. His publications include more than 30 international peer-reviewed papers and over 80 other articles, published reports, chapters, or specifications.

Syed Irfan Nabi, (PMP®) is an Assistant Professor at the Institute of Business Administration, Karachi, Pakistan, and also a Senior Researcher at Center of Excellence in Information Assurance (CoEIA) at King Saud University, Riyadh, Saudi Arabia. His areas of interest include information security management, information assurance, and softer issues concerning culture, organizational behavior, and people related to information security. He has extensive international teaching, research and consulting experience in the USA, Saudi Arabia, Pakistan, Bangladesh, and South Korea. He is author of numerous research publications in peer-reviewed journals and conferences. Currently he is pursuing his doctoral studies, and expects to complete them by December 2011.

Alessandro La Neve, PhD, is Full Professor at the Department of Electrical Engineering, of Centro Universitario da FEI, in São Bernardo do Campo, Brazil. He has Master's (1980) and Ph.D.(1982) degrees in Electrical Engineering, concentration in Digital Systems and Computer Architecture, from the Polytechnic School of Engineering, University of Sao Paulo, Brazil. At FEI, he has been director of the computer center, coordinator of the Graduate Program in Electrical Engineering, and academic director for the engineering courses. He has been active at undergraduate and graduate courses both as a teacher and advisor , and has worked at IPEI Research Institute, and as a consultant for industry as well, in the area of digital systems and automation, both hardware and software. He has several publications in national and international events. Areas of interest include: computer and network architectures, high speed computing algorithms, fuzzy systems, e-learning, and, more recently, security in computer networks and context-aware computing.

Daniel Oost was awarded his PhD (Management) from the University of Technology, Sydney in 2010. His PhD examined the following questions within the context of a large Australian company: How does analysis of the everyday discursive work of information security managers inform us about the phenomena that they constitute as 'information security? What does it mean to do information security? Prior to undertaking his PhD Daniel completed Honours in Information Systems at the University of Newcastle, and was awarded the University Medal. His professional experience includes security administration and analyst/programmer roles. Currently Daniel is working with Blueberry Paper, an Australian creative enterprise.

Alkesh Patel is a Senior Product Engineer in the Rediff.com since January, 2008. He is involved in designing and implementing large scale products at Rediff.com. He has done his Bachelor's in Engineering (Computer Science) from Maharaja Sayajirao University of Baroda and Master's in Information Technology with specialization in Intelligent Systems from Indian Institute of Information Technology, Allahabad. He has also served as a Lecturer in Saradar Vallabhbhai Patel Institute of Technology, Vasad during Nov-2004 to Jun-2006. He has authored several research papers which constitute areas of text/data mining, information retrieval, collective intelligence of users in social network, recommendation systems, machine learning, and natural language processing.

Mario Piattini has an MSc and PhD in Computer Science from the Technical University of Madrid and is a Certified Information System Auditor (CISA) and Certified Information Security Manager by ISACA (Information System Audit and Control Association). He is a Professor in the Department of Computer Science at the University of Castilla-La Mancha, in Ciudad Real, Spain. Author of several books and papers on databases, software engineering, and information systems, he leads the ALARCOS research group of the Department of Computer Science at the University of Castilla-La Mancha, in Ciudad Real, Spain. He is author of several books and papers on databases, security, software engineering, and Information Systems. He leads the ALARCOS research group of the Department of Computer Science at the University of Castilla- La Mancha, in Ciudad Real (Spain). His research interests are: advanced database design, database quality, software metrics, object-oriented metrics, and software maintenance.

Karen Renaud is a Senior Lecturer at the School of Computing, University of Glasgow. She has been working in the area of usable security for 9 years, and specialises in the development of usable authentication mechanisms. She chairs the Trust Security group in her school, and supervises a number of research students working on various aspects of information security.

Karim Mohammed Rezaul was awarded a PhD degree in Computing and Communications Technology from North East Wales Institute (NEWI) of Higher Education, University of Wales, UK in October 2007. He received his BSc. degree in the field of Naval Architecture and Marine Engineering from Bangladesh University of Engineering and Technology (BUET), Dhaka in 1998 and MSc. degree in Marine Technology from Norwegian University of Science and Technology (NTNU), Trondheim, Norway in 2001. His PhD research topic was "*Estimating Long-range dependent self-similar Network traffic: performance evaluation and control,*" supervised by Professor Vic Grout. He is a member of the Institute of Electrical and Electronics Engineers (IEEE), Association for Computing Machinery (ACM), Centre for Applied Internet Research (CAIR, UK), and a fellow of Institution of Engineers Bangladesh (IEB, Bangladesh). In February 2002, Dr. Karim was appointed as visiting Lecturer in the Department of Computing, Communications Technology and Mathematics at London Metropolitan University, and continued until June 2005. He is currently working as the Director of Studies and Senior Lecturer at St. Peter's College of London. He is the Founder and Director of Applied Research Centre for Business and Information Technology (ARCBIT). He is an author of a numerous scientific and business articles in scholarly & refereed publications which include books, book chapters, journals, and international conference papers. He is an Editor of several international journals and member of the technical program committee (TPC) of multiple international conferences. He is an Academic Advisor / Programme Director of various international colleges in UK. His research interests include e-business, network traffic engineering, long-range dependence phenomena (which appear in network traffic, stock markets, oil price, cardiology, economics, finance, hydrology, climate, weather etc.), time series analysis, quantitative development, business Information Systems & design, information security, designing algorithm & data structures, statistical computing, Internet technology & Grid Computing, Quality of Service (QoS) control, and traffic modelling & simulation. His Curriculum Vitae can be found at http://www.morekba.netii.net/cv.pdf.

Heiko Roßnagel is Senior Scientist at the Fraunhofer Institute for Industrial Engineering. He studied Computer Science at the Technical University of Darmstadt. He received a PhD in Business Administration and Economics at the Goethe-University Frankfurt. He has been participating in several European and national cooperative research projects such as the EC-funded projects Wireless Trust for mobile business (WiTness), Future of Identity in the Information Society (FIDIS), and Scoping the Single European Digital Identity Community (SSEDIC). His research interests are in the areas of security, privacy, and identity management with a focus on technology development and adoption.

Ian Rosewall is a new addition to Deakin, moving to Australia from Plymouth University in England. He now works with Professor Warren in the School of Information Systems, Deakin University, Australia. He has an MSc from Sheffield Hallam University in IT and Management. He is currently undertaking a PhD looking into information disclosure in the public and private sectors.

Luís Enrique Sánchez is PhD and MsC in Computer Science and is an Assistant Professor at the Escuela Superior de Informática of the Universidad de Castilla- La Mancha in Ciudad Real (Spain) (Computer Science Department, University of Castilla La Mancha, Ciudad Real, Spain), MSc in Information Systems Audit from the Polytechnic University of Madrid, and Certified Information System Auditor by ISACA. He is the Director of Professional Services and R&D departments of the company Sicaman Nuevas Tecnologías S.L. COIICLM board or committee member and responsible for the professional services committee. His research activities are management security system, security metrics, data mining, data cleaning, and business intelligence. He participates in the GSyA research group of the Department of Computer Science at the University of Castilla- LaMancha, in Ciudad Real (Spain). He belongs to various professional and research associations (COIICLM, ATI, ASIA, ISACA, eSEC, INTECO, etc).

Antonio Santos-Olmo has an MsC in Computer Science and is an Assistant Professor at the Escuela Superior de Informática of the Universidad de Castilla- La Mancha in Ciudad Real (Spain) (Computer Science Department, University ofCastilla La Mancha, Ciudad Real, Spain), MSc in Information Systems Audit from the Polytechnic University of Madrid, and Certified Information System Auditor by ISACA. He is the Director of Software Factory Department of the company Sicaman Nuevas Tecnologías S.L. His research activities are management security system, security metrics, data mining, data cleaning, and business intelligence. He participates in the GSyA research group of the Department of Computer Science at the University of Castilla- LaMancha, in Ciudad Real (Spain). He belongs to various professional and research associations (COIICLM, ATI, ASIA, ISACA, eSEC, INTECO, etc).

Margareth Stoll passed her PhD degree in Technical Sciences at the Vienna University of Technology (Austria) and worked for several years as collaborator, Lecturer, and consultant for different small, medium and great sized organizations in Austria, Germany, and Italy. Further, she is certified auditor for ISO 9001 quality management, ISO 27001 information security management, and ISO/IEC 20000-1 IT service management. She is project leader of COSEMA (cooperative security management) in the research group Quality Engineering (QE) at the University of Innsbruck. Her main research topics are holistic, interdisciplinary management systems for sustainable organizational development. She integrates most different research disciplines, such as strategic management, controlling, business process management, project management, IT management, information security management, quality management, knowledge management, and organizational learning.

Ivonne Thomas is a PhD student at Hasso Plattner Institute, University of Potsdam in Germany. She received her Master's degree in Software Systems Engineering in 2006. Ivonne Thomas has been working in the area of identity and trust management since more than four years including work placements at SAP Research in Brisbane, Australia as well as in the Security and Trust Group of SAP Research in Sophia Antipolis, France. Since three years she is working full-time on her PhD as a member of the HPI Research School on "Service-oriented Systems Engineering." For her PhD research, she is working on models and technologies towards a trustworthy and reliable management of digital identities in decentralized environments as SOA and the Internet.

Milena Tvrdíková works as an Assistant Professor in the Department of Applied Informatics at Faculty of Economics, VSB-Technical University of Ostrava. She also teaches at the WSB Poznan (Poland) and a Master of Business Administration (Faculty of Economics, Technical University of Ostrava and Liverpool John Moores University). She is President of The Moravian Society for Systems Integration, a member of the editorial board in Grada Publishing (Prague), a member of the editorial board of Systemic Integration magazine, Program Chairman of the Conference Information Technology for practice. She is also a member of the Executive Committee of the Association of EUNIS-CZ (European University Information Systems, Czech Republic) and coordinator of numerous projects in information systems and information technology.

Michael Van Hilst received his Master's and PhD in Computer Science from the University of Washington. He is a Research Professor at Florida Atlantic University. Formerly, he was a Vice President for a firewall company, worked for five years in the Software Technology Lab at HP Labs and for ten years at the Harvard/Smithsonian Center for Astrophysics, where he was a Senior Programmer and Software Architect. He has also worked for the French CNRS and at IBM TJ Watson Research Labs. He has numerous publications in security and software engineering, including OOPSLA and ACM SIGSOFT/FSE. Dr. Van Hilst is a member of the IEEE and a senior member of the ACM.

Matthew Warren is the Head of School and a Professor in the School of Information Systems, Deakin University, Australia. He has a PhD in Information Security Management from Plymouth University, UK. Professor Warren has received numerous prestigious research grants and has an international reputation for his scholarly work in the areas of information security, risk analysis, information warfare, and critical infrastructure protection. He has authored numerous books, book chapters, and journal articles.

Roel Wieringa is Chair of Information Systems at the University of Twente, the Netherlands. His research interests include value-based requirements engineering, business process modelling, conceptual modelling, and research methodology for requirements engineering. He is scientific director of the School for Information and Knowledge Systems (SIKS), which provides advanced education to all Dutch Ph.D. students in Information and Knowledge Systems. He has been Associate Editor in Chief of *IEEE Software* for the area of requirements engineering, and serves on the board of editors of the *Requirements Engineering Journal* and of the *Journal of Software and Systems Modelling.*

Tsang- Hung Wu has more than 8 years of engineering and management experience in information security, Internet, and e-commerce technologies. He is currently working a project manager within Cathay Securities Corporation. He passed Information Technology Infrastructure Library Foundation Certificate (ITIL Foundation), CompTIA Security+ Certification, and *Cisco Certified Network Associate* Routing & Switching (*CCNA*). Tsang- Hung Wu is a PhD student in the Department of Information Management at Yuan Ze University, Taiwan, Republic of China. He received the M.S degree in Department of Information Engineering from I-Shou University and B.S degree in Department of Applied Mathematics from Chinese Culture University. Tsang- Hung Wu is interested in information security, computer network, and IT management.

Jan Zibuschka is Senior Scientist at the Fraunhofer Institute for Industrial Engineering. He holds a Diploma in Computer Science from Technical University of Darmstadt. He participated in several national and international research projects dealing with security and privacy, such as the FP ICT projects PRIME, PrimeLife, and FIDIS. He published in several areas of economics of security, including the design of market-compliant solutions for privacy in location-based services and cost-efficient approaches for Web identity management and single sign on.

Index

E

F

G

H

I

K

L

M

N

O

P

R

S

T

U

V

W

CPSIA information can be obtained at www.ICGtesting.com
Printed in the USA
BVOW051916150112

280533BV00003B/5/P

9 781466 601970